ARTHUR SCHOPENHAUER
The World as Will and Representation

CW00819749

The purpose of the Cambridge Edition of the Works of Schopenhauer is to offer translations of the best modern German editions of
Schopenhauer's work in a uniform format suitable for Schopenhauer
scholars, together with philosophical introductions and full editorial
apparatus.

First published in 1818, *The World as Will and Representation*
contains Schopenhauer's entire philosophy, ranging through epistemology, metaphysics, philosophy of mind and action, aesthetics and
philosophy of art, to ethics, the meaning of life and the philosophy
of religion, in an attempt to account for the world in all its significant
aspects. It gives a unique and influential account of what is and is not
of value in existence, the striving and pain of the human condition
and the possibility of deliverance from it. This new translation of the
first volume of what later became a two-volume work reflects the elo-
quence and power of Schopenhauer's prose and renders philosophical
terms accurately and consistently. It offers an introduction, glossary
of names and bibliography, and succinct editorial notes, including
notes on the revisions of the text which Schopenhauer made in 1844
and 1859.

JUDITH NORMAN is Professor of Philosophy at Trinity University, Texas. She is co-editor of *The New Schelling* (2004) with Alistair Welchman. She has also previously translated works by Nietzsche including *Beyond Good and Evil* (Cambridge, 2002) and *The
Antichrist, Ecce Homo, Twilight of the Idols, The Case of Wagner and
Nietzsche Contra Wagner* (Cambridge, 2005).

ALISTAIR WELCHMAN is Assistant Professor of Philosophy at the
University of Texas at San Antonio. He is co-editor of *The New
Schelling* (2004), and has also published numerous articles on con-
temporary European thought.

CHRISTOPHER JANAWAY is Professor of Philosophy at the Uni-
versity of Southampton. His previous publications include *Self and
World in Schopenhauer's Philosophy* (1989) and *Schopenhauer: A Very
Short Introduction* (2002). He is editor of *The Cambridge Companion
to Schopenhauer* (1999) and has edited and translated *Schopenhauer:
The Two Fundamental Problems of Ethics* (2009).

THE CAMBRIDGE EDITION OF THE WORKS OF SCHOPENHAUER

GENERAL EDITOR

Christopher Janaway

Titles in this series:

The Two Fundamental Problems of Ethics
translated and edited by Christopher Janaway

The World as Will and Representation: Volume 1
translated and edited by Judith Norman, Alistair Welchman
and Christopher Janaway with an Introduction
by Christopher Janaway

ARTHUR SCHOPENHAUER

The World as Will and Representation

Volume I

TRANSLATED AND EDITED BY

JUDITH NORMAN

ALISTAIR WELCHMAN

CHRISTOPHER JANAWAY

with an Introduction by

CHRISTOPHER JANAWAY

CAMBRIDGE
UNIVERSITY PRESS

CAMBRIDGE
UNIVERSITY PRESS

University Printing House, Cambridge CB2 8BS, United Kingdom

Published in the United States of America by Cambridge University Press, New York

Cambridge University Press is part of the University of Cambridge.

It furthers the University's mission by disseminating knowledge in the pursuit of
education, learning and research at the highest international levels of excellence.

www.cambridge.org
Information on this title: www.cambridge.org/9781107414778

© Judith Norman, Alistair Welchman and Christopher Janaway 2010

This publication is in copyright. Subject to statutory exception
and to the provisions of relevant collective licensing agreements,
no reproduction of any part may take place without the written
permission of Cambridge University Press.

First published 2010
First paperback edition 2014

A catalogue record for this publication is available from the British Library

Library of Congress Cataloguing in Publication data
Schopenhauer, Arthur, 1788–1860.
[Welt als Wille und Vorstellung. English]
The world as will and representation / Arthur Schopenhauer ; translated and edited by Judith
Norman, Alistair Welchman, Christopher Janaway ; with an introduction by Christopher Janaway.
p. cm. – (The Cambridge edition of the works of Schopenhauer)
Includes bibliographical references and index.
ISBN 978-0-521-87184-6 (v. 1)
1. Philosophy. 2. Will. 3. Idea (Philosophy) 4. Knowledge, Theory of. I. Norman,
Judith, 1965– II. Welchman, Alistair. III. Janaway, Christopher. IV. Title.
B3138.E5N67 2010
193 – dc22 2010029486

ISBN 978-0-521-87184-6 Hardback
ISBN 978-1-107-41477-8 Paperback

Cambridge University Press has no responsibility for the persistence or accuracy of
URLs for external or third-party internet websites referred to in this publication,
and does not guarantee that any content on such websites is, or will remain, accurate
or appropriate.

Contents

v

Appendix: Critique of the Kantian Philosophy 441

General editor's preface

Schopenhauer is one of the great original writers of the nineteenth century, and a unique voice in the history of thought. His central concept of the will leads him to regard human beings as striving irrationally and suffering in a world that has no purpose, a condition redeemed by the elevation of aesthetic consciousness and finally overcome by the will's self-denial and a mystical vision of the self as one with the world as a whole. He is in some ways the most progressive post-Kantian, an atheist with profound ideas about the human essence and the meaning of existence which point forward to Nietzsche, Freud and existentialism. He was also the first major Western thinker to seek a synthesis with Eastern thought. Yet at the same time he undertakes an ambitious global metaphysics of a conservative, more or less pre-Kantian kind, and is driven by a Platonic vision of escape from empirical reality into a realm of higher knowledge.

Schopenhauer was born in 1788, and by 1809 had gone against his family's expectations of a career as a merchant and embarked on a university career. He completed his doctoral dissertation *On the Fourfold Root of the Principle of Sufficient Reason* in 1813, then spent several years in intensive preparation of what became the major work of his life, *The World as Will and Representation*, which was published at the end of 1818, with 1819 on the title page. Shortly afterwards his academic career suffered a setback when his only attempt at a lecture course ended in failure. Thereafter Schopenhauer adopted a stance of intellectual self-sufficiency and antagonism towards university philosophy, for which he was repaid by a singular lack of reaction to his writings. In 1835 he published *On the Will in Nature*, an attempt to corroborate his metaphysics with findings from the sciences, and in 1841 two self-standing essays on free will and moral philosophy, entitled *The Two Fundamental Problems of Ethics*. A large supplementary second volume to *The World as Will and Representation* appeared in 1844, accompanied by a revised version of the original which now appeared as Volume One; then in 1851 another two-volume work,

Parerga and Paralipomena, a collection of essays and observations. Only in the 1850s did serious interest in Schopenhauer's philosophy begin, with a favourable review appearing in an English journal and a few European universities offering courses on his work. In this final decade before his death in 1860 he published a third edition of *The World as Will and Representation* and a second edition of *The Two Fundamental Problems of Ethics*. After Schopenhauer's death his follower Julius Frauenstädt produced the first six-volume edition of his works in 1873, providing the basis for many subsequent German editions up to the *Sämtliche Werke* edited by Arthur Hübscher, which we use as the basis for our translations in the present edition.

Though Schopenhauer's life and the genesis of his philosophy belong to the early part of the nineteenth century, it is the latter half of the century that provides the context for his widespread reception and influence. In 1877 he was described by Wilhelm Wundt as 'the born leader of non-academic philosophy in Germany', and in that period many artists and intellectuals, prominent among them Richard Wagner, worked under the influence of his works. The single most important philosophical influence was on Nietzsche, who was in critical dialogue throughout his career with his 'great teacher Schopenhauer'. But many aspects of the period resonate with Schopenhauer's aesthetic theory, his pessimism, his championing of the *Upanishads* and Buddhism, and his theory of the self and the world as embodied striving.

Over the last three decades interest in Schopenhauer in the English-speaking world has been growing again, with a good number of mono-graphs, translations and collections of articles appearing, where before there were very few. More general trends in the study of the history of philosophy have played a part here. There has recently been a dramatic rise in philo-sophical interest in the period that immediately follows Kant (including the German Idealists and Romanticism), and the greater centrality now accorded to Nietzsche's philosophy has provided further motivation for attending to Schopenhauer. Yet until now there has been no complete English edition of his works. The present six-volume series of Schopen-hauer's published works aims to provide an up-to-date, reliable English translation that reflects the literary style of the original while maintaining linguistic accuracy and consistency over his philosophical vocabulary.

Almost all the English translations of Schopenhauer in use until now, published though they are by several different publishers, stem from a single translator, the remarkable E. F. J. Payne. These translations, which were done in the 1950s and 1960s, have stood the test of time quite well and performed a fine service in transmitting Schopenhauer to an English-speaking audience. Payne's single-handed achievement is all the greater given that he was not a philosopher or an academic, but a former military man who became a dedicated enthusiast. His translations are readable and lively and convey a distinct authorial voice. However, the case for new translations rests partly on the fact that Payne has a tendency towards circumlocution rather than directness and is often not as scrupulous as we might wish in translating philosophical vocabulary, partly on the fact that recent scholarship has probed many parts of Schopenhauer's thought with far greater precision than was known in Payne's day, and partly on the simple thought that after half a century of reading Schopenhauer almost solely through one translator, and with a wider and more demanding audience established, a change of voice is in order.

In the present edition the translators have striven to keep a tighter rein on philosophical terminology, especially that which is familiar from the study of Kant – though we should be on our guard here, for Schopenhauer's use of a Kantian word does not permit us to infer that he uses it in a sense Kant would have approved of. We have included explanatory introductions to each volume, and other aids to the reader: footnotes explaining some of Schopenhauer's original German vocabulary, a glossary of names to assist with his voluminous literary and philosophical references, a chronology of his life and a bibliography of German texts, existing English translations and selected further reading. We also give a breakdown of all passages that were added or altered by Schopenhauer in different editions of his works, especially noteworthy being the changes made to his earliest publications, *On the Fourfold Root* and the single-volume first edition of *The World as Will and Representation*. A further novel feature of this edition is our treatment of the many extracts Schopenhauer quotes in languages other than German. Our guiding policy here is, as far as possible, to translate material in any language into English. The reader will therefore not be detained by scanning through passages in other languages and having to resort to footnote translations. Nevertheless, the virtuoso manner in which Schopenhauer blends Latin, Greek, French, Italian and Spanish extracts with his own prose style is not entirely lost, since we have used footnotes to give all the original passages in full.

CHRISTOPHER JANAWAY

Editorial notes and references

Three kinds of notes occur in the translation:

(1) Footnotes marked with asterisks (*, ** and so on) are Schopenhauer's own notes.

(2) Footnotes marked with small letters (a, b, c) are editorial notes. These either give information about the original wording in Schopenhauer's text (in German or other languages), or provide additional editorial information. All (and only) such *additional* information is enclosed in brackets [ ]. All footnote material *not* in brackets consists of words from the original text.

(3) Endnotes marked with numerals 1, 2, 3. The endnotes are placed at the back of the book, and indicate variations between the different texts of the essays published during Schopenhauer's lifetime.

Schopenhauer's works are referred to by the following abbreviations:

Hübscher *SW* 1–7	*Sämtliche Werke*, ed. Arthur Hübscher (Mannheim: F. A. Brockhaus, 1988), vols. 1–7.
BM	*On the Basis of Morals* [*Über die Grundlage der Moral*].
FR	*On the Fourfold Root of the Principle of Sufficient Reason* [*Über die vierfache Wurzel des Satzes vom zureichenden Grunde*].
FW	*On the Freedom of the Will* [*Über die Freiheit des Willens*].
PP 1, 2	*Parerga and Paralipomena* [*Parerga und Paralipomena*], vols. 1 and 2.
WN	*On the Will in Nature* [*Über den Willen in der Natur*].
WWR 1, 2	*The World as Will and Representation* [*Die Welt als Wille und Vorstellung*], vols. 1 and 2.

Unpublished writings by Schopenhauer are referred to thus:

GB   *Gesammelte Briefe*, ed. Arthur Hübscher (Bonn: Bouvier, 1978).

HN 1–5   *Der handschriftliche Nachlaß*, ed. Arthur Hübscher (Frankfurt am Main: Kramer, 1970), vols. 1–5.

MR 1–4   *Manuscript Remains*, ed. Arthur Hübscher, trans. E. F. J. Payne (Oxford: Berg, 1988), vols. 1–4 [a translation of *HN* vols. 1–4].

Passages in Kant's *Critique of Pure Reason* are referred to by the standard method, using A and B marginal numbers corresponding to the first and second editions of the work. Other writings by Kant are referred to by volume and page number of the monumental '*Akademie*' edition (Berlin: Georg Reimer/Walter de Gruyter, 1900–), in the form Ak. 4: 397. Translations are based on those in the relevant volume of the Cambridge Edition of the Works of Immanuel Kant. References to works of Plato and Aristotle use the standard marginal annotations.

Introduction

Schopenhauer's *The World as Will and Representation* was first published in Leipzig at the end of 1818 (with 1819 as the date on its title page). It consisted of a single volume, and aimed, as its 30-year-old author stated in his preface, 'to convey a single thought'. He went on to confess, however, that 'in spite of all my efforts, I could not find a shorter way of conveying the thought than the whole of this book', a book that ran to over 700 pages and was not a little ambitious, ranging through epistemology, metaphysics, philosophy of mind and action, aesthetics and philosophy of art, to ethics, the meaning of life and the philosophy of religion, in an attempt to account for nothing less than *the world*: the nature of our cognition or knowledge of reality and how it relates to reality itself, the nature of our existence and the existence of everything in the world, what is and is not of value in existence, the pain of the human condition and the possibility of deliverance from it. Schopenhauer rounds off his book with a detailed and incisive critique of the philosophy of Kant, whom he admired and respected, but to whom he boldly applied Voltaire's saying '*C'est le privilège du vrai génie, et surtout du génie qui ouvre une carrière, de faire impunément de grandes fautes*' (It is the privilege of true genius, and above all the genius who opens a new path, to make great errors with impunity) – words we may well have occasion to apply to Schopenhauer himself.

This book is the major achievement of Schopenhauer's life, and the backbone of his intellectual career. What we have provided here is an English version, not of that 1818 text, but of the text as Schopenhauer reworked it cumulatively on two later occasions. In 1844 he republished *The World as Will and Representation* as a two-volume work, whose second volume runs parallel with the themes in the first and consists of fifty 'supplementary essays', some of them substantial and powerfully written pieces in their own right. At the same time he revised the original *World as Will and Representation*, which henceforth became known as Volume 1. Many passages are rewritten in this 1844 version and whole paragraphs are added, along with elaborations of Schopenhauer's original argument that were suggested by his copious reading of philosophy and literature – ancient, mediaeval and modern – and his knowledge of many of the expanding disciplines of the nineteenth century, including the perhaps unlikely pairing of the biological sciences and oriental scholarship. In 1859, the year before he died, Schopenhauer revised the book once more, and Volume 1 acquired yet more scholarly additions and clarificatory changes, though still without altering the essentials of his train of thought. The twice-revised version is longer, richer and denser than the original. Schopenhauer's approach is to accumulate inter-connecting passages and parallels, channelling a wide variety of cultural sources into a single synthetic vision, and by the same token directing the reader outwards to a wealth of intellectual reference points. The text we have used for this translation is essentially this last edition, subject to certain further revisions by various editors, starting with Julius Frauenstädt in 1873, through Paul Deussen's edition of 1911, to Arthur Hübscher's of 1988 which we treat as the standard text. Our endnotes give detailed information about changes between the different editions of Schopenhauer's lifetime.

The nature of the 'single thought' that Schopenhauer alleges is contained in this weighty work (and presumably also in the even greater supplementary material of later years) has been the subject of some slightly perplexed debate.[1] If there is a single thought, it must be highly elusive or highly complex, or both. But we can perhaps make an initial approach towards what Schopenhauer means if we examine the framework of four Books into which *The World as Will and Representation* is divided. Their titles and discursive subtitles are as follows:

(1) The world as representation, first consideration. Representation subject to the principle of sufficient reason: the object of experience and science.

(2) The world as will, first consideration. The objectivation of the will.

(3) The world as representation, second consideration. Representation independent of the principle of sufficient reason: the Platonic Idea: the object of art.

(4) The world as will, second consideration. With the achievement of self-knowledge, affirmation and negation of the will to life.

What we first notice here is an oscillation between the two key terms from the book's title. At the core of the single thought, then, is this: one and the

---

[1] For one substantial discussion see John E. Atwell, *Schopenhauer on the Character of the World: The Metaphysics of Will* (Berkeley: University of California Press, 1995), 18–31.

same world has two aspects, and we can learn about it by considering it as representation, then as will, then as representation in altered fashion, then as will in altered fashion. The two alterations in question introduce two more vital oppositions. With the world as representation, we can either consider it subject to the principle of sufficient reason, or independently of that principle. With the world as will, we can either consider it descriptively for what it is, or we can consider it on an evaluative dimension – with respect to its affirmation or negation. This, however, leaves us with an immense amount to explain. Let us next try to flesh out these bare bones a little, keeping in mind the four-part dynamic structure that any would-be 'single thought' really needs to have if it is to map on to the work as a whole.

Schopenhauer uses 'representation' (German *Vorstellung*) in the same way as his predecessor Kant uses it. It stands for anything that the mind is conscious of in its experience, knowledge, or cognition of any form – something that is present to the mind. So our first task in *The World as Will and Representation* is to consider the world as it presents itself to us in our minds. In ordinary human experience, and in the extension of this in the realm of scientific enquiry, we encounter objects, and these are ordered for us, necessarily, by space and time, and by relations of cause and effect. All the ways in which the world is thus ordered for us are species of the single principle 'Nothing is without a ground for its being rather than not being', otherwise known as the principle of sufficient reason. Every object is experienced as related to something else which grounds it. Everything in space and time has a determinate position in relation to other things in space and time, everything that happens has a determinate cause, every action relates back to a motive and to its agent's character, every truth is grounded in some other truth or in the evidence of the senses. So starting, as we must, from the world *as we find it* in everyday experience and empirical investigation, we see a multiplicity of objects related in necessary ways. But all of this tells us how the world must *appear* to us as subjects; it does not tell us how the world *is* when we try to consider it apart from the way it presents itself to our minds. We must next move on to consider the aspect of the world beyond representation, the world as 'thing in itself'.

In a word, Schopenhauer argues in his Second Book that the thing in itself – what the world is beyond the aspect of it that appears to us – is *will*. His guiding thought is that there is one single essence that underlies all objects and all phenomena, ourselves included, one single way in which the 'riddle' of all existence can be deciphered. The single world manifests itself to experience as a multiplicity of individual objects – Schopenhauer calls this the *objectivation* of the will – and each member of this multiplicity, embodying the same essence, strives towards existence and life. Human individuals are primarily beings who will and act, and share their ultimate nature with every other being in the world. Human rationality and consciousness are extremely useful, and give us an instrumental superiority over other beings, but are really only a froth on the surface, and do not distinguish humanity from the rest of nature at the most fundamental level. Indeed, our advanced capacities for cognition can be explained, for Schopenhauer, as serving the ends of willing: our ability to perceive and investigate the world functions primarily to enable us to manipulate objects that confront us, in order to continue existing and to reproduce ourselves. If we are really to understand the world and our place within it, we must not remain at the surface of the world as representation, but must delve into this deeper and darker aspect of reality, the world as will – darker because everything that wills or strives is necessarily at the mercy of suffering, and because this suffering has neither point nor end. As long as we will, we suffer; but that we will, and ultimately what we will, is a function of our inescapable essence, not something rationally chosen, and not something we have the means to put an end to by willing.

At the mid-point of *The World as Will and Representation* we return to a new, and brighter, consideration of the world as representation. It can happen, according to Schopenhauer, that we confront objects in a kind of experience that is out of the ordinary. We find all the usual kinds of relation – space, time and cause and effect – suspended, and lose ourselves in contemplation, forgetful of ourselves and of the distinction between ourselves and what we perceive. This is aesthetic experience, an extreme form of disinterestedness, a passive 'mirroring' of the world in which we cease to grapple with the world of objects, cease striving, and find temporary release from pain. While becoming as free as we can from subjectivity, we apprehend nature in a manner that takes our cognition as close as possible to the true essence of things: we perceive timeless features than run throughout nature, which Schopenhauer calls Ideas, intending us to take this notion in a sense close to Plato's (or to what are often called Platonic Forms nowadays). Art provides the best opportunity for this kind of experience because it gives us a view of nature mediated through the exceptionally objective mind of a genius. Art enables in us as spectators a state of calm passivity and enhanced objectivity, and the various art forms allow us to recognize diverse aspects of the will's manifestation in the world, from, as it were, a vantage point where our individual own will is not engaged.

The transition to the Fourth Book of *The World as Will and Representation* takes us back to the world as will, considered now with respect to its 'affirmation and negation', or at any rate the affirmation and negation of the 'will to life' that Schopenhauer finds to be the essence of each individual. This final part – by far the longest and, in Schopenhauer's words, the 'most serious' – is concerned with ethics, in both a narrower and broader sense. Building on the descriptive account of the will from the Second Book, Schopenhauer gives his own answers to conventional ethical questions: What are morally good and bad actions and characters? What is the nature of right and wrong? What constitutes compassion, and the virtues of justice and loving kindness? In what sense, if at all, are our actions free? But the main thrust of the Fourth Book is a broader ethical treatment of the value of human existence as such – a profound and troubling discussion that borders on religious territory while remaining resolutely atheist in its conviction. Schopenhauer has argued that the life of the human individual is inevitably one of striving and suffering, unredeemed by any final purpose or resting point for the will that is our essence. Now he argues that some salvation is needed from such an existence, but that it can only come from the restless will's becoming 'tranquillized' by a deep metaphysical insight that reveals individuality itself to be an illusion. The world in itself, outside of the forms of space and time that govern the world as representation for us, cannot be separated into individuals. The truly wise human being would comprehend this and would cease to be attached to the strivings of the particular individual manifestation of will he or she is. Such a redemptive state – sometimes reached intuitively through the painful experiences of life itself – is the will's 'self-negation' or 'self-abolition'. The will that is the human being's essence recoils from pursuing any of its goals, and the sense of individuality weakens to the point where reality can be contemplated with a serenity that is void of the usual pains of existence because the subject has become void of all striving and void of the usual sense of self.

THE WORLD OF OBJECTS AND SCHOPENHAUER'S
'INTRODUCTORY ESSAY'

From 1809 to 1813 Schopenhauer attended the universities of Göttingen and Berlin, studying philosophy among other subjects. He specialized early on in the work of Kant and Plato, both of whom had a profound formative influence on his thinking. He prepared *The World as Will and Representation* in the years 1814 to 1818, during which time he also began a life-long interest in Indian thought, starting with extracts from the *Upanishads* in a Latin version by A. H. Anquetil-Duperron entitled *Oupnek'hat*. In a notebook entry of 1816 Schopenhauer acknowledged the uniqueness of the mixture of influences on him: 'I do not believe my doctrine could have come about before the Upanishads, Plato and Kant could cast their rays simultaneously into the mind of one man.'[2]

Schopenhauer had published two works before *The World as Will and Representation*: a short treatise entitled *On Vision and Colours* (1816), and his doctoral dissertation *On the Fourfold Root of the Principle of Sufficient Reason* (1813). The latter is especially important to us here. In the first edition of *The World as Will* Schopenhauer referred to *On the Fourfold Root* throughout as 'the introductory essay', and went so far as to demand 'that the introduction be read before the book itself, even though it is not located inside the book but rather appeared five years earlier' (Preface to the first edition, 7). It will be helpful, therefore, to give an outline of the argument of the essay.

Two relatively simple ideas set the framework for *On the Fourfold Root*. One is the principle of sufficient reason itself – that 'nothing is without a ground for its being rather than not being'. In fact this principle could be translated more literally, if less conventionally, as 'principle of sufficient ground' (in German *Satz des zureichenden Grundes*). The idea is that everything is grounded in, explained or justified by, something else to which it is related in a variety of distinct ways. The second main idea is that all representation consists in the relation of subject and object. All cognition is by a subject and of an object. While the subject has cognition, and is presupposed wherever there is cognition, the subject itself is never cognized. What the subject is conscious of is always some object, but all objects are representations: 'To be an object for the subject and to be our representation are the same. All of our representations are objects for the subject, and all objects for the subject are our representations.'[3] Thus if we investigate the way our representations are organized, we shall at the same time be understanding the basic structure that pertains to objects of any kind. Schopenhauer now points out that our experience of objects is always of them in relation to one another. We never have cognition of anything 'subsisting for itself and independent . . . single and detached'. And whatever the particular content of our consciousness, there are certain kinds of relation between objects that are fundamental and necessary: 'all our representations stand to one another in a lawlike connection in respect of form, which can be determined *a priori*'. Discovering the necessary

---

[2] *MR* I, 467 (*HN* I, 422).
[3] *FR* § 16 (Hübscher *SW* I, 27). Following quotes are from the same passage.

kinds of connection between representations is discovering the necessary connections of all objects; and all these are connections of ground and consequent. All are forms of the principle of sufficient reason.

Schopenhauer shows how the principle of sufficient reason covers quite different species of ground–consequent relation and complains with some justification that previous philosophers have tended not to distinguish them clearly. Perhaps the most obvious of such species is the law of causality, the principle that everything that happens is the effect of some cause. This is the first form of the principle of sufficient reason for Schopenhauer, and it governs all our empirical representations in space and time. Everything we experience is spatially and temporally ordered, and whenever anything happens at a place at a time, something must have occurred to determine its happening. The relation between ground and consequent is always one of necessity, according to Schopenhauer. Hence any alteration, anything at all that 'becomes' or happens in the empirical realm of space and time (i.e. in our empirical representations) happens necessarily, according to a law, as a consequence of some particular cause which is also in space and time.

However, we human beings do not simply represent the spatio-temporal world to ourselves perceptually; we are able to form abstract concepts and use them to think, to make judgements and to perform sequences of reasoning. Any judgement we make, if it is to count as true, must also be grounded; but this form of grounding is quite distinct from that of causality, and so constitutes a second form of the principle of sufficient reason. It concerns what would usually be called not explanation, but justification. Under this second heading Schopenhauer locates in turn four ways in which judgements can be grounded, and expresses them also as four kinds of truth. There is logical (or formal) truth, where a judgement is grounded in another judgement from which it can be deduced. There is empirical truth, when a judgement is grounded in an immediate non-conceptual representation of experience. Then there is transcendental truth, for which Schopenhauer adopts the Kantian idea that we can know something to be true because it is a condition of the possibility of experience. These transcendental truths, for Kant, are synthetic *a priori*: known without requiring confirmation through experience, yet not deducible merely from concepts, i.e. neither logical nor empirical truths. Schopenhauer follows Kant closely here, giving the same sorts of examples of transcendental truth as Kant had done in the *Critique of Pure Reason*: 'Two straight lines do not enclose any space', 'Nothing happens without a cause', '$3 \times 7 = 21$'. Such judgements, Schopenhauer claims, have their truth grounded not in experience, nor in logical deduction, but in the conditions of the possibility of experience. Finally, he puts forward a fourth kind of truth, which he calls 'metalogical truth'. Truths of this kind supposedly express the conditions that make thinking possible as such, but they do not play any very prominent further role in Schopenhauer's philosophy.[4]

The third form of the principle of sufficient reason also trades directly on a position that Kant espoused in the *Critique of Pure Reason*. Schopenhauer has much to say in criticism of Kant, as we shall see, but the opening section of the *Critique* called the Transcendental Aesthetic is one for which he always has high praise. There Kant discusses space and time, and argues that they are, in effect, features contributed to experience by our own mind. Any world we can represent to ourselves must be in space and time: they constitute the formal structure that any objective world must take for us, whatever its particular content. Thus they are the subjective forms of all experience that we can gain through our senses, and we can know *a priori* that all experience must conform to them. All of this Schopenhauer adopts. But space and time, as well as providing this necessary framework for all experience, also give rise to another principle: that each part of space and of time is determined by its relation to the other parts. Every spatial position is determined by spatial positions distinct from it, and determines them, and likewise in the case of sequences of times. All parts of space and time stand in necessary relations to one another. Schopenhauer follows Kant in suggesting that there is a non-empirical, *a priori* form of cognition of the necessary properties of space and time, to be had in geometry and arithmetic. So he finds here a kind of ground–consequent relationship that is not one of causality, and not a matter of the relationship between judgements. This might be put by saying that a part of space or time is neither caused nor justified by its relation to other parts of space and time, but rather is constituted by such relations. So Schopenhauer talks here of the principle of the sufficient ground of *being*.

With the fourth class of grounds and consequents Schopenhauer broaches for the first time the subject of *willing*, which later becomes so central in his philosophy overall. He is here concerned with the relation of motive to action, which, however, turns out to be a special case of the first class, an example of cause and effect. Schopenhauer has much more to say about action and motive in his two later essays on ethics, as well as in

---

[4] There are four such truths, which Schopenhauer lists in *FR* § 33 (Hübscher *SW* 1, 109): 'a subject is identical to the sum of its predicates, or a=a'; 'a predicate cannot at the same time be attributed to and denied of a subject, or a=–a=o'; 'Of any two contradictory, opposing predicates one must belong to any subject'; 'Truth is the relation of a judgement to something outside it as its sufficient ground.'

The World as Will. The chief points he makes on the topic of willing in *On the Fourfold Root* are as follows. We have inner cognition as well as outer. That is, we not only have consciousness of the world of objects in space and time, but we have self-consciousness. And in this self-consciousness, Schopenhauer suggests, we are aware of ourselves as willing in different ways: acting, trying, deciding, desiring and registering a range of positive and negative affects and feelings that can also be called movements of the will. Outer consciousness and self-consciousness are quite distinct. And yet, when the will of which we are inwardly conscious is moved by some experience coming from outer consciousness (which is what Schopenhauer calls a *motive*: an experience that moves me to action), and when an act of will occurs, this sequence is at bottom no different from any relation of cause and effect. Motivation, he says, in a memorable phrase 'is causality seen from within'.[5] The insight that what we thus see from within (our will reacting to motives) belongs to the more general class of events being determined by their causes, and that the law of motivation is a version of the law of causality which governs the world of objects – this, he says, is the foundation stone of his whole metaphysics.

With this very quick sketch of the 'introductory essay' in place, let us now return to the four Books of *The World as Will and Representation*.

FIRST BOOK

Schopenhauer uses his first consideration of the world as representation to give a comprehensive account of cognition and its relation to reality. Three principal themes are worth commenting on here: idealism, the relation of subject and object, and the distinction between intuitive and conceptual cognition. All three themes are announced clearly in §§ 1–3. Schopenhauer firstly allies himself with *transcendental idealism*. According to this doctrine, originally developed by Kant in the *Critique of Pure Reason*, the objects that we experience as outside of us in space and time, causally interacting in lawlike ways, constitute a world of *appearance*, and we do not experience them *in themselves*. The objects of which any subject has conscious experience are a species of the subject's representations. The familiar world of empirical things is a world of objects *for a subject*, which is to say a world consisting of the subject's representations, and not a world that can be regarded as existing in itself, independently of the way it appears and must appear to an experiencing mind. The form of the mind itself necessarily

---

[5] *FR* § 43 (Hübscher *SW* 1, 145).

limits or shapes what this realm of objects can contain. The mind must organize its objects as related to one another in space, as contemporaneous or succeeding one another in time, and as entering into regular patterns of cause and effect. These, for Kant, and for Schopenhauer, are truths *a priori*, truths that we can know independently of confirmation through experience. They are ground rules for the possibility of experience itself.

Schopenhauer has various ways of arguing for transcendental idealism, but places his main trust in the proposition 'No object without subject'. This proposition, he says, is so obviously true that anyone who understands it must agree with it, and it establishes the truth of idealism at a stroke (had Kant acknowledged as much he would have saved himself and his readers a great deal of trouble, in Schopenhauer's view). There is more than a suspicion that Schopenhauer understands by 'object' simply something that presents itself to the mind of a subject – in which case 'No object without subject' is virtually a tautology – but that at the same time he takes the proposition to make a substantive claim by letting 'object' mean something like 'thing in the world', or at least 'cognizable thing in the world'. It is one thing to say that anything's being an object of cognition for me depends on my being there as subject of the cognition; it is another thing to say that anything I have cognition of could not exist except as cognized by me, or that anything human beings in general have cognition of could not exist except as cognized.

Representation, for Schopenhauer, consists essentially in the relation between subject and object, which are 'necessary correlates'. They are necessarily distinct: the subject of cognition can never itself be cognized as an object, and is rather the elusive 'point of view on the world' that we all, as experiencing individuals, 'finds ourselves as'. Subject and object are also mutually presupposing for Schopenhauer. 'No subject without object' is just as firm a truth, in his eyes, as 'No object without subject' – in other words, the subject cannot be there without having some cognitive content. 'Subject' does not mean the same for Schopenhauer as 'person' or 'human individual'. These terms refer to items in the world of objects. The body that each of us experiences as our own is likewise an object in space and time. But the subject is not an item in the world. So as person or embodied human individual each of us is in and of the world, something existing as an object among objects. But in addition we are the subject in whose consciousness all objects are present, but which cannot itself be conceived as existing among them. The notion that our existence and sense of self are poised between embodiment and pure subjecthood plays a vital role at many subsequent junctures in *The World as Will and Representation*:

different forms of consciousness are available to us as our sense of self alters.

For Schopenhauer, the human mind, and indeed any conscious mind, receives data through the bodily senses and structures them using what he calls the understanding (*Verstand*) or intellect (*Intellekt*). Without this structuring we would register only a conglomeration of subjective sensations, but with it we attain a picture of material objects persisting in time, occupying space and serving as the casual origins of observed changes and of our sensations themselves. However, Schopenhauer's account of cognition differs from Kant's superficially similar account, in that for Schopenhauer the understanding or intellect cognizes the world in a manner that is non-conceptual. Adopting another technical term of Kant's, but altering its use, Schopenhauer maintains that what the understanding gives us is intuition (*Anschauung*), which essentially means perceptual awareness of particular objects in space and time. For Kant, the senses give us an array of intuitions, and the understanding provides concepts under which it actively ordered the intuitions to produce an experience of a world of objects. Only creatures capable of forming concepts and making judgements could have such experience in the full sense. But for Schopenhauer animals such as a dog or a horse, who are incapable of forming concepts, are as much aware of a world of objects as any human subject: they perceive objects in space and time as we do, being simply incapable of making judgements, forming thoughts or carrying out reasoning, and hence being unable to comprehend anything more than what is immediately present in their perception.

§§ 4–7 fill out the picture of the world of objects that is available to the subject in empirical intuition. Empirical objects occupy space and time and causally interact with one another. The causally efficient occupant of any particular portion of space/time is simply *matter*. So if one were to take one's philosophical departure solely from the point of view of the object, one would arrive at *materialism*. However, to adopt this starting-point is one-sided: in this way one cannot account for the subject and its consciousness. Just as subject and object are mutually dependent and correlative, so too there is a correlativity between subjective and objective views of reality. Although he thinks materialism is correct as an account purely of objects, Schopenhauer argues that transcendental idealism is the only consistent view that takes the subject as its point of departure. For him it is also a mistake to contend that the subject is caused by objects or objects by the subject; they are not causally related at all, merely correlative components of representation. Causality is the form we impose on the interaction of objects with one another, but it has another function in Schopenhauer's account of cognition. When we register alterations in our bodily sense organs our understanding interprets these as the effects of external causes, thus giving rise to genuine representation of objects as opposed to mere sensations.

In §§ 8–15 Schopenhauer gives us a protracted discussion of reason and the kind of representations it gives rise to, namely concepts. Reason (*Vernunft*) for Schopenhauer is the capacity to form and manipulate concepts discursively to frame thoughts and arguments, and is quite distinct from understanding or intellect. Reason is closely linked to language, and is unique to human beings. For Schopenhauer concepts are secondary representations abstracted from the primary material given in intuition, i.e. immediate cognition through the senses of objects in space and time. Concepts are a kind of mediate cognition: they represent the world in a general way by omitting the particularities of immediate intuition, but remain dependent for any genuine content on those immediate intuitions from which they are abstracted. Reason itself is instrumental in value: it enables us, unlike other animals, to be guided in our actions by a vast range of motives that involve thoughts about what is not present immediately in intuition. Parts of Schopenhauer's discussion of reason and concepts are somewhat textbook-like in character, as he explains the way concepts combine into judgements, and the way judgements build up into syllogistic reasoning. He also puts forward an account of the manner in which the connotations of different concepts overlap and how this can be exploited in rhetorical persuasion, and talks about the vicissitudes peculiar to rational beings, such as foolishness, stupidity, pedantry and laughter.

The distinction made in § 12 between two kinds of cognition (*Erkenntniß*) has an importance that resonates throughout *The World as Will and Representation*. With concepts and judgements we are capable of *knowledge* (*Wissen*). Animals have immediate cognition of the world of object, but do not *know*. Reason confers on human beings, its sole possessors, many advantages. Because of it they can acquire, communicate and store knowledge, perform logical reasoning, be scientific investigators, found societies and undertake vast communal projects. Unlike animals, they can reflect and act upon past experience, work out likely future consequences and have a wide range of goals. However, this opens human beings to a much greater range of sufferings than animals; at the same time reason confers on humans no special 'dignity', nor does it have any special connection with freedom or morality. Schopenhauer rejects entirely Kant's conception of 'practical reason'.[6] The effective demotion of reason from any foundational role in characterizing human behaviour or explaining what has moral worth, and the consequent levelling that occurs between human beings and all other animals, are notable distinguishing features of Schopenhauer's philosophy. In § 16 Schopenhauer's positive account of the relation of reason to ethics limits it to the calm reflection of the Stoic stage, and the First Book ends, rather surprisingly, with a discussion of the strengths and weaknesses of Stoic ethics, full of characteristically scholarly citations from ancient texts.

SECOND BOOK

In the first of his oscillations between aspects, Schopenhauer now maintains that the account he has given of the world as representation, though true, is seriously inadequate. For by definition it does not tell us what we are in ourselves, nor what anything in the world apart from us is in itself. All this remains a 'riddle'. § 17 opens the Second Book by portraying the enquirer as searching for an 'inner essence' or a 'meaning' to the world. Already in § 18, probably the most important pivotal section in the whole of *The World as Will and Representation*, Schopenhauer proposes to solve the riddle, or decipher the meaning, by claiming that the essence, the very being in itself of all things, is will (*Wille*). The world that appears to us as representation is, in itself, will. Representation gives us the world as it is empirically, diverse, plural, spatio-temporal, lawlike and open to investigation. But we must make sense of the world and ourselves from within, not merely experience its manifestations from a detached standpoint. Will is what that same world and we ourselves are metaphysically – one and the same essence underlying all the many empirical appearances. This is the central message of the Second Book of *The World as Will and Representation*, and of Schopenhauer's philosophy as a whole.

In § 18 Schopenhauer begins by arguing from our immediate cognition of our own actions. Schopenhauer suggests that whenever we are conscious of ourselves, we are immediately conscious of ourselves as willing something. This is a unique inner consciousness, distinct in character from our 'outer' awareness of the world in representation, and it gives us the vital clue to our own essence: it is that we strive towards ends. The intrinsic core of our being is will. Schopenhauer makes a close connection between this and our essential embodiment. When we will, the action of our body in pursuit of

---

[6] This is best seen from the Appendix: Critique of the Kantian Philosophy (see 552); and from ch. 2 of *BM*.

an end is not the separate effect of an 'act of will': rather the body's action is the act of will become manifest in the objective realm of space and time. Even the body as such, whose function is to strive for ends, must be regarded as will become concrete, will become object, as Schopenhauer says in § 20. Thus the will that is our essence manifests itself in our body and its many functions, including the brain and nervous system, with the result that the self-conscious subject of cognition around which Kantian epistemology (and Schopenhauer's own First Book) is structured is to be explained as the result of physiology, but that physiology is ultimately explicable in metaphysical terms as the manifestation of an underlying striving force in nature. In the continuous discussion of §§ 19–22 Schopenhauer argues for an extension of the term 'will' to cover the essence of everything in the world. In the human case 'will' embraces not only desires, but actions, emotions and affects, and non-conscious or 'blind' physiological processes that can be described as end-directed. Schopenhauer then extends this idea to the whole of nature, claiming that we can make sense of the world as such by seeing its essence as a kind of blind striving manifesting itself in multiple instances within our experience. Thus, again, the one world is both representation and will.

A number of wide-reaching claims are made in § 23. One concerns the principle of individuation, or in the Latin phrase Schopenhauer likes to use, the *principium individuationis*. The issue here is what distinguishes one individual thing from all others, and hence what makes plurality, the existence of many distinct things, possible at all. For Schopenhauer the principle in question is that things are distinguished from one another by their position in space and time. But by the same token if we removed space and time there could be no distinct individuals, no multiplicity. Schopenhauer reasons that if the world as thing in itself must be conceived as existing outside the subjective forms of space and time, then the world as thing in itself must not be split up into separate individuals. This thought becomes of ever greater importance as *The World as Will and Representation* progresses, and the illusoriness of the individual is especially important in the ethics of the Fourth Book. Another central thought introduced in § 23 has to do with freedom. Nothing in the empirical realm of individuals is free, because everything is subject to cause and effect: everything that happens happens necessarily as the consequence of some ground. There are three different species of cause–effect relationship found in nature, in Schopenhauer's view: simple cause and effect, which occurs throughout nature at the level of physical and chemical explanation; stimulus and response, found in plants and animals; and finally motivation, where an effect is brought about by an event that occurs in cognition, a perceptual experience or thought. However, all these species are united in that in each of them the effect follows the cause with necessity, as specified by the principle of sufficient reason. On the other hand, once we reflect that the cause–effect relationship pertains only to the realm of the subject's representation, we can think of the world beyond its aspect as representation, the world in itself, as being free – another thought that Schopenhauer will capitalize on below in the Fourth Book.

In the latter half of the Second Book, in §§ 24–28, Schopenhauer confronts his account of the world as will with the accounts of nature given in the natural sciences. He is not hostile to science, and uses as many scientific findings as he can to support his metaphysical account. But science's picture of nature runs up against a crucial limitation, in his view. Its explanations always end with forces such as gravity or electricity which are capable of no further explanation. He argues that a single, comprehensive metaphysical explanation of all forces is needed. Schopenhauer's view of the natural world falls into the vitalist camp – there is a life force that can never be reduced to any form of mechanistic process – but, for him, the life force is just one manifestation of a universal unconscious end-seeking or striving that is present in all the forces of nature. He introduces the notion that nature is unified because it falls into certain universal kinds or Ideas (on a more or less Platonic model) that express the same essence at different degrees of clarity. Timelessly existing natural forces and natural species form a system of expressions of the will that has internal and external purposiveness (*Zweckmäßigkeit*): the parts of each organism fit together to enable it and its species to function, and the whole of nature exhibits a purposive fit between all the parts of the organic realm and between the organic and inorganic realms.

It is of the greatest importance to note that the will is nothing remotely like a mind or divine being for Schopenhauer: it lacks cognition or consciousness, cannot set itself goals or seek ends that are conceived as good. Nor is the will itself in any sense good. It merely strives away in perpetuity, producing countless transient individuals along the way as a matter of sheer brute fact. As *The World as Will and Representation* progresses the tone becomes more sombre. Willing goes on perpetually and without final purpose: it is built into us and into the whole fabric of the world. The individual's existence is dominated by will: incessant desires and needs shape all our perception and understanding of the world, ends can never finally be fulfilled, suffering is ever-present, but the will drives us on to strive and want more things that can never properly satisfy us even if we attain them.

Throughout nature one being dominates and destroys another, the world-will tearing itself apart, says Schopenhauer, because it is a hungry will and there is nothing for it to feed on but itself. This vision of existence, painted most vividly in § 27, has played a major part in earning Schopenhauer the title of the philosopher of pessimism.

§ 29 ends the Second Book by posing the following fundamental question: 'Every will is the will to something, it has an object, a goal of its willing: now the will that is presented to us as the essence in itself of the world: what does *it* ultimately will, or what does it strive for?' (187). And the answer is: Nothing. The very question is misplaced because the will, though always moving, is never really going anywhere:

In fact the absence of all goals, of all boundaries, belongs to the essence of the will in itself, which is an endless striving . . . [T]he striving of matter can always be merely impeded but never fulfilled or satisfied. But this is just how it is with all the strivings of all the appearances of the will. Every goal that is achieved is once again the beginning of a new course of action, and so on to infinity. The plant raises its appearance from the seed, through the stem and leaf to the flower and fruit, which is again only the beginning of a new seed, of a new individual which will run the whole course once again, and so on through infinite time. It is just the same with the life course of the animal: procreation is its highest point, and after this is attained the life of the first individual fades slowly or quickly away, while a new life repeats the same appearance and guarantees for nature that the species will be continued . . . [E]ternal becoming, endless flux belong to the revelation of the essence of the will. Finally, the same thing can also be seen in human endeavours and desires, which always delude us into believing that their fulfilment is the final goal of willing; but as soon as they are attained they no longer look the same and thus are soon forgotten, grow antiquated and are really, if not admittedly, always laid to the side as vanished delusions; we are lucky enough when there is still something left to desire and strive after, to carry on the game of constantly passing from desire to satisfaction and from this to a new desire, a game whose rapid course is called happiness and slow course is called suffering, so that the game might not come to a end, showing itself to be a fearful, life-destroying boredom, a wearied longing without a definite object, a deadening languor. (188–9)

The claim that 'the world is will' is fruitful and innovative in many ways, particularly for the historically forward-looking picture it allows Schopenhauer to paint of human life and its place within the natural world. But it is also frustrating for the reader. The term 'will' takes on such a wide use that we begin to wonder what sense it has, given that Schopenhauer asks us, on the one hand, to construe all the processes of nature as analogous to what we recognize in ourselves as willing, yet on the other hand rightly insists that it would be foolish to think of the rest of nature as acting on

conscious motives in the way human beings do. Another much-discussed
problem concerns the possibility of our having any cognition of the thing
in itself. If it is beyond our cognition, how could we succeed in knowing
anything about it? This question is not really addressed in Volume 1 of
The World as Will and Representation, but Schopenhauer turns to it in
chapter 18 of Volume 2, where he makes an important qualification: we
cannot know the world *absolutely* in itself, beyond all the forms of our
cognition, but we can make a generalization about the essence common to
all the phenomena we meet with in representation. Commentators have
suggested that, despite the terminology of 'gaining cognition of the thing
in itself', Schopenhauer might best be viewed, not as attempting to delve
into a realm of existence entirely beyond the empirical, but as offering a
figurative description of the empirical realm which allows us to make sense
of it and our own existence within it – though, as he reminds us from time
to time, that intended sense or meaning will not be fully available to us
until we reach the end of the book as a whole.

THIRD BOOK

The central notion of the Third Book of *The World as Will and Representation* is that of a transformed consciousness that removes us from the
everyday concerns of the will. Here the Platonic ancestry of Schopenhauer's
thought comes most clearly to the fore. In the alleged transformed consciousness we perceive a timeless Idea, one of the degrees in which the
will manifests itself throughout nature. To avoid confusion with Kantian
or Hegelian uses (or, as he thinks, misuses) of the word 'Idea' Schopenhauer typically adds a parenthesis and talks of '(Platonic) Ideas'. We can
think of the Ideas as universals that permeate nature and are accessible to
human cognition through the out-of-the-ordinary experience of will-less
consciousness. Schopenhauer's key thought is that in moments of intense
contemplation we lose our normal sense of self as an individual striving
after ends and employing cognition as a means to attain them, and instead
we 'mirror' the world passively, thereby coming to see the universal in the
particular object of intuitive perception (rather than attaining knowledge
of it through concepts or abstract reasoning). This kind of experience has a
higher cognitive value than that of ordinary everyday consciousness, which
is taken up with particular objects and their spatial, temporal and causal
inter-connections. Indeed, will-less consciousness is a more objective kind
of cognition than that of science, which only makes inferences about the
universal forces of nature, and does not intuit them directly. While this

elevated contemplative consciousness lasts, our will is in abeyance. We do not seek to understand the object we perceive in relation to what it can do for us, whether we desire or need it, what associations it has with other objects or with our emotions:

> we stop considering the Where, When, Why and Wherefore of things but simply and exclusively consider the *What*... we devote the entire power of our mind to intuition and immerse ourselves in this entirely, letting the whole of consciousness be filled with peaceful contemplation of the natural object that is directly present, a landscape, a tree, a cliff, a building, or whatever it might be, and, according to a suggestive figure of speech, we *lose* ourselves in this object completely, i.e. we forget our individuality, our will, and continue to exist only as pure subject, the clear mirror of the object, so that it is as if the object existed on its own, without anyone to perceive it, and we can no longer separate the intuited from the intuition as the two have become one, and the whole of consciousness is completely filled and engrossed by a single intuitive image. (201)

In such a state nothing troubles us, because no felt lack or need moves us at all. We are free of the will for some blissful moments, attaining a peace without which, Schopenhauer tells us, true well-being would be impossible.

The opening sections of the Third Book (§§ 30–32) provide a somewhat uneasy discussion of Ideas, which were introduced in the Second Book, but whose relationship to the will was left in some obscurity. Schopenhauer now links Ideas with the Kantian thing in itself. He says that the two 'are certainly not identical, but are nonetheless very closely related' (193), and then (quite implausibly) that Plato and Kant are 'compelled and inspired by the same world-view to do philosophy' and that 'both doctrines clearly mean exactly the same thing and have exactly the same ultimate goal' (196, 197). The positive use that Schopenhauer makes of this alleged trans-historical unanimity is as follows: the Ideas are to be construed as that form of cognitive representation that takes us *nearest* to the thing in itself. They are 'the most *adequate objecthood* of the will or thing in itself... the whole thing in itself, but in the form of representation' (198). When we are seeing the world most selflessly, in the out-of-the-ordinary kind of contemplation, we still cannot have cognition of the world purely in itself, but we are experiencing it in the most objective way.

After these preliminaries Schopenhauer embarks on an account of aesthetic contemplation. §§ 33–34 prepare for a stark contrast between aesthetic contemplation and 'viewing things in the ordinary way', where cognition is thoroughly imbued with the needs and perspectives of the will. In the transition from the ordinary cognitive state to that of will-less contemplation, both subject and object are transformed. The object is now not the individual thing, but a timeless Idea apprehended in the process of perceiving the individual thing. The subject also ceases to be the human individual or person, and becomes 'pure subject, the clear mirror of the object'. A will-less, disinterested consciousness is one in which, for a time, we are able to forget the self from consciousness altogether. After some evocative portrayals of the difference between timeless Ideas and their ever-changing, inessential appearances (§ 35), Schopenhauer reaches the core of his argument in this Book, the claim that Ideas come to be cognized uniquely in *art* (§ 36). The true artist is a genius, for Schopenhauer: someone who has to an abnormal degree the ability to remain in the state of will-less objectivity, to experience the world with an intensity of perception that enables him to transmit his knowledge of universals to the rest of humanity. Ideas are quite different from concepts (a contrast that Schopenhauer picks up later in § 49). Concepts are human abstractions from the experience of individual things through the senses. Ideas are features of reality discovered purely in immediate intuition, and are not (*contra* Plato) accessible to discursive, judgemental thought or reasoning. Hence, for Schopenhauer, genius proper is not found in science or mathematics, nor can one become an artistic genius by learning rules or precepts. Schopenhauer gives a generic character-portrait of the genius, and then (§ 36) moves sideways to an interesting account of madness, which he conceives as closely akin: 'Great wits to madness sure are near allied', as Dryden said.[7] On the other hand, he argues, the capacity for will-less, objective consciousness must be in all of us to some extent, since otherwise the artist would not be able to communicate the vision of the Ideas and enable us to see nature through his eyes (§ 37).

One of the most frequently cited passages in *The World as Will and Representation* occurs in § 38 where Schopenhauer brings to a climax the contrast between aesthetic contemplation and the ordinary way of viewing things, and evokes the peculiar worth of the out-of-the-ordinary experience for the human subject:

as long as our consciousness is filled by our will, as long as we are given over to the pressure of desires with their constant hopes and fears, as long as we are the subject of willing, we will never have lasting happiness or peace. Whether we hunt or we flee, whether we fear harm or chase pleasure, it is fundamentally all the same: concern for the constant demands of the will, whatever form they

---

[7] Though Schopenhauer misremembers this as from Byron. One should always be on the look-out for misquotation, misattribution and loose paraphrase in Schopenhauer's references.

take, continuously fills consciousness and keeps it in motion: but without peace, there can be no true well-being. So the subject of willing remains on the revolving wheel of Ixion, keeps drawing water from the sieve of the Danaids, is the eternally yearning Tantalus.

But when some occasion from the outside or a disposition from within suddenly lifts us out of the endless stream of willing, tearing cognition from its slavery to the will, our attention is no longer directed to the motives of willing but instead grasps things freed from their relation to the will, and hence considers them without interests, without subjectivity, purely objectively; we are given over to the things entirely, to the extent that they are mere representations, not to the extent that they are motives: then suddenly the peace that we always sought on the first path of willing but that always eluded us comes of its own accord, and all is well with us. It is the painless state that Epicurus prized as the highest good and the state of the gods: for that moment we are freed from the terrible pressure of the will, we celebrate the Sabbath of the penal servitude of willing, the wheel of Ixion stands still. (220)

In §§ 38–41 Schopenhauer makes the distinction (not unusual for his time of writing) between two kinds of aesthetic experience, the beautiful and the sublime. In a way everything in the world is beautiful, in that everything is the expression of some Idea, and everything can be contemplated purely objectively by a will-less consciousness. However, we tend to call beautiful especially those objects that best facilitate such contemplation and that express 'higher' Ideas such as those of humanity as such or of a particular human character, rather than those that express more primitive Ideas such as the force of gravity or a species of plant. The experience of something as sublime is, like the experience of it as beautiful, a case of gaining cognition of Ideas in a state of consciousness that is free of the will – and yet it requires in addition an awareness that the object contemplated is 'hostile to the will in general'. Clear examples would be the view of an inhospitable terrain such as a desert, or a violent storm – though Schopenhauer considers sublimity to be a matter of degree and gives more subtle examples too. Such cases require us to struggle mentally against our natural antagonism to the object and experience an elevation (*Erhebung*[8]) above it. By contrast, a most anti-aesthetic feeling occurs when an object is directly 'stimulating' (*reizend*) to our will. Under this heading Schopenhauer complains about painted depictions of food that appeal to our appetite and overtly desirable nudes (§ 40).

The latter half of the Third Book (§§ 42–52) is a long, detailed and often insightful account of the various art forms and genres: architecture

---

[8] Linked to *das Erhabene*, the German word for 'sublime' in this context.

and fountainry (§ 43); landscape gardening, landscape and animal painting (§ 44); historical painting and sculpture, the portrayal of human beauty and the nude (§§ 45–48); the literary arts, poetry, tragedy, and the aesthetic distinction between conceptual and intuitive cognition (§§ 49–51); and finally, in a class of its own, music (§ 52). In an evocative account that betrays a great personal intimacy with music (as much of the foregoing discussion does with the various other art forms, it must be said) Schopenhauer claims that music is a direct copy of the will itself. The world expresses the will directly, and so does music, without the need for mediation through any determinate Ideas. He has two principal thoughts here. One is that the course of a musical melody or harmonic progression is like the action of a willing being: it sets out in a direction, as it were, and strives through time from moment to moment to attain its goal. Its striving and its goal, like those of the will itself, have no determinate content, but long, slow pieces with delayed resolution directly mirror the state of a being whose will remains unfulfilled, and fast pieces with easy transitions between notes are expressive of the form taken by happiness. Schopenhauer's other thought is that the blend and interdependence of the voices in music (especially in classical Western harmony) is expressive of the fit between all the different levels at which the will manifests itself throughout nature, from elemental physical forces to the individuality of human character. Musicians have often admired Schopenhauer's theory and philosophers of music still discuss it, though it is perhaps unclear how much can be made of it beyond its undoubted metaphorical power.

With the exception of the case of music, Schopenhauer asserts that whenever we enter the aesthetic state of will-less, timeless consciousness we encounter universal Ideas, and that whenever we are in contact with universal Ideas we are in a state of will-less consciousness. However, when he comes to reflect on the many specific art forms, he admits that in some cases their value has more to do with will-less tranquillity and less to do with cognition of any very important universals, and at the other end of the spectrum more to do with the latter and less with tranquillity. A challenging case at this end of the spectrum is tragedy, whose portrayal of the frightening universal nature of humanity has its value in making us shudder before the truth of what is, or could well be, our own life. It is at least not obvious how the value of tragedy will also be found in the bliss of will-less, painless contemplation – but Schopenhauer's account is a significant intervention in the philosophical discussion of tragedy that has run from Plato and Aristotle until the present day.

Art, then, has for Schopenhauer a supreme value amid an otherwise troubled existence. Yet art does not provide an ultimate solution to the human predicament. Even the artist must return to the life of willing and suffering and is not permanently inured to it:

That pure, true, and profound cognition of the essence of the world . . . redeems him from life, not forever but rather only momentarily, and yet it is not his way out of life, but only an occasional source of comfort within it, until this intensifies his powers to the point where he finally grows tired of the game and seizes upon serious things. We can think of Raphael's St. Cecilia as a symbol of this transition. (295)

Thus at the end of the Third Book Schopenhauer sets the stage for the final monumental act of his four-part drama, whose ultimate transition points to a state of resignation in which the will is quietened altogether.

FOURTH BOOK

In § 53 Schopenhauer opens his Fourth Book with a general statement about ethics, which he sees as descriptive rather than prescriptive – we are not to expect from him any moral precepts or doctrines of duty. In general 'Virtue is as little taught as genius' (298), being a matter of the dispositions in one's character rather than the rational possession of rules. The overarching theme of the Fourth Book is ethical in the broadest sense: it is an attempt to say what is of value in human life – but given the explanation so far of the nature of the world as a blind will, little comfort is going to be available. The life of any human individual, as part of this world of will, is an inexorable striving that must remain unfulfilled while it briefly succeeds in postponing the inevitable end that awaits its transient existence. What attitudes can we have to this life, and to this will to life (*Wille zum Leben*) that constitutes our essence? What is it to 'affirm' the will, and what to 'negate' it? And which is the preferable condition?

In outline Schopenhauer's answer is as follows. Although we exist as empirical individuals separate from one another and so naturally regard the good as consisting in what we can attain through the activity of our own individual wills, from a metaphysical standpoint this is a mistaken view. When fully understood, the life of a human individual does not and cannot contain anything of true value. Worse, the existence of everything – as a manifestation of the pointlessly self-perpetuating and self-devouring will – is something ultimately to be lamented. To exist as a willing being is to strive without fulfilment, and hence to suffer. Because will is our essence, suffering is essential to all life – and consequently we are in need of 'salvation' or 'redemption', which can be achieved only by the will within us 'turning' and 'negating itself'. Schopenhauer argues that the notion of a 'highest good' makes no sense, but that if we wish to bring that expression back from retirement and apply it to anything, then it must be to the negation of the will:[9] cessation of desires and wants that relate to the individual we find ourselves as, loss of identification with this individual, elimination of one's personality or one's natural self with its in-built attachment to the ends of living and willing, and contemplation of the whole world, with all its strivings and pains, from a standpoint of emotional detachment. Calling on mystical pronouncements from diverse cultural traditions, Schopenhauer argues that only such a radical transformation, occasioned by a deep and rare knowledge of the ubiquity of suffering and the illusoriness of the individual, can restore any value to our existence.

The structure of the Fourth Book is initially hard to follow. It has very long sections that are especially rich in content, and is punctuated by deliberate postponements of the main argument. It is a matter for some debate whether the disjointedness is more than just presentational: we have the overarching vision of the worthlessness of human existence and the redemptive power of self-abolition, but how does this relate to what we might call Schopenhauer's more 'ordinary' ethical views concerning motivation, responsibility and the moral worth of compassionate, non-egoistic actions, all of which he interpolates into the discussion? § 55 announces a first postponement of the question about affirmation and negation, to discuss the issue of free will. The essentials of Schopenhauer's views on this topic are as follows.[10] No individual human actions are free. They are events in the world of appearance, and subject to the principle of sufficient reason. Motives occur and, given the character of the individual human being to whom they occur, the resulting actions are a necessary consequence. Human actions are indeed vastly different in character from all other instances of willing, by virtue of their potential to be rationally motivated. But this is not sufficient for free will, in Schopenhauer's view:

We see that a human being has the advantage over animals of possessing an *ability to choose* by virtue of abstract or rational cognition. But this only makes him a battleground for conflicting motives, and does not remove him from their control;

---

[9] See 389.

[10] The self-contained *Prize Essay on the Freedom of the Will* that Schopenhauer published in 1841 (as one of *The Two Fundamental Problems of Ethics*) is his best treatment of the question of free will, and when he came to revise *The World as Will and Representation* in 1844, he chose to refer the reader to that essay rather than attempt any major recasting (see 316).

thus, while this ability indeed conditions the possibility of the complete expression of the individual character, it can by no means be seen as a freedom of individual willing. That is, it does not signify any independence from the law of causality, whose necessity extends to human beings just as it does to every other appearance. (327)

It seems to us subjectively that we are free because we can reflect and are aware that no motive absolutely necessitates any action; however, each individual's character is fixed, and the combination of a present motive and the fixed disposition of our character necessitates what we will. Our character is empirical: we learn about it, in our own case as in that of others, only as it unfolds over time. But the empirical character is just the temporal reflection of our 'intelligible', non-empirical character that remains timelessly the same.

Schopenhauer takes the contrast of empirical and intelligible characters from Kant, and comments later that 'This is really the point where Kant's philosophy leads to my own, or where mine grows from the stem of Kant's'[11] – although the metaphor is apt only if we think of grafting on a plant of a different species, not least because Kant thinks of the intelligible aspect of the human character as purely rational and as antithetical to what the human being is by nature, both points on which Schopenhauer fundamentally disagrees. An important message from the discussion of free will in *The World as Will and Representation* is slipped in right at the beginning of § 55: it is that *the will as thing in itself is free*. Existing beyond the realm of representation, the will as thing in itself is not constrained by any of the forms of necessity that attach to the principle of sufficient reason. And if, as Schopenhauer insists, we define freedom negatively as the absence of necessity, then the will as thing in itself is free. Why one would want to say this in unclear, if one is focused in the usual way on the question whether my individual willing is free. But while he resolutely denies the latter kind of freedom, Schopenhauer here lights the long-burning fuse that leads to his final solution of the will's freely negating itself.

In § 56 Schopenhauer reminds us again that the theme is affirmation and negation of the will, but immediately side-steps once more, this time to examine the nature of willing and its satisfaction, in an important discussion that proceeds through §§ 57–59. Willing always occurs because something is felt as *lacking*: it is as such a form of *suffering*. But then attaining an

---

[11] See 531 in 'Appendix: Critique of the Kantian Philosophy'.

end through willing – what we call happiness – brings us nothing of positive value, because it just temporarily erases a painful lack or absence. New desires flood in almost immediately to plague us with their non-satisfaction. And if no new desires arrive we are tormented by boredom. We never reach a lasting satisfaction: there is no such thing in the life of a willing being. So human life is bound to be a strenuous, but ultimately empty game, 'dispositionally incapable of true happiness . . . essentially a multifaceted suffering and a thoroughly disastrous condition' (349). Schopenhauer claims to have shown this *a priori*: it applies constitutively to the very condition of living as an individual whose essence is willing, and is not the result of induction from empirical investigations of the world. Nonetheless, a tour through the specifics of human reality would lead one to the same conclusion:

if you led the most unrepentant optimist through the hospitals, military wards, and surgical theatres, through the prisons, torture chambers and slave stalls, through battlefields and places of judgment, and then open for him all the dark dwellings of misery that hide from cold curiosity, and finally let him peer into Ugolino's starvation chamber, then he too would surely come to see the nature of this best of all possible worlds. (351)

In § 60 the theme of affirmation and negation is addressed more squarely. It is natural for us to affirm the will to life, the bodily drive at the core of living things, all of which strive quite unreflectively to be alive and to produce more life beyond themselves. The drive to sexual activity in animals, including humans, is the most fundamental expression of the affirmation of the will to life (which is one reason why it is wrong to think of it merely as a will 'to live') and the genitals are the parts of the body in which will manifests itself in most concentrated form, almost free of any admixture of intellect. The sex drive, for Schopenhauer, is 'the ultimate purpose, the highest goal of life in the natural human being, as it is in the animal' (356). In affirming its will to life each living thing also naturally seeks its own well-being. This is what Schopenhauer calls *egoism*, and the discussion of it in § 61 leads him into his main treatment of justice, law and morality in *The World as Will and Representation*. Again there is a clearer and more concentrated account of these topics in Schopenhauer's essay *On the Basis of Morals*, though the essentials of both discussions are the same. Each individual regards him- or herself as the centre of the world, and in Schopenhauer's memorable image:

Just as a captain sits in a boat, trusting the weak little vessel as the raging, boundless sea raises up and casts down howling cliffs of waves; so the human individual sits calmly in a world full of sorrow, supported by and trusting in the *principium individuationis*, which is how the individual cognizes things as appearance. The boundless world, everywhere full of suffering, with its infinite past and infinite future, is alien to him – in fact, it is a fairy tale: his vanishing little person, his unextended present, his momentary comfort, these alone have reality for him. (379)

So we each strive primarily on our own behalf, and the affirmation of the will by one individual inevitably impinges harmfully on the sphere of expression of others' wills. An action that imposes on the will of other individuals in this way is *wrong*, and the institutions of law, justice and punishment exist to deter individuals from such wrongful affirmation of their wills. Right, meanwhile, is simply the negative correlate of this. In § 62 we hear about conscience, an inner pain felt by a perpetrator of wrong, which, according to Schopenhauer, reveals an awareness of the perpetrator's underlying identity with the wronged party.

After a discussion in § 63 of eternal justice – the notion that there is an equilibrium in the world between the amount of suffering inflicted and the amount endured, and that it is all deserved ('if human beings were not on the whole worthless, then their fate would not be on the whole so sad' (378)) – Schopenhauer turns in §§ 64–67 to his account of morality proper. Morality concerns affirmation and non-affirmation of the will in a particular sense. No egoistic action can have genuine moral worth, and still less an action out of malice, in which the exercise of one's own will is expressly aimed at negating the well-being of another, even with no gain to oneself. Moral worth is attained only when someone 'makes less of a distinction than is usually made between himself and others' (399). The resulting morally good actions, which meet with approbation from third parties and a particular kind of inner self-satisfaction, are of two kinds: they can arise either from a disposition to voluntary justice or from pure, unselfish love, or loving kindness (*Menschenliebe*), which Schopen-hauer equates with compassion (*Mitleid*).[12] The virtue of voluntary justice resides in an in-built sense of the capacity for suffering in other individuals that leads one to refrain from harming them or prevent their coming to harm. In the case of loving kindness, actual cognition of the suffering of others motivates one to alleviate it, often at the expense of suffering of one's own. The most extreme form of this, which has a paradigmatic status for Schopenhauer, is self-sacrifice for the good of others. Schopenhauer's explanation of these genuinely moral incentives is that they rest on being

---

[12] In *BM* (ch. III) Schopenhauer treats both voluntary justice and loving kindness as manifestations of *Mitleid*.

able to 'see through' the principle of individuation or the veil of *māyā* (illusion) that features in Indian thought. The morally good person glimpses in a direct and untutored way the unity of all expressions of the will, does not consider him- or herself as something apart from the whole, and hence sets everyone's suffering on a par or even attributes more significance to that of others than to his or her own.

In § 68 Schopenhauer finally arrives at the culmination of his argument and states 'I will now show how from the same source that gives rise to all goodness, love, virtue, and nobility there ultimately emerges also what I call the negation of the will to life' (405). This discussion then occupies him through to the end of the Fourth Book. This extreme conclusion to the book advocates a kind of extinction of the natural self, and although the technical details of this process are anything but clear, the intensity of Schopenhauer's conviction shines through his powerful prose in a manner that is both impressive and disquieting. The tone is close to being religious here, and the vocabulary is that of saintliness, conversion, redemption and grace. In Schopenhauer's view Christianity, Hinduism and Buddhism all contain elements of the same wisdom, provided one sets aside entirely all their accumulated clutter of deities, dogmas and fanciful metaphysics. There is no God, no creator; there are no divine entities, spirits or immortal souls, no intelligent plan, purpose or perfection to this world. But there is the possibility for human beings, albeit not for all, of an internal transformation which Schopenhauer calls the will's self-negation (*Selbstverneinung*) or self-abolition (*Selbstaufhebung*). The idea is that something stops the individual from willing on his or her own behalf at all. Experience of the world no longer motivates him or her to action in pursuit of goals or flight from harm. He or she attains an elevated state of passivity in which the world is seen as if from nowhere within it and his or her individual character, or 'person', is extinguished. This is, we are told, a blissful emptiness – no striving, no suffering – which may seem from the standpoint of our unaltered consciousness to be a dreadful state of 'nothing'. But Schopenhauer imagines that once one has made the transition our whole world of representation must also dwindle in significance, and indeed be seen as nothing.

Numerous questions can be raised about this account. One is this: if extinction of my 'person' is so blissful an occurrence, ought I not to commit suicide? Schopenhauer addresses this pressing issue in § 69. His answer is a resolute No: suicide is an error which solves nothing. The person who commits suicide because he has suffered greatly and sees no fulfilment in this world for his strivings, is deluded: he still regards fulfilment of his individual strivings as something in principle attainable and valuable. Greatly superior to this is continuing to exist with an attitude of resignation in the face of all suffering.

How, though, does the state of selfless redemption relate to moral goodness? In a letter to one of his most philosophically astute correspondents, Johann August Becker,[13] Schopenhauer explains that the value moral actions have for the one who performs them is a 'transcendental' one; such actions lead him on 'the sole path of salvation, i.e. deliverance from this world of being born, suffering and dying'.[14] The person who is so morally good that the distinction between him- or herself and others begins to fall away, feels all the suffering throughout the world as if it were his or her own. This leads to resignation, tranquillizing of the will, or its recoil away from life. One grasps the utter lack of value in living and willing as an individual at all. Only by undergoing such an extreme redemptive transformation in consciousness can the individual's existence attain genuine worth; and morality has value, ultimately, not in its own right, but because it is a step towards this self-denial of the will. When I feel compassion, rather than simply exercising my individual will and sensing there is something awry with so doing, I am alive to the will of others as having an import equal to mine or indeed greater than it. But this feeling ultimately has value only because it takes me a step nearer to an abandonment of my individuality, which Schopenhauer can express by saying that 'the will' which freely manifested itself as me, freely annuls itself in me.

It remains unclear how satisfactory this position is. Compassionate moral goodness and extreme will-lessness both involve a shift away from egoism, the natural affirmation of the will of the individual. Both involve removing the sense of uniqueness and security that the typical unenlightened human being invests in 'his vanishing little person, his unextended present, his momentary comfort'. But morality, as Schopenhauer conceives it, surely involves willing, often vehemently willing and acting on behalf of others. Choosing to sacrifice oneself in battle to save other lives is a passionate and personal act, not a lapse into impersonal will-less detachment. And, on the other side of the coin, why (or how) would the suffering of any living thing matter to the will-less subject whose individual personality and capacity to be motivated have been extinguished? Morality would seem to belong to what has been left behind by someone in the ultimate state of 'salvation'.

---

[13] See *GB*, 220, letter to Johann August Becker, 10 December 1944.
[14] He refers to *WWR* 1, § 68 (Hübscher *SW* 2, 448) and *WWR* 2, ch. 48 (Hübscher *SW* 3, 696).

There are further questions concerning the way in which such a state is supposed to come about. Schopenhauer says that someone who reaches the ultimate pitch of selfless love and benevolence, a saint or 'great soul', does so by attaining a kind of knowledge or cognition: he or she 'recognizes the whole, comprehends its essence, and finds that it is constantly passing away, caught up in vain strivings, inner conflict, and perpetual suffering' (405–6). This is a unique kind of insight in which one comes to see, not through argument or conceptual thinking, but intuitively, that all beings suffer and all beings are but deceptive manifestations of the same essence. This cognition, Schopenhauer says many times, acts as a *Quietiv*, a sedative or tranquillizer, of the will inside oneself. One recoils from all the goals and pleasures or the world, turns towards asceticism, and attains an inner peace and joy. It is exceptional to reach this insight through one's sheer degree of selfless saintliness. Another more frequent, secondary route (itself not exactly common, it must be said) is to gain the same cognitive enlightenment through experiencing suffering itself. The sheer brutality of one's particular life can 'purify' one's vision and lead to the same recoil of the will.

But does Schopenhauer think that such exceptional individuals will to become will-less? On the one hand Schopenhauer states that it is not an act of the individual's will that brings about the state of resigned will-lessness; rather

that negation of the will, that entrance into freedom cannot be forced by any intention or resolution, but rather emerges from the innermost relation of cognition to willing in human beings, and thus arrives suddenly, as if flying in from outside. That is precisely why the church calls it the *effect of divine grace*; but just as the church thinks that this is still dependent on the acceptance of grace, the effect of the tranquillizer is also ultimately an act of the freedom of the will. (432)

It is not the will of the particular human individual, caught up in space and time, that freely acquiesces in the insight into the world's suffering. Rather it is the will in itself, whose freedom Schopenhauer asserted earlier on. On Schopenhauer's account of cause and effect it is hard to see how cognition can literally be having an effect on the will, while at the same time the will is acting freely. But part of what he has in mind seems to be that the extraordinary form of cognition now fails outright to motivate the subject to act, and instead presents the world as an arena for pure contemplation. On the other hand, he talks of deliberately seeking out ascetic practices to assist in the will's self-abolition, and is sure that will-lessness is a difficult and unstable condition that one must struggle hard to maintain. So an absolutely clean break between willing and will-lessness seems in the end not to be achievable for human beings. Neither of the two aspects of the self that compete throughout *The World as Will and Representation* – self as embodied, will-driven individual, and self as pure, pain-free subject – yields entirely to the other, and we never escape the threat of some kind of inner turmoil.

THE CRITIQUE OF THE KANTIAN PHILOSOPHY

The Appendix to *The World as Will and Representation* that has this title amounts in size to a substantial fifth Book. It is a detailed critical reading of Kant, concentrating almost exclusively on Kant's theoretical philosophy, and following the structure of the *Critique of Pure Reason* in particular quite closely. Schopenhauer is complimentary about the greatness of Kant's achievements in the history of philosophy: he made the crucial distinction between appearance and thing in itself and realized that there could be *a priori* conditions of possibility attaching to the former; he placed ethics on the other, 'in-itself' side of the divide, and demolished the speculative (Christian) metaphysics that is associated primarily with mediaeval scholasticism, but persisted well into Kant's day, especially in the philosophical school initiated by Leibniz and Christian Wolff. The Transcendental Aesthetic section of the *Critique of Pure Reason* which treats of space and time as *a priori* forms of experience is, for Schopenhauer, brilliant and incontrovertible. Kant's proposed solution of the problem of free will set out in his Third Antinomy, where the distinction is made between empirical and intelligible characters, is also admirable. But Schopenhauer finds much to criticize, in general and in detail. In general, Kant's prose style and his obsession with architectonic patterns of threes and fours – particularly prominent in his doctrine of categories which repeatedly leads him to force his subject-matter under the headings of quantity, quality, relation and modality – make his writing obscure and artificial and show that he was not thinking clearly. Many readers of Kant have made such criticisms, but Schopenhauer's detailed and acerbic comments on this score are still fresh and a cut above most.

In terms of the content of Kant's position Schopenhauer must, given his own system, challenge Kant's negative attitude towards metaphysical enquiry. Metaphysics must not be a pseudo-science that attempts to leave behind all the teachings of experience, as Kant had said. It must be allowed to embrace empirical findings about the world, but also to attain genuine knowledge of a real essence underlying the empirical aspect of things. The presentation of some of Schopenhauer's other criticisms is complicated by the fact that when he first published *The World as Will and Representation* he had read only the second (1787) edition of Kant's *Critique of Pure Reason*, whereas by 1844 he had acquired and studied a copy of the then rare first edition of 1781, and had come to think that Kant's revisions only muddied the waters and exacerbated some systemic faults.[15] One such fault is Kant's alleged failure to distinguish between intuitive and conceptual cognition. Another is what Schopenhauer sees as a lack of clarity, or loss of nerve, in the way Kant presents his idealism.

Concerning intuition and concept the problem, as Schopenhauer sees it, is roughly as follows. Kant distinguishes intuition (*Anschauung*) and concept (*Begriff*) and holds that the combination of both is required for cognition. Concepts are general representations under which the mind may subsume many particulars given through the senses in intuition. Schopenhauer's first objection is: if we are already 'given' a particular object through intuition, why do we also need concepts for cognition of objects? His second objection is that Kant gives concepts the role of forming judgements – propositional thoughts that assert that things are thus and so in the world – but it is surely not the case that such thoughts play a role in all perception of objects. Much that we do, in Schopenhauer's view – such as striking a billiard ball adeptly, or applying a razor at the right angle for shaving (81) – involves an immediate perception of objects in the world of a kind in which conceptual judgement does not intervene. The mind does not just receive data passively: it imposes form upon what the senses receive, that form consisting of space, time and the cause–effect relation. But even the last of these, for Schopenhauer, is not essentially a matter of conceptual judgement, and he faults Kant for saying that it is, or perhaps implying so in an unclear way.

The issue of idealism is related. Our cognition reaches as far as appearances, which are a species of our representations, and we can have no cognition of things in themselves. So is Kant's not a straightforwardly idealist position? Kant wishes – especially in the second edition of the *Critique* – to

---

[15] The two editions of Kant's *Critique of Pure Reason* are now commonly known as A and B. In fact Schopenhauer's version of B was the fifth edition, which preserved all the changes Kant had made between the 1871 and 1878 editions. Schopenhauer made a detailed study of the differences between the two editions, and came to the view that Kant's later revisions had destroyed his superior presentation in A. He wrote to Johann Carl Friedrich Rosenkranz who was preparing a complete edition of Kant's works, and Rosenkranz was persuaded to print edition A as the main text of the *Critique*, with all the changes in B added as Supplements at the back of the volume (see below, 462). When Schopenhauer came to publish *his* second edition, he rewrote much of his Appendix to take account of Kant's edition A. All the relevant changes are listed in the endnotes to this volume.

combat that interpretation, but in Schopenhauer's eyes he struggles in vain against it, thereby spoiling the decisive idealism to be found in the first edition. Much hangs on the notion of an *object*. If the objects of our cognition are not things in themselves, they must be representations. But it is as if Kant cannot rest content with this, as if there must be a third thing between representation and thing in itself, an 'object in itself' (Schopenhauer's term) whose status must, however, remain shadowy and dubious. Schopenhauer penetrates here to some of the most complex and contentious issues in the interpretation of Kant. Some answers are needed to his objections, and even if there are answers more favourable to Kant (as other interpreters will no doubt suggest), those answers themselves are likely to be complex and subtle.

Schopenhauer's lengthy discussion moves through all the major sections of Kant's *Critique*. Another notable point of hostility is Kant's claim (in the Transcendental Dialectic) that there are certain 'ideas' built into reason itself – those of God, freedom and an immortal soul – because of a 'principle of reason' (*Vernunftprincip*) that something 'unconditioned' must always be sought by the rational mind as such. Schopenhauer regards any such principle as bogus, and comments that Kant here reverts to a version of the old Christian scholasticism, since these supposedly necessary ideas are in reality quite parochial and peculiar to one religious and philosophical tradition.

Schopenhauer then turns to the ethical side of Kant's philosophy, about which he is, if anything, even more dismissive – though here again the essay *On the Basis of Morals* provides a sharper and more thorough set of objections. (Chapter 2 of that essay in effect serves as the continuation of the Appendix.) Kant's whole approach to ethics is wrong, he insists: Kant invents a notion of 'practical reason' which is unfounded, and wrongly believes that reason and morality have something special to do with one another. A rationally motivated action is no more free than one motivated by fear, thirst or lust – it is just determined by a more complicated cause. And a rationally motivated action is not guaranteed to be any more morally good than one otherwise caused, nor is a habitually rational human being one of morally better character, nor a morally admirable human being especially rational. Schopenhauer suggests, for example, that Jesus of Nazareth, who is taken as a paradigm of a moral life, is not seen as having led a pre-eminently *rational* life. And many an evil tyrant has been assisted in attaining his ends by superior powers of reason. Kant's idea of an 'unconditional ought' is for Schopenhauer not just a big mistake, but a contradiction in terms. Aside from the fact that Schopenhauer himself considers ethics incapable of being prescriptive, and hence doubts whether it can legitimately speak about duties or oughts at all, he (in common with some other critics) finds the categorical imperative vacuous because of its pure formality, and is horrified at Kant's thought that

if a deed is to be truly good and deserving, it must be performed solely out of respect for recognized law and the concept of duty, and according to a maxim that reason is conscious of in the abstract, not from any inclination, not from any feeling of goodwill towards others, not from any tender-hearted compassion, sympathy or feelings from the heart . . . Rather, the deed must be done reluctantly and with self-restraint. (556–7)

He also argues that Kant's imperative is ultimately egoistic in nature, since Kant asks us to consider the consequences – for ourselves – of willing that a maxim (that of telling lies, in the well-known example) should become a universal law.

As for Kant's later publications, the *Critique of the Power of Judgement* (1790) and the *Doctrine of Right* and *Doctrine of Virtue* (1797: together comprising *The Metaphysics of Morals*), Schopenhauer tends to dismiss them rather summarily as products of rambling old age. This is especially surprising in the case of the *Critique of the Power of Judgement*, whose themes of aesthetics and teleology are both of such high importance for Schopenhauer.

SCHOPENHAUER'S WORKS AFTER 1818

In the first edition of *The World as Will and Representation* the only works of his own Schopenhauer had to refer to were *On the Fourfold Root* (the 'introductory essay') and *On Vision and Colours*. However, between the first edition and the two-volume re-release of 1844 he had produced two medium-length studies of note: *On the Will in Nature* (1836) and *The Two Fundamental Problems of Ethics* (1841), this latter volume comprising the two originally separate essays, *On the Freedom of the Will* and *On the Basis of Morals*. These works leave Schopenhauer's central position unchanged, but extend it in different directions. *On the Will in Nature* seeks confirmation of the theory of the will in scientific findings. The essays on ethics, as we have said, give self-contained accounts of the problem of free will and of the moral virtues, centring around the notion of compassion, and deal with these topics more fully and clearly than *The World as Will and Representation*. The 1840s proved a productive decade for Schopenhauer, for after *The Two Fundamental Problems of Ethics* and the new two-volume

World as Will, he published a substantially revised edition of *On the Fourfold Root* (1847) in which he made extensive changes to the text and renumbered its sections. In the final 1859 version of *The World as Will* that is before us in the present translation references to *On the Fourfold Root* are to this 1847 edition.[16] In 1851 came a new two-volume collection of essays and observations entitled *Parerga and Paralipomena*, and in 1854 a second edition of *On the Will in Nature*; and after Schopenhauer's final publication of *The World as Will and Representation* in 1859 the essays on ethics received a second publication in 1860, the year in which he died. The more he had written, the more Schopenhauer tended to cross-reference himself. So the 1859 version that we have before us acquired references to all of Schopenhauer's other works, sometimes in the spirit of 'if you want to know more about this, see such and such,' at other times with 'I presuppose that the reader is familiar with such and such.' Schopenhauer regarded all of his works as forming an organic whole, and said 'my philosophy is like Thebes with a hundred gates: one can enter from all sides and reach the centre point on a straight path through all of them'.[17] His thought certainly exhibits a remarkable unity across the different books and the decades in which they were written – but the one really essential guide to the 'city' he builds remains *The World as Will and Representation*, Volume 1.

BEGINNING AND END

We began with Schopenhauer's most extreme claim of unity in his first edition Preface, the 'single thought'. In the same place he also asks the following of his reader:

it is evident that the only way to completely fathom the thought presented here is to *read the book twice*, and in fact with considerable patience the first time, the sort of patience that only comes from a voluntary conviction that the beginning presupposes the end almost as much as the end presupposes the beginning, and similarly that all the earlier parts presuppose the later ones almost as much as the later ones presuppose the earlier. (6)

This is good advice for the otherwise unwary reader. The First Book (as well as being perhaps a little dry in places) seems to inhabit a relatively unchallenging landscape, familiar at least to anyone with a little knowledge of Kant. Schopenhauer seems primarily interested in the questions about knowledge and reality addressed by Kant in the *Critique of Pure Reason*,

---

[16] Our endnotes allow the reader to retrieve Schopenhauer's original references to *FR*'s first edition.
[17] *The Two Fundamental Problems of Ethics* (Cambridge edition, 2009), Preface to the first edition, 6.

and he tells us as much with regard to his opening account of idealism and his treatment of the different forms of human cognition, putting himself along with Kant in a narrative that starts with Descartes, Locke and Berkeley. But the significance of his initial account of the structure of our ordinary experience of the external world undergoes a vast shift at each further stage of the work, and we move further away from these points of reference. Metaphysics reveals an essence of the world to which cause and effect and the distinctness of individuals are alien; aesthetics provides a consciousness quite contrary to ordinary experience, and ethics shows us a world of misery and seeks to persuade us that we can salvage meaning for existence as a whole only through a profound withdrawal from the ways of ordinary experience, and a self-negation on the part of the very essence metaphysics has revealed. Although, at the end, Schopenhauer dismisses as empty verbiage Hinduism's talk of 're-absorption into Brahman' or the Buddhists' Nirvana, it is only because they are trying to say the unsayable. He is in sympathy with *what* they attempt to convey, an insight from which Europe has, in his view, become alienated, that 'for those in whom the will has turned and negated itself, this world of ours which is so very real with all its suns and galaxies is – nothing' (439). It is true, then, that we do not understand quite why Schopenhauer is telling us that the world as representation has the *a priori* forms of space, time and causality, or why we must recognize will as our essence, or why the thing in itself must be undivided, until we have seen the radical way in which his (single) train of thought unfolds.

Notes on text and translation

The translation in this volume is based on the German edition of Schopen-hauer's works edited by Arthur Hübscher, *Sämtliche Werke* (Mannheim: F. A. Brockhaus, 1988), Volume 2. Page numbers of that edition are given in the margins of the translation. Hübscher's definitive edition follows the first complete edition compiled by Julius Frauenstädt in 1873 and published by Brockhaus in Leipzig, with revisions taking account of numerous later editorial interventions. A paperback version of the Hübscher edition that preserves the same text, with different script and fewer editorial notes, is the so-called *Zürcher Ausgabe, Werke in zehn Bänden* (Zurich: Diogenes, 1977), in which *The World as Will and Representation* (Volume 1) appears in Volumes 1 and 2. (Those wishing to read the German text of the work that Schopenhauer himself last issued should consult Ludger Lütkehaus (ed.), *Arthur Schopenhauers Werke in fünf Bänden. Nach den Ausgaben letzter Hand* (Zurich: Haffmans, 1988), Vol. 1.) Arguments for using Hübscher as the basis for translation are given by Richard Aquila in his 'Introduc-tion' to Arthur Schopenhauer, *The World as Will and Presentation*, Vol. 1, trans. Richard E. Aquila in collaboration with David Carus (New York: Pearson/Longman, 2008), xli–xlii, the main reason being that Hübscher is commonly cited as the standard edition. When compiling our own edi-torial notes we have found it useful to consult those of Hübscher in the *Sämtliche Werke*, and also those in Paul Deussen (ed.), *Arthur Schopenhauers Sämtliche Werke* (Munich, 1911–12), whose notes are sometimes fuller. (We have also consulted editorial notes in the Aquila and Carus translation just mentioned.)

VOCABULARY

Many terms from the German text are given in editorial footnotes where this may be of help to the reader of a particular passage. Here we shall comment on some of the more important decisions that have been made about translating frequent items in Schopenhauer's vocabulary. The term *Vorstellung*, for whatever comes before the mind in consciousness, has been translated as 'representation'. This follows the most common rendering of the term in Kant's writings (Kant uses the Latin *repraesentatio* when he wishes to elucidate his use of *Vorstellung*[1]). A case could be made both for 'idea' and for 'presentation' as English translations of *Vorstellung*. The case for the former could be made, firstly, on the grounds of continuity with the use of 'idea' by Locke and other British empiricists; secondly, on the grounds that Schopenhauer himself uses 'idea' for *Vorstellung* in a sample of English translation composed in 1829, when he was proposing to translate Kant himself for an English audience;[2] and thirdly, 'idea' is simply a less clumsy word for the English reader.[3] Nonetheless, the mainstream translation in Kantian contexts nowadays is 'representation', and this continuity is arguably more important to preserve. Finally, particularly in his all-important aesthetic theory, Schopenhauer himself uses the term *Idee* – which is most comfortably translated as 'idea' (or 'Idea') – in a quite different sense, which he intends to be very close to a Platonic usage. We have chosen to avoid introducing the opposition of 'idea' versus 'Idea' and have opted instead for 'representation' versus 'Idea', which better reflects the opposition *Vorstellung* versus *Idee*.[4] The case for 'presentation' might be that, while 'representation' unnecessarily imports the connotation of a definite item in the mind that is a copy, depiction, or stand-in for something other than itself, 'presentation' resembles *Vorstellung* in suggesting simply the occurrence of something's coming before the mind or entering into its

---

[1] See *Critique of Pure Reason* A320 / B376.
[2] See Schopenhauer's letter 'To the author of Damiron's Analysis' (21 December 1829), in Arthur Hübscher (ed.), *Arthur Schopenhauer: Sämtliche Briefe* (*SB*), 122–3. In this letter, written in English, Schopenhauer advocates a 'transplantation of Kant's works into England' and promotes his own translating abilities, at one point commenting 'I hope . . . to render Kant more intelligible in English than he is in German: for I am naturally fond of clearness and precision, & Kant by the by was not' (120).
[3] See David Berman, 'Introduction', in Arthur Schopenhauer, *The World as Will and Idea: Abridged in One Volume* (London: Everyman, 1995), trans. Jill Berman, pp. xxxv–xxxvi.
[4] Paul F. H. Lauxtermann suggests 'Form' for *Idee*, in line with recent usage in translating Plato; but in the end he reverts to our policy of 'representation' versus 'Idea' (*Science and Philosophy: Schopenhauer's Broken World-View* (Dordrecht: Kluwer, 2000), 43 n.)

conscious experience.[5] However, this is a rather subtle difference, and since 'presentation' has to be construed as a term of art just as much as 'representation', we have not resisted the pull of the latter, more conventional term.

Already in the title of this work Schopenhauer presents the world as being both *Vorstellung* and *Wille*. This second central term in Schopenhauer's philosophy can only be translated 'will'. Some interpreters writing in English impose a distinction between 'will' and 'Will', intending by the latter *the* will, the will that Schopenhauer equates, or appears to equate with the world as a whole in itself. But there is in general no such orthographic differentiation in any of Schopenhauer's texts themselves, and we have not made any such distinction in the translation. (Arguably one would anyway need more variants than just two if one wanted to reflect the many nuanced roles that Schopenhauer gives to the term *Wille*: standing for the individual's will as manifested in his or her actions, for the underlying, non-empirical but individual character that is *my will*, for the one will that is common to all creatures, and so on.) The verb *wollen* is standardly translated as 'to will' (except in non-technical contexts where 'to want' is more appropriate) and *das Wollen* as 'willing'. The vital Schopenhauerian notion *Wille zum Leben* is always rendered as 'will to life'. It is not just a striving for individual survival, but also towards the end of propagating new life.

German has two words that are ordinarily translated as 'knowledge' – *Wissen* and *Erkenntniß*, and Schopenhauer makes a philosophical distinction between the two of them, arguing that *Wissen* is just one form of *Erkenntniß*. We have therefore tended to reserve the term 'knowledge' for *Wissen*, rendering *Erkenntniß* as 'cognition', its cognate verb *erkennen* as 'recognize', 'cognize' or 'have cognition of', and *erkennend* as 'cognitive' or 'cognizing' in contexts where they make a contribution to Schopenhauer's epistemology and theory of mind. This group of terms occurs very often in the text. One of Schopenhauer's major themes (from the very first line of § 1) is that *Erkenntniß* is common to human beings and other animals, but that animals have only an 'intuitive', immediate and non-conceptual understanding of the world, and lack the abstract, conceptual, or mediate kind of *Erkenntniß* that he calls *Wissen*. The other part of this theme is

---

[5] See the case made by Richard E. Aquila, 'Translator's Introduction', in Arthur Schopenhauer, *The World as Will and Presentation*, Volume I, trans. Richard E. Aquila in collaboration with David Carus (New York: Longman: 2008), pp. xii–xvi. Aquila acknowledges 'representation' as 'commonplace' in translating both Kant and Schopenhauer.

that the portion of cognition that we do not share with animals, conceptual thought, reasoning, *Vernunft*, is really of far less importance than philosophers have tended to think: it contains only what immediate cognition already contains, but in a more handy form. Schopenhauer ultimately argues that concepts and reason do not confer any particular 'dignity' or 'freedom' on human beings, and have nothing to do with moral value. This is all fairly radical in the post-Kantian climate. Schopenhauer certainly uses the Kantian terms *Sinnlichkeit*, *Verstand*, *Anschauung* and *Begriff* (which we translate conventionally as 'sensibility', 'understanding', 'intuition' and 'concept'), but he does so in order to present a theory of cognition that diverges markedly from Kant's in many ways. 'Intuition' is therefore to be understood as a term of art denoting an awareness of objects in space and time through the senses; and we translate *anschaulich* as 'intuitive' and so on.

In this usage we differ from Payne's well-known translation, which tended to translate *Anschauung* as 'perception'. We, again more standardly, use 'perception' to translate *Wahrnehmung*. A similar case is that of *Erscheinung*, where we normally use the customary 'appearance' (not 'phenomenon', except in cases where to talk of 'appearances' could be misleading in English). Schopenhauer accuses Kant of misusing the terms *phenomenon* and especially *noumenon*, and his own philosophy can be stated entirely without use of either term. Behind the world's aspect as appearance or representation lies the world as thing in itself (*Ding an sich*), and Schopenhauer uses somewhat novel expressions for the relation between thing in itself and appearance, saying that the latter is the *Objektivation*, or the *Objektität* of the former. The world of appearance is the world 'become object'. We coin the equally novel English words 'objectivation' and 'objecthood' for these two terms. In his revision of the text for the 1859 edition Schopenhauer frequently replaces *Objektität* with *Objektivation* – though the difference between the two is one of nuance, the latter suggesting more a process, the former more its product.

We have been fairly scrupulous with the cluster of terms *Mensch* ('human being'), *Person* ('person'), *Individuum* ('individual'), *Selbst* ('self') and *Ich* ('I'), all of which should be kept distinct from the ubiquitous term *Subjekt* ('subject'). Schopenhauer quite often talks about 'my person', 'my individual', and so on. I am the subject of cognition, while the individual that I am, unlike the subject, is something in the world that I experience. We translate *Leib* and *Körper* both as 'body'.

The frequently occurring *Grund* is translated as 'ground'. Sometimes this refers to a cause, at other times to a reason – and indeed there are four basic types of ground, as Schopenhauer had explained in his earlier essay *On the Fourfold Root of the Principle of Sufficient Reason*. In fact the principle referred to in that title, and throughout Schopenhauer's work, is *der Satz vom zureichenden Grunde* which should in strictness be rendered as 'the principle of sufficient ground'. However, in this one instance we have use 'principle of sufficient reason' simply as the more readily recognizable set phrase in English. Everywhere else *Grund* is 'ground'.

In Schopenhauer's discussion of aesthetics in the Third Book we have translated *reizend* as 'stimulating'. The German connotes something that provokes, tickles or arouses. As such, Schopenhauer argues that it essentially involves the will and therefore does not belong in art, which is supposed to inspire a disinterested contemplation, a contemplation free from the will. (Kant before him has also stated that *das Reizende* cannot be considered in a disinterested manner and therefore cannot be the object of pure judgements of taste.) Although the term is frequently translated as 'charming' in the context of the philosophy of art, we felt that this was too weak, failing to convey the sense of arousal that Schopenhauer objects to so strongly. Translating the term as 'stimulating' also makes comprehensible why Schopenhauer equates *das negativ Reizende*, 'what stimulates negatively', with 'the disgusting'. And finally, this translation allows us to maintain terminological continuity with Schopenhauer's use of the term in a biological context in the Second Book of his work.

German has two words that are commonly translated as 'poetry': *Poesie* and *Dichtkunst*. The English term 'poetry' has a somewhat narrower semantic field than either of these (the somewhat archaic 'poesie' corresponds more closely), but we decided to reserve 'poetry' for *Poesie* and translate *Dichtkunst* as 'literature'. This enables the reader to make sense of the fact that Schopenhauer refers to Shakespeare as a producer of *Dichtkunst* and the novel as a *Dichtungsart*.

The most important positive term in Schopenhauer's ethics is *Mitleid*. We translate it as 'compassion', not as 'pity'. The latter is in many contexts a legitimate rendering of the German term, but is a poor candidate for the fundamental incentive on which actions of moral worth are based, because instances of pitying often involve a sense of distance from or even superiority over those whose suffering one recognizes, whereas *Mitleid* for Schopenhauer must involve the collapse of any such distance or even distinction between the sufferer and the one who acts out of *Mitleid*. The two virtues in which *Mitleid* manifests itself are *Gerechtigkeit*, 'justice', and *Menschenliebe*, which we have translated as 'loving kindness'. It seems important that *Menschenliebe* is a species of *Liebe*, love. At some places in his text Schopenhauer originally had *Liebe*, but corrected it to *Menschenliebe*; and he glosses it as similar to the Christian concept of *agape*. Literally it is 'human-love', love of (and by) human beings. 'Philanthropy', though an exact parallel in Greek-based vocabulary, seems to refer less to a prevailing attitude of mind or incentive in one's character and more to the resultant good deeds.

In talking of human actions Schopenhauer varies his terminology without any detectable change in basic sense. Thus often he talks of *handeln* and *Handlung*, 'to act', 'action', then switches to *That, thun*, or *Thun* (modern German *Tat, tun, Tun*), which we generally translate as 'deed', 'to do', 'doing' or 'doings' to preserve a similar variation in style. The *th* for *t* here (see also *Theil, Werth* etc.) is one instance of divergence in spelling from that of the present day. All German words in editorial notes are given in the original orthography that the Hübscher edition preserves (other examples being *aa* for *a, ey* for *ei, ä* for *e*, and *dt* for *t*, thus *Spaaß, Daseyn, Säligkeit, gescheidt*).

The words *Moral* and *Moralität* are translated as 'morals' and 'morality' respectively. An immediate effect is to change the title of Schopenhauer's 1841 essay, sometimes referred to in footnotes in *The World as Will*, to *On the Basis of Morals* (when in Payne's version it was *On the Basis of Morality*). Schopenhauer tends to treat 'morals' as a theoretical study or philosophical enterprise for which the term 'ethics' is equivalent, while 'morality' describes people's real-life actions and judgements. The adjective *moralisch* is easily translated as 'moral' (and the adverb as 'morally'), *Ethik* and *ethisch* likewise as 'ethics' and 'ethical'. In his revisions Schopenhauer replaced many occurrences of 'ethical' with 'moral', though it is hard to say whether this is a mere change in stylistic preference.

The culmination of Schopenhauer's ethics is the idea of the will to life negating itself. There are a number of somewhat tricky terms in this area, which we translate as follows: *Bejahung*, 'affirmation', *Verneinung*, 'negation'; *Selbstbejahung, Selbstverneinung*, 'self-affirmation', 'self-negation'; *Selbstverleugnung*, 'self-denial'; *Selbstaufhebung*, 'self-abolition'. *Nichts* ('nothing') and its compounds become increasingly prominent as the book reaches its conclusion. We usually tend to translate *Vernichtung* as 'annihilation', *nichtig* as 'unreal', *Nichtigkeit* as 'nothingness'. Finally, when Schopenhauer talks in unique fashion of a metaphysical insight acting as the '*Quietiv* of the will', we have chosen to translate *Quietiv*, not as the rather ineffectual 'quieter', but as 'tranquillizer'.

Finally, we would like to thank Dr Richard Norman for his help in translating some of the scientific terms Schopenhauer uses in the Second Book of *The World as Will and Representation*.

STYLE, SYNTAX AND PUNCTUATION

Throughout this translation we have tried to render Schopenhauer into flowing, readable English. Schopenhauer is not a clumsy stylist – his German is fluent and very able. A translation that follows German syntax very closely might reflect the gross character of the original text quite accurately, but not its spirit. We aim for accuracy of translation in the sense of showing Schopenhauer for what he was, a clear and eloquent writer, successfully pursuing an ideal of clarity and readability. There are many factors to take into account in understanding Schopenhauer's stylistic decisions, but it is important to remember that he is positioning himself in relation to the constellation of post-Kantian thinkers. Kant had a notoriously dense style, which is famously taken up by Fichte and Hegel, whom Schopenhauer regards as his intellectual enemies. In making a point of writing fluently, Schopenhauer is explicitly breaking with this tradition, and announcing a new philosophical point of departure and a new function for philosophy, i.e. that it should not be confined to the academy, but should be a source of popular inspiration, something that Schopenhauer's work decidedly was in the latter part of the nineteenth century and into the twentieth century.

Schopenhauer writes German sentences of great variety in length and structure. Often he uses a direct and punchy statement, or a balanced classical sentence with two or three well-constructed clauses. But the greatest challenge for the translator is presented by those many occasions where Schopenhauer launches into a disproportionately long sentence. Helped by well-known features that distinguish German from English, notably the ability to frame long subordinate clauses with a verb postponed to the end, and three grammatical genders which allow nouns from earlier in the sentences to be picked up anaphorically without ambiguity, he can produce majestic sentences whose parts fit together perfectly and which make a powerful cumulative effect on the reader. In line with our policy of allowing Schopenhauer to speak eloquently to the English reader, we have frequently divided up such longer sentences and reordered clauses within a sentence, always with the aim of reflecting the overall structure of his argument more clearly.

Schopenhauer's punctuation, as transmitted by way of the Hübscher editions, is unlike standard present-day usage. One feature retained in the

translation is his use of a simple dash (–) between sentences to separate
out parts within a long paragraph. But we have tried to reflect his practice
of inserting commas, colons and semi-colons inside sentences loosely and
idiomatically rather than copying it. Another feature is Schopenhauer's
italicization of proper names, which we have tended to limit to occasions
when Schopenhauer first mentions someone in a given context, or shifts
back to discussing them.

SCHOPENHAUER'S USE OF OTHER LANGUAGES

A major decision has been made here which affects virtually every page
of Schopenhauer's published writings. Schopenhauer is a master of many
languages and delights in quoting extracts from other authors in Greek,
Latin, French, Italian and Spanish. These extracts vary in length from the
isolated phrase within a sentence to several unbroken pages of quotation
which he thinks will substantiate his own view. Very often he will round off
his argument with some apt words from Homer, Dante or Voltaire, always
in the original language. He also has the scholar's habit of incorporating
short tags in Latin or Greek into his own idiom (e.g. he will generally
refer to something as a *petitio principii* rather than saying that it begs the
question, or as a πρωτον ψευδος rather than 'a false first step' or 'primary
error'). Finally, when a substantial passage of Greek occurs Schopenhauer
helpfully adds his own Latin translation for the reader's benefit.

The cumulative effect gives Schopenhauer's style historical depth and a
pan-European literary flavour (with the occasional foray into transliterated
Sanskrit). The question is how to deal with all of this in an English
translation. Earlier versions have taken two different lines. One is simply
to reproduce all the non-German passages in their original languages and
leave it at that. This was done by R. B. Haldane and J. Kemp in their
translation of *The World as Will and Idea* in 1883 and by Madame Karl
Hillebrand in *On the Fourfold Root and On the Will in Nature* in 1891. While
it may have been a reasonable assumption in those days, as it may have
been for Schopenhauer himself, that anyone likely to read his book seriously
would have sufficient access to the requisite languages, at the present time of
writing such an assumption would appear misplaced. The second expedient
is to leave all the original language passages where they stand in the text,
but to add footnotes or parentheses giving English equivalents. This is
the method, adopted in Payne's translations, that readers of Schopenhauer
in English are now most familiar with. In the present translation, by
contrast, we have adopted a third strategy: with a few exceptions, everything

in the text is translated into English, and the original language version given in footnotes. This sacrifices some of the richness involved in reading Schopenhauer – but it arguably disadvantages only a reader who is a good linguist in several languages but not German. For all other readers of English, the relevance of Schopenhauer's quotations to his argument, and the overall flow of his writing, are better revealed by following the sense of quotations directly, especially on those many pages where he makes his point by way of a chunk of Greek followed by a chunk of Latin that gives a second version of the same, or where he quotes two or more pages in French. Nor is anything really lost by our policy, since every word of the original language extracts is given in footnotes on the same page.

Some exceptions to this practice occur where Schopenhauer specifically introduces a word in another language for discussion of its sense, or where he offers a Latin expression from the mediaeval scholastic tradition as especially apposite. In such cases the original language expression is retained in the text and the English equivalent offered in a footnote.

Where Schopenhauer quotes phrases and short sentences in Greek, he sometimes includes accents and sometimes omits them. We have followed his usage in all cases, despite the inconsistency.

Chronology

1788	Arthur Schopenhauer born on 22 February in the city of Danzig (now Gdansk), the son of the Hanseatic merchant Heinrich Floris Schopenhauer and Johanna Schopenhauer, née Trosiener
1793	Danzig is annexed by the Prussians. The Schopenhauer family moves to Hamburg
1797	His sister Adele is born. Schopenhauer begins a two-year stay in Le Havre with the family of one of his father's business partners
1799	Returns to Hamburg, and attends a private school for the next four years
1803–4	Agrees to enter career as a merchant and as a reward is taken by his parents on a tour of Europe (Holland, England, France, Switzerland, Austria). From June to September 1803 is a boarder in Thomas Lancaster's school in Wimbledon
1804	Is apprenticed to two Hanseatic merchants in Hamburg
1805	His father dies, probably by suicide
1806	Johanna Schopenhauer moves with Adele to Weimar, where she establishes herself as a popular novelist and literary hostess
1807	Schopenhauer abandons his commercial career for an academic one. Enters Gotha Gymnasium and then receives private tuition in Weimar
1809	Studies science and then philosophy (especially Plato and Kant) at the University of Göttingen
1811	Studies science and philosophy at the University of Berlin. Attends the lectures of Fichte and Schleiermacher
1813–14	Lives in Rudolstadt, writing his doctoral dissertation, *On the Fourfold Root of the Principle of Sufficient Reason*, which is accepted by the University of Jena and published in 1814. Conversations with Goethe on colour and vision

1814	Begins reading a translation of the *Upanishads*. Stays with his mother in Weimar, but breaks with her permanently after a final quarrel. Lives in Dresden until 1818
1814–18	Works on *The World as Will and Representation*
1816	Publishes *On Vision and Colours*
1818	March: completion of *The World as Will and Representation* by Brockhaus, published at the end of the year with '1819' on title page
1818–19	Travels in Italy (Florence, Rome, Naples, Venice) and returns to Dresden
1819	Is appointed as unsalaried lecturer (*Privatdozent*) at the University of Berlin
1820	Gives his only course of lectures, which is poorly attended
1822–3	Travels again to Italy (Milan, Florence, Venice). Returns from Italy to live in Munich. Is ill and depressed
1824	Lives in Bad Gastein, Mannheim and Dresden. Proposes to translate Hume's works on religion into German, but does not find a publisher
1826	Returns to Berlin
1829–30	Plans to translate Kant into English, without success
1831	Leaves Berlin because of the cholera epidemic. Moves to Frankfurt am Main
1831–2	Lives temporarily in Mannheim
1833	Settles in Frankfurt, where he remains for the rest of his life
1836	Publishes *On the Will in Nature*
1838	His mother dies
1839	Enters competition set by the Royal Norwegian Society of Sciences Scientific, and wins prize with his essay *On the Freedom of the Will*
1840	Submits *On the Basis of Morals* in a competition set by the Royal Danish Society of Sciences, and is not awarded a prize
1841	*On the Freedom of the Will* and *On the Basis of Morals* published under the title *The Two Fundamental Problems of Ethics*
1844	Publishes second, revised edition of *The World as Will and Representation*, adding a second volume consisting of fifty elaboratory essays
1847	Publishes second, revised edition of *On the Fourfold Root*
1851	Publishes *Parerga and Paralipomena* in two volumes

1853   An article on his philosophy by J. Oxenford in *Westminster and Foreign Quarterly Review* marks the beginning of his belated recognition

1854   Publishes second edition of *On the Will in Nature*. Julius Frauenstädt publishes *Letters on Schopenhauer's Philosophy*

1857   Schopenhauer's philosophy taught at Bonn University

1858   Declines invitation to be a member of Berlin Royal Academy

1859   Publishes third edition of *The World as Will and Representation*

1860   Publishes second edition of *The Two Fundamental Problems of Ethics*. Dies on 21 September in Frankfurt-am-Main

Bibliography

GERMAN EDITIONS OF SCHOPENHAUER'S WRITINGS

Der handschriftlicher Nachlaß, ed. Arthur Hübscher, 5 vols. (Frankfurt am Main: Kramer, 1970).

Faksimilenachdruck der 1. Auflage der Welt als Wille und Vorstellung, ed. Rudolf Malter (Frankfurt am Main: Insel, 1987).

Gesammelte Briefe, ed. Arthur Hübscher (Bonn: Bouvier, 1978).

Philosophische Vorlesungen, aus dem handschriftlichen Nachlaß, ed. Volker Spierling (Munich: R. Piper, 1984–6).

Sämtliche Werke, ed. Arthur Hübscher, 7 vols. (Mannheim: F. A. Brockhaus, 1988).

Schopenhauer's Sämtliche Werke, ed. Paul Deussen, 6 vols. (Munich: Piper Verlag, 1911–26).

Werke in fünf Bänden. Nach den Ausgaben letzter Hand, ed. Ludger Lütkehaus, 5 vols. (Zurich: Haffmans, 1988).

Werke in zehn Bänden (Zürcher Ausgabe), ed. Arthur Hübscher, 10 vols. (Zurich: Diogenes, 1977).

ENGLISH TRANSLATIONS OF SCHOPENHAUER'S WRITINGS

Essay on the Freedom of the Will, trans. Konstantin Kolenda (Indianapolis: Bobbs-Merrill, 1960).

Essays and Aphorisms, trans. R. J. Hollingdale (Harmondsworth: Penguin, 1970).

Manuscript Remains, trans. E. F. J. Payne, 4 vols. (Oxford: Berg, 1988).

On the Basis of Morality, ed. David E. Cartwright, trans. E. F. J. Payne (Oxford: Berghahn Books, 1995).

On the Fourfold Root of the Principle of Sufficient Reason, trans. E. F. J. Payne (La Salle, IL: Open Court, 1974).

On the Fourfold Root of the Principle of Sufficient Reason and On the Will in Nature, trans. Mme Karl Hillebrand (London: George Bell and Sons, 1891).

On the Will in Nature, ed. David E. Cartwright, trans. E. F. J. Payne (New York: Berg, 1992).

On Vision and Colors, ed. David E. Cartwright, trans. E. F. J. Payne (Oxford: Berg, 1994).

Parerga and Paralipomena, trans. E. F. J. Payne, 2 vols. (Oxford: Clarendon Press, 1974).

Prize Essay on the Freedom of the Will, ed. Günter Zöller, trans. E. F. J. Payne (Cambridge: Cambridge University Press, 1999).

Schopenhauer's Early Fourfold Root: Translation and Commentary, F. C. White (Aldershot: Avebury, 1997).

The Two Fundamental Problems of Ethics, ed. and trans. Christopher Janaway (Cambridge: Cambridge University Press, 2010).

The Two Fundamental Problems of Ethics, trans. David Cartwright and Edward Erdmann (Oxford: Oxford University Press, 2010).

The World as Will and Idea, trans. R. B. Haldane and J. Kemp, 3 vols. (London: Routledge and Kegan Paul, 1883).

The World as Will and Idea, abridged in one volume, trans. J. Berman, ed. D. Berman (London: Everyman, 1995).

The World as Will and Presentation, vol. 1, trans. Richard E. Aquila in collaboration with David Carus (New York: Pearson/Longman, 2008).

The World as Will and Representation, trans. E. F. J. Payne, 2 vols. (New York: Dover, 1969).

SELECTED BOOKS AND EDITED COLLECTIONS IN ENGLISH

Atwell, John E., *Schopenhauer on the Character of the World: The Metaphysics of Will* (Berkeley: University of California Press, 1995).

  Schopenhauer: The Human Character (Philadelphia: Temple University Press, 1990).

Cartwright, David E., *Historical Dictionary of Schopenhauer's Philosophy* (Lanham, MD: Scarecrow Press, 2005).

  Schopenhauer: A Biography (New York: Cambridge University Press, 2004).

Dauer, Dorothea, *Schopenhauer as Transmitter of Buddhist Ideas* (European University Papers, Series 1, vol. 15; Berne: Herbert Lang, 1969).

Fox, Michael (ed.), *Schopenhauer: His Philosophical Achievement* (Totowa, NJ: Barnes and Noble, 1980).

Gardiner, Patrick, *Schopenhauer* (Bristol: Thoemmes Press, 1997; originally pub. Penguin Books in 1963).

Hamlyn, D.W., *Schopenhauer* (London: Routledge and Kegan Paul, 1980).

Hannan, Barbara, *The Riddle of the World: A Reconstruction of Schopenhauer's Philosophy* (Oxford: Oxford University Press, 2009).

Hübscher, Arthur, *The Philosophy of Schopenhauer in its Intellectual Context*, trans. Joachim T. Baer and David E. Cartwright (Lewiston, NY: Edwin Mellen Press, 1989).

Jacquette, Dale, *The Philosophy of Schopenhauer* (London: Acumen, 2005).

Jacquette, Dale (ed.), *Schopenhauer, Philosophy, and the Arts* (Cambridge: Cambridge University Press, 1996).

Janaway, Christopher, *Schopenhauer: A Very Short Introduction* (Oxford: Oxford University Press, 2002).

  Self and World in Schopenhauer's Philosophy (Oxford: Clarendon Press, 1989).

Janaway, Christopher (ed.), *The Cambridge Companion to Schopenhauer* (Cambridge: Cambridge University Press University, 1999).
  Willing and Nothingness: Schopenhauer as Nietzsche's Educator (Oxford: Clarendon Press, 1998).
Janaway, Christopher and Alex Neill (eds.), *Better Consciousness: Schopenhauer's Philosophy of Value* (Oxford: Blackwell, 2009).
Jordan, Neil, *Schopenhauer's Ethics of Patience: Virtue, Salvation and Value* (Lewiston, NY: Edwin Mellen Press, 2009).
Lauxtermann, Paul F. H, *Science and Philosophy: Schopenhauer's Broken World-View* (Dordrecht: Kluwer, 2000).
Magee, Bryan, *The Philosophy of Schopenhauer* (Oxford: Clarendon Press, 1997).
Mannion, Gerard, *Schopenhauer, Religion and Morality: The Humble Path to Ethics* (London: Ashgate, 2003).
McGill, V. J., *Schopenhauer: Pessimist and Pagan* (New York: Haskell House, 1971).
Neeley, G. Steven, *Schopenhauer: A Consistent Reading* (Lewiston, NY: Edwin Mellen Press, 2003).
Ryan, Christopher, *Schopenhauer's Philosophy of Religion: The Death of God and the Oriental Renaissance* (Leuven: Peeters, 2010).
Safranksi, Rüdiger, *Schopenhauer and the Wild Years of Philosophy*, trans. Ewald Osers (London: Weidenfeld and Nicolson, 1989).
Simmel, Georg, *Schopenhauer and Nietzsche*, trans. Helmut Loikandl, Deena Weinstein and Michael Weinstein (Amherst: University of Massachusetts Press, 1986).
Tanner, Michael, *Schopenhauer: Metaphysics and Art* (London: Phoenix, 1998).
von der Luft, Eric (ed.), *Schopenhauer: New Essays in Honor of his 200th Birthday* (Lewiston, NY: Edwin Mellen Press, 1988).
White, F. C., *On Schopenhauer's Fourfold Root of the Principle of Sufficient Reason* (Leiden: E. J. Brill, 1992).
Wicks, Robert, *Schopenhauer* (Malden, MA and Oxford: Blackwell, 2008).
Young, Julian, *Schopenhauer* (London and New York: Routledge, 2005).
  Willing and Unwilling: A Study in the Philosophy of Arthur Schopenhauer (Dordrecht: Martinus Nijhoff, 1987).

The World as Will and Representation

Arthur Schopenhauer

Volume I

Four Books, with an Appendix
containing the Critique of the Kantian Philosophy

Ob nicht Natur zuletzt sich doch ergründe?
Goethe

['Might not nature finally fathom itself?' – from a
poem to Staatsminister von Voigt, 27 September 1816]

I

Contents of Volume 1

What I propose to do here is to specify how this book is to be read so as to be understood. – It aims to convey a single thought.[a] But in spite of all my efforts, I could not find a shorter way of conveying the thought than the whole of this book. – I believe it is the idea that people have sought out for such a long time under the heading of philosophy, which is why scholars of history have thought it to be as impossible to discover as the philosophers' stone, although Pliny had already told them: 'how much has been considered impossible before it has been done?' (*Natural History*, 7, 1).[b]

As this one thought is considered from different sides, it reveals itself respectively as what has been called metaphysics, what has been called ethics, and what has been called aesthetics; and it is only natural that it be all of these, if it really is what I claim it to be.

A *system of thoughts* must always have an architectonic coherence,[c] i.e. a coherence in which one part always supports another without the second VIII supporting the first, so the foundation stone will ultimately support all the parts without itself being supported by any of them, and the summit will be supported without itself supporting anything. *A single thought*, on the other hand, however comprehensive it might be, must preserve the most perfect unity. If it is divided up in order to be communicated, the various parts must still be organically coherent, i.e. each part containing the whole just as much as it is contained by the whole, with no part first and no part last, the whole thought rendered more distinct through each part, and even the smallest part incapable of being fully understood without a prior understanding of the whole. – But a book must have a first line and a last, and to this extent will always be very different from an organism,

---

[a] *Gedanke*
[b] *Quam multa fieri non posse, priusquam sint facta, judicantur?* (*Hist. nat.* 7, 1 [§ 6])
[c] *Zusammenhang*

however similar they might be in content: as a result, form and matter are in contradiction here.

In circumstances such as this, it is evident that the only way to completely fathom[a] the thought presented here is to *read the book twice*, and in fact with considerable patience the first time, the sort of patience that only comes from a voluntary conviction that the beginning presupposes the end almost as much as the end presupposes the beginning, and similarly that all the earlier parts presuppose the later ones almost as much as the later ones presuppose the earlier. I say 'almost': because this is by no means unconditionally so, and anything that could be done to give priority to what is explained only in the sequel – just as in general whatever could facilitate comprehensibility and clarity – has been honestly and conscientiously done. Indeed, I might have succeeded to some extent if it were not for the reader, who in reading the book thinks not only of what is being said but (which is only natural) of its possible consequences as well. As a result, the many places where the book really *is* in conflict with the opinions of the age (and, presumably, with those of the reader as well) can be joined by just as many more anticipated and imaginary points of conflict, so that what is in fact only a misunderstanding must look like lively disapproval. And although the painstakingly attained clarity of presentation and expression leaves no question about the immediate meaning[b] of what is said, such clarity cannot at the same time elucidate the relation between what is being said and everything else, which further exacerbates the problem. This is why the first reading requires, as I said, a patience that comes from the confidence that a second reading will put many things (if not everything) in a very different light. As to the rest, my serious attempts to render a very difficult topic fully and even easily comprehensible must justify occasional repetition. Even the structure of the whole, which is organic rather than chainlike, sometimes forces me to touch on the same point twice. This very structure, as well as the extremely close connections[c] between all of the parts, has not allowed me to divide the work into chapters and paragraphs, a division I otherwise find very valuable, but has instead required me to leave it in four main parts, four perspectives,[d] as it were, on the one thought. In each of these four Books, the reader must be particularly careful not to lose sight of the principal thought in the associated details that need to be treated along with it, or of the progress of the presentation

IX

---

[a] *Eindringen*
[b] *Sinn*
[c] *Zusammenhang*
[d] *Gesichtspunkten*

as a whole. – This, like the demands to follow, is absolutely essential for the hostile[a] reader (hostile, that is, to the philosopher, because he is one himself).

The second demand is that the introduction be read before the book itself, even though it is not located inside the book but rather appeared five years earlier under the title: *On the Fourfold Root of the Principle of Sufficient Reason: A Philosophical Essay*. – It is absolutely impossible to truly understand the present work unless the reader is familiar with this introduction and propaedeutic, and the contents of that essay are presupposed here as much as if they had been included in the book. Moreover, if the essay had not preceded the present work by several years, it would be incorporated into the First Book instead of standing in front of it as an introduction; there are gaps in the First Book where the material from that essay would have been, and the resulting incompleteness must be made good by constant appeal to that essay. But I have such a strong aversion to copying myself or struggling to find new words for what was said quite adequately the first time, that I preferred this method, despite the fact that I could now present the material in that essay rather better, particularly by cleansing it of many concepts that stem from my (then excessive) entanglement with the Kantian philosophy, concepts such as categories, outer and inner sense, and the like. Yet those concepts are there only because I had never really engaged with them on a very profound level, and thus only as side issues that do not touch on the main subject. This is why the reader who is familiar with the present work will automatically correct those passages in the essay. – But only after the reader has fully recognized (by means of this essay) what the principle of sufficient reason is and means, where it is valid and where it is not, the fact that it is not prior to all things and the whole world does not exist only in consequence of and according to this principle, as something like its correlate; only after the reader has fully recognized that this principle is really nothing more than the form in which an object (which is always conditioned by the subject) of whatever sort it may be, is always cognized, so long as the subject is a cognizing individual – only then is it possible to grasp[b] the method of philosophizing that is attempted here for the first time, and that is utterly distinct from all previous methods.

The same aversion to repeating myself verbatim or even saying the same thing a second time with different and less suitable words (having already used all the better ones) – this aversion is solely responsible for another gap

[a] *ungeneigten*
[b] *eingehen*

in the First Book of this work, since I have omitted everything written in the first chapter of my essay *On Vision and Colours*, which otherwise would have belonged here, word for word. So a familiarity with this short, earlier writing is also presupposed.

Finally, the third demand made of the reader could even have been left unstated, because it is nothing less than an acquaintance with the most important phenomenon[a] to emerge in philosophy over the past two thousand years, one that lies so close to us: I am talking about the principal works of Kant. I find that the effect of these works on a mind to which they truly speak is, as has already been said elsewhere, comparable to a cataract operation on a blind person: and if we were to continue this comparison,[b] my aim can be described as wanting to put cataract glasses into the hands of those who have successfully had this operation, since the operation is the most necessary condition for the use of those glasses. – However much I take the achievements of the great Kant as my point of departure, a serious study of his works has nonetheless enabled me to discover significant errors, and I have had to separate these errors out and show them to be unsound[c] so that I could then presuppose and apply what is true and excellent in his theories in a pure form, freed from these errors. So as not to interrupt and confuse my own discussion by frequent polemical remarks directed against Kant, I have put these into a special appendix. And my writing presupposes a familiarity with this appendix just as much as it presupposes, as I have said, a familiarity with the Kantian philosophy: so with this in mind, it is advisable to read the appendix first, and all the more so because its content refers directly to the First Book of the present work. On the other hand, given the nature of the material, the appendix inevitably makes occasional reference to the work itself; but all that follows from this is that it needs to be read twice, just like the main part of the work.

Thus, for the purpose of my discussion, I do not presuppose that the reader has a complete knowledge of any philosophy besides that of *Kant*. – But if in addition the reader has spent time in the school of the divine *Plato*, then he will be that much more prepared for and receptive to what I have to say. And if he has even shared in the blessing of the *Vedas*, which have been made accessible to us through the *Upanishads*, and which, to my mind, is the chief advantage that this still-young century enjoys over the previous one (and in fact, I expect the influence of the Sanskrit literature to have as profound an effect on us as the revival of Greek literature had on

XII

[a] *Erscheinung*
[b] *Gleichniß*
[c] *verwerflich*

the 15th century[1]) – so, as I was saying, if the reader has also already received and been receptive to the consecration of the ancient Indian wisdom, then he will be in the very best position to hear what I have to say to him. It will not strike him, as it will strike many others, as foreign or even inimical, since I would like to claim (if it does not sound arrogant) that each of the individual and disconnected remarks that form the *Upanishads* could   XIII be derived as a corollary[a] of the thoughts I will be imparting, although conversely my thoughts certainly cannot be found there.

But most readers will have already felt their impatience mounting and will have broken out into a rebuke that has been held back for some time with considerable effort: how dare I put a book before the public under demands and conditions, the first two of which are presumptuous and completely unreasonable, and this at a time when there is such a general abundance of distinctive thoughts that the press makes three thousand such thoughts into common property each year in Germany alone, in the form of estimable, original and completely indispensable works, as well as in countless periodicals, and even the daily papers? Particularly at a time when there is no lack of wholly original and profound philosophers; and in fact there are more of them living simultaneously in Germany alone than during the course of several centuries together? How, the indignant reader might ask, will there ever be an end to it if we have to do so much work for a single book?

Since I have absolutely nothing to say to such reproaches, I can only hope for some gratitude on the part of those readers for having warned them in time so that they do not waste a single hour with a book that it would be useless to read without fulfilling the stated demands and thus must be left entirely alone; this is particularly true since it is a fairly good bet that the book can have nothing to say to them, that it will only ever be a matter 'for few men'[b] and thus must wait calmly and modestly for the few whose   XIV uncommon way of thinking will find it palatable. Because even apart from its intricacies and wealth of detail, as well as the exertions that it expects of the reader, what well-informed person of this age, whose knowledge has approached the marvellous point where the paradoxical is the same as the false, could bear to encounter thoughts on almost every page that frankly contradict those that he himself had put down as true and established once and for all? And then, how unpleasantly disappointed people will be when

---

[a] *Folgesatz*
[b] *paucorum hominum* [Horace, *Satires* I. 9, 44]

they find absolutely no mention of the things that they believe they must look for here in particular, because their way of speculating coincides with that of a still-living great philosopher*,[2] who has written truly touching books and has only the small weakness of considering everything that he has learned and approved of before his fifteenth year as the innate and fundamental thoughts of the human spirit. Who wants to put up with all this? So my advice is simply to put down the book.

But I am afraid that even this will not let me off the hook. The reader who has come as far as the preface only to be rebuffed by it has paid good money for the book, and wants to know how he can be compensated. – My last resort now is to remind him that he knows other things to do with a book besides reading it. It can fill a space in his library as well as any other book, and it will look quite good there with its fresh, clean binding. Or he can leave it in the dressing room or on the tea table of his educated lady friend. Or finally, by far the best option of all and one that I would particularly advise, is for him to write a review of it.

XV   And so, after allowing myself this joke (and in this thoroughly ambiguous life there is hardly any page too serious to grant it a place), I offer up this book with profound seriousness and in the firm conviction that sooner or later it will reach those to whom alone it can be addressed. And as to the rest, I am calmly resigned to the fact that it will fully share the fate that truth has met with in every branch of knowledge, and most of all where the knowledge is most important, that of being granted only a short victory celebration between the two long periods of time when it is condemned as paradoxical or disparaged as trivial. The author of the truth usually meets with the first fate as well. – But life is short and the reach of the truth is long and long-lived: let us speak the truth.

(Written in Dresden in August 1818.)[3]

---

* F. H. Jacobi

It is not to my contemporaries, it is not to my compatriots – it is to humanity itself that I entrust my now-completed work, in the confidence that humanity will find some value in it, even if this value will only gain recognition belatedly, this being the inevitable fate of all good things. It can only be for humanity, not for the generation that hurries past, caught up in the delusions of the moment, that my mind has unceasingly devoted itself to its work, almost against my will, throughout the course of a long life. Even the lack of interest[a] could not shake my faith in its value during this time; I constantly saw the false, the bad, and finally the absurd and nonsensical* enjoying general admiration and esteem, and reflected that if people who know how to recognize what is genuine and true were not so rare as to be sought in vain for twenty years together, then those who are able to produce it would not be so few that their works afterwards constitute an exception to the transitory nature of earthly things, so that   XVII
we would lose the comforting prospect of posterity, which constitutes a necessary source of strength for everyone with a lofty goal. – Nobody who seriously takes on and pursues a problem[b] that does not result in material advantage can count on the sympathy[c] of his contemporaries. But in the meantime he will usually see the semblance of such a problem becoming accepted in the world and having its day: and this is as it should be. The problem itself must be pursued for its own sake or else it will fail, because intent[d] is always dangerous to insight.[e] Indeed, the whole of the history of literature testifies to the fact that everything worthwhile takes

---

* Hegelian philosophy

[a] *Theilnahme*
[b] *Sache*
[c] *Theilnahme*
[d] *Absicht*
[e] *Einsicht*

a long time to gain currency, particularly if its nature is instructive and
not entertaining: and in the meanwhile, falseness glitters and gleams. It
is difficult if not impossible to unite the problem with the semblance of
the problem. But this is just the curse of this world of misery and need:
everything must serve and slave for them; the world is not built to permit
any noble or sublime striving – such as a striving towards light and truth –
to thrive unchecked or to exist for its own sake. Rather, even if something
like this could ever assert itself, and its idea be thus introduced, material
interests[a] and personal goals will overpower it immediately and turn it into
their own tool or mask. Accordingly, after Kant gave renewed prestige to
philosophy, it was not long before this too had to become the instrument of
different goals, of state goals from above and personal ones from below; –
even if this was not philosophy in the strict sense, it was nonetheless its
look-alike and passed for philosophy. This should come as no surprise to
us, because the vast majority of people are constitutionally incapable of
XVIII   entertaining any goals except material ones, and cannot even imagine any
other kind. This is why to strive after truth alone is much too lofty and
eccentric an aspiration than can be expected to arouse the sincere interest
or real sympathy of all people, many people, or even just a few people. If,
nevertheless, you see a remarkable spirit of activity (such as in Germany at
the moment), a general bustle, people discussing and writing about matters
philosophical, you can confidently assume that the actual first mover,[b] the
hidden, driving force behind this activity, notwithstanding solemn looks
and assurances, is in fact real and not ideal goals. Specifically, it is personal,
official, ecclesiastical, political, and in short material interests that people
have in view. Consequently, it is purely partisan interests that set the many
pens of these supposed sages[c] so powerfully into motion, and so intent,
not insight, is the guiding star for these noise-makers,[d] and truth is really
the last thing they have on their minds. The truth does not find partisans:
rather, it can make its way through this sort of philosophical mêlée as
calmly and inconspicuously as through the winter night of the darkest
century that was held captive by the most rigid church doctrines, where
the truth was communicated like the esoteric doctrine of a few adepts, or
even entrusted to parchment alone. In fact I would say that no age can be
less propitious for philosophy than one in which it is shamefully misused

[a] *Interessen*
[b] *primum mobile*
[c] *Weltweisen*
[d] *Tumultuanten*

as an instrument of the state on the one side and as a meal ticket[a] on the other. Or do people really think that, given these sorts of aspirations and this sort of turmoil, the truth, which is not even at issue here, will somehow come to light? Truth is not a prostitute who throws her arms around the necks of people who do not want her: to the contrary, she is such a coy beauty that even someone who has sacrificed everything to her cannot be certain of her favours.

Now if governments make philosophy into the instrument of state goals, scholars on the other hand see a professorship of philosophy as an occupation that puts dinner on the table, just like any other occupation: so they clamour after this occupation in the assurance of their own good disposition, i.e. their intention to serve that goal. And they are as good as their word: not truth, not clarity, not Plato, not Aristotle, but rather the aims that they are meant to serve are their guiding star and instantly become the criterion of what is true, valuable, worthy of consideration, and of its opposite. So something that does not correspond to these aims, even if it is the most important and the most extraordinary achievement in their field, will either be condemned or, where this seems dangerous,[b] suffocated by being collectively ignored. Just look at their unanimous zeal in opposition to pantheism: will any fool believe that it comes from genuine conviction? – When philosophy is degraded into a money-earning trade,[c] how could it fail to degenerate into sophistry? Precisely because this is inevitable, and the rule 'he who pays the piper picks the tune'[d] has always held true, the ancients considered earning money from philosophy to be the mark of a sophist. – Now in addition, since nothing but mediocrity can be expected, demanded, or purchased for money in this world, we must resign ourselves to this fact even here. Accordingly, in all the German universities we see good old mediocrity struggling to create a philosophy that does not yet even remotely exist, using its own resources but accepting a prescribed standard and goal; – it would be almost cruel to make fun of such a spectacle.

For a long time, philosophy has been obliged to serve as a means to public ends on the one hand, and to private ends on the other; meanwhile, I have been pursuing my own train of thought for more than thirty years, undisturbed by all this, just because it is what I must do, and I could not do otherwise, out of an instinctive drive which is nonetheless supported

XIX

[a] *Erwerbsmittel*
[b] *bedenklich*
[c] *Brodgewerbe*
[d] [The German is more literally: 'Whose bread I eat, his song I sing.']

XX   by the confidence that what is thought truly and what throws light on obscurity will be grasped at some point by another thinking mind. It will appeal to him and give him pleasure and comfort: you speak to a mind like this just as we have been spoken to by those similar to us, who have become our consolation in this wasteland of life. In the meantime, we must pursue our problems for their own sake and on their own. But it is a strange fact about philosophical meditations that only what someone has thought through and investigated for himself can later be of use to someone else: not what was intended for others from the start. The former has the recognizable character of complete honesty, because people are not trying to fool themselves or offer themselves empty shells; this banishes all sophistications and verbiage, and so every sentence immediately repays the effort it takes to read it. Accordingly, my writings carry the stamp of honesty[a] and openness[b] so clearly and candidly that this in itself puts them into stark contrast with the three famous sophists of the post-Kantian period: I can always be found on the standpoint of *reflection*, i.e. of rational deliberation[c] and honest exchange of ideas,[d] never on that of *inspiration*, which is called intellectual intuition or even absolute thought, but whose true names are drivel and charlatanism. – So, working in this spirit and all the while seeing the false and the bad enjoying universal prestige, and in fact windbags' dronings* and charlatanism**,[4] held in the highest honour, I have long since renounced the approbation of my contemporaries. For twenty long years, these contemporaries have hailed a Hegel, this intellectual Caliban, as the greatest of philosophers, and indeed so loudly that it resounded throughout Europe – it is impossible for someone who has seen this to covet their approbation. They have no more wreaths of honour to

XXI   bestow: their approbation has been prostituted, and their censure means nothing. I can prove that I am serious about this, because if I were really after the approbation of my contemporaries I would have had to cross out some twenty passages that totally contradict all their views, and in fact must be somewhat offensive to them. But I would think it a dereliction on my part to sacrifice even a syllable for the sake of such approbation. My own guiding star has in all seriousness been the truth; to follow this I had

---

  * Fichte and Schelling
 ** Hegel

  [a] *Redlichkeit*
  [b] *Offenheit*
  [c] *Besinnung*
  [d] *Mittheilung*

to begin by thinking only of self-approbation, resolutely turning my back on an age that has sunk far when it comes to all higher intellectual pursuits, and a national literature that has been demoralized but for the exceptions, and in which the art of combining lofty expressions with lowly sentiments has reached a new high. Of course like everyone else, I can never escape the mistakes and weaknesses inherent in my nature, but I will not increase them with unworthy accommodations.–

Now as far as this second edition is concerned, I am pleased first of all that after twenty-five years I can find nothing to retract, and thus that my fundamental convictions have proved their worth, at least as far as I am concerned. The changes to the first volume (which contains only the text of the first edition) never touch on what is essential, but rather concern only secondary matters, and consist for the most part of short, explanatory addenda that have been inserted here and there. Only in the Critique of the Kantian Philosophy are there significant corrections and lengthy additions, because these could not be put into a supplementary Book as was the case with the four Books presenting my own teachings, where each Book received a supplement in the second volume. This supplementary volume is my preferred method for adding to and improving each Book, because the twenty-five years that have passed since they were written have made such a noticeable difference in my mode of presentation and tone of delivery that I could not really merge the content of the second XXII volume with that of the first into a unified whole, since such a fusion would be detrimental to both. So I offer the two works separately, and have often failed to change the earlier presentation at even those points where I would now express myself in an entirely different fashion; this is because I did not want to spoil the work of my younger years with the fault-finding of age. Whatever might stand in need of correction in this respect will rectify itself automatically in the readers' minds with the help of the second volume. Each volume supplements the other in the full sense of the term; namely, to the extent that this is due to one phase of a human life being an intellectual supplement to the other. Consequently, you will not only find each volume containing something the other does not, but you will also find that the advantages of the one consist in precisely what is lacking in the other. Thus, if the advantage of the first half of my work over the second lies in what only the fervour of youth and the energy of a first conception can bring, then the second half will surpass the first in the maturity and complete elaboration of the ideas, since these are fruits that follow only from a long life and much hard work. When I had the strength originally to grasp the basic idea of my system, to follow it immediately through its four ramifications,[a] to return from these to the unity of the trunk from which these four branches emerged, and then to give a clear presentation of the whole, I could not then be in a position to elaborate all the parts of the system with the completeness, thoroughness and detail that can only be attained by meditating on it over the course of many years; such meditations are required to test it out and illustrate it with countless facts, to support it with the greatest variety of proofs, to shed light on it from all angles, and then to place the different points of view into bold contrast in order to clearly separate the diversity of materials and put them into an orderly arrangement. So, although it would certainly be more pleasant to the reader to have my entire work in one piece rather than having it consist (as it does now) of two halves to be used together, the reader should take into account the fact that this would have required me to accomplish in one period of life what is possible only in two, since I would have needed to possess in a single period of life all the qualities that nature divided into two very different periods. Accordingly, the need to deliver my work in two mutually supplementary halves can be compared to the necessity that requires an achromatic object-glass (which cannot be made from a single piece) to be constructed by combining a convex lens of crown-glass with a concave lens of flint-glass, which only together produce the desired effect. Still, the reader will be compensated to some extent for the inconvenience of using two volumes simultaneously by the variety and diversion that comes when the same topic is treated by the same person in the same spirit but at very different ages. In the meantime I would strongly advise people who are unfamiliar with my philosophy to begin with the first volume without getting drawn into the supplements, and to use these only in a second reading; otherwise, it would be too difficult for them to grasp the coherence of the system which only the first volume presents, while the principal doctrines are justified more fully and developed completely on their own in the second. Even someone who has not decided whether to read the first volume twice will do better to read the second volume on its own, only after having read the first. He can do this by reading the chapters in order, since there is certainly a connection between the chapters of the second volume, albeit a looser one, and any gaps can be filled completely by recalling the first volume, provided this has been understood fully. Moreover, the reader will find references everywhere pointing back to the relevant passages in the first volume; this is why in

XXIII

XXIV

---

[a] *Verzweigungen*

the second edition of the first volume I numbered the sections which were separated only by lines in the first edition.

I have already explained in the preface to the first edition that my philosophy takes Kant as its point of departure and thus presupposes a thorough familiarity with that philosophy: I will reiterate that here. Kant's teaching so fundamentally alters every mind that has grasped it, that it can be considered an intellectual rebirth. It is the only thing capable of truly eliminating the inherent realism that comes from the original constitution[a] of the intellect. Neither Berkeley nor Malebranche could accomplish this, because they remain too strictly with the universal, while Kant enters into the particular and indeed in a way that has neither precedent nor successor. This results in an entirely idiosyncratic, one might say immediate, effect on the mind, which is then thoroughly disabused and henceforth sees everything in a new light. Only this will make the mind receptive to the more positive explanations I have to give. On the other hand, people who have not mastered Kant's philosophy are, whatever else they might have done, in something like a state of innocence, namely caught in that natural and childish realism into which we are all born, and which makes everything possible for us except philosophy. Consequently, this type of person is to the first what a minor is to an adult. The fact that this truth sounds paradoxical today, which would certainly not have been the case in the first thirty years after the appearance of the critique of reason, is due to the fact that a generation has grown up in the meantime that is not really familiar with Kant, having read him quickly and impatiently or having heard only a second-hand report. This again is due to the fact that the generation has been instructed poorly and as a result has wasted its time with the philosophemes of ordinary, and therefore officious minds, or even those of the windbag sophists who were irresponsibly recommended to it. This XXV explains the confusion with first concepts and, in general, the unspeakable crudity and crassness that peers out from under the shell of affectation and pretension in the philosophical efforts of the generation raised in this way. But anyone who thinks he can get to know Kant's philosophy from other people's accounts has made a terrible mistake. In fact, I would seriously warn people against accounts of this kind, particularly the more recent ones: and in these past few years I have come across descriptions of Kantian philosophy in the works of Hegelians that have entered the realm of complete fantasy. How could minds that have been disfigured and spoiled by Hegelian nonsense while still in the freshness of youth remain capable

---

[a] *Bestimmung*

of following Kant's profound investigations? They have been accustomed from early on to mistake the hollowest verbiage for philosophical ideas, the most miserable sophisms for sagacity, childish absurdities for dialectic, and their heads have been muddled by absorbing crazed word-combinations which torture and exhaust the mind that tries in vain to extract some meaning from them. Minds like these do not need a critique of reason, they do not need philosophy: first they need a medicine for the mind[a] as a purgative,[b] something like 'a short course in commonsensology',[c] and then we must wait and see whether there can ever be talk of philosophy with them. – It is futile to look for Kant's doctrine outside of Kant's own works: but these are thoroughly instructive, even where he is wrong, even where he is mistaken. His originality ensures that what holds for all real philosophers holds for him as well, and in the highest degree: you can get to know them only through their own writings, not through other people's accounts. This is because the thoughts of these extraordinary spirits cannot withstand filtration through a common mind. Born behind the broad, tall, beautifully arched brows from under which radiant eyes shine forth, they lose all strength and all life and no longer look like themselves when transplanted into the narrow dwellings and low housing of the narrow, depressed, thick-walled skulls where dull gazes peer out towards personal ends. We can even say that such heads act like uneven mirrors in which everything is twisted and distorted; things lose the regular proportions of their beauty and present a grimace. You can receive philosophical thoughts only from their authors: anyone who feels driven to philosophy needs to seek out its immortal teachers in the quiet sanctuary of their works. The main chapters of any one of these true philosophers will provide a hundred times more insight into that philosopher's teachings than the sluggish and cross-eyed accounts of these doctrines that are put out by ordinary minds who, in addition, are generally deeply enmeshed in whatever philosophy is currently in fashion, or in their own pet opinions.[d] But it is amazing how decidedly the public prefers these second-hand descriptions. In fact, an elective affinity seems to be at work here, drawing common natures to what is similar to them, so that they would rather hear from someone like themselves what even a great mind has said. This might be based on the same principle as the system of reciprocal instruction, according to which children learn best from other children.

XXVI

---

[a] *medicina mentis*
[b] *Kathartikon*
[c] *un petit cours de senscommunologie*
[d] *Herzensmeinung*

Now one more word for the professors of philosophy. – The sagacity, the proper and subtle tact with which they immediately knew that my philosophy was something completely different from – and in fact inimical to – their own efforts, and, to use a popular phrase, not their cup of tea;[a] the assured and sharp-witted political instinct[b] that told them exactly   XXVII
what to do with my philosophy, as well as the perfect unanimity with which they did it, and finally the persistence with which they kept it up, – I have always admired all this. This procedure they hit upon for dealing with my philosophy (which also has the advantage of being easy to put into effect) consists, as is known, in ignoring it completely and thereby secreting[c] it, – Goethe's malicious expression,[d] which really means holding back what is important and meaningful. This silent treatment is made all the more effective through the corybantic racket with which the birth of the intellectual children of like-minded types is reciprocally celebrated, and which grabs the public's attention so that they notice how important these types look when they greet each other over these births. Who could mistake the purpose of this procedure? For there can be no objection to the principle 'live first, then philosophize'.[e] The gentlemen wish to live and indeed to live by *philosophy*: and it is to *this* that they have been referred, with their wives and children, and they have dared to do so, in spite of Petrarch's 'poor and naked you walk along, Philosophy'.[f] But my philosophy is totally unsuitable for anyone to live by. It is completely devoid of the primary, indispensible prerequisite for the philosophy of a well-paid teacher: a speculative theology, which should and must be the principal theme of all philosophy – in spite of the troublesome Kant with his critique of reason –, even if this puts them in the position of always speaking about things they cannot know in the least. In fact, my philosophy never even sets down the fable so cleverly devised by (and now so indispensable to) the professors of philosophy, the fable of an immediately and absolutely cognizing, intuiting, or apprehending[g] reason; you only need to get the reader to swallow this idea at the very beginning in order to go on as comfortably as you please, in a coach and   XXVIII
four as it were, into the territory beyond the possibility of all experience, a territory Kant completely and forever blocked off to our cognition. There

[a] *etwas das nicht in ihren Kram paßt* [The German is more literally: 'something that doesn't suit their plans']
[b] *Politik*
[c] *Sekretiren*
[d] [in *Tag- und Jahreshefte*, 1821]
[e] *primum vivere, deinde philosophari*
[f] *povera e nuda vai filosofia* [Petrarch, *Il Canzoniere* [*The Songbook*], I, sonnet 7, 10]
[g] *vernehmenden*

you find precisely those fundamental dogmas of modern, Judaical, optimistic Christianity, immediately revealed and most beautifully arranged. Now what in the world could my own reckless, brooding, unprofitable philosophy have to do with that *alma mater*,[a] the good, productive university philosophy? My philosophy lacks that essential prerequisite and has no North Star except the truth, the naked, thankless, friendless, and often persecuted truth, and looking neither left nor right, heads towards this alone. University philosophy, on the other hand, burdened with a hundred interests and a thousand considerations, carefully manoeuvres its way, since it will always bear in mind the fear of the Lord, the will of the minister, the tenets of the established church, the wishes of the publisher, the encouragement of the students, the goodwill of colleagues, the course of the day's politics, the momentary inclination of the public, and whatever else. Or: what does my quiet, serious search for truth have in common with the shrill schoolroom bickering of the teachers' desks and benches, which are always fuelled by personal aims? In fact, these two types of philosophy are fundamentally different. This is why I brook no compromise, accept no fellowship, and take nobody into account, except perhaps someone who is looking for nothing but the truth; thus, none of the current philosophical partisans: they all follow their interests; but I have only insights to offer, and ones that do not suit any of them because they are not modelled on any of them. An entirely new age would have to dawn before my philosophy could ever be taught from the teacher's lectern. – That would be a fine thing, for a philosophy like this, which cannot be lived by, to come out into the open air and even win general admiration! That is why it had to be prevented, and had to be opposed to a man. But it is not

XXIX   such an easy game, this disputing and opposing: and it is also dangerous, because it calls the public's attention to the matter, and reading my works could spoil the public's taste for the lucubrations of philosophy professors. Anyone who has tasted seriousness will lose the taste for jokes, especially jokes of a tedious nature. This is why the system of silence that has been so universally adopted is the only correct system, and I can only advise people to stick with it and to keep it up for as long as it works, namely until ignoring something is taken to imply ignorance of it: then there will still be just enough time to think the better of it. Meanwhile, everyone is certainly free to pluck a little feather here or there for their own use, since there does not tend to be too oppressive a superfluity of thoughts at home. So the system of ignoring and silence can still hold up for quite a while, at

---

[a] [nourishing mother]

least for the span of time that I might have left to live; and this is quite a gain. And if in the meantime an indiscreet voice can occasionally be heard, then it will soon be drowned out by the loud lectures of the professors who know how to talk to the public about very different things and with important looks on their faces. Nonetheless I advise that the unanimity of the procedure be adhered to somewhat more strictly, and particularly for an eye to be kept on young people, who can sometimes be terribly indiscreet. Even so, I cannot guarantee that the commendable procedure can be kept up for ever, and I cannot vouch for the final outcome. It is after all a tricky business, directing the public, as good and obedient as the public usually is. Although we almost always see the Gorgias's and the Hippias's[a] in the ascendancy, and although the absurd usually rises to the top, and although it seems impossible for the voice of the individual to ever break through the chorus of the deluders and the deluded; – nonetheless, genuine works will always have an entirely distinctive, quiet, slow and powerful effect, and in the end they can be seen rising above the turmoil as if by a miracle, like a balloon that flies up above this planet's thick atmosphere into purer   XXX
regions, and having arrived there, stays put, and no one can pull it back down again.

Written in Frankfurt am Main in February 1844.

[a] [Gorgias and Hippias are two of the ancient Greek Sophists]

Preface to the third edition

What is true and genuine would gain ground in the world more easily if those who are incapable of expressing it would not at the same time conspire to suppress it. This circumstance has already delayed and impeded many things that could have done the world some good, even where it has not stifled them completely. The consequence of this to me has been that although I was only thirty when the first edition of this work appeared, I am only seeing this third edition in my seventy-second year. I find consolation for this in *Petrarch's* words: 'If someone who has been running all day arrives in the evening, it is enough' (*On True Wisdom*, p. 140).[a] I too have finally arrived and have the satisfaction of seeing the beginnings of my influence at the end of my career, with the hope that this influence, according to an old rule, will last all the longer, since it was so late starting out.–

XXXII   The reader will not miss anything in this third edition that was contained in the second, but will receive considerably more, since with all the additions it runs 136 pages longer than the second edition, although it has the same type.

Seven years after the appearance of the second edition I published the two volumes of *Parerga and Paralipomena*. What is understood by this latter name consists of additions to the systematic presentation of my philosophy which would have found their proper home in these volumes: but at that time I had to place them where I could, since it was very much an open question whether I would live to see this third edition. They are found in the second volume of the aforementioned *Parerga*, and will be easily recognized by the chapter titles.

Frankfurt am Main in September 1859.

---

[a]   *si quis, toto die currens, pervenit ad vesperam, satis est* (*de vera sapientia*, p. 140) [*Dialogo* I, B, in a Venetian edition of 1516. These dialogues are now not generally attributed to Petrarch]

FIRST BOOK

The world as representation, first consideration

Representation subject to the principle of sufficient reason: the object of experience and science

Sors de l'enfance, ami, réveille-toi!
Jean-Jacques Rousseau

['Wake up, my friend, and leave childish
things behind!'
– *La Nouvelle Héloïse*, V, I]

§ 1   3

'The world is my representation': – this holds true for every living, cognitive being, although only a human being can bring it to abstract, reflective consciousness: and if he actually does so he has become philosophically sound.[a] It immediately becomes clear and certain to him that he is not acquainted with either the sun or the earth, but rather only with an eye that sees a sun, with a hand that feels an earth, and that the surrounding world exists only as representation, that is, exclusively in relation to something else, the representing being that he himself is. – If any *a priori* truth can be asserted, then this is it; for this truth expresses the form of all possible and conceivable experience. This form is more universal than any other form, more universal than time, space and causality, which, in fact, presuppose it. If each of these forms (which we have recognized as so many particular forms of the principle of sufficient reason) applies only to a particular class of representations, then by contrast, subject / object dichotomy[b] is the general form of all these classes. It is the only form under which any representation – whatever kind it may be, abstract or intuitive, pure or empirical – is possible or even conceivable. Thus, no truth is more certain, no truth is more independent of all others and no truth is less in need of proof than this one: that everything there is for cognition (i.e. the whole

[a] *die philosophische Besonnenheit ist bei ihm eingetreten*
[b] *Zerfallen*

23

4   world) is only an object in relation to a subject, an intuition of a beholder,[a] is, in a word, representation. Of course this truth applies just as much to the past and future as to the present, and to the furthest as much as to what is close by: for it applies to time and space themselves, and it is only in time and space that such distinctions can be made. Everything that can or does belong in any way to the world is unavoidably afflicted with this dependence[b] on the subject and exists only for the subject. The world is representation.

This truth is not at all new. It was already present in the sceptical considerations that served as Descartes' point of departure.[1] Berkeley however was the first to express it definitely: he rendered an eternal service to philosophy by doing so, even though the rest of his teaching cannot survive. Kant's first mistake was to neglect this proposition, as is shown in the Appendix. – On the other hand, W. Jones (in the last of his papers 'On the Philosophy of the Asiatics', in *Asiatic Researches* Vol. IV, p. 164) testifies as to how early this basic truth was recognized by the wisdom of the Indians, appearing as it does as the fundamental tenet of the Vedanta philosophy (attributed to the *Vyasa*): 'the fundamental tenet of the Vedanta school consisted not in denying the existence of matter, that is of solidity, impenetrability, and extended figure (to deny which would be lunacy), but in correcting the popular notion of it, and in contending that it has no essence independent of mental perception; that existence and perceptibility are convertible terms.'[c] These words are quite sufficient to express the compatibility[d] of empirical reality with transcendental ideality.[2]

In this First Book we consider the world from this side alone, namely in so
5   far as it is representation. However, the inner reluctance with which anyone accepts that the world is merely their representation – even though the acceptance is inescapable – shows that, irrespective of its truth, this aspect is one-sided and hence the result of some arbitrary abstraction. We will make up for its one-sidedness in the next Book by means of another truth, a truth that is not as immediately certain as our present point of departure, and one that can only be achieved through more profound research, more difficult abstractions, separating what is different and unifying what is the same, – a truth that must be very serious and alarming, if not terrifying to anyone, a truth that can and must be maintained by him as well, namely this: 'The world is my will'. –

---

[a]   *Anschauung eines Anschauenden*
[b]   *Bedingtseyn*
[c]   [Schopenhauer quotes the passage in English and supplies a German translation in a footnote]
[d]   *Zusammenbestehen*

Until then however (i.e. in this First Book) we must steadfastly consider the world from the side where we have started, the side from which it can be known in cognition.[a] Accordingly, and without reluctance, we will consider all existing[b] objects – even our bodies themselves (as we will soon discuss in greater detail) – simply as representations and will call them mere representations. In so doing, we will abstract (as will hopefully become clear to everyone later) from the will, the sole constituent of the other side of the world. For the world is, on the one side, completely *representation*, just as it is, on the other side, completely *will*. However, a reality that would be neither of these, but rather an object in itself (and unfortunately this is what Kant's thing in itself has surreptitiously[c] degenerated into) is a fantastic absurdity[d] and to assume such a thing is a philosophical will-o'-the wisp.

§ 2

The *subject* is the seat of all cognition[e] but is itself not cognized by anything. Accordingly it is the support for the world and always presupposed as the general[f] condition of all appearances, of all objects: whatever exists, exists only for the subject. We all find ourselves as this subject, although only in so far as we have cognition of things, not in so far as we are objects of cognition. But the body is already an object, and, from this point of view, we call it too a representation. This is because the body is an object among objects, and must obey the laws of objects, even though it is an immediate object.*,3 Like all objects of intuition, it is situated within the forms of all cognition, in space and time (by means of which there is multiplicity). The subject, on the other hand, having cognition, but never cognized, is not situated within these forms, which in fact always already presuppose it. Neither multiplicity nor its opposite, unity, apply to the subject. We never have any cognition of it; rather, where there is cognition at all, it is what has that cognition.

There are two essential, necessary and inseparable halves to the world as representation (and here we are considering it only from this point

6

---

* *On the Principle of Sufficient Reason*, 2nd Edition, § 22.

[a] *Erkennbarkeit*
[b] *vorhandenen*
[c] *unter den Händen*
[d] *erträumtes Unding*
[e] *Alles erkennt*
[f] *durchgängige*

of view). The first is the *object*, whose form is space and time, and thus multiplicity. The other half, however, is the subject, which does not lie in either space or time because it is present complete and undivided in each representing being. From this it follows that a single such being with its object completes the world as representation just as much as the millions in existence do: and if this single representing being were to disappear, the world as representation would no longer exist. Consequently, these two halves are inseparable, even in thought, because each of them has meaning and exists only through and for the other. Each is present when the other is as well and disappears when the other disappears. They share a common border: where the object begins, the subject ends. That they share a border is shown by the fact that the most essential – and therefore most general – forms of all objects (space, time and causality) can be discovered and fully comprehended starting out from the subject even in the absence of any cognition of the object itself. In Kantian terms, these forms lie in our consciousness *a priori*. One of Kant's chief merits – and it is a very great one – is to have discovered this. But I go further and claim that the principle of sufficient reason is the common term for all these forms that objects have and that we are conscious of *a priori*; and so everything we know[a] purely *a priori* is nothing other than the very content of this principle and what can be deduced from it. This principle therefore expresses the totality of our *a priori* and certain cognition. In my essay *On the Principle of Sufficient Reason* I showed in detail how every possible object is subject to this principle, that is, how every such object stands in a necessary relation to other objects, on the one hand as determined and on the other hand as determining. This goes so far that the entire being[b] of all objects – in so far as they are objects, i.e. representations, and nothing else – can be exhaustively traced back to the necessary relation of objects to each other, so that the being of objects consists in nothing but this relation and is therefore completely relative (we will have more to say about this later). Moreover, I have shown that the necessary relation expressed in general by the principle of sufficient reason appears in different forms[c] corresponding to the classes into which objects fall according to their possibility; and again, this is what guarantees that the classification is correct. Here I assume throughout that the reader is presently familiar with what I said in that work, because if I had not already said it, it would necessarily belong at this point.

[a] *wissen*
[b] *Daseyn*
[c] *Gestalten*

§ 3

The most important division among all our representations is between the intuitive and the abstract. The latter form only *one* group of representations, namely concepts. Of all the creatures on earth, only human beings possess concepts, and the ability to conceptualize (which has always been referred to as *reason**) distinguishes humans from all animals. Later we will consider these abstract representations on their own; but first we will discuss only *intuitive representations*. These, then, encompass the entire visible world or the whole of experience, including the conditions for the possibility of experience. We have already mentioned Kant's highly significant discovery about these conditions, these forms of the visible world – i.e. about what is most universal in the perception[a] of the visible world, what belongs to all appearances of the visible world in the same way: time and space. He discovered that time and space can not only be conceived abstractly,[b] on their own and independently of their content, but they can also be intuited immediately.[c] This intuition is not some phantasm derived from repeated experience; rather, it is something independent of experience, and to such an extent that experience must in fact be conceived as dependent on it, since the properties of time and space, as they are known *a priori* in intuition, apply to all possible experience as laws that it must always come out in accordance with. This is the reason why, in my essay *On the Principle of Sufficient Reason*, I considered space and time as a special autonomous[d] group of representations, in so far as they are pure intuitions without content. Now Kant's discovery of this characteristic[e] of the universal forms of intuition is important in the following way: these universal forms are themselves intuitions[f] in their own right, independent of experience, and they can be recognized by their thorough conformity to law, which is the ground of the infallibility of mathematics. But it is also no less noteworthy a property of these forms that the principle of sufficient reason (which determines experience as the law of causality and motivation, while it determines thought as the law of the grounding of

8

---

* Kant was the only one to have mixed up this concept of reason. In this regard I refer to the Appendix as well as to my *Two Fundamental Problems of Ethics*, 'On the Basis of Morals', § 6.

[a] *Wahrnehmung*
[b] *in abstracto*
[c] *unmittelbar*
[d] *für sich bestehende*
[e] *Beschaffenheit*
[f] *anschaulich*

judgement) makes its appearance here in a most distinctive guise, which I call *the ground of being*.[a] In time, this ground is the succession of moments, and in space, the position of its parts that determine each other reciprocally *ad infinitum*.

Readers who see clearly from my introductory essay that the principle of sufficient reason has a unified content in spite of its different forms, will also be convinced how important cognition of the simplest of those forms (which we have identified as *time*) is for an insight into their own innermost essence. They will be convinced that each moment in time exists only in so far as it has annihilated the previous moment, its father, only to be annihilated just as quickly in its turn. They will be convinced that past and future (setting aside the consequences of their contents) are as unreal[b] as any dream; that the present is only the border between the two and so has neither extension nor duration. We will also recognize the same unreality[c] in all the other forms of the principle of sufficient reason. We will see that as it is with time, so it is with space, and as it is with space, so it is with everything that is in both space and time: everything therefore, that arises from cause or motive exists only relatively, exists only through and for something else similar to itself, i.e. something that has only the same relative existence.[d] In essence, this view is ancient: we see it in Heraclitus when he bemoans the eternal flux of things; in Plato's disparaging account of objects as eternally becoming but never being; in Spinoza's doctrine of the mere accidents of a single substance, which is the only thing that exists or endures; in the way Kant opposes what we have this kind of cognition of, as mere appearance, to things in themselves; in the end, it is the age-old wisdom of India that speaks here: 'It is *māyā*, the veil of deception that covers the eyes of mortals and lets them see a world that cannot be described as either being or not being: for it is like a dream; like sunlight reflected off sand that a distant traveller mistakes for water; or like a discarded rope that the traveller thinks is a snake.' (These comparisons are repeated countless times in the *Vedas* and the *Puranas*.) What all these meant, what they were speaking about, is the very thing we are considering here: the world as representation, subject to the principle of sufficient reason.

---

[a] *Grund des Seyns*
[b] *nichtig*
[c] *Nichtigkeit*
[d] *wieder nur eben so bestehendes*

§ 4

To recognize[a] the whole essence of time, it is enough to recognize the form of the principle of sufficient reason that appears in pure time as such (and is the basis for all counting and calculation). Time is, in fact, nothing over and above this very form; it has no other properties. The form of the principle of sufficient reason in time is succession; and succession is the whole essence of time. – Further, for exhaustive cognition of the whole essence of space, it is enough to recognize the principle of sufficient reason as it governs the pure intuition of space: space in its entirety is nothing other than the possibility of reciprocal determination of its parts, that is, *position*. The whole of geometry consists in considering this possibility in detail and laying down its consequences in abstract concepts for convenient application. – In just the same way, to recognize the entire essence of matter as such, it is enough to recognize the form of the principle of sufficient reason governing the content of the forms of space and time, what makes them perceptible, i.e. matter, that is to say, the law of causality: matter is, in its entirety, nothing other than causality, which is immediately apparent to anyone who thinks about it. This amounts to saying that for matter, its being[b] is its acting:[c] and it is inconceivable that matter has any other being. Only by acting can it fill space and time: its action on the immediate object (which is itself matter) is a condition for intuition, and matter can exist only in intuition. We can know the result of one material object acting upon[d] another only if the second object now has a different effect on the immediate object than it did before – indeed the effect[e] is nothing more than this. The whole being of matter therefore lies in cause and effect: for matter, its being is its acting. (For more details on this, see my essay *On the Principle of Sufficient Reason*, § 21, p. 77.)[4] It is very much to the point that the German term for the sum total[f] of everything material is *Wirklichkeit, actuality*,* a much more expressive word than *Realität*, reality. Matter acts only on matter, which is why the whole being and essence of

10

---

* *Mira in quibusdam rebus verborum proprietas est, et consuetudo sermonis antiqui quaedam efficacissimis notis signat* [It is astonishing how words are suitable to certain things, and the linguistic usage of the ancients designates many things in the most appropriate way]. *Seneca epist.* 81 [*Epistles*, Book X, 81, 9].

a *erkennen*
b *Daseyn*
c *Wirken*
d *Einwirkung*
e *Wirkung*
f *Inbegriff*

matter consists simply in the lawlike alteration[a] that *one* part of matter
brings about in another, and is therefore completely relative, according to
a relation that is valid only within its limits – just like space and just like
time.

Time and space however can each be represented on its own in intuition,
even without matter; matter, on the other hand, cannot be represented
without time and space. Even the form, which is inseparable from matter,
already presupposes space; and the activity of matter (which is its whole
being) always concerns alteration, and therefore always concerns a determination of *time*. But matter does not presuppose space and time merely
individually; rather the combination of the two constitutes the essence of
matter, precisely because the essence is, as has been demonstrated, action,
i.e. causality. This is because all the countless conceivable appearances
and states of affairs could coexist in infinite space without restricting each
other; or they could succeed each other in infinite time without mutual
disturbance. But in these cases there would not be any necessary relation between states of affairs and no need for a rule to determine that
relation – indeed, such a rule could never be applied. Consequently, even
with coexistence in space and change in time, there still would not be
causality as long as each of these two forms continued to run its own
course without any connection to the other; and since causality is in fact
the essence of matter, there would be no matter either. – But the law of
causality gets its meaning[b] and necessity from this alone: that the essence of
alteration is not mere change[c] of state itself, but rather lies in the fact that
one and the same position in space contains now *this* state of affairs, but then
later *another*; and the fact that at *one* and the same particular time there
is one state *here* but another state *over there*: only this mutual constraint
of space and time lends meaning, and at the same time necessity to the
rule that governs the way alterations must proceed. The law of causality
therefore does not determine the succession of states simply in time, but
in fact determines this succession with respect to a particular space; and it
does not determine the existence of states in a particular location, but in
fact in this location at a particular time. So alteration (i.e. change that takes
place according to causal law) always concerns a particular part of space
and, *simultaneously* and together with this, a particular part of time. Consequently, causality unites space with time. But we have found that the whole

[a] *Veränderung*
[b] *Bedeutung*
[c] *Wechsel*

essence of matter lies in action,[a] i.e. in causality: as a result, matter must also unify space and time, that is, matter must possess the properties of both time and space simultaneously, however much the two conflict with each other; matter must reconcile in itself what is impossible in each one: the fleeting course of time and the rigid and unchanging persistence of space (it derives infinite divisibility from both). Thus we find that matter involves, in the first place, *simultaneity*, which cannot take place either in mere time (which has no coexistence) or in mere space (which has no before, after, or now). But in fact the *simultaneous* existence of multiple states constitutes the essence of actuality because it first makes *duration* possible, in that duration itself can be known only in contrast to a change in something 12 present at the same time, and also because change can be characterized as alteration (that is, variation[b] of quality and form in a persistent *substance*, i.e. *matter*) only by means of what endures throughout the change.* If the world existed only in space, it would be rigid and unmoving; there would be no succession, no alteration, no activity – but with activity the representation of matter is also removed. On the other hand, if the world existed only in time, everything would be fleeting: there would be no persistence, no coexistence, thus no simultaneity, consequently no duration, and therefore, again, no matter. Only through the unification of time and space is there matter, i.e. the possibility of simultaneity, and through that, duration, and again through these, the persistence of substance during alteration of state.** Because it has its essence in the unification of space and time, matter clearly bears the marks of both. Matter attests to its origin in space partly through form (from which it is inseparable), but more particularly through its persistence (substance). This is because change is a property of time alone: there is nothing enduring in time considered on its own, which shows that the *a priori* certainty of persistence is derived entirely from the certainty of space.*** Matter reveals its origin in time through quality (accident): to appear at all, matter needs quality, which is in itself always causality, i.e. action on another piece of matter, and therefore alteration[c] – a temporal concept. The lawlikeness of the action however always

---

* That matter and substance are identical is shown in detail in the Appendix.

** This is also the reason for Kant's definition of matter as 'what is movable in space' [*Metaphysical Foundations of Natural Science*, Ak. 4: 480], because motion is nothing but the unification of space and time.

*** Not, as Kant has it, from cognition of time, as is shown in the Appendix.

[a] *Wirken*
[b] *Wandel*
[c] *Veränderung*

refers to both space and time: this is the only thing that gives it meaning. Causality can legislate nothing more than what kind of state occurs *at a particular time and in a particular place*. This derivation of the fundamental determinations of matter from forms of cognition that we are conscious of *a priori* is the basis for our recognition of certain properties of matter as *a priori*, namely: the ability to fill space[a] (that is, impenetrability, which is to say activity), as well as extension, infinite divisibility, persistence (i.e. indestructibility) and finally mobility. On the other hand, gravity is rather to be counted on the side of *a posteriori* cognition despite its universality and even though *Kant* treats it as cognizable *a priori* in *The Metaphysical Foundations of Natural Science*, p. 71 (Rosenkranz edition, p. 372).[b,5]

Just as the object exists only for the subject, as its representation, so each particular class of representations exists only for an equally specific disposition in the subject. These dispositions are called cognitive faculties and Kant's name for the subjective correlate of time and space (considered in themselves, as empty forms) is 'pure sensibility'. Since Kant broke new ground here, the expression may be retained even though it is not quite appropriate, since sensibility already presupposes matter. The subjective correlate of matter (or causality, since the two are the same) is the *understanding*,[c] and it is nothing other than this. To have cognition of causality is the understanding's only function, its single capability[d] – and it is a great and sweeping one with many applications and an unmistakable unity behind each of its manifestations. Conversely, all causality, and therefore all matter, and with it the whole of actuality, exists only for the understanding, through the understanding, and in the understanding. The first and simplest manifestation of the understanding which, in addition, is always present, is the intuition of the actual world, and this is absolutely nothing other than cognition of the cause based on the effect. Consequently, all intuition is intellectual.[e] Nonetheless we might never reach this if we were not immediately acquainted with some effect that could serve as a starting point: but there are in fact such effects on the animal body. To this extent, such bodies are the *immediate objects* of the subject: they mediate the intuition of all other objects. The changes that every animal body experiences are cognized immediately, that is, they are sensed;[f] and

---

[a] *Raumerfüllung*
[b] [Ak. 4: 518]
[c] *Verstand*
[d] *Kraft*
[e] *intellektual*
[f] *empfunden*

in so far as this effect is referred back to its cause, the intuition arises of this cause as an *object*. This referring is not a conclusion drawn from abstract concepts; it does not take place in reflection and is not voluntary; rather it is immediate, necessary and certain. It is the mode of cognition of the *pure understanding*. Without this, there would never be intuition and only a dull, plant-like consciousness of alterations in the immediate   14 object would remain. These alterations would follow one after the other in utterly meaningless succession unless, as pain or pleasure, they had some meaning for the will. But, just as the visible world is there as soon as the sun rises, so too the understanding with its one simple function transforms dull, meaningless sensation into intuition in *one* fell swoop. What the eye, the ear, the hand senses is not an intuition: it is merely data. Only when the understanding proceeds from the effect back to the cause is the world present in intuition, spread out in space, its form capable of change, its matter persisting throughout all time (because the understanding unites space and time in the representation of *matter*, i.e. activity). Just as the world as representation exists only through the understanding, it exists only for the understanding as well. In the first chapter of my essay *On Vision and Colours*, I have already discussed how the understanding creates an intuition out of the data supplied by the senses; how a child learns to have intuitions by comparing the impressions of the same object received by the various senses; how in fact this is the only thing that sheds light on so many sensory phenomena[a] such as seeing a single image with two eyes; or the experience of double vision when squinting or when viewing objects at different distances from the eye in a single glance; as well as all illusions caused by a sudden alteration in the sense organs. But I have gone into this important topic much more deeply and in much more detail in the second edition of my essay *On the Principle of Sufficient Reason* (§ 21).[6] Everything I wrote there in fact belongs at this point, and therefore really should be repeated here. But I am almost as averse to copying out my own work as someone else's, and I am not in a position to present it better here than I did there. So rather than repeat myself, I refer to that text and now assume that the reader is acquainted with it.

The way children (and congenitally blind people who recover their vision) learn to see; the fact that we see a single object but sense it twice, once with each eye; double vision and 'double touching'[b] when the sense organs are displaced from their usual position; the upright appearance of

---

[a] *Sinnenphänomene*
[b] [Schopenhauer uses the unusual word *Doppelttasten* on an analogy with double vision (*Doppeltsehn*)]

15   objects when their image in the eye is upside down;[7] the projection[a] of
colour (which is a purely internal function, a polarized distribution of
the eye's activity) onto external objects; and finally the stereoscope[8] – all
these are solid and irrefutable proofs that *intuition* is, in every case, not
based merely on the senses, but is intellectual: it is pure *understanding-
based cognition*[b] *of the cause, given the effect*, and hence it presupposes the
law of causality. As a result, the possibility of any intuition, and with it
any experience, is wholly and fundamentally dependent on cognition of
the law of causality; and conversely, this cognition is not dependent on
experience as Hume's scepticism maintains, a view that receives its first
refutation here. The fact that cognition of causation is independent of
all experience (i.e. the fact that it is *a priori*) can be clearly demonstrated
only by showing that experience is dependent on it; and this in turn
can happen only by proving (as I have done here and in the other places
referred to)[9] that cognition of causation is already contained in intuition in
general, which is where all experience lies, and therefore that cognition of
causation is completely *a priori* in relation to experience and presupposed
by experience as a condition, rather than itself presupposing experience.
This result cannot be proved in the way attempted by Kant, a method that
I criticize in my essay *On the Principle of Sufficient Reason* (§ 23).

§ 5

We must, however, guard against the gross misunderstanding of supposing
that because intuition is mediated by cognition of causality there must
therefore be a cause / effect relation between subject and object, whereas in
fact such a relation only ever exists between the immediate and the mediate
object, i.e. between objects. This is the false supposition at the heart of that
foolish dispute over the reality of the external world in which dogmatism
(appearing first as realism and then as idealism) and scepticism confront
each other. Realism posits the object as cause and locates the effect in the
subject. Fichtean[10] idealism makes the object into an effect of the subject.
16   But what cannot be emphasized enough is that in terms of the principle
of sufficient reason there is no relation at all between subject and object.
As a result, neither of the two claims was susceptible of any proof, and
scepticism launched successful attacks on both. – The law of causality is
already prior to intuition and experience (it is their condition) and thus

---

[a] *Uebertragen*
[b] *Verstandeserkenntniß*

cannot be gleaned from experience as Hume thought; similarly, subject and object are already prior to all cognition, and serve as its primary condition. This is why they are also prior to the principle of sufficient reason in general, since this is simply the form of all objects, the universal manner in which objects appear. But the object always presupposes the subject, so there can be no ground / consequent relation between them. My essay *On the Principle of Sufficient Reason* is intended to render the following service: it presents the content of this principle (the essential form of all objects, that is, the universal manner in which all objects exist) as something that belongs to the object as such. But the object as such always presupposes the subject as its necessary correlate: so the subject always remains outside the jurisdiction[a] of the principle of sufficient reason. The dispute over the reality of the external world is in fact based on this improper extension of the validity of the principle of sufficient reason to the subject: given this mistake, the dispute could make no sense, even on its own terms.[b] On the one side, dogmatic realism[c] claims to separate the representation from the object (even though they are one and the same) by treating the representation as the effect of the object. This involves assuming the existence of a cause that is completely distinct from the representation, an object in itself that is independent of the subject. But this is totally inconceivable because, as an object, it would always presuppose a subject and hence is only ever the representation of a subject. Using the same false assumption, scepticism opposes this position by arguing that in representation we only ever have the effect and never the cause, that we only know how the object *acts*, never what it *is*, that this action might not bear the least resemblance to what it *is*, and indeed that it may be completely wrong to assume that the object exists at all, since scepticism argues that the law of causality is derived from experience, but now claims that the reality of this experience is itself supposed to depend on the law of causality. – On this point, both doctrines would be well advised to note first, that representation and object are the same thing; and second, that for objects of intuition, their *being* simply is their acting. Acting is precisely what constitutes the actuality of a thing. To insist that objects exist outside the representation of a subject – and to insist that actual objects have a being distinct from their acting – these demands are completely meaningless and contradictory. It follows that all we know about an object of intuition (in so far as it is an object, i.e. a representation) is the way it acts: there is nothing left to

17

---

[a] *Gebiet der Gültigkeit*
[b] *konnte sich selbst nicht verstehen*
[c] *der realistische Dogmatismus*

know about an object apart from its representation. To this extent, the world intuited in space and time, which manifests itself as pure causality, is completely real.[a] The world is exactly as it presents itself and it presents itself completely and without reserve as representation, held together by the law of causality. This is its empirical reality.[b,11] But on the other hand, causality exists only in the understanding and for the understanding. Thus the understanding is always the condition for the actual (i.e. active) world[c] as such and in its entirety: without the understanding this world is nothing. But this is not the only reason why we must emphatically deny the dogmatist's declaration that the external world is real apart from the subject: the dogmatist is also wrong because it is impossible to consistently think any object at all apart from a subject. The entire world of objects is, and remains, representation; and precisely because of this, it is and will always be thoroughly conditioned by the subject, that is: the world has transcendental ideality.[12] But this is also why the world is not a lie or an illusion: it presents itself as what it is, as representation, and in fact as a series of representations bound together by the principle of sufficient reason. To those with common sense, this is how the world is: even its innermost meaning is comprehensible and speaks a language of utter clarity. Only a mind distorted by sophistry[d] would think to argue about its reality; and when that does happen, it is always the result of an invalid application of the principle of sufficient reason. This principle does indeed combine representations of whatever sort they may be; but it certainly does not combine representations with the subject, or with something that would be neither subject nor object, but rather merely the ground of the object. This concept is incomprehensible because only objects can act as grounds – and in fact they can only ground other objects. – Aside from this invalid extension of the principle of sufficient reason to something outside its province, further investigation into the source of the question of the reality of the external world reveals that there is also a quite specific confusion between the forms of the principle: namely, the form referring solely to concepts (or abstract representations) is transferred to intuitive representations (real objects), and a ground of cognition[e] is then required for objects, even though they can only have a ground of becoming. The principle of sufficient reason governs abstract representations – concepts

18

---

[a] *real*
[b] *Realität*
[c] *wirkliche, d.i. wirkende Welt*
[d] *Vernünfteln*
[e] *Grund des Erkennens*

linked to form judgements – in such a way that each judgement derives its value, its validity and its entire existence (here called *truth*) solely and completely by means of the relation of judgement to something external, its cognitive ground, and therefore we must always return to it. On the other hand, the principle of sufficient reason does not govern real objects (intuitive representations) as the principle of the ground of *cognition*, but rather of *becoming*, i.e. as the law of causality: all objects have already paid their debt to the principle of sufficient reason by coming to be at all, that is, by occurring as the effect of a cause: it is not valid nor is it even meaningful to demand a cognitive ground in this case; this demand is only appropriate for a completely different class of objects.[a] It follows that the intuitive world arouses neither scruple nor doubt in the beholder who remains with it: here we find neither truth nor error; these are confined to the domain of the abstract and reflective. Here the world lies open for the senses and for understanding; it presents itself with naïve truthfulness as just what it is: intuitive representation, developing in a lawlike manner according to the strictures of causality.

As we have treated the question of the reality of the external world up to this point, it always stemmed from an error of reasoning: one that went so far as a misunderstanding of reason itself. Accordingly, we could answer the question simply by clarifying its content.[b] The question had to resolve itself because there was no meaning[c] left in it after we investigated the whole essence of the principle of sufficient reason, the subject / object relation, and the actual character of sensory intuition. But the question has yet another source, quite distinct from the purely speculative one we have given up to now: this source is in fact empirical, although the question is also only ever raised from a speculative point of view; and in this sense[d] its meaning[e] is much easier to understand than it was with the first source. It is this:[13] we have dreams; is the whole of life not in some way a dream? – Or more specifically: is there a definitive criterion to distinguish between dream and reality? Between phantasms and real objects? – The claim that a dream is not as vivid and clear as a real intuition does not deserve any consideration at all: no one has ever held the two next to each other for comparison; the reality of the present moment can only be compared to

19

---

[a] *Objekten* [Schopenhauer here speaks of objects as equivalent to representations. As he explains in *FR*, §16, 'To be an object for the subject and to be our representation are the same. All of our representations are objects for the subject, and all objects for the subject are our representations']
[b] *Inhalt*
[c] *Bedeutung*
[d] *Bedeutung*
[e] *Sinn*

the *memory* of a dream. – Kant resolves the question this way: 'What distinguishes life from a dream is the way representations are connected to each other by the law of causality.'[a] But even in a dream, all the individual details are connected together by the principle of sufficient reason in all its different forms. This coherence is broken only between life and dreams or between individual dreams. So Kant's answer can really only be this: the *long* dream (life) is completely connected by the principle of sufficient reason, but only within itself, not with the *short* dreams – even though each of these is similarly consistent within itself. The bridge that leads from one to the other is therefore broken; and that is how we can tell them apart. – Nevertheless, it would be very difficult and often impossible to use this criterion to investigate whether something was a dream or a real event: we are in no position to follow the causal connections link by link from the present moment back to every event we have experienced; but we do not for that reason declare them to be dreams. As a result, this method of investigation is not generally used in real life to distinguish dream from reality. The only certain criterion for distinguishing between dream and actuality is in fact none other than the quite empirical one of waking up: when we wake up, the causal connection between dream events and events in waking life is expressly and perceptibly broken.[14] Hobbes makes a remark in chapter 2 of the *Leviathan* that is an excellent example of this, namely: after accidentally falling asleep in our clothes, we readily mistake dreams for reality, and are even more likely to do so when in addition our thoughts are all absorbed by some task or project which occupies us in the dream just as much as it does in waking life. In these cases we are no more aware of waking up than we were of falling asleep: dream runs together with reality and becomes mixed up with it. Then admittedly only Kant's criterion is left to use: but if a causal connection – or lack of connection – to the present cannot be discovered afterwards, as is often the case, then it must always remain undecided whether an occurrence was dreamed or really happened. – Now we are confronted at close quarters with the intimate relationship between living and dreaming: and we should not be ashamed to admit as much after it has been recognized and articulated by so many great minds. The closest comparison known to the *Vedas* and the *Puranas* for our whole knowledge of the actual world (which they call the web[b]

20

[a] [Schopenhauer gives no explicit reference, but *Prolegomena* § 13, note III contains the claim that the difference between truth and dreams is decided not through the quality of the representations, but 'through their connection according to the rules that determine the combination of representations in the concept of an object' (Ak 4: 290)]

[b] *Gewebe*

of *māyā*) is that of a dream – and this is the comparison they use most frequently. Plato often says that people live merely in a dream – and only the philosopher strives to wake up. Pindar writes (II. η, 135): 'Man is the dream of a shadow.'[a] And Sophocles:

> I see that we the living are nothing more than phantoms and ephemeral chimera.
>
> *Ajax*, 125[b]

Shakespeare stands most worthily in this company:

> We are such stuff
> As dreams are made of, and our little life
> Is rounded with a sleep. –
>
> *Tempest*, Act IV. sc.1

Lastly, Calderón was so deeply gripped by this view that he sought to   21 express it in a kind of metaphysical drama called *Life is a Dream*.[c]

Now, after so many poetic quotations, I may be pardoned for expressing myself figuratively as well. Life and dreams are the pages of one and the same book. In real life we read the pages in coherent order. But when the hour appointed for reading (i.e. the day) is done, and the time for rest has come, then we often leaf idly through the book, turning now to this page and now to another, in no particular order or sequence. Sometimes we turn to a page that we have already read, and sometimes to an unknown one – but they are always from the same book. So a page read separately is indeed out of sequence in comparison to the pages that have been read in order: but it is not so much the worse for that, especially when we bear in mind that a whole consecutive reading starts and finishes just as arbitrarily. In fact it should really be seen as itself only a single, separate, although larger, page.

Thus individual dreams are distinct from real life in that they do not mesh with the sequence[d] of experiences that always runs through real life (waking marks this difference). But real life has this inter-connection[e] of experiences because inter-connection is the form of experience; and in the same way, dreams also manifest inter-connection within themselves. But if we now adopt the point of view of a judge standing outside of both,

---

[a] σκιας οναρ ανθρωπος (*umbrae somnium homo*) [*Pythia* VIII, 135]

[b] Όρω γαρ ήμας ουδεν οντας αλλο, πλην | Ειδωλ', όσοιπερ ζωμεν, η κουφην σκιαν. (*Nos enim, quicunque vivimus, nihil aliud esse comperio, quam simulacra et levem umbram*)

[c] [*La Vida es Sueño* (1635)]

[d] *Zusammenhang*

[e] *Zusammenhang*

then there is no definitive way to distinguish between them, and we must concede to the poets that life is an extended dream.

Let us leave this separate empirical source for the question of the reality of the external world and return to its speculative source. We have found that this lies first in the invalid application of the principle of sufficient reason to the relation between subject and object. It also lies in a confusion of two forms of the principle of sufficient reason in which the principle of sufficient reason of cognition is transferred into an area in which the principle of sufficient reason of becoming applies. But this question could not have preoccupied philosophers so stubbornly if it were so devoid of any real content, if there was no truth, no meaning at all, in its innermost core, nothing lying at the bottom of it. Accordingly, we can assume that as this original sense became a subject for reflection and tried to express itself, it would have taken on these inverted forms and been posed in questions that do not make sense even on their own terms. This, anyway, is what I think happened; and for a pure expression of this innermost sense of the question (which the question itself did not know how to hit upon), I suggest the following: What is this world of intuition, apart from being my representation? I am conscious of this world only once, as representation. But is it in fact like my body, of which I am conscious twice over, once as *representation* and once as *will*? – The Second Book will consist of a clear explanation as to why the answer to this question is 'yes'; and the rest of this work will be concerned with the consequences of this discovery.

§ 6

Meanwhile, in this First Book, we will treat everything merely as representation, as an object for the subject: even the body itself, everyone's point of departure for intuition of the world, is no different from any other real object, and we will treat it too only to the extent that it can be known in cognition,[a] that is, it is for us merely a representation. Anyone who is already hostile to the idea that other objects are mere representations will be even more resistant to the idea that the body itself is also merely a representation. The reason is this: we have immediate cognition of the thing in itself when it appears to us as our own body; but our cognition is only indirect when the thing in itself is objectified in other objects of intuition. But the order of our exposition requires this abstract and one-sided perspective, forcibly separating things that belong together necessarily. So any hostility towards it must be temporarily stifled and appeased through

---

[a] *von der Seite der Erkennbarkeit*

the expectation that the one-sidedness of the present considerations will be balanced out by what follows to complete our cognition of the essence of the world.

So at this stage we will be treating the body[a] as immediate object, which is to say as the representation that serves as starting-point for the subject's cognition. The body is the starting-point because we are directly acquainted with the alterations it undergoes, and these alterations precede any application of the law of causality, and thus supply it with its initial data. As we have already shown, the essence of matter is action.[b] But cause and effect exist only for the understanding, which is nothing more than their subjective correlate. And the understanding could never be successfully applied without some other thing as a starting-point. This other thing is pure sensation,[c] an immediate consciousness of alterations in the body that makes the body an immediate object. Accordingly, there are two conditions for the possibility of cognition of the intuitive world. *Expressed objectively* the first condition is the ability of bodies[d] to act on each other and bring about alterations in each other. Without this universal property possessed by all bodies, no intuition would be possible, including the sensibility of animal bodies. On the other hand, if we want to find a *subjective expression* for this very same condition we must say this: the understanding makes intuition possible primarily because the law of causality, and so the possibility of cause and effect, has its source in, and is valid only for, the understanding: hence the intuitive world exists only for and through the understanding. The second condition is the sensibility of animal bodies – the property that certain bodies possess of being the immediate object for a subject. When something external acts in an appropriate way on the sense organs, the alterations they undergo deserve to be called representations only if they do not arouse pain or pleasure,[e] for if they have no immediate meaning for the will, then they can be perceived and exist only for *cognition*; so to this extent I claim that we have immediate cognition of the body and that it is *an immediate object*. In this context, however, the concept 'object' should not be taken in anything like its proper sense, because immediate cognition is really pure sensation. As such it is prior to the application of the understanding; and so the body is not really there as an *object* at all; rather, the bodies acting upon it are what are there as objects first and foremost. Cognition of proper objects (i.e. representations

23

[a] *Leib*
[b] *Wirken*
[c] *bloß sinnliche Empfindung*
[d] *Körper*
[e] *Wollust*

24   intuited in space) occurs only through and for the understanding and comes only after and not before application of the understanding. Consequently, cognition of the body as a proper object (i.e. an intuitive representation in space) is mediated, like that of all other objects, by a prior application of the law of causality to the action of one part of the body on another (for instance when the eye sees the body or the hand touches it). As a result, we cannot discover the shape of our own body just by using the sense of touch: even our own body presents itself as something extended, articulated and organic only through cognition, only as a representation, which means: only in the brain. Someone born blind attains this representation only gradually, by means of information supplied by touch.[15] A blind man without hands would never get to know the shape of his body; or might at best gradually construct and infer this knowledge from the action of other objects on the body. When we call the body an immediate object it should be understood with this caveat.

In addition, it also follows from what has been said above that all animal bodies are immediate objects, that is, starting points for intuition of the world by that seat of all cognition,[a] the subject, which for this very reason can never itself be known. So *cognition*, together with the movement upon motives which it makes possible, is the fundamental *characteristic of animal life*.[b] In just the same way, the characteristic of plants is movement according to stimuli.[c] Inorganic beings,[d] however, move only as a result of causes understood in the narrowest sense. I have explained all this in great detail in my essay *On the Principle of Sufficient Reason*, 2nd Edition § 20 as well as in my *Ethics*, 1st Edition, III, and 'On Vision and Colours' § 1. I therefore refer the reader to these texts.[16]

From what has been said it is clear that all animals, even the most imperfect, possess understanding: they all have cognition of objects, and this cognition serves as a motive that determines their movements. – Understanding is the same in all animals as well as in all human beings. It has the same unitary form in every case: cognition of causality, transition from effect to cause and from cause to effect and nothing else besides. But the acuity of the understanding and the scope of its knowledge vary enormously and are divided very finely into many different degrees. The lowest

25   degree recognizes only the causal relation between immediate and mediate objects and therefore succeeds only in progressing from the effect the body

---

[a]   *das Alles erkennende*
[b]   *Charakter der Thierheit*
[c]   *Reize*
[d]   *das Unorganisierte*

undergoes to its cause, thereby intuiting this cause as an object in space. The higher degrees involve knowledge of the causal nexus[a] merely of mediate objects in relation to each other, leading to an understanding of complex chains of causes and effects in nature. Even this latter is still a capacity of the understanding rather than reason: the abstract concepts of reason can serve only to take up what is immediately understood, to fix and combine it; they can never produce understanding itself. Every natural force and natural law, in every instance in which they are expressed, must first of all be immediately recognized and grasped intuitively by the understanding before it can enter abstractly[b] into reflective consciousness for reasoning. R. Hooke's[17] discovery of the law of gravitation was an immediate and intuitive comprehension that took place by means of the understanding, as was the derivation of so many important phenomena[c] from this law, which Newton's calculations later confirmed. Lavoisier's discovery of oxygen and the important role it plays in nature was the same; and so was Goethe's discovery of the origin of physical colours. All these discoveries simply move directly and accurately from effect to back to the cause, which leads directly to a recognition of the identity of the natural force that expresses itself in all causes of the same kind. And this whole insight is an expression of the same and sole function of the understanding that an animal uses to intuit the cause that acts on its body as an object in space, differing from it only in degree. It follows that all these great discoveries are, like intuition or every expression of the understanding, immediate insights, and as such, the work of a moment; they are *aperçus*, striking all at once, and are not the result of long chains of reasoning in the abstract.[d] Abstract reasoning serves rather to fix the immediate cognition of the understanding for reason by setting it down in abstract concepts, that is, by making it clear,[e] i.e. putting it into a state to be interpreted for others, to make it meaningful.[f] – This acuity of the understanding when it grasps the causal relations of objects that are themselves only indirectly known is of some application in the natural sciences – in fact it is responsible for all scientific discoveries. But it is also applied in practical life, where it is called *cleverness*, although in scientific applications it is better known as acumen, penetration or sagacity. Strictly speaking, *cleverness* refers only to the use of the understanding in

26

---

[a] *Zusammenhang*
[b] *in abstracto*
[c] *Erscheinungen*
[d] *in abstracto*
[e] *deutlich*
[f] *sie Andern zu deuten, zu bedeuten*

the service of the will.[18] But the distinction between the two concepts cannot be sharply drawn because in both cases it is a question of one and the same function of the understanding that is already active in animals when they intuit objects in space. At its highest degree of acuity, it can accurately investigate the unknown causes of natural phenomena[a] on the basis of their given effects and thereby provide reason with the material it requires to conceive of universal rules as natural laws; or it may invent complicated and ingenious machines by applying known causes to desired effects; or it may be applied to motivation, either to penetrate and frustrate subtle intrigues and machinations; or, on the other hand, to suitably arrange people and the motives they are susceptible to so that they can be set in motion like the levers and cogs of machines, and steered towards some desired goal. – Lack of understanding is *stupidity* in the original sense of the word. It is an *obtuseness in applying the law of causality*, an inability to gain an immediate grasp of the link between cause and effect, or between motive and action.[b] Stupid people cannot see the inter-connections between natural phenomena, either when these phenomena occur on their own or when they are consciously controlled, that is, pressed into service as machines; they therefore easily believe in magic and miracles. Stupid people do not notice that others who appear to be acting independently may in fact have made previous arrangements with each other. This is why they are quickly baffled and make easy targets for intrigues; they do not see that someone may have an ulterior motive when giving advice or proffering an opinion. But in each case, just one thing is always lacking: acuity, quickness and an effortless use of the law of causality, i.e. strength of understanding. – The best example of stupidity that I have come across, and the most informative in the present context, is that of a completely imbecilic boy of about eleven years who lived in an asylum. He was rational (since he could both speak and understand) but had a less developed understanding than many animals. Every time I visited he would stare at a monocle I wore around my neck: it reflected the windows of the room and the tops of the trees so that they appeared to be behind my neck. This he regarded with great surprise and joy every time I was there, and looked at the glass with unwavering astonishment: he could not understand the absolutely immediate causality of reflection.

There can be quite different degrees of acuity in human understanding, but there are even greater differences in acuity among the various species of

27

---

[a] *Erscheinungen der Natur*
[b] *Handlung*

animals. But all animals – even those that are closest to plants – have at least enough understanding to proceed from effects in the immediate object to a mediate object as cause, that is, to achieve the intuition or apprehension of an object. This level of understanding is what makes them animals in the first place; it permits movement on the basis of motives, and in so doing the possibility of searching for, or at least grasping at, nourishment. Plants on the other hand move only on the basis of a stimulus, and they must therefore either wait for it to influence them directly or else languish because they cannot go after or grasp at it. We are astonished at the great wisdom shown by the highest animals: dogs, elephants, apes and foxes (whose cunning was so masterfully described by Buffon). The cleverest animals allow us to measure quite precisely what the understanding can do without the aid of reason, that is, in the absence of abstract conceptual knowledge. We cannot recognize this so easily in ourselves because, in our case, reason and understanding always mutually support one another. As a result we find that displays of understanding in animals sometimes exceed, but at other times fall short of our expectations. For instance, we are surprised by the wisdom displayed by an elephant that had previously travelled in Europe and had therefore already crossed a number of bridges, but which refused to step onto one particular bridge, even though it could see the rest of the train of people and horses crossing. Because to it the bridge did not seem strong enough to bear its weight. On the other hand, we are astonished when the clever orang-utan finds a fire to warm itself but does not keep it going by adding wood. This shows that maintaining a fire requires deliberation[a] and cannot be achieved without abstract concepts. The universal form of   28 the understanding, cognition of cause and effect, is the prior condition for any intuitive cognition of the external world, for animals just as for us. But this fact already demonstrates with complete certainty that this form exists *a priori* even in animals. Yet, if another special proof is wanted, consider for example the following: even a very young dog does not dare to jump off a table, however much it wants to, because it foresees the effect of the weight of its body; and it will refrain even though it does not know anything about this specific case from experience. But in our assessment of animal understanding we must guard against attributing to understanding what is really a manifestation of instinct; instinct is a characteristic quite distinct from both understanding and reason, although it often operates in a way analogous to the combined efforts of these two. Discussion of this does not belong here, but will be undertaken instead when we consider the

[a] *Überlegung*

harmony or so-called teleology of nature in the Second Book. The 27th chapter of the supplementary volume is also devoted to this topic.[19]

Lack of *understanding* is *stupidity*; later we will see that an inability to use reason in the practical sphere is *folly* and that lack of *judgement* is *simple-mindedness*. Finally, loss of *memory*, whether partial or complete, is *madness*. Each of these will be considered in its rightful place. – What we have correct cognition of through *reason* is *truth*, i.e. an abstract judgement with an adequate ground (essay *On the Principle of Sufficient Reason* §§ 29ff.[20]); what we have correct cognition of through the *understanding* is *reality*,[a] i.e. the correct transition from an effect in the immediate object to its cause. *Error*[b] in contrast to *truth* is a deception of reason; and *illusion*[c] in contrast to *reality* is a deception of the understanding. The first chapter of my essay *On Vision and Colours* contains a more complete discussion of all these issues. – An *illusion* occurs when two very different causes are able to give rise to one and the same effect, and one of the causes occurs very frequently while the other does not. Since there is no datum the understanding can use to distinguish between the two causes (the effect is exactly the same in both cases), it supposes that the more frequent cause is at work. But because the understanding acts directly and immediately rather than discursively or reflectively, the wrong cause stands before us as an intuited object – and this is the illusion. In *On Vision and Colours* I also showed how double vision and 'double touching' result when the sense organs are put into an unusual position; and this proves beyond doubt that intuition can take place only through and for the understanding. Some examples of deception of the understanding, i.e. illusions include: a stick submerged in water appearing to be broken, and reflected images in spherical mirrors – when the surface of one of these mirrors is convex, the images appear to be partially behind the mirror and when the surface is concave they appear to be far in front of it. Another relevant example is the apparently greater size of the moon on the horizon compared with its size at the zenith. This is not an optical effect because a micrometer can be used to show that the moon actually encompasses a slightly greater angular area of the eye at its zenith than on the horizon. Rather it is the understanding that assumes that the reduced brightness of the moon (and all the stars) on the horizon is the effect of their greater remoteness; it treats them like objects on earth, according to atmospheric perspective,[d] and therefore

[a] *Realität*
[b] *Irrthum*
[c] *Schein*
[d] *Luftperspective*

takes the moon to be much larger on the horizon than at its zenith. For just the same reason, it takes the whole dome of the sky to be very much larger on the horizon, and therefore flattened out. When only the summit of a very high mountain is visible through clear and transparent air, this same invalid application of atmospheric perspective makes it appear closer than it really is, which detracts from its height. Mont Blanc looks like this, when viewed from Salenche. – All these deceptive illusions are right before our eyes in unmediated intuition. No amount of reasoning can remove them: reasoning can only prevent error, i.e. a judgement made without adequate ground, and replace it with a true judgement. For example, we can recognize in the abstract that the cause of the reduced brightness of the moon and stars is the duller haze on the horizon rather than their greater distance: but in all these cases, the illusion stubbornly persists despite this abstract recognition. The understanding is clearly and completely distinct from reason, the cognitive faculty specific to human beings; and even in human beings, the understanding, considered in itself, is unreasonable. Reason can only ever *know*;[a] intuition remains for the understanding alone and is free from the influence of reason.

§ 7

We must still make the following remark concerning our entire discussion so far: we did not start with either the *subject* or the *object*, but rather from the *representation*, and this already includes and presupposes the other two, because the subject / object dichotomy is the primary, most universal and essential form of representation. So we began by considering this form as such; only then (while referring the reader to the introductory essay[b] for the main point) did we consider its other, subordinate, forms, forms that concern only the object: time, space and causality. However, because these forms are essential to the object *as such*, and because the object is in turn essential to the subject *as such*, they can also be discovered starting out with the subject, i.e. they can be known *a priori*, and to this extent they should be viewed as the common border between subject and object. But they can all be traced back to a common expression: the principle of sufficient reason (as shown in detail in the introductory essay).

This procedure renders our approach utterly distinct from every philosophy that has even been attempted: these have all started out either

---

[a] *wissen*
[b] [i.e. *FR*, of which see esp. § 16]

from the subject or from the object, and have therefore sought to use the principle of sufficient reason to explain the one in terms of the other. We, by contrast, have removed the subject / object relation from the control[a] of this principle, leaving it to the object alone. – One philosophy, the Identity Philosophy, has arisen recently and become generally well known,[b] and could be viewed as an exception to the opposition we have just described: it uses neither the object nor the subject as its true initial point of departure, but rather a third thing, an Absolute that is neither object nor subject but rather the identity[c] of the two and can be known through rational intuition.[d] Since I am completely lacking in all rational intuition, I shall not venture to join a discussion of the aforementioned and reverend unity or of the Absolute. Nevertheless, I must observe (basing myself on the rational intuitionists' public record, which is available to all, even to laity like us) that this philosophy is no exception to the previously advanced pair of antithetical errors: its identity of subject and object is inconceivable and can only be intellectually intuited or experienced through personal immersion, so that, despite this identity, the philosophy does not avoid either of the two opposed errors. In fact it unites both errors in itself since it decomposes into two branches: on the one hand, the transcendental idealism of Fichte's doctrine of the I, which allows the object to be produced or spun out of the subject in accordance with the principle of sufficient reason; and on the other hand, the Philosophy of Nature[e] that, in just the same way, lets the subject come gradually into being out of the object by applying a method called construction. Very little is clear to me about this method, but enough to know that it proceeds according to the principle of sufficient reason in its various forms. Since rational intuition has passed me by completely, I forgo the deep wisdom that such construction contains and, to me, every procedure that depends upon it must remain like a book with seven seals.[f] Indeed, this is true to such an extent that – strange to say – whenever someone is teaching this deep wisdom, it is as if I can hear only the dronings of atrocious and extremely tedious windbags.[g,21]

Those systems that start from the object have always faced the problem of the intuitive world as a whole and of its order; but the object that

[a] *Herrschaft*
[b] [Schopenhauer is referring to the early work of F.W.J. Schelling]
[c] *Einerleiheit*
[d] *Vernunft-Anschauung*
[e] *Naturphilosophie* [also a reference to Schelling]
[f] [Schopenhauer is referring to Revelation 5 according to which the book of the seven seals will not be opened until doomsday]
[g] *Windbeuteleien*

they take as their actual starting-point is not always this intuitive world, or its fundamental constituent, i.e. matter. Rather, these systems may be divided according to the four classes of possible objects mentioned in the introductory essay. So we can say that Thales and the Ionians, Democritus, Epicurus, Giordano Bruno and the French materialists started out from the first of these classes, from the real world; Spinoza (who began with the purely abstract concept of a substance that exists only in his definition) and earlier, the Eleatics started out from the second class, from abstract concepts. The Pythagoreans and the Chinese philosophy of the *I Ching* started out from the third class, from time and hence number. And finally, the scholastics (who maintained that an otherworldly and personal being created out of nothing, through an act of the will) started out from the fourth class, namely an act of will motivated by knowledge.

The objective approach is at its most consistent, and can be taken furthest, when it presents itself as genuine materialism. This posits matter, and along with it time and space, as existing in themselves[a] and ignores the relation they have to the subject (which is the only thing that they can all exist in). Materialism also uses the law of causality as a thread to guide its progress; but by taking it as an intrinsically existing order of things, an eternal truth,[b] it ignores the understanding, since causality exists only in and for the understanding. Materialism attempts to find the simplest and the primary state of matter, and then to develop all other states out of it, ascending from mere mechanism to chemistry, to polarity,[c] vegetative life, animal life. If this should succeed, the last link in the chain would be animal sensibility or cognition, which materialism would then present as a mere modification of matter, a material state brought about by causality. If we were to follow materialism this far with clear notions,[d] we would, on reaching the summit, feel a sudden urge to laugh the unquenchable laughter of the Olympians: all at once, as if waking from a dream, we would realize that cognition, this final, painstaking achievement of materialism had already been presupposed as an indispensable condition from the very beginning, with mere matter, that in materialism we had indeed imagined we were thinking about matter, while in fact all we had been thinking of is the subject that represents matter, the eye that sees it, the hand that feels

32

---

[a] *schlechthin*
[b] *veritas aeterna*
[c] [See § 27 below, where Schopenhauer explains polarity as 'the separation of one force into two qualitatively different and opposed activities that strive to be reunited', and describes it as 'a basic type for almost all the appearances of nature']
[d] *mit anschaulichen Vorstellungen*

it, the understanding that knows it. This is how materialism's enormous begging of the question[a] would unexpectedly be exposed; the final link[22] would suddenly reveal itself as the support for the first, and the chain as circular. The materialist would be like the Baron von Münchhausen who, when riding through water, lifted his horse up with his legs while picking himself up by pulling his own pigtail over his head. So this is the fundamental absurdity of materialism: it starts out from something *objective* and takes something *objective* as its ultimate explanatory ground, whether it is *matter* in the abstract, i.e. the mere *thought* of matter, or whether it is an empirically given *material*[b] that has already been formed, such as chemical elements and their simplest compounds. Materialism considers something such as this to exist intrinsically and absolutely so that it can allow organic nature and eventually the cognitive subject to develop from it and be completely explained by it. – But the truth is that everything objective is as such already conditioned in a variety of ways by the cognitive subject and its cognitive forms; everything objective presupposes these forms and disappears completely if the subject is thought away. Materialism is therefore the attempt to explain what is given to us directly by means of what is given indirectly. It regards everything objective, extended and active,[c] everything material, as such a solid a foundation for its explanations that reducing everything to this foundation could leave nothing to be desired (even if the reduction were to go so far as action and reaction[d]). – My claim is that all this is given only very indirectly and conditionally and hence possesses a merely relative existence.[e] This is because it can only present itself as something extended in space and acting in time because it has gone through the production machinery of the brain and passed into its forms (time, space and causality). It is on the basis of things like that, given only indirectly, that materialism claims to explain representation, even though representation is directly given and in fact everything exists only within representation. In the end it goes so far as to claim to explain even the will on this basis, although in truth it is the will that explains all the fundamental forces that are guided by causes and hence express themselves in accordance with law.[23] – We could counter the claim that cognition is a modification of matter with the equally plausible claim that all matter, as representation of the subject, is just a modification of

[a] *petitio principi*
[b] *Stoff*
[c] *wirkend*
[d] *Stoß und Gegenstoß*
[e] *relativ Vorhandenes*

the subject's cognition. Nevertheless, the basic aim and ideal of all natural science is a fully realized materialism.[a] We can now see that this is obviously impossible, confirming another truth that will emerge in the course of our investigation: no science in the proper sense of the term (I mean: systematic cognition guided by the principle of sufficient reason) will ever reach its final goal or be able to achieve a fully satisfactory explanation. This is because science has nothing to do with the inner essence of the world and can never go beyond representation: in fact it really teaches us nothing more than to recognize the relation of one representation to another.

Every science invariably begins with two main pieces of data. The first is always some form of the principle of sufficient reason, as organon; the second is its particular object, as problem. So, for example, geometry poses the problem of space and has the ground of being in space as its organon; arithmetic poses the problem of time and has the ground of being in time as its organon; logic poses the problem of the combinations of concepts as such and has the ground of cognition as organon; history poses the problem of the past deeds of human beings as a whole and *en masse* and has the law of motivation as organon; and natural science poses the problem of matter and has the law of causality as organon. So the purpose and goal of natural science is to use causality as a guide in order to reduce all the possible states of matter to each other and ultimately to a single state; and then to deduce all the possible states of matter from each other and ultimately from a single state. Two states of matter therefore stand at opposite extremes of natural science: the one is the least immediate, and the other the most immediate object of the subject; in other words, the one is the crudest and most lifeless matter, its original element, and the other is the human organism. Natural science investigates the first as chemistry and the second as physiology; but neither extreme has been attained so far; only between the two has something been gained. And the prospects look quite bleak. Chemists are always trying to minimize the number of elements (it currently stands at about 60^{24}) on the assumption that the qualitative distinctions in matter will not go to infinity as its quantitative distinctions do: if they were to reach two, they would want to reduce these two to one. The law of homogeneity[b] implies the assumption that there is a primary chemical state of matter belonging to matter as such and prior to all others, and that these others are not essential to matter as such but only to its contingent forms and qualities. But it is

34

---

[a] *völlig durchgeführter Materialismus*

[b] [Kant discusses the law of homogeneity and uses the same example of chemistry in the *Critique of Pure Reason*, 'Regulative Employment of the Ideas of Pure Reason', A653f. / B681f.]

incomprehensible how this primary state could ever undergo a chemical alteration since there is no second state to act on it. So chemistry finds itself in the same predicament that Epicurus came across in mechanics when he had to specify how an individual atom could deviate from its original course. This contradiction, which develops completely of its own accord and can be neither avoided nor resolved, might quite properly be described as a chemical *antinomy*. Just as we have here discovered an antinomy in the first of the two extremes of natural science, so there is a corresponding counterpart at the other extreme. – There is just as little hope of reaching this other extreme of natural science because it is becoming increasingly clear that the chemical cannot be reduced to the mechanical, nor can the organic be reduced to the chemical or the electrical. Those who still take this venerable wrong turning today will soon have to creep back, silent and ashamed, just as all their predecessors have done.[25] The next Book will deal with this in more detail. The difficulties that we mention here merely in passing obstruct natural science in its own domain. Considered as a philosophy, natural science would be materialism: but, as we have seen, materialism is born with death in its heart because it bypasses the subject and the forms of cognition which are presupposed just as much by the crudest matter (where materialism would like to start) as by the organism (where materialism would like to end). 'No object without a subject' is the proposition that renders all materialism forever impossible. The sun and the planets without an eye to see them and without an understanding to cognize them – this can indeed be said with words; but for representation these words are wooden iron.[a] Conversely, however, the law of causality, as well as the treatment and investigation of nature that follow this law, still lead inexorably to the assumption that every more highly organized state of matter comes only after a cruder state. In other words: animals appeared before human beings, fish before land animals, plants before fish, and the inorganic before anything organic. Consequently, the primeval mass had to undergo a long series of alterations before the first eye could open. And yet the existence of the whole world still remains dependent on the opening of that first eye, even if it only belonged to an insect, since the eye is a necessary intermediary for cognition and the world only exists for and in cognition: without knowledge the world is quite inconceivable because it is essentially[b] representation and as such requires a cognitive subject to be the support of its existence. Indeed even this long expanse of time filled

---

[a] *Sideroxylon* [i.e. a contradiction in terms]
[b] *schlechthin*

with innumerable alterations through which matter advanced from form to form until finally the first knowing animal emerged; even this whole time itself can only be conceived in the identity of a consciousness: this time is the succession of its representations, the form of its cognition and in the absence of such identity, time loses all meaning and is nothing at all. So we can see that on the one hand the existence of the whole world necessarily depends on the first being with cognition, however imperfect it may be; but on the other hand we see with equal necessity that this first being with cognition depends on a long chain of causes and effects preceding it and is actually just one small link in this chain. Because we are drawn to them both with equal necessity, these two contradictory views could very well be called an *antinomy* of our cognitive faculty, and positioned as the counterparts to the antinomy we found in the first extreme of natural science. By contrast, Kant's fourfold antinomy is baseless shadow boxing,[a] as I show in the critique of his philosophy appearing as an appendix to the present work. – The contradiction that in the end is necessarily raised here can however be resolved because (in Kantian terms) time, space and causality do not belong to things in themselves but only to their appearance whose forms they are. In my terms, the objective world, the world as representation, is not the only side of the world, but, as it were, the external side of a world that has a completely different side in its most interior being, its kernel, in the thing in itself. We will consider this other side in the next Book, calling it 'will' after its most immediate[26] objectivation. But the world as representation, which is all we are considering here, certainly arises only with the opening of the first eye. The world as representation cannot exist in the absence of this cognitive medium, and therefore did not exist prior to it. But in the absence of this eye, that is, outside of cognition, there was no before, no   37
time. This does not however mean that time had a beginning; rather, all beginning takes place in time: but since time is the most universal form of the possibility of cognition, and all appearances must adapt themselves to it by means of the bond of causality, so time too is there with the first cognition, its infinity complete in both directions. The appearance that fills this first present must at the same time be recognized as causally connected with and dependent on a series of appearances stretching infinitely back into a past that is itself just as much conditioned by the present as the present is by the past. The past out of which the first present arises is just as dependent on the cognition of the subject as the first present itself is, and without such cognition, both are nothing. But necessity also dictates that

---

[a]   *Spiegelfechterei* [For the antinomy in Kant see *Critique of Pure Reason*, A405–567 / B432–595]

this first present does not portray itself as the first, as having no past for a mother, as the beginning of time; rather, in accordance with the ground of being in time, it must portray itself as a consequence of the past and hence must also, in accordance with the law of causality, portray the appearance that fills it as the effect of prior states that fill the past. – Those who are fond of mythological interpretations may take the birth of Kronos (χρονος[a]), the youngest Titan, as a symbol of the moment we are discussing here, when time appears even though it has no beginning: as Kronos castrates his father, the crude creations of heaven and earth come to an end and divine and human lineages now take the stage.[27]

The account we have arrived at by following materialism, the most consistent of philosophical systems that start out from the object, serves just as well to illustrate the inseparable reciprocal dependence of subject and object that goes with their irreconcilable opposition.[28] This recognition leads the search for the inner essence of the world, the thing in itself, away from these two components of representation towards something completely distinct that is not afflicted with such a primordial, essential and thereby insoluble opposition.

We have discussed the method of starting from the object and letting the subject arise out of it; the opposite method would be to start from a subject that is supposed to send forth[b] the object.[29] In all philosophy so far the second is as rare as the first is widespread and universal; in fact there is really only one example, and a very new one at that: the illusory philosophy[c] of J. G. Fichte.[30] We must comment upon it in this context, however little genuine worth and inner substance his doctrine actually had; indeed it was basically nothing more than shadow boxing, delivered with an air of the deepest seriousness, expressed in a measured tone and with lively enthusiasm, defending itself against weak opponents with eloquent polemics so that it could sparkle and seem to be something. But Fichte completely lacked any real seriousness, the type of seriousness that steadfastly holds the truth, its goal, before its eyes, impervious to any outside influence, as do all philosophers like him who adapt themselves to circumstances.[31] It clearly could not have been otherwise with Fichte. Anyone who becomes a philosopher does so because of a perplexity that he is trying to tear himself away from. Perplexity is Plato's θαυμαζειν,[d]

---

[a]   [*khronos*, i.e. time]
[b]   *hervortreiben will*
[c]   *Schein-Philosophie*
[d]   [*thaumazein*, wondering or bewilderment]

which he describes as 'a very philosophical feeling'.ᵃ But what distinguishes inauthentic from authentic philosophers is that in the latter, perplexity arises from their view of the world itself; whereas in the former, it arises only out of a book, out of an already existing system. This was what happened to Fichte, since he became a philosopher only as a result of Kant's thing in itself, and in its absence he would very probably have gone on to do something quite different, and with more success, because he possessed a striking talent for rhetoric.³² If he had delved only a little deeply into the meaning of the book that made him into a philosopher (the *Critique of Pure Reason*), then he would have understood that the spirit of its central teaching is this: the principle of sufficient reason is not, as the whole of scholastic philosophy has it, an eternal truth,ᵇ that is, it does not possess unconditional validity prior to, outside of, or above the world; but, whether it takes the form of the necessary nexus of space or time, or that of the law of the ground of causality or of cognition, the principle of sufficient reason has a merely relative and conditional validity within appearances alone. As a result, the inner being of the world, the thing in itself, can never be discovered using this as our guide, because everything it leads to is still dependent and relative, still only appearance and not thing in itself. Moreover, the principle of sufficient reason has nothing to do with the subject because it is merely the form of objects, which, for this very reason, are not things in themselves: the object is already there as soon as the subject is and *vice versa*, so the object cannot be added to the subject, nor can the subject be added to the object, as consequent to ground. But none of this had the slightest impact on Fichte: the only thing that interested him in the whole matter was the idea of *starting out from the subject*, which Kant had chosen in order to show that starting out from the object, as had been done previously, was the wrong approach and made the object into a thing in itself. Fichte took this approach of starting out from the subject as the crucial thing and thought, like all imitators, that in going further than Kant here he was also doing better than him;³³ but by going in this direction he was repeating the mistake made by the dogmatism of the past (the very thing that had occasioned Kant's critique), only in reverse. So the main issue was not affected and the same old and basic error remained just as before: namely, the assumption of a ground / consequent relation between object and subject; and hence the principle of sufficient reason too still retained an unconditional validity just as before. The thing in itself was

ᵃ μαλα φιλοσοφικον παθος [See *Theaetetus* 155d, though the wording is not exactly as Schopenhauer gives it]
ᵇ *veritas aeterna* [The term reoccurs below in this Latin form and its plural]

now displaced from the object where it lay previously onto the subject, but the complete relativity of these two,[a] showing that the thing in itself or the inner being of the world is not to be sought in them but outside of them, indeed outside of any thing with a merely relational existence – all this, as before, remained unrecognized. Just as if Kant had never existed, Fichte treats the principle of sufficient reason like the scholastics, as an eternal truth. Just as eternal fate ruled over the gods of the ancients, so these eternal truths (that is, metaphysical, mathematical and metalogical truths, and in some cases even the validity of the moral law) ruled over the god of the scholastics. Only these truths were completely independent, and both God and the world existed by virtue of their necessity. On Fichte's account, the I is the ground of the world (the not-I) in accordance with just such an eternal truth, the principle of sufficient reason: the object is actually a consequence or concoction[b] of the I. As a result, Fichte took care not to investigate or verify the principle of sufficient reason any further. If I had to
40   specify what form of that principle Fichte uses to allow the not-I to develop out of the I, like a web from a spider, I would say that it is the principle of sufficient reason of being in space. This is the only way to make some kind of meaningful sense[c] out of the excruciating deductions of the mode and manner in which the not-I is produced and fabricated out of the I – for this is the content of what is one of the most meaningless and hence also one of the most boring books ever written. – Fichte's philosophy is only of interest to us because, although it appears later, it is the genuine opposite of ancient materialism, which is the most consistent way of starting from the object, just as Fichte's philosophy is the most consistent way of starting from the subject. If it were not for this, his philosophy would not even be worth mentioning. Materialism overlooked the fact that with even the simplest object it had already and at once posited the subject as well. Similarly, Fichte overlooked not only the fact that with the subject (or whatever he prefers to call it) he had already and at once posited the object as well (because the subject is inconceivable without it) but he also overlooked the fact that all *a priori* derivation, indeed all proof of any kind, is based on necessity, and all necessity is based on the principle of sufficient reason, and nothing else, because to be necessary and to follow from a given ground – are interchangeable concepts.[*,34] He overlooked the fact that the principle

---

* On this see *The Fourfold Root of the Principle of Sufficient Reason*, 2nd Edition, § 49.

[a] *die gänzliche Relativiät dieser Beiden*
[b] *Machwerk*
[c] *Sinn und Bedeutung*

of sufficient reason is nothing other than the universal form of the object as such, and so already presupposes it, but is therefore not valid prior to or outside of the object and so cannot produce the object or give rise to it through its legislative force. Generally speaking, therefore, people make the same mistake when starting from the subject as when starting from the object, the mistake of presupposing what they claim to establish, namely the necessary correlative of the starting-point.

Our method is entirely[a] distinct in kind from both of these opposed misconceptions. We start out neither from the object nor the subject, but rather from *representation* as the primary fact of consciousness, whose most essential and primary form is the subject / object dichotomy, the form of the object being in turn the principle of sufficient reason in its various modes. Each of these governs its own class of representations so completely that recognizing the mode also amounts to recognition of the essence of the entire class itself: as representation, the class is in fact nothing other than the mode itself. Thus time itself is nothing other than the ground of being in time, i.e. succession; space is nothing other than the principle of sufficient reason in space, i.e. position; matter is nothing other than causality; the concept (as we will soon show) is nothing other than relation to the ground of cognition. The total and complete relativity of the world as representation, both in its most universal form (subject and object) and the form subordinate to this (the principle of sufficient reason), indicates, as we have already said, that the innermost being of the world is to be sought in a wholly different side of the world, in something *utterly distinct from representation*. The next Book will establish this by means of a fact just as immediately certain to every living being as the fact of representation.

Before we can do this, however, another class of representations, belonging only to human beings, must be considered: their material[b] is the *concept* and their subjective correlative is *reason*, just as the representations we have considered up to this point have had as their correlatives understanding and sensibility, which we share with the animals.*

§ 8

As if from the direct light of the sun into the borrowed reflection of the moon, we now pass from immediate, intuitive representation (which

---

* The first four chapters of the first book of the supplementary volume belong with the first seven paragraphs of this volume.

[a] *toto genere*
[b] *Stoff*

presents only itself[a] and is its own warrant) into reflection, the abstract, discursive concepts of reason (which derive their entire content only from and in relation to this intuitive cognition). As long as we maintain ourselves purely in intuition, everything is clear, stable and certain. There is no questioning, no doubting, no error: one does not want to go further, one cannot go further; in intuition one finds peace and in the present, satisfaction. Intuition is sufficient unto itself and so whatever has arisen from it alone and remained true to it can, like an authentic work of art, never be false or confuted by the passage of any amount of time: it does not offer opinions but rather the thing itself.[b,35] But with abstract cognition and reason came doubt and error, in the theoretical sphere, and in the practical, care and remorse. While *illusion* distorts reality for a moment, *error* can reign for millennia in abstractions, throw its iron yoke over whole peoples and stifle the noblest impulses of humanity; those it cannot deceive are left in chains by those it has, by its slaves. The wisest minds of all times have engaged this enemy, illusion, in unequal combat, and only what they have won from it has become the patrimony of humanity.[c] It is therefore a good idea to draw attention to error immediately, since we are setting foot on ground that lies within its territory. It is often said that one should track down the truth even when it has no discernible use because a use could arise indirectly, where it is least expected; to this I would like to add that one should strive just as much to discover and root out every error, even when it does no discernible harm, because this harm too could arise indirectly, where it is least expected since every error has a poison inside it.[36] If it is the mind,[d] if it is cognition that makes human beings into the lords of the earth, then there are no harmless errors, and still less any worthy of reverence, any holy errors. As a comfort to those who devote their life and strength in any way at all to the noble but onerous struggle against error, I cannot refrain here from adding that as long as truth is absent, error can indeed play its games in the night just as owls or bats do; nevertheless, it is more likely that these owls and bats will chase the sun back into the east than that a truth, once recognized and clearly and completely expressed, could be driven back so that some past error could once again occupy its broad seat without disturbance. That is the power of truth: its victory is difficult and troublesome, but once it is achieved, it can never be reversed.

---

[a] *sich selbst vertretend*
[b] *die Sache selbst*
[c] *Eigenthum der Menschheit*
[d] *Geist*

So far we have discussed only representations whose composition allows them to be traced back to time and space and matter (when we consider the object) or sensibility and understanding, i.e. cognition of causes (when we consider the subject); but in human beings alone, out of all the inhabitants of the earth, another cognitive power has appeared and a completely novel consciousness has arisen. This is very fittingly and correctly known as *reflection*[a] because it is in fact a mirroring,[b] something derived from intuitive cognition, although it has assumed a nature and constitution fundamentally different from such cognition and is ignorant of its forms; in it even the principle of sufficient reason, which governs all objects, takes on a completely different shape. This new, more highly potentialized consciousness, this abstract reflection of everything intuitive in the non-intuitive concepts of reason is the only thing that gives people the circumspection[c] that so completely distinguishes their consciousness from that of animals and which makes their stay on earth turn out so differently from that of their irrational brothers. People surpass animals as much in power as in suffering. Animals live only in the present; humans, meanwhile, live simultaneously in the future and the past. Animals satisfy their momentary needs; people use ingenious arrangements to provide for the future, even for times they will never experience. Animals are completely at the mercy both of momentary impressions and the effects of intuitive motives; people are determined by abstract concepts independent of the present moment. As a result, people can carry out considered plans and act on maxims without reference to the circumstances and contingent impressions of the moment; they can, for example, calmly make involved arrangements for their own death, they can dissemble to the point where a secret becomes unfathomable and accompanies them to the grave, and finally, they have a real choice between different motives. This is because it is only through abstraction[d] that the simultaneous presence of such motives in consciousness can lead to the knowledge that one motive excludes the other and hence permits a comparison of the relative force[e] each exerts on the will. Accordingly, the prevailing motive, in so far as it is decisive, 44 is the considered decision of the will and announces itself as a sure sign of the state[f] of the will. Animals on the other hand are determined by the

---

[a] *Reflexion*
[b] *Wiederschein*
[c] *Besonnenheit*
[d] *in abstracto*
[e] *Gewalt*
[f] *Beschaffenheit*

present impression: only fear of an equally present constraint can tame their desire, until in the end this fear becomes habitual and as such determines them (this is training). Animals sense and intuit;[a] humans *think* and *know*[b] as well: both *will*.[37] Animals communicate their sensations and moods through gesture and sound: humans communicate their thoughts, or dissimulate them, through language. Language is the first production as well as the necessary instrument of human reason. This is why the Greek and Italian languages use the same word to denote both language and reason: ὁ λόγος, *il discorso*, *Vernunft*, reason, is derived from *Vernehmen*, apprehending or understanding, which is not a synonym for hearing,[c] but rather signifies the internalization[d] of thoughts that have been communicated using words.[38] Reason accomplishes its greatest feats only by means of language: the co-ordinated action of many individuals, the systematic interplay of many thousands, civilization, the state; in addition: science, the preservation of past experience, the combination of commonalities into a single concept, the communication of truth, the dissemination of error, thought and poetry, dogmas and superstitions. Animals only learn what death is in death itself: but human beings are conscious of drawing nearer to death with each passing hour. This makes life sometimes a rather dubious[e] prospect even for those who have not recognized that incessant annihilation is characteristic of life itself. This is the main reason why human beings have philosophies and religions, though it is doubtful whether what we correctly esteem over all else in human action – namely nobility of character and voluntarily doing right – has ever resulted from either of them. On the contrary, what is to be found on this path, the only things that these two have given rise to, are the following creations of reason: the most eccentric and fantastic views of the various schools of philosophers and the strangest, sometimes even cruel, practices of the priests of the various religions.

The unanimous view of every age and people is that these various and far-reaching manifestations all spring from a common principle, from a special mental power that distinguishes humans from animals and that is called *reason*, ὁ λόγος, τὸ λογιστικον,[39] τὸ λογιμον, *ratio*. Everyone also knows very well how to recognize the manifestations of this faculty, and can tell what is rational and what is irrational; everyone can tell where reason

45

---

[a] *schaut an*
[b] *weiß*
[c] *Hören*
[d] *Innewerden*
[e] *bedenklich*

emerges in contrast to the other human capacities and characteristics; and, lastly, everyone knows that some things can never be expected from even the cleverest of animals, because animals lack this faculty. The philosophers of all ages also generally agree with this common knowledge of reason, and in addition emphasize several of its especially important manifestations: mastery of affects and passions, the ability to make inferences and to lay down universal principles, even those that can be ascertained prior to any experience, etc. However, all their explanations of the true essence of reason are wavering, vaguely delineated, long-winded, and lack both unity and focus; they stress first this manifestation and now that, and hence often deviate from one another. What is more, some of them start out from the opposition between reason and revelation, something completely foreign to philosophy that only serves to add to the confusion. It is striking in the extreme that up to now no philosopher has rigorously[40] traced all these various manifestations of reason back to a simple function, recognizable in each of them, that would explain each of them and that would accordingly constitute the true inner essence of reason. The excellent Locke does indeed correctly state (in his *Essay on Human Understanding*, Book 2, Chapter xi, §§ 10–11) that what characteristically distinguishes humans from animals is abstract universal concepts. And Leibniz repeats this, concurring whole-heartedly, in his *New Essays on Human Understanding*[a] (Book 2, Chapter 9, §§ 10 and 11). But when Locke comes to his actual explanation of reason in Book 4, Chapter 17, §§ 2–3, he completely loses sight of this simple and basic characteristic, and ends up giving a wavering, indeterminate, incomplete and disconnected account of the derivative manifestations of reason. Leibniz too does just the same thing in the corresponding section　46 of his work, only with more confusion and less clarity. In the Appendix I have detailed the extent to which Kant confused and falsified the concept of the essence of reason. And anyone who can be bothered to go through the mass of philosophical writings that have appeared since Kant will know that, just as the mistakes princes make are paid for by whole peoples, so the errors of great minds spread their malign influence over whole generations, even for hundreds of years, growing and proliferating until in the end they degenerate into monstrosities. All this can be derived from what Berkeley says: *Few men think; yet all will have opinions.*[b]

The understanding has only *one* function: the immediate cognition of relations of cause and effect. Intuition of the actual world, as well

---

[a] *Nouveaux essais sur l'entendement humain*
[b] [*Three Dialogues Between Hylas and Philonous*, No. 2. Schopenhauer quotes the English and gives a German translation in a footnote added in 1859]

as all cunning, sagacity and talent for discovery, however many different uses they have, are quite clearly nothing other than manifestations of this simple function. Similarly, reason has only *one* function: the formation of concepts; and all the phenomena[a] mentioned above can be very easily and in fact trivially explained on the basis on this simple function: it is what distinguishes the life of humans from that of animals; and everything that has been, at any time or place, described as rational or irrational points to the application or non-application of this function.*,41

§ 9

Concepts form a special class of representations that exist only in the human mind and are entirely different in kind[b] from the intuitive representations we have considered up to now. As a result, the cognition we attain of their essence can never be intuitive and truly evident,[c] but only abstract and discursive. It would therefore be absurd to demand that they be established through experience (if by this is meant the real world outside of us, itself an intuitive representation) or brought before the eyes or the imagination[d] like objects of intuition. Concepts can only be thought, not intuited, and only the effects that people bring about through concepts are objects of experience proper. These effects include: language, action that has been thought out and planned, science, and what results from all these. As an object of outer experience, speech is clearly nothing other than a highly perfected telegraph that communicates arbitrary signs with the greatest speed and the finest nuance. But what do the signs mean? How does their interpretation occur? While others speak, do we somehow instantaneously translate their speech into imaginative pictures that fly past us at lightning speed and move around and link themselves together, forming and colouring themselves according to the ever increasing stream of words and grammatical forms? What a tumult there would be in our heads while listening to a speech or reading a book! It does not happen like this at all. The meaning[e] of the speech is immediately understood, grasped exactly and determinately without, as a rule, being mixed up with

---

* This paragraph should be compared with §§ 26–27 of the 2nd edition of my essay *On the Principle of Sufficient Reason.*

[a] *Erscheinungen*
[b] toto genere *verschieden*
[c] *evident*
[d] *Phantasie*
[e] *Sinn*

any imaginative pictures.[a] Reason speaks to reason while remaining in its own province: it sends and receives abstract concepts, representations that cannot be intuited: it needs only a relatively small number of these, however, formed once and for all, to encompass, contain and represent all the innumerable objects of the actual world. This alone explains why animals can never speak or understand, even though they share both our speech organs and our intuitive representations: but words have no meaning or significance for animals precisely because they designate this very special class of representations (whose subjective correlative is reason). So, like every other phenomenon[b] that we ascribe to reason, and like everything that distinguishes humans from animals, language is to be explained in terms of a single and simple source: concepts, i.e. representations that are abstract rather than intuitive, and universal rather than individuated in space and time. Only in isolated cases do we pass from concepts over to   48 intuition, forming imaginative pictures for ourselves as intuitive *representatives*[c] *of concepts* (to which they can however never be adequate). I discuss these cases especially in § 28[42] of my essay *On the Principle of Sufficient Reason*, and so I do not want to repeat myself here. What I say there may be compared to what Hume says in the twelfth of his *Philosophical Essays* (p. 244) and what Herder says in his *Metakritik*, part I, p. 274 (which is otherwise a poor book). – The Platonic Idea, made possible by the unification of imagination and reason, comprises the main topic of the Third Book of the present work.

Although concepts are fundamentally different from intuitive representations, they nevertheless stand in a necessary relation to them; without this relation, concepts would be nothing, and so this relation constitutes their whole essence and existence. Reflection is necessarily a copy or repetition of the original intuitive world, although a copy of a very special kind in a completely heterogeneous material. Concepts may therefore be quite aptly termed representations of representations. In this case too the principle of sufficient reason has a particular form; and the form of the principle of sufficient reason governing a class of representations always in fact constitutes and exhausts the whole essence of the class itself, in so far as it is a class of representations. So, as we have seen, time is succession through and through, and nothing else; space is position through and through, and nothing else; and matter is causality through and through, and nothing else. In the same way, the whole essence of concepts, the class of abstract

---

[a] *Phantasmen*
[b] *Erscheinung*
[c] *Repräsentanten*

representations, consists of nothing other than the relation the principle of sufficient reason expresses in them; and since this is a relation to the ground of cognition, then the whole essence of an abstract representation lies in just one single thing: its relation to another representation, its cognitive ground. Now to start with, this ground can be another concept, i.e. another abstract representation; and even this concept can itself have another such abstract cognitive ground. But not forever: in the end, the series of cognitive grounds must terminate with a concept that has its ground in intuitive cognition. For the world of reflection as a whole is based on the intuitive world as its cognitive ground. The class of abstract representations is therefore distinguished from other classes in this way: in other classes, the principle of sufficient reason always demands some relation to another representation of the *same* class; but in the case of abstract representations, it ultimately demands a relation to a representation from *another* class.

For concepts related to intuitive cognition only indirectly (as described above), i.e. through the intermediary of one or more further concepts, the preferred term is *abstracta*; conversely, those that are grounded directly in the intuitive world are known as *concreta*. The latter term does not suit the concepts it designates very well at all because they are still *abstracta* and certainly not intuitive representations. These terms arise only from a very confused consciousness of the intended distinction; they can still be retained, but only with the interpretation[a] given to them here. Examples of the first kind, *abstracta* in the fullest sense, are concepts like: 'relation, virtue, investigation, beginning', etc. Examples of the second kind, inappropriately termed *concreta*, are the concepts 'person, stone, horse', etc. If the image were not too graphic, and thus somewhat facetious, the latter could be very aptly described as the ground floor of the edifice of reflection, and the former as its upper stories.*

It is not, as is often claimed, an essential property of a concept[b] that it includes[c] many things under it, i.e. that many intuitive (or even abstract) representations stand in the relation of cognitive ground to it, that is, are thought through it. This is, on the contrary, a derivative, secondary property of the concept and one that is in fact not always present, although it does always remain possible. The property stems from the fact that a concept is the representation of a representation, in other words, the whole essence of a concept lies in its relation to another representation

---

* See chapters 5 and 6 of the second volume.

[a] *Deutung*
[b] *Begriff*
[c] *begreift*

that is not the same as the concept itself. Indeed, this other representation usually belongs to a quite different class of representations, namely the intuitive representations, and can therefore possess temporal, spatial and other determinations, and quite generally have many other relations, that are not thought along with it in the concept. As a result, several representations, differing only in unessential details, can be thought through or subsumed under the same concept. However, 'holding true of many things' is not an essential but merely an accidental property of a concept. There can be concepts through which only a single real object is thought. Such concepts are still abstract and universal and quite unlike individual and intuitive representations. For example someone may be acquainted with a particular city only from geography and therefore possess a concept of it through which this single city is the only thing thought, even though a number of possible cities that are only partially different from it would all fit the concept. A concept does not possess universality because it is abstracted from many objects, but the other way around: it is because universality, that is, indeterminacy with respect to the individual,[a] is essential to the concept as an abstract rational representation, that different things can be thought through the same concept.

It follows from what has already been said that every concept has what may be termed an extension[b] or sphere, even in cases where only a single real object corresponds to it. The reason is that concepts are abstract and not intuitive, and are therefore not fully determinate representations. Now it often happens that the sphere of one concept has something in common with the spheres of others. In other words, what is thought in the one concept is partially the same as what is thought in the other, and what is thought in the other is partially the same as what is thought in the first. Nevertheless, if they are really distinct concepts, then each, or at least one, will contain something that the other does not: indeed, this is the relation that obtains between every subject and its predicate. To recognize this relation is *to judge*. The idea of presenting these spheres by means of spatial figures is very felicitous. It occurred first to Gottfried Ploucquet, who used squares to do it; Lambert, who came after him, used plain lines positioned under each other; but it was Euler who perfected the idea by using circles. I am unable to say what the ultimate basis is for this very exact analogy between the relations of concepts and those of spatial figures. But it is in any event a very fortunate circumstance for logic that the very

[a] *Nichtbestimmung des Einzelnen*
[b] *Umfang*

possibility of all conceptual relationships can, in the following way, be presented intuitively and *a priori* by means of such figures:

(1) The spheres of two concepts are exactly equal: for instance, the concept of necessity and that of following from a given ground; the concepts of *Ruminantia* and *Bisulca* (ruminants and animals with cloven hoofs) are of this kind; or those of vertebrates and red-blooded animals (although there may be some objection to this on account of the annelids). These are interchangeable concepts.[43] Such cases may be presented using a single circle that signifies the one as much as the other.

(2) The sphere of one concept completely encloses the sphere of another.

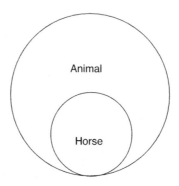

(3) A sphere includes two or more further spheres, which are mutually exclusive and at the same time exhaust the first sphere:

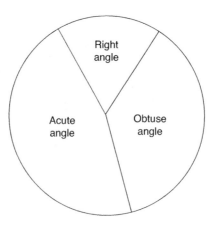

(4) Two spheres each include a part of the other:

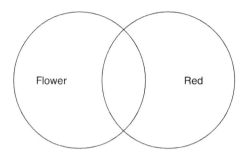

(5) Two spheres lie inside a third, but do not exhaust it: 52

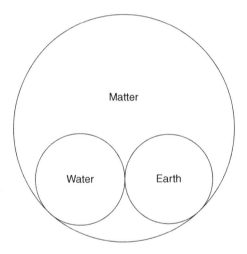

The last case applies to all concepts whose spheres do not have anything directly in common because there is always some third sphere that is perhaps very much wider and that includes both of them.

All combinations of concepts may be reduced to these cases, and the entire doctrine of judgement (with its conversion, contraposition, reciprocation and, as in Figure 3, disjunction) can be derived from them. The properties of judgements that Kant used to ground the supposed categories of the understanding can also be derived from them; although an exception must be made for the hypothetical form (because it does not combine just concepts, but judgements as well) and also for modality (the Appendix gives a thorough account of this and all the properties of judgements that are used to ground the categories). Concerning the possible combinations of concepts that we have just described, it only remains to observe that they can themselves be combined with each other in various ways: Figure 4, for example, can be combined with Figure 2. Only when a sphere that partly or wholly contains a second sphere is itself partly or wholly enclosed by a third does the ensemble present a syllogism of the first figure,[a] i.e. that combination of judgements through which it is recognized that a concept partly or wholly contained in a second concept is likewise contained within a third concept that itself contains the second. Negation is the reverse of this figure and its pictorial representation can only consist of two combined spheres that do not lie in a third. Long chains of syllogisms arise if many spheres are enclosed in this way. – This schematism of concepts, which is already explained quite well in many textbooks, can be used to ground the doctrine of judgement as well as the whole of syllogistic logic and makes it very easy and uncomplicated to teach them both. The reason is that this schematism gives insight into the origin of all their rules and allows them to be derived and explained. We do not have to burden our memory with all the rules, since logic can only be of theoretical interest and never of practical use for philosophy. It may be said that logic is to rational thought as the figured bass[b] is to music, or, more loosely, as ethics is to virtue or aesthetics to art; but it should be borne in mind that no one has ever become an artist by studying aesthetics or achieved nobility of character by studying ethics, that people composed music both beautifully and correctly long before Rameau and that we do not need to have mastered the system of figured bass to recognize dissonance. In just the same way, we do not need to know logic to avoid being deceived by sophisms.[c] Still, it must be conceded that the figured bass is very useful indeed for the practice of musical composition, if not for music criticism; aesthetics and even ethics might also have their practical uses, although to a much lesser extent and mainly negatively, so that we should not deny all practical value even to them. But logic cannot boast even this much, because it is merely abstract knowledge[d] of what everyone knows concretely.[e,44] We no more need logic to avoid false reasoning than we need its rules to help us reason correctly; and even the most learned logician completely puts it aside when actually thinking. The following remarks explain why. Every science consists of a system of universal and hence abstract truths,

53

---

[a] [Schopenhauer is not talking here about his diagrams, but about syllogisms of the first form, i.e. all As are B, C is an A, therefore C is a B]

[b] *Generalbaß* [also termed *basso continuo*]

[c] *Trugbeschlüsse*

[d] *Wissen* in abstracto

[e] in concreto *weiß*

laws and rules that relate to a particular kind of object. When a particular case then occurs, the question of whether or not it falls under the rules is always decided by using this universal knowledge (which applies once and for all) because it is infinitely easier to apply the universal than to have to start out again by investigating any particular case that might present itself on its own terms: once discovered, universal and abstract cognition 54 lies much closer to hand than the empirical investigation of particulars. But with logic it is just the other way around. Logic is universal knowledge[a] of the way reason proceeds, and is obtained when reason observes itself in abstraction from all content and expresses the result in the form of rules. But the way reason proceeds is necessary and essential to reason: left to itself, reason will never deviate from it. So it is both easier and safer to let reason proceed according to its nature in each individual case than to hold out in front of it an abstract knowledge of this very procedure, expressed in the form of an alien and externally imposed law. It is easier in the sense that in all other sciences, the general rule is more accessible than the investigation of a particular case by and through itself; but when using reason, it is the other way around: the procedure required in a given case is always more accessible than the general rule abstracted from this case because reason is just what it is in us that thinks. It is safer in the sense that it is much easier for an error to occur in abstract knowledge (or in its application)[45] than for a rational process[b] to take place running counter to its essence and nature. This accounts for the peculiar fact that in logic the rule is always verified by the individual case, whereas in other sciences, the truth of the individual case must be verified by the rule. When even the most practised logicians notice in a particular case that they have reached a different conclusion from the one dictated by the rule, they will look for a mistake in the rule before looking into the inference they have actually drawn. To want to make practical use of logic is to want to take something we are directly conscious of and completely certain about in each particular case and instead go to the indescribable trouble of deriving it from universal rules: this would be just like seeking the advice of mechanics in order to move or physiology in order to digest; learning logic for practical purposes is like training a beaver to build its own dam. – Even though it has no practical use, logic must nevertheless be preserved because of its philosophical interest as a special branch of knowledge concerning the orga- 55 nization and action of reason. We are justified in treating logic on its own terms, independently of all other sciences (as well as in teaching it in universities) because it is a self-contained, self-subsistent, internally

---

[a] *Wissen*
[b] *Verfahren der Vernunft*

complete and perfected discipline that achieves absolute certainty. But logic acquires its real value only in the context of philosophy as a whole, through its treatment of cognition, especially of the rational or abstract sort. Accordingly,[46] the teaching of logic should not take the form so much of a science oriented towards practice, and should not merely set down unembellished rules for the correct conversion of judgements and inferences etc.; instead it should be directed towards making known the essence of reason and concepts, and towards a detailed consideration of the principle of sufficient reason of cognition. After all, logic is merely a paraphrase of this principle, and indeed only for cases in which the ground for a judgement's truth is neither empirical nor metaphysical but rather logical or metalogical. In addition to the principle of sufficient reason of cognition, we must introduce three more fundamental laws of thought or judgements of metalogical truth that are just as closely related; the whole technique of reason emerges little by little from these.[47] The essence of thought proper, i.e. of judgement and inference, can be presented by combining conceptual spheres according to the spatial schema described above, and all the rules of judgement and inference can be derived from this schema by construction. The only practical use that can be made of logic is to prove that an opponent in debate is using intentional sophistries (not making genuine logical mistakes) by pointing out their technical names. By putting the practical orientation of logic into the background and foregrounding the inter-connection of logic with the whole of philosophy (as a chapter in its book)[48] we should not be making an acquaintance with logic less prevalent than it is now. For today anyone who does not want to remain uncultured[a] concerning what is most important, anyone who does not want to be counted among the ignorant masses, trapped as they are in darkness, must have studied speculative philosophy because this 19th century is a philosophical century. I do not mean by this that it possesses philosophy, or that philosophy dominates it; rather I mean that the century is ripe for philosophy, and therefore stands in need of it. This is a sign of a highly developed culture,[b] and even a fixed point on the cultural scale of the ages.*

Although logic can have little practical use, we cannot deny that it was invented for a practical purpose. My explanation of its origin is the following. As the taste for disputation became more and more developed among the Eleatics, the Megarics and the Sophists, rising by degrees almost to the point of a craving, the confusion that almost every dispute fell into

---

* See chapters 9 and 10 of the second volume.

[a] *roh*
[b] *hoch getriebene Bildung*

must have soon made them acutely aware of the need for a systematic procedure: they searched for a scientific dialectic as a guide to this procedure. The first thing they must have noticed was that both parties to a dispute must always agree about some proposition,[a] and their points of disagreement were to be traced back to this proposition in debate. A systematic procedure started to develop when these commonly recognized propositions were formally articulated as such and placed at the forefront of the enquiry. At first, these propositions only concerned the substance of the enquiry. But soon people realized that the way disputants referred back to an agreed-upon truth, and the way they tried to derive their claims from it, also had certain forms and obeyed certain laws that no one ever quarrelled about, even in the absence of any prior agreement concerning them. As a result, people saw that these must be the characteristic course taken by the essence of reason, the formal component of the enquiry. Now, although these were not exposed to doubt and disagreement, the thought nevertheless occurred to some brain[b] (who was systematic to the point of pedantry) that it would look very good, and complete the methodical dialectic, if the formal component of all disputation, the consistently law-like procedures used by reason itself were also to be expressed in abstract propositions. These could be placed at the forefront of any enquiry (just like the agreed-upon claims about its substance) as the permanent canon   57 of disputation itself, so that people could always refer and appeal to them. In this way, what people had previously followed as if by tacit agreement, or carried out as if instinctively, they now wanted to acknowledge consciously and express formally as law; in doing so, they gradually discovered more or less complete formulations for the fundamental principles of logic, such as the laws of non-contradiction, sufficient reason, and the excluded middle, the maxim of all and none,[c] as well as for the special rules of syllogisms, e.g. 'nothing follows from merely particular or negative premises', 'inference from the consequent to the ground is not valid',[d] etc. This was accomplished only slowly and with considerable difficulty, and prior to Aristotle, everything remained extremely incomplete, as can be seen partly from the long-winded and clumsy way that logical truths come to light in many Platonic dialogues, and even more clearly from what Sextus Empiricus tells us of the disputes the Megarics had about even the simplest and easiest of logical laws, as well as the laboured way they were brought

[a] *Satz*
[b] *Kopf*
[c] *dictum de omni et nullo* [The logical principle that what is predicated of any whole is predicated of any part of that whole, and what is not predicated of the whole is not predicated of any part of it: supposedly originating in Aristotle's *Prior Analytics* I, 1, 24b26]
[d] *ex meris particularibus aut negativis nihil sequitur, a rationato ad rationem non valet consequentia*

to clear expression (Sextus Empiricus, *Against the Mathematicians*, Book 8, pp. 112ff.[a]). Aristotle collected, ordered and corrected what he found, and brought it to an unparalleled level of completeness. If we consider in this fashion how the path taken by Greek culture prepared the ground for Aristotle's work and led up to it, we will not be particularly inclined to believe the claims of Persian authors[49] cited by *Jones* (who is rather taken with the idea himself) that Callisthenes came across a complete logic in India and sent it to his uncle, Aristotle (*Asiatic Researches*, Vol. 4, p. 163). – It is easy to see that Aristotle's logic must have been very welcome indeed to the scholastics of the dismal Middle Ages; their intellects[b] were hungry for debate but, for want of any real knowledge, they gnawed on formulas and words alone; even in its mutilated Arabic version, Aristotle's logic was grasped enthusiastically and soon established as the central plank of all science.[c] Although its reputation has subsequently diminished, nevertheless, even in our time, Aristotle's logic constitutes to its credit a self-subsistent, practical, and highly necessary scientific endeavour. Indeed Kant's philosophy, which in fact takes its foundation stone from logic, has awoken a lively new interest in it these days, an interest that, in this respect at least, logic has earned as an instrument for the cognition of the essence of reason.

58

Strictly accurate inferences are made through careful consideration of the relationships between conceptual spheres: only when one sphere is completely contained within a second, and this in turn is completely contained within a third, should we admit that the first is also completely contained within the third. On the other hand, the *art of persuasion*[d] depends on a merely cursory inspection of the relationships between conceptual spheres, which can then be determined as lying on either one side or the other according to the speaker's intentions. This generally happens in the following way: if the sphere of the concept under consideration lies only partly within a second sphere, but also partly within a third, completely different sphere, the first concept is declared to be completely contained within the second, or completely contained within the third, whichever suits the speaker's purpose. For example, when discussing passion, it can be subsumed at will either under the concept of the greatest force, the most powerful agency[e] in the world, or under the concept of the irrational, which is itself subsumed under that of the powerless or weak. This process can be repeated and reused on every concept the discussion leads to. Almost any

---

[a] *Sext Emp adv Math L. 8. p. 112 seqq.*
[b] *Geiste*
[c] *alles Wissens*
[d] *Ueberredungskunst*
[e] *Agens*

conceptual sphere is divided among many other concepts; each of these other concepts contains some area of overlap with the first, but includes much more that lies outside the first: the only sphere that the speaker allows to be illuminated is the one under which he wants to subsume the original concept; the others can be left in the dark, or even hidden. This trick is the basis of all the arts of persuasion and of all refined sophistry, since the purely logical sophisms, like *mentiens, velatus, cornatus,* etc.ᵃ are clearly too clumsy for practical application. I am not aware of anyone so far who has traced the essence of all sophistic reasoning and persuasion back to this, the most fundamental ground of their possibility, or shown how this possibility lies in what is most characteristic of concepts, i.e. in reason's own method of cognition. Since my presentation has led me to this point, I would like to make the issue even more clear (although it is not hard to comprehend) using the schema presented in the following table. This table is intended 59 to show how conceptual spheres overlap each other in such a multitude of ways that there is enough elbow-room to pass from one concept to any given other one at will. I do not want anyone to be misled by the table into lending more weight to this short incidental explanation than it naturally deserves. I have chosen the concept of *travel* as an explanatory example. Its sphere overlaps with four others so that a persuasive speaker may pass at will into any of them; these in turn overlap other spheres, many overlap two or more other spheres at once, and the speaker can continue plotting a course through them as he wishes, treating it as the only way, and finally ending up, according to his original intention, with either good or evil. The only requirement is to follow the spheres outwards from the centre (the main concept given) to the periphery without going backwards. Such a piece of sophistry can be dressed up either in continuous speech or as a rigorous syllogism, as the weakness of the listener suggests. At base, most scientific and in particular most philosophical proofs do not achieve much more than this. If it were not so, how could so many things, at so many different times have not been merely incorrectly understood (error has in fact a different origin), but actually demonstrated and proven, and then later discovered to be fundamentally false, e.g. the philosophy of Leibniz and Wolff, Ptolemaic astronomy, Stahl's chemistry, Newton's theory of colours, etc., etc.?*

---

* See chapter 11 of the second volume.

ᵃ [Literally: the liar, the veiled one, the horned one – all sophisms or paradoxes associated with the ancient Megarian philosopher Eubulides. The first is the familiar 'What I am saying now is a lie'; the second runs: 'Do you know this veiled man?' – 'No.' – 'But he is your father. So – do you not know your own father?'; the third 'What you have not lost, you have. But you have not lost horns. Therefore you have horns']

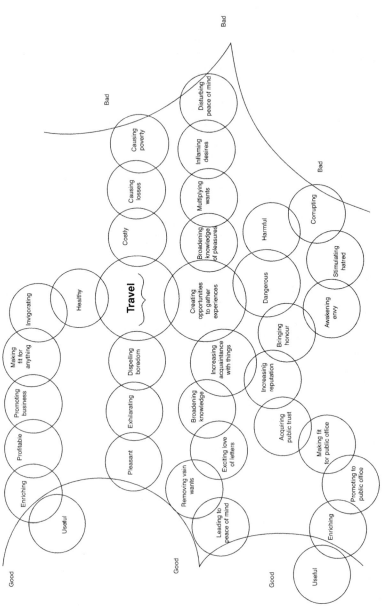

[Bonum; utile; ditans; quaestuosum; negotia promovens; ad quaelibet idoneum reddens; vigorans; salubre; jucundum; exhilarans; taedium expellens; Peregrinari; sumptuosum; damnosum; egestatis causa; Malum; animi tranquillitatem adducens; vana desideria sedans; litterarum amorem excitans; scientiam amplificans; peritiam augens; Experientiae latissimus campus; deliciarum cognitionem amplificans; desideria multiplicans; cupiditates incendens; animi tranquillitatem disturbans; utile; ditans; ad munera publica evehens; muneribus publicis idoneum reddens; fiduciam publicam comparans; auctoritatem concilians; honorificum; periculosum; invidiosum; odia suscitans; detrimentosum; exitiosum]

§ 10

All this brings us closer and closer to the question how we can achieve *certainty*;[a] how we can ground *judgements*; and what *knowledge*[b] and science[c] consist in. For these are acclaimed as the third greatest advantage conferred on us by reason, after language and circumspection in our actions.[d]

Reason is of a feminine nature: it can give only after it has received. On its own, it possesses nothing but the empty forms of its own operation. Completely pure rational cognition gives us in fact only four things, the very metalogical truths that I have already mentioned, namely: the laws of identity, non-contradiction, the excluded middle and sufficient cognitive ground. Even the rest of logic is not completely pure, rational cognition because it presupposes the relations and combinations of conceptual spheres; but intuitive representations are prior to the existence of concepts in general, whose essence is nothing but their relation to such representations, which they therefore presuppose. However, since this presupposition does not apply to any particular conceptual contents but only to the existence of concepts in general, logic taken as whole[50] can still be regarded as a pure rational science.[e] In all other sciences, reason has received its content from intuitive representations: in mathematics, from spatio-temporal relations which we are intuitively aware of prior to all experience; in pure natural science – i.e. in what we know about the course of nature prior to all experience –[51] scientific content springs from the pure understanding (i.e. from our *a priori* cognition of the law of causality and its connection to those pure spatio-temporal intuitions). In all other sciences, everything that is not borrowed from the sources already mentioned belongs to experience.[52] *To know*[f] in general means: to have the mental power to reproduce at will those judgements that have their sufficient cognitive ground in something external to themselves, i.e. those judgements that are *true*. Thus, only abstract cognition is knowledge; and since this is conditioned by reason, we cannot, strictly speaking, say that animals *know* anything, even though they possess intuitive cognition, memory (since this is required for intuitive cognition), and therefore even imagination,[g] as is shown by their dreams. We do attribute consciousness to animals; so the

60

[a] *Gewißheit*
[b] *Wissen*
[c] *Wissenschaft*
[d] *besonnenes Handeln*
[e] *reine Vernunftwissenschaft*
[f] *Wissen*
[g] *Phantasie*

concept of consciousness coincides with that of representation in general, of whatever kind, even though the word *Bewußtseyn*, consciousness, is derived from *Wissen*, knowledge. Consequently we do indeed attribute life to plants, but not consciousness. – So *knowledge* is abstract consciousness: it fixes in rational concepts what is cognized in other ways.

61

§ 11

In this respect, the true opposite of knowledge is feeling,[a] which we must therefore discuss at this point. The word *feeling* designates a concept with completely *negative* content, namely: something that is present to consciousness, but is *neither a concept nor abstract rational cognition*. No matter what it may otherwise be, it belongs to the concept *feeling*. As a result, the excessively broad sphere of this concept encompasses the most heterogeneous things so that no one can see how they come together without recognizing that they correspond to each other only in this negative respect: they are *not abstract concepts*. The most diverse, even hostile elements coexist peacefully in this concept, e.g. religious feeling, sensual feeling, moral feeling, the corporeal feeling of touch or pain or a feeling for colours, or sounds and their harmonies and disharmonies, the feeling of hatred, of disgust, of self-satisfaction, of honour, of disgrace, of right, of wrong,[53] the feeling for truth, aesthetic feeling, feeling of power, weakness, health, friendship, love, etc. etc. There is absolutely no common ground between these, except the negative ground that they are not abstract rational cognition. But what is most remarkable is when we bring even our intuitive *a priori* cognition of spatial relations, as well as our cognition of pure understanding, under this concept, and say quite generally we *feel* every cognition and every truth that we are as yet only intuitively conscious of, and have not set down in abstract concepts. By way of illustration I would like to give some examples of this usage from some recent publications, since they are a striking confirmation of my explanation. I remember reading in the introduction to a German translation of Euclid that beginners in geometry should be allowed to draw all the figures before going on to demonstrations because they would then have a *feeling* for geometrical truth before demonstration gives them full knowledge.[b] – Similarly, F. Schleiermacher talks about logical and mathematical feeling in his *Critique of the Doctrine*

---

[a] *Gefühl*
[b] *Erkenntniß*

of Ethics[a] (p. 339) and also about a feeling that two formulas are the same   62
or different (p. 342); moreover, in his *History of Philosophy*[b] (Vol. 1, p. 361),
Tennemann claims: 'one *felt* that the sophisms were incorrect, but could
not uncover the flaw'. – Because of the excessive breadth of its sphere
and its merely negative, completely one-sided and very meagre content,
failure to consider the concept of *feeling* from the right point of view or to
acknowledge the single negative characteristic essential to it will be a standing invitation to miscomprehension and disagreement. Since German also
possesses the nearly synonymous word *Empfindung*, sensation, it would
be expedient to commandeer it for the sub-category of corporeal feelings.
The origin of the concept of feeling, so disproportionate in comparison to
all other concepts, is doubtless this: concepts (and words, which designate
nothing but concepts) exist only for, and proceed from, reason; so with
concepts, we already have a one-sided point of view. But from a particular
point of view, what is nearby appears clear and is treated as something
positive; whereas things in the distance all flow into each other and are
soon regarded only negatively. This is why every nation calls all others
foreign, why the Greeks call everyone else a barbarian, why the English
term everything outside England *the continent* and whatever is not English,
continental,[c,54] why the believer calls everyone else heretic or heathen, why
the nobility call everyone else commoners,[d] why the student calls everyone
else philistine, and so on. Strange though it sounds, reason itself can be
regarded as guilty of the same one-sidedness, what we might call the same
crude ignorance stemming from pride: it is enough that a modification of
consciousness does not directly belong to *reason's* way of representing (i.e.
not be an *abstract concept*) for reason to place it under a *single* concept,
feeling. Up until now, reason has not had the thorough self-knowledge that
would render its own method clear to itself, and in consequence it has had
to pay for its sins through misunderstandings and confusions in its own
province, where some have even tried to set up a special faculty of feeling,
and are currently constructing theories about it.

§ 12   63

All abstract cognition, i.e. rational cognition, is a case of *knowledge*,[e] and,
as I have just explained, the concept of feeling is the diametric opposite

[a] *Kritik der Sittenlehre* [In fact *Grundlinien einer Kritik der bisherigen Sittenlehre* (1803)]
[b] *Geschichte der Philosophie*
[c] [In English in original]
[d] *roturiers*
[e] *ein Wissen*

of knowledge. Since reason only ever reproduces in cognition what had already been received by a different means, it does not actually extend our cognition, but only gives it a different form: it allows what is already cognized concretely[a] and intuitively to be cognized abstractly and universally, something incomparably more significant than a cursory glance at this formulation suggests. For the safe preservation of cognition, its communicability as well as its reliable and widespread practical application, all depend on its becoming knowledge[b] proper, or abstract cognition. Because sensibility and understanding can in fact only grasp *one* object at a time, intuitive cognition only ever applies to a particular case; it reaches only to what is nearest and no further. So every sustained, complex, systematic activity must start out from and be guided by fundamental principles, that is, abstract knowledge. For example, although the understanding's cognition of cause and effect is indeed intrinsically deeper, more complete, and more exhaustive than an abstract[c] thought of cause and effect (only the understanding has a full, immediate, intuitive cognition of the way a lever, or a block and pulley, or a cogwheel works, or of the self-supporting character of a vault etc.); yet, it is due precisely to the above-mentioned property of intuitive cognition (that it extends only to the immediate present), that understanding does not suffice on its own for the construction of machines or buildings: here it is rather reason that must come in to replace intuitions with abstract concepts, which it can then take as the guiding principle for the work; and, if they are correct, it will meet with success. Similarly, in pure intuition we are perfectly acquainted with the essence and lawlike nature of a parabola, a hyperbola or a spiral; but this cognition must be converted into abstract knowledge before it can be reliably applied in actuality: in the process, what is admittedly lost in intuitiveness is made up for in the reliability and precision of abstract knowledge. So differential calculus does not really extend our cognition of curves in any way; it contains nothing more than is already contained in the pure intuition of curves, taken on its own. But it does change the kind of cognition we have: it converts intuitive cognition into an abstract cognition that is so rich in consequences for practical application. Another peculiarity of our cognitive faculty is apparent here, one that could not be mentioned earlier because the distinction between intuitive and abstract cognition had not been fully clarified. It is this: spatial relations in themselves cannot be translated directly into abstract cognition; only temporal quantities, i.e. numbers, are suitable for

[a] *in concreto*
[b] *Wissen*
[c] *in abstracto*

this purpose. Only numbers, and not spatial quantities, can be expressed in abstract concepts that correspond exactly to them. The concept of a thousand is just as distinct from the concept of ten as the two temporal quantities are distinct from each other in intuition: when we think of a thousand, we think of a definite multiple of ten, into which we can at will decompose the thousand in temporal intuition, i.e. by counting. But, unless we appeal either to intuitive representation or to numbers, there is no exact distinction corresponding to the quantities themselves between the abstract concepts of a mile and a foot. Through both of these concepts, all that is thought is some spatial quantity in general, and if the two are to be adequately distinguished, we have absolutely no choice but to appeal to spatial intuition for help (and therefore leave the territory of abstract cognition), or to think the distinction in *numbers*. So if we want to obtain abstract cognition of spatial relations, they must first be translated into temporal relations, i.e. numbers: this is why the general doctrine of quantities is arithmetic and not geometry, and geometry must be translated into arithmetic if it is to be communicable, precisely determined, and applicable in practice. It is true that spatial relationships as such can be thought in the abstract, e.g. 'the sine increases in proportion to the angle'; but numbers are needed to specify the relationship quantitatively. The three dimensions of space must necessarily be translated into the single dimension of time   65 if we want to have abstract cognition of its relations (i.e. *knowledge*,[a] not mere intuition); and this necessity is what makes mathematics so difficult. This can be made very clear if we compare our intuition of curves to their analytical calculation, or if we compare logarithm tables for trigonometrical functions to our intuition of the changing relations of the parts of a triangle expressed by these tables. In one glance, intuition grasps things fully and with extreme precision: how the cosine decreases as the sine increases, how the cosine of one angle is the sine of the other, the inverse relations between the increase and decrease of the two angles, etc. But what a gargantuan network of numbers, what troublesome calculations are required to express the same things abstractly: how the *single* dimension of time must suffer, as it were, to reproduce the three dimensions of space! And yet this was just what had to happen if, for the sake of practical application, we wanted to gain possession of spatial relations laid down in abstract concepts: the former could not go into the latter directly, but only through the medium of pure temporal quantities (numbers) because these are the only things that can be directly connected to abstract cognition. It is also

[a] *Wissen*

worth noting that, while space is very well adapted to intuition, and its three dimensions allow even complex relationships to be easily surveyed, it nevertheless eludes abstract cognition; conversely, although time translates easily into abstract concepts, it yields very little to intuition: our intuition of numbers in their proper element (mere time, without the addition of space) scarcely reaches ten; beyond that we only have abstract concepts, not intuitive cognition, of numbers: but a precisely determined abstract concept is connected with every number word and algebraic sign.

In passing it may also be remarked at this point that many minds only find complete satisfaction in what is cognized intuitively. They seek an intuitive presentation of the ground and consequent of being in space: a Euclidean proof, or an arithmetic solution to a spatial problem, does not appeal to them. In contrast, other minds demand abstract concepts, the only things that can be used for practical application and communication: they have the patience and memory for abstract principles, formulas, proofs with long chains of reasoning and calculation (whose symbols represent the most complicated abstractions). The latter are looking for precision, the former for intuitiveness. The difference is characteristic.

Knowledge (abstract cognition) is most valuable because of its ability to be communicated and maintained in a fixed form: only this makes it so immeasurably important for practical application.[a] Someone may, in the understanding alone, have direct and intuitive cognition of the causal nexus of alterations in natural bodies as well as their motion, and be quite satisfied with it; but such cognition is only ready for communication after it has been fixed in concepts. Cognition of this first type is even sufficient for practical application, as long as the one who undertakes the task does so alone and the task can indeed be accomplished while the intuitive cognition is still fresh; but it is not sufficient if someone else's help is required, or the work is performed alone, but over the course of several different periods of time and therefore stands in need of a considered plan. For example, a practised billiards player can have a total familiarity with the laws governing the reciprocal impact of elastic bodies, albeit merely in the understanding, simply for immediate intuition, and it will be completely sufficient; but only a scientist who has studied mechanics has genuine knowledge of these laws, i.e. cognition of them in the abstract. Merely intuitive cognition based in the understanding[b] can even be enough to build machines, as long as the machine is built by its inventor alone, as is often seen with talented artisans

[a] *das Praktische*
[b] *bloß intuitive Verstandserkenntniß*

66

lacking scientific knowledge: but as soon as several people are necessary for the completion of a mechanical operation, machine or building, and the work requires co-ordinated activity spanning different points in time, then the manager will need to have sketched out a plan in the abstract: and this kind of co-operative activity is possible only through the use of reason. Strangely, however, when an individual person is to accomplish something in this first way, that is, alone and in one continuous action, then knowledge, the application of reason and reflection can actually be 67 a hindrance: e.g. in playing billiards, fencing, tuning an instrument or singing. In cases such as these, the activity must be managed directly by intuitive cognition: going by way of reflection makes the activity uncertain because attention is divided and the individual confused. This is why savages and people without culture,[a] who are very little accustomed to thinking, can perform many physical tasks (like fighting with animals or shooting arrows at targets, etc.) with a sureness and swiftness that the reflective European can never attain because his deliberateness leads to vacillation and hesitation: he tries, for example, to find the right place or time in the middle point between two false extremes; whereas the natural man[b] hits the target directly without reflecting on the wrong ways to go. Similarly, it is no help to me to know in the abstract how to give the exact angle in degrees and minutes at which my straight razor should be positioned, if I do not know it intuitively, i.e. have the knack of it.[55] The application of reason also disturbs our comprehension of physiognomy; for this too must take place directly by means of the understanding: and it is said that the expression and significance of someone's features can only be *felt*, which means precisely that they cannot be taken up into abstract concepts. Everyone has their own direct and intuitive physiognomics and pathognomics,[c] although some can recognize this signature of things[d] more clearly than others. But a physiognomics in the abstract, to be taught and learned, cannot be developed because in this area the nuances are so fine that concepts cannot reach them. As a result, abstract knowledge is to such nuances as a mosaic is to a *van der Werft* or a *Denner*: however fine the mosaic may be, there always remain borders between the stones, and so a continuous transition of one colour into another is impossible; in just the same way, however much the rigid and sharp boundaries between concepts

---

[a] *Wilde und rohe Menschen*
[b] *der näturliche Mensch*
[c] *Physiognomik und Pathognomik* [Techniques for accessing a person's interior (personality, emotions, etc.) through studying his / her exterior features]
[d] *signatura rerum* [The title of a book by Jacob Böhme]

are divided through increasingly minute definition, they will never be able to reach the fine modifications of the intuitive – but this is just the point we were making with our example of physiognomics.*

68　　This characteristic of concepts that makes them similar to the stones in a mosaic (and means that they always approach intuitions only asymptotically) is also the reason why nothing good can be achieved in art through concepts. If a singer or virtuoso wants to use reflection to guide a performance, it will remain lifeless. The same is true of composers, painters and even of poets: concepts are always unfruitful for art: they can only direct the purely technical aspects of art: their province is science. In the Third Book we will investigate in more detail why all genuine art stems from intuitive cognition and never from concepts. – Even in relation to behaviour and personal charm in one's dealings, concepts are only of negative benefit in suppressing crude outbreaks of egoism and brutality, so politeness is their laudable product; but no attractive, graceful or winning behaviour, nothing full of love or friendship can be attributed to concepts: otherwise:

> One feels the intent, and is annoyed.[a]

All dissimulation is the work of reflection; but it cannot be consistently maintained in the long run: 'no one can wear a mask for long',[b] as Seneca claims in his book *On Mercy*:[c,56] so it is also likely to be recognized and therefore lose its effectiveness. Reason is indeed necessary in the full urgency of life, where quick decisions, bold actions and swift, sure interventions are required; but it can easily ruin everything if it gains the upper hand and leads to indecisiveness because confusion prevented intuitive, direct, pure understanding from pinpointing and immediately undertaking the right act.

---

* For this reason it is my opinion that physiognomics cannot progress with any certainty beyond setting out a few quite general rules like the following: intellectual characteristics may be read in the brow and eyes, ethical ones (expressions of the will) in the mouth and the bottom half of the face; – brow and eye are mutually enlightening, but one seen without the other is only partially comprehensible; – there is no genius without a lofty, wide and finely arched brow; although these are often present without genius; – the uglier the face is, the more surely intellect [*Geist*] may be inferred from an intellectual [*geistreich*] appearance; the more beautiful the face, the more surely stupidity may be inferred from a stupid appearance; this is because beauty is conformity to the human type, and therefore already bears in and for itself the expression of mental clarity, whereas it is just the opposite with ugliness, etc.

[a] *fühlt man Absicht und man ist verstimmt* [Goethe, *Torquato Tasso*, II, I]
[b] *nemo potest personam diu ferre fictam*
[c] *de clementia* [I, i, 6, slightly paraphrased]

Finally, virtue and holiness do not stem from reflection either, but from   69
the inner depths of the will and its relation to cognition. This discussion
belongs at quite a different place in this work, so here I would only like
to make the following remark: the dogmas relating to ethics may be the
same in the reasoning[a] of entire nations, but the actions of each individual
can be different, and vice versa. Action occurs, as people say, according to
feelings: i.e. not according to concepts at all, but rather according to ethical
content. Dogmas keep idle reason occupied: but in the end actions go
forward on their own, not along the path of dogma; for the most part they
do not follow abstract maxims, but tacit ones, whose expression the whole
human being in fact is. So, however varied the religious dogmas of different
peoples are, a good deed is always accompanied by inexpressible satisfaction
and a bad one by infinite horror: no mockery can touch the former; no
father confessor's absolution can free us from the latter. This should not be
taken as denying that the application of reason is necessary for leading a
virtuous life: reason however is not its source, but has a subordinate role in
sustaining resolutions once they have been made and providing maxims to
struggle against the weakness of the moment, and lending consistency to
action. Ultimately, reason does the same for art, where it has just as little
to do with the essential business, but supports its execution, since genius
is not at one's beck and call, and yet the work must still be perfected in all
its parts and then rounded off into a whole.*

§ 13

All these discussions, of both the advantages and the disadvantages of applying reason, should serve to make the following clear: although abstract
knowledge reflects and is based on intuitive representation, it does not
coincide with intuitive representation so completely that it can substitute
for it in every case; in fact it never corresponds entirely to intuitive repre-   70
sentation, so that, as we have seen, many human achievements can only be
accomplished with the help of reason and a considered method, even while
some others can be better achieved without the application of reason. –
Just this incongruity of intuitive with abstract cognition, which means that
the latter only ever approximates the former, as a mosaic approximates
a painting, is the basis of an extremely peculiar phenomenon, as unique

---

* See chap. 7 of the second volume.

[a] *Vernunft*

to human beings as reason, and which, despite many attempts, has up to now never been satisfactorily explained: I mean *laughter*. Because of its origin, we cannot forgo an explanation of laughter at this point, even though it will hold up our progress once more. In every case, *laughter* arises from nothing other than the sudden perception of an incongruity between a concept and the real objects that are, in some respect, thought through the concept; in fact laughter itself is simply the expression of this incongruity. It often occurs when two or more real objects are thought through a *single* concept that transfers its identity to them; but their very great difference in other respects makes it conspicuously obvious that the concept only applied to the objects in a very one-sided way. However, we just as often suddenly become sensible of the incongruity between a single real object and the concept that has, for its part, correctly subsumed it.[57] The more correct the subsumption of such actual things[58] under a concept is on one side, and the greater and more glaring their unsuitability to it is on the other, so much the more powerful is the ridiculous effect that springs from this contrast. All laughter is occasioned by a paradoxical and hence unexpected subsumption, irrespective of whether it is expressed in words or deeds. This, in short, is the correct explanation of the ridiculous.[a,59]

I will not pause here to relate anecdotes as examples to make my explanation clear: it is so simple and easy to understand that it does not need examples, and anything ridiculous that the reader can think of will serve just as well for proof. But our explanation can certainly be confirmed and illustrated by dividing the ridiculous into the two types which in fact spring from that explanation. Either on the one hand two or more quite different real objects were first present to cognition as intuitive representations, and these were then voluntarily[b] identified with each other through the unity of a concept that included them both: this type of the ridiculous is called *wit*. Or, on the other hand, it is the concept that is first present in cognition, and the movement is now from the concept over to reality, over to the effect of the concept in reality, i.e. over to action: objects that are all thought by means of the same concept, but that are in other respects quite distinct, come now to be viewed and treated in the same way, until the extent of their differences comes to the fore, to the surprise and astonishment of the person performing the action: this type of the ridiculous is called *foolishness*. So everything ridiculous is either a witty conceit or

[a] *des Lächerlichen*
[b] *willkürlich*

an act of foolishness, according to whether there is a movement from the discrepancy between objects to the unity of a concept or the other way around: the former is always voluntary, the latter always involuntary and is forced on people only from outside. Now, the art of the court jester or the clown is to appear to switch these starting points around by masking wit as foolishness: such people are quite conscious of the differences between objects, but unify them under a single concept with tacit wit; then, starting out from this concept, they go on to discover the differences among the objects, and receive the very surprise that they had prepared for themselves. – It follows from this short but complete theory of the ridiculous that (setting aside this last case of the comedian) wit must always show itself in words, whereas foolishness shows itself mostly in actions, although it may also do so in words when only an intention is expressed without actually being carried out, or when it is expressed only in judgements and opinions.[60]

Pedantry is another kind of foolishness. It arises when people lack confidence in their own understanding and so do not want to let their understanding recognize what is right directly in the particular case; accordingly they place the understanding completely under the tutelage of reason, which they use in all cases. In other words, pedants always start out from universal concepts, rules and maxims and seek to hold themselves exactingly to these in life, in art and even in ethical conduct. The characteristic property of pedantry follows from this, namely its adherence to form, manner, expression and word at the expense of the heart of the matter.[61] This is where the incongruity of the concept with reality soon manifests itself: the concept never descends as far as the particular, the universality and rigid definition of the concept can never adapt themselves to the fine nuances and variety of modifications in the actual world. With their general maxims, pedants almost always come off badly in life, showing themselves to be unwise, insipid and of no use: in art, where concepts are unfruitful, pedants produce stiff, lifeless, mannered afterbirths. Even in relation to ethics, a resolution to act rightly and nobly cannot always be put into effect using abstract maxims: in many cases the infinitely finely nuanced nature of the situation means that the right choice must flow directly from character: the application of purely abstract maxims either gives the wrong result (because the maxims are only partly appropriate for the circumstances) or cannot be acted on at all (because the maxims are foreign to the individual actor's character, which cannot always be suppressed). This leads to inconsistencies. *Kant* cannot be completely cleared of the suspicion of provoking moral pedantry in so far as he makes it the condition of an action's moral

72

value that it take place on the basis of purely rational abstract maxims without any inclination or momentary emotion;[a] this charge is also the meaning of Schiller's epigram entitled 'Scruples of Conscience'.[b] – When, especially in political matters, people say 'doctrinaire', 'too theoretical', 'over-educated', they mean 'pedantic', because pedants know things very well in the abstract[c] but not concretely.[d] Abstraction involves thinking away fine distinctions: but practical application very much depends on exactly these.[62]

To complete the theory, we must also mention a spurious kind[e] of wit, namely wordplay, the *calembourg* or *pun*,[f] to which we can also add equivocation, *l'équivoque*, which is used mostly for obscene (indecent[g]) purposes.[63] Just as wit forces two quite distinct real objects under the same concept, so wordplay, by the use of chance, brings two different concepts under a single word: this arouses the same contrast, but it is much duller and more superficial because it does not stem from the nature of the things, but only from the arbitrariness of their names. With wit, the concept is identical and actuality diverse; but with wordplay, it is the concepts that are different and actuality (since words are actual) that is identical. It would be a rather too studied comparison to say that the play on words is to the witticism as the hyperbola[64] on a cone inverted upwards is to that on one inverted downwards. A verbal misunderstanding, or a *quid pro quo*,[h] is an unintentional *calembourg* and is related to the latter just as foolishness is to wit; as a result, the hard of hearing often give us as much amusement as the fool does, and bad comic writers use deafness rather than foolishness to arouse laughter.

Here I have treated laughter only from the psychical side; for the physical side, I refer the reader to what I have said on the topic in my *Parerga*, Volume 2, Chapter 6, § 92, p. 134 (1st edition).[*][65]

§ 14

I hope all these various enquiries have completely clarified the distinction and relation between, on the one hand, reason's mode of cognition

---

[*] See also chap. 8 of the second volume.

[a] *Aufwallung*

[b] *Gewissensskrupel* [The epigram, in *Die Philosophen* (*The Philosophers*) reads: 'Gladly I serve my friends, but unfortunately from inclination. So it eats at me often: I am not one who has virtue']

[c] *in abstracto*

[d] *in concreto*

[e] *Afterart*

[f] ['Pun' is in English in the original, and *calembourg* is the French for 'pun']

[g] *die Zote*

[h] [Literally 'one thing for the other', although usually used in English to describe a bargain]

(knowledge and concepts) and, on the other hand, immediate cognition in pure, sensible, mathematical intuition and apprehension in the understanding; moreover, our account of the peculiar relation between these two kinds of cognition almost unavoidably led us to parenthetical discussions about feeling and laughter. I now return from all this to a further discussion of science, the third most important advantage conferred upon us by reason, after language and judicious actions.[a] We must now give a general account of science, which will concern partly its form, partly the ground of its judgements, and finally its content.

We have seen that, apart from the basic principles of pure logic, knowledge in general never originates with reason itself. Rather, it is gained in a quite distinct way, as intuitive cognition, which is set down in the faculty of reason and thereby transformed into a completely different, abstract, kind of cognition. All *knowledge*[b] (i.e. cognition that has been elevated to abstract consciousness[c]) is related to true *science*[d] as the fragment is to the whole. Everyone has achieved knowledge about some things through experience and through investigation of the available particulars; but only those who set themselves the task of achieving complete and abstract cognition of some particular type of objects aspire to science. This type can be marked out only by means of a concept; and so, at the head of every science stands a concept that is used to think some fraction of things in general, and the corresponding science promises complete abstract cognition of just that fraction: e.g. the concept of spatial relations, or of the effects of inorganic bodies on each other, the constitution of plants, or animals, or the series of alterations to the surface of the earth,[66] or to the human race as a whole or the structure of a language, etc. If a science were to try to obtain knowledge[e] of its objects by individually investigating every single thing that is thought under its concept until it gradually came to know them all, then no human memory would be equal to the task and we could never be sure that the task was complete. So science makes use of the property of conceptual spheres mentioned above (the fact that they can encompass each other) and proceeds in the main to the wider spheres that lie within the concept of its object in general: by determining the relations of these spheres to each other, science at the same time determines everything thought within them in general; and this can be specified with increasing precision through the selection of narrower and narrower conceptual spheres. By this means, a

[a]　*besonnenes Handeln*
[b]　*Wissen*
[c]　*zum Bewußtseyn* in abstracto *erhobene Erkenntniß*
[d]　*Wissenschaft*
[e]　*Kenntniß*

science can comprehend its object completely. Science differentiates itself from everyday knowledge by means of the approach it takes to cognition, i.e. by progressing from the universal to the particular; and so systematic form is an essential and characteristic mark of science. The connection between each science's most universal conceptual spheres, i.e. familiarity with its most fundamental principles, is an indispensable condition for learning a science: how far to go from the most fundamental to the more specialized principles is a matter of choice, and does not increase the profundity but only the reach of that learning. – The number of fundamental principles (ones that subordinate all the others) varies greatly among the different sciences so that in some there is more subordination and in others more co-ordination; in this respect, the former make greater claims on our judgement[a] and the latter on our memory. The scholastics* already knew that because a syllogism must have two premises, no science can start out from a single fundamental and underivable principle, every science must rather have more than one, at least two of them. The properly classificatory sciences possess the most subordination, for instance zoology, botany and also physics and chemistry (in as much as they reduce all inorganic effects to a small number of fundamental forces); history on the other hand does not actually possess any subordination at all because historical universality consists in nothing more than an overview of important historical periods. But particular events cannot be derived from a historical period; they are subordinated to it only chronologically whereas conceptually they are co-ordinated with it. So, strictly speaking, history is a kind of knowledge[b] but not a science. In the Euclidean treatment of mathematics, only axioms are non-demonstrable first principles, and demonstrations are rigorously subordinated to these axioms at each step; but the Euclidean treatment is not essential to mathematics, and in fact every theorem introduces a new spatial construction that is in itself independent of its predecessors, and can also be known by itself and quite independently of them through pure spatial intuition, in which even the most involved construction is actually as immediately evident as an axiom (this will be discussed in more detail later). In any case, every mathematical principle always remains a universal truth, applicable to innumerable particular cases, and stepwise progress from simple to complex principles (which can be reduced to simple ones) is

---

* Suárez, *Disput[ationes] metaphysicae* [*Metaphysical Disputations*], *disp[utatio]* III, sect. 3, tit. 3.

[a] *Urtheilskraft*
[b] *ein Wissen*

also essential in mathematics, which is therefore in every respect a science. – 76
A science is complete as science (i.e. formally) when its principles possess as
much subordination as possible and as little co-ordination. A general talent
for science therefore requires the ability to subordinate conceptual spheres
according to their different determinations, so that, as Plato never tired of
warning against, the science does not become a mere universality with an
immense variety of particulars lined up directly underneath; instead our
knowledge must descend gradually from the most universal to the particular through intermediate concepts and classifications[a] comprising ever
more finer determinations. In Kant's words: the laws of homogeneity and
of specification must be satisfied simultaneously.[b] It follows from the fact
that this is the true nature of scientific completeness that greater certainty is
not the goal of science (since even the most isolated individual cognition[c]
can be extremely certain); but rather, science should aim to facilitate knowledge[d] through its formal presentation and the possibility this introduces
of the completeness of knowledge. So, although it is commonly believed
that the scientificity[e] of cognition consists in its greater certainty, this view
is wrong-headed; just as incorrect is the view (which in fact follows from
it) that only mathematics and logic are sciences in the proper sense of the
term, since only they, as completely *a priori*, contain incontestably certain
cognition. This advantage cannot be disputed, but it does not give them
any special claim to scientificity, which does not lie in security, but in
a systematic form of cognition grounded in a stepwise descent from the
universal to the particular. – It is characteristic of the sciences to approach
cognition by proceeding from the universal to the particular, and it implies
that a great deal of science is grounded in deduction from prior principles, i.e. on proof. This has resurrected an ancient misconception, that
only what has been proven is entirely true, and that every truth stands in
need of a proof; but the opposite is in fact the case: every proof stands in
need of some unproven truth either as its ultimate basis, or in turn as the
basis of its own proof. So an immediately grounded truth is preferable to
a truth that is grounded in proof, just as water from a spring[f] is preferable 77
to water from an aqueduct. Intuition, sometimes pure and *a priori* (as the
basis of mathematics) and sometimes empirical and *a posteriori* (as the basis

[a] *Eintheilungen*
[b] [See *Critique of Pure Reason* A657 / B685ff.]
[c] *einzelne Erkenntniß*
[d] *Wissen*
[e] *Wissenschaftlichkeit*
[f] *Quelle*

of all other sciences) is the source[a] of all truth and the foundation of all science. (The only exception is logic, which is based on the unmediated, although not intuitive, cognition reason has of its own laws.) Judgements are indeed to science what the sun is to the world: not however proven judgements or even their proofs, but rather judgements grounded in and drawn directly from intuition instead of from proof. It is these judgements that are the source of all light, and the others shine only because of their illumination. To establish the truth of such primary judgements directly in intuition, to raise such strongholds of science out of the immense mass of real things, is the task of *judgement*,[b] the faculty of translating intuitive cognition accurately and exactly into abstract consciousness, and the faculty that therefore plays the role of mediator between understanding and reason. Only an individual with an outstandingly strong sense of judgement, going beyond the common measure, is able to really advance the progress of the sciences; whereas anyone whose reason is healthy can deduce or prove or infer one proposition from another. By contrast, fixing something of which we have intuitive cognition into appropriate concepts and setting it down for reflection so that, on the one hand, the element common to many real objects is thought in *one* concept, and, on the other, their points of difference are thought through an equal number of concepts; recognizing and thinking different things just as different (despite their partial similarity), and also thinking identical things just as identical (despite their partial difference); and all in accordance with the aim and viewpoint that prevails on each occasion: all this is achieved by *judgement*. Lack of judgement is *simple-mindedness*. The simpleton sometimes misjudges the partial or relative diversity of things that are in some respect identical, and at other times misjudges the identity of things that are partially or relatively distinct. Moreover, Kant's division of judgement into reflective and subsumptive[c] can be applied to this explanation, according to whether it moves from the intuited objects to the concept or from the concept to the intuited objects, in both cases mediating between the intuitive cognition of the understanding and the reflective cognition of reason. – No truth can be produced through inferences entirely on their own; the necessity of establishing a truth inferentially is only ever relative, indeed subjective. Since all proofs are inferences, we should not look first for a proof of a new truth, but rather for immediate evidentness;[d] a proof should only be

[a] *Quelle*
[b] *Urtheilskraft*
[c] [See Kant, *Critique of the Power of Judgment*, Introduction, IV (Ak. 5: 179–80)]
[d] *Evidenz*

constructed as a temporary measure, while it is not yet evident. No science can be exhaustively proven, any more than a building can stand in mid air: all its proofs must lead back to something that is intuited and therefore no longer provable, for the whole world of reflection is based on and rooted in the world of intuition. All ultimate, i.e. original *evidentness* is *intuitive*: as the word already indicates.[a] Accordingly, evidentness is either empirical or it is based on *a priori* intuition of the conditions of possible experience: in both cases it yields only immanent and not transcendent cognition.[67] Every concept has value, indeed exists, only in relation (albeit sometimes very indirect) to an intuitive representation: and what applies to concepts also applies to the judgements made out of them, and to whole sciences. Consequently, every truth discovered through inferences and communicated through proofs could also, somehow, have been recognized directly, without inferences or proofs. This is certainly at its most difficult with some complicated mathematical claims only reached using chains of inference, e.g. the calculation of the chords and tangents to all the arcs using results derived from Pythagoras' theorem: but even a truth like this cannot rest essentially on abstract principles alone; it must also be possible to highlight for pure *a priori* intuition the spatial relations that it is based on, so that its abstract expression is directly grounded. But mathematical proofs will be discussed in more detail shortly.

People often talk in lofty tones about sciences that must be incontrovertibly true because they are based solely on correctly drawn inferences from watertight premises. But, however true its premises are, no chain of inferences ever contains anything more than a clarification and explication of what already lies, quite complete, within the premises: inference does no more than show explicitly[b] what was already understood implicitly.[c] When praising these sciences, people are thinking of the mathematical sciences in particular, and especially astronomy. But the certainty of astronomy stems from the fact that it is based on an *a priori*, and hence infallible, intuition of space: all spatial relations follow from one another with a necessity (ground of being) that affords *a priori* certainty; and they may therefore be derived from each other with certainty. To these mathematical properties we only have to add a single natural force, gravity (which acts precisely in proportion to mass and the square of distance) and then finally the law of inertia (guaranteed *a priori* because it follows from the law of causality) along with empirical data concerning the motion of each mass

79

---

[a] [*Anschaulich* (intuitive) is derived from *anschauen* meaning to look at]
[b] *explicite*
[c] *implicite*

resulting from its initial impetus. Nothing else is required for astronomy, which leads to solid results because of its simplicity and certainty, and these results are very interesting because of the size and importance of its objects. For instance, if I know the mass of a planet and the distance between it and its satellite, then I can reliably infer the orbital period of the satellite using Kepler's second law: this law is grounded in the fact that when the satellite is at a particular distance, only one velocity will keep it bound to the planet while at the same time preventing it from falling into the planet. – Consequently, it is only on this sort of a geometrical basis (i.e. by means of *a priori* intuition), and additionally only through the application of a natural law, that significant progress can be made with inferences. The reason is that they are, in this case, mere bridges from *one* intuitive apprehension to another; but this is not the case with pure inferences merely as such, i.e. inferences of an exclusively logical character. –[68] However, the origin of the primary and fundamental astronomical truths is actually induction, i.e. a correct, immediately grounded judgement that combines the content given in many intuitions: hypotheses are then constructed out of this, and the confirmation of these hypotheses by experience (as the induction approaches completeness) proves the initial judgement. For example, the apparent motion of the planets is recognized empirically; after many false hypotheses about the spatial sequence of this motion (the planetary orbit), the correct one was eventually discovered. Then the laws governing it (Kepler's laws) were discovered;[69] finally, so was the cause of these laws (universal gravitation). But empirical recognition of the fact that every observed case was in agreement both with all the hypotheses and with everything that followed from them, i.e. induction, lent them complete certainty. The discovery of the hypothesis was a matter of judgement correctly grasping and appropriately expressing the given facts;[70] but induction (i.e. repeated intuition) confirmed its truth. Even this truth however could have been established directly, with a single empirical intuition, if we could only travel freely through space and had telescopic eyes.[71] Here too, then, inferences are not the sole and essential source of cognition, but only really an expedient measure.

Finally, to give a third and quite different example, we would like to mention that so-called metaphysical truths[72] (i.e. the sort of truths Kant presents in his *Metaphysical Foundations of Natural Science*[a]) are indeed evident, but not because of any proofs. We have direct cognition of something *a priori* certain: we are conscious of it with the greatest necessity because

[a] *Metaphysische Anfangsgründe der Naturwissenschaft*

it is the form of all cognition. For instance we know directly as a negative truth that matter persists, i.e. can neither come to be nor pass away:[73] our pure intuition of space and time supplies the possibility of motion; through the law of causality, the understanding supplies the possibility of alteration in form and quality, but we lack any forms for representing the appearance and disappearance of matter. Consequently, this truth has been evident to everyone, everywhere and at all times, it has never yet been seriously doubted; but this could not have been the case if its cognitive ground were only a difficult and hair-splitting Kantian proof. Moreover, I have found Kant's proof to be false (as explained in the Appendix) and I have shown above that the permanence of matter is to be derived from the spatial and not the temporal component of the possibility of experience. The real basis of all truths that are in this sense called metaphysical[74] (i.e. that are abstract expressions of the necessary and universal forms of cognition) cannot lie in yet more abstract propositions; but instead only in direct conscious-ness of the forms of representation as they are registered *a priori* through apodictic statements that brook no refutation. If proof of these is however still desired, it can only amount to showing that what is to be proved is already partly contained in or presupposed by another truth that cannot be doubted: I have, for example, shown that every empirical intuition already involves the application of the law of causality; so our knowledge of this law is a condition of every experience and cannot therefore be, as Hume claimed, originally given in and conditioned by experience. – In general, proofs are not for those who want to learn so much as for those who want to argue.[a] The latter stubbornly deny even immediately grounded insight: but since only the truth can be completely consistent, they must be shown that what they directly deny in *one* form they admit indirectly in another; in other words: the logically necessary connection between what they deny and what they affirm.

In addition, scientific form (the subordination of all particulars to some-thing universal, and so on ever more universally) also implies that the truth of many propositions is grounded only in logic, that is, depends on other propositions, and therefore requires inferences, which at the same time emerge as proofs. But we should never forget that the whole of this form is only a way of facilitating cognition, not a means for achieving greater certainty. It is easier to know what characteristics an animal has on the basis of its species, and so on up through its *genus*, family, order and class, than to investigate each individually given animal on its own terms; but

81

---

[a] *disputiren*

the truth of any inferred claim is only ever conditional, and ultimately depends on some claim that is based not on inference, but on intuition. If intuition were always as accessible to us as derivation through inference, then it would be thoroughly preferable to the latter. For every deduction by means of concepts is extremely error prone because of the extensive overlap between conceptual spheres (mentioned above) and the often indefinite character of their contents; sophisms of all kinds and the many proofs of false doctrines are examples of this. – Regarded formally, syllogisms are indeed completely certain: but they are nevertheless very uncertain as a result of the concepts that are their content; on the one hand this is because their spheres are not delineated sharply enough, and on the other because they overlap so much that one sphere is partly contained in a multitude of others and one can choose to pass from the first sphere to this or that other one and then on to yet another one quite arbitrarily, as has already been shown. In other words: the minor term and the middle term can always be subordinated to a variety of concepts, from which the major term and the middle term can be chosen arbitrarily, thus causing the syllogism to turn out differently.[a] – As a result, immediate evidentness is always far preferable to proven truth and the latter should only be accepted when the former is too remote to be accessible and not when immediate evidentness is just as easy (or even easier) to obtain than proof. This is why, as we saw above, we always in fact use our immediate cognition of the laws of thought to guide our thinking, leaving logic unused: in this case, immediate cognition is more accessible in each and every case than derived scientific cognition.[*]

§ 15

Now we are convinced that all evidentness has its primary source in intuition and that absolute truth exists only in relation (be it immediate or mediate) to intuition; we are convinced moreover that the shortest route to truth is always the surest (since mediation through concepts is always very error prone); – if, I say, armed with this conviction, we turn to *mathematics*, as Euclid organized it into a science, and as it has, on the whole,

---

[*] See chap. 12 of the second volume.

[a] *terminus minor, medius, terminus major* [In a traditional syllogism the middle term occurs in both premises, the major term occurs in the first premise and the conclusion, the minor term in the second premise and as the subject of the conclusion. So in the inference 'All fruits are edible; all apples are fruits; therefore all apples are edible', *edible* is the major term, *fruits* is the middle term, *apples* the minor term]

remained up until today, then we cannot help finding that it has taken a peculiar route, indeed that it is going the wrong way. We expect every logical ground to be reduced to an intuitive one; but mathematics has devoted itself wholeheartedly to casting its own easily accessible intuitive　83 evidentness wilfully aside and replacing it with logical evidentness. We ought to treat this as akin to someone cutting off his legs so that he can go on crutches, or to the prince in 'The Triumph of Sensibility'[a] who flees from the actual beauty of nature to enjoy a theatre set that imitates nature. – Here I must recall what I said in the sixth chapter of my essay *On the Principle of Sufficient Reason*; I will assume that this is wholly present and fresh in the reader's memory, so that I can connect it directly with what I am going to say here without having to repeat my explanation of the distinction between the merely cognitive ground of a mathematical truth (which can be given logically) and its ground of being (which is the immediate inter-connection of the parts of space and time, and can be recognized only intuitively): true satisfaction and thoroughgoing knowledge are afforded only by insight into this ground of being, while the merely cognitive ground always remains superficial: the latter can indeed yield the knowledge[b] *that* something is as it is, but not *why* it is. Euclid chose this latter path, to the obvious detriment of the science. For example, at the very outset, Euclid should have used the form that the principle of sufficient reason adopts in pure space to show once and for all how the angles and sides of a triangle are mutually determining, both ground and consequent of each other: for here, as everywhere, the necessity that something is as it is because another quite different thing is as *it* is issues from this principle. But rather than giving us such a thoroughgoing insight into the nature[c] of the triangle, Euclid instead lays down a few fragmentary and arbitrarily selected propositions about it, and then presents a logical cognitive ground for them using a laborious logical proof in accordance with the principle of non-contradiction. Instead of an exhaustive knowledge of these spatial relations, we only get a few arbitrarily communicated results derived from them: we are in the same position as someone who is shown the various effects of an ingenious machine, whose inner workings and mechanism are withheld. The principle of non-contradiction compels us to admit that everything Euclid demonstrates is true: but we do not find out *why* it is so. We have almost the same uncomfortable sensation people feel after a　84

---

[a] *Triumph der Empfindsamkeit* [a satirical prose play by Goethe]
[b] *ein Wissen*
[c] *Wesen*

conjuring trick, and in fact most of Euclid's proofs are strikingly similar to tricks. The truth almost always emerges through a back door, the acciden- tal[a] result of some peripheral fact. An apagogic proof[b] often closes every door in turn, leaving open only one, through which we are forced simply because it is the only way to go. As in Pythagoras' theorem, lines are often drawn without any indication of why: later they show themselves to be traps that spring unexpectedly to capture the assent of students, who must admit in astonishment what remains completely incomprehensible in its inner workings, so much so that they can devote themselves to a thorough study of Euclid in its entirety without obtaining any real insight into the laws governing spatial relations – instead of the laws themselves, they only learn by rote a few of their consequences. This unscientific, genuinely empirical cognition is like that of the doctor who recognizes both the disease and the cure, but not the connection between them. All this is what happens when we capriciously reject the kind of grounding and evidentness appro- priate for a species of cognition, and instead forcibly introduce another kind that is essentially foreign to it. But in other respects, the way that Euclid achieved his results does warrant all the admiration that has been bestowed on him for so many centuries, and which stretches so far that his treatment of mathematics has been declared the paragon for any scientific exposition; and indeed all the other sciences have made an effort to model themselves on Euclid, although later on they gave up on it without really knowing why. Yet by our lights the Euclidean method can only appear as a brilliant piece of wrongheadedness. When any great aberration, whether in life or science, has been pursued intentionally and methodically, and has therefore been accompanied by general assent, the explanation always lies in the dominant philosophy of the time. – The Eleatics first discovered the distinction – indeed more often the conflict – between what is intuited, *phainomenon*, and what is thought, *nooumenon*,* and used it in a variety of ways both in their philosophical claims[c] and in their sophisms. The Megar- ics, the Dialecticians, the Sophists, the New Academics and the Sceptics all followed later and drew attention to illusion, i.e. deception of the senses (or better: deception of the understanding as it transforms the data of the senses into an intuition), which often lets us see things that reason is certain

85

---

* Here we may ignore Kant's misuse of these Greek expressions, which I criticize in the Appendix [Schopenhauer gives the expressions as φαινομενον, νοουμενον here and below in the text]

[a] *per accidens*

[b] *apagogischer Beweis* [An apagogic proof is an indirect form of proof like *reductio ad absurdum* that establishes a given proposition by showing that its negation leads to a contradiction]

[c] *Philosophemen*

are not real, e.g. a broken stick in water and other similar things. They recognized that sensory intuition is not to be trusted unconditionally, and then jumped to the conclusion that only rational and logical thought could establish the truth, even though Plato (in the *Parmenides*), along with the Megarics, Pyrrho and the New Academics showed by means of examples (of the same kind that Sextus Empiricus would later use) that, on the contrary, inferences and concepts were also misleading; indeed they may produce paralogisms and sophisms much more freely and in a way that is much more difficult to resolve than an illusion in sensory intuition. In any case, this rationalism, which emerged in opposition to empiricism, kept the upper hand, and Euclid adapted mathematics to its demands by using intuitive evidentness (*phainomenon*) to support only what he absolutely had to (the axioms), supporting everything else with inference (*nooumenon*). His method was dominant through the centuries, and was bound to remain dominant so long as pure *a priori* intuitions were not distinguished from empirical intuitions. Indeed Proclus (a commentator on Euclid) seems to have been fully aware of this distinction, as he shows in the passage of the commentary translated into Latin by Kepler in his book *On the Harmony of the World*; [a] however, he did not emphasize the issue enough and advanced it only in isolation so that he went unnoticed and did not achieve a breakthrough. Not until two thousand years later would there be a similar change in mathematics, this time occasioned by Kant's theories, which are destined to bring about such great changes in the knowledge, thought and action of all European peoples. For only after we have learned from this great mind that the intuitions of space and time are completely different from empirical intuitions, that they are quite independent of any sensory impression, that they are in fact the condition for sensory impressions, not the other way around, i.e. that they are *a priori* and hence not open to sensory deception; only then can we see that Euclid's logical way of treating mathematics is a useless precaution, a crutch for sound legs, that it is like a night traveller who, mistaking a clear and solid path for water, takes care not to tread on it and instead walks along the bumpy ground beside it, happy all the while to keep to the edge of the supposed water. Only now can we claim with certainty that what presents itself as necessary in the intuition of a figure does not come from the figure on paper (which could be very badly drawn), or from the abstract concept that we think as a result, but instead directly from the form of all cognition, something we are conscious of *a priori*. In every case, this form is the principle of sufficient reason; in this case, it is, as the form of intuition (i.e. space), the principle

86

---

[a] *De Harmonia Mundi* [*Harmonices mundi*, 1619]

of the ground of being; but it is just as directly evident and just as directly valid as the principle of the cognitive ground, i.e. logical certainty. Merely so as to put our trust in logical certainty, we do not have to (nor should we) leave the special province of mathematics in order to confirm it in the completely alien domain of concepts. Confining ourselves to specifically mathematical territory has this great advantage: mathematical knowledge *that* something is the case is the same thing as knowledge of *why* it is the case, even though the Euclidean method separates these two completely, letting us know only the former, not the latter. But, in Aristotle's splendid words from the *Posterior Analytics*, I, 27: 'A science is more exact and more excellent if it tells us simultaneously *what* something is and *why* it is, not *what* it is and *why* it is separately.'[a] In physics we are satisfied only when our recognition *that* something is the case is united with our recognition of *why* it is, so the fact that the mercury in a Torricelli tube is 28 inches high is a poor kind of knowledge if we do not add that it is held at this height to counterbalance the atmosphere. So why should we be satisfied in mathematics with the following occult quality[b] of the circle: the fact that the segments of any two intersecting chords always contain equal rectangles? Euclid certainly demonstrates it in the 35th proposition of the third book, but why it is so remains in doubt. Similarly, Pythagoras' theorem tells us about an occult quality of the right-angled triangle: Euclid's stilted, indeed underhand, proof leaves us without an explanation of why, while the following simple and well-known figure yields more insight into the matter in one glance than that proof, and also gives us a strong inner conviction of the necessity of this property and of its dependence on the right angle:

87

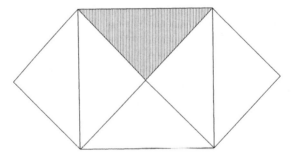

---

[a] Ακριβεστερα δ᾽ επιστημη επιστημης και προτερα, ἡτε του ὁτι και του διοτι ἡ αυτη, αλλα μη χωρις του ὁτι, της του διοτι. (*Subtilior autem et praestantior ea est scientia, quâ* quod *aliquid sit, et* cur *sit una simulque intelligimus, non separatim* quod, *et* cur *sit.*) [*Posterior Analytics* I, 27, 87a31–3]
[b] *qualitas occulta*

even when the sides at the right angle are unequal we must still be able to achieve this intuitive conviction, as we can generally with every possible geometrical truth, because the discovery of a geometrical truth always starts out from an intuition of the necessity, and the proof is only thought up later. So all that is required to intuitively recognize the necessity of a geometrical truth is an analysis of the thought process that first led to its discovery. For teaching mathematics, I altogether prefer the analytical method to Euclid's synthetic method, even though it runs into very serious – if not insuperable – problems in the case of complicated mathematical truths. Here and there in Germany, a start is already being made in changing the way mathematics is taught, and this analytical method is being increasingly adopted. The most decisive step in this direction has been taken by Herr *Kosack*, a teacher of physics and mathematics at the Nordhausen Gymnasium, who has added a thoroughgoing attempt to treat geometry according to my principles to the schedule for school examination on the 6th of April 1852.[75]

An improved method in mathematics requires first and foremost abandoning the prejudice that a proven truth is at all preferable to one that we have intuitive cognition of, or that a logical truth based on the principle of non-contradiction is preferable to an immediately evident metaphysical truth (for example, the pure intuition of space).

The content of the principle of sufficient reason is the most certain   88 and completely inexplicable, because in its various guises it designates the universal form of all our representations and cognitions. Every explanation is a reduction to the principle of sufficient reason, the identification of a particular instance of the connection between representations that the principle of sufficient reason expresses in general. Accordingly, it is the principle of all explanation, and hence is itself incapable of further explanation; nor does it need one, since such an explanation would in any case already presuppose it and gain meaning[a] only through it. No single form of the principle of sufficient reason has priority over any of the others: it is equally certain and equally incapable of proof whether it takes the form of the principle of the ground of being, becoming, action or cognition. The relation of ground to consequent is just as necessary in each one of these forms as it is in all the others: indeed this relation is the very origin as well as the only meaning that can be given to the concept of necessity. Nothing is necessary except a consequent when its ground is given; and nothing is a ground unless it leads necessarily to a consequent. The

---

[a] *Bedeutung*

ground of being in space conditions its consequent in space just as surely as the consequent expressed in a conclusion flows from its cognitive ground, given in the premises. If I have intuitively recognized the relation between a ground and consequent in space, then this relation is just as certain as any logical certainty. But any geometrical theorem expresses such a relation just as well as one of the twelve axioms does: a theorem is a metaphysical truth and as such is just as immediately certain as the principle of non-contradiction itself, the metalogical truth that is the universal basis for all logical argumentation. Anyone who denies the intuitively presented necessity of the spatial relations expressed in a theorem might just as well deny the axioms themselves, or deny that the conclusion of an argument follows from its premises, or even deny the principle of non-contradiction itself: for all of these are equally incapable of proof, and are immediately evident relations that we can have cognition of *a priori*. To want to derive the intuitively cognizable necessity of spatial relations from the principle of non-contradiction by means of a logical argument is like wanting to award

89 feudal rights over an estate to its immediate lord. Nevertheless, this is just what Euclid did. He supports only what he absolutely had to support (i.e. the axioms) on intuitive evidentness, and all subsequent geometrical truths are proven logically, that is, by presupposing the axioms and then by means of consistency with the assumptions made in a theorem or with a prior theorem, or by means of the inconsistency of the negation of a theorem with the assumptions, with the axioms, with prior theorems or even with itself.[76] But the axioms themselves are no more immediately evident than any other geometrical theorems; they are simply less complicated because they have less content.

When a criminal suspect[a] is examined, what he says is taken down as evidence so that its truth can be judged on the basis of the mutual consistency of his claims. But this is just a stopgap measure that does not put an end to the matter if we can directly investigate the truth of each of his claims for itself: after all, he could have been lying consistently from the start. However, this first method is the one used by Euclid to investigate space. It is true that he started out from the correct assumption that nature must always be consistent, and hence must also be consistent in its fundamental form, space; and, because the parts of space stand in the relation of ground and consequent to each other, there is not a single spatial determination that could be other than it is without coming into contradiction with all the rest. But it is a very burdensome and

---

[a] *Delinquent*

unsatisfactory detour to prefer mediate cognition to immediate cognition that is just as certain: this detour separates cognition *that* something is from cognition of *why* it is, constituting a great detriment to science and depriving students of any insight into the laws of space, indeed, it gets them quite out of the habit of investigating the ground and inner nexus of things, and teaches them instead to let themselves to be satisfied with the historical knowledge[a] *that* it is so. The exercise of acumen that wins Euclid's method such incessant praise amounts to no more than this: schoolchildren practise making inferences (i.e. applying the principle of non-contradiction), but more particularly they strain their memories remembering all the data whose mutual agreements have to be compared.

In addition it is worth mentioning that this method of proof has been applied only to geometry, and not arithmetic; in arithmetic, on the contrary, intuition alone (in this case, just counting) is allowed to make the truth clear. Intuition of numbers exists in *time alone*, and hence cannot be portrayed by any sensory schema akin to a geometrical figure, so the suspicion does not arise for arithmetic that intuition is merely empirical and might be subject to illusion; and the introduction of the logical mode of proof into geometry was due entirely to this suspicion. Because time has only a single dimension, counting is the only arithmetical operation; all others are reducible to it. Counting is nothing more than *a priori* intuition, but here no one has any hesitation about relying on it and it is the only way of verifying the rest of arithmetic: every calculation and every equation is ultimately verified through counting. We do not prove, for example that $\frac{(7 + 9) \times 8 - 2}{3} = 42$; on the contrary, we rely on pure intuition in time, i.e. counting, and transform every individual proposition into an axiom. Consequently, arithmetic and algebra are not taken up with the kind of proofs that fill geometry; rather, their whole content simply amounts to an abbreviated way of counting. As has already been mentioned, our direct intuition of numbers does not indeed reach much beyond ten: after that, an abstract concept of the number, fixed in a word, must take the place of intuition; the intuition is therefore no longer actually performed but merely designated determinately. Nevertheless, thanks to the invaluable expedient of a numbering system that always allows larger numbers to be represented through the repeated use of smaller ones, it is still possible to obtain intuitive evidentness for every calculation. This is true even where abstraction is used so extensively that not only numbers, but also indeterminate quantities and whole operations, like $\sqrt{r^{-b}}$, are thought

90

[a] *Wissen*

simply in the abstract,[a] and designated as such, so that they are not really performed but merely suggested.

Geometrical truth could be based exclusively on *a priori* intuition with just as much legitimacy as arithmetical truth, and the result would be just as certain. It is in fact always this intuitive cognition of necessity in accordance with the principle of the ground of being that makes geometry[77] so evident: this is also the basis for everyone's consciousness of the certainty of the claims of geometry, which never relies on the stilted march of a logical proof, since such a proof always misses the point and is usually soon forgotten without affecting anyone's conviction; we could even dispense with proof entirely and geometry would remain just as evident because it is quite independent of such proof, which only ever demonstrates something that we were already completely convinced of beforehand by a different kind of cognition. So logical proof is like a cowardly soldier who inflicts another wound on the corpse of an enemy already killed by someone else, but then boasts of finishing him off.*

After all this, I hope there is no longer any doubt that evidentness in mathematics, which has become the symbol and ideal of all evidentness, does not rest essentially on proof, but on immediate intuition: in this case therefore, as in all others, intuition is the ultimate ground and source of all truth. However, the intuition that forms the basis of mathematics has a great advantage in comparison with other kinds of intuition, and so also in comparison with empirical intuition, namely this: as an *a priori* intuition it is independent of experience (which is only ever given in a succession of parts) and everything is equally accessible to it so that it is possible to start out at will[b] from either a ground or a consequent. This insulates mathematics completely from deception because the consequent is known on the basis of the ground, and this is the only kind of cognition that possesses necessity: it is possible to know that sides are equal, for instance, because

---

* *Spinoza* always prided himself on proceeding *more geometrico* [in the geometrical way], and in fact he used this method more than he himself knew. He had an intuitive and immediate grasp of the essence of the world, which was settled and certain for him, and this he tries to demonstrate logically, i.e. independently of the knowledge he already had of it. He aims explicitly at this result, a result that he was already certain of in advance, but obviously he succeeds only because he arbitrarily chooses as a starting point a series of concepts that he has himself constructed (*substantia* [substance], *causa sui* [cause of itself] etc.) and makes free use in his proofs of the ready opportunities for every kind of arbitrariness that such broad conceptual spheres by their nature offer. What is true and excellent in his teaching is therefore quite independent of its proofs, just as it is in geometry. See also chap. 13 of the second volume.

[a] *in abstracto*
[b] *beliebig*

such cognition is grounded in the equality between angles; but all empirical
intuition, and most of experience,[78] proceed in the other direction, from
consequent to ground; and this kind of cognition is not infallible, because
necessity attaches only to the consequent (as long as the ground is given),
but not to cognition of the ground *from* the consequent (since the same
consequent can arise from different grounds). The latter kind of cognition
is nothing but induction, which treats the ground as certain on the basis
of several consequents that all point to it; but since the individual cases
can never occur all together, the truth here is also never unconditionally
certain. All cognition by way of sensory intuition, and most experience,
only ever has this kind of truth. The affecting of one of the senses makes
the understanding infer from the effect to the cause; but because inference
from the grounded back to the ground is never sure, false semblance, i.e.
sensory deception, is possible, and indeed often actual, as explained above.
Only when several or all five of the senses are affected in ways that indicate
the same cause does the possibility of illusion become extremely small;
although even here the possibility still exists, since in certain cases, like
that of counterfeit coins, all the senses are deceived at once.[79] All empirical
cognition is in the same situation, and as a result, so is the whole of natural
science, aside from its pure (or as Kant terms it, metaphysical) component.
In natural science too we come to know the cause from its effects, and so
every doctrine of nature is based on hypotheses that are often false and
must then gradually give way to better ones. Only in deliberately organized experiments does our cognition take a secure route, progressing from
the cause to the effect; but even experiments are undertaken only after
the formation of hypotheses.[80] As a result, no branch of natural science,
such as physics, astronomy or physiology could be discovered all at once,
as was possible in mathematics and logic; instead they required, and still
require, the collection and comparison of experiences over hundreds of
years. Only repeated empirical confirmation brings induction (on which
hypotheses rest) close enough to completeness that in practice it is treated
as certain, and the fact that a hypothesis originated through induction is
then considered as irrelevant as the incommensurability of straight and
crooked lines is to the application of geometry, or the fact that complete
precision can never be achieved in a logarithm is to arithmetic. Just as
the logarithm and the square of the circle can be brought infinitely close
to its correct value through infinite division, repeated experience brings
induction (i.e. cognition of the ground on the basis of the consequent),
if not infinitely close to the evidentness of mathematics (i.e. cognition of
the consequent on the basis of the ground), then close enough that the

possibility of deception is negligible.[81] But this possibility does still exist: for example, it is induction when an inference goes from countless cases to all cases, i.e. to a ground that is in fact unknown, that all the cases depend upon. What inference of this kind seems more certain than that all human beings have their hearts on the left-hand side? But there are very rare and completely isolated exceptions, i.e. human beings whose hearts lie on the right-hand side.[82] – Sensory intuition and empirical science[a] therefore share the same kind of evidentness. The advantage enjoyed by mathematics, pure natural science,[83] and logic (as cases of cognition[b] *a priori*) over these other two rests simply on this: their formal component,[c] the basis of all aprioricity is given in its entirety and all at once, so that here it is always possible to proceed from the ground to the consequent whereas in the other cases we can usually proceed only from the consequent to the ground. In other respects, the law of causality, or the principle of the ground of becoming, which guides empirical cognition, is in itself just as certain as any of the other forms of the principle of sufficient reason followed *a priori* by the sciences mentioned above. – Logical proofs from concepts (that is, inferences) have exactly the same advantage as cognition based on *a priori* intuition: they proceed from ground to consequent, and as a result they are intrinsically, i.e. formally, infallible. This fact has done much towards establishing the high repute generally enjoyed by proofs. But their infallibility is only relative; all they do is to subsume under the higher principles of a science. It is these principles that contain the entire fund of the science's truth, and they cannot themselves merely be proven in their turn; instead they must be based on intuition, which is pure *a priori* intuition in the case of the small number of *a priori* sciences mentioned above, but otherwise it is always an empirical intuition that can be elevated to universality only through induction. So, although experiential sciences also prove the particular from the universal, the universal has itself been verified only by means of particulars: it is only a warehouse of accumulated provisions, not a self-producing soil.

94

So much for the grounding of truth. – As regards the origin and possibility of *error*,[d] there have been many attempts to explain it since Plato's figurative solution of the dovecot that catches the wrong doves (*Theaetetus*, pp. 167ff.[e]). *Kant's* vague and indeterminate explanation of the origin of

---

[a] *Erfahrungswissenschaft*
[b] *Erkenntnisse*
[c] *das Formelle der Erkenntnisse*
[d] *Irrthum*
[e] [See 197c. Schopenhauer refers to the Bipont edition]

error using the image of diagonal motion can be found in the *Critique of Pure Reason*, p. 294 of the first edition and p. 350 of the 5th edition.[a,84] – Since truth is the relation of a judgement to its cognitive ground, the problem is how someone making a judgement can really believe that he has such a ground when he does not, i.e. how error, or the deception of reason, is possible. I think this possibility is wholly analogous to the possibility of illusion, or deception of the understanding, as I discussed it above. In my opinion (and this also shows why the explanation belongs exactly at this point), *every error is an inference from consequent to ground.* Such an inference is indeed valid when you know that the consequent can have only this and no other ground, but otherwise it is not. In making an error, someone either assigns to a consequent a ground that it cannot possibly have (which shows a real lack of understanding, i.e. of the capacity for immediate recognition of the connection between cause and effect), or, more often, the ground assigned to the consequent is indeed a possible one, but a major premise[b] is added to the inference from consequent to ground stating that this consequent *always* arises from the assigned ground; only a fully-fledged induction could justify such a premise, but this induction is presupposed rather than performed. The *always* is therefore too broad a concept, and should be replaced by a *sometimes* or an *often*; had these been used, the conclusion would turn out to be problematic,[c] and, as such, no longer erroneous. The fact that people who make errors act like this is due to either excessive haste or an inadequate awareness of what is possible, so that they do not understand[d] the need for the induction that has to be made. Error is therefore wholly analogous to illusion. Both are inferences from consequent to ground: in illusion the inference follows the law of causality and is performed by the understanding alone, i.e. immediately and in intuition itself; in error the inference follows all the forms of the principle of sufficient reason and is performed by reason in the act of thinking, although it most frequently follows the law of causality, as the following three examples show (they may be viewed as the types or representatives of the three species of error).[85] (1) Sensory illusion (deception of the understanding) gives rise to error (deception of the reason) when for instance someone mistakes a painting for a high relief[e] and then really takes it for one; the error results from a syllogism with the following major

95

---

[a] [See A294–5 / B350–1]
[b] *Obersatz*
[c] [i.e. in Kant's sense, possibly true rather than actually true. See *Critique of Pure Reason* A74 / B100]
[d] *nicht weiß*
[e] *ein Haut-Relief*

premise: 'if there are places where dark grey gradually fades into white, then this is *always* caused by light illuminating peaks and troughs unequally: therefore[a] –.' (2) 'If money is missing from my cashbox, then the cause is *always* my servant having a duplicate key: therefore –.' (3) 'If the sun's image is refracted through a prism (i.e. bent upwards or downwards) so that it now appears oblong and coloured instead of round and white as before, then on this as on every occasion the cause must be that the light has several homogeneous but differently coloured rays hidden in it, each with a different degree of refraction, and that these light rays are bent apart from each other because of these different degrees of refraction so that they now present an oblong and multicoloured image: therefore – let us drink!'[b] – Every error must be traceable back to this kind of inference from a hypothetical major premise that is often simply a false generalization and[86] arises from the assumption that there is a single ground for this consequent; the only exceptions are mistakes in calculation, which are in fact not really errors at all, but mere mistakes:[c] the operation indicated by the numerical concepts has not actually been carried out in pure intuition (i.e. by counting) but rather another one has been carried out instead.

As for the *content* of the sciences in general, this is in fact always the relation between the appearances of the world, in accordance with the principle of sufficient reason and guided by the question 'Why?', a question whose validity and meaning are derived from this principle alone. To establish such a relation is to *explain*. So explanation cannot go any further than to show that the relation between two representations is that of the particular form of the principle of sufficient reason governing the class to which the representations belong. If an explanation achieves this, it is no longer possible to ask 'why?', because the relation that has been established absolutely cannot be imagined[d] otherwise than as it is, i.e. it is the form of all cognition. So no one asks why $2 + 2 = 4$, or why the equality of angles in a triangle determines the equality of its sides, or why a particular cause is followed by its effect, or why the truth of the conclusion is manifest given the truth of the premises. Every explanation that does not lead back to such a relation, one where it is no longer possible to ask why, must end up assuming some occult quality,[e] and this is the character

96

---

[a] *ergo*
[b] *ergo – bibamus* [Schopenhauer is parodying an argument for Newton's theory of light, which he had attacked in *On Vision and Colours*, first published in 1816]
[c] *Fehler*
[d] *vorgestellt*
[e] *qualitas occulta*

of every original force of nature. Every natural scientific explanation must ultimately end up in an occult quality, and hence in something completely obscure: natural science must therefore leave the inner essence[a] of a stone just as unexplained as that of a human being; it can give just as little account of the gravity, cohesion and chemical properties[87] etc. expressed by the one as of the cognition and action[b] expressed by the other. Gravity for instance is an occult quality because it can be thought away and thus does not come from the form of cognition as something necessary, as is the case with the law of inertia, which follows from the law of causality; hence tracing something back to this law furnishes a completely satisfactory explanation.[88] So two things are absolutely inexplicable, that is, cannot be traced back to a relation expressed by the principle of sufficient reason: first, the principle of sufficient reason itself in all four of its forms, which cannot be explained because it is the principle of all explanation, indeed explanation only makes sense in relation to this principle; and second that which the principle of sufficient reason does not reach, although what is original[c] in all appearances stems from it: the thing in itself,[89] our cognition of which is not subject to that principle. At this point we must leave the thing in itself without understanding it at all, for it can be made comprehensible only in the next Book, when we will return to our discussion of the possible achievements of the sciences. There comes a point where natural science, indeed every science, leaves things as they are because its explanation of things, indeed the principle of sufficient reason, the very principle of its explanation, cannot reach any further; this is the point where philosophy really takes things up again and considers them from its own point of view, which is quite distinct from that of the sciences. – In my essay *On the Principle of Sufficient Reason* (§ 51),[90] I showed how the guiding thread for each of the different sciences is one or another form of this principle: in fact this may perhaps be the most appropriate way to categorize the sciences. But an explanation according to one of these guiding threads is, as already mentioned, always merely relative: it explains things in relation to each other, but always presupposes something that is left unexplained: in mathematics, for example, it is space and time; in mechanics, physics and chemistry, it is matter, qualities, original forces and natural laws; in botany and zoology it is the variety of the species and life itself; in history it is the human race, with all its peculiarities of thought and will; – and in all of these, it is the principle of sufficient reason, in the form applied to each

97

[a] *Wesen*
[b] *Handeln*
[c] *das Ursprungliche*

case, that is left unexplained. – *Philosophy* has the peculiarity that it does not presuppose anything as already known;[a] everything is equally foreign and equally problematic to it: not only relations between appearances, but also the appearances themselves, and even the principle of sufficient reason itself. The other sciences are happy to reduce everything to this principle, but for philosophy the reduction would achieve nothing because one member of the series is just as foreign to it as another. Furthermore, the way in which appearances are connected together is itself as much of a problem as what is thereby linked, and this problem is in its turn as severe after the linkage as it was before. As we have already said, the very thing that the sciences presuppose and posit as the basis and limit of their explanations is exactly what constitutes the real problem for philosophy: so the latter starts just where the sciences stop. Proofs cannot be the foundation of philosophy, because proofs derive unknown propositions from known ones, whereas for philosophy everything is equally foreign and unknown. There cannot be a principle that would result in the very beginning of the world with all its appearances: so a philosophy cannot be derived by demonstration from stable principles,[b] as Spinoza wanted. Philosophy is also the most universal kind of knowledge[c] and its fundamental principles cannot therefore be the consequences of some other kind of yet more universal knowledge. The principle of non-contradiction only establishes the mutual consistency of concepts, but does not specify the concepts themselves. The principle of sufficient reason explains the connections between appearances, but not the appearances themselves. So philosophy cannot use these principles to search for either an efficient cause or a final cause[d] of the world as a whole. The present philosophy at least is not remotely concerned with *where the world came from* or *what it is for*, but only with *what* it is. Here the Why is subordinate to the What because the former question already belongs to the world: it arises only through the form of the world's appearance (the principle of sufficient reason), applies to it alone and is meaningful only within it. It could indeed be said that each of us knows *what* the world is without any further instruction because each of us is that very cognitive subject whose representation the world is; and this would in fact be true, as far as it goes. But such cognition is intuitive, concrete cognition:[e] philosophy's task is to reproduce this in the abstract,[f] to elevate

98

---

[a] *bekannt*
[b] *ex firmis principiis*
[c] *Wissen*
[d] *causa efficiens . . . causa finalis*
[e] *in concreto*
[f] *in abstracto*

the succession of transient intuitions and in general everything that the wide-ranging concept of *feeling* includes (and designates merely negatively as knowledge that is neither abstract nor clear) into permanent knowledge. Accordingly, philosophy must be an abstract statement of the essence of the entire world, of the whole as well as of all its parts. However, to avoid getting lost in an infinite mass of particular judgements, philosophy must make use of abstraction and think everything particular in the light of the universal, and rethink its differences in the light of the universal too: as a result, it will sometimes divide and sometimes unite, condensing all the variety in the world as a whole into a few abstract concepts in accordance with its nature, and handing them over to knowledge. The concepts used by philosophy to fix the essence of the world must, however, facilitate cognition of what is completely particular just as much as cognition of the universal: cognition of the one must be tied to cognition of the other down to the last detail. As a result, philosophical ability consists, as Plato put it, of recognizing the one in the many and the many in the one. Philosophy will therefore be a collection[a] of very universal judgements that have their cognitive ground directly in the world itself in its entirety, without excluding anything, in other words, in everything that is to be found in human consciousness; philosophy will be *a complete recapitulation, a reflection, as it were, of the world, in abstract concepts.* This can be achieved only by unifying things that are essentially identical in a *single* concept and sorting out what differs into another. Bacon of Verulam already set this as the task for philosophy when he said: 'Only that philosophy is the true one, which reproduces the testimony of the world most accurately and, as it were, transcribes the dictation of the world, and is nothing other than the *copy and reflection* of the world, and does not add anything of its own, but just reproduces and repeats' (*On the Dignity and Advancement of Learning*, Book 2, ch. 13).[b] We take what he says however in a more extended sense than he could then have contemplated.

99

   All the parts and aspects of the world agree with each other because they belong to a single whole; and this agreement must also be rediscovered in philosophy's abstract copy[c] of the world. So some of the judgements contained in philosophy's collection could, to a certain extent, be derived

---

[a] *Summe*
[b] *Ea demum vera est philosophia, quae mundi ipsius voces fidelissime reddit, et veluti dicante mundo conscripta est, et nihil aliud est, quam ejusdem* simulacrum et reflectio, *neque addit quidquam de proprio, sed tantum iterat et resonat* (de augm. scient., L. 2, c. 13) [Francis Bacon, *De Dignitate et augmentis scientiarum* – although Schopenhauer's reference to this specific passage is questionable]
[c] *Abbild*

from others and this must in fact always be reciprocal. But all the other judgements must be there for the first one to exist, and so they must be set up beforehand and grounded immediately in concrete cognition of the world, and the more so as immediate grounding is more secure than mediate grounding. Their mutual harmony, which ensures that they flow together in the unity of a *single* thought, arises from the harmony and unity of the intuitive world itself (their common cognitive ground); so this harmony will not be used as the first thing for grounding them, but rather only as an additional corroboration of their truth. – The task itself can only become fully clear when it has been completed.*

§16

After this whole discussion of reason as a special cognitive power peculiar to human beings, and of the achievements and characteristic phenomena of human nature that it brings about, all that remains now for me to discuss is reason in so far as it guides human action, which, in this respect, can be termed *practical*. Much of the topic to be addressed here has been covered elsewhere, in the Appendix to this work, where I contested the existence of what Kant calls practical reason, which he presents (very conveniently of course) as the immediate source of all virtue and the seat of an absolute *ought*, i.e. one that has fallen from heaven. I later provided the detailed and thorough rebuttal of this Kantian principle of morals in my *Fundamental Problems of Ethics*.[a],[91] – As a result, I do not have much more to say here about the actual influence of reason, in the true sense of the word, on action. At the outset of our discussion of reason we already remarked in general how very different the deeds and conduct of human beings are from those of animals, and that this difference should be regarded as due entirely to the presence of abstract concepts in consciousness. Concepts have such a sweeping and significant influence on our whole existence that they put us in much the same relation to animals in general as animals with vision have to those without eyes (certain larvae, worms and zoophytes): only through touch can such animals recognize what is immediately present to them in space, i.e. what is in contact with them; seeing animals on the other hand can recognize a broad sphere of things that are both near and far. In the same way, lack of reason confines animals to intuitive representations,

---

* See chap. 17 of the second volume.

[a] [See ch. 2 of *BM*]

which are immediately present to them in time, i.e. real objects: on the other hand, thanks to our abstract[a] cognition, we grasp not only what is narrowly and actually present, but also the whole of the past and the future and the whole wide realm of possibility: we can freely survey life on all sides, far beyond what is present and actual. So, to a certain extent, reason is for inner cognition in time what the eye is for sensory intuition in space. However, just as the ability to see objects is valuable and significant only because it announces how they will feel, so the whole value of abstract cognition always lies in its relation to intuitive cognition. This is also why the natural human being always puts much more emphasis on what is   101 cognized immediately in intuition than he does on abstract concepts (i.e. things that are merely thought) and prefers empirical[92] to logical cognition. Those who live more in word than deed, those who have seen more on paper and in books than they have in the actual world, are otherwise inclined, and in their most degenerate form they become pedants and literalists.[b] This is the only way to understand how Leibniz, Wolff[c] and all their followers could have been lead so far astray by the example of Duns Scotus[93] as to explain intuitive cognition as merely a confused kind of abstract cognition! To his credit, I must mention that Spinoza's good sense led him to do the reverse and explain that all general concepts come from a confusion of something we have cognition of intuitively (*Ethics* II, prop. 40, Schol. 1.). – This perverse frame of mind has also given rise to several other things: in mathematics, the rejection of the kind of evidentness specific to it in favour of logical evidentness alone; the deprecation of non-abstract cognition by subsuming it all, quite generally, under a term as wide as 'feeling'; and finally, Kant's declaration, in his ethics, that pure, good will, of the kind that speaks to us directly from cognition of circumstances and leads to beneficent and benevolent deeds, is a mere feeling, a worthless and vain paroxysm,[d] and his desire to attribute moral worth only to action undertaken on the basis of abstract maxims.

The panoramic view of life as a whole, which gives human beings our advantage over the animals, can also be compared to a colourless, abstract, geometrical miniature of life's course. Armed with this sketch, we have the same relation to the animals that a ship's pilot (who, thanks to nautical chart, compass and quadrant, always knows with precision his ship's heading and position on the sea) has to the unskilled crew who see

---

[a] *in abstracto*
[b] *Buchstabenmenschen*
[c] *Wolf*
[d] *Aufwallung*

only waves and sky. So it is noteworthy, indeed marvellous, that we human beings always lead a second, abstract life alongside our concrete life.[a] In the first we are subject to all the storms of reality and are prey to the influence of the present: we must strive, suffer and die, just as animals do. But our abstract life, as it appears before us in rational contemplation, is the calm reflection of the first life and the world it is lived in; it is that miniature sketch just mentioned. In this realm of peaceful deliberation what had previously possessed us completely and moved us deeply, now appears cold, colourless and strange to the eye: here we are simply onlookers and spectators. In this retreat into reflection we are like actors who have played our scene, and now take our seats among the audience before we have to return to the stage; anything may now happen on the stage, even the preparation of our own death, and, looking out from the audience, we view it with equanimity;[b] but then we return to act and suffer as we must. The equanimity[c] we human beings experience, so different from the thoughtlessness of animals, stems from this second life; it is this equanimity that, after prior deliberation, calm resolution, or acknowledged necessity, allows us to endure coolly something that is of the utmost importance for us, often something quite terrible – or even to undertake it ourselves: as in suicide, execution, duelling, all kinds of life-threatening deeds of daring, and in general things that make our animal nature rise up in rebellion. This is where we can see to what extent reason dominates our animal nature and calls out to the strong: 'Verily, you have a heart of iron' (*Iliad*, 24, 521).[d] Here we can really say that reason is expressing itself *practically*: where reason guides deeds, where abstract concepts furnish the motive, where deeds are not determined by individual intuitive representations or the impressions of the moment that guide animals – this is where *practical reason* shows itself. In the Appendix I have given a detailed explanation, clarified by the use of examples, of the fact that all this is quite distinct from the ethical value of action and totally independent of it; that rational action and virtuous action are two completely different things; that reason can find itself in alliance with great wickedness[e] just as well as with great goodness, and that both the one and the other are only really effective with the addition of reason; that reason stands just as readily in the service of the methodical and consistent execution of noble intentions as it does in

[a] *Leben* in concreto . . . in abstracto
[b] *gelassen*
[c] *Gelassenheit*
[d] σιδηρειον νυ τοι ητορ! (*ferreum certe tibi cor!*)
[e] *Bosheit*

the service of bad intentions, serving both maxims of prudence as well as maxims of ignorance (something that results from the feminine, receptive and preservative rather than self-creative nature of reason). What I say in the Appendix should have its rightful place here, but had to be put off on account of my polemic against Kant's spurious practical reason; I therefore refer the reader here to that Appendix.   103

The *Stoic sage* presents in an ideal form the most complete development of *practical reason* in the true and authentic sense of the word, the highest peak a human being can attain using only reason, where the distinction between humans and animals shows itself most clearly. For originally and essentially Stoic ethics is not a doctrine of virtue at all, but simply a guide for rational living: its end and aim is the achievement of happiness[a] through peace of mind,[b] and virtuous conduct is included only as it were accidentally,[c] as a means rather than an end. Consequently, Stoic ethics is fundamentally different in both its point of view and its whole essence from ethical systems that insist directly on virtue, such as the doctrines of the *Vedas*, Plato, Christianity and Kant. The end of Stoic ethics is the achievement of happiness: 'the end of all virtue is happiness',[d] according to Stobaeus' account of the Stoics (*Eclogues*, Book II, ch. 7, p. 114 and p. 138).[e,94] But Stoic ethics also shows that happiness can only be assured through inner tranquillity and peace of mind (*ataraxia*[f]), and that these in turn can only be achieved through virtue: this is all that is meant by the expression: virtue is the highest good. But, of course, if the means gradually makes us forget the end, and virtue is commended in such a way that it betrays an interest quite different from our own happiness and indeed blatantly contradicts it, then this is one of those inconsistencies where, in every system, immediately recognized truth (or, as people say, felt truth) leads back to the right track even while doing violence to logical inferences. This is clearly visible in Spinoza's ethics, for instance, which uses palpable sophisms to derive a pure doctrine of virtue from the egoistic maxim: to seek what is useful to oneself.[g] According to my understanding of the spirit of Stoic ethics, its origin lies in this thought: whether reason, the great human prerogative, which appreciably though indirectly (through

---

[a] *Glück*
[b] *Geistesruhe*
[c] *per accidens*
[d] τελος το ευδαιμονειν (*virtutes omnes finem habere beatitudinem*)
[e] [See *Eclogues* II, 6. Schopenhauer's reference is inaccurate. His page references are to the 1792 edition of Arnold Heeren]
[f] αταραξια [imperturbability]
[g] *suum utile quaerere* [*Ethics* 4. prop. 20]

the planning of action and all that follows from this) lightens our lives and loads, might not also be capable of directly (i.e. using nothing but cognition) eliminating at once all the different kinds of suffering and sorrow that fill life – either completely, or at least for the most part. It was not considered fitting that a being endowed with the privilege of reason, who can use it to survey and take in an infinity of things and situations, should, in the present moment and in the events contained in the few years of a short, fleeting, and uncertain life, nonetheless be exposed to the sort of intense anxiety and suffering that spring from the violent strain of desire and revulsion; it was thought that the proper application of reason must raise human beings above all this and be capable of making them invulnerable. This is why Antisthenes claimed: 'We must obtain either understanding or the noose' (Plutarch, *On the Stoic Self-contradictions*, ch. 14),[a] i.e. life is so full of troubles and vexations that we must either rise above it by correcting our beliefs, or we must leave it.[95] The Stoic insight was that privation and suffering do not follow immediately and necessarily from not-having, but rather from wanting-to-have and yet not having; consequently, this wanting-to-have is the necessary condition under which not-having becomes privation and gives rise to pain: 'cupidity and not poverty causes pain'[b],[96] (Epictetus, fragment 25). Moreover, experience shows that it is only hope, the claim to something, that gives birth to the wish and nourishes it; so we are not disturbed or troubled by the many unavoidable ills[c] that are common to everyone nor by goods no one can attain, but only by the trivial More and Less of what the individual can avoid or attain. Indeed experience also shows that not only what is absolutely unattainable but also what is relatively unattainable or unavoidable does not disturb us in the least; therefore, the ills we start out with as individuals and also the goods that must necessarily be denied us are regarded with indifference, so that, true to this human peculiarity, every wish soon dies and cannot arouse any more pain, as long as there is no hope for it to feed on. It followed from this that all happiness depends on the proportion between what we claim and what we receive: it does not matter how big or small the quantities in this proportion are, since it can be produced just as easily by reducing the first quantity as by increasing the second. Equally, it followed that all suffering in fact springs from a disproportion between what we demand and expect, and what we get; but this disproportion is

---

[a] Δει κτασθαι νουν, η βροχον (*aut mentem parandam, aut laqueum. Plut. de stoic[orum] repugn[antiis]*, c. 14 [1039E])

[b] Ου πενια λυπην εργαζεται, αλλα επιθυμια (*non paupertas dolorem efficit, sed cupiditas*)

[c] *Uebel*

clearly located in our cognition* and, given more insight, could be removed completely. This is why Chrysippus claimed: 'we must live according to the experience of what usually happens'[a] (Stobaeus, *Eclogues*, Book II, ch. 7, p. 134), i.e. one ought to live with a proper acquaintance with the course of the things of the world.[97] Every time people are put out by something, or misfortune[b] leaves them dumbstruck, or they get angry or they despair, then the very fact that things turn out differently from their expectations shows that they were in error and that they were not acquainted with life and the world, and do not know how at every step inanimate nature thwarts the will of the individual through chance, just as animate nature does so through conflicting purposes as well as through wickedness. Such people have either failed to use their reason to gain general knowledge about this characteristic of life, or they lack judgement, that is, they cannot recognize in the particular case what they know in general and are therefore surprised and put out by it.[**,98] In the same way, every lively pleasure is also an error, a delusion,[c] because getting what you want can never be permanently satisfying, as well as because possessions and happiness are on indefinite loan to us from chance, and can therefore be recalled at a moment's notice. Every pain rests on the disappearance of such a delusion: and so both arise from faulty cognition; the sage therefore is always as aloof from jubilation as from pain and nothing that happens disturbs his *ataraxia*.

 106

In keeping with the end and spirit of the Stoics, *Epictetus* begins with one idea and constantly keeps returning to it as the core of his wisdom. The idea is this: we should ponder very carefully indeed and distinguish between what depends on us and what does not. If we take no account at all of the latter, we can be sure to remain free of all pain, suffering and anxiety. But the only thing that depends on us is the will; and this is where the gradual transition to a doctrine of virtue takes place. This

---

*   *Omnes perturbationes judicio censent fieri et opinione* [All bad moods are, so they teach, based on judgement and opinion] Cicero, *Tusculan Disputations* 4, 6 [more correctly 4, 7, 14] Ταρασσει τους ανθρωπους ου τα πραγματα, αλλα τα περι των πραγματων δογματα. (*Perturbant homines non res ipsae, sed de rebus opiniones.*) [Things themselves do not disturb human beings, but rather opinions about things.] Epictetus, [*Enchiridion* (*Manual*)] ch. V.

**   Τουτο γαρ εστι το αιτιον τοις ανθρωποις παντων των κακων, το τας προληψεις τας κοινας μη δυνασθαι εφαρμοζειν ταις επι μερους. (*Haec est causa mortalibus omnium malorum, non posse communes notiones aptare singularibus.*) [The cause of all ills for human beings is this: that they cannot apply the general concept to the particular case.] Epictetus, *Dissert[ationes]* (*Discourses*), III, 26 [more correctly IV, 1, 42]

[a] δει ζην κατ' εμπειριαν των φυσει συμβαινοντων [In fact p. 134 is in *Eclogues* II, 6]
[b] *Unglück*
[c] *Wahn*

is because people noticed that, just as the external world independent of us produces good and bad fortune,[a] so the will gives rise to inner satisfaction or dissatisfaction with ourselves. Then later on they asked whether the names *bonum et malum*[b] should be given to the first pair or the second one. The choice was actually arbitrary and irrelevant, but the Stoics argued incessantly with the Peripatetics and the Epicureans about the issue, entertaining themselves with an inadmissible comparison between these two wholly incommensurable quantities and with the conflicting, paradoxical claims that follow from it, which they accused each other of making. Cicero's *Paradoxes*[c] give us an interesting collection of these claims, from the Stoic point of view.[99]

Zeno, the founder,[d] seems to have originally taken a somewhat different route. His starting point was this: in order to achieve the highest good, i.e. bliss[e] through peace of mind, one must live in harmony with oneself. ('To live in harmony: that is, to live according to a single fundamental principle and in harmony with oneself', Stobaeus, *Ethical Eclogues*, Book II, ch. 7, p. 132. Similarly: 'Virtue consists in the harmony of mental behaviour with itself throughout the whole of life', ibid., p. 104).[f,100] Now, this is possible only if we conduct ourselves completely *rationally*, according to concepts, not according to transitory impressions or moods; but only the maxims of our actions lie within our power (not their success or external circumstances), so, if we want to remain completely consistent, we must make the maxims our end rather than the other things – and this reintroduces the doctrine of virtue.

Zeno's immediate followers already regarded his moral principle – to live in harmony – as too formal and lacking in content. So they gave it substance by adding: 'to live in harmony with nature' (ὁμολογουμένως τῇ φύσει ζῆν). According to Stobaeus (*loc. cit.*), this was first inserted by *Cleanthes* and it made the whole issue much more nebulous, because of the size of the conceptual spheres and the indeterminacy of the terms, because *Cleanthes* meant the whole of nature in general, while *Chrysippus*

107

---

[a] *Glück und Unglück*
[b] [Good and evil]
[c] *Paradoxa*
[d] [of Stoicism]
[e] *Glückseligkeit*
[f] ὁμολογουμένως ζῆν· τουτο δ᾽ εστι καθ᾽ ἑνα λογον και συμφωνον ζῆν. – *Consonanter vivere: hoc est secundum unam rationem et concordem sibi vivere. Stob. Ecl. eth. L. II, c. 7, p. 132....* ἀρετην διαθεσιν ειναι ψυχης συμφωνον ἑαυτῃ περι ὁλον τον βιον. *Virtutem esse animi affectionem secum per totam vitam consentientem, ibid. p. 104* [but again both page references are in fact in *Eclogues* II, 6]

meant human nature in particular (Diogenes Laertius,[a] 7, 89). Virtue is then supposed to be the only thing appropriate to human nature, just as the satisfaction of animal drives is the only thing appropriate to animal nature. Again, this brings us forcibly back to the doctrine of virtue, and ethics is supposed to be grounded in physics, no matter how much this distorts or even destroys it. The Stoics generally set great store by unity of principle, since they did not see God and world as separate at all.

Taken as a whole, Stoic ethics is in fact a very valuable and estimable attempt to adapt that great privilege of humanity, reason, to an important and salutary end, namely that of raising us above the suffering and pain that every life encounters, by means of this advice:

By which reason may you be able to pass your life gently: may desire, ever needy, never disturb and vex you, nor fear nor hope for things of little use.[b]

and this allows us to participate to the highest degree in that dignity which attaches to us as rational beings distinct from animals (in fact there is no other sense in which we can talk of dignity). – This is my view of Stoic ethics and it shows why I had to mention it here, in my presentation of what *reason* is and what it can achieve. To a certain extent, we can achieve this end through the application of reason and a purely rational ethic, and experience does show that the happiest people are those purely rational types we generally call practical philosophers (rightly so, because true, i.e. theoretical, philosophers carry life over into concepts, whereas practical philosophers carry concepts over into life); nevertheless we are still very far from achieving anything perfect in this respect, where the correct use of reason is really able to eliminate all the burdens and suffering of life and lead to bliss. It is rather completely contradictory to want to live without suffering, a contradiction also contained in the common expression 'a blessed life',[c] as will certainly be clear to anyone who has read my exposition through to the end. This contradiction is also revealed in the ethics of pure reason itself, since the Stoics are forced to include in their guide for a blessed life (because this is what their ethics always remains) a recommendation for suicide in the case of excessive and incurable bodily suffering incapable of being philosophized away with principles and inferences, just as oriental despots include a fine vial of poison among their splendid jewels and utensils. In this case, bliss, the only purpose of life, has been thwarted and

108

---

[a] [*Lives of Eminent Philosophers*]
[b] *Qua ratione queas traducere leniter aevum:* | *Ne te semper inops agitet vexetque cupido,* | *Ne pavor et rerum mediocriter utilium spes.* [Horace *Epistles*, I, 18, 97]
[c] *säliges Leben*

suffering can now only be evaded through death, which should itself be undertaken with indifference, like any course of medication. This reveals a stark contrast between Stoic ethics and all the other ethical systems mentioned above, the ones that make virtue directly and in itself their end, even if it is accompanied by the most extreme suffering: these ethical systems do not allow people to end their lives to escape suffering, even though none of their proponents knew how to express the true ground for this rejection of suicide, and instead painstakingly gathered together any number of illusory grounds. The true ground will emerge in the context of the discussion in the Fourth Book. But the contrast mentioned above reveals and confirms the essential difference between the fundamental principle of the Stoics (which is actually only a special form of eudaimonism) and that of the other doctrines we have discussed, despite the fact that the two often have the same results and seem to be related. The inner contradiction, mentioned above, that affects Stoic ethics even in its basic idea, can also be discerned in the fact that the Stoics were never able to present their ideal, the Stoic sage, as a living being with inner poetic truth; he remains stiff and wooden, a mannequin that no one can engage with and who does not himself know what to do with his own wisdom. His perfect composure, peace and bliss really contradict the essence of humanity, so that we are unable to form any intuitive representation of him. How completely different they seem, next to the Stoic sage, those who the wisdom of India sets before us and has actually brought forth, those voluntary penitents who overcome the world; or even the Christian saviour, that splendid figure, full of the depths of life, of the greatest poetical truth and highest significance, but who, with perfect virtue, holiness and sublimity, nevertheless stands before us in a state of the utmost suffering.*

---

* See chap. 16 of the second volume.

SECOND BOOK

The world as will, first consideration

The objectivation of the will

Nos habitat, non tartara, sed nec sidera coeli:
Spiritus, in nobis qui viget, illa facit.

['It dwells in us, not in the underworld, nor in the
heavenly stars: All this is brought to pass by the living
spirit in us.' Agrippa von Nettesheim][1]

In the First Book we considered representation only as such, which is to say
only with respect to its general form. Of course when it comes to abstract
representations (concepts), we are familiar with their content as well, since
they acquire this content and meaning only through their connection to
intuitive representation and would be worthless and empty without it.
This is why we will have to focus exclusively on intuitive representation in
order to learn anything about its content, its more precise determinations,
or the configurations it presents to us. We will be particularly interested in
discovering the true meaning of intuitive representation; we have only ever
felt this meaning before, but this has ensured that the images do not pass by
us strange and meaningless as they would otherwise necessarily have done;
rather, they speak and are immediately understood and have an interest
that engages our entire being.[a]

We turn to mathematics, natural science and philosophy, each of which
raises our hope that it might shed some light on the problem. – But first we
find that philosophy is a many-headed monster with each head speaking a
different language. Of course they do not all disagree on the point at issue,
the meaning of intuitive representation: with the exception of sceptics
and idealists, they speak fairly consistently about an *object* that *grounds*   114
representation, an object whose entire being and essence is of course totally

[a] *Wesen*

different from representation, while at the same time being as similar to it as one egg to another. But this is not very helpful: we do not know how to distinguish such an object from representation; in fact, we find that they are one and the same, since any object will always and forever presuppose a subject, which is why it continues to be a representation; similarly, we have recognized that being-an-object[a] belongs to the most general form of representation, which is just the subject/object dichotomy. Similarly, the principle of sufficient reason (to which we here refer) can be nothing more to us than the form of representation, which is to say the lawlike connection of one representation with another, not the connection of the whole finite or infinite series of representations with something totally unlike representation and therefore totally unrepresentable. – We discussed the sceptics and idealists earlier[b] when we were talking about the dispute over the reality of the external world.

If we now look to mathematics to fill in our entirely general and exclusively formal knowledge of intuitive representation, we will hear more about these representations only to the extent that they occupy space and time, i.e. to the extent that they are quantities. Mathematics will specify 'how many?' and 'how large?' with the most exacting precision: but since this is only ever relative, i.e. a comparison between one representation and another, and in fact only one-sided, i.e. merely with respect to quantity, this is not the sort of elucidation we are really looking for.

Looking at last to the broad area of natural science with its many subdisciplines, we can draw an initial distinction between sciences that deal with the description of forms,[c] which I will call *morphology*, and those that deal with the explanation of alterations, which I will call *aetiology*. The morphological sciences look at static forms and the aetiological sciences at changing matter and the laws governing its transition from one form into another. The morphological sciences include the entire range of disciplines known as natural history (though this is not the literal meaning of the term). With botany and zoology in particular, natural history shows us the variety of determinate organic forms that remain fixed and stable despite constant change to the individual. These forms constitute a large fraction of the content of intuitive representation: natural history classifies, separates, combines and arranges these forms into natural and artificial systems, bringing them under concepts that make possible an overview and cognition of the whole. Further, these sciences demonstrate that a

115

[a] *Objektseyn*
[b] [See § 5 above]
[c] *Gestalten*

ubiquitous, infinitely fine-grained analogy is present in both the whole and the parts (unity of plan[a,2]), which makes them similar to a set of exceedingly diverse variations on an unspecified theme. These sciences are not primarily concerned with the transition of matter into those forms, i.e. the genesis of the individual, since each individual originates from others similar to itself through procreation, which is equally mysterious everywhere and has so far eluded attempts at clear knowledge: but the little we do know of the matter is properly found in physiology, which is already included among the aetiological sciences. Mineralogy, which belongs for the most part to morphology, tends towards aetiology as well, particularly at the point where it becomes geology. All the branches of science that deal primarily with knowledge of cause and effect are true aetiologies: these teach us how *one* state of matter necessarily gives rise to another determinate state according to an infallible rule: how one determinate alteration necessarily conditions and gives rise to another: and this account is what we call an *explanation*. Here we find principally mechanics, physics, chemistry and physiology.

But if we devote ourselves to this teaching we soon realize that the information we are looking for does not belong to aetiology any more than it belongs to morphology. The latter presents us with an infinite variety of innumerable forms that are clearly related through an unmistakable family resemblance; these are representations that will forever remain foreign to us if we approach them along this path; looking at them only in this way, they stand before us like hieroglyphs we do not comprehend. – Aetiology, for its part, tells us that some one determinate state of matter will lead to some other, according to the law of cause and effect, and with this it has explained this second state of matter and done its job. But in fact it has 　116 done nothing more than establish the lawlike order in which states emerge in space and time, and tell us in each case what appearance will necessarily emerge at any given time and place: so it determines their position in time and space according to a law whose determinate content has been given by experience, and yet whose general form and necessity we are aware of independently of experience. But this does not shed any light at all on the inner essence of any of these appearances: this inner essence[b] is called a *natural force*,[c] and lies outside of the ambit of aetiological explanation; what aetiology calls a *natural law*[d] is the unchanging constancy with which such a force expresses itself, whenever its known conditions are present. But all

---

[a] *unité de plan*
[b] *das innere Wesen*
[c] *Naturkraft*
[d] *Naturgesetz*

that it knows or could ever know is this natural law, these conditions, this emergence at a particular time and place. The force that is itself expressed, the inner essence of the appearances that emerge according to these laws will remain an eternal mystery to it, something as entirely foreign and unfamiliar in the simplest phenomenon[a] as in the most complicated. So far, aetiology has achieved its aims most completely in mechanics and least completely in physiology; still, as far as its inner essence is concerned, the force that makes a stone fall to the ground or one body repel another is no less foreign or mysterious to us than the force that produces movement and growth in an animal. Mechanics assumes matter, gravity, impenetrability, transfer of motion through impact, rigidity, etc. to be inscrutable; it calls them forces of nature, and calls their necessary and regular appearance under certain conditions laws of nature; only then does it start giving explanations. These explanations consist in specifying faithfully and with mathematical precision how, where and when each force expresses itself, and tracing each appearance that mechanics comes across back to natural forces. Physics, chemistry and physiology each do the same in their own fields, except that they presuppose much more while accomplishing less. Consequently, even the best aetiological explanation of the whole of nature 117 would really be nothing more than a catalogue of inexplicable forces and an authoritative specification of the rule according to which they emerge, succeed one another, and displace one another in space and time: but it must always leave unexplained the inner essence of the forces that thus appear, and content itself with appearances and their arrangement. This is because the law aetiology follows does not go further than this. As such, it can be compared to the cross-section of a piece of marble, which shows all sorts of veins next to one another but does not let us see the course each vein runs in the interior of the marble before reaching the surface. Or, if I can be permitted a humorous analogy (because it is more striking), – given a complete aetiological account of the whole of nature, the philosophical investigator would always feel like someone who finds himself in completely unfamiliar company without knowing how, and where each person in turn introduces another as his friend or cousin, thus making them sufficiently acquainted: in the meantime, however, the man himself, while expressing his pleasure at each new acquaintance, keeps asking himself: 'But how the devil do *I* fit in to this whole group?'

So when it comes to those appearances we know merely as our representations, aetiology can never give us the sort of elucidation we want,

---

[a] *Erscheinung*

the sort of explanation that would lead us beyond them. This is because once all its explanations are complete, they are still mere representations, which is to say perfect strangers whose meaning we do not understand. The causal connection merely specifies the rule and relative order of their emergence in space and time, but does not give us any greater insight into what actually emerges. Furthermore, the law of causation is itself only valid for representations, for objects of a determinate class, and is meaningful only on this presupposition: thus, like the objects themselves, it exists only in relation to a subject, which is to say conditionally; this is why we can know it just as well when we proceed from the subject, i.e. *a priori*, as when we proceed from the object, i.e. *a posteriori*, which is what Kant has taught us.

But what goads us to further research is simply the fact that we are not satisfied with knowing that we have representations, that they are such and such, and that they are joined according to this or that law whose general   118
expression is always the principle of sufficient reason. We want to know the meaning[a] of those representations: we ask if this world is nothing more than representation; in which case it would have to pass over us like an insubstantial dream or a ghostly phantasm,[b] not worth our notice; or in fact whether it is something else, something more, and if so, what this could be. This much is certain: what we are looking for would have to be wholly and completely different from representation, and so its forms and laws could be nothing at all like those of representation; this is why we could never use representation as a guide to discover its laws, since the laws of representation only connect objects and representations to each other; and these are the forms of the principle of sufficient reason.

Now we are already in a position to see that we can never reach the essence of things *from the outside*: no matter how much we look, we find nothing but images and names. We are like someone who walks around a castle, looking in vain for an entrance and occasionally sketching the façade. And yet this is the path that all philosophers before me have taken.[3]

§ 18

What I am searching for, the meaning of the world that confronts me as a mere representation, and the transition from this world as mere representation of the cognizing subject to whatever it may be besides, could indeed never be discovered if the enquirer were himself nothing more than a pure

[a] *Bedeutung*
[b] *Luftgebilde*

subject of cognition (a winged cherub's head without a body). But he is rooted in this world and finds himself in it as an *individual*, i.e. his cognition, which upholds and conditions the entire world as representation, is nonetheless completely mediated through a body whose affections, as we have shown, are the starting point for the understanding as it intuits this world. To the pure subject of cognition as such, this body is a representation like any other, an object among objects: to this extent, the subject is familiar with its movements and its actions[a] in the same way he is familiar with the alterations that take place in other objects of intuition; and these movements would be just as foreign and incomprehensible as these other objects if their meaning were not unriddled[b] in an entirely different way. Otherwise the pure subject of cognition would see his own actions[c] as following from motives presented to him with the constancy of a natural law, just like the alterations that occur in other objects due to causes, stimuli and motives. But he would not understand the motives' influence any more intimately than he would understand the connection between any other effect and its cause. He would have no understanding of the inner essence of his body's actions[d] and expressions; he would refer to this essence variously as a force, a quality, or a character, but he would have no more insight than this. But none of this is the case: rather the subject of cognition, appearing as an individual, is given the solution to the riddle:[e] and this solution is *will*. This and this alone gives him the key to his own appearance, reveals to him the meaning and shows him the inner workings of his essence, his deeds, his movements. The body is given in two entirely different ways to the subject of cognition, who emerges as an individual only through his identity with it: in the first place it is given as a representation in intuition by the understanding,[f] as an object among objects and liable to the same laws; but at the same time the body is also given in an entirely different way, namely as something immediately familiar to everyone, something designated by the word *will*. Every true act of his will[g] is immediately and inevitably a movement of his body as well: he cannot truly will an act without simultaneously perceiving it as a motion of the body. An act of the will and an act of the body are not two different states cognized objectively, linked together in a causal chain, they do not stand in

---

[a] *Aktionen*
[b] *enträthselt*
[c] *Handeln*
[d] *Handlungen*
[e] *Räthsel*
[f] *in verständiger Anschauung*
[g] *Akt seines Willens*

a relation of cause and effect; they are one and the same thing, only given in two entirely different ways: in one case immediately and in the other case to the understanding in intuition. An action of the body[a] is nothing but an objectified act of will, i.e. an act of will that has entered intuition. Furthermore, we will see that this is true of all bodily motion, not just motivated action, but even involuntary acts[4] in response to simple stimuli; indeed, that the entire body is nothing but objectified will, i.e. will that has become representation; all of which will be clarified in the discussion to come. That is why I will now call the body the *objecthood of the will*,[b] although in the previous Book and in the essay *On the Principle of Sufficient Reason* I called it the *immediate object*, in keeping with the intentionally one-sided standpoint I adopted there (that of representation). And thus we can also say, in a sense: the will is *a priori* cognition of the body, and the body is *a posteriori* cognition of the will. – Resolutions of the will concerning events in the future are really just rational deliberations over things that will be willed later, they are not true acts of will: a decision is stamped only in the execution, and until that time it remains an unsettled design and exists only in reason, abstractly.[c] Willing and doing are different only for reflection: in actuality they are one. Every true, genuine and immediate act of will is instantly and immediately also the appearance of an act of the body: correspondingly, any effect on the body is instantly and immediately an effect on the will as well: it is called pain when it is contrary to the will; and it is called comfort or pleasure[d] when it is in accordance with the will. The gradations of the two are very different. But it is quite wrong to call pain[e] and pleasure representations: they are nothing of the sort, but rather immediate affections of the will in its appearance, the body: a forced, momentary willing or not-willing of the impression the body is undergoing. There are only a few, specific impressions on the body that can be immediately considered as mere representations and are thus exceptions to what has just been said; these impressions do not stimulate the will and it is only through them that the body becomes an immediate object of cognition, because, as an intuition in understanding, the body is mediated just like all other objects. What I have in mind are the affections of the purely objective senses: sight, hearing and touch, and only to the extent that these organs are affected in ways that are specific, natural and fitting

---

[a] *Aktion des Leibes*
[b] *Objektität des Willens*
[c] *in abstracto*
[d] *Wohlbehagen, Wollust*
[e] *Schmerz*

for each of them. This involves such an exceptionally weak stimulation to the enhanced and specifically modified sensibility of these parts that it does not affect the will; and since no stimulation disturbs the will, this simply delivers to the understanding the data that become intuition. But any stronger or atypical affection of the sense organs causes pain, i.e. is contrary to the will, and so these organs are also part of the will's object-hood. – Weakness of nerves manifests itself when impressions that should have just enough strength to serve as data for the understanding are in fact strong enough to move the will, i.e. produce pain or happiness,[a] although more often pain. This pain is somewhat dull and indistinct, so not only are certain noises and strong lights perceived as painful but a general sort of sickly, hypochondriac temper arises too, which is not clearly recognized as such. – The identity of body and will is demonstrated in many other ways as well, such as the fact that every violent and excessive movement of the will, i.e. every affect immediately agitates the body and its inner workings and disturbs the course of its vital functions. This is specifically discussed in *On the Will in Nature*, p. 27 of the second edition.[b,5]

Finally, the cognition I have of my will, although it is immediate, cannot be separated from that of my body. I do not have cognition of my will as a whole, in its unity, in perfect accordance with its essence; rather I cognize it only in its individual acts, which is to say in time, time being the form in which my body (like every other object) appears: this is why the body is the condition of cognition of my will. Consequently, I cannot truly imagine[c] my will without my body. In the essay *On the Principle of Sufficient Reason*, the will, or rather the subject of willing, is indeed treated as a special class of representations or objects: but even there we saw that this object coincides with the subject, i.e. ceases to be an object; there we called this coinciding the miracle *par excellence*:[d] the entirety of the present work is, to some degree, an explanation of this. To the extent that I really cognize my will as an object, I cognize it as a body: but this brings me back again to the first class of representations described in that essay, that of real objects. In what follows, we will increasingly realize that this first class of representations can be explained and unriddled only through the *fourth* class described there, which no longer really confront the subject as object. Accordingly, we will realize that we need to use the law of motivation governing that

---

[a] *Wohlgefühl*
[b] [See Hübscher *SW* 4, 28]
[c] *vorstellen*
[d] κατ᾽ εξοχην

fourth class in order to understand the inner essence of the law of causation (valid in the first class) and what takes place according to this law.

We have presented the identity of the will and the body only provisionally; but this identity can only really be established in the way we are doing here – indeed, for the first time – and will be doing even more as we proceed; that is, it can only be established by raising immediate consciousness, concrete cognition,[a] to rational knowledge or transferring it to abstract cognition.[b] On the other hand, by its nature it can never be demonstrated, i.e. derived as mediate cognition from some other immediate source, precisely because it is itself the most immediate cognition there is; if we do not grasp it as such and keep hold of it we will wait in vain to get it back again somehow in a mediate way, as derived cognition. It is an entirely distinctive mode of cognition and this is precisely why its truth cannot really be placed into one of the four rubrics I used to classify all truths in the essay *On the Principle of Sufficient Reason*, §§29ff.,[6] those rubrics being logical, empirical, transcendental and metalogical.[c] The reason is that it, unlike those others, is not the connection between an abstract representation and another representation, or the necessary form of intuitive or abstract representing; rather it is the connection between a judgement and the relationship an intuitive representation, the body, has to something that is not a representation at all, but is rather entirely different in kind[d] from this: will. I would therefore like to distinguish this truth above all others, and call it *philosophical truth par excellence*.[e] This can be expressed in different ways, and we can say: my body and my will are one; – or: what (as intuitive representation) I call my body, I call my will to the extent that I am aware of it in an entirely different and utterly incomparable manner; – or: my body is the *objecthood* of my will; – or: besides being my representation, my body is also my will; etc.[*]

123

§ 19

In the First Book we were reluctantly driven to describe our own body as being (like all other objects in this world of intuition) simply a representation of the cognizing subject. But now we see what in each of our

---

[*] See chap. 18 of the second volume.

[a] *Erkenntniß* in concreto
[b] *Erkenntniß* in abstracto
[c] [See Introduction above, xviii–xix]
[d] *ein . . . toto genere Verschiedenes*
[e] κατ' εξοχην

consciousnesses distinguishes the representation of our own body from all representations that are, in other respects, exactly the same: first, we are conscious of the body in quite another manner, completely different in kind, indicated by the word *will*. And second, precisely this double cognition we have of our own body elucidates for us the body itself, the way it is motivated to act and move, the way external influences cause it to suffer, and, in a word, what the body is, not as a representation, but apart from that, *in itself* – elucidation that we do not immediately have concerning the essence of any other real object, what it does and what it undergoes.

The subject of cognition is an individual precisely because of this special relation with the one body that, aside from all this, is only a representation like any other. But this is just the reason why this relationship (which makes the subject of cognition an *individual*) exists between the subject of cognition and only one of all his many representations; and this in turn is why the body is the only representation of which he is conscious not just as a representation but at the same time in an entirely different way, as a will. However, if we abstract away from this special relationship, from that twofold and completely heterogeneous cognition of one and the same thing, then this one thing – the body – is a representation like any other. Therefore, in order to orient himself here, the knowing individual must choose between two assumptions: on the one hand, he could assume that the distinctive feature of this one representation is just that it is the only one he knows in this double way, that only this *one* object in intuition is simultaneously accessible via two avenues of insight, and that this is not due to any difference between this one object and all others, but rather it is due to a difference between the relationship his cognition has to this one object and the relation it has to all other objects. Alternatively, the cognizing individual could assume that this one object is essentially different from all other objects, that it is unique among objects in being simultaneously will and representation, that all other representations are mere representations, i.e. mere phantoms, and therefore, that his body is the only real individual in the world, i.e. the only appearance of the will, and the only immediate object of the subject. – The fact that other objects, when considered as mere representations, *are* like the body, i.e. they too occupy and act in space (itself perhaps merely a representation), is demonstrably certain given the *a priori* guarantee of the law of causality which does not allow for there to be effects without causes: but apart from the fact that this only allows us to infer a cause in general – not the same cause – from some effect, we are still left in the realm of mere representation, since it is

only there that the law of causation holds valid, and it can never lead us beyond. But as to whether the objects familiar to the individual only as representations are, like his own body, appearances of a will; as mentioned in the previous Book, this is what is really at stake in the question of the reality of the external world: to deny it is *theoretical egoism*, which considers all appearances outside of the individual to be phantoms. Practical egoism does exactly the same thing in practice, namely considering and treating one's own person as the only actual one, and others as mere phantoms. Of course theoretical egoism can never be disproved: still, it is only ever used in philosophy as a sceptical sophism, i.e. for show. As a genuine conviction it can only be found in a madhouse: accordingly, it should be treated with medication, not refutation. So we will not go into it any further except to regard it as the last stronghold of scepticism, which is always polemical. Since our knowledge will always be bound up with and limited by our   125
individuality, everyone can necessarily *be* only one thing while *having cognition of* everything else; and in fact, this limitation of cognition is what gives rise to the need for philosophy. Moreover, since we are trying, for this very reason, to use philosophy to expand the limits of our cognition, we will look upon the sceptical arguments of theoretical egoism as a little frontier-fortress that will undeniably be forever invincible, but whose garrison can never leave, so we may go safely past it and not be afraid to leave it behind us.

We now clearly understand our double cognition of the essence and operation[a] of our own body, a cognition that we are given in two completely different ways; and we will go on to use this cognition as a key to the essence of every appearance in nature; and when it comes to objects other than our own body, objects that have not been given to us in this double manner but only as representations in our consciousness, we will judge them on the analogy with our body, assuming that, since they are on the one hand representations just like the body and are in this respect homogeneous with it, then on the other hand, what remains after disregarding their existence as representation of a subject must have the same inner essence as what we call *will*. After all, what other sort of existence or reality could we attribute to the rest of the corporeal world? Where could we get the elements to construct such a world? We do not know anything – we cannot even think anything – besides will and representation. The corporeal world exists immediately only in our representation, and if we want to credit it with the greatest reality we know then we attribute to it the reality that

---

[a] *Wirken*

our own body has for each of us: because everyone considers this to be the most real thing.[a] But if we analyse the reality of this body and its actions, then apart from the fact that it is our representation, the only thing we discover in it is the will: this exhausts its reality. There is no other reality we could attribute to the corporeal world. If the corporeal world is therefore to be more than simply our representation, we must say that apart from representation, i.e. in itself and according to its innermost essence, it is what we find immediately in ourselves as will.[7] I say 'according to its innermost essence', but we must first get to know this essence of the will better so that we can distinguish what it is in itself from the many degrees[b] of its appearance. For instance the will's being accompanied by cognition and its determination by motives that are conditioned by this: these, as we will see in what follows, do not belong to its essence but only to its clearest appearance as animals and human beings. So when I say: the force propelling a stone to earth is – according to its essence, in itself, and aside from all representation – will, then this should not be given the absurd meaning[c] that the stone is moved by a motive in cognition just because that is how the will appears in human beings.*,[8] – But now we want to take what has been presented so far in a broad and provisional way and establish and justify it more clearly and in greater detail, developing it to its fullest extent.**

§ 20

The *will* makes itself known as the essence in itself of our own body, as that which it is besides being an object of intuition, a representation, primarily, as we have said, in the voluntary movements of this body. These bodily movements are nothing other than the visible manifestation of particular

---

* So we could never agree with Bacon of Verulam when (in *De Augm. Scient. L. 4 in fine* [*De Dignitate et augmentis scientiarum, On the Dignity and Advancement of Learning*, Book 4 at the end]) he claims that all mechanical and physical movements of bodies [*Körper*] follow only from previous perceptions of these bodies, even if this false claim was inspired by some inkling of the truth. It is the same with Kepler's assertion in his essay *De Planeta Martis* [*On the Planet Mars*] that the planets must have cognition to allow them to follow their elliptical orbits so accurately, and to be able to measure the velocity of their motion so that the triangle of the surface of their orbit is always proportional to the time in which they traverse their bases.
** See chap. 18 of the second volume.

[a] *das Realste*
[b] *Grade*
[c] *tolle Meinung*

acts of will;[a] they coincide perfectly and immediately with the acts of will   127
as one and the same thing, distinguished only by the form of cognition
into which they have passed, i.e. become representation.

These acts of will[b] continue to have a ground outside themselves, in
motives. But these motives do not determine anything more than what I
will at *this* time, in *this* place, under *these* circumstances; not *that* or *what* I
will in general, i.e. the maxims that characterize the whole of my willing.[c]
This is why motives cannot explain the complete essence of my will; rather,
they only determine its expression at a given point in time, they are only
the occasion for my will to present itself; the will itself lies outside the
jurisdiction[d] of the law of motivation, which necessarily determines only
its appearance at each moment in time. The motive provides sufficient
grounds for explaining my actions only when my empirical character is
taken into account; when I abstract away from my character and ask why
in general I will this and not that, there can be no answer, because the
principle of sufficient reason[e] governs only the *appearance* of the will, not
the will itself, which should accordingly be considered *groundless*.[f] I am, in
part, presupposing Kant's doctrine of empirical and intelligible character
here, as well as the relevant discussions from my *Fundamental Problems
of Ethics*, pp. 48–58, and again on pp. 178ff. of the first edition.[g,9] But
in addition, this is a theme that we will need to discuss more thoroughly
in the Fourth Book. For now I need only call attention to the fact that
the grounding of one appearance in another, in this case the deed in the
motive, in no way contradicts the claim that the essence in itself of that
appearance is the will, which is itself groundless. Since the principle of
sufficient reason in all of its forms is nothing other than the pure form
of cognition, it is valid only for representation, for appearance, for the
visible manifestation[h] of the will, and not for the will that itself becomes
visible.

Every action of my body, then, is the appearance of an act of will: and
this act is just my will itself, in general and in its entirety (and therefore

---

[a] *Willensakte*
[b] *Akte des Willens*
[c] *mein gesammtes Wollen*
[d] *außerhalb des Gebietes*
[e] *Satz vom Grunde*
[f] *grundlos*
[g] [See *FW*, ch. II, and *BM*, §10 (Hübscher *SW* 4, 46–57 and 174–8; Cambridge edition of *The Two
Fundamental Problems of Ethics*, 66–76 and 172–5)]
[h] *Sichtbarkeit*

also my character) expressing itself again in the presence of certain motives. But if this is so, then the indispensable condition and presupposition of my body's action would have to be the appearance of the will. This is because only what exists directly and solely through the will can condition the will's appearance; otherwise the condition would be merely accidental[a] and make the will's appearance a mere accident: but this condition is the entire body itself. Therefore the entire body must itself be an appearance of the will, and must be related to my will as a whole, i.e. to my intelligible character (whose appearance in time is my empirical character) in the same way that an individual action of the body is related to an individual act of the will. So the entire body must be nothing other than my will made visible, it must be my will itself to the extent that my will is an intuitive object, a representation of the first class. – We have already mentioned in confirmation of this point that every impression made on my body also instantly and immediately affects my will, with what in this respect is called pain or pleasure (at lower grades of the will these are agreeable or disagreeable feelings), and that, conversely, every violent movement of the will – which is to say affects and passions – agitates the body and disturbs the course of its functioning. – And in fact it is possible to give an (albeit imperfect) aetiological account of the genesis of my body, and a somewhat better account of its development and maintenance; this is precisely what physiology does: but this only explains its subject-matter in the same way that the motive explains the action. So the fact that we can ground an individual action in a motive and trace its necessary consequences does not remotely contradict the fact that action in general and in its essence is simply the appearance of an intrinsically groundless will; likewise, the physiological explanation of bodily functions[10] does not do the slightest damage to the philosophical truth that the entire existence of this body and the sum total of its functions are only the objectification[b] of the will that appears in the external actions of this body in accordance with motives. The physiologist will try to trace these external actions, the immediately voluntary movements, back to causes in the organism, e.g. attributing motion in muscles to an influx of humours[c] ('like the contraction of a rope that has become wet' says Reil in his *Archiv für Physiologie*, Vol. 6, p. 153); even supposing a thorough explanation of this

[a] *zufällig*
[b] *Objektivirung*
[c] *Säften*

sort were possible, this would still never invalidate the immediately certain   129
truth that every voluntary motion (animal functions[a]) is the appearance
of an act of will. Nor can the physiological explanation of vegetative life
(natural, life functions[b]), however far it extends, ever abolish the truth that
this whole, highly developed animal life is only the appearance of the will.
Indeed, as mentioned above, no aetiological explanation can ever provide
more than the necessarily determined position in time and space of an
individual appearance, its necessary emergence according to a fixed rule:
but this would leave the inner essence of any appearance forever inscrutable;
it is presupposed in every aetiological explanation and simply labelled 'force'
or 'law of nature', or, when speaking about actions, 'character' or 'will'. –
Although every individual action necessarily follows from the given motive
(presupposing a determined character), and although growth, nutrition
and all the alterations in an animal body take place according to causes
that operate necessarily (stimuli), nonetheless the whole series of actions,
and consequently each individual act, and its condition that performs these
actions (the entire body itself), and consequently also the process of which
it consists and through which it exists – all this is nothing other than the
appearance of the will, the will becoming visible, the *objecthood* of the *will*.
This is why human and animal bodies are so perfectly suited to human
and animal wills in general, which is similar, though far superior, to the
way a tailor-made tool is suited to the will of its maker, and thus appears as
purposiveness,[c] i.e. the possibility of teleological explanations of the body.
The parts of the body must therefore correspond perfectly to the principal
desires[d] through which the will manifests itself, these parts must be the
visible expression of these desires: teeth, throat and intestines are objectified
hunger; the genitals are objectified sex drive; prehensile hands and swift
feet correspond to the more indirect strivings[e] of the will they present.
In the same way, the general human form corresponds to the general
human will, the individual body structure[f] corresponds to the individually   130
modified will – the individual's character – which for this reason is utterly
and in all aspects characteristic and expressive. It is most remarkable that
Parmenides had already expressed this thought in the following verses,
quoted by Aristotle (*Metaphysics* III, 5):

[a] *functiones animales*
[b] *functiones naturales, vitales*
[c] *Zweckmäßigkeit*
[d] *Hauptbegehrungen*
[e] *Streben*
[f] *Korporisation*

For as in each case is the blending of the the much-bent limbs, so stands thought for men; for it is the same thing which thinks – the nature of the limbs – for each and every man; for what exceeds is thought.*,a

§ 21

These considerations should give rise to a clear and certain recognition in the abstract[b] of what everyone immediately feels concretely,[c] namely that the essence in itself[d] of our own appearance is *will*, and this is presented to us as a representation by our actions as well as by their permanent substrate, the body. The will is the most immediate thing in our consciousness, and thus has not passed completely into the form of representation in which object and subject stand opposed to each other; rather, it announces itself immediately and in such a way that subject and object are not distinguished with complete clarity, and it becomes known to the individual only in its separate acts, not as a whole. Anyone who has reached these conclusions with me will automatically have the key to knowledge of the innermost essence of nature as a whole; all that needs to be done is to apply this insight to appearances that are not given in an immediate as well as mediated way (as is the case with our own appearance), but are only given in a mediated and one-sided form, as *representation*. We will recognize that same will as the inner essence, but not only of people and animals, which are appearances very similar to our own; rather, the continuation of this reflection will lead us to recognize this will as the driving and vegetating force in plants, the force growing in crystals, turning magnets north, delivering a shock when heterogeneous metals strike each other; it appears as repulsion and

131

---

* Cf. chap. 20 of the second volume; also in my work *On the Will in Nature* under the headings 'Physiology' and 'Comparative Anatomy' where what has just been briefly mentioned here is treated in greater depth.

a

Ὡς γαρ ἑκαστος εχει κρασιν μελεων πολυκαμπτων,
Τως νοος ανθρωποισι παρεστηκεν· το γαρ αυτο
Εστιν, ὁπερ φρονεει, μελεων φυσις ανθρωποισι,
Και πασιν και παντι· το γαρ πλεον εστι νοημα.

(*Ut enim cuique complexio membrorum flexibilium se habet, ita mens hominibus adest: idem namque est, quod sapit, membrorum natura hominibus, et omnibus et omni: quod enim plus est, intelligentia est.*)

[What Schopenhauer cites as Book III is *Metaphysics* Γ (IV), 5, 1009b21. The quoted passage is fragment 16 of Parmenides, English translation slightly adapted from that of Jonathan Barnes]

b *in abstracto*

c *in concreto*

d *Wesen an sich*

attraction, separation and unification in the elective affinities of matter, and finally, even as gravity, struggling so forcefully in all of matter, pulling stones to the earth and the earth to the sun, – all these are different only in the way they appear; in their innermost essence, they are the same thing we know so intimately and so much better than anything else, the thing that, when it occurs most clearly, we call *will*. Because we are using reflection in this manner we do not have to remain with appearances but can pass over to the *thing in itself*. Appearance means representation and nothing more: all representations, of whatever sort they may be, all *objects*, are *appearances*. Only the will is *thing in itself*: as such, the will is by no means a representation, it is quite different in kind[a] from representation: all representations, all objects are the appearance, the visible manifestation,[b] the *objecthood* of the will. The will is the innermost, the kernel of every individual thing and likewise of the whole: it appears in every blind operation of a force of nature: it also appears in deliberative human action; these differ from each other only in the grade of their appearing, not in the essence of what appears.

§ 22

This *thing in itself* (we will retain the Kantian expression as a standing formula) can never be an object, because an object is only its appearance and not what it really is. If we are to think objectively about this thing in itself, it must borrow its name and concept from an object, from something   132 that is somehow objectively given, and thus from one of its appearances: but if this is to further our understanding, it can be nothing other than the most complete of all its appearances, i.e. the clearest, most highly developed appearance, the one that is illuminated immediately by knowledge: but this is just the human *will*. It is nonetheless fair to say that we are only using a denomination from the superior term[c] that gives the concept of will a broader scope than it has had before. As Plato has so often remarked, recognizing the identical in different appearances and the different in similar appearances is the precondition for philosophy. But until now, people have not recognized the identity that obtains between the will and the essence of all the striving and acting forces in nature, and have therefore failed to notice that the many and varied kinds of appearances are only different species of the same genus; instead, people have seen

[a] toto genere . . . *verschieden*
[b] *Sichtbarkeit*
[c] *denominatio a potiori*

them as heterogeneous: this is why there could be no word to designate the concept of this genus. Accordingly, I will name the genus after its most important species; the more intimate and immediate cognition we have of this species leads to the mediated cognition we have of all the others. But anyone incapable of broadening the concept in the way we require will remain in a state of perpetual misunderstanding, using the word *will* to mean just the one species that has borne the name so far, the will that is accompanied by cognition and is expressed exclusively in accordance with motives – and indeed only through abstract motives, under the guidance of reason; however, as we have said, this is only the most distinct appearance of the will. We need to take this appearance and isolate in thought its innermost essence (which we will find immediately familiar); then we need to attribute this essence to all the weaker, less distinct appearances of the same essence; this procedure will lead to the requisite broadening of the concept of will. – Conversely, however, I will be misunderstood by anyone who thinks it is ultimately a matter of indifference whether the word will or some other word is used to designate the essence in itself of all appearance. This would be the case if that thing in itself were something whose existence we merely *inferred*, and thus only knew it in a mediated way, merely abstractly:[a] in which case we could certainly call it whatever we wanted: the name would just symbolize some unknown quantity. But the word *will*, which is supposed to unlock the innermost essence of all things in nature for us like a magic spell – this word does not have the slightest connotation of an unknown quantity or the result of an inference; rather, it refers to something of which we have immediate cognition, something so thoroughly familiar that we know and understand what will is much better than anything else, whatever it may be. – Until now people have subsumed the concept of *will* under the concept of *force*:[b] I will do precisely the opposite, and let every force in nature be known as will. Do not think that this is just a quibble over terms or a matter of indifference: it is in fact a matter of the greatest significance and importance. This is because intuitive cognition of the objective world, i.e. appearance, representation, is at the root of the concept of *force* – just as it is at the root of all other concepts – and the concept of force is created from such cognition.[11] It is abstracted from the realm governed by cause and effect, and thus from intuitive representation, and signifies simply the causal nature[c] of a cause at the point where, aetiologically, it can do no more explanatory work,

133

---

[a] *in abstracto*
[b] *Kraft*
[c] *Ursachseyn*

but rather is the necessary presupposition of all aetiological explanation. On the other hand, the concept of *will* is unique among all possible concepts in that it does *not* come from appearance, it does *not* come from mere intuitive representation, but rather comes from within, springs from everyone's most immediate consciousness. We immediately recognize our own individuality[a] in the essence of this immediate consciousness that has no form, not even that of subject and object; but at the same time we *are* this, since here what cognizes coincides with what is cognized. So when we trace the concept of *force* back to that of *will* we are only tracing an unknown back to something infinitely better known, indeed, to the only thing that we have actual, immediate and absolute knowledge of, and we have very greatly extended our cognition. If on the other hand, we subsume the concept of *will* under that of *force*, as people used to do; then we relinquish the only immediate cognition we have of the inner essence of the world by sinking it under a concept abstracted from appearance – a concept which, for that reason, would never let us escape from appearances.

§ 23

134

As thing in itself, the *will* is completely different from its appearance, and entirely free of all forms of appearance. The will only takes on these forms when it appears, which is why these forms concern only its *objecthood* and are foreign to the will itself. The will has nothing to do with even the most general form of all representation, that of being an object for a subject, and it has even less to do with the subordinate forms that are collectively expressed in the principle of sufficient reason. As we know, space and time belong to the principle of sufficient reason, and so, in consequence, does multiplicity, which exists and is made possible only through these. With respect to this last point, I would borrow an old scholastic expression and call time and space the *principium individuationis*[b] and I ask the reader always to bear this in mind. It is only by virtue of time and space that something that is one and the same in essence and concept can nonetheless appear as different, as a multiplicity of coexistent and successive things: time and space are thus the *principium individuationis*, the object of so much hair-splitting and controversy among the scholastics, which you can find collected together in Suárez (*Disputatio* 5, section 3). – As we have been saying, the will as thing in itself lies outside the province of the principle of

[a] *sein eigenes Individuum*
[b] [principle of individuation]

sufficient reason in all its forms, and therefore has absolutely no ground,[a] although each of its appearances is entirely subject to the principle of sufficient reason: it is moreover free of all *multiplicity*, notwithstanding its innumerable appearances in time and space. It is itself one, but not in the manner of an object, since an object's unity is known in contrast to a possible multiplicity: nor is it one in the way a concept is, since a concept arises only through abstraction from multiplicity: rather, it is one in the sense that it lies outside of time and space, outside the *principium individuationis*, i.e. the possibility of multiplicity. Only after the following reflections on appearances and the different manifestations of the will have completely clarified all this – only then will we truly understand the meaning of Kant's doctrine that time, space and causation have no bearing on the thing in itself but are only forms of cognition.

135   People have actually recognized the groundlessness of the will where it manifests itself most clearly, as human will, which is deemed to be free and independent. But given the groundlessness of the will itself, people have at the same time overlooked the necessity that governs it wherever it appears, and declared deeds to be free when they were not, since every individual action follows with strict necessity from the effect of a motive on the character. As we have already said, necessity is the relation of consequent to ground, nothing more. The principle of sufficient reason is the general form of all appearance; and human activities, like all other appearances, must be subject to it. But because in self-consciousness the will is known immediately and in itself, this consciousness is also a consciousness of freedom. However, this overlooks the fact that the individual, the person, is not will as a thing in itself, but rather an *appearance* of the will and, as such, is determined, and has entered into the form of appearance, the principle of sufficient reason. Hence the remarkable fact that everyone considers themselves to be *a priori* completely free, even in their individual actions, and thinks they can change their lives at any moment, which basically means turning into someone else. It is only *a posteriori*, through experience that they are astonished to discover that they are not free but instead subject to necessity, and that, intentions and reflections notwithstanding, they do not change their behaviour; from the beginning of their lives to the end they have to bear with the same character that they themselves condemn, and, as it were, play to the end the part they have undertaken. I cannot pursue these ideas any further just now, since they concern ethics and therefore belong to a different part of this work. In the meantime, I simply want to

[a] *ist schlechthin grundlos*

point out here that although the will is in itself groundless, its *appearance* is very much subject to the law of necessity, i.e. the principle of sufficient reason; and I call attention to this fact so that the necessity exhibited in the appearances of nature might not prevent us from recognizing in them the manifestations of the will.

So far we have regarded as appearances of the will only those alterations that have no ground other than a motive, i.e. a representation; that is why when it comes to nature, only human beings (and possibly animals) have been credited with wills; because as I have already discussed elsewhere, cognition, representation is certainly the genuine and exclusive characteristic of animal existence.[a] But the instincts and creative drives[b] of animals show us at once that the will is at work even where it is not guided by cognition.* The fact that animals do have representations and cognition is not at issue here, since they work towards a goal as if it were a known motive, although they have no cognition of it whatsoever; that is why their actions here take place without motives, unguided by representation, and show us first and most clearly how the will is active even in the complete absence of cognition. The one-year-old bird has no representation of the eggs it builds its nest for; the young spider has no representation of the prey it spins its web for; nor is the antlion thinking of ants when it digs a hole for the first time; the larva of the stag beetle chews a hole into the wood where its metamorphosis will take place, and the hole is twice as big if it is going to be male than if it is going to be female, in order to accommodate the horns it has no idea[c] it will acquire. The will is clearly at work in this kind of animal behaviour as it is in the rest of their behaviour: but it is in blind activity,[d] which, although accompanied by cognition, is not guided by it. If, however, we have now come to realize that representation as a motive is not a necessary or essential condition for the activity of the will, we will be in a better position to recognize the operation of the will in cases where it is less striking, and be as little inclined, for instance, to attribute a snail's house to a will that is foreign to the snail but guided by cognition, as to think that the house we ourselves build comes into existence through a will other than our own. Rather, we will recognize both houses as works of the will objectifying itself in both sets of appearances, a will that operates

136

---

* Chap. 27 of the second volume has a discussion of this.

[a] *Thierheit*
[b] *Kunsttrieben*
[c] *Vorstellung*
[d] *Thätigkeit*

in us according to motives, but blindly in the snail, as a formative drive[a] directed outwards. The same will often acts blindly in us as well: in all our bodily functions that are not guided by cognition, in all the body's vital and vegetative processes, digestion, circulation of the blood, secretion, growth, reproduction. Not only actions of the body but the whole body itself, as we established above, is appearance of the will, objectified will, concrete will: everything that occurs in it must therefore occur through will, although this will is not guided by cognition here, not determined by motives, but rather acts blindly, according to causes that in this case are called *stimuli*.[b]

What I call *cause*[c] in the narrowest sense of the term is that state of matter which, in necessarily bringing about another state, itself sustains just as great an alteration as the one it causes, a state of affairs that is expressed in the rule 'action and reaction[d] are equal'. Further, in a true cause, the effect intensifies in exact proportion to the cause, and thus the reaction as well; so that, if we ever know what type of effect it is, we can measure and calculate the degree of the effect from the degree of intensity of the cause, and vice versa. True causes like this are in effect in all the phenomena[e] of mechanics, chemistry, etc., in short, in all alterations in inorganic bodies. On the other hand, what I call *stimuli* are those causes that do not themselves sustain a reaction proportionate to their action and whose degree of intensity is in no way parallel to the intensity of the effect, and thus the effect cannot be measured from it: rather, a small increase in stimulus can result in a very large increase in the effect, or can, conversely, do away with the previous effect entirely, etc. All effects on organic bodies as such are of this kind: thus, all true organic and vegetative alterations in animal bodies are due to stimuli, not to mere causes. But a stimulus, like every cause and every motive in general, determines nothing more than the point of entry for the expression of each force in time and space, not the inner essence of the force that expresses itself; given our previous discussion, we know this essence to be the will, and we therefore ascribe to it the alterations in the body that occur without consciousness as much as those that occur with it. The stimulus mediates, it bridges the gap between motive (which is causality that has passed through cognition) and cause in the narrowest sense. In individual cases it is sometimes closer to motive, sometimes closer to cause, but it is nonetheless always distinct

---

[a] *Bildungstrieb*
[b] *Reize*
[c] *Ursache*
[d] *Wirkung und Gegenwirkung* ['effect and counter-effect']
[e] *Erscheinungen*

from both: so for instance, sap rises in the plants because of stimuli, and this cannot be explained by citing mere causes working according to the laws of hydraulics or capillary tubes: but it is certainly assisted by these, and in general is very close to being a purely causal alteration. By contrast, although the movements of the *Hedysarum gyrans* and the *Mimosa pudica* take place in response to mere stimuli, they are nonetheless very similar to movements that are motivated and almost seem to want to make the transition.[a] It is a stimulus-response when an increase in light makes our pupils contract, but this turns into motivated movement, because it occurs when the retina would be hurt by too much light, and we try to avoid it by contracting our pupils. – Erections are occasioned by a motive, which is to say a representation; but it acts with the necessity of a stimulus: i.e. it cannot be resisted but must be removed to become ineffective. It is the same with disgusting objects that make people feel sick. We have just been considering animal instincts as an actual but completely different type of intermediary between movement due to stimuli and actions from a motive in cognition.[12] We might be tempted to see respiration as another intermediary along these lines: it is a matter of dispute whether this is a voluntary or involuntary motion, i.e. whether it really comes from motives or from stimuli, a fact that would perhaps argue in favour of its being an intermediary between the two. *Marshall Hall* (*On the Diseases of the Nervous System* §§ 293 *seq.*)[b] describes it as a mixed function, since it is controlled in part by the cerebral (voluntary) nerves and in part by the spinal (involuntary) nerves.[13] But ultimately we must consider it one of the expressions of the will that follows from motives. This is because other motives, i.e. mere representations, can determine the will to inhibit or accelerate it, and, as with all other voluntary actions, it seems you are free to stop breathing altogether and suffocate. In fact this can really happen, as soon as some other motive is strong enough to determine the will to overcome the urgent need for air. Several accounts have claimed that Diogenes really ended his life this way (*Diogenes Laertius* VI, 76). Negroes are also said to have done this (F.B. Osiander *On Suicide*,[c] 1813, pp. 170–80). This would be a strong example of the influence of abstract motives, i.e. of genuinely rational willing overpowering merely animal willing. The notion that breathing is at least somewhat conditioned by cerebral activity is supported by the fact that prussic acid kills by first paralysing the brain,[14] thus indirectly inhibiting breathing: but if breathing is continued artificially

139

---

[a] [These plants are commonly known as Telegraph Plant (or Semaphore Plant) and Sensitive Plant]
[b] [Presumably *Lectures on the Nervous System and its Diseases*, 1836]
[c] *Ueber den Selbstmord* [1813]

until the narcotic effect on the brain is over, death does not occur at all. While we are on the subject, respiration gives us the most striking example of the fact that motives act with just as much necessity as do stimuli and mere causes (in the narrowest sense of the term), and can only be rendered inoperative[a] by opposing motives, like action being counteracted by reaction.[b] Because with breathing, the feeling that you could simply stop is incomparably weaker than with other movements due to motives; the motive here is very urgent, very close, and very easy to satisfy, since the muscles used to carry it out do not get tired; further, it usually has no impediments, and the whole process is supported by the individual's most inveterate habit. But in fact all motives act with the same necessity. Recognizing that motives give rise to motion with just as much necessity as stimuli do will enable us to see more clearly that what occurs in the organic body in a completely lawlike manner due to stimuli is nonetheless, in its inner essence, the will; although this will is in itself never subject to the principle of sufficient reason (i.e. to necessity), it is in all its appearances.[*][15]

140   We therefore will not stop at the recognition that animals are appearances of the will in their actions and their whole existence, body structure[c] and organization; rather we will take our privileged, immediate cognition of the essence in itself of things and extend it to plants as well. Plants are moved only by stimuli, and the only essential difference between plants and animals is that plants lack cognition and the motivated movement that is conditioned by cognition. Thus what appears in representation as plant, as mere vegetation and blindly driving force, we will treat, as regards its essence in itself, as will, and recognize it as what constitutes the basis of our own appearance as it expresses itself in our deeds as well as in the entire existence of our body itself.

All that remains is for us to take the final step and extend this way of approaching things to all the forces in nature that act according to those universal, immutable laws; these laws dictate the movements of all bodies that, lacking organs, have no receptivity to stimuli or cognition of motives. We must therefore take the key to the understanding of the essence in itself of things, a key provided only by the immediate cognition of our own

---

[*] This knowledge is fully established in my prize essay *On the Freedom of the Human Will*, where for this reason, the relation between *cause, stimulus, and motive* is discussed in detail (pp. 30–44 of the *Fundamental Problems of Ethics*) [See Hübscher *SW* 4, 29–41; Cambridge edition of *The Two Fundamental Problems*, 52–62]

[a] *außer Wirksamkeit gesetzt*
[b] *Druck durch Gegendruck*
[c] *Korporisation*

essence, and apply it to these appearances in the inorganic world as well, appearances that are more remote from us than any others. – Now let us turn to them with an enquiring eye; let us look at the violent, inexorable impulse of masses of water rushing down to the depths, the perseverance of the magnet that always returns to the North Pole, the longing with which iron flies to the magnet, the vehemence of two poles in an electric current striving to reunite (as with human desires, this striving is only intensified by obstacles).[16] Let us look at how the crystal suddenly and rapidly forms with such regularity in its development, a development that is clearly only a striving in different directions (albeit an exceptionally staunch and precisely determined striving) that is constrained and held fast in the grip of rigidity. Let us notice the selectivity with which bodies attract and repel, unite and separate when they are in a fluid state and freed from the bonds of rigidity. Finally, let us feel immediately how encumbered our bodies are when some burden is striving towards the earth, incessantly   141 pushing and pressing our bodies in pursuit of its only endeavour. – Once we have seen all this it will not take any great stretch of the imagination to recognize (despite its distance from our own essence) the very same thing that in us pursues its goal illuminated by cognition while here, in the weakest of its appearances, it is blind, dull, one-sided and unalterable in its striving. Nonetheless, because it is everywhere one and the same, – just as the first light of dawn shares the name sunlight with the bright rays of noon, – it must be called *will* here as well as there, a name signifying the being in itself of every thing in the world and the sole kernel of every appearance.

But the distance, indeed the semblance[a] of a complete difference between the appearances of inorganic nature and the appearances of the will (which we perceive as the core of our own essence), originates mainly from the contrast between the fully determined lawlikeness in the one and the seemingly lawless arbitrariness in the other type of appearance. Because individuality is powerfully evident in human beings (everyone having his or her own character), the same motive does not possess the same power[b] over each of us, and its effect is modified by the thousands of minor circumstances that come into play in the individual's broad sphere of knowledge, circumstances that other people know nothing about. This is why actions cannot be predetermined from motives alone, because the other factor is missing, namely a precise familiarity with the individual character

[a] *Schein*
[b] *Gewalt*

and the knowledge that goes with it. By contrast, the appearances of natural forces represent the other extreme: they operate according to universal laws, without deviation or individuality, in accordance with readily apparent conditions, subject to the most precise predetermination, and the same force of nature will express itself in the millions of its appearances in exactly the same way. To clarify this point, to establish the identity of the *one* and indivisible will in all its exceedingly diverse appearances, in the weakest as in the strongest, we must begin by considering the relation between the will as thing in itself and its appearance, i.e. between the world as will and the world as representation; this will open up for us the best path to a deeper and more probing investigation of the whole theme of this Second Book.*,17

142

§ 24

The great Kant has taught us that time, space and causality are present in our consciousness with respect to their lawlikeness and the possibility of all their forms; and that their presence in consciousness is entirely independent of the objects that appear in them and constitute their content. In other words: time, space and causality can be found just as easily by proceeding from the subject as from the object, which is why it is just as correct to call them the subject's mode of intuition as it is to call them characteristics of the object, *in so far as it is an object* (or as Kant would say: appearance), i.e. *representation*. These forms can even be seen as the indivisible boundary between object and subject: this certainly explains why all objects must appear in them, but also why the subject possesses and examines them thoroughly without reference to the appearing object. – Now if the objects that appear in these forms are not just empty phantoms, that is, if they are to be significant, then they need to signify or express something that is not just another object or representation (as they are), something whose existence is not just relative to a subject, something that can exist without an external support as its essential condition, i.e. something that is *not a representation* but rather a *thing in itself*. So we might at least ask: are these representations, these objects, anything besides or apart from representations or objects of the subject? And what else could they be, in this sense?

---

* See chap. 23 of the second volume, likewise the chapters on 'Plant Physiology' and 'Physical Astronomy' in my work *On the Will in Nature*, the latter being of such supreme importance for the essence of my metaphysics.

What is this aspect that is totally distinct in kind[a] from representation? What is the thing in itself? – *The will*: this has been our answer, but I will set it aside for the moment.

Whatever the thing in itself might be, Kant reached the correct con-   143
clusion that time, space and causality (which we have since recognized as forms[b] of the principle of sufficient reason, this being the general expression of the forms[c] of appearance) cannot be properties of it; rather, time, space and causality can be associated with the thing in itself only after, and to the extent that, it has become a representation, i.e. they belong only to its appearance, not to it itself. Since the subject cognizes and constructs them entirely from itself, independent of any object, they must be connected to the *being of representation* as such, not to what becomes a representation. They must be the form of the representation as such, not qualities of whatever it is that has assumed this form. They must already be given with the mere opposition of subject and object (not notionally,[d] but in fact), and therefore must be simply the more exact determination of the form of cognition in general, whose most general determination is that opposition itself. An aspect of appearance (of the object) is conditioned by space, time and causality (since it can only be represented by means of these) – namely *multiplicity* (conditioned by coexistence and succession), *change and persistence* (conditioned by the law of causality), and matter (the representation of which presupposes causality), and finally everything that can only be represented by means of these. But all this taken together does not belong essentially to *what* appears, *what* enters into the form of representation, but rather adheres only to the form itself. Conversely, however, the aspect of appearance that is *not* conditioned by time, space and causality, that cannot be reduced to or explained by them, is precisely where what appears, the thing in itself, immediately declares itself. Accordingly, what is most completely open to cognition, i.e. has the greatest clarity, distinctness and susceptibility to exhaustive enquiry, is necessarily what accrues to cognition *as such*, i.e. to the *form* of cognition; it does not accrue to something that is *not* in itself a representation, *not* an object, and can only become cognized by entering into these forms, i.e. has become a representation, an object. Thus, only what depends exclusively on being cognized, on being a representation in general and as such (not on what is cognized and has only become representation), which therefore belongs without distinction   144

[a] toto genere *verschieden*
[b] *Gestaltungen*
[c] *Formen*
[d] *im Begriff*

to everything that is cognized, and which for precisely this reason can be found just as easily by proceeding from the subject as from the object – only this can, regardless of all else, afford a sufficient, fully exhaustive, fundamentally clear cognition. But this consists in nothing other than the forms of all appearance, forms that we are conscious of *a priori* and that are collectively expressed in the principle of sufficient reason. The forms of this principle – time, space and causality – refer to intuitive cognition (which, at the moment, is our exclusive concern). The whole of pure mathematics and pure *a priori* natural science is grounded in them alone. Thus, only in these sciences is cognition safeguarded from all obscurity, from any encounter with the unfathomable (the groundless, i.e. the will),[a] which cannot be derived from anything else; in this respect even Kant, as mentioned earlier, considered this sort of cognition (along with logic) to be particularly – indeed exclusively – scientific. But on the other hand this sort of cognition shows us nothing other than mere connections, relationships between one representation and another, form divorced entirely from content. Any content the form receives, every appearance that fills it contains something whose essence is no longer completely cognizable, and can no longer be explained entirely through something else, which is to say it contains something ungrounded; at which point cognition immediately loses its perfect clarity and transparency. But what eludes investigation[b] is precisely the thing in itself which, in its essence, is not a representation, not an object of cognition; rather, it can only become cognized by assuming that form. The form is originally alien to it, and it can never become entirely one with it, it can never be reduced to mere form, and, since this is the principle of sufficient reason, it can never be entirely *fathomed*.[c] So although mathematics gives us exhaustive cognition of what appears as quantity, position, number – in short, spatial and temporal relations – and although the whole of aetiology gives us a perfect account of the lawlike conditions under which appearances, with all their properties, emerge in time and space – all this does nothing more than tell us why any given 145 determinate appearance needs to manifest itself now here and now there. It will never help us penetrate the inner essence of things; something is always left over that no explanation will dare to give, but rather must always presuppose, namely the forces of nature, the determinate manner in which things act, the quality, the character of each appearance, the ungrounded that does not depend on that form of appearance, the principle of sufficient

---

[a]   *das Unergründliche (Grundlose d. i. Wille)*
[b]   *Ergründung*
[c]   *ergründet*

reason, which is intrinsically alien to that form but which enters into that form and now comes forward according to its law. This law, to be sure, determines only the coming forward itself, not *what* comes forward, only the How, not the What of what appears, simply the form, not the content. – Mechanics, physics and chemistry dictate the rules and laws according to which the forces of impenetrability, gravity, rigidity, fluidity, cohesion, elasticity, heat, light, elective affinities, magnetism, electricity, etc. operate, i.e. the laws, the rules that these forces follow every time they emerge in space and time: but no matter what we do, the forces themselves remain occult qualities.[a] It is precisely the thing in itself that displays those phenomena when it enters appearance; it is utterly different from the phenomena, although its appearance is completely subject to the principle of sufficient reason as the form of representation. Still, it can itself never be traced back to this form, and therefore it cannot be fully explained aetiologically or completely grounded. Of course it is completely comprehensible to the extent that it has assumed that form, i.e. to the extent that it is appearance; but this comprehensibility does not remotely explain its inner essence. Thus, as the necessity accruing to some cognition increases, and our ability to think or represent it any other way (for instance, through spatial relations) decreases, – then the cognition itself becomes proportionately more distinct and sufficient, but it diminishes in purely objective content and genuine reality. Conversely, the more the content of cognition reveals itself as purely accidental and strikes us as merely empirically given, then this is a sign that there is more genuinely objective and truly real content to it, but also more that is inexplicable, i.e. not derivable from anything else.[18]

Throughout the ages, to be sure, aetiology has failed to understand its own purpose and has tried to reduce the whole of organic life to chemistry or electricity, and then the whole of chemistry (i.e. quality) to mechanism (action[b] through the shape of atoms), and then finally mechanism to the object of phoronomy (i.e. time and space united for the possibility of motion), or alternatively to the object of mere geometry (i.e. position in space). (In much the same way, people rightly calculate the decrease of an effect in a purely geometrical manner, according to the square of the distance and the theory of the lever.) In the end, geometry is reduced to arithmetic which, because it has a single dimension, is the most comprehensible, clear and thoroughly fathomable form of the principle of sufficient reason. Examples of the general method I have in

[a] *qualitates occultae*
[b] *Wirkung*

mind here include: Democritus' atoms, Descartes' vortex, the mechanistic physics of *Le Sage*, which at the end of the eighteenth century tried to give mechanistic explanations for chemical affinities as well as gravitation, using the concepts of impact and pressure, as may be seen more closely in the 'Newtonian Lucretius'.[a] Reil's use of form and mixture as the cause of animal life tends in this direction as well. Finally, we see the same tendencies in the crude materialism that is being rehashed now, in the middle of the 19th century, and ignorantly believes itself to be original. First of all, by stupidly denying the life force,[b] it tries to explain the phenomena of life using physical and chemical forces, which in turn are supposed to come from the mechanical operations of matter, the position, shape and movement of imagined atoms; in this way, it tries to trace all forces of nature back to impact and counter-impact,[c] which serve as its 'thing in itself'. Even light is supposed to be a mechanical vibration or even undulation of an imaginary ether (postulated for this purpose) which reaches the retina and drums on it four hundred and eighty-three trillion beats a second for red, or seven hundred and twenty-seven trillion for violet, etc. So colour-blindness is when people cannot count the drumbeats, right? Such crass, mechanical, Democritean, flimsy and truly clumsy theories are no less than we expect from people who, fifty years after the appearance of Goethe's theory of colours, still believe in Newton's homogeneous light and are not ashamed to say so. They will learn that what can be pardoned in the child (Democritus) will not be forgiven in the man. They might even come to an ignominious end some day: but then everyone would slink away and pretend they had nothing to do with it.[19] We will soon have more to say about the false reduction of the original forces of nature to each other: but this is enough for now. If this reduction were to succeed, then of course everything would be explained and grounded, and ultimately reduced to a problem of arithmetic, which would then be the holiest of holies in the temple of wisdom where the principle of sufficient reason happily leads us in the end. But all the content of appearance would disappear and only form would be left: *what* it is that appears would be reduced to *how* it appears, and this *how* could also be cognized *a priori*, and thus depend entirely on the subject, and thus only be for the subject, and thus in the end be simply a phantom, representation and form of representation through and through: it would be pointless to ask for a thing in itself. – If this were really to happen, the entire world could be derived

[a] *Lucrèce Neutonien*
[b] *Lebenskraft*
[c] *Stoß und Gegenstoß*

from the subject and we would in fact achieve what Fichte wanted to *seem* to achieve through his windbag dronings.[a] – But this will not happen: this is how fantasies, sophistries, castles in the air come about, but not science. People have been successful in reducing the many and manifold appearances in nature to particular original forces, and these successes have always brought real progress: people have taken a number of forces and qualities that were initially considered different, and derived them from each other (for instance, magnetism from electricity),[20] thus reducing their number: aetiology will achieve its aim when it recognizes all the original forces of nature for what they are, arranging them and establishing the way they operate, i.e. the rule by which, guided by causality, their appearances emerge in time and space and determine their positions with respect to one another. But original forces will always remain, the content of appearance will always be left over as an indissoluble residuum that cannot be reduced to form, and thus cannot be explained from something else in accordance with the principle of sufficient reason. – This is because there is an aspect to every single thing in nature that can never be assigned a sufficient reason,[b] that can never be explained, something for which no further cause can be found: this something is the specific mode of its operation, i.e. the very mode of its being, its essence. Of course a cause can be established for each particular effect of a thing, and this cause dictates that the thing must act precisely now, precisely here: but there is never a cause for it to act in general and in precisely this manner. If it had no other qualities, if it were a mote in a sunbeam, it would still exhibit that unfathomable something, at least as gravity and impenetrability: but this, I say, is to the mote what a man's *will* is to the man, and like the will, it is in its inner essence not subject to explanation; in fact, it is in itself identical to the will. Of course a motive can be established for every manifestation of the will, for every particular act of will at this time, in this place; the manifestation of will necessarily follows from some motive on the presupposition of someone's character. But the fact that the person has this character, that he wills in the first place, that out of several motives, precisely this one and no other – indeed, that any motive at all – moves his will, no ground can ever be given for this. What a person considers to be his unfathomable character, a character that is presupposed in every explanation of his deeds from motives; just this is the essential quality of every inorganic body, its manner of operation whose manifestations arise due to some external influence, while

148

[a] *Windbeuteleien*
[b] *Grund*

it itself is not determined – and therefore not explained – by any external source: its particular appearances, through which alone it is manifest, are subject to the principle of sufficient reason: it itself is groundless. The scholastics had already recognized this in all its essentials and designated it as *forma substantialis*.[a] (See Suárez, *Metaphysical Disputations*,[b] Disputatio XV, sect. I.)[21]

It is as great an error as it is a common one to believe that we understand the most common, universal and simple phenomena the best; these are simply the phenomena we are most used to seeing, and so have grown accustomed to our ignorance. It is just as inexplicable to us that a stone falls to earth as that an animal moves. As mentioned before, people believe that the most universal forces of nature (e.g. gravitation, cohesion, impenetrability) are the starting point for explaining forces that occur less frequently and only in complex circumstances (e.g. chemical qualities, electricity, magnetism), and finally that these are used to understand organisms and animal life, or even human cognition and willing. The operation of occult qualities[c] is tacitly assumed although no enlightenment is expected on that score, since people had intended to build upon them, not beneath them. This sort of thing, as we have said, cannot work. But apart from this, such structures are always built on air. What use are explanations that in the end lead back to something just as unfamiliar as the initial problem had been? In the last analysis, do we understand the inner essence of those universal forces of nature any more than we do the inner essence of an animal? Isn't the one just as unexamined as the other? Unfathomable because it is groundless, because it is the content, the What of appearance that can never be reduced to its form, the How, the principle of sufficient reason. But we who are pursuing philosophy and not aetiology, i.e. unconditioned rather than relative knowledge of the essence of the world, we take the opposite path and start from what we know immediately and most perfectly and have complete and utter confidence in, from what is closest to us, in order to understand what we know only distantly, in a one-sided and indirect manner: from the most powerful, most meaningful, and clearest appearance we will come to understand the less complete and weaker ones. With the exception of my own body, I know only *one* side of things, that of representation: the inner essence of things is closed to me and remains a deep mystery, even when I know everything that causes alterations in them. Only by comparison with what happens in myself when, swayed

149

---

[a] [substantial form]
[b] *Disputationes Metaphisicae*
[c] *qualitates occultae*

by a motive, my body performs an action, the inner essence of my own alterations determined by external grounds, can I gain insight into the manner in which those inanimate bodies alter themselves according to causes, and thus understand their inner essence. Knowing the cause of the inner essence's appearance only gives me the rule for how it enters time and space, nothing more. I can know this because my body is the only object where I do not just know the *one* side, that of representation, but also the other, which is called *will*. Thus, instead of believing that I would better understand my own organization, and thus my cognition and willing and motivated movements if I could only reduce them to movements from causes through electricity, chemistry, mechanism, – since I am doing philosophy, not aetiology, I must instead take the opposite tack, and take my own motivated movements as a starting point for understanding the simplest and most common movements of inorganic bodies (movements that follow from causes); I must recognize that the unfathomable forces manifesting themselves in all natural bodies are identical in kind to what in me is the will, differing only in degree. This means: the fourth class of representations that I treated in the essay *On the Principle of Sufficient Reason* must be my key to the knowledge of the inner essence of the first class, and I must use the law of motivation to understand the inner meaning of the law of causality.

Spinoza says (Letter 62) that if a stone thrown flying through the air were conscious it would think it was flying of its own will. I only add that the stone would be right. Projectile thrust plays the same role for it that motive does for me; and what in the case of the stone appears as cohesion, gravity, persistence in the assumed state is, in its inner essence, just what I recognize in myself as will, and what the stone would also recognize as will if it were to attain cognition too. In this passage Spinoza focuses on the necessity with which the stone flies and rightly wants to apply it to the necessity in a person's individual act of will. I, on the other hand, think that the inner essence presupposed by all real necessity (i.e. effects of causes) is what gives necessity its meaning and validity in the first place. It is called character in the case of people and quality in the case of stones, but it is the same in both. Where it is known immediately it is called *will*; it has its weakest degree of manifestation, of objecthood, in stones, and its strongest in humans. – Even St Augustine expressed with proper feeling this striving of all things that is identical with our will, and I cannot help setting down his naïve expression of the matter: 'If we were animals, then we would love the life of the flesh and what corresponds to its meaning; we would be satisfied with this as our good, and if everything were going well for us we would demand nothing more. Likewise, if we were trees, then we certainly could not perceive or move towards anything, but there is a sense in which we would *strive* towards that which makes us more fruitful or brings us richer yields. If we were stones, or waves, or wind, or flame, or anything like this, without any consciousness or life, then we still would not be without a sort of *striving* for our position and order. For *love*, as it were, is expressed in the weight of inanimate bodies, whether they strive downwards by virtue of weight or upwards by virtue of levity: for bodies are driven where they will go through their weight, as the spirit is through love' (*City of God*, XI, 28).[a,22]

It is also worth noting that *Euler* saw that the essence of gravitation must ultimately be reduced to the 'inclination and appetite' (and thus will) that is distinctive to bodies (in the 68th of his *Letters to a German Princess*). In fact this is precisely what makes him hostile to Newton's concept of gravitation, and he is inclined to attempt a modification of it in accordance with the earlier Cartesian theory, and thus deduce gravitation from ether pushing on the body, considering this 'more rational' and more suitable 'for those who like clear and intelligible principles'. He wants to see attraction banished from physics as an occult quality.[b] This is in keeping with the dead view of nature which, as the correlate of the immaterial soul, was dominant in Euler's age. This is noteworthy with respect to the basic truth I have established, which even at that time this fine mind saw shimmering in the distance; he hurried to turn back in time, and in his anxiety, seeing all the contemporary fundamental views threatened, even sought refuge in old absurdities that had already been debunked.[23]

§ 25

We know that *multiplicity* in general is necessarily conditioned by time and space and is thinkable only through them; in this respect, we call them the *principium individuationis*. But we have recognized time and space as forms of the principle of sufficient reason, a principle that expresses all

---

[a] *Si pecora essemus, carnalem vitam et quod secundum sensum ejusdem est amaremus, idque esset sufficiens bonum nostrum, et secundum hoc si esset nobis bene, nihil aliud quaereremus. Item, si arbores essemus, nihil quidem sentientes motu amare possemus: verum tamen id quasi appetere videremur, quo feracius essemus, uberiusque fructuosae. Si essemus lapides, aut fluctus, aut ventus, aut flamma, vel quid ejusmodi, sine ullo quidem sensu atque vita, non tamen nobis deesset quasi quidam nostrorum locorum atque ordinis appetitus. Nam velut amores corporum momenta sunt ponderum, sive deorsum gravitate, sive sursum levitate nitantur: ita enim corpus pondere, sicut animus amore fertur quocunque fertur (De civ. Dei, XI, 28)*

[b] *qualitas occulta*

our *a priori* cognition. However, as we discussed earlier, this only affects whether things can be cognized, it does not affect the things themselves, i.e. it is only the form of our cognition, not a property of the thing in itself; as such, the thing in itself is free of every form of cognition, even the most general, that of being an object for a subject, i.e. it is something wholly and completely distinct from representation. If then, as I believe I have adequately proven and made abundantly clear, this thing in itself is *the will*, then as such and considered apart from its appearance, it lies outside of time and space, and thus knows no multiplicity, and is consequently *one*, though, as already mentioned, not in the way an individual or a concept is one. Rather, it is one in the manner of something to which the condition for the possibility of multiplicity, the *principium individuationis*, is foreign. Thus, the multiplicity of things in space and time, which together constitute the *objecthood* of the will, fails to affect the will itself, and it remains indivisible in spite of them. It is not as if there is a smaller part of the will in a stone and a larger part in a person, since the relation between part and whole belongs exclusively to space and no longer makes sense apart from this form of intuition.[24] Rather, even more and less are relevant only for appearance, i.e. manifestation, objectivation. There is a higher degree[a] of objectivation in plants than in rocks, a higher degree in animals than in plants: indeed, the will becomes manifest, it enters into objectivation in as infinite a number of gradations as can be found between the weakest twilight and the brightest sunshine, between the loudest sound and the most distant echo. We will return later to consider the degrees of manifestation that belong to its objectivation, to the image[b] of its essence. But as the gradations[c] of its objectivation do not directly concern the will itself, still less is it concerned with the multiplicity of appearances at these different levels, i.e. the masses of individuals of every form, or the particular expressions of every force, since this multiplicity is immediately conditioned by time and space which the will itself never enters. It reveals itself just as fully and completely   153 in a *single* oak tree as in millions: their quantity, their multiplication in space and time have no meaning when it comes to the will, they are only meaningful with regard to the multiplicity of the individuals who have cognition in space and time and are themselves multiplied and dispersed in it, but whose plurality concerns only its appearance, not it itself. Thus one could say that if, impossibly,[d] a single being, however insignificant,

---

[a] *Grad*
[b] *Abbilde*
[c] *Abstufungen*
[d] *per impossibile*

were to be totally annihilated, the whole world would necessarily go down along with it. The great mystic Angelus Silesius feels this when he says:

> I know God cannot live a moment without me:
> If I would perish he must also to cease to be.[a]

People have tried in different ways to get us each to grasp the immeasurable size of the universe, and have used the opportunity to make edifying observations, for instance concerning the relative smallness of the earth and indeed of human beings, and then again, by contrast, concerning the greatness of the mind[b] in such a small creature that can conceive, grasp, and even measure the size of this universe, etc. Fair enough! But when I consider the immeasurability of the world, the most important thing about it is that the essence in itself, whose appearance is the world (whatever else it might be) cannot in its true self be stretched out and divided in endless space in this way, but this infinite extension belongs instead only to its appearance, while it itself is present whole and undivided in every single thing in nature, in all of life; thus we lose nothing if we stop with any given individual, and true wisdom is not to be attained by measuring the boundless world or, what would be more to the point, by personally flying through endless space; but rather by completely investigating some given individual and trying to fully know and understand its true and distinctive essence.[25]

Accordingly, the next Book will contain a detailed discussion of a topic that will already have impressed itself on every student of Plato, namely, that those different levels of objectivation of the will that exist as the unattained models of the countless individuals in which they are expressed, or the eternal forms of things, do not themselves enter time and space, the medium of individuals; rather, they stand fast and are not subject to any change, always being and never becoming, while the individuals arise and pass away, always becoming and never being. These *levels of the objectivation of the will* are, I say, nothing other than *Plato's Ideas*. I mention it here in passing in order to be able to use the word *Idea* in this sense later on. Accordingly, I always understand this word in the true and original sense that Plato gave it. Ideas must never be thought of as abstract productions of scholastic, dogmatizing reason. Kant used the term incorrectly as well as illegitimately in describing this scholastic notion, despite the fact that Plato had already taken possession of it and used it most aptly. Thus I understand

154

---

[a] [*Der Cherubinischer Wandersmann* (*The Cherubinic Wanderer*), I, 8]
[b] *Geist*

by *Idea* every determinate and fixed *level of the will's objectification*, to the extent that it is a thing in itself and thus foreign to all multiplicity; indeed, these levels relate to individual things as their eternal forms or archetypes. Diogenes Laertius provides the shortest and most concise statement of this famous Platonic dogma (III, 12): 'Plato teaches that the Ideas exist in nature as archetypes, as it were, and that other things only resemble them and exist as their copies.'[a,26] I will take no further notice of Kant's abuse of this word: what I need to say on this account I say in the Appendix.

§ 26

The most universal forces of nature present themselves as the lowest levels of objectivation of the will; for one thing, they appear in all matter without exception, as gravity and impenetrability; for another, they divide the matter we generally encounter amongst themselves. Accordingly, some of them will dominate this piece of matter and others will dominate that one, as rigidity, fluidity, elasticity, electricity, magnetism, chemical properties and qualities of every sort, and this is just how matter acquires its specificity. In themselves, they are just as much the immediate appearances of the will as a person's deeds, and, like a person's character, are groundless. As with human behaviour, only their individual appearances are subject to the principle of sufficient reason; they themselves can never be called either effect or cause, but are only the preceding and presupposed conditions of all cause and effect, through which their own essence unfolds and reveals itself. This is why it does not make sense to look for a cause of gravity or electricity: these are original forces whose expressions indeed take place according to cause and effect, so that each one of their individual appearances has a cause which is itself in turn just such an individual appearance and which determines that this force express itself here and emerge in time and space, while the force itself is in no way the effect of a cause or the cause of an effect. – This is why it is incorrect to say: 'gravity causes a stone to fall'; the cause here is rather the proximity of the earth, since this is what pulls on the stone. Take the earth away and the stone would not fall, although gravity would still be there.[27] The force itself lies entirely outside the chain of causes and effects that presupposes time, since the chain is meaningful only in relation to time: but the force lies outside of time as well. Individual

---

[a] ὁ Πλατων φησι, εν τη φυσει τας ιδεας ἑστανaι, καθαπερ παραδειγματα· τα δαλλα ταυταις εοικεναι, τουτων ὁμοιωματα καθεστωτα. (*Plato ideas in natura velut exemplaria dixit subsistere; cetera his esse similia, ad istarum similitudinem consistentia.*) [Diogenes Laertius, *Lives and Opinions of Eminent Philosophers*, III, 12, §13; the passage paraphrases Plato's *Parmenides* 132d]

alterations are always caused by alterations that are just as individual; they are not caused by the force whose expression they are. Because, however many times it may occur, a cause derives its efficacy from a force of nature which is groundless as such, i.e. lies completely outside the chain of causes and the province of the principle of sufficient reason in general, and is known to philosophy as the immediate objecthood of the will, the in-itself[a] of the whole of nature; but aetiology (physics in this case) establishes it as an original force, i.e. an occult quality.[b]

On the higher levels of the will's objecthood – and with people in particular – we see individuality displayed prominently in the vast differences between individual characters, i.e. in the complete personality which is already expressed outwardly through strongly delineated individual physiognomies that include the whole of corporeality.[c] No animal has anything like this degree of individuality; only the highest animals have any semblance of it, and even there the species character is entirely dominant. This is why there is very little individuality in their physiognomies. The further we descend the more any trace of individual character is lost in the generality of the species; even in the physiognomy, this generality is all that remains. When we are familiar with the psychological character of the species we know precisely what to expect from the individual; by contrast, in the human species each individual needs to be studied and fathomed on its own, and this is extremely difficult if we are to predict in advance the behaviour of any given individual with any degree of certainty, on account of the possibility of dissimulation (which begins only with reason). This distinction between the human species and all others is probably related to the fact that the furrows and convolutions in the brain, which are entirely absent in birds and only very weakly present in rodents, are (even in higher animals) far more symmetrical and consistently the same in each individual than they are in humans.[*,28] This phenomenon of the particularization of individual character distinguishes people from animals; and this is illustrated by the fact that in animals the sex drive seeks satisfaction without noticeable selection, while with people this selection is instinctively and unreflectively pursued to the point of violent passion. Thus, every human being is a particularly determined and characteristic appearance of the will,

---

* Wenzel, *De structura cerebri hominis et brutorum* [*On the structure of the brain in humans and animals*] 1812, chap. 3. – Cuvier, *Leçons d'anat. comp.* [*Lessons in comparative anatomy*], lesson 9, articles 4 and 5. – Vicq d'Azyr, *Hist de l'acad. de sciences de Paris* [*History of the academy of sciences in Paris*] 1783, pp. 470 and 483.

[a] *das Ansich*
[b] *qualitas occulta*
[c] *Korporisation*

and can even be viewed as his or her own individual Idea. Animals, on the other hand, do not have any individual character at all since only the species is distinctive; the trace of the individual becomes fainter and fainter the further we go from human beings, and finally plants have no other individual peculiarities than those that can be fully accounted for by the favourable or unfavourable external influences of the soil, the climate or other contingencies. Individuality vanishes once and for all when we come to the realm of inorganic nature. Only the crystal can to a certain extent be seen as an individual: it is a unity of striving in specific directions in the grip of a rigidity that makes the trace of this striving permanent. It is at the same time an aggregate of its basic shape, unified by an Idea, just as a tree is an aggregate of the individual shooting fibres that display and repeat themselves in every vein of the leaf, in every leaf, in every branch. Indeed, to a certain extent each of these can be seen as a separate plant that feeds parasitically off the larger plant, so that the tree, like the crystal, is a systematic aggregate of small plants, although only the whole is the complete exhibition of an indivisible Idea, i.e. of this determinate level of the will's objectivation. But individual members of the same species of crystal are indistinguishable except for markings provided by external contingencies: we can even make any species of crystals sprout large or small, at will. But we cannot find any individual as such – that is, with traces of an individual character – in inorganic nature. All appearances in inorganic nature are expressions of universal forces of nature, i.e. levels of the will's objectivation that do not objectify themselves by means of the differences between individualities, partially expressing the entirety of the Idea (as is the case in organic nature); instead, the appearances of inorganic nature exhibit themselves only in the species, and do so fully and without deviation in every individual appearance. Since time, space, multiplicity and causal determination belong to neither the will nor the Ideas (the levels of objectivation of the will), but rather only to the individual appearances of these, a force of nature (gravity or electricity, for instance) will be precisely the same throughout all its millions of appearances; only external circumstances can modify its appearance. This unity of its essence in all of its appearances, the inalterable constancy of its emergence as soon as the conditions for it are present (following the guide of causality), is called a *law of nature*. If such a law is ever known through experience then the appearance of that force of nature whose character is expressed and laid down in it can be predicted and calculated exactly. This lawlikeness is precisely why the appearances of the lower levels of the will's objectivation seem so different from the appearances of the same will on the higher, i.e. clearer levels of its objectivation, in animals, humans, and their actions. There, the stronger or weaker emergence of the individual character and the susceptibility to motives that often remain hidden from the observer (because they reside in knowledge), have so far completely prevented people from recognizing that the inner essence of both types of appearance is identical.

There is something surprising, indeed almost terror-inspiring[a] about the infallibility of the laws of nature if we start with cognition of the individual rather than the Idea. We are amazed that nature never forgets its laws even once: that when nature operates according to a law of nature once; when certain materials come together under determinate conditions, a chemical bond, a production of gas, a combustion takes place, regardless of whether the conditions are staged or obtain wholly by chance (in which case the precision is all the more surprising for being unexpected); the determinate appearance arises immediately and without delay, today as much as a thousand years ago. We are most vividly impressed by this marvel in the case of rare phenomena[b] that come about only under highly contrived conditions, but are nonetheless expected under these conditions; an example would be that when certain metals placed in an alternating formation in an acidic solution come into contact with each other, silver leaf brought between the extremes of this series will immediately erupt into green flame; or when hard diamonds under certain conditions are transformed into carbonic acid. What surprises us is the eerie[c] ubiquity of the forces of nature; we are struck here by something that has become a commonplace in everyday phenomena, namely how the connection between cause and effect is really just as mysterious as any connection imagined to hold between a magic incantation and the spirit[d] it seems necessarily to conjure up. But we must penetrate through to the philosophical knowledge that a force of nature is a particular level of objectivation of the will (which we also know to be our innermost essence), and this will (in itself and apart from its appearance and the forms of this appearance) lies outside of time and space; accordingly the plurality conditioned by space and time does not belong to the will itself or to the levels of its objectivation, i.e. the Idea (in any direct manner), but only to its appearances. We must realize as well that the law of causality is only meaningful in relation to time and space, since the multiple appearances of the different Ideas in which the will manifests itself are positioned in time and space, and there they are given an order in which to emerge. And once we have penetrated through to this knowledge, the inner meaning of Kant's great doctrine will dawn on

<hr>

[a] *Schaudererregendes*
[b] *Erscheinungen*
[c] *geistermässig*
[d] *Geist*

us: space, time and causality do not apply to the thing in itself but only to the appearance, they are only forms of our knowledge, not qualities of the thing in itself. Then we will be in a position to see that our astonishment over the lawlike and precise operations of the forces of nature, over the perfect uniformity of all their millions of appearances, over the infallibility of their emergence, can be compared to the astonishment of a child or a savage[a] who sees a flower through a many-faceted glass for the first time and wonders over the perfect uniformity of the countless flowers that he sees, counting the leaves of each one separately.

Each universal, original force of nature is thus in its inner essence nothing other than the objectivation of the will at a low level: we call each of these levels an eternal *Idea* in Plato's sense. A *law of nature* however is the relation of the Idea to the form of its appearance. This form is time, space and causality, which are necessarily and inseparably connected and related to each other. The Idea multiplies itself into countless appearances in space and time: but the order in which the Ideas emerge in those forms of multiplicity is firmly determined by the law of causality: this is, as it were, the rule[b] for the limit points of those appearances of the different Ideas, and it regulates how space, time and matter are distributed among them. This rule is thus necessarily related to the identity of all existing matter, matter being the substrate shared by all the different appearances. If these were not all referred to and divided among the same material substrate, there would be no need for such a law to determine their claims: the appearances could all fill infinite space and infinite time, coexisting and simultaneous. It is only because all these appearances of the eternal Ideas are referred to one and the same matter that it is necessary for there to be a rule[c] for their appearing and disappearing: otherwise none of them would leave room for any of the others. The law of causality is thus essentially linked to the law of permanence of substance: each acquires its meaning only reciprocally, from the other: again, space and time are related to them in the same way. Time is the mere possibility of opposite determinations in the same matter: space is the mere possibility of the same matter given opposite determinations. Thus in the previous Book we described matter as the unification of time and space, and this unification shows itself when substance persists while accidents change; causality or becoming is simply the general possibility of this happening. This is why we also said that matter is causality through and through. We described the understanding as the subjective correlate of causality, and said that matter (and thus the whole world as representation)

160

[a] *eines Wilden*
[b] *Norm*
[c] *Regel*

exists only for the understanding – that it is the condition of matter, its support, as its necessary correlate. All this is only a passing reminder of what was covered in the First Book. The two Books can be rendered completely intelligible only by paying close attention to their inner agreement: this is because the will and representation, which are inseparably united as the two sides of the real world, are torn apart from each other in these two Books in order to examine each more clearly in isolation.

An example might be in order here to clarify how the law of causality is meaningful[a] only in relation to time, space and matter (which consists in their unification), since this law determines the limits according to which the appearances of the natural forces are distributed in the possession of matter. The original natural forces themselves, on the other hand, as immediate objectivations of the will (which, as thing in itself, is not subject to the principle of sufficient reason), lie outside the forms that give validity and meaning to aetiological explanations and which, for this reason, can never lead to the inner essence of nature. – With this in mind, let us consider a machine that has been constructed according to the laws of mechanics. Movement is initiated by the gravity of iron weights; resistance is provided by the rigidity of copper wheels that push and lift each other and the levers by virtue of their impenetrability, etc. Here, gravity, rigidity and impenetrability are original, unexplained forces: mechanics merely indicates the conditions under which, and the manner in which, they express themselves, come forward, and take charge of determinate matter, time and place. Now a strong magnet can affect the iron of the weights and overcome gravity: the machine will stop and the matter instantly becomes the scene of an entirely different force of nature, namely magnetism, but aetiological explanation will never do more than specify the conditions of its entrance. Or let the copper discs of the machine be laid on zinc plates with an acid solution between them: the same matter of the machine is immediately left to another original force, galvanism, which now governs the matter according to its own laws, and reveals itself in that matter through its appearances; aetiology can do no more than give the conditions under which, and the laws according to which, they will show themselves. Now if we raised the temperature and introduced pure oxygen, the whole machine would burn: i.e. an entirely different force of nature, chemical force,[b] has once again inexorably laid claim to this matter at this time and in this place, and revealed itself in the matter as an Idea, as a specific level

---

[a] *Bedeutung hat*
[b] *Chemismus*

of the objectivation of the will. – Suppose that the resulting lime now binds itself with an acid: a salt forms, crystals start to sprout: they mark the appearance of another Idea, which is itself completely unfathomable, while the entrance of its appearance depends on conditions that aetiology   162
knows how to give. The crystals disintegrate and mix with other materials, and vegetation rises out of this: a new appearance of the will: – and the same persisting matter can be followed *ad infinitum*; we will see how now this and now that force of nature asserts its rights over it and inevitably seizes it in order to step forward and reveal its essence. The law of causality is what determines this right, and gives the point in time and space where it is valid; but the explanation based on this law goes no further than this. The force itself is the appearance of the will and as such it is not subject to the forms of the principle of sufficient reason, i.e. it is groundless. It lies outside of all time, it is omnipresent[29] and seems to be constantly waiting for the circumstances to arise under which it can step forth and seize control over a particular piece of matter, repressing the forces that had been in charge up to this point. Time exists only for the appearance of this force and is without meaning for the force itself: chemical forces can slumber in a piece of matter for millennia until contact with reagents sets them free; then they appear, but time exists only for this appearance, not for the forces themselves. Galvanism slumbers for millennia in copper and zinc and they lie peacefully next to silver, but as soon as they all come into contact under the right conditions they necessarily go up in flames. Even in the organic realm we see a dry seed preserve a slumbering force for three thousand years until finally, with the arrival of favourable conditions, it grows into a plant. –*,[30]

---

* On 16 September, 1840, at the Literary and Scientific Institute of the City of London, Mr Pettigrew, at a lecture on Egyptian antiquities, showed grains of wheat that Sir G. Wilkinson had found in a grave at Thebes, where they must have been lying for three thousand years. They were found in a hermetically sealed vase. He sowed twelve grains, and a plant emerged and grew to a height of five feet, and whose seeds are now fully mature. From the *Times* of 21 September 1840. – Likewise, at the Medical Botanical Society in London in the year 1830, Mr Haulton produced a tuberous root that had been found in the hand of an Egyptian mummy. The root may have been included for religious reasons, and was at least 2,000 years old. He planted it in a flower pot where it immediately turned green and started to grow. This was quoted from the *Medical Journal* of 1830 in the *Journal of the Royal Institution of Great Britain*, October 1830, p. 196. – 'In the garden of Mr Grimstone of the Herbarium, Highgate, in London, there is a pea plant in full flower that comes from a pea that Mr Pettigrew and the officials of the British Museum took from a vase found in an Egyptian sarcophagus where it must have been lying for 2844 years.' – From the *Times*, of 16 August 1844. – In fact, the living toads that have been found in limestone lead to the conclusion that even animal life is capable of being suspended this way for thousands of years, if the suspension begins during hibernation and is sustained by special conditions.

163   If these considerations have clarified the distinction between the forces of nature and all their appearances; if we have seen that the former is the will itself on a particular level of its objectivation, but that multiplicity comes to appearances only through time and space, and the law of causation is nothing other than the determination of the location in time and space of individual appearances, then we recognize the perfect truth and the profound meaning of *Malebranche's* doctrine of occasional causes, *causes occasionelles*. It is well worth the effort to compare this doctrine as he expresses it in the *The Search after Truth*[a] (particularly in the third chapter of the second part of the sixth book and in the elucidations that follow) with my present exposition and to perceive the most perfect agreement between the two doctrines, in spite of the enormous differences in our trains of thought. Indeed, it is remarkable to me how Malebranche, who was entirely wrapped up in the positive dogmas inexorably forced upon him by his age, nonetheless, in such bonds and under such a burden, would so fortuitously and correctly hit upon the truth, and know to reconcile it with these very dogmas, or at any rate with the language of dogmatism.

The force of truth is unbelievably strong and makes a lasting impact. Its traces spread far and wide and can be found in all the dogmas of different
164   ages and countries, even the most bizarre and absurd of these dogmas, often in strange company and peculiar admixtures, but recognizable nonetheless. In this sense it is like a plant that sprouts under a pile of large stones, but still keeps growing towards the light, working its way through many detours and bends, disfigured, pale and stunted, but towards the light all the same.

But Malebranche is right: every natural cause is only an occasional cause, it only gives the occasion, the opportunity for the appearance of that one and indivisible will that is the in-itself[b] of all things and whose gradual objectivation is this whole visible world. The cause only brings about the emergence of the will, allows it to become visible at this place, in this time. To this extent, the emergence is dependent on the cause; but the entirety of appearance, its inner essence, is not: this essence is the will itself, which the principle of sufficient reason does not apply to, and which is, accordingly, groundless. No thing in the world has a cause of its existence *per se* and in general; rather, there is only a cause for it to be precisely here and precisely now. Why a stone exhibits gravity at a certain point, rigidity at another, electricity at another, and chemical properties at yet another, this depends

[a] *Recherches de la vérité*
[b] *das Ansich*

on causes, on external influences, and can be explained accordingly: but these properties themselves, and thus the stone's whole essence (which consists of these properties and consequently expresses itself in all the ways just mentioned), the general fact that it is what it is, that it exists at all, for this there is no ground; rather it is the manifestation of the groundless will. Thus, all causes are occasional causes. This is what we have found in that part of nature that is devoid of cognition: but it is precisely the same when we are no longer dealing with causes and stimuli, but instead with motives that determine the entrance of appearances in the behaviour of animals and people. Because in both cases it is one and the same will that appears, highly diverse in the degrees of its manifestation, multiplied in their appearances, subject to the principle of sufficient reason with respect to these appearances, but in itself free from it all. Motives do not determine people's characters, but rather only the appearance of their characters, and thus their deeds; motives determine the external shape of the course of a life, not its inner meaning and substance: these follow from the character, which is the immediate appearance of the will and thus groundless. Why one person is evil and another good is not a matter of motives or external influences (such as education or sermons), and in this sense it is strictly inexplicable. But whether an evil person displays his evil in petty injustices, cowardly schemes and dirty tricks performed in his immediate surroundings, or whether he is a conqueror who oppresses whole peoples and plunges the world into misery, shedding the blood of millions; this is the outer form of his appearance, the inessential aspect of it, and depends on the circumstances in which fate has placed him, on the surroundings, on the external influences, on the motives; but his decisions based on these motives can never be explained by them: they flow from the will, whose appearance this man is. More about this in the Fourth Book. The manner in which the character develops its qualities can be compared precisely to the way each body in that part of nature devoid of cognition displays its own qualities. Water remains water, with the qualities inherent to it; but whether it is a still lake reflecting its shores, or whether it plummets foaming from a cliff, or whether it is artificially made to spray in long jets into the sky: this depends on external causes: the one state is as natural to water as the other; but it will always display one or the other according to the circumstances, equally ready to show any of them, but in each case staying true to the character it always, and exclusively, reveals. Similarly, every human character will reveal itself in all circumstances: but the appearances that emerge from it will be in keeping with the circumstances.

165

§ 27

All these observations concerning the forces of nature and their appearances should make clear to us how far we can go with causal explanations, but also where we must stop to avoid foolishly attempting to reduce the content of appearances to their mere form, so that ultimately only the form remains. Now, we will also be able to determine what we can generally expect of 166 aetiology. Aetiology will look for the causes of all the appearances in nature, i.e. the conditions under which they reliably emerge: but then it will reduce the many types of appearances arising under diverse circumstances to what operates in all appearances and what is presupposed by their cause: the original forces of nature. It will ascertain whether a difference between appearances is due to a difference in forces or whether it is only due to different circumstances under which the one force expresses itself. It will be sure not to regard the expression of one and the same force under different circumstances as the appearance of different forces; but conversely, it will be just as careful not to consider appearances belonging to originally different forces as the expressions of a single force. Now this is clearly the province of judgement,[a] which is why in physics so few people are capable of broadening our insight, although everyone can enlarge the field of experience. Inertia and ignorance lead people to appeal to original forces too readily: this was exaggerated almost to the point of irony in the entities and quiddities of the scholastics. The last thing I want to do is to enable a return to these concepts. We cannot appeal to the objectivation of the will in lieu of a physical explication any more than we can appeal to the creative power of God. This is because physics requires causes and the will is never a cause: its relation to appearance could never be put in terms of the principle of sufficient reason. Instead, something that is in itself will exists on the other hand as representation, i.e. it is appearance. As such, it observes the laws that constitute the form of appearance. So for instance, although each motion is an appearance of the will, it must nonetheless have a cause that situates it in relation to a particular time and place, which is to say: not in general, according to its inner essence, but rather as a *particular* appearance. In the case of a stone, this cause is a mechanical one; in the case of human movement it is a motive: but it must always be there. However, what is universal, the common essence of all appearances of a particular sort, what must be presupposed if causal explanation is to have sense or meaning, is the universal force of nature, which can never

---

[a] *Urtheilskraft*

be more than an occult quality[a] for physics, precisely because this is where aetiological explanation ends and metaphysical explanation[31] begins. But we will never interrupt the chain of causes and effects with an appeal to some original force; this chain does not run back to such a force as if it were its first link; rather, the nearest link in the chain already presupposes the original force as much as the most distant one does, and could not explain anything otherwise. A series of causes and effects can mark the appearance of the most diverse forces, whose successive entrance becomes visible in the series, as I have explained above with the example of a metal machine. But the differences between these original forces (forces that can never be derived from one another) in no way interrupts the unity of that chain of causes and the connections between all its links. The aetiology of nature and the philosophy of nature will never detract from one another; they go hand in hand, observing the same object from different points of view. Aetiology accounts for the causes that necessarily give rise to the particular appearances to be explained. As the basis for all its explanations, it points to the universal forces that are active in all these causes and effects. It determines these forces exactly, their number, the differences between them, and then all the effects in which each respective force emerges differently, given the differences in circumstances; the force will always emerge in accordance with its distinctive character, which is developed according to an infallible rule called a *law of nature*. When physics has accomplished all this it will be complete: then no force of inorganic nature will remain unknown and there will no longer be any effect that has not been explained as the appearance of one of these forces under particular circumstances according to a law of nature. Nonetheless, a law of nature will still be just a rule observed by nature, a rule it operates under in certain circumstances, whenever these circumstances arise. Thus a law of nature can always be defined as a universally expressed fact, *un fait généralisé*, and thus the complete presentation of all laws of nature would only be a complete register of facts.[b,32] – *Morphology* would then complete the investigation of the whole of nature by enumerating, comparing and classifying all the enduring configurations of organic nature: it has little to say about the cause of the emergence of the individual being, since this is always procreation which has a separate theory, and in rare cases is a spontaneous generation.[c] But strictly speaking, this is how all the lower levels of the objecthood of the will (thus physical and chemical appearances) emerge in individual cases,

167

168

[a] *qualitas occulta*
[b] *Thatsachenregister*
[c] *generatio aequivoca*

and the task of aetiology is just to give the conditions for this emergence. Philosophy however only thinks about universals, even in nature: here, the original forces themselves are its object,[a] and it sees in them the different levels of objectivation of the will, which is the inner essence, the in-itself, of this world, which it declares to be the mere representation of the subject when it regards the world apart from that essence. – But if, instead of laying the ground for philosophy and applying its teachings to particular examples, aetiology instead thinks its goal is to get rid of all the original forces until only *one* is left, the most universal one (impenetrability for instance), which it imagines it understands completely, and forcibly tries to reduce all the others to it[33] – if aetiology does this, it abandons its own foundations and can give only error instead of truth. The substance of nature is now repressed by the form, everything is attributed to the influence of circumstances, nothing to the inner essence of things. If this method were actually to succeed, then the riddle of existence, as we said earlier, would be solved like an arithmetic problem. But this is what people do when, as mentioned before, all physiological effects are thought to be reducible to form and mixture, and thus to electricity, and electricity to chemistry, and chemistry to mechanism. This was the mistake of Descartes and all the atomists, for instance, when they reduced the motion of heavenly bodies[34] to the impact of a fluid, and reduced qualities to the connection and configuration of atoms, and tried accordingly to explain all appearances of nature as mere phenomena of impenetrability and cohesion. This has been abandoned, but our electrical, chemical and mechanical physiologists still do essentially the same thing these days when they keep trying to

169 explain the whole of life and all the functions of the organism from the 'form and mixture' of its component parts. Physiology's explanatory goal of reducing organic life to the universal forces observed by physics can even be found explicitly in Meckel's *Archive for Physiology*,[b] 1820, vol. 5, p. 185. – Also *Lamarck*, in his *Zoological Philosophy*,[c] vol. 2, chap. 3, describes life as the simple effect of heat and electricity: 'heat and electrical matter together are all we need to explain this essential cause of life' (p. 16).[d] This would make heat and electricity the thing in itself and the animal and plant kingdoms its appearance. The absurdity of this opinion comes into sharp relief on pp. 306ff. of that work.[35] It is well known that in

[a] *Gegenstand*
[b] *Archiv für Physiologie*
[c] *Philosophie zoologique*
[d] *Le calorique et la matière électrique suffisent parfaitement pour composer ensemble cette cause essentielle de la vie.*

recent times all these views that have been so often debunked return with renewed audacity.[36] Looked at closely, they ultimately presuppose that the organism is only an aggregate of the appearances of physical, chemical and mechanical forces, which, coming accidentally into contact, create the organism as a freak of nature[a] without any greater significance. Viewed philosophically, the organism of an animal or human being would not be the presentation of a particular Idea, i.e. it would not be the immediate objecthood of the will on a certain higher level; rather, it would mark the appearance of only those Ideas that objectify the will in electricity, chemistry and mechanism. And so the organism would be accidentally blown together from the conjunction of these forces, like the shapes of people and animals in clouds or stalactites, and have no greater intrinsic interest. – However, we will soon see the extent to which this application of physical and chemical modes of explanation to the organism might be allowable and useful within certain parameters: I will show that the life force certainly makes use of the forces of inorganic nature, even though it in no way consists in them, any more than the blacksmith consists in the hammer and anvil. That is why even the simplest plant life cannot be explained by them (from something like capillary attraction and endosmosis), much less animal life.[37] The following observations will prepare the way for that rather difficult discussion.   170

Given what we have said, the natural sciences are certainly wrong to try to reduce the higher levels of the will's objecthood to the lower ones. It is just as mistaken to fail to recognize the original, self-sufficient forces of nature and to deny their existence as it is to assume the existence of specific forces (in the absence of any grounds for doing so) when faced only with known forces appearing in a special manner. This is why Kant is quite correct when he says that it is absurd to expect there to be a Newton for a blade of grass, i.e. someone who would reduce a blade of grass to the appearances of physical and chemical forces whose accidental concretion (a mere freak of nature) would fail to display a characteristic Idea (i.e. the will would not immediately reveal itself on a higher and distinctive level), but rather would only accidentally assume this form, like the appearances of inorganic nature. The scholastics, who certainly would not have permitted anything like this, would have correctly called this a full-fledged denial of the substantial form, and a degradation to the status of a mere accidental form.[b] Aristotle's term 'substantial form' designates precisely what I call the

---

[a] *Naturspiel*
[b] *forma substantialis . . . forma accidentalis*

level of objectivation of the will in a thing.[38] – On the other hand, however, we must not overlook the fact that in all the Ideas, i.e. in all the forces of inorganic nature and all the configurations of organic nature, it is *one and the same will* revealing itself, i.e. entering into the form of representation, into *objecthood*. Thus, the unity of the will must make itself known through an inner relationship between all its appearances. Now this reveals itself on the higher levels of the will's objecthood, where the entire appearance has greater clarity (which is to say: in the plant and animal kingdoms) through the universally prevailing analogy of all forms, the basic type[a] that can be traced through all appearances. Accordingly, this basic type is the guiding principle of the excellent systems of zoology that have been developed during this century by the French, and is most fully established in comparative anatomy as 'unity of plan', 'uniformity of the anatomical element'.[b,39] Locating this basic type is a main concern and certainly the most laudable endeavour of the philosophers of nature working within Schelling's school[40] too; they have done good work here, although at the same time their hunt for analogies in nature often degenerates into a bad joke. But they are right to detect those universal relationships and family resemblances in even the Ideas of inorganic nature, e.g. between electricity and magnetism (whose identity was established later),[41] between chemical attraction and gravity, etc. They have drawn particular attention to the fact that *polarity* (i.e. the separation of one force into two qualitatively different and opposed activities[c] that strive to be reunited), which generally reveals itself spatially by separating into opposite directions, is a basic type for almost all the appearances of nature, from the magnet and the crystal up to human beings. In China, on the other hand, this knowledge has been evident since ancient times in the doctrine of the opposition of *Yin* and *Yang*.[42] – In fact, since everything in the world is the objecthood of one and the same will, and consequently identical with respect to its inner essence, there must not only be an unmistakable analogy between all things, with everything less perfect already showing the trace, outline and plan of the next most perfect thing – in addition, since all those forms only belong to the world as *representation*, we can even assume that in the most universal forms of representation, in the true scaffolding of the appearance world, that is, in space and time, it is already possible to discover and establish the basic type, the outline and plan of everything that fills the forms. A dim awareness of this seems to have inspired the Kabbala and the mathematical

---

[a] *Grundtypus*
[b] *l'unité de plan, l'uniformité de l'élément anatomique*
[c] *Thätigkeiten*

philosophy of the Pythagoreans, and even the Chinese in the *I Ching*.[43] And we find it in Schelling's school as well, with its many different attempts to bring to light an analogy between all the appearances of nature, and its many, albeit ill-fated, endeavours to derive the laws of nature from the mere laws of space and time. But you never know how far some genius will some day go towards realizing both projects.

Now we must never lose sight of the difference between appearance and thing in itself, and thus never dare to distort the identity of the will that is objectified in all Ideas (because it has particular levels of its objecthood), misrepresenting it as an identity between the particular Ideas themselves (in which the will appears). Accordingly, we must never dare to reduce chemical or electrical attraction to gravitational attraction (for instance) even though their inner analogy is known and the first can be seen as the higher potency of the latter, as it were. We would be just as little justified in using the inner analogy in the structure of all animals as an excuse for mixing and identifying the species, and explaining the more perfect as a variation of the less perfect. Ultimately, even physiological functions are never reducible to chemical or physical processes; yet by way of justifying this procedure within certain limits, the following can be considered as highly likely.

Sometimes several of the appearances of the will at the lower levels of its objectivation – the inorganic levels – come into conflict with one another since each, guided by causality, wants to take control of the matter at hand. The appearance of a higher Idea will emerge from this conflict and overpower all the less perfect Ideas that were there before, in such a way that it lets their essence continue to exist in a subordinate manner by taking an analogue of them into itself. This process is intelligible only given the identity of the appearing will in all the Ideas and its striving for higher and higher objectivation. Thus in the solidification of bones (for instance) we see an unmistakable analogy with crystallization, which controlled the calcium originally, although ossification can never be reduced to crystallization. This analogy is weaker in the solidification of flesh. Similarly, the combination of humours[a] in the animal body, and secretion as well, are analogues of chemical combination and separation. The laws of chemistry do continue to operate here, although they are subordinate, highly modified and overpowered by a higher Idea. That is why merely chemical forces outside of an organism will never yield such humours; rather

[a] *Säfte*

172

Encheiresin naturae chemists call it now,
Mocking themselves, they know not how.[a,44]

173   A more perfect Idea will result from such a victory over several lower
Ideas or objectivations of the will; and by absorbing an analogue of higher
power from each of the Ideas it overpowers, it will gain an entirely new
character: the will is objectified in a new and clearer fashion. It first arises
through spontaneous generation[b] and subsequently through assimilation
to the existing germ, organic humour, plant, animal, human being. The
higher appearance thus stems from the conflict between lower appearances,
swallowing the others up but also realizing all of their striving to the highest
degree. – Accordingly, here the law is already: 'a serpent can become a
dragon only by devouring a serpent'.[c]

I wish it had been possible by dint of clarity of presentation to overcome the obscurity that clings to the substance of these thoughts: but
it is only too clear to me that I will have to enlist the aid of the
reader's own observations if I am not to remain incomprehensible, or be
misunderstood. – Given the standpoint we have adopted, we will certainly find traces of chemical and physical interactions in the organism,
but we will never be able to base an explanation of the organism in these
interactions; this is because the organism is absolutely not a phenomenon
that has arisen through the unified operations of such forces, which is to
say accidentally.[d] Rather, it comes from a higher Idea that has subjugated
all the lower ones though an *overwhelming assimilation*. This is because
the *one* will objectifies itself in all Ideas; and in striving for the highest
possible objectivation, it now abandons the lower levels of its appearance
after a conflict between them, in order to appear on a higher and thus
more powerful level. No victory without a struggle: since the higher Idea
or objectivation of the will can come forward only by overpowering the
lower Ideas, it encounters resistance on their part. Even when the lower
Ideas are quickly brought into submission, they nonetheless keep striving
to express their essence in a complete and self-sufficient manner. When a
magnet lifts a piece of iron it is engaged in an ongoing struggle against
gravity which, as the lowest objectivation of the will, has a more original
right to the matter in the iron; the magnet even gathers strength through

---

[a]   [Goethe, *Faust* I, 1940f. *Encheiresis naturae* (Greek and Latin): taking-in-hand or manipulation of
nature]

[b]   *generatio aequivoca*

[c]   *Serpens, nisi serpentem comederit, non fit draco.* [Bacon, *Sermones fideles* 38 (or *Essays*, 40), 'De fortuna'
('Of fortune')].

[d]   *zufällig*

this constant struggle, since resistance spurs it on to greater efforts, as it were. This is how it is with all of them, even the appearance of the will   174
that presents itself in the human organism: an ongoing struggle against the many physical and chemical forces which, as lower Ideas, have a prior right to that matter. Thus the arm that overpowers gravity and is raised for a while sinks back down. And thus the contented feeling of health that expresses the victory of the Idea of the organism that is conscious of itself over the physical and chemical laws that originally controlled the bodily humours: of course this feeling is so often interrupted – and in point of fact always accompanied – by a varying degree of discontent, a feeling that arises from the resistance put up by those forces and which ensures that even the vegetative part of our life is always accompanied by a quiet suffering. Thus digestion depresses all animal functions by calling upon the whole of the life force to overpower the chemical forces of nature through assimilation. Thus the burden of physical life in general, the necessity of sleep and ultimately of death in which, favoured by circumstances, those subjugated forces of nature overpower the organism that is wearied even by constant victory, winning back the matter that was torn from them, and succeed in presenting their essence without hindrance. It can thus also be said that each organism presents the Idea that it is modelled on,[a] but only after discounting the part of its force used for overpowering the lower Ideas that compete with it for matter. Jacob Böhme seems to have thought of this when he says somewhere that all human and animal bodies, indeed all plants, are really half dead. Now an organism will be a more or less perfect expression of its Idea in proportion to its success in overpowering the natural forces that express the lower levels of the objecthood of the will; that is, it will be closer to or further from the *ideal* that is the mark of beauty in the species.

Everywhere in nature we see conflict, we see struggle, we see victory changing hands; later we will recognize this more clearly as the internal rupture[b] that is essential to the will. Each level of the will's objectivation is in conflict with the others over matter, space and time. The underlying,   175
persisting matter must constantly change form as mechanical, physical, chemical and organic appearances, following the guiding thread of causality, all crowd around, greedy to emerge and tear the matter away from the others so they can each reveal their own Idea. This conflict can be traced through the whole of nature, indeed nature exists only through this

---

[a] *deren Abbild er ist*
[b] *Entzweiung mit sich selbst*

conflict: 'because if strife were not inherent in things then all would be one, as Empedocles said',[a] Aristotle, *Metaphysics*, B, 5.[45] In fact, this conflict is itself only the revelation[46] of the internal rupture that is essential to the will. This universal struggle is most clearly visible in the animal kingdom, which feeds off the plant kingdom, and in which every animal in turn becomes food and prey for another; i.e. the matter in which its Idea presents itself must give way to the presentation of another, since every animal can maintain itself in being only by constantly destroying[b] another. So the will to life constantly lives and feeds off itself in its different forms up to the human race, which overpowers[47] all others and regards nature as constructed[c] for its own use. But in the Fourth Book we will also find that this is the same human race in which this struggle, this self-rupturing of the will, reveals itself with the most terrible clarity and *man is a wolf to man*.[d,48] In the meantime, we will recognize the same conflict, the same overpowering just as clearly on the lower levels of the objecthood of the will. Many insects (in particular the *Ichneumonidae* wasps) lay their eggs on the skin, in fact in the bodies of other insects' larvae; the first thing the hatching brood does is to slowly destroy the larvae as they emerge. The young hydra grows out of the old one like a branch and later separates off; while the two are still connected, they fight for whatever prey comes along, even to the point where one will tear it out of the other's mouth (Trembley, *Polyps*,[e] II, p. 110, and III, p. 165). The bulldog ant of Australia provides the most glaring example of this sort: when cut in half, the tail and the head begin to fight: the head attacks the tail with its teeth and the tail bravely defends itself by stinging the head: the fight usually takes about half an hour until they die or are dragged off by other ants. This always happens. (Taken from a letter by Howitt in the *Weekly Journal*, printed in Galignani's *Messenger* on 17 Nov. 1855.) On the banks of the Missouri the stem and all the branches of a mighty oak tree are sometimes so entangled and bound up in a gigantic, wild vine that it withers away as if suffocated. You can see the same thing even at the lowest levels,[49] when water and carbon are converted into plant saps by organic assimilation, or plants or bread are converted into blood, and also wherever animal secretions take

176

---

[a] ει γαρ μη ην το νεικος εν τοις πραγμασιν, ἐν αν ην ἅπαντα, ὡς φησιν Εμπεδοκλης· (*Nam si non inesset in rebus contentio, unum omnia essent, ut ait Empedocles*) [In fact see *Metaphysics* B (III), 4, 1000b1]

[b] *Aufhebung*

[c] *ein Fabrikat*

[d] *Homo homini lupus* [See Plautus, *Asinaria* (*The Comedy of Asses*), II, line 495]

[e] *Polypod.* [Abraham Trembley, *Mémoires pour servir à l'histoire d'un genre de polypes d'eau douce* (*Memoirs for a history of a species of freshwater polyps*), 1744, German edn. 1791]

place by limiting chemical forces to a subordinate field of activity. So too in inorganic nature when, for instance, sprouting crystals come into contact, clash, and interfere with each other to the point where they cannot exhibit a purely crystalline form; almost every druse is the copy of this sort of conflict of the will at that low level of its objectivation. Or also when a magnet forces magnetism onto a piece of iron in order to present its Idea there as well, or when galvanism, overpowering elective affinity and undermining the strongest bonds, abrogates the laws of chemistry to the point where the acid of a salt decomposed at the negative pole has to pass to the positive pole without binding to the alkalis it passes through on its way, or without even being able to turn the litmus paper it touches red. On a grander scale, this is seen in the relation between a central body and a planet: although the planet is more or less dependent, it always resists, just like chemical forces in the organism; this is how the constant tension between centripetal and centrifugal forces arises, a tension that keeps the globe in motion and is itself the expression of the universal conflict that is essential to the appearance of the will, and which we are now considering. Since every body must be seen as the appearance[50] of a will, but will must necessarily present itself as a striving, the original condition of every spherical heavenly body cannot be rest but rather motion, striving forwards into infinite space without pause or goal. This contradicts neither the law of inertia nor that of causality; according to the former, matter as such is indifferent to rest or motion, so motion could be its original condition just as well as rest. Thus, when we find matter in motion we are just as little justified in assuming that this was proceeded by a state of rest and looking for a cause of the movement as we would be if, conversely, we were to find it at rest and assume this to be preceded by motion and then went looking for the cause of the movement's cessation.[51] Thus we must not look for something that started the centrifugal force. Rather, in the case of the planets it is (according to Kant's and Laplace's hypothesis) a remnant of the original rotation of the central body whose contraction caused the planets to separate off. But motion is essential to the central body itself: it is constantly rotating, and simultaneously flying around through endless space, or perhaps circulating around a greater central body that we cannot see.[52] This view is in perfect agreement with astronomers' speculations about a central sun, as well as with the displacement we perceive of our entire solar system, or perhaps of the entire star cluster to which our sun belongs – which would ultimately entail a universal displacement of all fixed stars together with the central sun. Of course this loses all meaning in infinite space (since in absolute space motion cannot be distinguished from

177

rest),[53] but precisely through this striving and aimless flight, it becomes the expression of that nothingness, that absence of a final goal which we will be compelled to recognize at the end of this book as the striving of the will in all its appearances; once again, endless space and endless time had to be the most universal and essential forms of the will's complete appearance, which exists to express its whole essence. – Finally, we can even recognize this mutual conflict of all the appearances of the will in mere matter regarded as such, to the extent that the essence of its appearance is correctly described by Kant as repulsive and attractive force; so that even matter exists only in the conflict of opposed forces. If we abstract away from all the chemical differences in matter, or think back in the chain of cause and effect to the point where chemical difference did not yet exist, we are left with mere matter, the world balled up in a sphere. Its life, i.e. objectivation of the will, now consists of that struggle between the forces of attraction and repulsion, the one as gravity, pulling towards the centre from all sides, the other as impenetrability, resisting the former (whether through rigidity or elasticity), and whose steady pressure[a] and resistance can be regarded as the objecthood of the will on the very lowest level, and expresses its character even there.

Here, on the lowest level, we see the will presenting itself as a blind impulse,[b] a dark, dull driving,[c] remote from any direct knowledge. This is the simplest and the weakest mode of its objectivation. But it still appears in the whole of inorganic nature as this sort of blind impulse and striving in the absence of knowledge, in all the original forces that physics and chemistry are busy seeking out, and whose laws they are trying to learn. Each of these forces presents itself to us in millions of identical, lawlike appearances which do not register a single trace of individual character, but rather are simply multiplied in time and space, i.e. through the *principium individuationis*, as an image is multiplied in the facets of a glass.

The will is at work in the plant kingdom, objectifying itself more clearly from level to level, and here its appearances are bound together by stimuli rather than causes as such. The will is of course still wholly devoid of cognition, a dark, driving force, even in the vegetative aspect of animal appearance, in the creation and development of every animal and in the maintenance of its inner economy, where its appearance is still necessarily determined by nothing more than mere stimuli. The objecthood of the will rises to higher and higher levels, and finally reaches the point where the

---

[a] *Drang*
[b] *Drang*
[c] *ein finsteres, dumpfes Treiben*

individual presenting the Idea can no longer obtain food for assimilation simply by moving in response to stimuli; this is because it needs to wait for these stimuli, but here the food is more specifically determined, and given the increasing multiplicity of the appearances, the crowding and confusion has grown so great that appearances disrupt each other. This means that the chance event that would bring food to an individual that is moved by mere stimuli has become too improbable. Thus, from that point on, when the animal tears itself from the egg or womb where it vegetated without cognition, food must be sought after and chosen. This calls for movement upon motives, which in turn calls for cognition, which thus enters as an assistant,[a] a mechanism[b] and this is required at this level of objectivation of the will for the preservation of the individual and the propagation of the species. It enters the scene, with the brain or one of the larger ganglia as its representative,[c] just as every other effort or determination of the self-objectifying will is represented by an organ, i.e. presented for representation[d] as an organ.[*,54] – But given this assistance, this mechanism, the *world as representation* stands forth in one fell swoop, together with all of its forms, object and subject, time, space, multiplicity and causality. The world now shows its second side. Merely *will* so far, it is now at the same time *representation*, the object of the subject of cognition. The will, which until now had pursued its drives in the dark with the utmost certainty and infallibility, has lit a light for itself on this level, a means that had become necessary to neutralize the disadvantage arising from the crowding and the complications of its appearances, and in fact precisely the most perfect of them. The infallible certainty and lawlikeness that had characterized its operations so far in inorganic and merely vegetative nature relied on the fact that it alone was active in its original essence, as blind impulse, will, unaided but also undisturbed by a second, entirely different world, the world as representation. The world of representation is indeed only the copy of the will's own essence, but nonetheless has an entirely different nature, and now intervenes in the nexus of the will's appearances. This puts an end to its infallible certainty. Animals are already exposed to illusion, to deception. But they have only intuitive representations, not concepts or

179

180

---

* See chap. 22 of volume 2, as well as my essay *On the Will in Nature*, p. 54 and pp. 70–9 of the first edition, or pp. 46ff. and pp. 63–72 of the second edition. [See Hübscher *SW* 4, 48ff. and 69–77]

[a] *Hülfsmittel*
[b] μηχανη
[c] *repräsentirt*
[d] *Vorstellung*

reflection, and are thus tied to the present and cannot take the future into consideration. – It seems that this sort of non-rational cognition might not always be enough and might sometimes require some help. We are struck by two types of phenomena in which the will working blindly and the will enlightened by cognition encroach on each other's territory in a very surprising way. In the one case, among those animal deeds guided by intuitive cognition and its motives, we find a group of deeds that are not guided in this way, deeds that take place with all the necessity of the blind operations of the will. These are the creative drives;[a] they are not guided by motives or cognition, but seem to perform their tasks from abstract, rational motives. The other case, which is the opposite of this first, is when, conversely, the light of cognition penetrates the workshop of the blind operations of the will, and illuminates the vegetative functions of the human organism – namely, in magnetic clairvoyance.[b,55] – Finally, where the will has achieved the highest degree of objectivation, the cognition from the understanding that arises in animals, and that the senses supply with data, and from which arise mere intuitions that are tied to the present – this cognition is no longer sufficient. The complicated, multifaceted, malleable, extremely needy being who is exposed to countless injuries – the human – had to be illuminated by a twofold cognition in order to exist; a higher potency of intuitive cognition, as it were, had to be added, a reflection of that intuitive cognition: reason as the faculty of abstract concepts. With this came soundness of mind,[c] which entails the ability to survey the future and the past; and this introduces deliberation, concern and the ability to act in a premeditated manner, abstracted from the present; and finally, it also introduces a completely transparent consciousness of the decisions of one's own will as such. But if the possibility of illusion and deception has already arrived on the scene with mere intuitive cognition, which has dispelled the former infallibility that the drives of the will enjoyed in the absence of cognition, and instinct and creative drive (as expressions of the will in the absence of cognition) must come to its aid in the midst of the drives that *are* guided by cognition, – then the entrance of reason means that the certainty and assurance of the expressions of the will (which at the other extreme, in inorganic nature, even appear as strict lawlikeness) are almost entirely lost: instinct retreats completely, deliberation, which is now supposed to replace everything,[56] gives rise (as was argued in the First Book) to indecision and uncertainty: error becomes possible, and in many

181

[a] *Kunsttrieben*
[b] *magnetischen Hellsehn*
[c] *Besonnenheit*

cases hinders the adequate objectivation of the will through deeds. Even if the will has already taken its definite and unalterable course[57] in the form of a character, and willing itself infallibly occurs on the occasion of a motive, error can falsify its expressions. This is because delusive motives similar to the real ones can slip in and suppress them:[*,58] so for instance when superstition imposes imaginary motives that compel someone to adopt a course of action entirely opposed to what his will would otherwise adopt under the circumstances: Agamemnon kills his daughter, a miser distributes alms out of pure egoism in the hope of one day being paid back a hundredfold,[59] etc.

Thus cognition in general, rational as well as merely intuitive, proceeds originally from the will itself and belongs to the essence of the higher levels of its objectivation as a mere mechanism,[a] a means for the preservation of the individual and the species as much as any organ of the body. Originally in the service of the will and determined by the accomplishment of its aim, cognition remains almost entirely in its service throughout: this is the case in all animals and in almost all human beings. Nonetheless, in the Third Book we will see how in certain people knowledge evades this servitude, throws off its yoke and can exist free from any purposes of the will and purely for itself, simply as a clear mirror of the world; and this is the origin of art. Finally, in the Fourth Book we will see how this sort of cognition, acting back on the will, can bring about the will's self-abolition,[b] i.e. the resignation that is the final goal, indeed the innermost essence of all virtue and holiness and is redemption from the world.

182

§ 28

We have considered the great quantity and diversity of appearances in which the will objectifies itself; indeed, we have looked at the endless and implacable struggle among these appearances. Nevertheless, according to the whole of our presentation up to this point, the will itself, as thing in itself, has no share in that multiplicity or change. The diversity of the (Platonic)[60] Ideas, i.e. the gradations of the will's objectivation, the number

---

* Thus the scholastics correctly said: *Causa finalis movet non secundum suum esse reale, sed secundum esse cognitum* [The final cause does not operate according to its actual essence, but rather according to its known essence]. See Suárez, *Disp[utationes] Metaph[isicae]*, Disputatio XXIII, sections 7 and 8. [No exact passage in the *Metaphysical Disputations* corresponds with Schopenhauer's reference, though the beginning of section 8 is close]

[a] μηχανή
[b] *Selbstaufhebung*

of individuals in which each of the Ideas presents itself, the struggle of the forms over the matter: none of these things make any difference to the will, but are rather just ways in which it is objectified; these things have only a mediated relation to the will, mediated, that is, by its objectivation, which also ensures that they belong to the expression of the will's essence for representation. Just as a magic lantern exhibits many different images while one and the same flame makes them all visible, so too in all the diversity of appearances that fill the world alongside each other, or (as events) follow each other and push each other out of the way, there is just *the one* will that appears; everything is its manifestation, its objecthood, and it remains unmoved in the midst of that change: it alone is the thing in itself, while all objects are appearance, phenomenon as Kant puts it. – Although it is in the human being, as (Platonic) Idea, that the will finds its clearest and most perfect objectivation, nonetheless, this Idea could not express its essence on its own. In order to appear in its proper significance, the Idea of a human being cannot be presented alone and in isolation but rather must be accompanied by the stepwise descent through all animal forms,[a] through the plant kingdom, and down to the inorganic: only taken together do they complete the objectivation of the will; they are presupposed in the Idea of a person as the flowers of a tree presuppose leaves, branches, trunks and roots:

183   they form a pyramid with human beings at the very top. But if you like a good comparison you can also say: their appearance accompanies that of humans just as necessarily as a full light is accompanied by all the gradations of half-shadow through which it loses itself in darkness: or you can also call these lower appearances the echo of humans and say: the animal and plant are the descending fifth and third of human beings, and the inorganic realm is the lower octave. The complete truth of this final simile will only become clear to us when, in the following Book, we attempt to uncover the profound significance of music, and show ourselves how the melody that progresses by connecting high, swiftly moving tones can in a certain sense be seen as presenting human lives and strivings, connected by reflection; on the other hand, the disconnected ripienos and heavy-moving bass (that make up the harmony so vital to the perfection of the music) depict the rest of animal nature and that part of nature which is devoid of cognition. More of that in its place, where it will not sound so paradoxical. – But we also find the *inner necessity* in the sequence of the will's appearances (which are inseparable from the adequate objecthood of the will) expressed through an *outer necessity* in the whole of these appearances themselves,

---

[a] *Gestaltungen*

which entails that humans are in need of animals for their maintenance, and animals at each level are in need of one another, and also of plants, which in turn need soil, water, chemical elements and their combinations, the planet, the sun, rotation and circulation around the sun, the slope of the ecliptic, etc. – This basically stems from the fact that the will needs to live off itself because there is nothing outside of it and it is a hungry will. Thus, pursuit, anxiety and suffering.[61]

Just as the knowledge of the unity of the will (as thing in itself) through the infinite variety and multiplicity of appearances is the only thing that really sheds light on that remarkable, unmistakable analogy between all the productions of nature, the family resemblance that can be regarded as variations on the same, un-given theme, – in the same way, the clear and deeply grasped knowledge of that harmony, that essential connection of   184 all the parts in the world, that necessity of their gradation which we have just been considering – all these open to us a true and adequate insight into the inner essence and significance of the undeniable *purposiveness*[a] of all the products of organic nature, a purposiveness which must even be presupposed *a priori* when we think and make judgements about them.

This *purposiveness* is twofold: it is in part an *internal* purposiveness, i.e. an agreement between all the parts of an individual organism which are arranged so that the maintenance of the organism itself as well as its genus results, and thus presents itself as the goal of the arrangement. But it is an *external* purposiveness as well, namely a relation of inorganic nature to organic nature in general, or of the individual parts of organic nature to each other, which makes possible the maintenance of the whole of organic nature or even the genera of the individual animals, and thus confronts our judgement as the means to this goal.

Internal purposiveness now enters the course of our discussion in the following way. If, as we have been saying, none of the differences in the forms of nature and none of the variations among individuals belong to the will but rather only to its objecthood and the form of its objecthood, then it necessarily follows that the will is indivisible and wholly present in every appearance, although the degrees of its objectivation, the (Platonic)[62] Ideas, are very different. To make this easier to grasp, we can view these different Ideas as separate and intrinsically simple acts of the will, in which its essence expresses itself to a greater or lesser extent: but the individuals are themselves appearances of Ideas (and thus of these acts), in time, space and multiplicity. – Now, on the lowest levels of objecthood, such an act

---

[a] *Zweckmäßigkeit*

(or Idea) retains its unity, even in appearance; while on the higher levels it needs a whole series of states and developments in time in order to appear; only taken together do these states and developments complete the expression of its essence. So, for instance, the Idea that reveals itself in some universal force of nature presents only a simple expression, even if this presentation differs according to external circumstances: otherwise its identity could not be established at all, since it is identified by abstracting away the difference introduced by these external circumstances. That is why the crystal has only *one* life expression,[a] its crystallization, which is fully and exhaustively expressed afterwards in the congealed form, the corpse of that momentary life. But even the plant does not express the Idea (whose appearance it is) all at once and through a simple expression, but rather in the temporal succession of the development of its organs. The animal not only develops its organism in the same way, through a succession of often very different forms (metamorphosis) – the form itself, despite being the objecthood of the will on this level, is not sufficient for a perfect presentation of its Idea. This is rather completed only through the actions of the animal, in which its empirical character (which is the same for the whole species) expresses itself and completes the perfect revelation of the Idea, and this presupposes the definite organism as a basic condition. In humans, each individual already has a distinctive empirical character (indeed, as we will see in the Fourth Book, to the point of abolishing[b] the character of the species completely, namely through the self-abolition[c] of the whole of willing). What is recognized as the empirical character through the individual's necessary development in time and temporally conditioned division into individual actions, is, abstracting from its temporal form of appearance, the *intelligible character*, as Kant expressed it. Kant's immortal contribution assumed a particularly brilliant form when he established this distinction and presented the relationship between freedom and necessity, i.e. between the will as thing in itself and its appearance in time.*,[63] The intelligible character coincides with the Idea, or more specifically with the original act of will revealed in the Idea: to this extent, not only the

---

* See *Critique of Pure Reason*, 'Resolution of the cosmological idea of the totality of the derivation of occurrences in the world from their causes', pp. 560–86ff. of the fifth edition and pp. 532ff. of the first edition [A532–558 / B560–586]; and *Critique of Practical Reason*, fourth edition, pp. 169–79; Rosenkranz edition, pp. 224ff. [Ak. 5: 94–103]. Compare with my essay *On the Principle of Sufficient Reason*, §43.

[a] *Lebensäußerung*
[b] *Aufhebung*
[c] *Selbstaufhebung*

empirical character of every person but also of every species of animal, indeed every species of plant, and even every original force of inorganic nature, can be seen as the appearance of an intelligible character, i.e. of an extra-temporal, indivisible act of will. – I would like to call attention in passing to the naïvety with which every plant expresses and lays before us its entire character merely through its shape, and reveals its entire being and willing, which is what makes the physiognomies of plants so interesting; on the other hand, we must observe an animal's deeds and drives in order to know it according to its Idea; and human beings need to be fully researched and investigated, since reason makes them capable of a very high degree of deception. The animal is as much more naïve than a human, as the plant is than the animal. In animals we see the will to life as it were more naked than in humans, where it is clothed in so much cognition and veiled so thoroughly by the capacity for deception that their true essence comes to light almost by accident or in isolated incidents. The will shows itself completely naked though also much weaker in the plant, as a purely blind impulse to exist, without purpose or goal. Plants reveal their whole essence at first glance and with a perfect innocence unimpaired by the fact that they display their genitalia at their pinnacle, while all animals keep them in the most concealed place. This innocence of plants is based on their lack of cognition: guilt[a] does not lie in willing but rather in willing accompanied by cognition. Every plant will begin by telling us about its native land, its native climate, and the nature of the soil from which it emerged. That is why even the untrained eye will be able to tell whether an exotic plant comes from the tropics or from the temperate zone, and whether it grows in water, in a swamp, on the mountains, or on the moors. But apart from this, every plant expresses the particular will of its species and says what cannot be expressed in any other language.[64] – But now let us apply these ideas to the teleological consideration of the organism, to the extent that it concerns the organism's internal purposiveness. In inorganic nature, the Idea that must always be regarded as a single act of will only reveals itself in a single and always identical expression, and one can thus say that here   187 the empirical character shares in the unity of the intelligible character and coincides with it, as it were, so that no internal purposiveness is evident here. All organisms, by contrast, present their Idea through a sequence of consecutive developments conditioned by a diversity of different and coexisting parts, and thus only when combined do the expressions of their empirical characters express their intelligible characters. But this necessary

[a] *Schuld*

coexistence of the parts and sequential nature of the development does not cancel out the unity of the appearing Idea, the unity of the act of will that expresses itself. Rather, the unity now finds its expression in the necessary relation and concatenation of those parts and developments with each other, according to the law of causality. Since it is the single and indivisible (and therefore perfectly self-coherent) will that reveals itself in the entire Idea as in an act, then although its appearance divides into different parts and states, it must nonetheless exhibit that unity as a general coherence among these parts and states: all the parts are necessarily related to and dependent on each other, and this reproduces the unity of the Idea in appearance. Accordingly, we now recognize these different parts and functions of the organism as means and ends in relation to each other, and the organism itself as the ultimate end of them all. The intrinsically simple Idea divides itself into the multiplicity of parts and states of the organism, and its unity is reproduced through the necessary connection of those parts and functions, such that these are both cause and effect, and thus both means and ends of one another – but neither this division nor this unification is characteristic of or essential to the appearing will as such (as thing in itself) but rather only to its appearance in space, time and causality (pure modes of the principle of sufficient reason, the form of appearance). They belong to the world as representation, not the world as will: they belong to the manner in which the will becomes an object, i.e.

188   representation, on this level of its objecthood. Anyone who has entered into the spirit of this perhaps somewhat difficult discussion will now correctly understand Kant's doctrine, which claims that both the purposiveness of the organic as well as the lawlikeness of the inorganic are imported into nature only by our own understanding, and thus both concern only appearances, not things in themselves. The astonishment we expressed earlier over the infallible consistency of the lawlikeness of inorganic nature is essentially the same as astonishment over the purposiveness of organic nature: in both cases we are only being surprised by the sight of the original unity of the Idea which has assumed the form of multiplicity and diversity for appearance.*

Now as far as the second type of purposiveness goes (recalling the classification introduced above), *external* purposiveness, this does not show itself in the internal economy of organisms but rather in the support and assistance they receive from the outside, both from inorganic nature as well as from other organisms. Here we find the same general explanation as was

---

* Compare *On the Will in Nature*, at the conclusion of the section entitled 'Comparative Anatomy'.

given in the discussion immediately above, since the whole world with all of its appearances is the objecthood of the one and indivisible will, the Idea, which stands in the same relation to all other Ideas as a harmony does to the individual voices; thus, that unity of the will must also show itself in the coherence of all its appearances with each other. But we could gain much greater clarity concerning this unity if we were to look more closely at the appearances of external purposiveness and the coherence between the different parts of nature, a discussion that will at the same time retrospectively illuminate the preceding remarks. We will best succeed in this by considering the following analogy.

Since the character of any particular person is thoroughly individual and not entirely subsumed[a] under that of the species, it can be seen as a specific Idea corresponding to a distinctive act of the will's objectivation. This act itself would then be the person's intelligible character, and the empirical character would be its appearance. The empirical character is   189 utterly and completely determined by the intelligible character, which is groundless will, i.e. will as thing in itself, not subject to the principle of sufficient reason (the form of appearance). Over the course of a lifetime, the empirical character must provide a copy of the intelligible character, and cannot turn out differently from what is required by the essence of the intelligible character. But this determination extends only to what is essential, not to what is inessential in the way the life appears. The inessential factors include a more precise determination of the events and actions that constitute the material in which the empirical character shows itself. These are determined by external circumstances, which supply the motives that the character reacts to according to its nature; and since these can be very dissimilar, the outer shape of the empirical character's appearance (and thus the particular factual or historical course of the life) will necessarily be directed by their influence. These might turn out very differently, even if the content that is essential to this appearance remains the same: so, for instance, it does not matter whether we play for matches[b] or for crowns; but whether we cheat at the game or go about it honestly, that is the essential thing: the latter is determined by the intelligible character, the former by external influences. Just as the same theme can be presented in a hundred variations, so too the same character can be presented in a hundred very different life histories.[65] But as different as the external influences may be, the empirical character that expresses itself in the course

---

[a] *begriffen*
[b] [The German has 'nuts']

of a life must, however it turns out, objectify the intelligible character precisely, since it adapts its objectivation to the given material of factual circumstances. – Now the course of one's life is essentially determined by character, but influenced by external circumstances; and we need to assume that something analogous takes place when the will, in the original act of its objectivation, determines the different Ideas in which it objectifies itself, i.e. the different configurations of the natural beings among which it parcels out its objectivation (and for this reason, the Ideas will necessarily be related to each other in appearance). We must assume that there was a universal and reciprocal adaptation and conformity between all those appearances of the *one* will, albeit a conformity removed from all temporal determination (as we will soon see more clearly), since the Idea lies outside of time. Therefore every appearance has had to conform to the environment in which it entered, but the environment has also had to conform to the appearance, even when it occupied a much later position in time; and we see this consensus of nature[a] everywhere.[66] Every plant is suited to its soil and climate, every animal to its element and the prey that is to become its food, and it is also to some extent protected against its natural predators; the eye is suited to light and its refrangibility,[b,67] lungs and blood are suited to the air, the airbladder is suited to the water, the eye of the seal to the change of medium, the hydrous cells in the stomach of a camel to the drought of the African desert, the sail of the nautilus to the wind that is to drive its little ship,[68] and so forth down to the most specific and surprising instances of external purposiveness.* But here we need to abstract from all temporal relation, since this concerns only the appearance of the Idea, not the Idea itself. Accordingly, this type of explanation can also be used retrospectively, and we must not only assume that each species adjusts itself to the given circumstances, but that these temporally prior circumstances themselves likewise took into account the being that was yet to come. This is because it is indeed one and the same will that objectifies itself in the whole world: the will knows nothing of time, since this form of the principle of sufficient reason does not belong to it or to its original objecthood, the Ideas, but only to the manner in which the will is cognized by the individuals who are themselves transient, i.e. to the appearance of the Ideas. Thus for our present purposes, the temporal sequence is entirely meaningless with respect to the manner in which the

190

---

* See *On the Will in Nature*, the section on 'Comparative Anatomy'.

[a] *consensus naturae*
[b] *Brechbarkeit*

objectivation of the will distributes itself among the Ideas, and the Ideas whose *appearances* entered into the temporal sequence earlier, in accordance with the law of causality (to which they are subject), gain no advantage over those whose appearance enters later, which are rather precisely the most perfect objectivations of the will; the earlier ones needed to adapt to them just as much as they needed to adapt to the earlier ones. Thus the course of the planets, the gradient of the ecliptic, the rotation of the earth, the division of solid land and ocean, the atmosphere, light, heat, and all similar appearances that are in nature what the ground bass is in harmony – all these adjusted themselves, anticipatorily, to the future races of living beings that they would be carrying and maintaining. Similarly the soil adjusts itself for the nourishment of plants, and these for the nourishment of animals, and these for the nourishment of other animals, just as much as the other way around. All parts of nature accommodate themselves to each other because it is *one* will that appears in them all, but the temporal sequence is entirely foreign to its original and only *adequate objecthood* (this expression is explained in the following Book), the Ideas. Even now that the species are already in existence and only need to maintain themselves, we still occasionally see such a future-oriented concern in nature, truly abstracted from the order of time, a self-accommodation of what exists to what is yet to come. Thus the bird builds a nest for young it does not yet know; the beaver builds a dam without knowing its purpose; the ant, the hamster, the bee all stock up for a winter they know nothing about; the spider, the antlion set traps with what looks like intentional cunning for unknown future prey; insects lay their eggs where the future brood will be able to find its future nourishment. In the flowering season, the female flower of the dioecious *Vallisneria* unwinds the spiral thread of the stem that had been holding it at the bottom of the water, and uses it to rise to the surface. At just the same time, the male flower tears itself away from the short stem on which it had been growing at the bottom of the water, and so by sacrificing its life it reaches the surface and swims around looking for the female flower. Then, after pollination, the female contracts its spirals and withdraws back to the bottom where the fruit develops.*,[69] And here I also need to mention the larva of the male stag beetle, which, for its metamorphosis, chews a hole in the wood that is twice as big as that of the female, in order to have room for its future horns. Thus in general, animal instinct gives us the best explanation for the other instances of teleology in

191

192

---

* *Chatin*, 'Sur la Valisneria spiralis' in *Comptes Rendus de l'Academie des Sciences*, No. 13, 1855. ['On Valisneria spiralis', in *Reports of the Academy of Sciences*]

nature. Instinct looks like an action that follows the concept of a purpose, although it is entirely devoid of any purpose; and so too all formations in nature look like purposive ones, although they are entirely devoid of any purpose. This is because in the external as well as the internal teleology of nature, what we necessarily think of as means and ends is everywhere only *the appearance of the unity of the one, internally coherent will* that has been broken up into space and time for our mode of cognition.

Nonetheless, the reciprocal adaptation and accommodation of the appearances that spring from this unity cannot eradicate the inner conflict described above, which appears in the universal struggle of nature, and which is essential to the will. That harmony only goes far enough to make the *continuation* of the world and its beings possible, since otherwise they would have perished long ago. That is why this applies only to the continuation of the species and the general conditions of life, not to the continuation of individuals.[70] Accordingly, if, by virtue of this harmony and accommodation, the *species* in the organic and the *universal forces of nature* in the inorganic continue to exist alongside each other and even support each other, the inner conflict of the will objectified through all those Ideas shows itself in the endless battle for extermination of the *individuals* of those species, and the constant struggle of the *appearances* of those forces of nature with each other, as we explained before. The scene and the object of this struggle is the matter that they each strive to tear away from the other, as well as space and time, whose unification through the form of causality is really matter, as was explained in the First Book.[*,71]

193

§ 29

Here, I bring the second main section of my presentation to a close. This has been the very first communication of an entirely novel thought, one that is too new to be entirely free of all traces of the individuality in which it arose; still, I hope I have succeeded in communicating as much as possible the clear certainty that this world in which we live and have our being is, in its whole essence, the *will* through and through, and at the same time *representation* through and through; that this representation as such already presupposes a form, namely object and subject, and is therefore relative; and if we ask what is left over after we get rid of this form along with all the subordinate forms that are expressed by the principle of sufficient

* See chs. 26 and 27 of the second volume.

reason – as something quite different in kind[a] from representation – it can be nothing other than *will*, which is therefore the true *thing in itself*. Everyone finds that he is this will that makes up the inner essence of the world, and he also finds that he is the cognitive subject; the whole world is only the representation of the subject and to this extent it exists only in relation to his consciousness, as its necessary bearer. Thus in this twofold view everyone is the whole world itself, the microcosm, and finds in himself both sides of the world whole and complete. What he recognizes as his own essence is the same thing that constitutes the essence of the world in its entirety, the essence of the macrocosm: and thus it is, like himself, both will through and through and representation through and through; nothing more remains. Thus, we see here that the philosophy of Thales, who investigated the macrocosm, coincides with the philosophy of Socrates, who investigated the microcosm, since the object of both proves to be the same. – But all the knowledge communicated in the first two Books will become more complete and thus more certain in the two Books that follow, and hopefully many of the questions that may have arisen more or less clearly in the discussion to this point will find a satisfying response.

In the meantime, *one* such question deserves special mention, since it really only arises to the extent that we have not completely revealed the   194 meaning of the discussion so far; indeed, it can even serve to clarify what has already been said. This question is the following. Every will is the will to something, it has an object, a goal of its willing: now the will that is presented to us as the essence in itself of the world: what does *it* ultimately will, or what does it strive for? – This question, like so many others, comes from confusing the thing in itself with appearance. The principle of sufficient reason (one of the forms of which is the law of motivation) extends only to the latter, not the former. Everywhere, a ground can only be given for appearances as such, for particular things, never for the will itself or for the Idea in which it is adequately objectified. So we can look for a cause for every individual movement or alteration in nature (i.e. a state that necessarily brings it about) but never for the natural force itself that is revealed in this and in countless other similar appearances: and it is real ignorance, born of a lack of clear-headedness,[b] when people look for the cause of gravity, of electricity, etc. Only if it had somehow been shown that gravity, electricity, were not original, characteristic forces of nature but rather only the manner in which a more universal, previously

---

[a] *ein . . .* toto genere *Verschiedenes*
[b] *Besonnenheit*

known force of nature appeared – only then we could look for the cause why this force of nature gave rise here to the appearance of gravity, or electricity. All this has already been extensively discussed. But likewise, every particular act of will of a cognizing individual (which is itself only the appearance of will as thing in itself) necessarily has a motive without which the act would never arise. Now the material cause[72] only contains the determination that the expression of this or that force of nature needs to arise at this time, in this place, on this matter; and similarly the motive only determines the act of will of a cognizing being at this time, in this place, under these circumstances, as something entirely particular; it in no way determines that this being wills at all and wills in this way: this is the expression of its intelligible character which, as the will itself, the thing in itself, is groundless, lying outside the province of the principle of sufficient reason. This is why every human being always has purposes and motives guiding his actions, and always knows how to account for his particular deeds: but when asked why he wills in general, or why in general he wills to exist, he would not have an answer and in fact the question would make no sense to him; and this is really just an expression of his consciousness that he himself is nothing but will whose willing in general thus goes without saying and requires a more precise determination through motives only in its particular acts at each point in time.

In fact the absence of all goals, of all boundaries, belongs to the essence of the will in itself, which is an endless striving. We touched on this before, in our discussion of centrifugal force: it is also revealed most simply on the very lowest level of the objecthood of the will, namely in gravity, whose constant striving is clear to see, despite the evident impossibility of its final goal. Even if all the matter that exists were compressed together into a clump, as gravity wills it to be, gravity would still strive towards the middle point within this clump, always struggling against impenetrability, as rigidity or elasticity. Thus, the striving of matter can always be merely impeded but never fulfilled or satisfied. But this is just how it is with all the strivings of all the appearances of the will. Every goal that is achieved is once again the beginning of a new course of action, and so on to infinity. The plant raises its appearance from the seed, through the stem and leaf to the flower and fruit, which is again only the beginning of a new seed, of a new individual which will run the whole course once again, and so on through infinite time. It is just the same with the life course of the animal: procreation is its highest point, and after this is attained the life of the first individual fades slowly or quickly away, while a new life repeats the same appearance and guarantees for nature that the species will be continued. Indeed, the constant renewal of matter in each organism can also be seen as the simple appearance of this constant pressure[a] and change; physiologists have stopped considering this to be the necessary replacement of the material[b] consumed in movement, since the possible wear and tear of the machine is not remotely equivalent to the constant influx through nutrition: eternal becoming, endless flux belong to the revelation of the essence of the will. Finally, the same thing can also be seen in human endeavours[c] and desires, which always delude us into believing that their fulfilment is the final goal of willing; but as soon as they are attained they no longer look the same and thus are soon forgotten, grow antiquated and are really, if not admittedly, always laid to the side as vanished delusions; we are lucky enough when there is still something left to desire and strive after, to carry on the game of constantly passing from desire to satisfaction and from this to a new desire, a game whose rapid course is called happiness and slow course is called suffering, so that the game might not come to an end, showing itself to be a fearful, life-destroying boredom, a wearied longing without a definite object, a deadening languor. – According to all we have said, when the will is illuminated by cognition it always knows what it wills here, what it wills now; but never what it wills in general: every particular act has a goal; but the whole of willing has none: just as every particular appearance of nature is determined by a sufficient cause to enter at this place, in this time, but the force manifesting itself in general in the appearance does not have a cause, because such a force is a level of appearance of the thing in itself, of the groundless will. – But the only self-cognition of the will as a whole is representation as a whole, the entire intuitive world. This is its objecthood, its revelation, its mirror. What it expresses in this capacity will be the subject of our further discussion.*

196

---

* See chap. 28 of the second volume.

[a] *Drang*
[b] *Stoff*
[c] *Bestrebungen*

THIRD BOOK

The world as representation, second consideration

Representation independent of the principle of sufficient reason: the Platonic Idea: the object of art

Τί τὸ ὂν μὲν ἀεὶ, γένεσιν δὲ οὐκ ἔχον; καὶ τί τὸ γιγνόμενον μὲν καὶ
ἀπολλύμενον, ὄντως δὲ οὐδέποτε ὄν;

Plato

['What is it that always is, and has no becoming; and what is it that becomes and passes away but never truly is?' – Based on *Timaeus* 27d–28a]

§ 30

In the First Book, the world was presented as mere *representation*, object for a subject; in the Second Book we considered this world from its other side and found that it is also *will*, and this proved to be the only thing the world is, apart from representation. In recognition of this fact we went on to name the world as representation (both as a whole and in its parts) the *objecthood of the will*, which accordingly means: the will become object, i.e. representation.[1] We may further recall that such an objectivation of the will had many, albeit determinate, levels at which the essence of the will enters representation (i.e. presents itself as an object) with gradually increasing degrees of clarity and perfection. We already recognized these levels as Plato's Ideas, in so far as they are nothing but particular species, or the original, unchanging forms and qualities of all natural bodies, inorganic no less than organic, as well as the universal forces that manifest themselves according to natural laws. Taken together, these Ideas present themselves in countless individuals and details, relating to these as model[a] to imitations.[b] The multiplicity of such individuals can be represented only through time and space, and their arising and passing away only through causality, and we know that all of these forms are nothing but the different configurations

---

[a] *Vorbild*
[b] *Nachbildern*

of the principle^a of sufficient reason, which is the ultimate principle^b of all
finitude and individuation, as well as the universal form of representation
200   as it comes under the cognition of the individual as such. By contrast,
the Idea does not enter into that principle; hence, neither multiplicity
nor change applies to it. While presenting itself in countless individuals
that ceaselessly become and pass away, the Idea itself remains the same,
unchanged; the principle of sufficient reason has no meaning for it. But
since this is the form of the whole of the subject's cognition (to the extent
that the subject has cognition as an *individual*), the Ideas also lie entirely
outside the cognitive sphere of the subject as such. Thus, if the Ideas are
supposed to be the object of cognition, then cognition will be possible only
when individuality is suppressed in the cognitive subject. We will now turn
to a closer and more thorough examination of this issue.

§ 31

But first, the following, very important remark. I hope that my argument
in the previous Book was convincing: what Kant's philosophy calls the
thing in itself (which appears as a doctrine that is so meaningful and yet
obscure and paradoxical, particularly² given the way Kant introduces it
through an inference from grounded to ground) was seen as a stumbling
block^c and in fact, as the weak point of his philosophy – as I was saying, if
you approach this thing in itself along a completely different path, the path
we have taken, it is nothing other than the *will*, given our determination
of the expanded scope of this concept. I hope further that after what has
been said, there will be no reservations about recognizing what Plato calls
the *eternal Ideas* or the unchanging forms (εἰδῆ) in the particular levels
of the objectivation of the will that constitutes the in-itself of the world.
These forms are admittedly the principal, though at the same time the
most obscure and paradoxical dogma of his doctrine, and have been a
source of reflection, a bone of contention, an object of ridicule, and also
of admiration for so many and such different minds over the course of
centuries.

201   Now if we consider the will to be the *thing in itself*, and the *Idea* to be
the immediate objecthood of that will on a specific level, then we see that
Kant's thing in itself and Plato's Idea, which for him is the only thing that

^a *Satz*
^b *Princip*
^c *Stein des Anstoßes*

truly is,[a] these two great, obscure paradoxes of the two greatest philosophers of the West, – are certainly not identical, but are nonetheless very closely related and distinct in only one respect. And precisely because these two great paradoxes, for all their inner harmony and affinity,[b] seem so different as a result of the radical differences between their authors, they are in fact the best commentaries on each other, since they are like two completely different paths leading to a *single* goal. – This can be readily explained. What *Kant* said was essentially the following: 'time, space and causality are not determinations of the thing in itself, but instead belong only to its appearance, since they are nothing but the forms of our cognition. And since multiplicity and all arising and passing away are possible only through time, space and causality, it follows that these too belong only to appearances and not at all to things in themselves. But given that our cognition is conditioned by these forms, the whole of experience is only cognition of appearance, not of the thing in itself: and so the laws of experience cannot be considered valid for the thing in itself. This holds true even for our own I,[c] which we can cognize only as appearance, not as what it might be in itself.' This is the meaning and content of Kant's doctrine for the important point at issue. But now Plato says: 'the things of this world, which our senses perceive, have absolutely no true being:[d] *they always become and never are*: they have only relative being, and altogether exist[e] only in and through their relation to each other: which is why their entire existence[f] can just as well be called a non-existence. So they too are not objects of genuine cognition (επιστημη), because there can only be cognition of what exists in and for itself and always in the same way: they on the other hand are the object of mere opinion[g] arising from sensation (δοξα μετ' αισθησεως αλογου). So long as we are restricted to perceiving these, we are like men sitting in a dark cave, who are bound up so tightly that they cannot even turn their heads; they can only see the wall in front of them, which, by the light of a fire burning behind them, shows the shadow images of actual things being carried between themselves and the fire. They cannot see each other or, in fact, themselves, only their shadows on the wall. Their wisdom consists in having learned from experience to predict the sequence of those shadows. However, the

202

---

[a] οντως ον
[b] *Verwandtschaft*
[c] *Ich*
[d] *Seyn*
[e] *sind*
[f] *Daseyn*
[g] *Dafürhalten*

only things deserving the name of truly being[a] (οντως ον), because *they always are and never become or pass out of existence*, are the real archetypes[b] of those shadow images: they are the eternal Ideas, the primordial forms[c] of all things. *Multiplicity* does not apply to them, because each is, in its essence, only one, being the archetype itself whose copies[d] or shadows are all the particular, transitory things of the same sort and with the same name. Neither does *arising or passing away* apply to them because they truly exist, never becoming nor passing away, like their vanishing copies. (Both these negative determinations necessarily presuppose that time, space and causality have neither meaning nor validity for the Ideas, which do not exist in them.) So there can be genuine cognition only of the Ideas, since the object of such cognition can only be what is eternally and in every respect (and thus in itself); it cannot be what is, but then again is not, according to how you look at it.' – This is Plato's doctrine. It is obvious and requires no further proof that both doctrines have precisely the same inner sense, that both explain the visible world as an appearance that is unreal in itself, and that has meaning and borrowed reality only by virtue of what is expressed in it (the thing in itself for the one, the Idea for the other); but this reality, true existence, is, according to both doctrines, utterly foreign to all appearance, even the most universal and essential forms of that appearance. Kant disallowed these forms by grasping them directly in abstract expressions and baldly denying time, space and causality, as mere forms of appearance, to the thing in itself: Plato, on the other hand, did not achieve the highest expression, and only indirectly denied these forms to his Ideas by refusing to the Ideas what is possible only through these forms, namely the multiplicity of things of the same sort as well as the processes of arising and passing away. Although it is not necessary, I will use an example to shed light on this remarkable and important agreement. Suppose a living animal were standing before us. Plato would say: 'This animal does not really exist, but only appears to exist; it is a constant becoming, a relative existence[e] that could just as well be called a non-being as a being.[f] The only thing that truly is, is the Idea that shows itself[g] in this animal, or the animal in itself (αυτο το 9ηριον) which is independent

---

[a] *wahrhaft Seiend*
[b] *Urbilder*
[c] *Urformen*
[d] *Nachbilder*
[e] *Daseyn*
[f] *Seyn*
[g] *abbildet*

of everything and exists in and for itself (καθ᾽ ἑαυτο, αει ὡσαυτως),[a] not becoming, not coming to an end, but rather always existing in the same way (αει ον, και μηδεποτε ουτε γιγνομενον, ουτε απολλυμενον). Now to the extent that we recognize the Idea in this animal, it is irrelevant and a matter of complete indifference whether what we have in front of us is this animal or its ancestor from a thousand years ago, whether it is here or in a distant country, whether it presents itself in this or that manner, place, action, and finally whether it is this or some other individual of its type: all this is unreal and concerns only appearance: the Idea of the animal is the only thing that has true being and is the object of actual cognition.' – Thus Plato. Kant would say something like: 'This animal is an appearance in time, space and causality, which are the sum total of *a priori* conditions of the possibility of experience that lie in our cognitive faculty, and are not determinations of the thing in itself. Therefore, this animal, as we perceive it at this determinate time, in this given place, as an individual that has become and will likewise necessarily pass away in the nexus[b] of experience, i.e. in the chain of causes and effects, is not a thing in itself, but rather an appearance that is valid only with respect to our cognition. To have any cognition of it as it may be in itself, and consequently independently of all determinations in time, space and causality, we would need a mode of cognition different from the only one possible for us, that is, cognition through sense and understanding.'

To bring Kant's language even closer to Plato's, we could also say: time, space and causality are the structure of our intellect by means of which the *one* essence[c] that genuinely exists for each type presents itself to us as a multiplicity of similar beings[d] in endless succession, beings that are always arising anew and passing away again. The view of things made possible by (and according to) this structure is *immanent*; on the other hand, the view that becomes aware of its own condition is the *transcendental*. This transcendental view is found abstractly[e] in the *Critique of Pure Reason*; but in exceptional cases it can arise intuitively as well. This last point is my own addition, which I will try to explain right here, in the Third Book.[3]

If people had ever understood and grasped Kant's doctrine, if people since Kant had really understood and grasped Plato, if they had faithfully and earnestly reflected on the inner sense and content of the doctrines of

---

[a] [Compare Plato, *Phaedo* 78d]
[b] *Zusammenhang*
[c] *Wesen*
[d] *Wesen*
[e] *in abstracto*

both these great masters, instead of throwing around the jargon of the one and parodying the style of the other – then they could not fail finally to notice how much these two great sages are in agreement and that both doctrines clearly mean exactly the same thing and have exactly the same ultimate goal. They would *not* keep comparing Plato with Leibniz, a man on whom his intellect certainly did not rest, much less compare him with a certain well-known and still-living gentleman,*,4 as if determined to mock the shades of the great thinkers of antiquity; rather, they would be much further along than they actually are, or rather they would not have regressed as disgracefully far as they have over the past forty years;5 they would not be led by the nose by one windbag today and another tomorrow. The 19th century in Germany – a century of such significant portents – would not have been inaugurated with philosophical burlesques (similar to ones the ancients performed at family funerals) played out on Kant's grave, exciting the justified scorn of other nations, because these sorts of things are very poorly suited to the serious and even stiff Germans. But the real public for genuine philosophers is so small that even students who can comprehend are meted out sparingly by the centuries. – 'Many carry the *thyrsos*, but few become bacchants.' 'Philosophy therefore fell into disrepute, because people did not engage with it as was due to its honour: because it was not bastards who should have concerned themselves with philosophy, but the rightful heirs.' Plato.a

People only paid attention to words like: 'representations *a priori*, conscious forms of intuition and thinking that are independent of experience, basic concepts of the pure understanding', etc., – and then asked whether in fact Plato's Ideas (which are also basic concepts and moreover are supposed to be recollections of an intuition of truly existing things stemming from before their lifetime) – whether these are not the same as Kant's forms of intuition and thought, which lie *a priori* in our consciousness: these two wildly dissimilar doctrines, the Kantian doctrine of the forms that restrict the individual's cognition to appearance, and the Platonic doctrine of the Ideas, cognition of which explicitly negates these forms, – because these doctrines (which are, to this extent, diametrically opposed) use slightly

205

---

* F. H. Jacobi

a Εισι δη ναρθηκοφοροι μεν πολλοι, βακχοι δε γε παυροι. (*Thyrsigeri quidem multi, Bacchi vero pauci.*) [*Phaedo* 69c–d]. Ἡ ατιμια φιλοσοφια δια ταυτα προσπεπτωκεν, ὁτι ου κατ'αξιαν αυτης ἁπτονται· ου γαρ νοθους εδει ἁπτεσθαι, αλλα γνησιους·: (*Eam ob rem philosophia in infamiam incidit, quod non pro dignitate ipsam attingunt: neque enim a spuriis, sed a legitimis erat attrectanda*) [*Republic*, VII, 535c]

similar expressions, they were closely compared; people deliberated and debated whether they constituted a single doctrine, and ultimately discovered that they were not the same after all, deciding that there were no points of agreement between Plato's doctrine of Ideas and Kant's critique of reason.* But enough about this.

§ 32

Despite the inner agreement between Kant and Plato, and despite the fact that both men have the same goal in mind and are compelled and inspired by the same world-view to do philosophy, we do not believe, given our discussion to this point, that Idea and thing in itself are simply one and the same: for us rather, the Idea is only the immediate and therefore adequate objecthood of the thing in itself, which is however itself the *will*,   206 to the extent that it (the will) has not yet been objectified and become representation. This is because, just as Kant claimed, the thing in itself is supposed to be free of all the forms that are attached to cognition as such: and (as will be shown in the appendix) Kant was simply mistaken in failing to consider being-an-object-for-a-subject as one of these forms, and indeed before all others, since precisely this is the first and most universal form of all appearance, i.e. representation; he should therefore have explicitly denied that his thing in itself was an object, as this would have saved him from that great inconsistency, an inconsistency that was discovered quite early. By contrast, the Platonic Idea is necessarily an object, something cognized,[a] a representation and, for precisely this reason (but for only this reason), distinct from the thing in itself. It has merely shed the subordinate forms of appearance (which are all comprehended under the principle of sufficient reason) – or rather it has not yet entered into these forms; but it has retained the first and most general form, that of representation in general, of being an object for a subject. It is the forms that are subordinated to representation (whose universal expression is the principle of sufficient reason) that multiply the Idea into particular and transient individuals, and as far as the Idea is concerned, it is a matter of complete indifference how many of these individuals there are. The principle of sufficient reason is thus the form into which the Idea enters when it comes under the cognition of the subject as individual. The individual thing that appears in

---

* See for instance *Immanuel Kant: ein Denkmal* [*Immanuel Kant, A Memorial*] by Fr. Bouterweck, p. 49, – and Buhle's *Geschichte der Philosophie* [*History of Philosophy*], Vol. 6, pp. 802–15 and 823.

[a] *ein Erkanntes*

conformity with the principle of sufficient reason is thus only an indirect objectivation of the thing in itself (which is the will), and the Idea stands between this individual and the will as the only immediate objecthood of the will, since it has not taken on any other form belonging to cognition as such apart from that of representation in general, i.e. of being an object for a subject. Thus it alone is also the most *adequate objecthood* of the will or the thing in itself, and is itself the whole thing in itself, but in the form of representation: and here is where the ground of the great agreement between Plato and Kant lies, although speaking very strictly, they are not talking about the same thing. Individual things do not constitute a wholly adequate objecthood of the will; rather, objecthood is already obscured by the forms whose common expression is the principle of sufficient reason, 207 and which are conditions for cognition as it is possible for the individual as such. – If it were permissible to draw conclusions from an impossible premise, we would in fact no longer recognize particular things, events, change or multiplicity, but only Ideas, only the steps on the ladder of the objectivation of that one will, of the true thing in itself, grasped in pure, unclouded cognition, and consequently, our world would be a *Nunc stans*,ª – all this would be the case if, as the subject of cognition, we were not at the same time individuals, i.e. if our intuition were not mediated by a body whose affections constitute its starting-point, and which is itself only willing made concrete, objecthood of the will, and thus an object among other objects, and as such can only enter into cognitive consciousness in the forms of the principle of sufficient reason, consequently already presupposing and hence introducing time and all the other forms that this principle expresses. Time is merely the scattered and dismembered perspective that an individual beingᵇ has of the Ideas that are outside of time and therefore *eternal*: Plato thus says that time is the moving image of eternity: αιωνος εικων κινητη ὁ χρονος.*,⁶

§ 33

The only type of cognition that we as individuals possess is subordinate to the principle of sufficient reason, which excludes cognition of Ideas; as a result, it is certain that, if it is possible for us to raise ourselves from cognition of particular things to cognition of the Ideas, this can only take

---

* See chapter 29 of the second volume. [Greek extract here is after *Timaeus*, 37d]

ª [A persisting Now, a continuing present: Albertus Magnus, *Summa theologiae*, I, 5, 22]
ᵇ *Wesen*

place by means of an alteration in the subject that corresponds to and is analogous with that radical change in the whole nature of the object, and by virtue of which the subject, in so far as it has cognition of an Idea, is no longer an individual.

We may remember from the previous Book that cognition in general belongs to the objectivation of the will on its higher levels, and that the sensibility, nerves and brain are, just like the other parts of organic beings, expressions of the will at this degree of its objecthood, and consequently that the representation which arises through them also serves the will as a means (μηχανη) for achieving its now complicated (πολυτελεστερα) ends of maintaining a creature[a] with diverse needs. Originally and essentially therefore cognition is entirely in the service of the will, and just as the immediate object (which becomes the starting-point for cognition through application of the principle of causality) is nothing but objectified will, so all cognition that follows the principle of sufficient reason also maintains more or less of a relationship to the will. This is because the individual finds his body to be one object among the many to which it entertains a variety of relationships and connections[b] in accordance with the principle of sufficient reason, and observation of these always leads back (whether the road is a long or a short one) to his body, and thus to his will. Since it is the principle of sufficient reason that places the objects in this relationship to the body and thus to the will, the cognition that serves this principle will similarly only aim to come to know of objects just those connections posited by the principle of sufficient reason, and thus pursue their various relationships in time, space and causality. This is because it is only through these that the object is of *interest* to the individual, i.e. that it has a connection to will. That is why cognition in the service of the will does not have cognition of objects beyond their relations, and has cognition of objects only as far as they exist at this time, in this place, under these circumstances, through these causes, with these effects, and, in a word, as individual things: if we were to remove all these relations, then objects would disappear as well for such cognition, precisely because it has nothing other than this to cognize in them. – Nor can we conceal that the sciences also view things in essentially the same way, namely as nothing other than relations, connections of time, of space, the causes of natural alterations, the comparison of shapes, motives for events, and thus simply relations. What differentiates science from ordinary cognition is merely its

208

---

[a] *Wesen*

[b] [In this passage we translate *Beziehung* as 'relationship', *Verhältniß* as 'connection', and *Relation* as 'relation'. These distinctions are not always observed elsewhere in the translation]

form, systematic nature, the way it facilitates cognition by assembling all particulars under universals through subordination to concepts, thereby allowing cognition to attain completeness. All relations themselves possess only a relative existence: for instance, all being in time is a non-being as well, because time is just what enables the same thing to assume opposite qualities: thus every appearance in time is, in turn, *not*: because what distinguishes its beginning from its end is only time itself, something essentially vanishing, relative, and not enduring, here called permanence.[a] But time is the most general form of all objects of cognition in the service of the will, and the fundamental type of the remaining forms of cognition.

For the most part, cognition always remains subordinated to the service of the will, as it in fact developed in this service, and indeed sprang from the will as the head springs from the trunk of the body. With animals this servitude of cognition to the will can never be overcome.[b] With human beings, such an overcoming appears only as an exception, as we will now be considering more closely. This distinction between humans and animals is expressed outwardly by the differing relationships between the head[c] and the trunk. In the lower[7] animals, the two are still completely united: in all of them, the head faces the ground where the objects of the will can be found: even in the higher animals the head and trunk are still much more unified than in humans, whose head[d] seems to be placed freely on the body, borne by it without serving it. This prerogative of humans is displayed by the Apollo Belvedere to the highest degree: the far-seeing[e] head of the god of the Muses sits so freely on its shoulders that it seems entirely wrenched away from the body and no longer subject to its cares.

§ 34

As we have said, it is possible – although only in exceptional cases – to go from the ordinary cognition of particular things to cognition of the Idea. This transition occurs suddenly when cognition tears itself free from the service of the will so that the subject ceases to be merely individual and now becomes the pure, will-less subject of cognition, no longer concerned with relations following the principle of sufficient reason but instead resting and

---

[a] *Dauer*
[b] *aufzuheben*
[c] *Kopf*
[d] *Haupt*
[e] *weitumherblickende*

becoming absorbed in[a] a steady contemplation of the object presented, aside from its inter-connections[b] with any other object.

This requires a detailed explanation if it is to become clear, and the reader must temporarily suspend his astonishment until it dies away of its own accord, which will happen once he has grasped the complete thought being communicated in this work.

When elevated by strength of mind to stop viewing things in the ordinary way, no longer led by the forms of the principle of sufficient reason to pursue merely the relations between things (which in the end always aims at their relation to our own will), if we stop considering the Where, When, Why and Wherefore of things but simply and exclusively consider the *What*, if we do not allow our consciousness to become engrossed by abstract thinking, concepts of reason; but if, instead of all this, we devote the entire power of our mind to intuition and immerse ourselves in this entirely, letting the whole of consciousness be filled with peaceful contemplation of the natural object[c] that is directly present, a landscape, a tree, a cliff, a building, or whatever it might be, and, according to a suggestive figure of speech,[d] we *lose* ourselves in this object completely, i.e. we forget our individuality, our will, and continue to exist only as pure subject, the clear mirror of the object,[e] so that it is as if the object[f] existed on its own, without anyone to perceive it, and we can no longer separate the intuited from the intuition[8] as the two have become one, and the whole of consciousness is completely filled and engrossed by a single intuitive image – if, therefore, the object[g] is in this manner removed from any relation to things outside of itself, and the subject is removed from any relation to the will, then what we thus cognize is no longer the individual thing as such, but rather the *Idea*, the eternal form, the immediate objecthood of the will at this level: and this is precisely how someone gripped by this intuition is at the same time no longer an individual: the individual has lost himself in this very intuition: rather, he is the *pure*, will-less, painless, timeless *subject of cognition*. All this may seem quite peculiar at present (and I know very well that it confirms Thomas Paine's observation[9] that 'from the sublime to the   211

---

[a] *aufgehen in*
[b] *Zusammenhange*
[c] *Gegenstand*
[d] *nach einer sinnvollen Deutschen Redensart*
[e] *Objekt*
[f] *Gegenstand*
[g] *Objekt*

ridiculous there is only one step'ᵃ) but it will become gradually clearer and less surprising in the sequel. It is also what Spinoza had in mind when he wrote: 'the mind is eternal to the extent that it conceives things under the form of eternity',ᵇ (*Ethics*, V, Prop. 31, Scholium).*,¹⁰ In this kind of contemplation the particular thing instantly becomes the *Idea* of its species and the intuiting individual becomes *the pure subject of cognition*. The individual as such has cognition only of particularᶜ things; the pure subject of cognition only of Ideas. This is because the individual is the subject of cognition in its relation to a certain particular appearance of the will it serves. This particular appearance of the will is, as such, subordinated to the principle of sufficient reason in all its forms: all cognition related to this individual thus follows the principle of sufficient reason as well, and since this kind of cognition only ever has relations as its object, no other kind is suitable for the will's purpose. As such, the cognizing individual and the particular thing he has cognition of are links in the chain of causes and effects, always located in some place and at some time. The pure subject of cognition and its correlate, the Idea, have left behind all those forms of the principle of sufficient reason: time, place, the cognizing individual and the individual he has cognition of have no meaning for it. Only when a cognizing individual raises himself to pure subject of cognition in the manner described, and in so doing raises the object observed to an Idea, does the *world as representation* step forward, purely and in its entirety, completely objectifying the will, since only the Idea is its *adequate objecthood*. This includes in itself and in the same way both object and

212   subject, since these constitute its only form: but they both have equal weight in the Idea; and just as even here the objectᵈ is nothing but the representation of the subject, so the subject also, being entirely absorbed into the intuited object,ᵉ has become this object itself, so that its entire consciousness is no longer anything but this object's clearest image. This very consciousness in fact constitutes the entire *world as representation*, if we imagine all the Ideas, or levels of the objecthood of the will, passing

* For clarification of the mode of cognition under discussion I also recommend what he says in the same work at Book II, Prop. 40, Schol., 2, and Book V, Prop. 25 to 38 about the *cognitio tertii generis, sive intuitiva* [third form of cognition, or intuitive cognition], and most especially Prop. 29, Schol.; Prop. 36, Schol., and Prop. 38, Proof and Scholium.

ᵃ *du sublime au ridicule il n'y a qu'un pas* [See *The Age of Reason*, Part II, Conclusion: 'When authors and critics talk of the sublime, they see not how nearly it borders on the ridiculous']
ᵇ *mens aeterna est, quatenus res sub aeternitatis specie concipit*
ᶜ *einzelne*
ᵈ *Objekt*
ᵉ *Gegenstand*

through it in succession. In all times and all places,[a] particular things are nothing but Ideas multiplied by means of the principle of sufficient reason (the form of cognition for individuals as such), a process that obscures their pure objecthood. When the Idea emerges, subject and object can no longer be distinguished within it because the Idea, the adequate objecthood of the will, the genuine world as representation, arises only to the extent that subject and object reciprocally fill and completely permeate each other; in just the same way, the individual cognizing and the individual thing thus cognized are, as things in themselves, indistinguishable. This is because if we abstract completely from that genuine *world as representation*, nothing remains except the *world as will*. The will is the in-itself of the Idea, which completely objectifies it; it is also the in-itself of the particular thing, and of the individual cognizing it, which together objectify it incompletely. As will, outside of representation and all of its forms, it is one and the same thing in the object of contemplation and in the individual who soars upwards in this contemplation, becoming conscious of himself as pure subject: the two are thus not in themselves distinct, because in themselves they are the will, which cognizes itself here. Multiplicity and difference exist only as the manner in which they are cognized by the will, i.e. only in appearance, by virtue of its form, which is the principle of sufficient reason. Without the object, without the representation, I am not a cognizing subject but rather mere blind will; and similarly, without me as the subject of cognition, the thing cognized is not an object but rather mere will, blind urge.[b] In itself, i.e. outside of representation, this will is one and the same thing as my own will: only in the world as representation, whose form is always minimally that of subject and object, are we separate from each other as the cognizing individual and the individual cognized. As soon as cognition, the world of representation, is suppressed, absolutely nothing is left but mere will, blind urge. The fact that it retains its objecthood and becomes representation presupposes at once both subject and object:[c] but the fact that this objecthood is the pure, complete and adequate objecthood of the will presupposes the object as Idea, free from the forms of the principle of sufficient reason, and the subject as pure subject of cognition, free from individuality and servitude to the will.

213

Now anyone who has become so engrossed and lost in the intuition of nature that he continues to exist only as the pure, cognitive subject will thus be immediately aware that as such he is the condition, which is to say

[a] *Räume*
[b] *Drang*
[c] *setzt, mit Einem Schlage, sowohl Subjekt als Objekt*

the bearer, of the world of all objective being,[a] because this now presents itself as dependent on him. He thus draws nature into himself, so that he feels it only as an accident of his being.[b] It is in this sense that *Byron* said:

> Are not the mountains, waves and skies, a part
> Of me and of my soul, as I of them?[c]

But how could anyone who feels this way consider himself absolutely transient in contrast to everlasting nature? He will rather be seized with the consciousness of what the *Upanishad* of the *Veda* expresses: 'I am all these creations taken together, and there is no other being besides me',[d] (*Oupnek'hat*, I, 122).*,[II]

§ 35

If we are to acquire deeper insight into the essence of the world, it is absolutely necessary to learn to distinguish the will as thing in itself from its adequate objecthood, and the different levels on which this objecthood emerges with increasing clarity and perfection, i.e. the Ideas themselves, from the mere appearance of the Ideas in the forms of the principle of sufficient reason, the individual's constricted[e] mode of cognition. Then we will agree with Plato when he accords genuine being to the Ideas alone, while granting only an apparent, dream-like existence to things in space and time, to this world that is real for the individual. Then we will realize how the same Idea manifests itself in so many different appearances and presents its essence to cognizing individuals only bit by bit, one aspect after the other. We will then also differentiate the Idea itself from the manner in which its appearance comes to be observed by the individual, knowing that the former is essential and the latter inessential. We will consider this using examples from the least significant cases and then from the most significant. – When clouds drift, the figures they form are not essential to the clouds themselves, which are indifferent to such figures:

214

---

* For this see chapter 30 of the second volume.

[a] *Daseyn*
[b] *Wesen*
[c] *Childe Harold*, III, 75 [Schopenhauer quotes the lines in English and gives a translation in a footnote]
[d] *Hae omnes creaturae in totum ego sum, et praeter me aliud ens non est* [Deussen notes that the corresponding passage is *Brihadâranyaka Upanishad*, I, 4, 1, but that no wording there is exactly equivalent to the Latin version in the volume *Oupnek'hat*. The Persian editors of the text on which *Oupnek'hat* is based had the tendency to run together passages from different places in the *Upanishads*]
[e] *befangene*

but the fact that they are buoyant vapours which are pressed together, driven away, spread out, and torn apart by the impact of the wind, this is their nature, it is the essence of the forces that objectify themselves in clouds, it is the Idea: each of the figures formed by the clouds exists only for the individual observer. – The stream that tumbles over the stones is indifferent to the eddies, waves and masses of foam that can be seen in it, these being inessential: the fact that it obeys gravity, and behaves as an inelastic, completely mobile, formless, transparent fluid is its essence and is, *if cognized intuitively*, the Idea: the forms it gives rise to (the eddies, waves and foam) exist only for us, to the extent that we have cognition as individuals. – The ice on the window-pane forms crystals according to the laws of crystallization, which reveal the essence of the natural forces that emerge here and present the Idea; but the images of trees and flowers formed by the ice are inessential and exist only for us. – What appears in clouds, streams and crystals is the weakest echo of the will that emerges more perfectly in plants, still more perfectly in animals, and most perfectly of all in human beings. But only what is *essential* in all these levels of its objectivation constitutes the *Idea*: by contrast, the unfolding of the Idea, its separation into a variety of multifarious appearances in the forms of the principle of sufficient reason – this is not essential to the Idea, it lies only in the individual mode of cognition and is real for this alone. Now the same thing necessarily holds for the unfolding of that Idea which constitutes the most complete objecthood of the will: i.e. the history of the human race, the thronging of events, the changing times, the many shapes that the form of human life takes in different countries and centuries – all this is only the accidental form of appearance of the Idea; it does not belong to the Idea itself, in which alone is found the adequate objecthood of the will, but only to the appearance, which comes under individual cognition, and is as alien, inessential and indifferent to the Idea itself as the figures are to the clouds that show them, the shapes of the eddies and foam are to the stream, and the images of trees and flowers are to the ice.

For anyone who has really comprehended this and knows how to distinguish the will from the Idea and the Idea from its appearance, worldly events will not be meaningful in and of themselves, but only to the extent that they are characters in which the Idea of humanity can be read. People like this will not believe, as others do, that time can produce anything that is actually new or meaningful, that something categorically[a] real can come into existence in or through time, or even that time itself as a whole has a

215

---

[a] *schlechthin*

beginning or end, plan or developmental tendency,[a] or has for its ultimate
goal something like the highest perfection (according to their ideas) of the
latest generation that has been around for thirty years. These people are as
unlikely to join Homer in setting up a whole Olympia full of gods to guide
events in time as they are to join Ossian in considering the figures in the
clouds to be individual beings, since, in relation to the Idea that appears
in each, as we have said, the one is about as meaningful as the other. In
the diverse forms of human life and the ceaseless change of events, they
will regard only the Idea as enduring and essential, since the will to life
has its most perfect objecthood in the Idea, whose different aspects are
demonstrated in the qualities, passions, errors and strengths of the human
race, in selfishness,[b] hatred, love, fear, courage, frivolity, stupidity, slyness,
wit, genius, etc., all of which, converging and coalescing in a thousand
different shapes (individuals), ceaselessly stage the history of the world in
both large and small scale, so that it is very much the same whether it was
set in motion by matches or by crowns. They will find in the end that
216 the world is like Gozzi's dramas, always populated by the same characters
with the same plans and the same destinies: although naturally the motives
and events differ from play to play; nevertheless, the spirit of the events
is the same: the characters of one play know nothing of the proceedings
in the other, although they had themselves acted in it: and so, after all
that was experienced in the earlier plays, Pantalone is no more nimble or
generous, Tartaglia no more conscientious, Brighella no more courageous
and Columbine no more modest. –

If we were ever given a clear view into the realm of possibility and all
the chains of causes and effects, if the spirit of the earth[c] were to rise up
and show us an image of the most excellent individuals, the heroes and
illuminators of the world, people who chance had destroyed before the full
force of their vigour could be felt, – and if it were then to show us the great
events that would have altered world history and ushered in periods of the
highest culture and enlightenment, but that had been nipped in the bud
by the blindest chance and the most meaningless accidents, and finally if
it were to show us the majestic strength of great individuals, strength that
would have caused whole ages to bear fruit had not these individuals been
led by mistakes or passions or forced by necessity to squander it uselessly
on unworthy and unfruitful objects, or even to fritter it away in games: – if
we were to see all this, we would shudder and grieve over the lost treasures

[a] *Entwicklung*
[b] *Eigennutz*
[c] *der Erdgeist*

of entire ages. But the spirit of the earth would smile and say: 'The source from which both the individuals and their strength flow is inexhaustible and infinite, like time and space: because these, just like these forms of all appearance, are also only the appearance, the visibility of the will. No finite measure can exhaust that endless source: and so infinity will always stand open, undiminished, for the return of any event or work that was strangled in its infancy. True loss is just as impossible as true gain in this world of appearance. Only the will exists: it, the thing in itself, is the source of all those appearances. Its self-knowledge[a] and its consequent decision to affirm or negate is the only event in itself.'*

217

§36

History traces the thread of events: it is pragmatic to the extent that it derives them in accordance with the law of motivation, a law that determines the appearing will where it is illuminated by cognition. On the lowest levels of its objecthood, where the will still operates without cognition, natural science in the form of aetiology is concerned with the laws of the alterations of its appearances, and natural science in the form of morphology is concerned with what is permanent in its appearances; approaching its almost infinite task with the help of concepts that include the universal in order to deduce the particular from it. Finally, mathematics is concerned with the mere forms (i.e. time and space) in which the Ideas appear pulled apart into multiplicity, so they can be cognized by the subject as individual. All these, which are collectively known as science, follow the principle of sufficient reason in its different forms, and their theme remains appearance, its laws, connections and the relations that arise from these. – But now what mode of cognition is concerned with the truly essential aspect of the world alone, an aspect that exists outside and independently of all relations, the true content[b] of the world's appearances, an essence that is not subjected to change and is thus cognized at all times with the same degree of truth, – in a word, the *Ideas*, which are the immediate and adequate objecthood of the thing in itself, the will? – It is *art*, the work of genius. Art repeats the eternal Ideas grasped through pure contemplation, it repeats what is essential and enduring in all the appearances of the world, and, depending on the medium in which it repeats the Ideas, it

---

* This last sentence cannot be understood without familiarity with the following Book.

[a] *Selbsterkenntniß*
[b] *Gehalt*

takes the form of either the visual arts,[a] poetry[b] or music; art originates in the cognition of the Ideas alone; and its only goal is the communication of this cognition. – Science, following the restless and insubstantial current of the four types of ground and consequent, is always ushered onward with each goal it attains, and can no more find a final goal or complete satisfaction than we can walk to the point where the clouds touch the horizon; art, on the other hand, is always at its goal because it wrests the object of its contemplation out from the current of worldly affairs,[c] and the object stands before it in isolation: and this particular thing, which played such a vanishingly small role in that current of worldly affairs, becomes for art a representative of a whole, an equivalent of what is multiplied to infinity in space and time: thus art remains at rest with this particular: it stops the wheel of time: relations vanish for it: only what is essential, the Idea, is its object. – Thus we can directly describe it as *the way of regarding things independently from the principle of sufficient reason*, as opposed to the way of regarding things that closely follows this principle, which is the path of experience and science. This latter way of regarding things can be compared to an infinite horizontal line; the former can be compared to a vertical line that bisects it at any given point. The rational way of regarding things follows the principle of sufficient reason, and it alone is valid and useful in practical life as it is in science: a genius's way of regarding things turns away from the content of the principle of sufficient reason, and it alone is valid and useful in art. The first way of regarding things is that of Aristotle, the second is, on the whole, that of Plato. The first is like a violent storm that drives onward without a starting point or a goal, bending, moving and tearing up everything it encounters; the second is like a peaceful ray of sunlight that cuts through the path of this storm, completely unmoved by it. The first is like the countless, violently moving drops of the waterfall, which always change and do not stand still for a single instant: the second is like the rainbow that rests peacefully on top of this raging tumult. – The Ideas are grasped only through what we already described as a pure contemplation[d] that is completely absorbed by its object, and the essence of *genius* consists simply in the prevalence of a capacity for such contemplation. Now since this calls for a complete forgetting of one's own person and its relationships, *genius*[e] is nothing

---

[a] *bildende Kunst*
[b] *Poesie*
[c] *Strohme des Weltlaufs*
[d] *Kontemplation*
[e] *Genialität*

other than the most perfect *objectivity*,[a] i.e. an objective orientation of the mind, as opposed to a subjective orientation that is directed to one's own person, i.e. the will. Accordingly, genius is the capacity to maintain oneself in a purely intuitive state, to lose oneself in intuition and to withdraw cognition that originally only existed in its service to the will from this   219 service, i.e. temporarily to put one's interests, willing and purposes entirely out of mind, and consequently, fully to relinquish one's personality in order to remain as the *pure cognitive subject*, the clear eye of the world: and this not just momentarily, but for as long and with as much clarity of mind[b] as is necessary to repeat what has been grasped in the form of well-considered art and 'what floats in wavering appearance to fasten down in enduring thoughts'.[c] – For genius to emerge in an individual, it is as if a degree of cognitive power had been granted to him that is far in excess of the amount required for the service of the individual will; and, when liberated, this surplus of cognition now turns into the subject purified of all will, the bright mirror of the essence of the world. – This explains why individuals of genius tend to be lively to the point of distraction:[d] the present is rarely enough for them because it does not fully engage their consciousness: this is what gives them their restless zeal; they are constantly on the look-out for new objects that would be worth considering, and they long, almost always in vain, for the company of creatures similar to themselves, equals in whom they can really confide; in the meantime, ordinary mortals are completely engaged with and satisfied by the ordinary present, entering into it and finding people like themselves everywhere, deriving a sort of contentment from everyday life that is denied to genius. – Imagination[e] has been recognized as an essential feature of genius, and the two are sometimes even considered identical: the first conclusion is correct but not the second. Since the objects of genius as such are the eternal Ideas, the permanent, essential forms of the world and all its appearances, and since cognition of the Idea is necessarily intuitive and not abstract, the genius's cognition would be restricted to the Ideas of objects actually present to him, and would depend on the chain of circumstances that leads him to these objects, if imagination did not broaden his horizon far beyond what he actually experiences personally, and enable him to take the few things that come into his actual apperception and construct everything

[a] *Objektivität*
[b] *Besonnenheit*
[c] [Goethe, *Faust* I, 348–9 slightly altered by Schopenhauer]
[d] *Unruhe*
[e] *Phantasie*

220 else, thus allowing almost all the possible scenes of life to pass through him. Moreover, actual objects are almost always very deficient exemplars of the Idea presented in them: hence the genius needs imagination in order to see in things not what nature actually created,[a] but rather what it was trying unsuccessfully to create, a failure due to that struggle between its forms that we discussed in the previous Book. We will return to this later when we examine sculpture. Thus, imagination broadens, as much in quality as in quantity, the genius's field of vision beyond the objects that are actually presented to him. This is why an uncommonly strong imagination is the companion – in fact the condition – of genius. But the converse is not true: the former is not a sign of the latter since even people without any genius at all can have a great deal of imagination. An actual object can be regarded in two opposite ways: purely objectively, the way a genius does, grasping its Idea; or ordinarily, simply in its relations to other objects and to one's own will in accordance with the principle of sufficient reason; similarly, a figment of the imagination[b] can be intuited in two ways as well: regarded in the first way, it becomes a means for cognizing the Idea (and the artwork is the communication of this Idea): in the second case, the figment is used to create day-dreams[c] that gratify the individual's mood and conceit, momentarily deceiving and amusing him so that all he really comes to know are the relations between the figments of the imagination. Someone who plays this game is a day-dreamer:[d] he will easily blend the images of his solitary self-amusement together with reality, for which he will then be unfit: he might write down the phantasmagoria[e] of his imagination, where they become the ordinary novels of all genres, and entertain people like himself and the general public, since the reader pictures himself in the place of the hero and then finds the description very 'pleasant'.[f]

The ordinary person, a factory product of nature that is made each day by the thousand, is, as we have said, not remotely capable of maintaining an attitude that is fully disinterested[g] (in every sense of the term), even if he can assume such an attitude to begin with: yet this attitude is that of true contemplation.[h] The ordinary person can only pay attention to things
221 that stand in some sort of relation to his will, even if it is a very indirect

---

[a] *gebildet*
[b] *ein Phantasma*
[c] *Luftschlösser*
[d] *ein Phantast*
[e] *Gaukeleien*
[f] *gemütlich*
[g] *uninteressierte Betrachtung*
[h] *Beschaulichkeit*

one. The abstract concept of something is sufficient and even (for the most part) more suitable for this perspective, which only ever affords cognition of relations; so the ordinary person does not linger for very long with mere intuition, or gaze too long at an object; rather, whenever something presents itself to him, he quickly looks for a concept to bring it under, just as a lazy person[a] looks for a chair and then loses interest in it. That is why he finishes with everything so quickly, with artworks, with beautiful objects in nature, and with the truly and universally significant view of all the scenes of life. But he does not take the time: he looks only to his own course through life, or at most to anything that could be on his course, which is to say topographical signs in the broadest sense: he does not spend any time observing life itself as such. The genius, on the other hand, has such an excess of cognitive power that it can be temporarily withdrawn from service to his will; accordingly, he takes the time to observe life itself, and strives to grasp the Idea of each thing, not its relations to other things: as a result he often fails to think about his own course of life, and generally pursues it rather clumsily. For the ordinary person, the cognitive faculty is a lantern that lights the way, while for the genius it is the sun that reveals the world. Such different ways of looking at life are quickly evident even in outward appearances. The man in which genius lives and works is easily distinguished by his gaze; both lively and steadfast, it bears the character of thoughtfulness,[b] of contemplation,[c] as we can see in the portraits of the few faces belonging to the geniuses that nature now and then brings forth among the untold millions: on the other hand, a prying look[d] – the true opposite of contemplation – can be seen in the gazes of other people, when they are not simply dull or commonplace, as they usually are. Accordingly, the 'expression of genius' in a face consists in the decided preponderance of cognition over will that is visible in it, and consequently also expresses cognition that is unrelated to willing, i.e. *pure cognition*. By contrast, in ordinary faces the expression of willing is dominant, and you can see that   222 cognition only ever comes into action under the impulse of willing, and is thus directed exclusively towards motives.[12]

Since cognition in a genius (i.e. cognition of the Idea) does not follow the principle of sufficient reason, and since cognition that does follow this principle confers cleverness and rationality in the affairs of life and gives rise to science, geniuses suffer from defects arising from neglect of

[a]   *Träge*
[b]   *Beschaulichkeit*
[c]   *Kontemplation*
[d]   *das Spähen*

that latter mode of cognition. Nonetheless we must add the qualification that what I say in this context is true only to the extent and during the time that they are really in the grips of the genius's mode of cognition, and this is by no means the case for every moment of their lives, since the great, though spontaneous exertion required for an apprehension of the Ideas that is free of the will necessarily wears off, and there are long intervals in which geniuses are rather similar to ordinary people in both their merits and their flaws. This is why people have always considered the activity[a] of genius as inspiration (as in fact the name itself indicates), the activity of a superhuman being distinct from the individual himself and which takes possession of the individual only periodically. Genius's aversion to paying attention to the content of the principle of sufficient reason will show itself initially in relation to the ground of being as an aversion to mathematics; mathematics considers the most general forms of appearance, space and time (which are themselves only forms of the principle of sufficient reason), and is thus the complete opposite of the way of looking at things[b] that disregards all relations and looks immediately and exclusively for the content of appearance, for the Idea that expresses itself there. Besides, genius will resist the logical method of mathematics, since this shuts out genuine insight and is unsatisfying; this method consists merely of a chain of inferences that presents itself according to the principle of the ground of cognition, and calls on memory more than any other power of the intellect in order to constantly keep in mind all the earlier principles that serve as premises. In addition, experience has confirmed that the great geniuses of art have not had any aptitude for mathematics: nobody has ever

223   excelled in both at the same time. Alfieri claims that he was never even able to comprehend Euclid's fourth theorem. Goethe has been reproached often enough by the ignorant opponents of his doctrine of colours for his lack of familiarity with mathematics; of course in this case, where it is not a matter of calculations or measurements according to hypothetical data but rather immediate cognition of cause and effect based in the understanding,[c] this reproach was so slanted and off-target that it put into sharp relief the total lack of judgement on the part of these opponents just as much as the rest of their Midas remarks did. The fact that even today, almost half a century after the appearance of Goethe's theory of colours, Newton's nonsense[d] remains in undisturbed possession of the professorships even in Germany,

[a] *Wirken*
[b] *Betrachtung*
[c] *unmittelbare Verstandeserkenntniß der Ursache und Wirkung*
[d] *Flausen*

and people still talk seriously about the seven types of homogeneous light and their different degrees of refraction,[a] – one day this will be numbered among the great intellectual peculiarities[b] of people in general and Germans in particular.[13] – The reason just given also explains the equally well-known fact that superior mathematicians, for their part, have little sensitivity to beautiful works of art, a fact that is expressed particularly naïvely in the well-known anecdote about the French mathematician who, after reading through Racine's *Iphigenia*, shrugged his shoulders and asked: 'What does that prove?'[c] – Further, since a firm grasp of relations in accordance with the laws of causality and motivation really does constitute shrewdness, and the genius's cognition is not directed to relations, then a shrewd person, in so far as and at the time he is being shrewd, will not be a genius, and a genius, in so far as and at the time he is being a genius, will not be shrewd. – Finally, intuitive cognition, the field that contains the Ideas entirely, is directly opposed to rational or abstract cognition, which is guided by the principle of sufficient reason of cognition.[d] It is a well-known fact that great genius is seldom paired with a preponderance of rationality; rather, the converse is generally the case and geniuses are often subject to violent affects and irrational passions. Still, the explanation[e] for this is not the weakness of reason, but rather in part the extraordinary energy of the whole appearance of the will that the individual of genius is, and that expresses itself through the intensity of all his acts of the will, and in part the prevalence of intuitive cognition (through sense and understanding) over abstract cognition, and hence the decisive orientation towards the intuitive, whose highly energetic impression so eclipses the colourless concepts for the genius that the former rather than the latter becomes the guide for his actions, and these become correspondingly irrational: this is why the present always makes a very powerful impression on geniuses and goads them on towards thoughtlessness, affect and passion. And, since a portion of their cognition has been withdrawn from the service of the will, they will, in the course of a conversation, not think so much about the person they are speaking *to*, as the things they are speaking *about*, which they bear vividly in mind: thus they will judge or narrate too objectively for their own good and talk about things that it would be shrewder not to mention, etc. Finally, they are inclined to monologues and

224

[a] *Brechbarkeit*
[b] *Charakterzügen*
[c] *Qu'est-ce que cela prouve?*
[d] *Satz vom Grunde des Erkennens*
[e] *Grund*

in general can exhibit many weaknesses that actually verge on madness. It has been frequently noted that genius[a] and madness are two sides of the same coin and blend into each other, and poetic enthusiasm[b] has even been called a type of madness:[c] Horace calls it 'amiable madness'[d] (*Odes*, III, 4), and Wieland 'sweet madness'[e] at the beginning of *Oberon*.[14] Even Aristotle, according to a passage in Seneca (*On Tranquility of the Mind*,[f] 15, 16) said: 'There is no great genius without an admixture of madness.'[g] Plato expressed this in the myth of the dark cave cited above (*Republic* VII) by saying that those who have been outside the cave and seen the true sunlight and actually existing things (the Ideas) can no longer see inside the cave because their eyes have become unaccustomed to the darkness; they can no longer properly recognize the shadow images down below, and will be ridiculed for their mistakes by the others who have never been out of the cave and away from these shadow images. In the *Phaedrus* he also says (p. 317) that there could be no true poets without a certain madness, and in fact (p. 327) that anyone who recognizes the eternal Ideas in transient things will seem mad.[h] Cicero too says: 'Democritus claims that there can be no great poets without madness, and Plato says the same' (*On Divination*, I, 37).[i] And finally, Pope says:

225

> Great wits to madness sure are near allied,
> And thin partitions do their bounds divide[j,15]

Particularly instructive in this regard is Goethe's *Torquato Tasso*, where he presents us not only with the suffering and essential martyrdom of genius as such, but also with its continual transition into madness. Finally, the fact that genius and madness are in direct contact is confirmed on the one hand by the biographies of men of great genius, such as Rousseau, Byron,[16] Alfieri, and by anecdotes from lives of others; but, on the other hand, I must mention that in frequent visits to madhouses I have found individual subjects with unmistakably great talents, whose genius was clearly visible through their madness, although in these cases madness retained the upper

---

[a] *Genialität*
[b] *dichterische Begeisterung*
[c] *Wahnsinn*
[d] *amabilis insania* [*Odes* III, 4, 5–6]
[e] *holden Wahnsinn*
[f] *De Tranquillitate Animi* [correct reference is 17, 10]
[g] *Nullum magnum ingenium sine mixtura dementiae fuit*
[h] [*Phaedrus* 245a and 249d]
[i] *Negat enim, sine furore, Democritus, quemquam poëtam magnum esse posse; quod idem dicit Plato* (*de divin*[*atione*]. I, 37 [80]) [See also Plato, *Phaedrus*, 245a]
[j] [In fact this is from Dryden: *Absalom and Achitophel*, I, 163]

hand entirely. This cannot be ascribed to chance, because on the one hand, there are relatively very few people who are mad, and on the other hand, genius is rare beyond all ordinary measures and appears only as the greatest exception in nature; we can convince ourselves of this merely by counting the really great geniuses produced in all of civilized Europe during the whole of antiquity and modernity (although only those who have left behind works that have retained an enduring value for humanity are to be included), – counting these individuals and comparing their number with the 250 million[17] who, by renewing themselves every thirty years, constantly populate Europe. Indeed, I do not want to fail to mention that I have known people of decisive although certainly not outstanding intellectual[a] superiority who at the same time betrayed a faint tinge of insanity.[b] It might thus seem that every increase in intellect beyond the ordinary measure is an abnormality that disposes one to madness.[18] In the meantime, I want to give my opinion as briefly as possible as to the purely intellectual[19] grounds for this relation between genius and madness, because this discussion would certainly help explain the true essence of genius, i.e. that intellectual quality[c] that alone can create genuine works of art. But this requires a brief discussion of madness itself.*   226

A clear and complete insight into the essence of madness, an accurate and distinct conception of what really distinguishes the mad from the healthy, has, in my opinion, yet to be found. – Neither reason nor understanding can be denied to people who are mad: because they speak and perceive, they often draw perfectly correct inferences; as a rule, they intuit what is present to them quite correctly and understand the connection between cause and effect. Visions, like febrile hallucinations, are not usually symptoms of madness: delirium distorts intuition, madness distorts thought. For the most part, people who are mad are not at all mistaken in their understanding of what is immediately *present*; rather their ravings[d] always refer to what is *absent* or *past*, and only through these does it refer to its connection with the present. That is why their illness seems to me to affect the *memory* in particular; not, of course, to the point where they have none at all: because many of them know a great deal by heart, and sometimes recognize people they have not seen in a long time; rather it has the effect

---

* For this see chapter 31 of the second volume.

[a] *geistig*
[b] *Verrücktheit*
[c] *Geisteseigenschaft*
[d] *Irrereden*

of tearing apart the threads of memory, so that the continuous connections in the memory are abolished and a uniform or coherent recollection of the past becomes impossible. Individual scenes from the past are still accurate, as is the singular present; but there are gaps in their recollection which they then fill out with fictions that are either always the same and turn into fixed ideas (this being a fixed delusion, melancholy) or always different, ideas of the moment (which is then called folly,[a] *fatuitas*). This is why, when he enters an insane asylum,[20] it is so difficult to ask a mad person about his earlier life. The true and the false become increasingly blended in his memory. Although the immediate present is recognized accurately, it is distorted by a fabricated connection to a delusional[b] past: thus the mad will identify themselves and others with people from out of their fabricated past, utterly failing to recognize some of the people they know, and, though they have an accurate representation of the individual who is present, all the connections they draw between this individual and anything absent will be false. If the madness is more advanced, there is a complete loss of memory, and the madman will then be incapable of referring to anything absent or past, and will be entirely determined by his present mood together with the fictions that fill out the past in his mind: we will never be safe for a single moment from maltreatment or murder with someone like this, unless we keep reminding him of our superior power. – The cognition of the mad is like that of animals in that both are restricted to the present: but they are distinguished by the fact that the animal really has no representation of the past as such, although the past has an effect on the animal through the medium of habit, which is why, for instance, a dog will recognize his earlier master even after many years (i.e. will receive a familiar impression upon seeing him); but the dog has no recollection of the time that has elapsed in the interim. The madman, on the contrary, always carries around a past in the abstract[c] in his reason, but a false one, one that exists for him alone whether constantly or only momentarily: the influence of this false past also prevents him from making use of the present that *is* recognized correctly, as animals do. I can explain the fact that intense mental suffering and unexpected but terrible events often cause madness in the following way. All such suffering is always restricted to the present as an actual event, and is thus only temporary and to this extent not yet excessively burdensome: it only becomes immoderate when it is a lasting pain: but this only

227

---

[a] *Narrheit*
[b] *gewähnt*
[c] *in abstracto*

happens in thought and hence in the *memory*: now, when this sort of sorrow or painful knowledge[a] or remembrance is so agonizing that it becomes absolutely unbearable and the individual succumbs to it, – then a being[b] who is experiencing this degree of anguish will seize upon *madness* as a last resort to save his life: the mind so profoundly tormented will tear apart the threads of his memory, as it were, and fill in the gaps with fictions, and thus escape into madness from the mental pain that exceeds its strength, – just as someone might remove a limb afflicted by gangrene and replace it with a wooden one.[21] – As examples, consider the raving Ajax, or King Lear, or Ophelia, because the creations of authentic genius (which are the only examples that can be appealed to here as generally familiar) are just as true as real people: and frequent actual experience in this also shows exactly the same thing. A weak analogy for this way of passing from pain to madness is the fact that we all often try (as if mechanically) to dispel a suddenly occurring and painful memory by making a motion or exclaiming out loud, to distract ourselves from it or to disperse it by force. –

228

From what has been said, we can now see that people who are mad correctly recognize particular things in the present and also many particular things from the past, but fail to understand their inter-connection, their relations, and thus are mistaken and talk nonsense;[c] and this is precisely their point of contact with genius: because geniuses also abandon cognition of the connection between things, because it is cognition of relations, which is cognition in accordance with the principle of sufficient reason, and they do this in order to see and seek only the Ideas in things, to grasp their genuine, intuitively expressed essence, with respect to which *one* thing represents its entire species and thus, as Goethe says, one case is valid for thousands, – geniuses too lose sight of cognition of the inter-connection between things: the particular object of their contemplation,[d] or the present that they grasp with exaggerated vividness appears in such a bright light that the rest of the links in the chain to which it belongs retreat into darkness as it were, and this results in the phenomena that have been likened to madness for so long. What exists only incompletely in the particular thing at hand and is weakened by modifications, is raised to its Idea, to completeness, by the genius's way of viewing things: thus he sees extremes everywhere, and this is precisely why his actions tend towards the extremes as well: he does not know how to achieve the correct balance,

[a] *Wissen*
[b] *Natur*
[c] *irren und irrereden*
[d] *Beschauung*

he lacks sobriety, and the result is as we have described. He has complete
229 cognition of the Ideas, but not of individuals. Thus, as has been remarked,
a poet can know *humanity* thoroughly and profoundly, but *human beings*
very badly; he is easy to deceive, and a plaything in the hands of people of
cunning.*

§ 37

As our discussion has shown, genius consists in the capacity for cognition
independent of the principle of sufficient reason, and hence in the capacity
for cognition of the Ideas of things rather than cognition of individual
things themselves that exist only in their relations; and genius consists in
the capacity to be the correlate of the Idea over and against these individual
things, which is to say, the capacity to be the pure subject of cognition
and no longer an individual. Yet this capacity must reside in all people to a
different and lesser degree; otherwise, they would be no more able to enjoy
works of art than to produce them, and would be absolutely insensitive to
beauty and sublimity – in fact these words would be meaningless for them.
We must therefore assume that this faculty is present in everyone (unless
perhaps there are some who are entirely incapable of aesthetic pleasure[a]),
and that everyone can have cognition of the Ideas of things in the particular
things and in so doing momentarily put aside their own personality. The
genius only has the advantage of being capable of sustaining this mode
of cognition much longer and to a much higher degree, allowing him to
maintain the clarity of mind[b] needed to repeat what he has thus cognized
in an intentional work,[c] this repetition being the work of art itself. In the
work of art he communicates the Idea he has grasped to others. It remains
the same and unchanging throughout: and hence the nature[d] of aesthetic
pleasure is the same whether it is called forth by a work of art or directly
through the intuition of nature and life. The artwork merely facilitates the
kind of cognition in which the pleasure consists. That we encounter the
Idea more readily in the artwork than we do directly in nature and reality is
230 due solely to the fact that the artist has cognition of only the Idea and not
reality and so has replicated only the pure Idea in his work, separating it off

---

* For this see chapter 32 of the second volume.

[a] *Wohlgefallen*
[b] *Besonnenheit*
[c] *in einem willkürlichen Werk*
[d] *Wesen*

from reality and omitting all distracting contingencies. The artist allows us to look into the world through his eyes. The fact that he has these eyes, that he has cognition of the essential aspect of things lying outside of all relations, is precisely the gift of genius, and it is innate; but the fact that he also can lend this gift to us and allow us to use his eyes: this is acquired, it is the technical aspect of art. This is why, now that I have presented the inner essence of the aesthetic mode of cognition in its most general outline, the more thorough philosophical consideration of the beautiful and the sublime that follows will discuss them both in nature and in art simultaneously, without separating these any further. I will next consider what takes place when people are moved[a] by the beautiful, when we are moved by the sublime: the question of whether this emotion[b] proceeds directly from nature, from life, or whether it can be passed on to them only through the medium of art makes no real difference, only a superficial one.

§ 38

We have discovered that there are *two inseparable components* of the aesthetic way of looking at things: cognition of the object, not as a particular thing but rather as a Platonic *Idea*, i.e. as a permanent form of this whole genus of things;[22] and then the self-consciousness of the one who has this cognition, not as an individual, but as *pure, will-less subject of cognition*. The condition under which both components always emerge together was the abandonment of the mode of cognition bound up with the principle of sufficient reason, which is the only mode suitable for the service of the will, as well as for science. – We will see that even the *pleasure* that is excited by the sight of the beautiful arises from both of those components, and in fact sometimes more from the one, and sometimes more from the other, according to the object of aesthetic contemplation.

All *willing* springs from need, and thus from lack, and thus from suffer-   231
ing. Fulfilment brings this to an end; but for every wish[c] that is fulfilled, at least ten are left denied: moreover, desire[d] lasts a long time and demands go on forever; fulfilment is brief and sparsely meted out. But even final satisfaction itself is only illusory: the fulfilled wish quickly gives way to a new one: the former is known to be a mistake, the latter is not yet known to be one. No achieved object of willing gives lasting, unwavering satisfaction;

[a] *rührt*
[b] *Rührung*
[c] *Wunsch*
[d] *Begehren*

rather, it is only ever like the alms thrown to a beggar that spares his life today so that his agony can be prolonged until tomorrow. – Thus, as long as our consciousness is filled by our will, as long as we are given over to the pressure[a] of desires with their constant hopes and fears, as long as we are the subject of willing, we will never have lasting happiness or peace. Whether we hunt or we flee, whether we fear harm or chase pleasure, it is fundamentally all the same: concern for the constant demands of the will, whatever form they take, continuously fills consciousness and keeps it in motion: but without peace, there can be no true well-being.[b] So the subject of willing remains on the revolving wheel of Ixion, keeps drawing water from the sieve of the Danaids, is the eternally yearning Tantalus.

But when some occasion from the outside or a disposition[c] from within suddenly lifts us out of the endless stream of willing, tearing cognition from its slavery to the will, our attention is no longer directed to the motives of willing but instead grasps things freed from their relation to the will, and hence considers them without interests, without subjectivity, purely objectively; we are given over to the things entirely, to the extent that they are mere representations, not to the extent that they are motives: then suddenly the peace that we always sought on the first path of willing but that always eluded us comes of its own accord, and all is well with us. It is the painless state that Epicurus prized as the highest good and the state of the gods: for that moment we are freed from the terrible pressure of the will, we celebrate the Sabbath of the penal servitude of willing, the wheel of Ixion stands still.

232   But this is precisely the state that I described above as being essential for cognition of the Idea, as a state of pure contemplation, absorption in intuition, losing oneself in the object, forgetting all individuality, abolishing the mode of cognition that follows the principle of sufficient reason and grasps only relations; in so doing, the particular intuited thing is at once and inseparably raised to the Idea of its type, and the cognizing individual is raised to the pure subject of will-less cognition; as such, neither stands in the stream of time or of any other relations. It is then all the same whether we see the setting of the sun from a prison or from a palace.

Inner disposition, a preponderance of cognition over willing, can produce this state in any surroundings. We see this in those excellent Dutch masters[d] who directed this sort of purely objective intuition towards the

[a] *Drange*
[b] *Wohlseyn*
[c] *Stimmung*
[d] *Niederländer*

most insignificant objects and have erected a lasting monument to their own objectivity[a] and mental tranquillity in the *still life*. The aesthetic spectator cannot consider this without emotion, since it puts before him[b] the artist's peaceful, quiet, will-less state of mind, the state of mind that was needed to intuit such insignificant things in such an objective way, to consider them so attentively and to repeat this intuition with such clarity of vision:[c] and since the picture invites the spectator to share in this state, his emotion is often even augmented by the contrast to the uneasy mental state,[d] clouded by intense willing, in which he finds himself. Landscape painters, particularly Ruisdael, have often painted utterly insignificant landscapes in the same spirit and so produced the same effect in an even more gratifying manner.

An artist's inner mental strength can achieve this much entirely on its own: but the purely objective frame of mind[e] can be facilitated and promoted from the outside by the right sort of objects, by the richness of beautiful nature that invites intuition of them, and indeed does so insistently. Whenever nature suddenly rises to meet our gaze, it almost always succeeds, if only for a few moments, in snatching us away from subjectivity, from our slavery to the will, and transporting us into the state of pure cognition. This also explains why people who are tormented by passions or needs and worries are so suddenly refreshed, cheered and comforted by a single free glimpse into nature: the storm of passions, the   233
stress[f] of wishes and fears as well as all the torment of willing are then immediately and miraculously calmed. For at the moment when, torn free from willing, we surrender ourselves to pure, will-less cognition, we enter into another world, as it were, where everything that moves our will and agitates us so powerfully no longer exists. That liberation of cognition lifts us out of all this as profoundly and as completely as sleep and dreaming do: happiness and unhappiness disappear: we are no longer the individual, this is forgotten, we are only the pure subject of cognition: we continue to exist only as the *one* eye of the world that gazes out from all cognizing creatures, although it can only become completely freed from service to the will in human beings when all individual differences have vanished, and indeed so completely that it is then a matter of indifference whether this

[a] *Objektität*
[b] *vergegenwärtigt*
[c] *besonnen*
[d] *Gemütsverfassung*
[e] *Gemütsstimmung*
[f] *Drang*

seeing eye belongs to a powerful king or a suffering beggar. This is because neither happiness nor misery is taken with us across this border. We are always so close to a realm where we have escaped all our misery completely; but who has enough strength to survive there for long? As soon as any relation between even that purely intuitive object and our own will, our own person, re-enters our consciousness, the magic is over: we fall back into cognition governed by the principle of sufficient reason, we no longer recognize the Idea but only the particular thing, the link in a chain to which we too belong, and we are once again given over to all our misery. – The majority of people almost always occupy this standpoint because they have absolutely no objectivity, i.e. genius. This is why they do not like to be alone in nature: they need company, or at least a book. Their cognition is still in the service of the will, so what they look for in an object is some sort of connection with their will, and if something lacks any such connection there sounds within them, like a ground bass,[a] a constant, hopeless 'it's no use to me': which means that even the most beautiful surroundings will have a desolate, gloomy, alien, hostile appearance for them when they are alone.

234   Finally, it is also the blessing of a will-less intuition[b] that, through an act of self-deception, it casts such a wonderful spell over things in the past or far away, presenting them to us in a so much rosier light. This is because when we picture days long past spent in a distant place, our imagination recalls only the objects, not the subject of the will, a subject that carried its incurable sufferings around with it then as well as now: but these have been forgotten because they have since made way for so many others. Now objective intuition[c] operates in memory just as intuition of the present *would* operate if we were able to free ourselves from the will and surrender ourselves to intuition. That is why sudden memories of past and distant scenes fly past us like a lost paradise, especially when some difficulty troubles us more than usual. Imagination[d] recalls only what is objective, not what is individual-subjective, and we imagine[e] that the objective scene once stood before us as pure and unclouded by any relation to the will as we picture it now in the imagination: but in fact, the relation of objects to our willing was as painful to us then as it is now. We can avoid all the suffering that comes from objects in the present just as well as we

---

[a] *Grundbaß*
[b] *Anschauen*
[c] *Anschauung*
[d] *Phantasie*
[e] *wir bilden uns ein*

can avoid it from those that are remote as soon as we raise ourselves to viewing them in a purely objective way, thus creating the illusion that these objects alone are present and we are not: then, as pure subject of cognition, we are rid of our suffering selves and fully one with the objects, and in such moments our needs are as alien to us as they are to the objects. The world as representation is then all that remains, and the world as will has vanished.

I hope that all these remarks have enabled me to make clear the nature[a] of the subjective condition for aesthetic pleasure, and how great a role this subjective condition plays in the pleasure itself, namely the liberation of cognition from service to the will, forgetting oneself as an individual, and the elevation of consciousness to the pure, will-less, timeless subject of cognition, independent of all relations. The objective side of aesthetic spectatorship, the intuitive apprehension of the Platonic[23] Idea always occurs simultaneously with and as a necessary correlate to this subjec-   235
tive side. But before we turn to a closer examination of this objective side and its contribution to art, it is more to the purpose to remain with the subjective side of aesthetic pleasure somewhat longer, in order to con-clude our examination of it by discussing the impression of the *sublime*, which depends on it alone and arises through a modification of it. After this, an examination of the objective side will complete our investigation of aesthetic pleasure.

But first, the following remarks belong with what has already been said. Light is the most joyful thing there is: it has become the symbol of everything good and salutary.[b] It signifies eternal salvation in all religions, while darkness symbolizes damnation. Ormuzd lives in the purest light, Ahriman in eternal night. Dante's paradise looks something like Vauxhall in London in that all the blessed spirits appear as points of light that arrange themselves in orderly figures.[24] An absence of light makes us immediately sad; we are happy when it returns: colours immediately excite our lively enjoyment[c] which reaches a climax when they are transparent.[25] All this comes solely from the fact that light is the correlate and condition of the most perfect intuitive mode of cognition, the only mode that has absolutely no direct effect on the will. In contrast to the affection of the other senses, the sensuous operation of vision is in itself and immediately completely incapable of giving rise to a pleasing[d] or unpleasing *sensation* in the organ,

[a] *Art*
[b] *heilbringend*
[c] *Ergötzen*
[d] *Annehmlichkeit*

i.e. it has no immediate connection to the will: only the intuition that comes from the understanding can give rise to this sensation, which then lies in the object's relation to the will. Even hearing is different: tones can give immediate pain and can also be immediately and sensuously pleasant[a] without reference to harmony or melody. Since touch is united with the feeling of the entire body, it is even more subordinate to the immediate influence of the body on the will, although there are still some sensations of touch free from either pain or pleasure. Smells however are always pleasant or unpleasant: tastes even more so. These two last senses are thus the ones most contaminated by the will: hence, they are always the most vulgar[b] and Kant calls them the subjective senses. The delight[c] we take in light is therefore in fact nothing other than a delight in the objective possibility of the purest and most perfect intuitive mode of cognition, and as such can be derived from the fact that pure cognition, liberated from and rid of all willing, is highly gratifying[d] and already as such has a great share in aesthetic enjoyment.[e] – This perspective on light allows us further to derive the incredible degree of beauty that we attribute to the reflection of objects in water. That lightest, fastest, finest sort of interaction of bodies, to which we owe the most perfect and pure of our perceptions by far: the effect produced by reflected beams of light: here it is brought before our eyes clearly, openly and completely, in cause and effect, and indeed on a large scale:[26] hence the aesthetic delight we take in this, which is for the most part rooted entirely in the subjective ground of aesthetic pleasure, and is a delight in pure cognition and its ways.*

§ 39

All of these considerations are meant to emphasize the subjective component of aesthetic pleasure, which is to say this pleasure to the extent that it is a delight in simple, intuitive cognition as such, as opposed to the will, – these considerations naturally include, and are directly related to the following explanation of the disposition called the feeling of the sublime.[f]

---

* For this see chapter 33 of the second volume.

[a] *angenehm*
[b] *unedelsten*
[c] *Freude*
[d] *erfreulich*
[e] *Genusse*
[f] *Erhabenen*

We have already noted above that our transport[a] into the state of pure contemplative intuition[b] occurs most easily when objects meet that state halfway,[c] i.e. when they turn readily into representatives of their Ideas by virtue of their intricate and at the same time clear and determinate form, which constitutes beauty in the objective sense. We find this quality   237
above all in natural beauty, which gives even the most insensitive people at least a fleeting sense of aesthetic pleasure: in fact, it is striking how the plant kingdom in particular invites us to assume an aesthetic perspective, insists upon it, as it were; we could say that this obliging character[d] of plants is connected with the fact that unlike animal bodies, these organic beings are not themselves the immediate object of cognition and thus require an outside[e] individual who is endowed with understanding if they are to quit the world of blind willing for that of representation, which is why they long for this exit, so that they can attain at least indirectly what is denied to them directly. In any event, I will leave this bold and somewhat rambling conjecture entirely undecided, since only a very ardent and devoted consideration of nature can inspire or justify it.*,[27] Nature has this obliging character, a significance and clarity in its forms that enables the Ideas individuated in them to address us readily, – and as long as it is this obliging character that transports us from cognition of mere relations in the service of the will into aesthetic contemplation, and in so doing elevates us to the subject of cognition that is free of the will: as long as this is the case, it is only the *beautiful* that affects us, and the feeling of beauty that is aroused. But if the very objects whose significant forms invite us to pure contemplation have a hostile relation to the human will in general (as it presents itself in its objecthood, the human body) and oppose it, threatening it with a superior power that suppresses all resistance, or reducing it to nothing with its immense size; and if the spectator pays no attention to this obtrusive, hostile relation to his will, but   238
rather, although perceiving and acknowledging it, consciously turns away

---

* I am all the more delighted and astonished now, 40 years after I so timidly and hesitantly recorded the idea above, to have discovered that St Augustine has already expressed it: *Arbusta formas suas varias, quibus mundi hujus visibilis structura formosa est, sentiendas sensibus praebent; ut, pro eo quod* nosse *non possunt, quasi* innotescere *velle videantur* [Plants offer the senses for perception their manifold forms through which the visible structure of this world is beautifully shaped, since, being themselves incapable of *cognition*, they seem to want to *be known*] (*De civ. Dei* [*City of God*], XI, 27).

[a] *Versetzen*
[b] *Anschauen*
[c] *Gegenstände demselben entgegenkommen*
[d] *dieses Entgegenkommen*
[e] *fremd*

from it by violently wrenching himself free from his will and its relations and surrendering himself to cognition alone, peacefully contemplating those very objects that are terrible to the will as pure, will-less subject of cognition, grasping only their Ideas (Ideas being foreign to every relation) and thus gladly lingering over their contemplation,[a] and consequently being raised above[b] himself, his own person, his willing, and all willing: – then he is filled with the feeling of the *sublime*,[c] he is in a state of elevation,[d] which is why the object that gives rise to this state is also called *sublime*. Hence what distinguishes the feeling of the sublime from the feeling of the beautiful is this: with the beautiful, pure cognition has won the upper hand without a struggle, since the beauty of the object (i.e. that quality in the object that facilitates cognition of its Idea), has expelled from consciousness both the will and the cognition of relations that toils in its service, and has done so without resistance and thus imperceptibly, leaving consciousness as the pure subject of cognition, so that not even a memory of the will remains. With the sublime, on the other hand, that state of pure cognition is gained only by means of a conscious and violent tearing free from relationships between the same object and the will (relationships that are recognized as unfavourable) by means of a free and conscious elevation over the will and the cognition relating to it. This elevation must not only be achieved consciously, it must also be sustained and is therefore accompanied by a constant recollection of the will, although not of a particular, individual willing, such as fear or desire,[e] but rather of human willing in general, to the extent that it is universally expressed through its objecthood, the human body. If a real, particular act of will were to enter consciousness through some actual personal distress or danger from the object, then the individual will that was actually moved in this way would quickly gain the upper hand, the tranquillity of contemplation would be rendered impossible, and the impression of the sublime would be lost, since it would give way to anxiety, in which the individual's attempts to save himself would supersede any other thought. – Some examples will clarify this theory of the aesthetic sublime considerably and place it beyond doubt; at the same time they will demonstrate the differences between the various grades of the feeling of the sublime. The feeling of the sublime is the same as the feeling of the beautiful in its most important respect, namely pure

239

---

[a] *Betrachtung*
[b] *hinausgehoben*
[c] *Erhabenen*
[d] *Erhebung*
[e] *Wunsch*

cognition free from the will and the cognition that necessarily appears along with this, of the Ideas that stand outside of all relations determined by the principle of sufficient reason. The feeling of the sublime is distinct from the feeling of the beautiful only by virtue of an additional element, namely an elevation above the relationship[a] – recognized as hostile – between the object contemplated and the will in general. Several different degrees of sublimity are thus apparent depending on whether this additional element is strong, loud, urgent, close, or only weak, distant, merely intimated – in fact, this is the origin of the transition from the beautiful to the sublime. I think it is relevant to this account to illustrate this transition as well as the weaker grades of the impression of the sublime by means of examples, although people without much aesthetic sensitivity and whose imaginations are not very lively will only understand the later examples of the higher, clearer degrees of the impression of the sublime; accordingly, they should focus on these later examples and disregard the ones that will be discussed first of the very weak degrees of the impression under examination.

Just as a human being is dark and vehement impulse[b] of willing (signified by the pole of the genitals as the focal point of willing) and at the same time eternal, free, serene[c] subject of pure cognition (signified by the pole of the brain), similarly and corresponding to this contrast, the sun is a source of both *light*, the condition for the most perfect type of cognition, and for precisely this reason the most joyful[d] of things, – and *heat*, the primary condition for all life, i.e. of all appearance of the will on its higher levels. Thus, what heat is for the will, light is for cognition. Light is for this very reason the greatest diamond in the crown of beauty, and has the most decisive effect on the cognition of every beautiful object: its general presence is an indispensible condition; when placed to advantage, it enhances the beauty of even the most beautiful. It enhances architectural beauty above all else, although it can turn even the most insignificant thing into a beautiful object. – Now if in the dead of winter, when all of nature is frozen, we look at the rays of the sun, low in the sky and reflected by stony masses they illuminate without warmth, and which thus only favour the purest mode of cognition, not the will, then contemplation[e] of the beautiful effect of light on these masses transports us, as all beauty does, into the state of pure cognition, a state however that here calls for a certain

240

---

[a] *Verhältnis*
[b] *Drang*
[c] *heiter*
[d] *erfreulichste*
[e] *Betrachtung*

elevation above the interest of the will through our faint recollection of how little warmth (the principle of life) is provided by these very rays, – and contains a gentle invitation to persist in pure cognition, turned away from all willing, and is in precisely this way a transition from the feeling of beautiful to that of the sublime. It is the faintest intimation of the sublime in the beautiful, and beauty itself only emerges here at a low degree. The following example is almost as faint.

Let us transport ourselves to a very solitary region with a boundless horizon under a completely cloudless sky, with trees and plants in completely still air, no animals, no people, no moving water, the deepest calm; – surroundings like these are like a summons to seriousness, to contemplation, to tear oneself free from all willing with its pressing needs: but this is precisely what gives such a lonely and deeply tranquil environment a tinge of the sublime. The will needs to keep striving and attaining, and since this environment does not offer it any objects either favourable or unfavourable, then only the state of pure contemplation remains, and anyone incapable of this is abandoned with shameful degradation to the emptiness of the idle will, the misery of boredom.

Accordingly, such surroundings provide a standard for measuring our own intellectual value, which can be gauged by our ability to tolerate or even love solitude. Thus, the environment described above offers an example of the sublime at a low degree, since the state of pure cognition, in its peacefulness and total sufficiency, is blended with a contrasting memory of the dependence and poverty of a will in need of constant activity.[a] – The view out over endless prairies in the North American interior is renowned for this species of the sublime.[28]

241   Now if we allow this sort of environment to be devoid of plant life and to exhibit only barren rocks, then the will becomes quickly alarmed by the complete absence of organic material necessary for our subsistence. The desert assumes a terrible aspect:[b] our mood becomes more tragic: the elevation to pure cognition takes place with a decided tearing away from the interests of the will, and as long as we persist in the state of pure cognition, the feeling of the sublime comes clearly to the fore.

The feeling of the sublime can be occasioned at still higher gradations by the following environment. Nature in stormy motion; the gloaming[c] through threatening black storm clouds; enormous, barren, hanging rocks that interlock so as to cut off our view; rushing, foaming masses of water;

[a] *Treiben*
[b] *Charakter*
[c] *Helldunkel*

complete desolation; the howling of the wind as it cuts through a ravine. Our dependency, our struggle with hostile nature, our will which is broken in this struggle, these now come vividly[a] before our eyes: but as long as our personal troubles do not gain the upper hand and we remain in a state of aesthetic contemplation,[b] the pure subject of cognition peers through that struggle of nature, through that image of the broken will, and calmly, in a manner both unperturbed and unconcerned[c] grasps the Ideas in those very objects that are threatening and terrible to the will. The feeling of the sublime lies in precisely this contrast.

But the impression becomes even more powerful when we find ourselves face to face with the struggle of enraged forces of nature in all their grandeur, when in those surroundings, the rage of a plunging stream prevents us from hearing our own voices; – or if we are on the high seas, in a raging storm, with waves as tall as houses rising up and sinking back down again, violently breaking against steep cliffs on the shore, spraying foam high into the air, the storm howling, the ocean roaring, lightning flashing from black clouds, and thunderclaps drowning out the storm and the sea. Then the untroubled spectator will experience the twofold character of his consciousness most clearly: he feels himself to be both an individual, a frail appearance of the will that can be crushed by the slightest blow of those forces, helpless against the might of nature, dependent, abandoned to chance, a vanishing nothing in the face of enormous powers; and yet at the same time the eternal, tranquil subject of cognition that, as the condition of all objects, carries and supports just this entire world, with the terrible struggles of nature merely as its representation, while the subject itself calmly apprehends the Ideas, free from and foreign to all need and all willing. This is the full impression of the sublime. Here it is occasioned by the sight of a power that is incomparably superior to the individual and that threatens him with annihilation.

242

This impression can arise in a completely different manner, from the presence of a mere magnitude in space and time, a magnitude immense enough to reduce the individual to nothingness. We can call the first type the dynamic sublime and the second the mathematical sublime, retaining Kant's terms and his correct classification,[d] although we part ways with him completely when it comes to the explanation of the inner essence of

---

[a] *anschaulich*
[b] *Beschauung*
[c] [Schopenhauer inserts the English term in parentheses, after the German term '*nicht mitgetroffen*']
[d] [Kant, *Critique of the Power of Judgment* §§ 24ff, Ak. 5: 247ff.]

this impression, and allow neither moral reflections nor hypotheses from scholastic philosophy to play a role.

When we lose ourselves in the contemplation[a] of the infinite extent of the world in space and time, reflecting on the millennia past and the millennia to come, – or indeed when the night sky actually brings countless worlds before our eyes, so that we become forcibly aware of the immensity of the world, – then we feel ourselves reduced to nothing, feel ourselves as individuals, as living bodies, as transient appearances of the will, like drops in the ocean, fading away, melting away into nothing. But at the same time, rising up[b] against such a spectre of our own nothingness, against such a slanderous impossibility, is our immediate consciousness that all these worlds really exist only in our representation, only as modifications of the eternal subject of pure cognition, which is what we find ourselves to be as soon as we forget our individuality, and which is the necessary, the conditioning bearer and support of all worlds and all times. The magnitude of the world, which we used to find unsettling, is now settled securely within ourselves: our dependence on it is nullified by its dependence on us. – Yet we do not reflect on all this straight away; instead it appears only as the felt consciousness that we are, in some sense (that only philosophy makes clear), one with the world, and thus not brought down, but rather elevated,[c] by its immensity. It is the felt consciousness of what the *Upanishads* of the *Vedas* repeatedly express in so many ways, but most exquisitely in that dictum already cited above: 'I am all these creations taken together, and there is no other being besides me'[d] (*Oupnek'hat*, Vol. I, p. 122). This is an elevation above one's own individuality,[e] the feeling of the sublime.

We can get a direct impression of the mathematical sublime from a space that is certainly small in comparison with the whole world, but that becomes immediately and completely perceptible so that its entire magnitude has an effect on us in all three dimensions sufficient to make the size of our own body almost infinitely small. A space that is empty for perception (such as an open space) can never have this effect, only a space that can be immediately perceived because it is bounded in all dimensions, and thus only a huge and very high dome, such as St Peter's in Rome or St Paul's in London. In these cases the feeling of the sublime arises through

---

[a] *Betrachtung*
[b] *erhebt sich*
[c] *gehoben*
[d] *Hae omnes creaturae in totum ego sum, et praeter me aliud ens non est* [Quoted above, 204: See note there]
[e] *das eigene Individuum*

an awareness of the vanishing nothingness of our own bodies in the face of a magnitude that is on the other hand found only in our representation and that, as the subject of cognition, we support, and so in this as in all other cases, the feeling arises through the contrast between the insignificance and dependency of our self as an individual, as an appearance of the will, over and against the consciousness of ourselves as the pure subject of cognition. Even the dome of the starry heavens, when regarded in the absence of reflection, operates no differently from those domes made of stone, and thus only with its apparent magnitude, not its real one. – Many objects of our intuition arouse the impression of the sublime by reducing us to nothingness in the face of their spatial magnitude or their advanced age, i.e. their temporal duration, and yet we revel in the pleasure of seeing them: very high mountains, the pyramids of Egypt, colossal ruins of early   244
antiquity are all of this type.

Indeed, our explanation of the sublime can even be applied to the ethical, namely to what has been called the sublime character. This too arises from the fact that the will is not aroused by objects that are clearly well suited to arouse it, but instead cognition retains the upper hand even here. Consequently, such a character will regard human beings purely objectively, and not in terms of whatever relations they might have to his will: for instance, he will observe their failings, even their hatred and injustice towards him, but without being himself moved to hatred; he will look upon their happiness without feeling envy; he will recognize their good qualities without wanting to be more closely associated with them; he will perceive the beauty of women without desiring them. His personal happiness and unhappiness will not affect him strongly, rather he will be such as Hamlet described Horatio:

> for thou hast been
> As one, in suffering all, that suffers nothing;
> A man, that fortune's buffets and rewards
> Hast ta'en with equal thanks, etc. (act 3, scene 2).

This is because when he looks over the course of his own life with all its misfortunes he will not see his own individual fate so much as the fate of humanity in general, and thus he will conduct himself more as a knower than as a sufferer.[a,29]

---

[a] *erkennend*

§ 40

Because opposites shed light on each other, we should perhaps remark here that the true opposite of the sublime will certainly not be recognized as such at first glance: it is the *stimulating*. I understand by this something that arouses the will with the prospect of immediate satisfaction,[a] fulfilment. If the feeling of the sublime comes about when something[b] directly unfavourable to the will becomes an object[c] of pure contemplation, and this contemplation is sustained only by constantly turning away from the will and rising[d] above its interests, this constituting the sublimity of disposition; then the stimulating[e] by contrast drags the viewer down from the pure contemplation required for any apprehension of the beautiful, since it necessarily stimulates[f] his will with the same immediately agreeable objects, so that the viewer no longer remains the pure subject of cognition, but instead turns into the needy, dependent subject of willing. – Every cheerful type of beauty is generally called stimulating, but this concept is too broad and in need of further distinctions, so I must put it entirely to the side and in fact reject it.[30] – But in the sense we have specified and clarified, I can find only two species of the stimulating in the field of art, and both are unworthy of art. The first is very low, and can be found in Dutch still lifes when they make the mistake of portraying objects that are edible and whose illusory presentation necessarily stirs the appetite, which is just the sort of stimulation of the will that puts an end to any aesthetic contemplation of an object. Paintings of fruit are still admissible, since fruit is a further development of the flower and presents itself through form and colour as a beautiful product of nature without necessarily reminding us of its edibility; but unfortunately we often find deceptively natural portrayals of prepared and table-ready dishes, oysters, herring, lobster, bread and butter, beer, wine, etc., and this is totally objectionable. – In historical painting and sculpture the stimulating consists in nudes whose posture, dishabille, and whole manner of treatment are calculated to arouse lust in the viewer; this instantly annuls any purely aesthetic contemplation, and thus works counter to the goal of art. This mistake corresponds precisely to the mistake we just criticized in the Dutch. The ancients almost never commit

---

[a] *Gewährung*
[b] *Gegenstand*
[c] *Objekt*
[d] *Erhebung*
[e] *Reizende*
[f] *aufreizt*

this error, for all the beauty and complete nudity of their figures, because the artist himself created them with a purely objective spirit, filled with ideal beauty, not in a subjective spirit of base desire.[a] – The stimulating is 246 therefore to be universally avoided in art.

There is a negative stimulation too, which is even more objectionable than the positive stimulation just mentioned, and this is the disgusting. Just as with genuine stimulation, it stimulates the viewer's will, destroying any purely aesthetic contemplation. But what it arouses is an intense negative willing,[b] a repugnance: it stimulates the will by showing it objects it detests. This is why people have always known that it is not at all permissible in art, while even ugliness can be tolerated in the right place as long as it is not disgusting, as we shall see further below.

§ 41

The course of our investigations required us to insert a discussion of the sublime into the middle of our discussion of the beautiful, having investigated only its subjective side.

This is because it was only a special modification of this subjective side that distinguished the sublime from the beautiful. Whether the state of pure, will-less cognition that is presupposed and required by all aesthetic contemplation came about as if on its own and without resistance, invited and drawn forward by the object, with the will simply disappearing from consciousness; or whether this state was first achieved only through a free and conscious elevation above the will – and the contemplated object has an unfavourable and hostile relation to this will, which would annul contemplation if we gave ourselves over to it; – this is the difference between the beautiful and the sublime. There is no essential distinction between them in the object, because in every instance, the object of aesthetic contemplation is not the particular thing but rather the Idea striving to be revealed in it, i.e. the adequate objecthood of the will at a particular level; its necessary correlate is the pure subject of cognition that, like the Idea, has withdrawn from the principle of sufficient reason, just as the correlate of the individual thing is the cognizing individual, both of which lie within the sphere of the principle of sufficient reason.   247

[a] *Begierde*
[b] *Nichtwollen*

234 The World as Will and Representation

When we call something[a] *beautiful*, we are expressing the fact that it is the object[b] of our aesthetic contemplation, and this entails two things: first, that we become *objective* in viewing it, i.e.[31] that in contemplating it we are no longer conscious of ourselves as individuals but as the pure will-less subject of cognition; and second, that what we cognize in the individual object[c] is not the individual thing but rather an Idea, and this can only take place to the extent that our contemplation of the object is not given over to the principle of sufficient reason and does not pursue the object's relation to something external to it (which is always ultimately linked up with its relations to our willing), but instead rests with the object itself. This is because the Idea and the pure subject of cognition always enter consciousness at the same time, as necessary correlates, and when they enter, all temporal distinctions also vanish at once, since both are completely alien to the principle of sufficient reason in all of its forms and lie outside the relations that are introduced through this principle, just as the rainbow and the sun have no part in the steady movement and succession of falling droplets. Thus, when I regard (for instance) a tree aesthetically, i.e. with artist's eyes, and thus do not have cognition of it but of its Idea, then suddenly it does not matter whether it is this tree or some ancestor of this tree that blossomed thousands of years ago, or similarly whether the viewer is this or some other individual living in some place and at some time; the individual thing and the cognizing individual are suppressed along with the principle of sufficient reason, and nothing is left except the Idea and the pure subject of cognition, which together constitute the adequate objecthood of the will on this level. And the Idea is exempt from space as well as time, since the genuine Idea is not this spatial figure before my eyes but rather the expression, the pure meaning of this figure, its innermost essence that opens itself up and speaks to me, and this can remain the same through vast differences in the spatial relations of the figure.

Since on the one hand, every existing thing[d] can be considered purely objectively and apart from all relation, and since on the other hand, the will appears in every thing on some level of its objecthood, making the thing an expression of an Idea; so it follows that everything is *beautiful*. – Dutch still lifes, which we have already mentioned above (§ 38) in this connection,

[a] *Gegenstand*
[b] *Objekt*
[c] *Gegenstand*
[d] *jedes vorhandene Ding*

testify to the fact that even the most insignificant thing can be viewed in a purely objective and will-less manner, and hence prove to be beautiful. But one thing is more beautiful than another when it facilitates that purely objective contemplation,[a] meeting it halfway and indeed compelling it to take place, in which case we call the thing very beautiful. This happens in part because, as an individual thing, it expresses the Idea of its species[b] very purely, through the very clear, pure and determinate relation between its parts (a relation that is saturated with significance); it reveals its Idea perfectly because it completely unites all the possible expressions of its species and thus greatly facilitates the viewer's transition from the individual thing to the Idea and thereby to a state of pure contemplation.[c] This advantage of a particularly beautiful object also lies in part in the fact that the Idea itself which addresses us from the object is at a high level of the objecthood of the will and is thus saturated in significance and highly suggestive. This is why human beings are more beautiful than anything else, and the revelation of the human essence is the highest goal of art. The human figure and expression are the most significant objects for the visual arts,[d] just as human action is the most significant object for poetry. – Still, each and every thing has its own distinctive beauty: not only every organic thing that presents itself in the unity of an individuality; but even inorganic things that lack form, and in fact all artefacts as well. This is because all these things reveal the Ideas in which the will objectifies itself on the lowest levels, and at the same time contribute the deepest, lingering bass-tones of nature, as it were. Gravity, rigidity, fluidity, light, etc. are the Ideas that express themselves in rocks, buildings, bodies of water. Fine landscape gardening[e] and architecture can do nothing more than help these things display their qualities clearly, completely, and in many different ways, giving them the opportunity to express themselves purely, by means of which they invite us to contemplate them aesthetically[f] and facilitate such contemplation. On the other hand, inferior buildings and areas neglected by nature or ruined by art have very little or no chance for success in this: all the same, the universal, fundamental Ideas of nature cannot disappear from them entirely. Even in these cases, they address the viewer who looks for   249

[a] *Betrachtung*
[b] *Gattung*
[c] *Beschaulichkeit*
[d] *bildenden Kunst*
[e] *schöne Gartenkunst*
[f] *zur ästhetischen Beschauung*

them, and even inferior buildings and the like are capable of being viewed aesthetically: the Ideas of the most universal qualities of their materials[a] are still recognizable in them, it is only that the artificial[b] form they have been given does not facilitate aesthetic contemplation, but in fact makes it more difficult. Consequently, even artefacts serve to express Ideas: only it is not the Idea of the artefact that speaks from them, but rather the Idea of the material[c] that has been given this artificial form. Scholastic terminology offers two phrases that handily express this thought, namely that the Idea expressed is that of the artefact's *forma substantialis*[d] and not its *forma accidentalis,*[e] and the latter does not lead to any Idea but only to a human concept, which is where it originated. It goes without saying that in this context we expressly do not mean by artefact a work of plastic art.[f] Moreover, what the scholastics actually understood by *forma substantialis* is what I refer to as the degree of objectivation of the will in a thing. We will come back to the expression of the Idea of material shortly, when we consider architectural beauty. – Given our view, we cannot agree with Plato when he claims (*Republic* X, pp. 284–5, and *Parmenides*, p. 79, Bipont edition[g]) that tables and chairs express the Ideas of Table and Chair; rather, we say that they express the Ideas that already announce themselves[h] as such in their bare material. According to Aristotle (*Metaphysics* XI, chapter 3) Plato himself only allowed for Ideas of natural beings: 'Plato says that there are as many Ideas as there are natural things',[i] and in chapter 5 it says that according to the Platonists, there are no Ideas of House or Ring. In any case,[32] even Plato's closest students denied that there were Ideas of artefacts, as Alcinous reports (*The Handbook of Platonism,*[j] chapter 9). He says specifically: 'But they define the *Idea* as a timeless archetype of natural things. For most of Plato's followers do not admit there to be Ideas of artificial products, e.g. of shields and lyres, nor of things that are contrary to nature, such as fever or cholera, nor of particular beings such as Socrates or Plato, nor of petty things such as dirt or fragments, nor of relations, such as being greater or taller; for the Ideas are the eternal thoughts of

250

---

[a] *Stoff*
[b] *künstlich*
[c] *Material*
[d] [substantial form]
[e] [accidental form]
[f] *Werk der bildenden Kunst*
[g] [See *Republic* 596b–597d, *Parmenides* 130b–e]
[h] *sich aussprechen*
[i] ὁ Πλατων εφη, ὅτι ειδη εστιν ὁποσα φυσει. (*Plato dixit, quod ideae eorum sunt, quae natura sunt*) [*Metaphysics* Λ (XII), 3, 1070a18]
[j] *introductio in Platonicam philosophiam*

God and are perfect in themselves.'[a,33] – This gives me the opportunity to mention another point in which our doctrine of the Ideas deviates quite radically from Plato's. He teaches (*Republic* X, p. 288[b]) that the object fine art[c] aims to depict, the model for painting and poetry, is not the Idea but the particular thing. The whole of our discussion up to this point claims precisely the opposite, and Plato's opinion is not so much misleading for us as it is the source of one of the greatest and acknowledged errors of that great man, namely his disdain and dismissal of art, and poetry in particular: he directly connects his false judgement in this matter to the passage cited here.

§ 42

I return to our discussion of the aesthetic impression. Cognition of the beautiful always posits the pure cognizing subject at the same time as, and inseparably from, the cognition of the Idea as object. And yet the source of aesthetic pleasure will sometimes be located more in the apprehension of the Ideas that are cognized, and sometimes more in the happiness and peace of mind of pure cognition that has been liberated from all willing and thus from all individuality and the pain that comes from it: and certainly this preponderance of one or the other component of aesthetic pleasure will depend on whether the intuitively apprehended Idea is a higher or lower level of the objecthood of the will. So with aesthetic contemplation of natural beauty in the inorganic realm, in the vegetable world, or in beautiful works of architecture (either in reality, or through the medium of art), the pleasure of pure will-less cognition will predominate, because the Ideas apprehended here are only the low levels of the objecthood of the will, and thus these appearances do not have any profound meaning or interpretive richness. By contrast, when animals or people are the object of aesthetic contemplation or presentation, the

251

---

[a] Ὁρίζονται δε την ιδεαν, παραδειγμα των κατα φυσιν αιωνιον. Ουτε γαρ τοις πλειστοις των απο Πλατωνος αρεσκει, των τεχνικων ειναι ιδεας, οἷον ασπιδος η λυρας, ουτε μην των παρα φυσιν, οἷον πυρετου και χολερας, ουτε των κατα μερος, οἷον Σωκρατους και Πλατωνος, αλλ᾽ ουτε των ευτελων τινος, οἷον ρυπου και καρφους, ουτε των προς τι, οἷον μειζονος και ὑπερεχοντος· ειναι γαρ τας ιδεας νοησεις Θεου αιωνιους τε και αυτοτελεις. – (*Definiunt autem* ideam *exemplar aeternum eorum, quae secundum naturam existunt. Nam plurimis ex iis, qui Platonem secuti sunt, minime placuit, arte factorum ideas esse, ut clypei atque lyrae; neque rursus eorum, quae praeter naturam, ut febris et cholerae; neque particularium, ceu Socratis et Platonis; neque etiam rerum vilium, veluti sordium et festucae; neque relationum, ut majoris et excedentis: esse namque ideas intellectiones dei aeternas, ac seipsis perfectas.*)

[b] [See *Republic* 600e–602c]

[c] *schöne Kunst*

pleasure will consist more in the objective apprehension of these Ideas, which are the clearest manifestations[a] of the will; this is because these exhibit the greatest multitude of forms, as well as a wealth of profoundly significant appearances, and reveal[b] the essence of the will to us most completely, whether in its intensity, horror, satisfaction, or broken state (this last in tragic portrayals), or finally even in its turning[c] or self-abolition,[d] which is the theme of Christian painting in particular, just as historical painting and drama generally have as their object the Idea of the will illuminated by complete cognition. – We will now review the arts one by one, which will lend completion and clarity to the theory of beauty we have presented.

§ 43

Matter as such cannot be the presentation of an Idea. This is because, as we discovered in the First Book, it is causality through and through: its being is nothing but acting.[e] Now causality is a form of the principle of sufficient reason: cognition of the Idea, by contrast, essentially excludes the content of that principle. And in the Second Book we discovered matter to be the common substrate of all particular appearances of the Ideas, and consequently to be the link between the Idea and the appearance or particular thing. Thus for the one reason as much as for the other, matter by itself cannot present any Ideas. This is also confirmed *a posteriori* by the fact that there can be absolutely no intuitive representation of matter as such but only an abstract concept: intuitive representations present only the forms and qualities supported by matter, and in all of which Ideas reveal themselves. This also corresponds to the fact that only a particular causal connection can be presented in intuition, not causality itself (the entire essence of matter). – But on the other hand, every *appearance* of an Idea, since it has entered as such into the form of the principle of sufficient reason, or into the *principium individuationis*, must present itself in matter as a material quality. To this extent, as we have said, matter is the link connecting the Idea with the *principium individuationis* (which is the individual's form of cognition), or the principle of sufficient reason. – Hence, Plato quite correctly established matter as a third thing, alongside but distinct from the

252

---

[a] *Offenbarungen*
[b] *offenbaren*
[c] *Wendung*
[d] *Selbstaufhebung*
[e] *Wirken*

Idea and its appearance (the individual thing), which together account for everything else in the world (*Timaeus*, p. 345[a]). As appearance of the Idea, the individual is always material.[b] Every quality of matter is also always the appearance of an Idea, and as such is able to be the object of aesthetic contemplation as well, i.e. we can have cognition of the Idea presented in it. This applies even to the most general[c] qualities of matter, qualities that it never lacks and whose Ideas are the weakest objecthood of the will. These are: gravity, cohesion, rigidity, fluidity, reaction to light, etc.

When we consider *architecture*[d] merely as a fine art,[e] leaving aside its utilitarian function, where it serves the will rather than pure cognition, and is thus no longer art in our sense; then the only intention we can attribute to it is that of bringing some of the Ideas at the lowest levels of the objecthood of the will more clearly into intuition, namely: gravity, cohesion, rigidity, hardness, these universal qualities of stone, those first, simplest and dullest visibilities of the will, the sounds of the ground bass of nature;[f] and then, alongside these, light, which is in many respects their opposite. Even at this low level of the objecthood of the will we already see its essence manifesting itself in discord: because the struggle between gravity and rigidity is in fact the only aesthetic content of fine architecture:[g] its task is to let this content come to the fore with complete clarity and in a variety of different ways. It performs this task by depriving these indestructible forces of their shortest path to fulfilment, and detaining them along a detour that prolongs the   253
struggle and makes the inexhaustible striving of both forces visible in a variety of different ways. – If left to its original inclination, the building's entire mass would present a mere lump clinging to the surface of the earth as tightly as possible, urged ceaselessly in this direction by gravity (which is how the will appears here) while resisted by rigidity, which is likewise the objecthood of the will. But this very inclination, this striving, is what architecture prevents from attaining immediate satisfaction, allowing it only indirect and roundabout satisfaction. So for instance a beam can press towards the ground only by means of a column; the dome has to be its own support, and can only satisfy its striving towards the mass of the earth by means of pillars, etc. But it is precisely along these forced detours, through these very obstacles, that the forces subsisting in the mass of raw stone

[a] [*Timaeus* 48–9]
[b] *Materie*
[c] *allgemeinsten*
[d] *Baukunst*
[e] *schöne Kunst*
[f] *Grundbaßtöne der Natur*
[g] *schönen Architektur*

develop themselves in the clearest and most varied way: and the purely aesthetic goal of architecture can go no further than this. Thus the beauty of a building certainly lies in the conspicuous purposiveness[a] of each part, not for some external and arbitrary human purpose (to this extent, the work belongs to practical architecture), but rather immediately for the existence[b] of the whole; the relation of the position, size and form of each part to this whole must be so necessary that, as far as possible, the removal of any part would bring it down. Because only when each part supports as much as it properly can, and each is supported exactly where and exactly as much as it needs to be, does that opposition,[c] that struggle between rigidity and gravity which constitutes both the stone's life and expressions of will, develop itself to the most complete visibility, and these lowest levels of the objecthood of the will reveal themselves clearly. Similarly, the shape of each part must be determined only by its purpose and relation to the whole rather than arbitrarily. Columns are the very simplest form of support, determined solely by their goal: winding columns are tasteless: square pillars are in fact not as simple, although they happen to be easier to make than round columns. The forms of the frieze, the joist, the arch and the dome[d] are likewise determined entirely by their immediate goals and are self-explanatory given these goals. Ornamentation of the capital etc. belongs to sculpture, not architecture, and, as added decoration, is merely tolerated but can be omitted as well. – Given what we have said, in order to understand or take aesthetic pleasure in a work of architecture it is indispensably necessary to have an immediate and intuitive acquaintance[e] with the weight, rigidity and cohesion of its material, and our enjoyment of such a work is suddenly and sharply diminished by the disclosure that the building is made of pumice-stone,[34] because then it would strike us as a kind of fake building.[f] It would almost be the same if we were to find out that it is only made of wood when we had thought it was stone, precisely because this now alters and shifts the relation between rigidity and gravity, and thus the significance and necessity of all the parts, since those natural forces reveal themselves much more weakly in buildings made of wood. This is also why works of fine architecture really cannot be made of wood, however many forms it can assume: our theory is the only one

[a] *Zweckmäßigkeit*
[b] *Bestand*
[c] *Widerspiel*
[d] *Kuppel*
[e] *Kenntniss*
[f] *Scheingebäude*

able to explain this. But also: if we are told that the building we enjoy looking at is made of very diverse materials with wildly disparate weights and consistencies, but which cannot be told apart by sight, the whole building would become as disagreeable to us as a poem in a language we do not understand. All this goes to show that architecture operates not only mathematically but also dynamically, and[35] that what speaks to us in architecture is not just something like form and symmetry, but those basic forces of nature, those primary Ideas, those lowest levels of the objecthood of the will. – The regularity of a building and its parts is brought about in part by the immediate purposiveness of each part for the existence[a] of the whole; but in part the regularity also helps facilitate an overview and understanding of the whole; and finally, in part, the regularity of the figures contributes to its beauty by revealing the lawlike character[b] of space as such. But all of this has only subordinate value and necessity and is by no means the main point; even symmetry is not indispensable, since ruins can be beautiful as well.

255

Now works of architecture have a very special relation to light: they double their beauty in full sunlight with blue sky in the background, and have a completely different effect again in moonlight. Thus, when a work of fine architecture is being built, particular attention is paid to the effects of light and the celestial orientation.[c] The main reason for this is that all the parts and their relations really only become visible in bright clear light: but besides this, it is my opinion that architecture is not only meant to reveal gravity and rigidity, but also at the same time it is meant to reveal the essence of light, which is the complete opposite of these. Since light is intercepted, blocked and reflected by the huge, opaque, clearly delineated and multiform masses, its nature and properties are unfolded most purely and distinctly, and this to the great pleasure of the viewer, since light is the most enjoyable of things, as the condition and the objective correlate of the most perfect mode of intuitive cognition.

Now because the Ideas that are brought into clear intuition through architecture are the lowest levels of the objecthood of the will, and consequently the objective significance of what architecture reveals to us is relatively small, the aesthetic pleasure we feel in looking at a beautiful and favourably illuminated building lies not so much in the apprehension of the Idea as in the subjective correlate introduced along with this apprehension, and thus consists predominantly in the fact that this sight tears

[a] *Bestand*
[b] *Gesetzmäßigkeit*
[c] *Himmelsgegenden*

the viewer away from – and raises him above – the mode of cognition that individuals possess, a mode that serves the will and follows the principle of sufficient reason, to that of the pure subject of cognition, free from the will, and thus to pure contemplation itself which is freed from all the suffering of willing and individuality. – In this respect, the converse of architecture and the opposite extreme in the series of fine arts is drama, which brings to cognition the most significant Ideas of all. This is why the objective side is overwhelmingly dominant in the sense of aesthetic pleasure we feel with drama.

256   Architecture is distinct from the visual arts[a] and poetry in that it does not produce an *imitation*[b] but rather the thing itself: it does not repeat the Idea that is cognized, as those other arts do in which the artist lends the viewer his eyes; rather, in this case the artist orients the object properly for the viewer and facilitates his apprehension of the Idea by making the actual individual object express its essence clearly and completely.

Unlike other works of fine art, works of architecture are very seldom constructed for purely aesthetic purposes: instead, these are subordinated to other, practical purposes that are foreign to art itself, and so the great merit of the architect consists in carrying through the purely aesthetic goals in spite of their subordination to foreign ones, and achieving them by skilfully adapting them in a variety of different ways to each of the arbitrary goals, and judging correctly which aesthetic-architectonic beauty would suit and be joined to a temple, which to a palace, which to an armoury,[c] etc. The more a harsh climate steps up the demands of necessity, of practicality, determining them more tightly and prescribing them more imperatively, the less room there is for beauty in architecture. In the mild climates of India, Egypt, Greece and Rome, where the demands of necessity were fewer in number and more loosely determined, architecture was most at liberty to follow its aesthetic goals: these were tightly constrained under the northern skies. Here, where coffers,[d] pointed roofs and towers were required, architecture could develop its own beauty only in very restricted quarters, and had instead to embellish itself all the more with decorative elements borrowed from sculpture, as can be seen in fine Gothic architecture.

If, in this way, architecture suffers under great restrictions through the demands of necessity and practicality; then on the other hand, this provided

---

[a] *bildenden Künsten*
[b] *Nachbild*
[c] *Zeughause*
[d] *Kasten*

it with a powerful support, since, given the scope and the expense of its works and the narrow sphere of its aesthetic effect, it could not sustain itself purely as a fine art if it did not at the same time have a secure and honourable position among the human professions as a useful and necessary occupation. It is a deficiency in this regard that prevents another art from standing at its side as its sister, although from an aesthetic perspective it would certainly stand as the partner of architecture: I am talking about fountainry as a fine art.[a] This is because architecture is to the Idea of gravity (where this appears combined with rigidity) what fountainry is to that same Idea where it is associated with fluidity, i.e. formlessness, transparency, the most effortless mobility. Foaming and roaring waterfalls that plunge over rocks, peaceful cascades dispersing into spray, springs gushing upwards as high columns of water, and clear reflective lakes reveal the Ideas of fluid and heavy matter just as architectural works exhibit the Ideas of rigid matter. Practical hydraulics[b] offers no support to fountainry as a fine art, since the goal of the latter generally cannot be united with that of the former, apart from certain exceptional cases, for instance in the Trevi Fountain[c] in Rome.[*,36]

257

§ 44

In a certain way, landscape gardening[d] performs the same service for the higher levels of vegetable nature that the artforms just mentioned perform for the lowest levels of the objecthood of the will. For the most part the scenic[e] beauty of a spot depends on the diversity of the natural objects found together in it, and thus on the fact that these objects are clearly separated from each other and emerge distinctly while presenting themselves in an appropriate combination and variation. These are the two conditions that landscape gardening promotes;[37] nonetheless it does not exert nearly as much control over its material as architecture does over its material, and so its effect is limited. The beauty landscape gardening displays belongs almost entirely to nature: landscape gardening itself adds little to it: and on the other hand, it cannot accomplish very much in the

---

[*] For this see chapter 35 of the second volume.

[a] *schöne Wasserleitungskunst*
[b] *nützliche Wasserleitungskunst*
[c] *Cascata di Trevi*
[d] *schöne Gartenkunst*
[e] *landschaftliche*

face of unfavourable natural conditions; when nature is its adversary and not its ally, its achievements are meagre.

Since the plant kingdom offers itself everywhere to aesthetic pleasure without the intervention of art, it belongs primarily to landscape painting to the extent that it *is* an object of art. The rest of nature, in as much as it lacks cognition, also falls, along with the plant kingdom, into the province of landscape painting. – With still lifes and paintings of unadorned architecture, ruins, church interiors and the like, the subjective side of aesthetic pleasure predominates: that is to say, our delight in them does not lie primarily in the immediate apprehension of the Ideas presented, but rather more in the subjective correlate of this apprehension, in pure cognition free of the will; since the painter allows us to see things through his eyes, we share both in the sensation here as well as in the afterglow[a] of the profound peace of mind and complete silencing of the will that were needed to submerge cognition so completely in those lifeless objects and to apprehend them with such affection, i.e. with such a degree of objectivity.[b] – Now on the whole, genuine landscape painting has this sort of effect as well: but because the Ideas it presents are higher levels of the objecthood of the will and are thus more significant and substantial, the objective aspect of aesthetic pleasure comes more to the fore and balances out the subjective side. Pure cognition as such is no longer completely the principal concern; instead, the Idea that is cognized, the world as representation on a significant level of the objectivation[38] of the will, operates with equal power.

But a much higher level is revealed in paintings and sculptures of animals, and this latter can be found in important ancient relics, such as the horses in Venice, on Monte Cavallo,[c] on the Elgin marbles, but also in Florence in bronze and marble, as well as the ancient boar there, the howling wolves, the lions in the Arsenal in Venice, and also an entire room in the Vatican filled mostly with ancient animals, etc. The objective side of aesthetic pleasure has a decisive preponderance over the subjective in these portrayals.[39] The tranquillity of the subject who cognizes these Ideas, who has quieted his own will, is indeed present, just as it is in every aesthetic experience:[d] but we do not perceive its effect because we are occupied with the restlessness[e] and intensity of the will that is portrayed. It is that willing, a willing that constitutes our own being as well, that now comes before our eyes, and

[a] *eine Mitempfindung und das Nachgefühl*
[b] *Objektivität*
[c] [in Rome]
[d] *Betrachtung*
[e] *Unruhe*

258

does so in shapes where the will's appearance is not controlled or tempered   259
by thoughtfulness[a] (as it is with us); rather, it presents itself with stronger
features and a clarity that verges on the grotesque and monstrous, but also
without disguise, naïvely and openly, in the clear light of day, which is
precisely why we take an interest in animals.[40] What is characteristic in the
species came to the fore even in the portrayal of plants, but appeared in
their forms alone: here it is much more significant, and expresses itself not
only in shape, but in action, position and gesture, although only ever as the
character of the type, not of the individual. – This cognition of the Ideas
of higher levels, which we obtain through a foreign medium in painting, is
something we can share in directly[b] as well, through a purely contemplative
intuition of plants and observation of animals, and indeed of animals in
their free, natural and comfortable state. An objective view[c] of their diverse
and remarkable forms and their comings and goings[d] is an instructive
lesson from the great book of nature, deciphering the true signature of all
things.[*,e] We see in it the many different grades and modes of manifestation
of the will, which is one and the same in all beings, and wills the same
thing everywhere, objectifying itself as life, as existence, in such endless
variation, such diversity of forms, all of which are accommodations to the
diversity of external conditions, like so many variations on the same theme.
But if we wanted to explain their inner essence to the spectator's reflection
and communicate it in a single phrase, we could do no better than to use
the Sanskrit formula that occurs so often in the Hindu holy book and is
called *Mahavakya*, the great word: *'tat tvam asi'*,[f,41] which means 'You are   260
this living thing.'

§ 45

Finally, the great task of historical painting and of sculpture is the immediate and intuitive presentation of the Idea in which the will reaches the

---

* Jacob Böhme, in his book *de Signatura rerum* [*The Signature of All Things*, 1622], ch. 1, §§ 15, 16,
  17, says: 'There is nothing in nature that does not also reveal its inner form outwardly: because the
  inner always works towards revelation.... Everything has a mouth for revelation.... And this is the
  language of nature in which every thing speaks from out of its own quality and always reveals and
  presents itself.... For everything reveals its mother who therefore provides the *essence and will* for
  formation.'

[a] *Besonnenheit*
[b] *unmittelbar theilhaft*
[c] *Betrachtung*
[d] *Thun und Treiben*
[e] *signatura rerum*
[f] [From *Chândogya-Upanishad*, 6, 7, 8]

highest grade of its objectivation. The objective aspect of delight in beauty is completely predominant here, and the subjective side has retreated into the background. It should also be noted that in animal painting (the level immediately below this one), what is characteristic is entirely identical with what is beautiful: the most characteristic lion, wolf, horse, sheep, bull has always been the most beautiful as well. This is because animals do not have character as individuals – their only character is that of the species. But in the portrayal of human beings, the species character is separate from the character of the individual: the former is called beauty (entirely in the objective sense), while the latter retains the name character or expression, and the new difficulty emerges of portraying both of them together fully in any given individual.

Human beauty is an objective expression that signifies the most complete objectivation of the will on the highest level at which it can be cognized, the complete expression in intuitive form of the Idea of a human being as such. But however strongly the objective side of beauty comes to the fore here, the subjective side remains its constant companion. No object draws us into purely aesthetic intuition[a] as readily as the most beautiful human face and figure, the sight of which immediately suffuses us with an inexpressible pleasure[b] and raises us above ourselves and all that ails us;[c] but this is possible only by virtue of the fact that this clearest and purest susceptibility of the will to cognition[d] is also what transports us most quickly and readily into the state of pure cognition, a state in which our personality, our willing with its constant agony, disappears for as long as the pure, aesthetic delight continues: thus Goethe says: 'Whoever looks on human beauty cannot be touched by evils: he feels himself in harmony with the world and with himself.'[e] – We must explain how nature can achieve a beautiful human figure by means of the fact that the will objectifies itself at this highest level in an individual and thereby completely overwhelms (both through fortunate circumstances as well as through its own force) all the obstacles and resistance put up against it by the lower levels of the will's appearance, which are the natural forces,[42] from which the will must first win over and wrest away the matter that belongs to all of them. Furthermore, the appearance of the will on the highest levels always possesses multiplicity in its form: even the tree is only a systematic aggregate of innumerably

261

---

[a] *Anschauen*
[b] *Wohlgefallen*
[c] *Alles was uns quält*
[d] *Erkennbarkeit des Willens*
[e] [*Die Wahlverwandtschaften* (*Elective Affinities*), I, 6]

repeated sprouting fibres: this compounding of structure[a] increases more and more the higher we ascend, and the human body is a highly intricate[b] system of very different parts, each of which lives in subordination to the whole while also possessing its own distinctive life, its *vita propria*: but the fact that all these parts are subordinated to the whole and co-ordinated with each other in precisely the right way, the fact that they conspire to present the whole in a harmonious manner, with nothing excessive and nothing curtailed; – together, these are the rare conditions that result in beauty, the perfect expression[c] of the species character. – Thus nature. But what of art? – It is said to be the imitation[d] of nature. – But how is the artist supposed to recognize the successful work of nature that is to be imitated and to find it among the unsuccessful works unless he anticipates the beautiful *prior to experience*? Moreover, has nature ever really produced a human being every part of whom was completely beautiful? – This is why it is said that the artist has to sort through many people to find scattered, individual beautiful parts and combine them into a beautiful whole: an absurd and meaningless view, since it refers us right back to the question of how he is supposed to recognize precisely these forms as beautiful and the others not? – We can see how far the old German painters got with beauty by means of the imitation of nature. Just look at their nudes. – No cognition of beauty is possible purely *a posteriori* and from mere experience: it is always at least partly *a priori*, although it is entirely different from the modes of the principle of sufficient reason that we are conscious of *a priori*. These concern the universal form of appearance as such, in so far as this form grounds the possibility of cognition in general, the universal *How* of appearing, which allows for no exceptions:[43] both mathematics and the pure natural sciences proceed from this cognition. By contrast, the other type of cognition *a priori*, which makes possible the presentation of the beautiful, concerns the content of appearances instead of the form, the *What* of appearing instead of the *How*. We all recognize human beauty when we see it, but in true artists this recognition takes place with such clarity that they show us beauty they themselves have never seen and surpass nature in their portrayals; this is possible only because *we ourselves* are the will whose adequate objectivation on its highest level should be judged and discovered here. This alone allows us to anticipate what nature (which is of course the very will that constitutes our own essence) is at pains to present; in a

262

---

[a] *Zusammensetzung*
[b] *kombiniert*
[c] *vollkommen ausgeprägt*
[d] *Nachahmung*

true genius this anticipation is accompanied by a degree of mental clarity[a] that enables him to look at particular things and recognize the *Idea*, as if he *understands nature's half-spoken words*, and then clearly enunciates what nature only stutters, imprinting in solid marble the beauty of the form that nature fails to achieve after a thousand attempts, confronting nature as if to call out to her: 'This is what you wanted to say!' and 'Yes, that was it!' is the reply of the knowing connoisseur.[b,44] – This is the only way the geniuses of Greece could discover the prototype[c] of the human figure and establish it as the canon for the school of sculpture; and only by virtue of such anticipation is it possible for all of us to recognize beauty where nature really has achieved it in an individual thing. This anticipation is the *Ideal*: it is the *Idea* to the extent that it is at least partially recognized *a priori* and becomes practical for art by supplementing what is given *a posteriori* through nature. The possibility of this sort of *a priori* anticipation of the beautiful in the artist, as well as its *a posteriori* acknowledgement in the connoisseur, lies in the fact that both the artist and the connoisseur are themselves the in-itself of nature, the self-objectifying will. As Empedocles[45] said, like is known[d] only by like: only nature can understand itself; only nature will fathom itself; but also mind can learn[e] only from mind.*,[46]

The absurd belief (although it is held by Xenophon's Socrates: Stobaeus, *Anthology*,[f] Vol. 2, p. 384)[47] that the Greeks discovered the established Ideal of human beauty in an entirely empirical manner, by combining individual beautiful parts, exposing and noting down a knee here, an arm there – this belief has a direct analogy in literature,[g] namely the assumption that Shakespeare, for instance, noted down and then reproduced from his own experience of the world the countless variety of characters in his dramas, characters that are so true, so sustained, and elaborated in such depth. The impossibility and absurdity of such an assumption needs no argument: it is

263

---

* The last sentence is the translation of Helvetius' *il n'y a que l'esprit qui sente l'esprit* [*De l'esprit*, (*On Mind*), discourse II, 4], which I did not need to point out in the first edition. But since then the age has been so reduced and made so crude by the stultifying influence of Hegelian would-be wisdom [*Afterweisheit*] that many people might well imagine that I am alluding to the opposition between 'mind and nature': this is why I need to explicitly guard against having such vulgar philosophemes attributed to me.

[a] *Besonnenheit*
[b] *hallt es aus dem Kenner wider*
[c] *Urtypus*
[d] *erkannt*
[e] *vernommen*
[f] *Flori[legium]*
[g] *Dichtkunst*

obvious that just as the genius produces the work of visual art only through a prescient anticipation of beauty, he produces poetic works only through the same sort of anticipation of the characteristic, although both require experience as a schema; it is only through this schema that what they are both conscious of obscurely and *a priori* is called into full clarity, and the possibility of insightful[a] portrayal begins.

Human beauty was explained above as the most complete objectivation of the will at the highest level on which it can be cognized. It expresses itself through form, which lies only in space, and has no necessary reference to time, as does motion, for instance. To this extent we can say: beauty in the objective sense is the adequate objectivation of the will through a purely spatial appearance. Plants are nothing other than such purely spatial appearances of the will; the expression of their essence does not entail motion, and consequently makes no reference to time (apart from their development): their mere shape[b] expresses their essence and exhibits it openly. But a complete revelation of the will appearing in animals and human beings requires in addition a series of actions through which their appearing is referred immediately to time. All this was mentioned already in the previous Book: it is relevant to our present discussion in the following way. Just as the purely spatial appearance of the will can objectify the will more or less completely on every particular level (thereby constituting beauty or ugliness), so too the temporal objectivation of the will (i.e. action, and indeed immediate action, which is to say movement) can correspond purely and completely to the will that objectifies itself in it, with no foreign admixture, nothing superfluous, no deficiencies, expressing precisely the particular act of will in question; – or it can all happen the other way around. In the first case the motion is *graceful*;[c] in the second it is not. Thus, just as beauty is the fitting[d] presentation of the will in general through its purely spatial appearance, *grace* is the fitting presentation of the will through its temporal appearance, i.e. the absolutely correct and appropriate expression of that act of will through the movement and posture[e] objectified in it. Since movement and posture already presuppose the body, Winckelmann expresses himself very correctly and aptly when he says: 'grace is the proper relation of the person who acts to the action' (*Works*, Vol. 1, p. 258). It is obvious that while plants can certainly be

[a]   *besonnenes*
[b]   *Gestalt*
[c]   *mit Grazie*
[d]   *entsprechende*
[e]   *Stellung*

considered beautiful, they can only be described as graceful in a figurative sense; but animals and human beings can be both beautiful and graceful. According to what we have said, grace consists in the fact that every movement and posture is executed in the easiest, most appropriate and most comfortable manner, and is thus the entirely fitting expression of its intention, or the act of will, without anything superfluous (which would present itself in the form of a self-defeating and unnecessary busyness or contorted posture) or anything lacking (which would present itself as wooden stiffness). Grace presupposes as its condition a correct proportion of all limbs and a regular and harmonious physique; only in this way is complete ease and evident purposiveness in all postures and movements possible: grace is therefore never without a certain degree of corporeal beauty. When the two are complete and united they are the clearest appearance of the will at the highest level of its objectivation.[48]

As mentioned above, one of the distinguishing features of humanity is that the character of the species is separate from that of the individual so that to a certain extent, as we said in the previous Book, each human being presents a completely distinctive Idea. Thus, along with beauty as the character of the species, the arts devoted to the presentation of the Idea of humanity are also concerned with the character of the individual, which is what we really mean by *character*. But this is true only to the extent that character is not seen as something contingent, something wholly and completely idiosyncratic to the individual in his particularity,[a] but rather as an aspect of the Idea of humanity that happens to be particularly pronounced in this individual so that the presentation of this individual serves to reveal this aspect of the Idea. Thus, although character as such is individual, it must nonetheless be apprehended and presented in ideal terms, i.e. with an emphasis on its significance to the Idea of humanity in general (it contributes in its own way to the objectivation of this Idea): if this is not done, then the presentation becomes a portrait, a repetition of the particular as such, with all its contingencies. And as Winckelmann says, even the portrait should be the ideal of the individual.

This *character*, which is to be apprehended in ideal terms and which emphasizes one of the particular aspects of the Idea of humanity, presents itself visibly, in part through the enduring physiognomy and body structure[b] and in part through fleeting emotion and passion, the reciprocal modification of cognition and willing, all of which is expressed through

[a] *Einzelheit*
[b] *Korporisation*

facial expression and movement. The individual always belongs to humanity and humanity, for its part, is always revealed in the individual (indeed in
the particular and ideal significance of that individual); as a result, beauty
ought not to be annulled by character, nor character by beauty because
if the species character were annulled by that of the individual, the result
would be caricature, and were the individual character to be annulled by
that of the species, the result would be insignificant. Thus, a portrayal[a]
that is intended to be beautiful (as is primarily the case with sculpture)   266
will nonetheless always modify the species character to some extent by the
individual character and always express the Idea of humanity in a determinate, individualized manner, emphasizing a particular aspect of this Idea;
this is because to a certain extent, the human individual as such has the
dignity[b] of an Idea of his own, and it is essential to the Idea of humanity
that it present itself in individuals of particular significance. Hence we find
in the works of the ancients that the beauty they apprehend so clearly is
not expressed through a single form but rather through many forms that
bear different characters, as if it was always grasped from a different side,
and, accordingly, displayed differently in Apollo, differently in Bacchus,
differently in Hercules, and differently in Antinous: indeed, what is characteristic can constrain the beautiful and ultimately even cross over into
ugliness in the drunken Silenus, in fauns, etc. But if what is characteristic
is really taken to the point of annulling the character of the species, which
is to say to the point of being unnatural, then it becomes caricature. – But
we must prevent the characteristic from detracting from grace even more
than from beauty, because expression of character requires graceful posture
and movement as well, and so it must be carried out in a way that is easiest
and most expedient[c] for the person concerned. Not only the sculptor and
the painter but every good playwright will observe this: otherwise here too
you will only get caricature in the form of distortion and contortion.

  Sculpture is concerned primarily with beauty and grace. The true character of the spirit, which comes forward in affect, passion, interplay of
cognition and willing, and which can only be portrayed through gesture
and facial expression, is chiefly the province of *painting*. Although eyes and
colouring (which lie outside the purview of sculpture) contribute greatly
to beauty, they are much more essential to character. Moreover, beauty
unfolds itself more completely when observed from several points of view:

[a] *Darstellung*
[b] *Dignität*
[c] *zweckmäßigste*

by contrast, the expression, the character can be apprehended perfectly from even a *single* standpoint.

267   Because beauty is clearly the prime purpose of sculpture, *Lessing* tried to explain the fact that *Laocoön does not cry out* by claiming that crying out is incompatible with beauty. But since Lessing made this the theme, or at least the starting-point, of one of his books, and since so much has been written about it both before and after him, I may be forgiven for adding my opinion here in passing, although a special topic such as this does not really belong in the context of our discussion, which is exclusively oriented towards the universal.

§ 46

It is obvious that Laocoön, in the famous group, does not cry out, and the universal, ever-recurring astonishment on that score must be based on the fact that anyone in his place would cry out, and this is what nature demands as well: when in the throes of the most intense physical pain, with the sudden onset of the greatest bodily anguish, any reflection that could lead to anything like a silent endurance[a] is pushed out of consciousness, and nature gives vent to a cry that simultaneously expresses the pain and the anguish, calls for help and frightens the attacker. Thus even Winckelmann was sorry not to see the expression of a cry: but in trying to vindicate the artist, he really made Laocoön into a Stoic who considers it beneath his dignity[b] to cry out in accordance with nature,[c] and instead adds to his pain the useless compulsion[d] of stifling it: thus Winckelmann sees in him 'the tried spirit of a great man writhing in agony who tries to hold back the expression of feeling[e] and shuts it up within himself: he does not break out into a loud scream, as in Virgil; only worried sighs escape from him' etc. (*Works*, Vol. 7, p. 98. – The same thing in more detail in Vol. 6, pp. 104ff.). In his *Laocoön*, Lessing criticizes Winckelmann's view and improves on it in the manner mentioned above: in place of a psychological ground he posits a purely aesthetic one, namely that beauty, the principle of ancient art, does

268 not permit the expression of a cry. He provides another argument, namely that a stationary work of art cannot portray a wholly ephemeral state that is incapable of duration; but there are hundreds of counter-examples of

[a] *Dulden*
[b] *Würde*
[c] *secundum naturam*
[d] *Zwang*
[e] *Empfindung*

superb figures held fast in fleeting movements, dancing, wrestling, playing catch, etc. In fact, in the essay on the *Laocoön* at the beginning of the *Propyläen* (p. 8), Goethe considers the choice of such an entirely ephemeral moment as precisely what is needed. – In the present day, *Hirt* (*Horen*, 1797, No. 7.) reduced everything to the highest truth of the expression, and decided the matter by claiming that Laocoön does not cry out because he cannot, since he is in the process of suffocating to death. Finally, *Fernow* (*Roman Studies*, Vol. 1, pp. 426ff.) discussed and weighed all three opinions, not adding anything new himself, but instead reconciled and unified all three.

I cannot help but be surprised that such thoughtful and astute men struggle to bring in far-fetched and inadequate reasons, resorting to psychological, even physiological arguments to explain a matter whose reasons are quite close at hand and are obvious to the unbiased, – and in particular that Lessing, who came so close to the correct explanation, nevertheless completely missed the real point.

Prior to all psychological or physiological investigation as to whether Laocoön would cry out given his situation (which by the way I utterly and completely agree he would) we must pronounce that the group cannot be portrayed as crying out for the simple reason that portrayal of this lies entirely outside the province of sculpture. A Laocoön that cries out could not be cut from marble, only a Laocoön with his mouth open wide vainly trying to cry out, a Laocoön whose voice has stuck in his throat, *vox faucibus haesit*.[a],[49] The essence of crying out and consequently its effect on the spectator is bound up exclusively with the sound, not the gaping mouth. This latter phenomenon necessarily accompanies the cry but must first be motivated and justified by the sound it produces: then, as characteristic of the action, it is permissible and in fact necessary, even if it detracts from the beauty. But the portrayal of crying out is entirely foreign to – and in fact impossible in – the visual arts: it would be truly incomprehensible to portray a gaping mouth, the violent means of crying out that disturbs all the features and the usual expression, while omitting its end, the cry itself along with its effect on the mind.[b] What is more, this would produce the always ridiculous spectacle of a permanent exertion without effect, which really can be compared with the trickster who stops up the horn of a sleeping night watchman with wax, wakes him up with calls of a fire, and laughs over his unsuccessful attempts at blowing the

269

---

[a] [Virgil, *Aeneid*, II, 774]
[b] *Gemüth*

horn. – By contrast, it is entirely permissible to present the cry when it falls within the province of the art depicting it,[a] because it serves the truth, i.e. the complete presentation of the Idea. This is how it is in poetry, which makes use of the reader's imagination[b] for its intuitive portrayal: this is why, in Virgil, Laocoön cries out like a bull that has broken free after being struck by the axe: this is why Homer (*Iliad*, XX, 48–53) has Mars and Minerva cry out so terrifyingly without detracting from their divine dignity or beauty. It is just the same in the theatre:[c] Laocoön on stage would simply have to cry out; Sophocles lets Philoctetes cry out, and he surely would have actually cried out on the ancient stage. In the same vein, I remember in London seeing the famous actor *Kemble* in *Pizarro*, a play translated from the German; he was playing the American Rolla, a half savage with a very noble character: still, he cried out loudly and vehemently when wounded, and this had a grand and excellent effect because, being highly characteristic, it contributed significantly to the verisimilitude.[d] – By contrast, a silent screamer in painting or stone would be far more ridiculous than the painted music that was already criticized in Goethe's *Propyläen*, because screaming detracts from beauty and normal expressions much more than music does, since music for the most part involves only hands and arms and should be regarded as an action characteristic of the person, and can therefore be painted quite properly as long as it does not call for any violent movement of the body or distortion of the mouth: so for instance there is St Cecilia at the organ, Raphael's *Violin Player* in the Sciarra gallery in Rome,[50] and many others. – And so, because the limitations of art do not permit Laocoön's pain to be expressed by crying out, the artist needed to evoke[e] every other expression of pain: and this he has done with consummate perfection, as Winckelmann (*Works*, Vol. 6, pp. 104ff.) demonstrated so masterfully, his superb description retaining its full value and truth once you abstract out his attribution of a Stoic disposition.*

§ 47

Because sculpture is concerned primarily with beauty and grace, it loves the nude and tolerates clothing only when it does not conceal the forms.

* This digression has its own supplement in chapter 36 of volume 2.

[a] *der darstellenden Kunst*
[b] *Phantasie*
[c] *Schauspielkunst*
[d] *Wahrheit*
[e] *in Bewegung setzen*

It uses drapery not as covering but as an indirect presentation of form: this way of presenting form occupies the understanding a great deal since it can intuit the cause, namely the form of the body, only through the immediately given effect, the cast of the drapery. Accordingly, drapery is to sculpture what foreshortening is to painting. Both are significations,[a] but not symbolic ones; rather, when they succeed they immediately compel the understanding to intuit what is signified just as if it had actually been given.

I may be permitted to introduce in passing a simile appropriate for the rhetorical arts. Just as the beauty of the bodily form[b] is shown to greatest advantage when it is most lightly clad, or even totally unclad, and thus a very beautiful person who also has taste and was permitted to indulge it would rather walk around practically naked, dressed only as people did in antiquity; – likewise, any beautiful mind, full of ideas, would always express itself in the most natural, simple and straightforward way, anxious   271 to communicate its thoughts to others (if this is at all possible) and thus relieve the solitude that he must experience in a world such as this: but conversely, intellectual poverty, confusion and wrong-headedness,[c] clothe themselves in the most laboured expressions and obscure turns of phrase in order to conceal petty, trivial, bland or trite thoughts in difficult and pompous expressions, just as someone who lacks the majesty of beauty wants to compensate for this deficiency with clothing and tries to hide the triviality or ugliness of his person beneath barbaric adornments, sequins, feathers, ruffles, puffs and cloaks. There are many authors who, if forced to translate their pompous, obscure books into their petty, straightforward content, would be as embarrassed as this overdressed man would be if he were to go naked.

§ 48

The primary concern of *historical painting* is beauty and grace but also character, by which is understood the portrayal of the will at the highest level of its objectivation, where the individual has special significance[d] in emphasizing a particular aspect of the Idea of humanity. We do not recognize this significance only through the mere form[e] of the individual,

---

[a] *Andeutungen*
[b] *Körperform*
[c] *Verschrobenheit*
[d] *Bedeutsamkeit*
[e] *Gestalt*

but rather through actions of every sort and through the modifications of
cognition and willing that occasion and accompany these actions, made
visible in gestures and facial expression.[a] Since the Idea of humanity is to be
portrayed in this sphere, the many facets of this Idea will have to be unfolded
before our eyes through significant individuals; and the significance of these
individuals can, in turn, be made apparent only through a variety of scenes,
events and actions. Historical painting solves this infinite task by bringing
before our eyes scenes of life of every sort, whether their significance is
great or small. There are no insignificant individuals or actions: the Idea
of humanity unfolds itself more and more in all and through all. As a
result, absolutely no event in human life is to be excluded from painting.
Consequently, people do the excellent painters of the Dutch school a
great injustice when they esteem only their technical proficiency while
disparaging everything else because the school usually portrays themes from
everyday life while they on the other hand think that only world historical
or biblical events are significant. We should first pause to consider that the
inner significance of an action is entirely distinct from its outer significance,
and the two often go their separate ways. The outer significance is the
importance of an action in relation to its consequences in and for the
actual world, and thus according to the principle of sufficient reason. Inner
significance is the depth of insight into the Idea of humanity that the
action opens up by bringing to light the aspects of that Idea that appear
less frequently. It does this by clearly and decisively allowing self-expressing
individualities[b] to unfold their distinctive traits in circumstances that have
been arranged to facilitate this. Only inner significance is relevant for art:
outer significance is relevant for history. But they are totally independent
of each other; they can appear together, but each can also appear on its
own. An action that is highly significant for history can be very common
and ordinary with respect to its inner significance: and conversely, a scene
from everyday life can have immense inner significance if it allows even
the most hidden furrows of human individuality and human deeds and
willing to appear in a bright and clear light. In addition, events whose
outer significances are very dissimilar can have the same inner significance;
for instance, it is very much the same with respect to inner significance
whether ministers with their maps fight over countries and peoples, or
whether peasants in the tavern stake their claims over cards and dice, just
as it makes no difference whether you play chess with figures made of gold

272

[a] *Miene*
[b] *Individualitäten*

or of wood.[51] Moreover, the scenes and events that make up the lives of so many millions of people, their comings and goings,[a] their hardships and their joys,[b] are for that very reason important enough to be the subject-matter of art, and through their rich variety must provide sufficient material for unfolding the many-sided Idea of humanity. Even the fleeting nature of the moment, which art has fixed in such a painting (called a *genre*-painting these days), excites a quiet, distinctive emotion,[c] because holding fast the fleeting and constantly changing world in an enduring image of individual events that nevertheless represent the whole is an accomplishment of the art of painting that seems to bring time itself to a standstill by raising the particular to the Idea of its species.[52] Finally, the historical and externally significant subjects of painting often have the disadvantage that precisely what is significant about them is not intuitively presentable but must be added in thought. In this respect, the nominal significance[d] of the painting must be distinguished from its real significance: the former is the outer significance added only as a concept; the latter is the aspect of the Idea of humanity that is revealed to intuition through the painting. An example of the former might be Moses as he is found by the Egyptian princess, an extremely important moment for history: the real significance on the other hand, which is actually given to intuition, is a foundling being saved by a noble woman from his floating cradle – an event that could well have frequently taken place. Only costume can alert the scholar to the particular historical case here; but dress only makes a difference with respect to the nominal significance, and is a matter of indifference for the real, because this latter knows[e] only human beings as such, not the arbitrary forms. Subjects drawn from history have no advantage over those drawn from mere possibility (which can therefore only be termed general, not individual) because what is genuinely significant in historical subjects is not in fact what is individual, not the particular event as such, but rather what is universal in it, the aspect of the Idea of humanity that expresses itself through it. On the other hand even particular historical themes are certainly not to be rejected on this account: it is just that the genuinely artistic insight that they offer, as much for the painter as for the viewer, is never tied to their individual and particular aspects (these in fact constitute what is the historical about them) but rather to the universal that expresses

273

[a] *Thun und Treiben*
[b] *Freude*
[c] *Rührung*
[d] *Bedeutung*
[e] *kennt*

itself in them, to the Idea. In addition, the only historical themes that should be chosen are those in which the principal subject can actually be portrayed rather than having to be added in thought: otherwise, the nominal significance is too remote from the real significance: what is merely thought in the painting becomes the most important element and detracts 274   from what is intuited. It is a problem even with theatre when the central event takes place behind the scenes (as is the case with French tragedy), but this is clearly a much greater flaw in a picture. Historical subjects have a decisively detrimental effect only when they restrict the painter to a field that is chosen arbitrarily, for purposes other than artistic ones; but their effect is entirely detrimental when this field is poor in painterly or significant themes, for instance if the subject is the history of a petty, isolated, stubborn, hierarchical (i.e. ruled by delusion) and obscure group of people[a] such as the Jews, who are despised by their contemporaries, the great peoples of the Orient and Occident. – A mass migration[b] took place between our time and that of all ancient peoples, just as a change of the sea bed separates the present surface of the earth from the one whose organisms[c] can only be seen in fossilized form,[d] and it should therefore be regarded as a great misfortune that the people whose past culture is supposed to provide the primary underpinning for our own should not be, for instance, the Indians or the Greeks or even the Romans, but rather precisely these Jews. It was an unlucky star for the geniuses of Italian painting of the 15th and 16th centuries in particular that in the narrow sphere to which they were arbitrarily referred for their choice of subject-matter, they had to grasp at miserable wretches of every sort; the historical sections of the New Testament are almost less propitious for painting than the Old, and the subsequent history of martyrs and teachers of the church is a thoroughly unhappy topic. Nonetheless, we must clearly distinguish the pictures that take as their subject the historical or mythological aspect of Judaism or Christianity from those in which the genuine, i.e. ethical spirit of Christianity is revealed to intuition through the portrayal of people who are full of this spirit. These portrayals are in fact the highest and most admirable achievements in the art of painting: only the greatest masters of this art, particularly Raphael and Correggio (above all in his earlier pictures) have succeeded at them. Paintings of this sort should in point of fact not be considered historical, because they typically do not portray any events

[a] *Winkelvolk*
[b] *Völkerwanderung*
[c] *Organisationen*
[d] *versteinert*

or actions, but are only groupings of saints, of the redeemer himself, often   275
still a child, with his mother, angels, etc. In their faces, and particularly
in the eyes, we see the expression, the reflection[a] of the most complete
cognition, namely cognition not oriented towards individual things but
rather towards the Ideas, and that has therefore completely apprehended
the whole essence of the world and of life; in them, this cognition reacts
back upon the will, not supplying it with *motives* as other cognition does,
but on the contrary becoming a *tranquillizer* of all willing, from which
complete resignation (which is the innermost spirit of both Christian as
well as Indian wisdom) has proceeded, the relinquishing of all willing,
the turning back and abolition of the will, and with it the abolition of
the entire essence of this world, and hence redemption. In this way the
eternally praiseworthy masters of art express the highest wisdom through
their works, in intuitive form.[b] And here is the summit of all art which,
after it has followed the will in its adequate objecthood (the Ideas) through
all levels from the very lowest, where it first unfolds its essence and is moved
in so many ways by causes, and then to stimuli, and finally to motives,
now finishes by presenting its free self-abolition through the one great
tranquillizer that arises for it from the most complete cognition of its own
essence.[*]

§ 49

All of our observations so far concerning art are grounded in the truth that
the object of art that the artist aims to portray and that the artist must
cognize prior to his work as its seed and origin, – is absolutely nothing
other than an *Idea* in Plato's sense:[53] it is not the individual thing, the object
of our common apprehension, nor is it the concept, the object of rational
thought and science. Although Idea and concept have something in common, namely the fact that as unities both stand for[c] a multiplicity of actual
things, yet the great difference between the two will have become clear and
convincing enough from what was said in the First Book about the concept
and what is being said in the present Book about the Idea. I certainly do   276
not mean to say that Plato had a clear conception of this distinction: in
fact, many of his examples and descriptions of Ideas are applicable only to

---

[*] This passage will be entirely incomprehensible without the following Book.

[a] *Wiederschein*
[b] *anschaulich*
[c] *vertreten*

concepts. For now we will leave this as it is and go our own way, glad whenever we come across the trace of a great and noble mind, but nonetheless
following our goal instead of his footsteps. – *Concepts* are abstract, discursive; they are determinate only with respect to their boundaries, within
their spheres they are completely indeterminate. They are accessible and
comprehensible to anyone in possession of reason; they can be communicated verbally without any further mediation, and are entirely exhausted
by their definitions. By contrast, Ideas, which are perhaps best defined as
adequate representatives[a] of concepts, are thoroughly intuitive and, despite
the fact that they stand for an infinite number of particular things, they are
nonetheless thoroughly determinate: they are never cognized by individuals as such, but only by someone who has raised himself above all willing
and all individuality to become the pure subject of cognition: accordingly,
they are accessible only to the genius and hence also to someone who,
through an elevation of his cognitive powers usually occasioned by the
works of a genius, is in the same state of mind as a genius:[b] this is why
the Ideas are not absolutely but only conditionally communicable, since
the Idea grasped and repeated in the work of art speaks to people only in
proportion to their own intellectual value; which is why precisely the most
excellent works of every art, the noblest products of genius, will always
and necessarily remain closed books for the obtuse majority, inaccessible
to them and separated from them by a wide gulf, just as the society of the
prince is inaccessible to the rabble. Of course even the dullest accept on
authority works acknowledged to be great so as not to betray their own
weakness: still, they are always quietly ready to condemn such works as
soon as they can hope to do so without exposing themselves, at which point
they gladly give vent to their long-concealed hatred of everything great and
beautiful, of works that humiliated them by never speaking to them, and
their hatred of the authors of these works. In general, one must have value
oneself in order freely and willingly to acknowledge value in another. This
is the basis for the requirement that modesty accompany all merits, as well
as the disproportionately loud praise for this virtue which alone, among
all its sisters, is always added to the praise of anyone distinguished in some
way by the person who dares to praise him, so as to conciliate the worthless
and silence their wrath. For what is modesty if not false humility which
someone with merits and advantages in a world teeming with perfidious
envy uses to beg the pardon of those who have none? Someone who does

277

---

[a] *Repräsentant*
[b] *in einer genialen Stimmung*

not lay claim to merit because he in fact has none is being honest, not modest.[54]

The *Idea* is unity shattered into multiplicity through the temporal and spatial form of our intuitive[a] apprehension: the *concept* on the other hand is unity reassembled from plurality by means of the abstraction of our reason: it can be designated as unity after the fact, and the Idea as unity before the fact.[b,55] Finally, the distinction between concept and Idea can be expressed figuratively by saying: *concepts* are like dead receptacles; what we place inside actually lies next to each other, and we cannot take out more (through analytic judgements) than we have put in (through synthetic reflection): in those who have grasped them, on the other hand, *Ideas* develop representations that are novel with respect to concepts sharing the same name: the Idea is like a living and developing organism endowed with generative powers, an organism that can produce things that were not already packaged up inside it.

Now it follows from everything we have said that as useful as the concept is for life, and as practical, necessary and fruitful as it is for science, it will always be barren for art. By contrast, the apprehended Idea is the true and unique source for every genuine work of art. In its forceful originality it is drawn only from life itself, from nature, from the world, and also only from true genius or someone momentarily inspired[c] to the point of genius. Genuine works bearing eternal life arise only from such an immediate conception.[d]

Precisely because the Idea is and remains intuitive, the artist is not conscious of the intent and purpose of his work abstractly;[e] an Idea rather than a concept hovers before him: this is why he cannot give an account of what he does: he is driven merely by feelings, as people like to say, and works unconsciously, even instinctively. By contrast, imitators,[f] mannerists, *imitatores, servum pecus*,[g] approach art from the concept: they take note of what is effective and pleasing in genuine works of art, clarify this to themselves, grasp it in a concept and hence abstractly, and then imitate it, overtly or covertly, with shrewd intent. They suck nourishment from the works of others like parasitic plants, and they take on the colours of this nutriment like polyps. In fact, we could take this comparison even

278

---

[a] *intuitiv*
[b] *unitas post rem . . . unitas ante rem*
[c] *Begeisterten*
[d] *unmittelbare Empfängniß*
[e] *in abstracto*
[f] *Nachahmer*
[g] [imitators, servile herd: Horace, *Letters*, I, 19, 19]

further and assert that they are like machines that can certainly grind and mix together whatever is put in them, but can never digest it, so that the foreign components can always be rediscovered, picked out of the mixture, and separated: only the genius is like an organic body[a] that assimilates, transforms and produces. He is certainly cultivated and educated by his predecessors and their works, but it is only by life and the world itself that he is made directly fertile, only by the impression of what can be intuited: thus, even the highest level of cultivation will never detract from his originality. All imitators and mannerists grasp the essence of other people's exemplary achievements in concepts; but concepts can never endow a work with inner life. The age, which is to say the dull and obtuse multitude always found in the age, is familiar with concepts alone and clings to them, so that it receives mannerist works with ready and noisy approval: but these same works will be unpalatable after a few years, because the spirit of the age, i.e. the predominant concepts in which alone these works are rooted, will themselves have changed. Only genuine works that are drawn directly from nature and from life remain forever young and eternally forceful,[b] like nature and life themselves. They do not belong to any age, but rather to humanity itself, which is why they are met with lukewarm receptions in their own ages (to which they disdain to conform); and since they indirectly and negatively exposed the errors of their own ages, they received only belated and grudging recognition. Yet this is also why they do not grow old but instead retain a fresh and new appeal for even the most distant ages: then they are no longer exposed to neglect and misunderstanding, because they are crowned and sanctioned by the approval of the few minds[c] capable of judging, minds that appear at rare and isolated times through the centuries* and cast the ballots that slowly accumulate and thus ground the authority that alone constitutes the seat of judgement people have in mind when they appeal to posterity. It is only those successively appearing individuals, because the masses and mobs of posterity will for all times be and remain just as wrong-headed and stupid as the masses and mobs of the contemporary world always are and have always been. – Just read the complaints of the great minds[d] of every century concerning their

---

* *Apparent rari, nantes in gurgite vasto.* ['They appear singly, swimming on the desolate waves', Virgil, *Aeneid* I, 118]

[a] *Leib*
[b] *urkräftig*
[c] *Köpfe*
[d] *Geister*

contemporaries: they always sound the same as they do today, because the human race is always the same. In every age and in every art, style[a] takes the place of the spirit,[b] which is only ever the property of the few: but style is the old, discarded garb of the last known appearance of spirit. In view of all this, the approval of posterity is only purchased as a rule at the cost of the approval of the present, and vice versa.*,56

§ 50

Now if all art aims to communicate the apprehended Idea, which appears in isolation, cleansed of all foreign elements through the intermediary of the artist's mind so that it can be grasped by someone with weaker susceptibility and no productive ability; and if, further, it is objectionable for art to take the concept as its point of departure, then we will not be able to approve of deliberately and avowedly intending an artwork to express a concept, as is the case with *allegory*. An allegory is a work of art that means[c] something other than what it portrays. But something that can be intuited (and consequently the Idea) expresses itself immediately and quite completely, and does not need to be signified[d] by some intermediary. On the other hand, something that must be signified and represented[e] (i.e. by   280
means of another, completely different thing), because it cannot itself be brought before intuition in this way, is clearly a concept. So an allegory is always supposed to designate a concept, and consequently direct the mind of the spectator away from the intuitive representation[f] being presented to a totally different, abstract, non-intuitive representation lying entirely outside of the artwork:57 here the picture or statue is supposed to do the same thing as writing does much more completely. The goal in this case is not what we claim the purpose of art to be, namely the presentation of an Idea that can only be apprehended intuitively. No great perfection on the part of the artwork is required for what is intended in this case: it is enough that one sees what the thing is supposed to be, since the goal is achieved as soon as this is revealed, and the mind is then guided to an

---

* See chapter 34 of the second volume.

[a] *Manier*
[b] *Geist*
[c] *bedeuten*
[d] *andeuten*
[e] *repräsentiert*
[f] *Vorstellung*

entirely different sort of representation,[a] to the abstract concept that was the presupposed aim. Consequently, allegories in the visual arts are nothing other than hieroglyphics: whatever incidental artistic value they might possess as intuitive presentations does not accrue to them *as* allegories, but for other reasons. The fact that Correggio's *Night*,[b] Annibale Carracci's *Genius of Fame*, Poussin's *Horae*[c] are very beautiful pictures must be clearly separated from the fact that they are allegories. As allegories they accomplish nothing more than an inscription might, and in fact rather less. We are reminded here of the distinction made above between the real and the nominal significance[d] of a painting. The nominal significance here is just the allegorical as such, e.g. the genius of fame; the real significance is what is actually depicted: in this case, a beautiful winged youth with beautiful boys flying around him: this expresses an Idea: but this real significance is only effective so long as the nominal, allegorical significance is forgotten: when thinking about the latter, intuition is left behind and your mind is occupied with an abstract concept: but the transition from Idea to concept is always a descent. In fact the nominal significance, the allegorical intent, frequently detracts from the real significance, the intuitive truth: so, for instance, the unnatural lighting in Correggio's *Night*, which, however beautifully it is executed, is motivated by purely allegorical considerations and could not possibly be real. Thus, if an allegorical picture has artistic value as well, this is completely separate and independent from its accomplishments as an allegory: artwork such as this serves two purposes simultaneously, namely the expression of a concept, and the expression of an Idea: only the latter can be an artistic goal; the other is a goal foreign to art, a playful diversion that allows a painting to perform the office of an inscription and hieroglyph at the same time, a device invented for the benefit of those to whom the authentic essence of art can never speak. It is the same when an artwork is also a useful tool, where it also serves two purposes at once, such as a statue that is at the same time a candelabra or caryatid, or a bas-relief that is at the same time Achilles' shield. The pure art-lover will not tolerate either one. Of course an allegorical image can make a vivid impression on our mind even in its capacity as allegory: but an inscription would have had the same effect in similar circumstances. For instance, when the desire for fame has taken firm and lasting hold in a man's mind, and he looks on fame even as his rightful possession, withheld from him only as long as he has not yet produced the title deeds: and if he were now to stand before

281

---

[a] *Vorstellung*

[b] [The piece is known as *Nativity* or *Holy Night* or *Adoration of the Shepherds*]

[c] [The painting is *Dance to the Music of Time*]

[d] *Bedeutung*

The Genius of Fame with its laurels, his emotions[a] would be stirred and his strength called into action: but the same thing would also happen if he were suddenly to see the word 'fame' written on the wall in large, clear letters. Or if someone has proclaimed a truth that is important either as a maxim for practical life or as an insight for science, but it has fallen on deaf ears, then an allegorical image portraying the age as lifting up the veil and revealing the naked truth will have a powerful effect on him: but the same effect would also be accomplished with the motto: 'the age discovers the truth'[b] because only the abstract thought is really ever effective here, not what is intuited.

Now if, as we have said, allegory in the visual arts is a mistaken endeavour serving a cause quite foreign to art, then it will be absolutely intolerable if it reaches the point where the portrayal of forced and violently far-fetched subtleties descends into foolishness. This is seen, for instance, when a turtle 282 is made to indicate womanly modesty or seclusion;[c] Nemesis looking down into the bosom of her robe indicates that she sees into hidden things as well; Bellori's explanation that Annibale Carracci dressed Lust[d] in yellow robes because he wanted to indicate that its pleasures are quick to fade and become yellow like straw. – Now, when there is absolutely no connection between what is being portrayed and the concept that it indicates[e] – that is, no connection based either in subsumption under the concept or in an association of ideas – and instead the sign and the signified[f] are linked together entirely by convention, by positive and arbitrary stipulation, I call this degenerate variety of allegory a *symbol*. Thus the rose is the symbol of discretion, the laurel the symbol of fame, the palm the symbol of victory, the mussel the symbol of pilgrimage,[58] the cross the symbol of the Christian religion: symbols also include colours when they are used as such to indicate something, such as yellow as the colour of falseness and blue as the colour of fidelity. Symbols such as these may often be useful in life, but their value is foreign to art: they should be regarded as hieroglyphs or even Chinese calligraphy, and in fact belong together with coats of arms, the bushes that signify an inn, the key that enables you to recognize the gentleman in waiting, or the leather that identifies the miner. – Finally, when certain historical or mythic people or personified concepts are identified with a fixed and established symbol, these should really be called *emblems*:

[a] *Gemüth*
[b] *Le tem[p]s découvre la verité.*
[c] *Eingezogenheit*
[d] *Wollust*
[e] *dadurch angedeuteten Begriff*
[f] *Zeichen und Bezeichnetes*

examples are the animals of the evangelists, the owl of Minerva, the apple of Paris, the anchor of hope, etc. Meanwhile people generally take emblems to be those simple, symbolic portrayals that are explained through a motto and are supposed to illustrate a moral truth; there are large collections of these by J. Camerarius, Alciati and others: they provide the transition to poetic allegory, a topic that we will discuss further below. – Greek sculpture appeals to intuition and is thus *aesthetic*; Hindustani sculpture appeals to the concept and is therefore merely *symbolic*.[59]

283 This judgement on allegory is grounded in our previous discussion of the inner essence of art, and it is entirely consistent with that discussion; but it is diametrically opposed to Winckelmann's view which, far from regarding allegory as entirely foreign to the purpose of art and often interfering with this purpose (as we have done), promotes it everywhere, and even locates the highest goal of art in the 'presentation of universal concepts and non-sensuous things' (*Works*, Vol. 1, pp. 55ff.). We must all decide for ourselves which view to accept. Given these and similar views of Winckelmann concerning the authentic metaphysics of beauty, I am struck by the truth that one can have the greatest susceptibility and the best judgement concerning artistic beauty without being able to give an abstract and authentically philosophical account of the essence of beauty and of art: just as one can be very noble and virtuous and possess a very tender conscience that weighs particular cases with the precision of a gold-scale without this enabling one to fathom philosophically the ethical meaning of actions and present them abstractly.[a]

Allegory has an entirely different relation to *poetry* than it does to the visual arts, and although it is objectionable in the latter case, it is entirely permissible and most useful in the former. This is because in the visual arts, allegory proceeds from the given intuitive material, the true subject-matter of all art, to what is thought abstractly; in poetry however, the relation is reversed: in poetry, what is immediately given in language is the concept, and the foremost aim of poetry is always to proceed from this immediately given concept to what is intuited, which the listener's imagination[b] must undertake to present. When in the visual arts we are directed from what is immediately given to something else, this other thing must always be a concept, because in this case only what is abstract cannot be immediately given; but a concept can never be the origin of a work of art and the communication of a concept can never be its goal. In poetry by contrast, the concept is the material, the immediately given, which we may very

[a] *in abstracto*
[b] *Phantasie*

well leave behind in order to evoke something intuitive, which is entirely different and in which the goal is reached. In the context of a poem[a] many concepts or abstract thoughts might be indispensable that are in themselves and immediately wholly incapable of being intuited: these thoughts will   284 then often be rendered intuitable through examples that are subsumed under them. This is already the case with figurative expressions and takes place in every metaphor, simile, parable and allegory, all of which can be differentiated only by the length and detail of their portrayals. This is why similes and allegories are so superbly effective in the rhetorical arts. How beautifully Cervantes says of sleep that 'it is a cloak that covers the whole man' in order to express how it rids us of all mental and physical suffering. How well Kleist uses allegory in the following verse to express the thought that philosophers and scholars enlighten the human race:

The ones whose night lamp illuminates the whole of the earth.[b,60]

How forcefully and vividly[c] Homer describes Ate, the bringer of disaster, by saying: 'she has tender feet, for she does not walk upon the hard earth but steps only on the heads of men.' (*Iliad*, XIX, 91). What a strong effect Menenius Agrippa's fable about the stomach and limbs had on the Roman people in their wanderings. What a fine expression of a highly abstract philosophical dogma we find in Plato's allegory of the cave, an allegory that we have already mentioned, found at the beginning of the seventh book of the *Republic*. The myth of Persephone should likewise be seen as a profound allegory with a philosophical tendency, an allegory in which Persephone, by eating a pomegranate in the underworld, falls prey to it: this is made particularly clear by Goethe's treatment of the myth, a treatment beyond praise, inserted in passing as an episode into his *Triumph of Sensibility*.[d] I know of three extended allegorical works: one obvious and admitted example is the incomparable *Criticon* of Balthasar Gracián,[e] which consists of an immense and rich tapestry of inter-connected and highly ingenious allegories that clothe moral truths in bright garb; the author uses this device to bring the greatest vivacity[f] to the work and astonish us with the wealth of his inventions. Two veiled allegories are *Don Quixote* and *Gulliver in Lilliput*. The first is an allegory of the life of everyone who does not look

---

[a] *Dichtung*
[b] [Ewald von Kleist, *Der Frühling* (*Spring*), *Works* (1803) I, 236]
[c] *anschaulich*
[d] *Triumph der Empfindsamkeit*
[e] [Baltasar Gracián, *El Criticón* (*The Faultfinder*) published between 1651 and 1657. Schopenhauer translates a substantial excerpt from this work in the Preface to the first edition of his *Two Fundamental Problems of Ethics*]
[f] *anschaulichkeit*

merely to his own welfare, as others do, but pursues an objective, ideal
purpose that has seized hold of his thinking and willing and which of
course makes him appear peculiar in this world. With *Gulliver* we only
need to regard everything physical as intellectual to see what the *satirical
rogue*[a] (as Hamlet would call him) has in mind.[61] – Now since the concept
is always what is given in poetic allegory, and the allegory tries to illustrate
this graphically[b] through an image, the allegory might therefore sometimes
be expressed or supported by a painted image: as a result, this image would
not be regarded as a work of visual art, but rather only as a hieroglyphic
designation that makes no claim to painterly, but rather only to poetic
value. Lavater's beautiful allegorical vignette is of this type, a vignette that
must have such a heartening effect on every noble champion of truth: a
hand holding a candle is being stung by a wasp, while above the flame
gnats are being burned: underneath is the motto:

> Although it might singe the gnats' wings to the veins,
> Destroying their skulls and consuming their brains;
> Light still remains light;
> The fiercest of wasps could sting me with its might,
> I still hold it tight.

The same sort of thing can be seen in the gravestone with the extinguished,
smoking candle and the inscription:

> When the candle's out we soon shall know,
> Whether wax or tallow made it glow

Finally, we can include the example of the old German family tree on
which the final offshoot of a very old family expressed his resolve to lead
the rest of his life in complete abstinence and chastity and thus allow
the lineage to die out by portraying himself at the root of the tree with
many branches and cutting off the tree above himself with shears. The
symbols we have mentioned, which are usually called emblems, belong
here, and we could also describe them as short, painted fables with an
explicit moral.[62] – Allegories of this sort are always to be considered as
poetic, not painterly, and are justified as such: the pictorial execution always
remains of secondary importance here, and nothing more is expected of it
than that it portray its subject in a recognizable fashion. But as in visual arts,
so too in poetry, allegory becomes symbol when there is only an arbitrary
connection between what is shown in intuition and the abstraction thus

---

[a] [Schopenhauer uses the English phrase. See *Hamlet* Act II, scene 2]
[b] *anschaulich machen*

indicated. Since everything symbolic fundamentally rests on convention,[63] the symbol has among its other disadvantages that over time its meaning is forgotten, leaving it entirely mute: who would guess, if they did not already know, why the fish is the symbol of Christianity? Only a Champollion, because it is a phonetic hieroglyph through and through.[64] Thus, as a poetic allegory, the Revelation of John is in approximately the same position as the reliefs with the great sun-god Mithra,[a] – always still being interpreted.[*,65]

§ 51

Now if we take what we have said so far about art in general and turn from the visual arts to *poetry*,[b] we will have no doubt that it too aims to reveal the Ideas, the levels of objectivation of the will, and to communicate them to the listener with the clarity and vivacity with which the poetic mind[c] grasps them. Ideas are essentially intuitive: if, therefore, only abstract concepts are directly communicated by means of words in poetry, it is nevertheless clear that the aim is still to allow the listener to intuit the Ideas of life in the representatives[d] of these concepts, something that can take place only with the help of the listener's own imagination.[e] But in order to put this into effect given the goal, the abstract concepts (which are the immediate material of poetry just as they are of the driest prose) must be arranged in such a way that the pattern of intersection of their spheres ensures that no concept can persist in its abstract generality; instead an intuitive representative appears before the imagination and the poet's words continually modify this in keeping with his intentions. Just as the chemist is able to distil out solid precipitates by combining completely clear and transparent liquids, similarly the poet understands how to connect the abstract, transparent generality of concepts in order to precipitate out, as   287 it were, what is concrete and individual, the intuitive representation. This is because the Idea can be cognized only intuitively, and knowledge of the Idea is the goal of all art. Excellence in poetry, as in chemistry, allows one to consistently obtain precisely the precipitate one has in mind. The many epithets of poetry serve this end, epithets that keep restricting the generality of some concept to the point where it can be intuited. For almost every

---

[*] See chapter 36 of the second volume.

[a] *magnus Deus sol Mithra*
[b] *Poesie*
[c] *das dichterische Gemüth*
[d] *Repräsentanten*
[e] *Phantasie*

noun, Homer introduces an adjective whose concept divides the sphere of the noun, at once greatly reducing the sphere of its concept and bringing it that much closer to intuition. For instance:

> Helios' glowing lamp sank into the ocean,
> Pulling the dark night over the food-growing earth.[a,66]

And

> Soft blows the wind that breathes from that blue sky!
> Still stands the myrtle and the laurel high[b]

uses only a few concepts to precipitate out before the imagination the full bliss of a southern climate.

Rhythm and rhyme are very special resources for poetry. I can think of no other way to explain their incredibly powerful effect than this: owing to their fundamental connection to time, our representational faculties[c] have a peculiarity that makes us follow any regularly recurring sound internally and join in, as it were. Rhythm and rhyme thus become a way of holding our attention, since we follow the performance more willingly; but also they lead us, blindly and prior to any judgement, to chime in with the performance – and this gives it a definite and emphatic power of persuasion, independent of all reasons.

Because poetry communicates the Ideas using material that is general, i.e. concepts, it covers a considerable amount of territory. The whole of nature, the Ideas of all levels can be portrayed by poetry which, according to the standard of the Idea to be communicated, proceeds sometimes with descriptions, sometimes with narrations, and sometimes with direct dramatic portrayals. The visual arts typically surpass poetry in the portrayal of the lower levels of the objecthood of the will because nature devoid of cognition, as well as merely animal nature, reveals almost its entire essence in a single well-chosen moment. By contrast, human beings are the principal concern of poetry to the extent that they do not express themselves merely through their figure and face, but through a chain of actions and the thoughts and affects that accompany these actions. No other art can equal poetry in this, because it can make use of progressive change, while the visual arts cannot.

The great subject-matter of poetry is thus the revelation of the Idea that is the highest level of the will's objecthood, the presentation of human

---

[a] Εν δ' επεσ' Ωκεανω λαμπρον φαος ηελιοιο, | Ἑλκον νυκτα μελαιναν επι ζειδωρον αρουραν. (*Occidit vero in Oceanum splendidum lumen solis,* | *Trahens noctem nigram super almam terram.*) [*Iliad* VIII, 485]

[b] [Goethe, *Balladen*, 'Mignon', translation by Coleridge]

[c] *Vorstellungskräfte*

beings in the inter-connected series of their actions and endeavours. – Of course we get to know humanity through experience and history as well, but these tell us more about *human beings*[a] than about *humanity* itself:[b] i.e. they furnish empirical information about human behaviour (from which we can derive rules for our own conduct) rather than allowing us to look deeply into the inner essence of humanity. Of course nothing prevents experience and history from undertaking this: nevertheless, when it is the essence of humanity itself that is unlocked for us through history or through our own experience, then we have already grasped the latter (and the historian the former) with artistic eyes, already grasped it poetically, i.e. according to the Idea and not the appearance, according to its inner essence and not its relations. Our own experience is as indispensable a condition for understanding literature[c] as it is for history because it is, as it were, the lexicon of the language spoken by both. But history really is to poetry what portrait painting is to historical painting: the former gives what is true in particular, the latter what is true in general; the former has the truth of appearance, and can attest to it on this basis; the latter has the truth of the Idea, which cannot be found in any individual appearance but nonetheless speaks out of all of them. Poets are selective and deliberative in placing significant characters in significant situations: historians take both as they come. In fact, they must examine and select events and people not according to their inner, true significance, expressive of the Idea, but according to the outer, illusory,[d] relative significance that is important with reference to its connections, its consequences. They cannot consider anything in and of itself, according to its essential character and expression, but must always consider everything according to its relations, within a network, in its influence on what follows and indeed particularly on their own age. So they will not skip over an insignificant action on the part of a king, an act in itself quite ordinary, because this act has consequences and influences. On the other hand, they will not mention actions of very distinguished individuals that might be quite significant in themselves but have no consequences, no influence. This is because their view conforms to the principle of sufficient reason and takes hold of appearance, whose form this principle is. Poets however grasp the Idea, the essence of humanity, outside of all relations, outside of all time, the adequate objecthood of the thing in itself on its highest level. Even if the inner essence, the significance of appearances, the kernel of all those shells can never be completely lost

289

---

[a] die *Menschen*
[b] den *Menschen*
[c] *Dichtkunst*
[d] *scheinbar*

in the historian's way of looking at things, and can still be found and recognized (at least by those who are looking for it); nonetheless, what is significant in itself and not in its relations, the authentic unfolding of the Idea, can be found with far greater accuracy and much more clarity in poetry than in history, and so, as paradoxical as it might sound, poetry can be credited with much more authentic, genuine, inner truth than can be attributed to history. This is because historians are supposed to track down the individual event precisely as it occurs in real life, as it develops in time through the intricately inter-connected chains of grounds and consequents; but they cannot possibly possess all the relevant information to enable them to see or discover everything; at every turn the original of their image either abandons them or a false image slips in unnoticed, and this happens so often that I think I may assume there is more that is false in history than true. Poets on the other hand have grasped the Idea of humanity from just the aspect that is to be portrayed, and it is the essence of their own self that is objectified for them in it: as we argued above in the case of sculpture, their cognition is partly *a priori*: their model stands firm, clear and brightly illuminated before their mind[a] and cannot desert them: this is why they show us the Idea purely and clearly in the mirror of their mind and their description is as true as life itself, down to the last detail.* The great ancient historians are therefore poets when it comes to particulars, where they have

290

---

* It goes without saying that I am only ever talking about the rare, great, true poets [*Dichter*] and nobody could be further from my mind than that shallow tribe of mediocre poets [*Poeten*], rhymesters and tellers of fairy tales that proliferate so wildly in Germany, particularly nowadays, and whose ears should be ceaselessly and from all sides assailed with:

> Neither gods nor people
> nor the advertising columns permit anyone to be a mediocre poet
> [*Mediocribus esse poëtis*
> *Non homines, non Di, non concessere columnae*
> Horace, *Ars poetica*, 372].

It is indeed worth seriously considering the quantity of time and papers – both their own and those of others – that have been wasted by this swarm of mediocre poets, and how harmful their influence is, given that the public in part always reaches for novelty, but in part also has by nature more of an inclination for perversity and banality, for which it has a greater affinity; thus, these works of the mediocre poets draw the public away and hold it back from those true masterpieces and any cultivation it would receive from them, and consequently they have an effect that is precisely counter to the favourable influence of geniuses, increasingly ruining taste and holding back the progress of the age. This is why critics and satirists should pitilessly and mercilessly castigate the mediocre poets until, for their own sakes, they are compelled to employ their spare time in reading something good rather than writing something bad. – Because if the botched efforts of the talentless could put even the gentle god of the Muses [Apollo] into such a rage that he could flay Marsyas, I do not see what mediocre poetry could ground its demands for tolerance on.

[a] *Geist* [and in the rest of this paragraph]

no information, e.g. in the speeches of their heroes; indeed, the whole way in which they treat their material tends towards the epic: but this is just what lends unity to their portrayal and lets them retain the inner truth even where the outer is inaccessible to them, or even falsified. And if we have just compared history with portraiture in contrast to poetry, which would correspond to historical painting, then we find Winckelmann's dictum that a portrait should be the ideal of the individual[a] is also observed by the ancient historians since they portray the individual[b] so that the aspect of the Idea of humanity expressed in it comes to the fore: modern historians, by contrast, with few exceptions provide for the most part only: 'a rubbish bin and a lumber room and at best a mock-heroic play'.[c] – Thus for anyone wanting to know[d] humanity in its inner essence (an essence that is identical in all appearances and developments), to grasp it according to its Idea, the works of the great, immortal poets hold out a much truer and clearer image than the historians ever could: because even the best among them are far from being the first among poets, and their hands are tied. In this respect, the relation between the two can also be illustrated by the following simile. The pure historian who works exclusively from data is like someone who does not know anything about mathematics and who takes figures he happens upon by chance and examines the relations between them by measuring them; the empirically discovered results of this research will therefore be tainted by all the errors of the figures as drawn: the poet on the other hand is like the mathematician who constructs these relations *a priori* in pure intuition and expresses them, not as they actually are in figures as drawn, but as they are in the Idea that the drawing is supposed to render visible.[e] – Thus Schiller says:

291

> What has never anywhere taken place,
> That alone will never age.[f,67]

I must say that even biographies, particularly autobiographies, have a greater value than authentic history with respect to knowledge[g] of the essence of humanity, at least the way history is typically treated. In part this is because biographical information can be assembled more accurately and completely than historical information; and in part because the agents of

---

[a] *Individuum*
[b] *Einzelne*
[c] [Goethe, *Faust* I, 582–3]
[d] *erkennen*
[e] *versinnlichen*
[f] [Schiller, *An die Freunde* (*To Friends*), 49–50]
[g] *Erkenntniß*

authentic history are not so much human beings as peoples and armies, and the individuals who do crop up seem so far away, have so much surrounding them, such a great retinue, and in addition are wrapped in the stiff clothing of state or heavy and inflexible suits of armour, so that it is truly difficult to recognize human movement through it all. By contrast, a true description of the life of the individual within a narrow sphere will show all the forms and nuances of the way human beings act, the excellence, virtue, indeed the holiness of particular individuals, the perversity, misery, perfidy of most, the iniquity of many. In fact, from the only point of view we are considering here, namely the inner significance of what appears, it

292   makes absolutely no difference whether the objects that action turns on are, viewed relatively, trivialities or matters of importance, farmyards or kingdoms: for in themselves, none of these things have any significance and they acquire it only through the fact that and in so far as they set the will into motion: a motive has significance only in relation to the will; on the other hand, the relations that, as a thing, it possesses to other similar things do not come into consideration at all. Just as a circle with a one-inch diameter and a circle with a diameter of 40 million miles will have exactly the same geometrical properties, so the events and the history of a village and those of a kingdom will be the same in their essentials; and we can study and come to know humanity in the one just as in the other.[68] It is also wrong to assert that autobiographies are full of deceit and dissimulation. Rather, lying (although possible anywhere) is perhaps more difficult there than elsewhere. Dissimulation is easiest in simple conversation; in fact, paradoxical as it might sound, it is actually more difficult even in a letter, because in writing a letter we are left to ourselves and look within, not to the outside, so that, finding it difficult to bring the unfamiliar and the distant up close, we will not have the tools to gauge the other person's impressions; and the recipient, for his part, will calmly review the letter in a mood foreign to the writer, reading it repeatedly and at different times, and easily discovering the concealed intent. We get to know an author as a human being most easily from his book, because these conditions all work even more strongly and consistently in this case. And dissimulation is so difficult in autobiography that perhaps there has never been one that was not on the whole truer than any other piece of recorded history. The man who writes his life surveys it in general terms, details grow small, what is close grows distant, what is distant comes close again, and the field of consideration shrinks: he seats himself at the confessional and does so voluntarily: here the spirit of the lie does not grab hold of him so easily because everyone also has a tendency to truth that must be

overpowered with every lie and that is in an unusually strong position in just this case. The relation between biography and the history of a people[a] can be made clear through the following simile. History shows us humanity in the way a look-out point on a tall mountain shows us nature: we see a great deal all at once, wide stretches, great masses; but nothing is clearly recognizable according to its whole and authentic essence. By contrast, the portrayal of the life of the individual shows us human beings in the same way that we become familiar with nature when we walk among trees, plants, cliffs, rivers and lakes. But just as in the case of landscape painting, in which the artist lets us look into nature through his eyes, greatly facilitating our recognition of its Ideas and the state of pure, will-less cognition that is required for this, so too is literature vastly superior to both history and biography for the presentation of the Ideas that we can look for in them: because here too, genius holds before us the clarifying mirror in which we are faced with everything essential and significant, arranged together and placed in the brightest light, omitting what is contingent and foreign.*

Now the poet can carry out his task of portraying the Idea of humanity in one of two ways: either what is portrayed is at the same time the portrayer (this is what happens in lyric poetry, in the song proper,[b] where the poetry-writer[c] vividly intuits and describes only his own state[69]); because of this, therefore, i.e. through its object, a certain subjectivity is essential to this genre; – or, on the other hand, what is being portrayed is wholly different from the portrayer, as in all the other genres, where the portrayer is concealed to a greater or lesser degree behind what is portrayed, even to the point of vanishing entirely. In the romance, the portrayer still expresses his own situation to some extent through the tone and attitude of the whole: because of this, although it is much more objective than the song, the romance still has some elements of subjectivity, but these become increasingly faint in the idyll, still more so in the novel, are almost entirely gone in the epic proper, and finally vanish without a trace in the drama, which is the most objective and most perfect genre of poetry in more than one respect, as well as the most difficult. The lyrical genre is for this reason the easiest, and if art otherwise belongs only to the rare and true genius, even someone who is not particularly distinguished can produce a

---

* See chapter 38 of the second volume.

[a] *Völkergeschichte*
[b] *im eigentlichen Liede*
[c] *der Dichtende*

294   lovely song when some strong, external source of inspiration,[a] some burst
of enthusiasm intensifies his mental powers: because all that is needed for
this is a lively intuition of his own state in the moment of exhilaration.
This is confirmed by the many isolated songs by otherwise unknown and
random individuals, particularly the German folk-songs assembled in the
superb collection *The Boy's Magic Horn*,[b] and the equally innumerable love
songs and other popular songs in all languages. The whole achievement of
this poetic genre is to grasp the mood of the moment and embody it in a
song. Still, the lyric poetry[c] of true poets[d] forms an image of the interior of
humanity as a whole, and everything that millions of people past, present
and future have felt and will feel (because the same situations keep recurring) finds its proper expression in the lyric. Because these situations keep
recurring, they are as permanent as humanity itself, and always evoke the
same feelings; so the lyric products of true poets continue to ring true and
retain their freshness and power over thousands of years. Now if, in general,
the poet is the universal human being, then everything that has moved a
human heart, whatever issues forth from human nature in any situation,
whatever dwells or broods in the breast of man, – this is his theme and
his material; and along with these, all the rest of nature. Thus the poet
can sing of the sensual just as well as of the mystical, can be Anacreon or
Angelus Silesius, can write tragedies or comedies, can present a sublime
disposition or a common one, according to his mood and mission. This is
why nobody can tell the poet that he should be noble or sublime, moral,
pious, Christian, this or that, or even less reproach him for being this and
not that. He is the mirror of humanity and brings what it feels and does[e]
to its own consciousness.[70]

Now if we consider more closely the essence of the song proper and take
as our examples the models of this genre that are both outstanding and pure,
not those that in any way approximate another genre, such as romances,
elegies, hymns, epigrams, etc., then we will find that the distinctive essence
295   of the song in the narrowest sense is the following. – It is the subject of the
will, i.e. one's own willing, that fills the consciousness of the singer, often
as a liberated, satisfied willing (joy[f]), but even more often as a frustrated[g]

---

[a] *Anregung*
[b] *Wunderhorn* [the full title is *Des Knaben Wunderhorn*]
[c] *Poesie*
[d] *ächter Dichter*
[e] *treibt*
[f] *Freude*
[g] *ein gehemmtes*

willing (sorrow[a]), always as affect, passion, as an excited state of mind. Besides this however and together with it, the sight of nature around him makes the singer aware of himself as the subject of pure, will-less cognition, whose imperturbable, blissful peace now forms a contrast with the pressure of ever-restricted, always needy willing: the sensation of this contrast, of this back-and-forth, is what the song as a whole really expresses and what in general constitutes the lyrical state. In this state, pure cognition draws towards us, as it were, to deliver us from willing and the stress of willing:[b] we follow, but only for a moment: we are always torn back again from peaceful contemplation[c] by willing, by the memory of our personal aims; but again and again we are enticed from willing the next time we are in beautiful surroundings in which pure, will-less cognition presents itself to us. That is why in song and in the lyrical mood, willing (the personal interest of goals) and pure intuiting of the surroundings presented, are wonderfully imbricated with each other: the relationships between the two are sought out and imagined; the subjective mood, the affecting of the will colours the intuited surroundings in reflection, and these surroundings in turn colour the mood: the song proper is the imprint of the whole state of mind that is mixed and shared in this way. – Any of Goethe's immortal songs can be cited as an example to clarify this abstract analysis of a state that is very remote from all abstraction; I will recommend only a few as particularly clear about this point: 'Shepherd's Lament', 'Welcome and Farewell', 'To the Moon', 'On the Lake', 'Autumn Feeling';[d] the genuine songs in 'The Boy's Magic Horn' are excellent examples as well, and in particular the one that begins: 'O Bremen, I must leave you now.'[e] – As a comic and truly apt parody of the lyrical character, I am particularly struck by a song of Voß in which he describes the feelings of a drunken lead-roofer who has fallen off a tower and, in falling, makes a very strange observation for someone in his situation, one associated with cognition that is free of the will, namely that the tower clock shows the time to be half past eleven. – Whoever shares the view I have presented of the lyrical state will also admit that this state is really the intuitive and poetic recognition of the claim advanced in my essay *On the Principle of Sufficient Reason* and also mentioned in the present writing, that the identity of the subject of cognition with the subject of willing can be called a miracle *par excellence*:[f] so that in the

296

---

[a] *Trauer*
[b] *Wollen und seinem Drange*
[c] *Beschauung*
[d] 'Schäfers Klagelied', 'Willkommen und Abschied', 'An den Mond', 'Auf dem See', 'Herbstgefühl'
[e] 'O Bremen, ich muß dich nun lassen'
[f] κατ' εξοχην

end, the poetic effect of the song really rests on the truth of that claim. – Over the course of a life, these two subjects or, more colloquially, the head and the heart, grow increasingly distinct: more and more, people separate their subjective sensations from their objective cognition. In children the two are still completely merged together: children barely know how to distinguish themselves from their environment; they blend in with it. In young men, perceptions always strike sensation and mood first, and are in fact mingled in with them; *Byron* has expressed this very well:

> I live not in myself, but I become
> Portion of that around me; and to me
> High mountains are a feeling.[a,71]

This is why young men cling so firmly to the outer, intuitive aspect of things; this is why they are not suited for anything except lyric poetry and are not ready for dramatic poetry until they are men. We can imagine the elderly as at best epic poets, as with Ossian and Homer, because narration belongs to the character of the elderly.

In the more objective types of literature,[b] especially the novel, epic and drama, there are two ways in particular of achieving the goal, the revelation of the Idea of humanity: first, through the apt and profoundly conceived depiction of significant characters, and second, through the invention of significant situations in which these characters can develop themselves. Just as it is incumbent on chemists not only to give a clear and true presentation of the basic materials and their principal combinations, but also to expose them to the influence of reagents that show their distinctive qualities clearly and conspicuously – similarly, it is incumbent on the poet not only to present us truthfully and faithfully with significant characters, as nature itself does, but also to familiarize us with these characters by putting them into situations in which their distinctive qualities can completely display themselves and the characters can be shown clearly and in sharp relief; such situations are, accordingly, referred to as significant ones. In real life as in history, chance rarely introduces situations of this type, and they are isolated, lost and hidden in the mass of insignificant situations. The novel, the epic and the drama are distinguished from real life as much in the arrangement and selection of significant characters as in the fact that the situations they present are completely suffused with significance. Both however are effective only under the condition of the strictest truthfulness,

297

---

[a] [*Childe Harold*, III, 72]
[b] *Dichtungsarten*

and a lack of unity in the characters, contradictions of the characters among themselves or with human nature in general, as well as the impossibility of the events (or an improbability approaching impossibility), even in matters of secondary importance, are just as offensive in poetry as distorted figures, false perspectives and bad lighting are in painting. This is because in both cases we demand a true mirror of life, of humanity, of the world, only clarified by the presentation and lent significance by means of its arrangement. Since there is only one goal for all the arts, presentation of the Ideas, and the only essential distinction between the various arts is the level of the objectivation of the will at which the Idea to be presented is found, which in turn determines the material of the presentation, so too the most dissimilar arts can be elucidated through comparison with each other. Thus, for instance, in order to grasp fully the Ideas that express themselves in water, it is not enough to look at water in a quiet pond or evenly flowing stream; rather those Ideas are developed completely only when water appears in all those conditions and with all the obstacles that, working on it, bring about the full expression of all of its properties. This is why we find water beautiful when it plunges downwards, roars, foams, springs up into the air again, or turns into spray as it falls, or finally, forced by artificial means, rises upwards in a jet: and although it manifests itself differently in different conditions, it always states its 298 character truthfully: it is just as natural for water to spray upwards as it is for it to reflect calmly; it is just as prepared for the one as for the other, as soon as the conditions emerge. Now what the artist who works with fountainry achieves with fluid matter is achieved by the architect with rigid matter, and again in the very same way by the epic or dramatic poet with the Idea of humanity. The development and clarification of the Idea that expresses itself in the objects of each art, of the will that objectifies itself on every level, is the common goal of all the arts. A human life, as it usually shows itself in reality, is like water as it usually shows itself in ponds and rivers: but in epics, novels and tragedies, selected characters are transposed into circumstances that allow them to display all their distinctive features and reveal the depths of the human mind that become visible in significant and extraordinary actions. Thus literature objectifies the Idea of humanity, whose distinguishing characteristic is to present itself in highly individualized characters.

Tragedy[a] should be viewed, and is in fact recognized, as the pinnacle of literature, both in relation to the grandeur of its effect and the difficulty

---

[a] *das Trauerspiel*

of achieving it. It is of great significance for the whole of our discussion and also important to bear in mind that the goal of this highest of poetic achievements is the portrayal of the terrible aspect of life, that the unspeakable pain, the misery of humanity, the triumph of wickedness,[a] the scornful domination of chance, and the hopeless fall of the righteous and the innocent are brought before us here: for here we find a significant intimation as to the nature[b] of the world and of existence.[72] What emerges horribly is the conflict of the will with itself, displaying itself most fully here, at the highest level of its objecthood. It becomes visible in human suffering, which is brought about in part through chance and error, which step forward as rulers of the world and through their treachery (which goes so far as to appear intentional) are personified as fate; and in part it is brought about by humanity itself, through the clashes between the strivings of individual wills, through the wickedness and perversity of the majority. It is one and the same will that lives and appears in them all, but whose appearances battle amongst themselves and tear themselves apart. The will emerges violently in this individual, more weakly in this other, it is brought to its senses and attenuated by the light of cognition more over here, less over there, until finally, in isolated cases, this cognition, clarified and intensified through suffering itself, reaches the point where it is no longer deceived by appearance, the veil of *māyā*; it sees through the form of appearance, the *principium individuationis*,[c] and the egoism that rests on this principle slowly dies away, so that *motives* that had previously been so violent lose their power, and in their place, complete cognition of the essence of the world acts as a *tranquillizer* of the will and leads to resignation, the abandonment not only of life, but of the whole will to life. So in tragedy we see that, after a long struggle and much suffering, the noblest people eventually renounce forever the goals they had, up to that point, pursued so intensely, as well as renouncing all the pleasures of life, or even willingly and joyfully giving them up: thus Calderón's steadfast prince; thus Gretchen in *Faust*; thus Hamlet, whom Horatio would gladly follow, but who calls upon him to stay and breathe on painfully for a while longer in this harsh world, to cast light on Hamlet's fate and clear his memory; – thus the Maid of Orleans, the Bride of Messina:[d] they all die, purified by suffering, i.e. after the will to live[e] has already died out inside them; in Voltaire's *Mahomet*

---

[a] *Bosheit*
[b] *Beschaffenheit*
[c] [principle of individuation]
[d] [these last two are plays by Schiller]
[e] *Wille zu leben*

this is stated literally in the final words that the dying Palmira cries out to Mahomet: 'The world is for tyrants: live!' – By contrast, the demand for so-called poetic justice rests on a complete failure to recognize the essence of tragedy and in fact the essence of the world. This demand appears in its full triteness and impertinence in the criticisms that Dr Samuel Johnson has offered of some of Shakespeare's plays, complaining with true naïvety about the thorough neglect of poetic justice; which is certainly the case: after all, what have the Ophelias, Desdemonas and Cordelias done wrong? – But only the trite, optimistic, Protestant-rationalist or actually Jewish world-view would demand poetic justice and find its own satisfaction in the satisfaction of this demand. The true sense of tragedy is the   300 deeper insight that the hero does not atone for his particular sins, but for original sin instead, i.e. the guilt of existence itself:

> Because the greatest offence of man,
> Is that he was born[a]

as Calderón says with perfect frankness.[73]

I will allow myself only one remark concerning the detailed treatment of tragedy. The only thing essential to tragedy is the portrayal of a great misfortune. But the many different ways in which the poet can accomplish this can be organized into three specific categories.[b] It can take place through extraordinary evil, an evil that reaches the limits of the possible and is attributable to the one character that is the author of the misfortune; examples of this type are: Richard III, Iago in *Othello*, Shylock in *The Merchant of Venice*, Franz Moor, Euripides' Phaedra, Creon in *Antigone*,[74] and the like. It can also take place through blind fate, i.e. chance and error: a true model for this type is Sophocles' *Oedipus Rex* as well as the *Women of Trachis*,[75] and in general most of the tragedies of the ancients belong here: modern examples include: *Romeo and Juliet*, Voltaire's *Tancred*, and *The Bride of Messina*. Finally, the misfortune can also be introduced simply by means of people's positioning with respect to each other, through their relationships; so that there is no need for a terrible mistake or unheard-of accident or even for a character whose evilness extends to the limits of human possibility; instead, morally ordinary characters in everyday circumstances are positioned with respect to each other in such a way that their situation forces them knowingly and clear-sightedly to cause each other the greatest harm without the injustice falling on one side or

---

[a] *Pues el delito mayor | Del hombre es haber nacido* [*La Vida es Sueño* (*Life is a Dream*), I, 2]
[b] *Artbegriffe*

the other. This last type seems to me much preferable to the other two, because it shows us the greatest misfortune not as an exception, not as something brought about by rare circumstances or monstrous characters, but rather as something that develops effortlessly and spontaneously out of people's deeds and characters, almost as if it were essential, thereby bringing it terrifyingly close to us. And if in both the other categories of tragedy we catch sight of an appalling fate and horrific evil as powers that are indeed terrible but that threaten us only from a great distance so that we ourselves will probably escape them without being driven to renunciation, – then this last genre shows us the sort of powers that destroy life and happiness and that can at any moment make their way towards us as well, where the greatest suffering is brought about by entanglements essentially the same as those assumed by our own fate, and through actions that we too might perhaps be capable of committing, so that we may not complain of injustice: then we shudder as we feel ourselves already in the middle of hell. But the execution of this final type of tragedy brings with it the greatest difficulties because it has to produce the greatest effect merely by positioning and distribution, with the least expenditure of means and the smallest number of causes of action:[a] thus even some of the best tragedies evade this difficulty. A perfect specimen of this type of tragedy is nonetheless to be found in a work that in other respects is greatly surpassed by many others of the same great master: it is *Clavigo*.[b] To a certain extent *Hamlet* belongs here, if you look only at his relation to Laertes and Ophelia; *Wallenstein*[c] has this merit as well; *Faust* is entirely of this type, if you consider as the principal action only the events with Gretchen and her brother; likewise Corneille's *Cid*, except that this lacks a tragic end, which, by contrast, you find in the analogous relation of Max to Thecla.[*,d,76]

§ 52

Now that we have considered all the fine arts with the universality proper to our point of view, beginning with fine architecture (whose goal as such is to make the objectivation of the will clear at the lowest level of its visibility, where it shows itself as the dull striving of mass, conforming to

---

[*] See chapter 37 of the second volume.

[a] *Bewegungsursachen*
[b] [by Goethe]
[c] [by Schiller]
[d] [characters in *Wallenstein*]

law but with no cognition, but nonetheless still revealing self-dichotomy and struggle, namely between gravity and rigidity) – and concluding our investigation with tragedy at the highest level of the objectivation of the will, and which puts that very schism before our eyes in fearful grandeur and clarity; – we find that one fine art still remained, and must remain excluded from our consideration since there was absolutely no suitable place for it in the systematic context of our presentation: and this is *music*. It stands completely apart from all the others. What we recognize in it is not an imitation[a] or repetition of some Idea of the essence of the world: nonetheless, it is such a great and magisterial art, it exercises so powerful an effect within us, is understood so deeply and entirely by us as a wholly universal language whose clarity exceeds even that of the intuitive world itself; – that we can certainly look to it for more than an 'unconscious exercise in arithmetic in which the mind does not know that it is counting',[b] which is what Leibniz took it to be,* although he was entirely correct to the extent that he considered only its immediate and external significance, its outer shell. But if it were nothing more, then the satisfaction that it affords would be similar to the feeling we have when some mathematical problem comes out right, and would not be that heartfelt joy with which we see the deepest recesses of our being[c] given voice. Thus,[77] from our perspective, focusing on the aesthetic effect, we must grant it a much more serious and profound significance, one that refers to the innermost essence of the world and our self, and in this respect the numerical relations into which it can be resolved are not the signified but, even in the first instance, the sign. By analogy with the rest of the arts, we can conclude that music must in some sense relate to the world as presentation to presented, as copy to original,[d] since all of the other arts share this distinctive feature, and music has an effect on us that is, on the whole, similar to theirs, but stronger, quicker, more necessary and more unerring. Its imitative[e] relation   303
to the world must also be very intimate,[f] infinitely true and strikingly apt, because it is instantaneously comprehensible to everyone and has a certain infallibility recognizable from the fact that its form can be reduced to completely determinate rules that can be expressed numerically, and

---

* *Leibnitii epistolae, collectio Kortholti* [*Letters of Leibniz*, edited by Christian Kortholt], letter 154

[a] *Nachbildung*
[b] *exercitium arithmeticae occultum nescientis se numerare animi*
[c] *Wesen*
[d] *wie Nachbild zum Vorbilde*
[e] *nachbildliche*
[f] *innige*

from which it cannot deviate in the least without entirely ceasing to be music. – Nonetheless the point of comparison between music and the world, the respect in which the former acts as an imitation or repetition of the latter, is very deeply hidden. In every age, people have played music without being able to give an account of it: content with an immediate understanding of music, people did without an abstract conceptualization of this immediate understanding.

By devoting my mind entirely to the impression made by the art of music[a] in its many different forms, and then returning to reflection and to the train of thought expounded in the present work, an explanation came to me of the inner essence of music and its mimetic relation to the world, a relation that must be necessarily presupposed by analogy. This explanation is entirely sufficient for me as well as satisfactory for my investigation, and will be equally insightful to those who have followed me thus far and agreed with my view of the world; nonetheless, I recognize that the explanation is fundamentally incapable of proof, since it assumes and lays down a relationship between music as a representation and something that can fundamentally never be a representation; it claims to regard music as the copy of an original that cannot itself ever be directly presented. Here, therefore, at the conclusion of this Third Book, devoted primarily to the arts, I cannot do more than to present the explanation that I find personally satisfying of the marvellous musical art,[b] and I must leave the acceptance or rejection of my view to the overall effect on readers of, on the one hand, music itself, as well as, on the other, the whole of the single thought that I have communicated in this text. Beyond that, in order for readers to be genuinely convinced by my explanation of the significance of music, I consider it necessary that they listen to music frequently and with sustained reflection; and in order to do so it is again necessary that they should already be very familiar with the whole of the thought I am presenting here.

The (Platonic)[78] Ideas are the adequate objectivation of the will; the goal of all the other arts is to arouse cognition of these Ideas through the presentation of particular things (artworks themselves are always such things) – something that is possible only given a corresponding alteration in the subject of cognition. As a result, they all objectify the will only indirectly, namely by means of the Ideas: and since our world is nothing other than the appearance of the Ideas in multiplicity as a result of those

[a] *Tonkunst*
[b] *Kunst der Töne*

Ideas entering into the *principium individuationis* (the form of cognition possible for the individual as such); then, since it passes over the Ideas, music is also wholly independent of the appearing world, simply ignoring it, so that it could in a sense still exist even if there were no world at all, something that cannot be said of the other arts. In fact, music is an *unmediated*[a] objectivation and copy[b] of the entire *will*, just as the world itself is, just as in fact the Ideas themselves are, whose multiplied appearance constitutes the world of particular things. Therefore, unlike the other arts, music is in no way a copy of the Ideas; instead, it is a *copy of the will itself*, whose objecthood the Ideas are as well: this is precisely why the effect of music is so much more powerful and urgent than that of the other arts: the other arts speak only of shadows while music speaks of the essence.[79] But since it is the same will that objectifies itself in the Ideas as much as in music (albeit completely differently in each of them) then there must be a parallelism between them even if there is absolutely no direct similarity, there must still be an analogy between music and the Ideas whose multiplied, incomplete appearance makes up the visible world. Evidence for this analogy will clarify these points better, since understanding here is hindered by the obscurity of its object.

In the lowest notes of harmony, in the ground bass, I recognize the lowest levels of the objectivation of the will, inorganic nature, the mass of the planet. All the higher notes, which are brisk, sprightly and die away more quickly, are known to originate from the secondary vibrations[c] of the deep tonic note[d] (they always resonate softly with this tonic note) and   305
it is the law of harmony that a bass note may be accompanied only by those high notes that actually already sound with it on their own (its *sons harmoniques*[e]) through these secondary vibrations. Now this is analogous to the fact that all the natural bodies and organizations must be seen as arising from a stepwise development out of the planetary mass: this mass is both their support and their source: and this is the same relationship that the higher notes have to the ground bass. – There is a limit to the depth at which tones are still audible: this corresponds to the fact that matter is not perceptible in the absence of form and quality (i.e. without the expression of a force that cannot itself be further explained, precisely one in which an Idea expresses itself), and more generally to the fact that no matter can be

---

[a] *unmittelbar*
[b] *Abbild*
[c] *Nebenschwingungen*
[d] *Grundton*
[e] [harmonics]

entirely without will: thus, just as a certain pitch is inseparable from tone as such, so a certain grade of expression of the will is inseparable from matter. – For us, as a result, ground bass is to harmony what inorganic nature is to the world, the crudest mass on which everything rests and from which all things arise and develop. – Now, further, in all the ripienos that produce harmony between the bass and the leading voice that sings the melody, I recognize the entire sequence of levels[a] of Ideas in which the will objectifies itself. Those closer to the bass are the lower of these levels, bodies that are still inorganic but that already express themselves in a variety of ways: to me, the higher voices represent the plant and animal kingdoms. – The particular intervals of the scales parallel the particular levels of the objectivation of the will, the particular natural species. Deviation from the arithmetical correctness of the intervals either through some sort of tempering[b] or when it is produced by key selection, is analogous to the deviation of the individual from the type of the species: indeed, impure dissonances yielding no determinate interval can be compared to the monstrous hybrids[c] between two species of animals or between humans and animals. – But these bass and ripieno voices that make up the *harmony* lack the coherent forward motion found only in the upper voice

306   singing the *melody*; this is the only voice that moves quickly and lightly, in modulations and runs, while the harmonic voices all move more slowly and without any intrinsic coherence. The deep bass, representative of the crudest mass, moves most ponderously: it rises and falls only in large intervals, in thirds, fourths, fifths, never by a *single* tone, unless it is a bass transposed by a double counterpoint.[80] It is also physically[81] essential for the deep bass to move slowly: a rapid run or trill here cannot even be imagined. The upper voices of the ripieno move more quickly, although still without any melodic coherence or significant forward movement, and this has a parallel in the animal kingdom. All ripienos voices proceed in a way that is at once disconnected but also conforms to law; and this is analogous to the fact that in the whole of the irrational world, from the crystal to the most perfect animal, no being has a genuinely coherent consciousness[82] that would make its life into a meaningful whole, no creature has the experience of a succession of mental developments, no creature improves itself[d] through education; instead everything stays

---

[a] *Stufenfolge*
[b] *Temperatur* [this term, tempering, as in Bach's *Well-Tempered Clavier*, describes the process of deviating from pure intervals]
[c] *Mißgeburten*
[d] *sich vervollkommnet*

the same all the time for them, as determined for their species by fixed law. – Finally, in *melody*, the high-singing, principal voice that guides the whole, moving forward with unhindered freedom[a] so as to join everything from beginning to end seamlessly together into a *single*, meaningful thought, a principal voice presenting a whole, – in this I recognize the highest level of the objectivation of the will, the thoughtful[b] living and striving of human beings. Only human beings, being endowed with reason, keep looking forwards and backwards over the course of their actual life as well as their countless possibilities, thereby achieving a life course that, in being thoughtful, is a coherent whole: – correspondingly, only *melody* is joined up from beginning to end in a way that is full both of purpose and significance. As such, it narrates the story of the will as it is illuminated by thoughtfulness, the will whose imprint in reality is the sequence of its deeds; but it says more, it tells the will's most secret story, it paints every emotion, every striving, every movement of the will, everything that reason collects under the broad and negative concept of feeling and cannot grasp any further with its abstractions. Thus music has always   307 been described as the language of feeling and of passion, just as words are the language of reason: Plato already describes music as: 'the movement of melodies that imitates the emotions of the soul',[c] *Laws*, VIII, and Aristotle too says: 'Why are rhythm and melody, which are only sounds, similar to states of soul?' *Problems*, ch. 19.[d,83]

Now the essence of a human being consists in the fact that his will strives, is satisfied, and strives anew, and so on and on, and in fact his happiness and well-being are nothing more than the rapid progress of this transition from desire to satisfaction and from this to a new desire, since the absence of satisfaction is suffering and the absence of a new desire is empty longing, languor,[e] boredom; correspondingly, the essence of the melody is a constant departure, deviation from the tonic[f] in a thousand ways, not only to the harmonic intervals, to the third and dominant, but to every note, to the dissonant seventh and to the augmented intervals, always followed however by an eventual return to the tonic: in all these ways

---

[a] *mit ungebundener Willkür*
[b] *besonnene*
[c] ἡ των μελων κινησις μεμιμημενη, εν τοις παθημασιν ὁταν ψυχη γινηται (*melodiarum motus, animi affectus imitans*) [*Laws* VIII, 812c; though not an accurate quotation]
[d] δια τι οἱ ρυθμοι και τα μελη, φωνη ουσα, η θεσιν εοικε; (*cur numeri musici et modi, qui voces sunt, moribus similes sese exhibent?*) [920b29 is a somewhat similar passage to Schopenhauer's suggested quotation. *Problems* is a work traditionally in the Aristotelian corpus, whose authorship has been seriously doubted]
[e] [*languor* in English, or Latin, in the original]
[f] *Grundton*

the melody expresses the many different forms of the striving of the will, but it always also expresses satisfaction by eventually regaining a harmonic interval and, even more, the tonic. The creation of melody, the discovery of all the deepest secrets of human willing and sensation in it is the work of the genius, whose activity, here more than anywhere else, is more obviously remote from any reflection or conscious intentionality, and could be termed inspiration. The concept is barren here, as it is everywhere else in art: the composer reveals the innermost essence of the world and expresses the deepest wisdom in a language that his reason does not understand, just as a magnetic somnambulist explains things that he has no idea about when awake. Thus, in a composer more than in any other artist, the human being and the artist are entirely separate and distinct. The poverty and limitations of the concept are obvious even in our explanation of this marvellous art: nevertheless, I want to try to take our analogy further. – Just as a more

308   rapid transition from desire to satisfaction and from satisfaction to a new desire comprise happiness and well-being, so brisk melodies without long deviations are cheerful; slow melodies that fall into painful dissonances and take many bars before they wind their way back to the tonic are sad, by analogy with delayed and hard-won satisfaction. Languor, delay in finding something new to excite the will, can be expressed in no way other than as a protracted tonic, whose effect is soon unbearable: very monotonous, inane[a] melodies already come close to this. The short, easy phrases of swift dance music seem to speak only of common happiness that is easy to come by; by contrast, the *allegro maestoso* with its grand phrases, long passages and extended deviations[b] describes a grander, nobler striving after, and eventual accomplishment of, a distant goal. The *adagio* speaks of the suffering of a great and noble striving that scorns all petty happiness. But what a wonderful effect there is with the *minor* and the *major*! How astonishing that the change of a semitone, the introduction of the minor third instead of the major, instantly and inevitably urges an anxious, awkward sensation on us from which we are just as instantaneously rescued by the major. An *adagio* in the minor achieves an expression of the highest pain and becomes a most deeply moving lament. Dance music in the minor seems to describe the absence of a petty happiness that we ought rather to disdain; it seems to speak of the achievement of a lower goal through toil and drudgery. – The inexhaustibility of the possible melodies corresponds to the inexhaustibility of nature in the variety of individuals, physiognomies and life histories.

[a] *nichtssagende*
[b] *Abwirrungen*

Modulation from one key into another, completely different one entirely abolishes any connection to what preceded it, and so[84] is like death in so far as death brings the individual to an end; but the will that appeared in the individual lives on afterwards, just as it was alive before, appearing in other individuals whose consciousnesses nonetheless have no connection to that of the first.

Still, despite the evidence of all these analogies, we must never forget that music has only an indirect relation to them, not a direct one, because it never expresses appearance but only the inner essence, the in-itself of all appearance, the will itself. Therefore it does not express this or that individual and particular joy, this or that sorrow or pain or horror or exaltation or cheerfulness or peace of mind, but rather joy, sorrow, pain, horror, exaltation, cheerfulness and peace of mind as such *in themselves*, abstractly,[a] as it were, the essential in all these without anything superfluous, and thus also in the absence of any motives for them. Nevertheless, we understand them perfectly in this pared-down quintessence. This is why our imagination is so easily excited by them and tries to take that invisible and yet so vividly aroused spiritual world, a world that speaks to us directly, and to form it, to clothe it in flesh and bone and thus embody it in an analogous example. This is the origin of songs with words and ultimately of opera, – whose libretto, for this very reason, should never depart from this subordinate position to assume the principal role, making music into a mere means for its expression, which is a bad mistake and seriously wrong-headed. For music everywhere expresses only the quintessence of life and of the events taking place in it, never these themselves, and so distinctions within these do not always influence it. Precisely this universality, exclusive as it is to music, together with the most exact precision gives music its high value as the panacea for all our suffering. Thus if music ties itself too closely to words or tries to model itself on events, it is trying to speak a language that is not its own. Nobody has avoided this error as completely as *Rossini*: which is why his music speaks its *own* language so clearly and purely that it has no need of words at all and retains its full effect when performed on instruments alone.

Given all we have said,[85] we can view the appearing world (or nature) and music as two different expressions of the same thing; this thing itself is thus the only middle term of their analogy, and it must be cognized before we can have any insight into this analogy. Seen as the expression of the world, music is therefore a universal language to the highest degree, indeed it is to

309

---

[a] *in abstracto*

the universality of concepts almost what these are to particular things. But
its universality is in no way the empty universality of abstraction; rather, it
is of a different sort altogether, and is united with thorough and clear-cut
determinateness.[a] In this respect it is comparable to numbers and geometric
figures, which, as the universal forms of – and *a priori* applicable to – all
possible objects of experience, are not for that matter abstract, but rather
intuitive and thoroughly determinate. All possible endeavours, excitations
and expressions of the will, all processes that take place within human beings
and that reason throws into the broad and negative concept of feeling, can
be expressed through the infinitely large number of possible melodies, but
always in the universality of mere form and without matter, only ever
according to the in-itself, not according to appearance, its innermost soul,
as it were, without the body. From this inner relationship of music to the
true essence of all things, we can also explain how it is that if an appropriate
piece of music is played with some scene, action, event, surrounding, it
seems to disclose to us its most secret sense, and acts as the clearest and
most apt commentary on it; moreover, we can also explain that if someone
surrenders himself completely to the impression made by a symphony, it
is as if he sees all the possible events of life and the world passing before
him: yet if he pauses and reflects on this,[b] he cannot specify any point
of similarity between the play of notes[c] and the things he has in mind.
For[86] music is, as we have said, different from all other arts in that it is
not a copy[d] of appearance, or better, of the adequate objecthood of the
will, but is instead a direct copy of the will itself, and thus presents what
is metaphysical in all that is physical in the world, the thing in itself for
all appearance.[87] We could therefore just as well call the world embodied
music as embodied will: this also explains why music causes every painting,
and in fact every scene from real life and the world, suddenly to emerge
in a state of heightened significance; and of course the more so the greater
the analogy there is between the melody and the inner spirit of[88] the
given appearance. This is why we can set a poem to music as a song, or
a graphic[e] presentation to music as a pantomime, or the two together to
music as an opera. Such individual images of human life, set to the universal
language of music, are never connected to music or correspond to it with
complete necessity; rather they are to music what an arbitrary example is
to a universal concept: they present in the determinateness of reality what

[a] *Bestimmtheit*
[b] *sich besinnt*
[c] *Tonspiel*
[d] *Abbild*
[e] *anschauliche*

310

311

music expresses in the universality of mere form. This is because melodies are to a certain extent like universal concepts, being abstractions from reality.[a] Reality, and hence the world of specific[b] things, provides what is intuitive, what is particular and individual, the specific case both for the universality of concepts as well as for the universality of melodies, although these two universalities are opposed in a certain respect: concepts contain simply the very first forms[c] abstracted from intuition, the outer shells that have been stripped off things, as it were, and are thus wholly authentic *abstracta*; music on the other hand provides the innermost kernel, prior to all form[d] – the heart of things. This relationship can be expressed extremely well in the language of the Scholastics, where it is said that concepts are the *universalia post rem*, while music gives the *universalia ante rem*, and reality gives *universalia in re*.[e,89] The universal sense of a melody accompanying one literary text[f] could correspond to the same degree to other, equally arbitrarily selected examples of the universality expressed in it: this is why the same composition is suitable for many verses, and hence also *vaudeville*. But the very possibility of a relationship between a composition and a graphic[g] presentation rests, as we have said, on the fact that both are expressions of the same inner essence of the world, only quite different ones. Now when such a relationship is really at hand in a particular case, when the composer knew how to express the stirrings of the will (which constitutes the kernel of an event) in the universal language of music, then the melody of the song, the music of the opera is expressive. But the analogy the composer has discovered between the two must proceed from direct cognition of the essence of the world, unbeknownst to his reason; it must not be an imitation[h] mediated through concepts with conscious intentionality: otherwise music would not express the inner essence, the will itself, but would instead give only an unsatisfactory imitation of the will's appearance; this is what happens in all authentically imitative[i] music, such as Haydn's *The Seasons* as well as his *Creation* in many places, where appearances of the intuitive world are imitated[j] directly; it is the same with all battle pieces, something that is to be rejected entirely.

312

---

[a] *Wirklichkeit*
[b] *einzelne*
[c] *Formen*
[d] *Gestaltung*
[e] [universals after the fact, universals before the fact, universals in the fact]
[f] *Dichtung*
[g] *anschaulichen*
[h] *Nachahmung*
[i] *nachbildende*
[j] *nachgeahmt*

The inexpressible intimacy[a] of all music, which allows it to pass before us like a paradise that is so utterly familiar and yet eternally foreign, so entirely comprehensible and yet so inexplicable, rests on the fact that it renders all the impulses[b] of our innermost essence but without any reality and removed from their pain. Similarly, its essential seriousness,[90] which completely excludes the ridiculous from its own, immediate vicinity, can be explained by the fact that its object is not representation (it is only in relation to this that deception and ridiculousness are possible) – but rather, its object is directly the will, which is in its essence the most serious thing of all, as that on which everything depends. – Even repetition signs, including *da capo*, attest to the richness of content and meaningfulness of the language of music; these would be intolerable in works written in the language of words, and yet these signs are entirely to the point and pleasing in music, because in order to grasp it fully, we must listen to it twice.[91]

Throughout this discussion of music, I have tried to make clear that music uses a highly universal language to express the inner essence, the in-itself of the world (which we think through the concept of will, after its clearest expression) and does so in a distinctive[c] material, namely pure tones, and with the greatest determinateness and truth; moreover, in my view and according to my endeavours, philosophy is nothing other than a complete and correct repetition and expression of the essence of the world in very general concepts, since only through such concepts is it possible to survey that whole essence in a way that is both universally adequate and applicable; as a result, anyone who has followed me and entered into my way of thinking will not think it so very paradoxical when I say that if we succeed in giving a perfectly correct, complete and detailed explanation of music, which is to say a thorough repetition, in concepts, of what it expresses, this would at the same time be a satisfactory repetition and explanation of the world in concepts, or something wholly in agreement with it, and thus would be the true philosophy; accordingly, we could parody that saying of Leibniz quoted above (which is quite right from an inferior perspective) in the sense of our superior insight into music as follows: 'Music is an unconscious exercise in metaphysics,[92] in which the mind does not know that it is philosophizing.'[d] Because *scire*, to know, always means to have put into abstract concepts. But further and apart from its aesthetic or inner significance but considered merely externally and purely empirically

313

---

[a] *Innige*
[b] *Regungen*
[c] *einartig*
[d] *Musica est exercitium metaphysices occultum nescientis se philosophari animi*

music is, thanks to the abundantly confirmed truth of Leibniz's saying, nothing other than the means for grasping (immediately and *in concreto*) larger numbers and more orderly numerical ratios, all of which we would otherwise be able to cognize only indirectly, by grasping them in concepts. So, by uniting these two very different and yet correct views of music we can create for ourselves the idea of the possibility of a philosophy of numbers, like that of Pythagoras or the Chinese in the *I Ching*, and then interpret in this sense the Pythagorean saying quoted by Sextus Empiricus (*Against the Mathematicians*,[a] Book VII), the saying that reads: 'with respect to numbers, all things are similar'.[b] And finally, if we bring this view to bear on our interpretation of harmony and melody given above, we will find that a mere moral philosophy without an explanation of nature, such as Socrates tried to introduce, is entirely analogous to a melody without harmony, which is all that Rousseau wanted to have, and that conversely a mere physics and metaphysics without an ethics would correspond to a mere harmony without melody. – If I may be permitted, I will add to these informal remarks a few more observations concerning the analogy between music and the appearing world. In the previous Book we found that the highest level of the objectivation of the will, the human being, cannot appear alone and isolated, but presupposes the levels beneath him and these always presuppose still lower levels: likewise music which, like the world, immediately objectifies the will, is perfect[c] only in complete[d] harmony. In order to complete its impression, the high, leading voice of melody needs the accompaniment of all the other voices down to the deepest bass, which is to be seen as the origin of them all: melody intervenes as an integral component of harmony, and vice versa: and just as it is only   314 in the full-voiced whole that music expresses what it aims to express, so, the one, extra-temporal will finds its complete objectivation only in the complete unification of all the levels, which reveal its essence in countless grades of ascending clarity. – The following analogy is also very remarkable. In the previous Book we saw that, notwithstanding the mutual adaptation of all the appearances of the will to each other as species (an adaptation that occasions a teleological perspective on them), there nevertheless remains a conflict between those appearances as individuals; this conflict cannot be abolished, it is visible on all the levels of appearances, and it makes the world into a standing battleground of all those appearances of one and the

---

[a] *Adv[ersus] Math[ematicos]*
[b] τῷ αριϑμῷ δε τα παντ' επεοικεν (*numero cuncta assimilantur*)
[c] *vollkommen*
[d] *vollständig*

same will, rendering visible its inner self-contradiction. There is something in music that corresponds even to this. A completely pure harmonic system of notes is both physically as well as arithmetically impossible. The very numbers through which notes are expressed have insoluble irrationalities: we cannot even compute a scale within which each fifth would relate to the tonic as 2 to 3, each major third as 4 to 5, each minor third as 5 to 6, etc. This is because when the notes are related correctly to the tonic, they are no longer related correctly to each other, since for instance the fifth would have to be the minor third to the third, etc.: the notes of the scale are like actors who sometimes have to play one role and sometimes another.[93] Thus, completely correct music cannot even be conceived, much less performed; and this is why every possible piece of music deviates from complete purity: the best it can do is to hide its essential dissonances by distributing them among all the notes, i.e. through tempering. Just look at Chladni's *Acoustics*, § 30, and his *Short Overview of the Theory of Sounds and Tones*,[a] p. 12.*

I could add something more concerning the way music is perceived, namely entirely and only in and through time, completely excluding space, and without being at all influenced by any cognition of causality (or there-fore by the understanding), because notes make their aesthetic impression already as an effect; we do not have to refer them back to a cause, as we must with intuition. – But I do not want to prolong these observations further, since I have perhaps already treated some of these topics at somewhat too great a length in this Third Book, or become too involved in details. But my purpose required this, and it will be less subject to disapproval if one bears in mind the importance and high value of art (which are seldom suffi-ciently recognized), and considers that if, as we have said, the whole visible world is only the objectivation, the mirror of the will, accompanying it for its self-cognition and indeed, as we will soon see, for the possibility of its redemption; and if, at the same time, the world as representation, viewed on its own by breaking it free from the will, letting it be the only thing occupying one's consciousness, is the most joyful and the only innocent side of life; – we have to consider art as the greater intensification,[b] the more complete development of all this, since it essentially accomplishes the same thing as the visible world itself, only more concentratedly, with

315

---

* See chapter 39 of volume 2.

[a] *Akustik ... Kurze Uebersicht der Schall-und Klanglehre*
[b] *als die höhere Steigerung*

deliberateness and clarity of mind,[a] and it therefore may be called the blossom of life in the full sense of the term. If the whole world as representation is only the visibility of the will, then art is the clarification of this visibility, the *camera obscura* that shows objects with greater purity and allows them to be surveyed and summarized more readily, the play within a play, *Hamlet*'s stage upon the stage.

The pleasure of all beautiful things, the consolation that art affords, the enthusiasm that allows the artist to forget the difficulties of life, this one advantage the genius possesses over other people and the only thing that compensates him for his suffering (which is increased in proportion to his clarity of consciousness) and also for his desolate solitude among a race so different from him, – all this is due to the fact that, as we will continue to show, the in-itself of life, the will, existence itself, is a constant suffering, partly miserable, partly horrible; on the other hand, the same thing as representation alone, purely intuited, or repeated in art, free from pain, affords a meaningful spectacle.[b] This aspect of the world (which can be cognized purely) and its repetition in some art or another is the artist's element. He is riveted by his observations of the spectacle of the will's objectification: he comes to a stop with it, does not tire of observing it and repeating it as a presentation, and in so doing himself bears the cost of the performance of this spectacle, i.e. he is himself the will that has thus objectified itself and remains in a state of constant suffering. For him that pure, true and profound cognition of the essence of the world becomes a goal in itself: he comes to a stop there. Hence, this cognition does not become a tranquillizer of the will for him, as we will see in the next Book with the saints who have achieved resignation; for him, it redeems him from life, not forever but rather only momentarily, and it is not yet his way out of life, but only an occasional source of comfort within life itself, until this intensifies his powers to the point where he finally grows tired of the game and seizes upon serious things. We can think of Raphael's St Cecilia as a symbol of this transition.[94] And now, in the following Book, we will turn to serious things as well.

[a]   *mit Absicht und Besonnenheit*
[b]   *Schauspiel*

FOURTH BOOK

The world as will, second consideration

With the achievement of self-knowledge, affirmation and negation of the will to life

Tempore quo cognitio simul advenit, amor e medio supersurrexit
Oupnek'hat, studio Anquetil-Duperron, vol. II, p. 216

['When knowledge asserted itself, thence arose desire.' *Oupnek'hat* is a Latin version of the *Upanishads* (1801). The passage corresponds to *Ātma Upanishad*, 3, though as Deussen points out, no equivalent words are found there]

§ 53

The final part of our discussion declares that it will be the most serious, since it deals with human actions,[a] which are of direct concern to everyone; no one is unfamiliar with or indifferent to such a topic. In fact, it is so natural for people to relate everything to action that they will always consider that part of any systematic discussion which concerns deeds[b] to be the culmination of the whole work, at least to the extent that it is of interest to them, and will accordingly pay serious attention to this part, if to no other. – In the present context, the discussion that follows is what is generally referred to as practical philosophy, in contrast to the theoretical philosophy that has so far been our concern. But in my opinion, philosophy is always theoretical, since what is essential to it is that it treats and investigates its subject-matter (whatever that may be) in a purely contemplative manner, describing without prescribing. On the other hand, for it to become practical, guide action,[c] shape character – these are long-standing demands, and mature insight should encourage us to give them up once and for all. Because here, where the worth or worthlessness of an existence, where salvation or damnation is in question, the issue cannot be resolved with dead concepts, but only by the innermost essence of the man

[a] *Handlungen*
[b] *Thun*
[c] *Handeln*

himself, the daemon that leads him and has not chosen him but rather has been chosen *by* him (as Plato would have it), or his intelligible character (as

320 Kant says). Virtue is as little taught as genius: indeed, concepts are just as barren for it as they are for art, and useful for both only as tools. It would be just as absurd to expect our systems of morals and ethics to inspire virtuous, noble and holy men as it would be to think that our aesthetics could create poets, painters and musicians.

Philosophy can never do more than to interpret and explain what is present, to bring the essence of the world – that essence which speaks intelligibly to everyone in a concrete fashion,[a] which is to say as a feeling – to the clear and abstract cognition of reason, and to do so in every possible respect and from every point of view. In the preceding three Books we tried to accomplish this from other points of view, with the generality proper to philosophy; now, in the present Book, human action will be treated in the same way. This aspect of the world might well prove to be the most important of all, not only (as I remarked previously) according to subjective judgement, but objectively as well. As we proceed, I will remain strictly faithful to the method we have been using so far, and presuppose what has already been advanced, which is really just the one thought that has been the content of this whole work. I will now explain human action just as I have explained all the other topics so far, thus doing everything I can to communicate this idea as fully as possible.

The perspective we have adopted and the method we have specified should discourage any expectation that this ethical Book will contain precepts[b] or a doctrine of duty; still less will there be any general moral principle, a universal formula, as it were, for generating virtue. There will be no talk of an '*unconditional ought*',[c] because (as we will argue in the Appendix) it entails a contradiction; nor will we be discussing a 'law of freedom', which is in the same situation. We will not talk about 'oughts' at all: that is how you talk to children, or to nations in their infancy, not to those who have acquired all the culture of a mature age. It is of course

321 a manifest contradiction to call the will free and then to prescribe laws that it ought to will by: – 'ought to will' – wooden iron! But our whole point has been that the will is not only free, but omnipotent: it gives rise, not only to its actions, but to its world as well; and as *it* is, so does its acting appear, so does its world appear: both are the self-cognition of the will and nothing besides: it determines itself and in so doing determines

[a]   *in concreto*
[b]   *Vorschriften*
[c]   *unbedingten Sollen*

both its action and its world: this is because there is nothing besides the will, and these are the will itself: only in this way is it truly autonomous; it would be heteronomous on any other view. Our philosophical efforts can extend only to an interpretation and explanation of human action and the innermost essence and content of the very different and even conflicting maxims which are its living expression. We will do this in the context of our discussion so far, and in the same way that we have tried to interpret the other appearances of the world and bring their innermost essence to clear, abstract cognition. In so doing, our philosophy will continue to assert the same *immanence* that it has maintained all along: it will not oppose Kant's great doctrine by trying to use the forms of appearance (whose common expression is the principle of sufficient reason) as a pole for vaulting over the appearances themselves (which are the only things that give these forms their meaning), and landing in the boundless realm of empty fictions. Rather, this real world of the cognizable, in which we are and which is in us, will remain both the material and the limit of our discussion: it is so rich in content that it could never be exhausted by even the deepest investigation of which the human spirit is capable. Now, since the real, cognizable world will continue to provide as rich a source of material and reality for our ethical investigations as it did for our previous investigations, it will be entirely unnecessary for us to take refuge in insubstantial negative concepts, and then somehow make even ourselves believe that we are saying something when we raise our eyebrows and talk about the 'Absolute', the 'infinite', the 'supersensible' or any other mere negations ('it is nothing but a negative expression combined with an unclear representation':[a] Julian, *Orations*, 5),[1] instead of which we could just say: 'Cloud Cuckoo-land' (νεφελοκοκκυγια):[b] but we will not need to serve up 322 these sorts of empty, covered dishes. – Finally, we will not be doing history and calling it philosophy any more than we did previously. This is because we feel that people are infinitely remote from a philosophical knowledge[c] of the world when they imagine that its essence can somehow (however delicately concealed) be grasped *historically*. Yet this is the case with anyone whose views of the intrinsic essence of the world include a *becoming* or a *having-become*[d] or *becoming-becoming*,[e] anyone who attributes the

---

[a] ουδεν εστι, η το της στερησεως ονομα, μετα αμυδρας επινοιας. – *nihil est, nisi negationis nomen, cum obscura notione.*

[b] See Aristophanes, *Clouds*

[c] *Erkenntniß*

[d] *Gewordenseyn*

[e] *Werdenwerden*

slightest significance to the concepts of earlier or later, and consequently, who implicitly or explicitly looks for and locates a beginning and an end-point for the world together with a path between them, along which the philosophizing individual can recognize his own location. In most cases, such *historical philosophizing* produces a cosmogony, which admits of many variations, or else a system of emanation, or a doctrine of the fall; or ultimately, if fruitless efforts along these paths drive the desperate philosopher to the final path, such a historical philosophy will turn tail and produce a doctrine of steady becoming, springing up, originating, emerging into the light from the darkness, from the dark and gloomy ground, primal ground,[a] groundlessness,[b] or some such drivel. This, by the way, can be dismissed most readily by noting that an entire eternity, i.e. an infinite time has elapsed before the present moment, and thus everything that could or should have become already necessarily *has* become.[2] All such historical philosophy, whatever airs it gives itself, acts as if Kant never existed, and treats *time* as a determination of things in themselves, thus remaining in what Kant called appearance (as opposed to the thing in itself), or what Plato called that which becomes and never is (as opposed to what is and never becomes), or finally what the Indians call the web of *māyā*. Cognition made possible by the principle of sufficient reason can never allow anyone to gain access to the inner essence of things; all we do is chase appearances to infinity, moving without end or goal like a squirrel on a wheel, until tired at last, whether on the top or the bottom, we stop at some arbitrary

323   point and want people to respect us for it. The truly philosophical way of looking at the world, i.e. the way that leads beyond appearance and provides cognition of the inner essence of the world, does not ask where or whence or why, but instead, always and everywhere, asks only for the *what* of the world. In other words, it does not look at things according to some relation, or as becoming and passing away – in short, according to one of the four forms of the principle of sufficient reason; on the contrary, it divorces itself from the whole tendency to view things according to the principle of sufficient reason, and focuses on what remains, namely the essence of the world that always stays the same, appearing in all relations itself but never subject to them, the Ideas themselves. Both philosophy and art take this cognition as their point of departure, as does that state of mind which alone leads to true holiness and redemption from the world, as we will discover in this Book.

[a] *Urgrund*
[b] *Ungrund*

§ 54

Hopefully the first three Books will have led to clear and certain knowledge[a] that in the world as representation, the will finds a mirror in which it can cognize itself with an increasing clarity and perfection that culminates in the human being; the human essence is, however, completely expressed only through the connected series of our actions. The self-conscious connection of these actions is made possible by reason, which continually allows us to survey the whole in the abstract.[b]

Regarded simply in itself, the will is just a blind and inexorable impulse,[c] devoid of cognition; this is how we have seen it appear in inorganic and vegetative nature and their laws, as well as in the vegetative aspect of our own lives. With the emergence of the world as representation (which has developed to serve the will) the will obtains cognition of its willing and what it wills: namely, nothing other than this world, life, precisely as it exists. That is why we called the appearing world the mirror of the will, its objecthood: and since what the will wills is always life, precisely because life is nothing but the presentation of that willing for representation, it is a mere pleonasm and amounts to the same thing if, instead of simply saying 'the will', we say 'the will to life'.[d]

324

Since the will is the thing in itself, the inner content, the essential aspect of the world, while life, the visible world, appearance, is only the mirror of the will; life will be as inseparable from the will as a shadow from its body. And where there is will, there will be life and world as well. So for the will to life, life is a certainty, and as long as we are filled with life-will,[e] we do not need to worry about our existence, even in the face of death. It is true we see the individual come into being and pass away: but the individual is only appearance, it exists only for cognition that is caught up in the principle of sufficient reason, the *principium individuationis*. Certainly, for this kind of cognition, the individual receives life as a gift, emerges out of nothing, and then suffers the loss of this gift through death, returning back into nothing. But we want to look at life philosophically, i.e. according to its Ideas, and so we will find that neither the will, the thing in itself in all appearances, nor the subject of cognition, the spectator of all appearances, are in any way touched by birth or death. Birth and death belong to the

[a] *Erkenntniß*
[b] *in abstracto*
[c] *Drang*
[d] *der Wille zum Leben*
[e] *Lebenswillen*

appearance of the will, and thus to life, and an essential aspect of life is
that it presents itself in individuals that come into being and pass away;
these are fleeting appearances that have emerged in the form of time –
appearances of what has no cognition of time but needs to present itself
in precisely this manner in order to objectify its true essence. Birth and
death both belong to life, and balance each other as reciprocal conditions
or, if you like the expression, as poles of the whole appearance of life. The
wisest of all mythologies, that of India, expresses this by taking Shiva,[3]
the very god who symbolizes destruction and death (just as Brahma, the
lowest and most sinful god of the Trimurti symbolizes procreation and
generation, and Vishnu symbolizes preservation) – and, I say, giving him,
along with a necklace of skulls, the attribute of the lingam as well, this
symbol of procreation, which thus emerges here as a compensation for
death, suggesting that procreation and death are essential correlates that
neutralize and cancel each other out. – The very same attitude compelled
the Greeks and Romans to adorn their costly sarcophaguses as we see them
today, with festivals, dances, weddings, hunts, fights between animals, and
bacchanalia, which is to say with images of the strongest urges of life.
These are shown not only in diversions and entertainments like this, but in
voluptuous groupings as well, even to the point of showing us satyrs mating
with goats. Clearly, the intention was to point away from the death of the
mourned individual as emphatically as possible, and towards the immortal
life of nature; and to indicate, though without abstract knowledge,[a] that the
whole of nature is the appearance and also the fulfilment of the will to life.
The form of this appearance is time, space, causality, and (by means of these)
individuation, which entails that the individual must come into being and
pass away, but which does not disturb the will to life (the individual is, as
it were, just a single example or specimen of its appearance) any more than
the death of a single individual harms the whole of nature. This is because
nature does not care about the individual but only about the species, and
pursues its preservation so seriously, lavishing such extravagant care on it
through an enormous overabundance of seed and the great power of the
fertilizing drive. By contrast, the individual holds no value for nature, nor
could it hold any, since nature's kingdom is infinite time, infinite space,
and in these an infinite number of possible individuals; thus, it is always
ready to let go of the individual, which is why the individual is not only
exposed to destruction in a thousand ways through the most meaningless
accidents, but is even destined for destruction from the first, and is led

[a] *Wissen*

towards destruction by nature itself, from the moment it has served to maintain the species. In so doing, nature itself in all naïvety speaks the great truth that only Ideas, not individuals, have genuine reality, i.e. are the complete objecthood of the will. Now since human beings are nature itself, and in fact nature at the highest degree of its self-consciousness, but nature is only objectified will to life, then anyone who has grasped and retained this perspective can certainly and rightly console himself over his own death and that of his friends by looking at the immortal life of nature that he himself is. This is how we can understand Shiva with the lingam, as well as those ancient sarcophaguses that call out to the lamenting viewer with images of the most ardent life: Nature does not grieve.[a]

That procreation and death are to be thought of as belonging to life and essential to the appearance of the will is also apparent from the fact that both present themselves to us merely as the expressions at higher potencies of the source of all the rest of life. But this is absolutely nothing other than the constant change of matter beneath the steady persistence of form: and this is itself just the transience of individuals in relation to the permanence of the species. Constant nutrition and reproduction differ only in degree from procreation; and constant excretion differs only in degree from death. The former is seen most simply and clearly in plants. A plant is nothing but the constant repetition of the same drive of its simplest fibre, which groups itself into leaves and branches; it is a systematic aggregate of similar, mutually supporting plants, whose only drive is constant reproduction. Through a stepwise metamorphosis, it finally rises to a complete satisfaction of this drive, to the blossom and the fruit, that compendium of its being and striving in which it achieves its single goal through a short path, completing a thousand times in a single stroke what it had been doing in the particular case so far: repeating itself. Its drive to the fruit stage is related to the fruit itself as writing is to printing. And it is clearly the same with animals. The process of nutrition is always just procreation, the process of procreation is nutrition at a higher potency; pleasure in procreation is enjoyment of the feeling of life[b] at a higher potency. On the other side, excretion, the constant removal and disposal of matter, is just what death (the opposite of procreation) is in a higher potency. Here, we are always content to retain the form without missing the discarded matter; and this should be our attitude towards death, which is just the same thing (at a higher potency and in the whole) that takes place daily and hourly (on a

---

[a] *natura non contristatur*
[b] *Behaglichkeit des Lebensgefühls*

smaller scale) with excretion: as we are indifferent to the one, we should not recoil from the other. From this perspective, it is just as absurd to demand the continuation of the individual who will be replaced by other individuals as it is to demand the continued existence of the matter of his body that is constantly being replaced with new matter: it seems just as foolish to embalm corpses as it would be to carefully preserve our bodily secretions. As for the individual consciousness that is bound up with the individual body, this is completely interrupted every day by sleep. Deep sleep cannot be distinguished from death (into which it often steadily passes – e.g. in the case of freezing to death) with respect to the present; they are distinguishable only with respect to the future, namely when it comes to waking up. Death is a sleep in which the individual is forgotten: everything else wakes up again, or rather has never slept.*

Above all, we need to recognize clearly that the form of the will's appearance (which is to say: the form of life or of reality) is really just the *present*, not the future or the past: these are only conceptual,[a] they exist only in the context of cognition, to the extent that it follows the principle of sufficient reason. Nobody has ever lived in the past, and nobody will ever live in the future; the *present* is the only form of all life, and it is also life's most secure possession, and can never be torn away from it. The present always exists, together with its content: both are fixed in place and do not waver, like the rainbow on the waterfall. Because[4] for the will it is life, and for life it is the present that is certain and secure. – Of course, when we think back on bygone millennia, on the millions of people then alive, we ask: What were they? What has become of them? – But on the other hand, we need only look back on the past of our own life and play back its scenes vividly in our imagination and now ask again: What was all that? What has become of it? – As with our life, so it is with the lives of those millions. Or should we think that the past takes on a new existence when it has been sealed by

---

* For those who do not find it too subtle, the following consideration can also help clarify the fact that the individual is only appearance, not the thing in itself. Every individual is on the one hand the cognitive subject, i.e. the complementary condition for the possibility of the whole objective world, and on the other hand a single appearance of the will, which is precisely what objectifies itself in every thing. But this duality of our essence does not remain in a self-subsisting unity: otherwise we would be able to be aware of ourselves *in ourselves and independent of the objects of cognition and willing*; but this is absolutely impossible. Rather, as soon as we try for once to understand ourselves, and to do so by turning in on ourselves and directing our cognition inwardly, we lose ourselves in a bottomless void and find ourselves like hollow, transparent spheres from whose void a voice is speaking, while the cause of it is not to be found within, and in wanting to grasp ourselves we shudder as we catch nothing but an insubstantial phantom.

[a] *im Begriff*

death? Our own past, even the most recent past, even yesterday, is nothing but an unreal dream of the imagination, and the same holds true for the past of all those millions. What was? What is? – the will, whose mirror is life, and cognition free of the will, which sees the will clearly in that mirror. Anyone who has not or will not recognize this will have to add another question to the ones just posed about the fate of past generations: why is the person asking these questions, of all people, lucky enough to occupy this precious, fleeting present, the only thing that is real, while those hundreds of generations of humanity, and indeed the heroes and wise men of those ages, have sunk into the night of the past, becoming nothing; while he, his insignificant I,[a] really exists? – or more concisely, if just as oddly: why is this now, his now, – precisely what *is* now, and has not already *been* long ago? – In asking such strange questions, he views his existence and his time as mutually independent and the former as having been thrown into the latter. He really assumes the existence of two nows, the first belonging to the object, the other to the subject, and is surprised by the happy accident that has brought them together. But in truth (as is demonstrated in my essay *On the Principle of Sufficient Reason*) the present is only formed at the point of contact between the object, whose form is time, and the subject, which does not have any of the modes of the principle of sufficient reason for its form. But every object is the will to the extent that it has become a representation, and the subject is the necessary correlative of all objects; but real objects exist only in the present: past and future contain only concepts and phantasms, and thus the present is the essential form of the appearance of the will and is inseparable from it. Only the present is always there and fixed immovably in place. Empirically grasped as the most fleeting thing of all, it presents itself to the metaphysical outlook (which sees beyond the forms of empirical intuition) as the only thing that persists, the *Nunc stans*[b] of the scholastics. The source and the bearer of its content is the will to life or thing in itself – which is us. That which forever becomes and passes away, since it has either already been, or is still to come, belongs to appearance as such, by virtue of its forms, which are what make coming to be and passing away possible. Thus let us think: 'What was? – What is. – What will be? – What was';[c] and take it in the strict sense of the words, understanding it not as similar[d] but rather as identical.[e] Because for the

329

---

[a] *sein unbedeutendes Ich*
[b] [enduring Now]
[c] *Quid fuit? – Quod est. – Quid erit? – Quod fuit.*
[d] *simile*
[e] *idem*

will, life is a certainty, and for life, the present is a certainty. That is why everyone can say: 'I am lord of the present once and for all, and it will accompany me through all eternity like my shadow: that is why I do not wonder where it comes from and how it happens to be precisely now.'[5] – We can compare time to an endlessly spinning circle: the half that is always sinking would be the past, the half that is always rising would be the future; but on top, the indivisible point that touches the tangent would be the extensionless[a] present: as the tangent does not roll with the circle, the present, the object's point of contact (whose form is time) does not roll with the subject (which has no form) because it does not itself belong to what can be cognized but is rather the condition for everything that is. Or: time is like an unstoppable stream, and the present is like the rock that it breaks on but does not carry away.[6] The will, as thing in itself, is no more subordinate to the principle of sufficient reason than is the subject of cognition, which, in a certain respect, is ultimately the will itself, or its expression; and as the will is certain of life, of its own appearance, it is also certain of the present, the only form of real life. That is why we do not have to investigate the past before life or the future after death: what we instead need to know[b] is the *present*, the only form in which the will appears;* the present will not escape from the will, but neither will the will escape from the present. So someone who is satisfied with life, who affirms it in every way, can confidently regard it as endless and banish any fear of death as a deception that gives him the irrational fear that he could ever be deprived of the present, or that there could ever be a time that did not contain a present: a deception about time similar to another one about space, in which people think that wherever on the earth's surface they happen to be is at the top, and everywhere else is below: in the same way, everyone attaches the present to their individuality and thinks that the whole of the present will be extinguished along with it, leaving past and future without a present. But just as every point on the earth is the top, the *present* is the form of all life, and to fear death because it robs us of the present is as foolish as fearing that you could slide to the bottom of the earth's surface from the top where you are lucky enough

---

* *Scholastici docuerunt quod aeternitas non sit temporis sine fine aut principio successio, sed* Nunc stans; i.e. *idem nobis* Nunc *esse, quod erat* Nunc *Adamo: i.e. inter* nunc *et* tunc *nullam esse differentiam.* [The scholastics taught that eternity is not a succession without end or beginning, but rather an *enduring Now*, i.e. that we possess the same *Now* that was the *Now* for Adam; i.e. that there is no difference between the *Now* and the *Then*.] Hobbes, *Leviathan*, ch. 46.

[a] *ausdehnungslos*
[b] *erkennen*

to be standing at the moment. The form of the present is essential to the objectivation[7] of the will; as an unextended point, the present cuts time (which extends infinitely in both directions) and is fixed immovably in place, like an everlasting noon without the cool of evening, just as the real sun burns incessantly while only seeming to sink into the bosom of the night. That is why fearing death as an annihilation is like thinking that the evening sun could complain: 'Woe is me! I am sinking into eternal night.' –*,[8] Conversely, someone who is oppressed by the burdens of life, who certainly desires life and affirms it, but detests its sufferings and in particular does not want to put up with the difficult lot that has fallen to him any longer: a person like this cannot hope for liberation in death, and cannot save himself through suicide; the temptation of cool, dark Orcus as a haven of peace is just a false illusion. The earth turns from day into night; the individual dies: but the sun itself burns its eternal noontime without pause. For the will to life, life is a certainty: the form of life is the endless present; it does not matter how individuals, appearances of the Idea, come into existence in time and pass away like fleeting dreams. – Even here, suicide already appears to us as a futile and therefore foolish act: when we have gone further in our discussion, it will appear in an even less favourable light.

Dogmas change and our knowledge[a] is deceptive; but nature does not err: its course is certain and lies in plain sight. Everything is completely in nature, and nature is completely in everything. It has its centre in every animal: the animal has found its way into existence with certainty, and it will find its way out with certainty too: in the meantime, it lives without concern or fear of annihilation, supported by a consciousness that it is nature itself and, like nature, immortal. Only humans with their abstract concepts carry around the certainty of their own deaths: yet only very rarely can this frighten them, and only for a moment, when some occasion brings it before the imagination. Reflection can do little against

331

332

---

* In Eckermann's *Conversations with Goethe* (2nd edition, Vol. I, p. 154) Goethe says: 'Our spirit is a being of an entirely indestructible nature: it is a continuous operation from eternity to eternity. It is like the sun which only seems to set to our mundane eyes, but which really never sets and continually shines on.' – *Goethe* got this simile from me; I did not get it from him. Doubtless he used it, in this conversation from 1824, following a (perhaps unconscious) recollection of the passage above; since that, in the same words as this, is how it read in the first edition, p. 401; and it also occurs there again on p. 528, and here at the end of § 65. That first edition was sent to him in December 1818, and in March 1819 he sent (through my sister) a letter to me in Naples (where I was at that point), in which he reported his approval of it, and included a slip of paper where he had noted the numbers of a couple of pages that he had particularly liked: so he had read my book.

a *Wissen*

the powerful voice of nature. People have the certainty, springing from their innermost consciousness, that they are nature, the world itself, and this certainty constitutes an enduring state, at work in people as it is in unthinking animals. Because of this, nobody is made visibly uneasy by the thought of a certain and none-too-distant death; rather everyone lives on as if they were going to live forever. We can go so far as to say that nobody has a genuine and lively conviction of the certainty of his death, since otherwise there could not be so great a difference between his state of mind and that of a condemned criminal; of course everyone acknowledges the certainty abstractly[a] and theoretically, but nonetheless puts it aside without taking it into vivid consciousness, like other theoretical truths that have no practical application. Anyone who has observed this peculiarity of the human mentality will see that psychological explanations, which cite habit and an acquiescence in the inevitable, are utterly insufficient. Rather, the reason for this is the deeper one we have given. This can also explain why, in all ages and among all peoples, you find dogmas of some kind, dogmas that are held in esteem, about the continuation of the individual after death, although evidence in their favour must always be extremely inadequate, while the proofs against them are strong and numerous. But in truth, this does not really require proof; common sense knows it as a fact and it is fortified as such by the confidence that nature lies as little as it errs; nature presents its deeds and essence openly, it even expresses them naïvely, while we ourselves obscure them with our delusions so that we can read into them what is congenial to our limited viewpoint.

We have now brought to clear consciousness the fact that, although particular appearances of the will have a temporal beginning and temporal end, the will itself, as thing in itself, is not affected by this, nor is the correlative of all objects, the subject that has cognition but is itself never cognized, and that for the will to life, life is always a certainty: – but this should not be considered a doctrine of continual existence.[b] Permanence does not belong to the will, considered as thing in itself (or to the pure subject of cognition, the eternal eye of the world) any more than does passing away, since these determinations are valid only in time, and both the will and the pure subject of cognition lie outside time. The egoism of the individual (that particular appearance of the will illuminated by the subject of cognition) cherishes the wish to persist through infinite time – but the views we have set forth do not furnish this wish with any more

333

[a] *in abstracto*
[b] *Fortdauer*

nourishment or comfort than could be derived from the cognition that the rest of the external world will continue to exist in time after his death, which is just the expression of the same view but regarded objectively and thus temporally. Of course everyone is transient, but only as appearance; as thing in itself everyone is timeless, and thus endless as well; but also, it is only as appearance that he is different from other things in the world, while as thing in itself he is the will that appears in everything, and death annuls the deception that separates his consciousness from everything else: this is continued existence.[9] The fact that he is untouched by death, which is true for him only as thing in itself, coincides (for appearance) with the continued existence of the rest of the external world.* This is also why the fervent and merely felt consciousness of what we have just raised to clear cognition in fact (as we have said) prevents the thought of death from poisoning the life even of rational beings. Such consciousness is the basis of that thirst for life[a] that sustains all living things and allows them to pursue their lives with vigour, as if there were no such thing as death – that is, as long as they keep their eyes fixed on life and are engaged with it. But this does not prevent the individual from being seized by a fear of death and doing everything possible to escape it when he is confronted with death in an actual particular case (even if it is only imagined) and is forced to look it in the eye. As long as his cognition was directed to life as such, he had to recognize also the imperishability in it – but similarly, when death looks him in the eye he has to recognize it for what it is, the temporal end to the particular temporal appearance. It is not pain that we fear in death, partly because pain clearly lies on this side of death, and partly because we take refuge in death from pain just as, conversely, we sometimes endure the most horrible pain just to escape death for a while longer, however quick and easy it would be. Thus, we distinguish between pain and death as two quite different evils: what we fear in death is in fact the termination of the individual, which it openly admits itself to be, and since the individual is one particular objectivation of the will to life itself, he resists death with his entire being. – Now where feeling reveals us to be so helpless, reason

334

* In the *Veda* this is expressed by saying that when someone dies, his vision becomes one with the sun, his sense of smell with the earth, his taste with water, his hearing with the air, his speech with fire, etc. (*Oupnek'hat*, Vol. I, pp. 249ff.) – and also through the fact that in a certain ritual, the dying person entrusts his senses and all his faculties one by one to his son, in whom they are supposed to live on (ibid., Vol. II, pp. 82ff.) [Deussen gives as corresponding passages *Brihadāranyaka Upanishad* 4, 4, 2 and *Kaushītaki Upanishad*, 2, 15: though in the former case no exact passage corresponds to Schopenhauer's paraphrase]

[a] *Lebensmuth*

can nonetheless step in and overcome this adverse impression to a great extent by placing us at a higher standpoint where we can take in the whole picture instead of the details. That is why a philosophical knowledge[a] of the essence of the world that reaches the point we have now reached (but goes no further), could overcome the horror of death, even from this standpoint, to the extent that reflection has power over immediate feeling in any given individual. Someone who has thoroughly integrated the truths stated so far into his way of thinking, without at the same time having any personal experience or far-reaching insight into the continuous suffering that is essential to all life; someone, rather, who is perfectly happy and content with life and who, after calm reflection, could wish that his life as he has experienced it so far would be of endless duration, or of perpetually new recurrence, and whose thirst for life is so great that he would gladly and willingly take on all the pain and hardships that life is subject to in return for its pleasures; such a person would stand 'with firm, strong bones on the well-grounded, enduring earth',[b] and would have nothing to fear: armed with the knowledge[c] that we have given him, he would look at death with indifference as it rushed towards him on the wings of time, regarding it as a false illusion,[d] an impotent phantom, frightening to the weak, but powerless against anyone who knows that he himself is that will whose objectivation or image is the whole world, and to which, for this reason, life and the present will always remain certainties, the true and only form of appearance of the will; the thought of an infinite past or future without him can hold no horror for him, since he regards this as an empty illusion and the web of *māyā*, and thus has as little to fear from death as the sun has to fear from the night. – In the *Bhagavad Gita*, Krishna introduces this perspective to his future pupil, Arjuna, as Arjuna, seized with grief at the sight of the armies ready for war (somewhat like Xerxes[e]) loses heart, and wants to give up the fight to avoid the destruction of so many thousands: Krishna leads Arjuna to this perspective, and the deaths of those thousands cannot restrain him any more; he gives the sign for battle. – Goethe's Prometheus describes this perspective too, particularly when he says:

> Here I sit, forming men
> In my image,
> A race like me,

[a] *Erkenntniß*
[b] Goethe, *Grenzen der Menschheit* [Boundaries of Humanity]
[c] *Erkenntniß*
[d] *Schein*
[e] [In Aeschylus' play *The Persians*]

To suffer, to weep,
To take pleasure and be happy,
And not to heed you,
Like me!^a

The philosophies of Bruno and Spinoza could also lead people to this perspective, if their conviction is not shaken or weakened by the errors and imperfections of these systems. Bruno's philosophy does not have a genuine ethics, and the ethics in Spinoza's, although praiseworthy and attractive in itself, does not come from the essence of his doctrine at all but is just tacked onto it with weak and obvious sophisms. – Finally, many people would   336 adopt the perspective we have described if their cognition kept pace with their willing, i.e. if they were free from errors and in a position to become clearly and distinctly themselves. For cognition this is the perspective of the complete *affirmation of the will to life*.

The will affirms itself, which means that while in its objectivity (i.e. in the world and life) its own essence is given to it completely and distinctly as representation, this cognition is no impediment to its willing; rather, consciously, deliberately, and with cognition, it wills the life that it thus recognizes as such, just as it did as a blind urge before it had this cognition. – The opposite of this, the *negation of the will to life*, is manifest when willing comes to an end with that cognition. The particular, known appearances no longer act as *motives* for willing, but instead, cognition of the essence of the world (which mirrors the will) – cognition that has arisen by grasping the *Ideas* – becomes a *tranquillizer*^b of the will and the will freely abolishes itself. All these unfamiliar concepts, which are difficult to understand given this general manner of expression, will hopefully become clear through the presentation of the phenomena that will soon follow, namely ways of acting that express on the one hand affirmation in its different degrees, and on the other hand negation. Both take *cognition* as their point of departure – not an abstract cognition that is expressed verbally, but rather a living cognition that is expressed only through deeds and behaviour and remains independent of dogmas which, as abstract cognition, are preoccupations of reason. My only goal can be to present both and bring them to the clear cognition of reason, but without prescribing or recommending one or the other, which would be as foolish as it would be pointless, since the will in itself is absolutely free and wholly self-determining, and there is no law for it. – First of all, before we proceed to this argument, we must discuss and

^a [The last stanza of Goethe's poem *Prometheus*]
^b *Quietiv*

determine more precisely this *freedom* and its relation to necessity, and we
must also add a few general remarks concerning the will and its objects,
337   particularly as regards life, whose affirmation and negation is our problem.
All of this will enable us to illuminate the knowledge[a] we have in mind of
the ethical meaning of ways of acting, in their innermost essence.

Since, as we said, this whole work is just the unfolding of a single
thought, it follows that all its parts are bound together most intimately;
each one does not just stand in a necessary connection to the one before,
presupposing only that the reader has remembered it (as is the case with
all philosophies that consist merely of a series of inferences); rather, every
part of the entire work is related to every other and presupposes it, which
requires that the reader bear in mind not only what has just been said
but all the earlier parts of the work as well, so that he can connect them
with the present part at any moment, however much might have come in
between. Plato placed this exacting demand on his reader as well, through
the tortuous labyrinth of his dialogues, which come back to the main
point only after long, albeit ultimately clarifying episodes. We need to
make this exacting demand because, although we need to dissect our one
and only thought into many discussions for the purpose of communication,
this is an artificial form and in no way essential to the thought itself. –
Presentation and comprehension are both made easer by the separation of
four principal perspectives into four Books, connecting what is related and
homogeneous with the utmost of care. Nonetheless, the material does not
by any means allow for a linear progression, as is the case with history, but
rather requires a more intricate presentation. Thus it is necessary to study
the book repeatedly, since this alone will clarify the connection of each part
to the other; only then will they all reciprocally illuminate each other and
become perfectly clear.*

§ 55

That the will as such is *free* follows from our view that it is the thing in
338   itself, the content of all appearance. But we also recognize that appearance
is completely subordinate to the principle of sufficient reason in its four
forms: and since we know that necessity is absolutely identical with being
a consequent from a given ground, since the two concepts are equivalent,
then everything that belongs to appearance, i.e. is an object for the subject

---

* See chapters 41–4 of the second volume.

[a] *Erkenntniß*

of cognition as an individual, is on the one hand a ground, on the other hand a consequent, and in this last capacity is thoroughly and necessarily determined, which is to say: there is no sense in which it can be other than it is. The whole content of nature, all of its appearances, is thus thoroughly necessary, and the necessity of each part, each appearance, each event, can in every case be demonstrated, since there must be a ground on which it depends as a consequent. There are no exceptions: it follows from the unrestricted validity of the principle of sufficient reason. But on the other hand, this very same world in all its appearances is for us the objecthood of the will; and since the will is not itself appearance, representation, or object, but rather thing in itself, it is not subordinate to the principle of sufficient reason, the form of all objects, and thus not determined as a consequent by a ground, which means it knows[a] no necessity, i.e. it is *free*. The concept of freedom is thus in fact a negative one, since its content is merely the negation of necessity, i.e. of the relation of consequent to its ground as dictated by the principle of sufficient reason. – We have before us, in its clearest form, the point of unity of that great opposition, the unity of freedom with necessity; this has often been discussed in recent times, although as far as I know it has never been clearly or properly articulated. As appearance, as object, each thing is thoroughly necessary: *in itself*, this same thing is will, which is completely free for all eternity. The appearance, the object, is necessarily and irrevocably determined in the uninterrupted chain of grounds and consequents. But the existence of this object in general, and the manner of its existence, i.e. the Idea that reveals itself in the object or, in other words, its character, is an immediate appearance of the will. In accordance with the freedom of this will, it could fail to exist at all, or even be originally and essentially something entirely different; in which case the entire chain of which it is a link (and which is itself the appearance of the same will) would be entirely different. But once it is present, it has entered into the series of grounds and consequents and is always necessarily determined within this series; therefore, it cannot become something different, i.e. alter itself, nor can it step out of that series, i.e. disappear. Human beings, like every other part of nature, are the objecthood of the will: so everything we have said holds true for them as well. Just as each thing in nature possesses forces and qualities that react to determinate influences in a determinate way and constitute the character of the thing, a human being has his *character* as well, from which motives call forth his actions with necessity. Empirical character is revealed in the

339

---

[a] *kennt*

way he acts, but intelligible character, the will in itself whose determinate appearance he is, is revealed in turn in the empirical character. But a human being is the most perfect appearance of the will, whose existence (as we showed in the Second Book) requires illumination by such a high degree of cognition, that a fully adequate repetition of the essence of the world under the form of representation becomes possible in this cognition; and this, as we learned in the Third Book, is the apprehension of the Ideas, the pure mirror of the world. Thus, in human beings the will can achieve full self-consciousness, clear and exhaustive cognition of its own essence as it is mirrored in the whole world. As we saw in the previous Book, art arises from the actual existence of this degree of cognition.[10] At the very end of our discussion it will also be established that, since the will relates it to itself, the same cognition makes possible an abolition[a] and self-negation[b] of the will in its most perfect appearance; so that freedom, which otherwise applies only to the thing in itself and can never show itself in appearance, can then also emerge into appearance; by abolishing the essence that grounds appearance (while appearance itself continues in time) it can generate a self-contradiction within appearance and in so doing present the phenomena of holiness and self-denial.[c] But this can only become fully comprehensible at the end of this Book. – In the meantime, we will explain only in a general way that human beings are to be distinguished from all other appearances of the will by the fact that freedom, i.e. independence of the principle of sufficient reason (an independence that applies only to the will as thing in itself and contradicts appearance) might nevertheless be able to emerge into appearance through them. In doing so, it will necessarily present itself as a self-contradiction within appearance. In this sense, it is not only the will in itself that can be called free but human beings can as well, and this distinguishes them from all other beings. But how we are to understand this can only become clear in the following discussion, and at the moment we will have to put it completely to the side. In fact, we must first guard against the mistake of thinking that the actions of a particular, determinate human being are not subject to necessity, i.e. that the force of a motive is less sure than the force of a cause, or than the derivation of a conclusion from premises. If we disregard the entirely exceptional case mentioned above, freedom of the will as thing in itself in no way translates directly into appearance, not even where it has reached the highest level of manifestation, in rational animals

340

---

[a] *Aufhebung*
[b] *Selbstverneinung*
[c] *Selbstverleugnung*

with individual characters, i.e. in persons. The person is never free, even though it is an appearance of a free will, because it is the already determined appearance of the free willing of that will. And since this appearance enters into the form of all objects, the principle of sufficient reason, it develops the unity of the will through a multiplicity of actions. But because the unity of that will in itself lies outside of time, the multiplicity of actions presents itself with the lawlikeness of a force of nature. Since, however, it is nonetheless a free willing that is manifest in the person and the whole of his conduct,[a] relating itself to him like a concept to its definition, each of his particular deeds can be ascribed to the free will and registers itself as such directly in consciousness: that is why, as we mentioned in the Second Book, we all consider ourselves free *a priori* (i.e. in accordance with our original feeling), even in our individual actions, in the sense that in any given case every course of action is open to us, and we only come to know[b] *a posteriori*, through experience and reflecting on experience, that our acting takes place with complete necessity, from the meeting of character and motives. Thus it happens that the most vulgar people[c] always follow their feelings and zealously defend the complete freedom of individual actions, while the great thinkers of all ages, and indeed even the more profound religious doctrines, have denied it. But the whole essence of a human being is will, and people themselves are only appearances of this will; moreover, the necessary form of such appearances is the principle of sufficient reason, which can be discerned from even the subject, and which in this case assumes the form of the law of motivation – for someone who realizes all this, any doubts about the inevitability of a deed from a given character with a present motive will seem like doubts that the angles of a triangle add up to two right angles. – Priestley gives a very satisfactory treatment of the necessity of individual acts in his *Doctrine of Philosophical Necessity*; but Kant, whose merit here was particularly great, was the first to demonstrate the compatibility of this necessity with the freedom of the will in itself, i.e. outside of appearance,* by establishing the distinction between intelligible and empirical character. I fully support this distinction, since the former (intelligible character) is the will as thing in itself, to the extent that it

341

---

* *Critique of Pure Reason*, first edition pp. 532–58; fifth edition, pp. 560–86 [i.e. A532–58 / B560–86]; and *Critique of Practical Reason*, fourth edition, pp. 169–79. – Rosenkranz edition, pp. 224–31 [Ak. 5: 94–100].

[a] *Wandel*
[b] *erkennt*
[c] *jeder Roheste*

appears in a particular individual, to a particular degree, while the latter (empirical character) is this appearance as it presents itself temporally in ways of acting and even spatially, in bodily structure.[a] I already used the best expression for clarifying the relationship between them in the introductory essay, namely that the intelligible character of each human being can be regarded as an extra-temporal and thus indivisible and unchanging act of will,[b] whose appearance, when developed and drawn out in time, space, and all the forms of the principle of sufficient reason, is the empirical character, as it presents itself to experience in the human being's whole pattern of behaviour[c] and life history. Just as the entire tree is simply the constantly repeated appearance of one and the same drive, which presents itself most simply in the fibre and recurs and is easily recognized in the construction of the leaf, stem, branch and trunk, similarly all human deeds are just the constantly repeated expression of the intelligible character, only somewhat varied in form, and the empirical character is an induction based on the summation of these expressions. I will not repeat Kant's masterly presentation here, but rather presuppose it as known.

342

In 1840 I gave a thorough and detailed treatment of the important subject of the freedom of the will in my crowned prize essay on the subject, and showed the reason why people mistakenly think they have found an empirically given, absolute freedom of the will, a *liberum arbitrium indifferentiae*[d] as a fact in self-consciousness: the question set for the essay was very insightfully directed to this very point. Since I can now refer the reader to this work, as well as to §10 of the prize essay *On the Basis of Morals* that was published in the same volume under the title *The Two Fundamental Problems of Ethics*, I will omit the incomplete presentation of the necessity of the act of will that I published at this point in the first edition; instead I will explain the reason for the above-mentioned mistake in a brief discussion that presupposes the nineteenth chapter of the second volume, and thus could not appear in the prize essay we have just mentioned.

Since the will, as true thing in itself, is genuinely primordial[e] and independent, a feeling of originality and independence[f] must accompany its acts[g] in self-consciousness, even though these acts are already determined.

---

[a] *Korporisation*
[b] *Willensakt*
[c] *Handlungsweise*
[d] [free choice of indifference]
[e] *Ursprüngliches*
[f] *Eigenmächtigkeit*
[g] *Akte*

But apart from all this, the illusion of empirical freedom of the will (as opposed to the transcendental freedom that can alone be attributed to it), and thus the illusion of a freedom in the individual deed, arises from the separation of the intellect from the will, and its subordinate position with respect to the will. This is demonstrated in the nineteenth chapter of the second volume, particularly under no. 3. The intellect first experiences the will's resolutions *a posteriori* and empirically. Thus, when faced with a choice, it has no information about how the will is going to decide. For the intelligible character, when motives are given, only *one* decision is possible 343 and it is, accordingly, a necessary one. For this reason, the intelligible character does not fall within the sphere of cognition of the intellect, which is only familiar with the empirical character, and this through its successive, individual acts. That is why it also seems to the cognizing consciousness (intellect) that two opposed decisions are equally possible for the will in any given case. But this is just the same as if we were to look at a vertical pole that has come unbalanced and is wobbling and say 'it can fall to the right or to the left', where the force of the word '*can*' is clearly only subjective, and really means 'with respect to the data we have on hand': because objectively, the direction it will fall was necessarily determined as soon as the wobbling began. Likewise, the decision of our own will is indeterminate only for the spectator, our own intellect, and thus only relatively and subjectively, namely for the subject of cognition; on the other hand, in every choice the subject is faced with, its decision is both determined and necessary, objectively and in itself. But this determination only enters consciousness with the successful decision. We even have empirical proof of this when we are faced with any sort of difficult and important decision, although only under a condition that we are hoping will materialize, but has not done so yet; in this situation there is nothing we can do for the time being, and we have to be passive. For now, we think about what we will choose to do when the circumstances change and grant us free activity[a] and a decision. Far-sighted, rational deliberation usually comes out in favour of one decision, while immediate inclination comes out for the other. As long as we have to be passive, the balance seems tilted in favour of reason; but we can see in advance how strongly we will be pulled by the other side when the opportunity for acting arises. Until then, we are anxious to clarify the motives for both sides as much as possible through calm meditation on the pros and cons,[b] so that each one can exert its full influence upon

---

[a] *freie Thätigkeit*
[b] *pro et contra*

the will when the time comes, and the will won't be skewed by a mistake on the part of the intellect into making a different decision than it would make if both motives were equally effective. But this clear display of the motives on both sides is all that the intellect can contribute to the choice. It waits for the true decision as passively and with the same eager curiosity as if it were someone else's will. From the standpoint of the intellect, both decisions appear equally possible: and this is precisely the illusion of the will's empirical freedom. Of course the decision enters the sphere of the intellect quite empirically, as an end to the matter; and yet it emerges from the constitution,[a] the intelligible character of the individual will in its conflict with given motives, and thus it comes about with complete necessity. The only contribution the intellect can make to all this is to put the constitution of the motives into sharp relief; it cannot determine the will itself because, as far as it is concerned, the will is utterly inaccessible, and even, as we have seen, unfathomable.

If, in the same circumstances, a person could act one way at one time and another way at another time, then his will itself would have to have altered in the interval, which means the will would have to be in time, since alteration is possible only in time. So either the will would be a mere appearance, or time would be a determination of the thing in itself.[11] This is why the conflict over the freedom of individual deeds, over the *liberum arbitrium indifferentiae*, really turns on the question of whether or not the will is in time. If the will as thing in itself is really outside of time and every form of the principle of sufficient reason (which is necessary according to Kant's doctrine as well as my whole presentation) then not only will the individual act in the same way in the same situation, and not only will every evil deed stand surety for countless other evil deeds that the individual *must* perform and *cannot* omit; but also, as Kant has said, if the empirical character and the motives are fully given, we could calculate how people will behave in the future just as we calculate eclipses of the sun or moon. Nature is consistent, and so is character: every individual action must follow from the character, just as every phenomenon follows from a law of nature: the cause in the latter case, and the motive in the former, are only occasional causes, as was shown in the Second Book. The will, whose appearance is the whole being and life of a human being, cannot deny itself in the particular case, and what a human being wills on the whole, he also wills always in the particular.

---

[a] *Beschaffenheit*

The claim that the will is empirically free, a *liberum arbitrium indiffer-entiae*, is intimately connected with the idea that the human essence[a] is located in a *soul*,[b] which is originally a *cognizing* thing,[c] even an abstract *thinking* one and, only as a result of this, a thing that *wills*; this puts the will in a secondary position, although in fact it is cognition that is secondary. The will was even regarded as an act of thought[d] and identified with judgement, especially by Descartes and Spinoza. From this we could infer that each human being is what he is only as a result of his *cognition*: that he enters the world as a moral cipher, gets to cognize things in the world, and resolves accordingly to be such and so, to act in such a way; or as a result of fresh cognition, he could even adopt a new way of acting and become someone different. Moreover, he would recognize that something is *good* and will it only as a result of this, instead of *willing* it first and calling it *good* as a result of that. But according to my whole fundamental outlook this is a reversal of the true relation. The will is first and primordial; cognition only comes in later, since it belongs to the appearance of the will as its instrument. Accordingly, everyone is what he is through his will and his character is primordial, since willing is the basis of his being. Through the cognition he then acquires, he experiences *what* he is, i.e. he becomes acquainted with his character. So he *cognizes* himself as a result of, and according to, the constitution of his will; and does not, as the old view would have it, *will* in consequence of and according to his cognition. On that view, he would need merely to consider *what* he would most like to be, and then he would be it: that is freedom of the will on this view. So this doctrine is really that a human being is his own work, in the light of cognition. I say, on the contrary: he is his own work prior to any cognition, which is added only later, in order to throw light on what he has done. That is why he cannot decide to be such and such, and cannot become someone different; rather he *is*, once and for all, and only then comes to cognize *what* he is. The old doctrine holds that he *wills* what he cognizes; I say he *cognizes* what he wills.[12]

    346

The Greeks called character ηθος and the expression of character, i.e. ethics[e] ηθη; but this word comes from εθος, habit: they chose it to express the constancy of character metaphorically, through the constancy of habit. 'Since the word ηθος (character) is named after εθος (habit); then ethics

---

[a] *Wesen*
[b] *Seele*
[c] *Wesen*
[d] *Denkakt*
[e] *Sitten*

gets its name from habit,' says Aristotle (*Ethica Magna*, I, 6, p. 1186, and *Eudemian Ethics*, p. 1220, and *Nicomachean Ethics*, p. 1103).[a] Stobaeus states: 'The followers of Zeno explain ethics figuratively as the spring of life from which flow particular actions',[b] II, ch. 7.[13] – In the articles of Christian faith we find the dogma of predestination as a result of[14] election or non-election by grace[c](Romans 9:11–24), which is clearly inspired by the insight that people do not change; rather, their lives and behaviour, i.e. their empirical characters, are only the unfolding of their intelligible characters, the development of decided, unalterable dispositions that are already recognizable in the child; thus, behaviour is fixed and determined even at birth, and in its essentials stays the same to the very end. We agree with this too; but I will certainly not attempt to defend the consequences that follow from combining this perfectly correct insight with the dogmas of Jewish articles of faith, and that give rise to the greatest difficulties, the Gordian knot, never to be untied, at the centre of most of the controversies in the church.[15] Even the Apostle Paul himself was barely able to defend it using the parable of the potter he developed for this purpose; and the result he reached was ultimately nothing other than:

347   The human race should fear the gods! They hold the power in their eternal hands, and they can use it as they like. –[d]

But considerations like this are not really germane to our subject. It would be more to the point to offer some remarks about the relation between character and cognition, which is where all its motives have their place.

The motives that determine the appearance of character, or action, influence it through the medium of cognition; but cognition is changeable, often shifting to and fro between error and truth, although as a rule it is increasingly set right over the course of a life – to very different degrees, of course. But this being the case, someone's way of acting can be visibly altered without warranting the conclusion that his character itself has altered. What someone truly wills, the striving from his innermost essence and the goal he pursues accordingly – this is something we could never alter

[a] Το γαρ ηθος απο του εθους εχει την επωνυμιαν. ηθιχη γαρ καλειται δια το εθιζεσθαι (*a voce* εθος, *i.e. consuetudo,* ηθος *est appellatum: ethica ergo dicta est* απο του εθιζεσθαι, *sive ab assuescendo*) [See *Ethica Magna* (or *Magna Moralia*: a work now regarded as not by Aristotle), I, 6, 1186a1–3; *Eudemian Ethics* II, 2, 1220a–b; *Nicomachean Ethics* II, ch. 1, 1103a17–18. The Greek terms at issue are *êthos* and *ethos*]
[b] οι δε κατα Ζηνωνα τροπικως· ηθος εστι πηγη βιου, αφ' ης αι κατα μερος πραξεις ρεουσι (Stoici autem, Zenonis castra sequentes, metaphorice ethos definiunt vitae fontem, e quo singulae manant actiones.) [*Eclogues*, more correctly II, ch. 6]
[c] *Gnadenwahl und Ungnadenwahl*
[d] [Goethe, *Iphigenie*, IV, 5.]

with external influences such as instruction: otherwise we could recreate him. Seneca makes the apposite remark: '*velle non discitur*';[a] which shows that he preferred the truth over his fellow Stoics, who said that virtue can be taught.[b,16] Only motives can affect the will externally. But they can never alter the will itself, because their power is based on the presupposition that the will is precisely what it is. All that they can do is to alter the direction of its striving, i.e. get the will to use a different path to search for the thing that it invariably seeks. This is why instruction and improved knowledge,[c] i.e. external influence, can certainly teach the will that it is using the wrong means to an end, and move it onto an entirely different path towards the goal that it strives for in accordance with its inner essence, or even get it to adopt a different object altogether: but such external influence can never get the will to will something genuinely different from what it has willed before. This remains fixed and invariable, because it is nothing other than the willing itself, which would otherwise have to be annulled. But looking at the first case, modifying deeds by modifying knowledge,[d] this can go as far as taking the always invariable goal, let us say Mohammed's paradise, and trying this time to achieve it in the real world, and at another time to achieve it in an imaginary world; this would entail modifying the means as well, using cunning, violence and deceit the first time, and using abstinence, justice, alms-giving and pilgrimages to Mecca the next. But the striving itself has not altered as a result, still less the will itself. So even if its actions certainly appear very different at different times, its willing has remained exactly the same. *Velle non discitur.*

348

To be effective, a motive does not just need to be present, it must be recognized:[17] according to a very apt Scholastic expression that we have already mentioned once before, 'the final cause operates not according to its real essence, but rather according to its known essence'.[e] For the relationship between (for instance) egoism and compassion to emerge in any given person, it is not enough for that person to possess wealth and see others in need;[18] he must also know[f] what wealth can do both for himself and for others; the suffering of others must not only present itself, he must also know what suffering is, as well as enjoyment. Perhaps he did not know all this the first time he was in a given situation as well as he

---

[a] [willing cannot be taught. *Epistles*, 81, 14]
[b] διδακτην ειναι την αρετην (*doceri posse virtutem*) [Diogenes Laertius, *Lives of Eminent Philosophers*, VII, 91]
[c] *Erkenntniß*
[d] *Erkenntniß*
[e] *causa finalis movet non secundum suum esse reale; sed secundum esse cognitum.*
[f] *wissen*

did the second time; and so if he acts differently in the same situation, this is because the circumstances were actually different, even though they seem the same, the difference being the man's cognition of the circumstances. – Just as ignorance of actually existing circumstances renders them ineffective, completely imaginary circumstances can operate like real ones, not only in the case of a single illusion, but even overall and permanently. For instance, if someone is firmly convinced that every good deed will be repaid a hundred times over in a future life, this conviction will operate just like a secure, long-term bank draft, and he can give things away out of egoism just as he would appropriate things out of egoism if he held different views. But he has not altered: *velle non discitur*. Since cognition has such a great influence on action (given the inalterability of the will), the different tendencies of character develop only gradually. This is why character appears different at each time of life, and a passionate and wild youth can be followed by a sedate, temperate, manhood. In particular, any evil in a person's character emerges more powerfully with age; but sometimes passions that were indulged in youth are later voluntarily restrained simply because conflicting motives have only just entered cognition. So we are all innocent in the beginning, which just means that neither we nor anyone else recognizes the evil of our own natures: the evil arises only with motives, and we only come to recognize the motives in time. Ultimately, we come to recognize ourselves as quite different from what we imagined ourselves to be *a priori*, and we are often frightened by ourselves.

Remorse[a] never comes from alterations in the will (which would be impossible) but rather from the fact that cognition has altered. I must continue to will the essential and real aspect of what I have willed previously, because I am myself this will lying outside time and alteration. That is why I can never regret[b] what I have willed, although I can regret what I have done, because I was led by false conceptions to do something that was out of keeping with my will. The insight that comes from correcting our cognition is *remorse*. This is not just limited to worldly wisdom, i.e. to selecting the means and judging whether the end is in keeping with my true will; it extends to the truly ethical as well. So for instance I can act more selfishly than is in my character, led astray by exaggerated ideas[c] of my needs or another person's cunning, falseness or evil, or because I am in too great a hurry, i.e. I act without thinking, determined not by

---

[a] *Reue*
[b] *bereuen*
[c] *Vorstellungen*

motives recognized clearly in the abstract,[a] but rather by merely intuited motives, through an impression of the present which excites an affect strong enough to rob me of the full use of my reason. Here too, coming back to my senses just means correcting my cognition, and this can give rise to remorse, something that always reveals itself in making amends for what happened as much as possible. It can be noted that people deceive themselves by staging apparent cases of hastiness that are really secretly deliberate actions. For we fool and flatter no one more than ourselves with little games like this. – The converse can take place as well: I can be led to act less selfishly than is strictly consistent with my character because I have too much confidence in other people, or because I do not know the relative value of the good things in life, or because I used to hold some sort of abstract dogma that I then lost faith in; these would set me up for a different sort of remorse. Remorse is always recognition of the relationship between deed and true intention, but recognition that has been corrected. – When the will reveals its Ideas in space alone, i.e. through mere shape, it comes into conflict with the matter that is already governed by other Ideas, in this case forces of nature, and the shape that is striving for manifestation rarely emerges as perfectly pure and clear, i.e. beautiful. The will finds an analogous obstacle as it reveals itself in time alone, i.e. through actions: since the information provided by cognition is seldom entirely correct, the deed does not correspond perfectly to the will, and this sets the stage for remorse. Thus remorse always proceeds from recognition that has been corrected, not from a change of will, which would be impossible. The anguish of conscience[b] over what has been done is nothing like remorse; it is the pain of recognizing yourself as such, i.e. as will. It is squarely based on the certainty that you still have the same will. If the will were altered and the anguish of conscience were just remorse, then it would be abolished: the past could no longer cause any anxiety, since it would present the expression of a will that was no longer that of the person experiencing remorse. Later we will have a detailed discussion of the meaning of anguish of conscience.

Cognition is the medium of motives, and its influence – not on the will itself, but on the emergence of the will into actions – also underlies the fundamental difference between human and animal deeds, since humans and animals have different modes of cognition. The animal cognizes only intuitively while humans, through reason, have abstract representations or

[a] *in abstracto*
[b] *Gewissensangst*

350

351   concepts as well. Although animals and humans are determined through motives with the same degree of necessity, humans have an absolute *ability to choose*[a] that gives them an advantage over animals and has often been regarded as a freedom of the will in particular deeds; in truth, however, it is nothing other than the possibility of a full-fledged battle between several motives, where the stronger motive determines the will with necessity. For this to happen, the motives must assume the form of abstract thoughts, because this is the only way genuine deliberation is possible, i.e. a weighing of opposing grounds for action. With animals the choice can only be between intuitively available motives, and this is why animals are limited to the narrow sphere of their present, intuitive apprehension.[19] Accordingly, it is only in animals that the necessity of the determination of the will through the motive, which is the same as that of the effect through the cause, can be intuitively and immediately presented; here the spectator too can see the motive as directly as he can see its effect. With humans, on the other hand, motives are almost always abstract representations that the spectator does not have access to, and the necessity of their operation is hidden from even the agent himself behind their conflict. This is because it is only abstractly[b] that several representations can lie side by side in consciousness, as judgements and chains of inferences, and operate against each other, free from all temporal determination, until the stronger among them overpowers the rest and determines the will. This is the absolute *ability to choose*, or deliberative capacity, which raises humans above animals and leads us to credit ourselves with freedom of the will, believing that human willing is the mere result of the operations of the intellect and that the intellect is not based in any particular drive.[c] In truth, a motive is effective only when it has the person's own particular drive as its foundation and presupposition, the drive in his case being an individual one, i.e. a character. You will find a fuller presentation of this deliberative capacity and the resulting difference between human and animal choice[d] in *The Two Fundamental Problems of Ethics* (1st edn., pp. 35ff.), which I refer to

352   here. In fact, people's deliberative capacity is one of the things[20] that makes their existence so much more harrowing than that of animals, because generally speaking, our greatest sufferings do not lie in the present, as intuitive representations or immediate feeling, but rather in reason, as abstract concepts, tormenting thoughts. Animals are completely free from

---

[a]   *Wahlentscheidung*
[b]   *in abstracto*
[c]   *Trieb*
[d]   *Willkür*

these, because they live only in the present and are thus in an enviably carefree condition.[21]

We have shown that the human deliberative ability is dependent on the faculty of thinking abstractly, and thus on the faculties of judgement and inference; and this dependence seems to have been what misled Descartes as well as Spinoza into identifying[22] the decisions of the will with the faculty of affirmation and negation (the power of judgement). Descartes concluded from this that what he regarded as the free and indifferent will is responsible for all theoretical errors too: Spinoza on the other hand concluded that the will is necessarily determined by motives, just as judgement is determined by grounds;* this last claim having some truth to it, although it is that of a true conclusion drawn from false premises.[23]

The dissimilarity we have demonstrated between the ways humans and animals are moved by motives has profound consequences for the nature[a] of each, and is what is primarily responsible for the striking and radical difference between the existence[b] of the two. While an animal is only ever motivated by intuitive representations, a human being is at pains to exclude this sort of motivation altogether, to allow himself to be determined only by abstract representations. By this means he makes use of the privilege of reason to the greatest possible advantage, and independently of the present, does not choose or avoid temporary bouts of pleasure or pain, but considers the consequences of each. Most of the time, apart from completely trivial actions, we are determined by abstract, thought-out motives, not by our current impressions. That is why we find every individual, momentary privation quite easy to bear, but every renunciation terribly difficult: the former affects only the passing present, while the latter concerns the future and thus comprises countless privations, to which it is equivalent. The causes of our pains and pleasures are not generally found in the real present[24] but instead in abstract thoughts, and these often strike us as unbearable, inflicting torments that dwarf all the sufferings of animals in comparison, since they can often block out even our own physical pain. In fact, when we are experiencing acute mental suffering we inflict physical suffering on ourselves just to distract ourselves from the mental suffering. This is why people in extreme mental pain will tear their hair, beat their chests, scratch their faces, and throw themselves on the ground; all of which are really just a violent means of distraction from an unbearable thought. It is precisely

353

---

* Descartes, *Meditations* 4. – Spinoza, *Ethics*, Part II, Prop. 48 and 49 *etc.*

[a] *Wesen*
[b] *Daseyns*

because mental pain makes us insensible to physical pain, being by far the greater of the two, that suicide is very easy for someone who is in despair or is consumed by pathological depression,[a] even if he would have found the thought shocking in earlier, happier days. Besides,[25] worries and passions, i.e. the play of thoughts, are a greater and more frequent strain on the body than physical hardship. In keeping with this, Epictetus rightly says: 'It is not things themselves that disturb people but opinions about things' (V)[b] and Seneca: 'there is more to frighten than to oppress us, and we suffer more frequently from ideas than from reality' (*Epistles*, 5).[c] Even Eulenspiegel offered a wonderful satire on human nature by laughing uphill and crying downhill. In fact, children who hurt themselves often do not cry at the pain but only start crying when somebody comforts them, because this makes them think about the pain. These great differences in behaviour and in suffering derive from differences between the human and animal modes of cognition. Only abstract concepts make it possible for people to choose between several motives; and this is the condition for a clear and decisive individual character, which is the primary distinction between people and animals (since animals have almost no character except the character of their species). It is only after a choice has been made that the resulting decisions, which vary from individual to individual, become a sign of

354 individual character, which is different in everyone; animal behaviour, on the other hand, depends only on the presence or absence of an impression, supposing that the impression is a motive for its species at all. That is why for people, only the decision and not merely the desire[d] is a valid token of a person's character, both for himself and for others. But the decision only becomes certain through the action, both for himself as for others. The desire is simply the necessary consequence of the present impression, whether it is the impression of an external stimulus or of a transient inner mood; for this reason it is just as immediately necessary and lacking in deliberation as the act of an animal: that is why desire only expresses the character of the species, as in animals, and not the individual, i.e. it merely signifies what *human beings in general*, not the *individual* who experiences this desire, would be able to do. Because it is already a human action, the deed always requires a certain amount of deliberation,

---

[a] *Unmuth*
[b] Ταρασσει τους ανθρωπους ου τα πραγματα, αλλα τα περι των πραγματων δογματα (*Perturbant homines non res ipsae, sed de rebus decreta*) [*Handbook* (or *Encheiridion*), ch. 5]
[c] *Plura sunt, quae nos terrent, quam quae premunt, et saepius opinione quam re laboramus (Ep. 5)* [though 13, 4 is the correct reference]
[d] *Wunsch* [elsewhere 'wish']

and because people are generally in control of their reason, which is to say they are thoughtful,[a] i.e. they make decisions according to well-considered, abstract motives, only the action is the expression of the intelligible maxim of their acting, the result of their innermost willing. As such, it is related as a letter is to the word that describes their empirical character, which is itself only the temporal expression of the intelligible character. That is why only deeds, not desires or thoughts, weigh on the consciences of people with healthy minds. Only our deeds hold before us a mirror of our will. The thoroughly ill-considered and blindly emotional[b] deed that we mentioned before is, to a certain extent, a cross between simple desire and decision: that is why true remorse, when manifested in deeds, can erase it from the image of our will that is our course through life, as if it were nothing more than a badly drawn line. – By the way, this might be the place to note an odd likeness: the relation between desire and deed has a completely accidental but nonetheless exact analogy in the relation between electrical accumulation and electrical discharge.

As a result of this whole discussion of the freedom of the will and related topics, we find that, although the will can be called free, even omnipotent, when we are regarding it in itself and outside appearance, nevertheless in its particular appearances illuminated by cognition, which is to say in human beings and in animals, it is determined by motives, and these motives ensure that the same character will always react in the same lawlike and necessary way. We see that a human being has the advantage over animals of possessing an *ability to choose* by virtue of abstract or rational cognition. But this only makes him a battleground for conflicting motives, and does not remove him from their control; thus, while this ability indeed conditions the possibility of the complete expression of the individual character, it can by no means be seen as a freedom of individual willing. That is, it does not signify any independence from the law of causality,[26] whose necessity extends to human beings just as it does to every other appearance. The difference between willing in humans and in animals – itself introduced by reason, or conceptual cognition – extends this far and no further. But an entirely different phenomenon of the human will, one that is impossible in animals, can arise when a human being abandons all cognition of individual things as such, cognition that is subject to the principle of sufficient reason, and instead uses cognition of the Ideas to see through the *principium individuationis*; this

355

[a] *besonnen*
[b] *im blinden Affekt begangen*

makes possible a true emergence of genuine freedom of the will as thing in itself, and thus leads to a certain self-contradiction in appearance, a contradiction indicated by the word self-denial;[a] and in fact, the in-itself of its essence finally abolishes itself.[b] – We are not yet in a position to clearly present this true, unique and immediate expression of the freedom of the will in itself, even in appearance, but it will be the final subject of our discussion.

The present arguments have clarified the unalterable nature[c] of the empirical character for us (which is merely the unfolding of the extra-temporal, intelligible character) as well as the necessity of the action that takes place when the intelligible character encounters a motive. But now that this has been accomplished, we need to dispel an inference that can easily be drawn from this in support of objectionable tendencies. Our character is to be seen as the temporal unfolding of an extra-temporal and

356   thus indivisible and unalterable act of will, or an intelligible character; and this act irrevocably determines everything essential, i.e. the ethical content of how we conduct our lives, which must express itself as such in its appearance, the empirical character. At the same time, only the inessential features of this appearance, the outer shape of our life's course, depend on the forms in which the motives present themselves. And someone could conclude from all this that it is a waste of time to work at improving his character or resisting the force of evil inclinations, and that he would be better advised to submit to the inevitable, and immediately give in to every inclination, no matter how evil. – But this is just the same as the theory of an inexorable fate and the consequences that can be drawn from it are known as 'lazy reasoning',[d] or more recently, the Turkish faith, and the correct refutation of it is attributed to Chrysippus and presented by Cicero in the book *On Fate*,[e] chapters 12 and 13.

But although everything can be seen as irrevocably predetermined by fate, this is only by means of the chain of causes. There is no case in which it can be determined that an effect takes place without its cause. It is not simply the event that is predetermined, but the event as the result of a previous cause: thus fate not only determines the result, but the means that determines the occurrence of the result. If the means do not take place, then the result certainly will not take place either: both always exist

---

[a] *Selbstverleugnung*
[b] *sich aufhebt*
[c] *Unveränderlichkeit*
[d] αργος λογος
[e] *de fato*

according to the determination of fate, although we only ever find this out after the fact.

Just as events always take place according to fate, i.e. the endless chain of causes, our deeds too must always take place according to our intelligible character: but just as we do not recognize the former in advance, we also have no *a priori* insight into the latter; it is only *a posteriori*, through experience that we get to know ourselves,[a] just as we get to know other people. If our intelligible character entails that we will reach a good decision only after a protracted struggle with an evil inclination, then this struggle must take place, and we must wait it out. Reflections on the inalterability of character and the unity of the source of all our deeds cannot mislead us into forestalling the decision of character in favour of one side or the other: when the decision is made we will find out which type we are, and mirror ourselves in our deeds. This explains the satisfaction or, alternatively, the mental anguish we experience when looking back over the course of our lives: neither response emerges from the supposition that these past deeds still have any being: they are past, they were, and are now no more. Their great importance for us comes from their significance, the fact that these deeds are the cast of our character, the mirror of our will, and in looking at them we recognize our innermost self, the kernel of our will. Because we do not experience this in advance but only after the fact, it is right that we should strive and struggle in time so that the image we create through our deeds will be a source of reassurance rather than concern, to the fullest extent possible. As we have said, the significance of this reassurance (or mental anguish) will be further investigated below. The following, self-subsistent remarks are what belong at the present juncture.

Besides the intelligible and empirical characters, we can mention a third that is distinct from those others, the *acquired character*, which is only acquired over the course of a life and through contact with the world. This is what people have in mind when they praise someone as a man of character or censure him as characterless. – Of course someone could say that empirical character is unalterable since it is the appearance of the intelligible character, and, like every phenomenon in nature,[b] internally consistent; and as a result, a human being must also appear internally consistent and self-identical and thus cannot need to acquire a character artificially, through experience and reflection. But this is not how it seems

357

---

[a] *lernen wir... uns selbst kennen*
[b] *Naturerscheinung*

to that person, and although people might always be the same, they do not understand themselves at every moment; in fact, they frequently misunderstand themselves until they have acquired a certain degree of genuine self-knowledge.[a] As a simple drive of nature, empirical character is intrinsically irrational: in fact, reason interferes with how it expresses itself, and its interference is proportionate to the thoughtfulness and intelligence of the person involved. This is because these rational qualities show him and even reproach him with what is appropriate for *human beings in general*, as a species character, and what is possible in willing and doing. This impedes his insight into what he alone wills and what he alone can do, by virtue of his individuality. He finds in himself a disposition for all the many human aspirations and abilities; but without experience, he is not aware of the extent to which these are present in his individuality: and if he now limits himself to projects that are in keeping with his character, there will be certain moods and moments when he will feel impelled in the opposite direction, towards incompatible schemes that must be entirely repressed if he wants to pursue the first set of projects without disruption. Just as our physical path on earth is always a line and never a plane, similarly, when we want to accomplish and possess one thing in life we need to give up countless other things, right and left, and leave them undone. If we could act like children at a fair, grabbing at everything that tickles our fancy without stopping to make up our minds, this would be a wrong-headed attempt to change our line into a plane: we would zigzag all over the place without getting anything done. – Or, to use another comparison, it is like Hobbes' doctrine of right, where everyone originally had a right to everything but exclusive right to nothing; but someone could acquire an exclusive right to a particular thing by renouncing the right to everything else, while the others do the same thing in relation to what the first person has chosen. This is exactly how it is with life: we can only seriously and successfully pursue one particular project – whether it is pleasure, honour, wealth, science, art, or virtue – by giving up all claims that are foreign to it and renouncing everything else. That is why it is not enough simply to will something, or even to be able to do it; a human being must also *know*[b] what he is willing, and *know* what he can do: only then does he begin to show character, and only then can he achieve anything properly. Prior to this he is indeed characterless, despite the natural consistency of the empirical character, and although in general he must be true to himself

---

[a] *Selbsterkenntniß*
[b] *wissen*

and run his course, he will not set off on a straight line but rather take a
shaky, crooked line, deviating, wavering, turning back, and setting himself
up for pain and remorse: and this is all because he sees before himself,
in matters both great and small, everything that human beings can and
do achieve, and does not yet know what portion of this is appropriate or
practicable or even just enjoyable for himself. He will envy other people
for positions and circumstances that are suited only to the other people's
characters, not to his own, and in which he himself would be unhappy, or
even unable to cope. Just as fish do well only in water, birds in the air, and
moles underground, everybody can do well only in the atmosphere they
find congenial; not everyone, for instance, can breathe in the atmosphere
of a court. Many a person has no insight into these matters and will make
all sorts of failed attempts,[27] doing violence to his character in many small
respects and being forced to yield to it again overall: and what he achieves
so painfully and against his nature will not give him any pleasure; what
he learns in this way will remain dead; even from an ethical perspective,
if someone performs a deed that is too noble for their character, that does
not arise from a pure and direct impulse but instead from a concept, a
dogma, then subsequent egoistic remorse will rob it of all value, even in
the person's own eyes. *Velle non discitur.* We realize only through experience how inflexible other people's characters really are, and until then
we harbour a childish faith that we can move them with irrational ideas,[a]
with pleas and entreaties, with examples and noble actions, and make some
one of them abandon his type, alter his way of acting, forgo his way of
thinking, or even widen the scope of his abilities; and we do the same with
ourselves. We must first learn through experiences what we want and what
we can do: until then we do not know[b] it, we are characterless, and we will
frequently have to be driven back onto our own true path by sharp blows
from the outside. – But if we finally learn this lesson, we will have achieved
what the world calls character, the *acquired character*. This is nothing other
than the greatest possible familiarity with our own individuality: it is the
abstract and therefore clear knowledge[c] of the invariable qualities of our
own empirical character, of the dimensions and directions of our mental
and physical abilities, and thus of the total strengths and weaknesses of
our own individuality. This enables us to organize the unalterable role
of our own person in a thoughtful and methodical manner (a role that
we had previously acted out naturally, without any rules) and under the

360

^a *Vorstellungen*
^b *wissen*
^c *Wissen*

direction of solid concepts, we can also fill gaps in it left by whims or weaknesses. We have now put the ways of acting that are necessitated by our individual natures into clear and conscious maxims, maxims that are always present to us. We follow these maxims as deliberately as if they had been learned, without ever being led astray by a present impression or the fleeting influence of mood, without being hindered by the bitterness or sweetness of some particular thing that we meet along our way, without hesitating, without wavering, without inconsistency. We will no longer act like novices, waiting, trying, fumbling around to see what we really want and are capable of doing; we know[a] it once and for all, and every time we make a choice we only have to apply general principles to the individual case in order to reach a decision right away. We are acquainted[b] with our will on a general level, and we will not let ourselves be misled by moods or external demands into deciding on something in a particular case that runs contrary to the will as a whole. We are aware of the nature[c] and extent of our abilities and our weaknesses, and this saves us a great deal of suffering. This is because there is really no other pleasure than the use and feeling of our own powers,[d] and the greatest pain is the feeling that we lack strength when we need it. Now if we have investigated where our strengths and weaknesses are, we will develop our salient natural talents, make use of them, try to apply them however we can, and go where they are appropriate and effective; at the same time, we will always exercise self-restraint and avoid projects where we do not have much natural aptitude; we will guard against unsuccessful efforts. Only someone who has achieved this will always be calmly and confidently himself; he will never let himself down, because he always knows what he can expect of himself. He will often enjoy the feeling of his strengths, and rarely experience the pain of being reminded of his weaknesses. This is the experience of humiliation, which is perhaps the cause of our greatest mental anguish: it is why people find it much easier to think about their misfortunes than their blunders. – Now, if we are fully aware of our strengths and weaknesses, we will not try to display abilities that we do not have, playing with false coins, because such mirror tricks will always fall short of their goal. Since the whole human being is only the appearance of his will, nothing can be more mistaken than for him, starting from reflection, to will to be something

361

---

[a] *wissen*
[b] *kennen*
[c] *Art*
[d] *Kräfte*

other than he is: this is a direct contradiction of the will with itself. Imitating other people's qualities and idiosyncrasies is much more shameful than wearing other people's clothes, because it is a judgement we ourselves pass on our own worthlessness. Knowing our own minds and all of our abilities with their fixed and unchanging limits is, in this respect, the safest path to the greatest possible satisfaction with ourselves. This is because it is as true for inner states as it is for outer ones that we take greatest comfort in the full certainty of irrevocable necessity. Nothing exacerbates a trouble we have experienced so much as thinking about the ways in which it could have been avoided; accordingly, nothing can give us greater peace of mind than observing what happened from the perspective of necessity, where all accidents appear as tools of an active fate, and recognizing the trouble as an inevitable result of the conflict of inner and outer circumstances, which is fatalism.[28] We really only rant and rage for as long as we hope to affect others or drive ourselves to unprecedented exertions. But children and adults both know very well how to give in as soon as it is clear to them that things are not going to change:

> Forcefully holding back the rancour nurtured in the breast.
> (Homer, *Iliad*, XVIII, 113[a])

We are like elephants in captivity who struggle and rage horribly for many   362
days until they see that it is fruitless and suddenly offer their necks for the yoke, tame forever. We are like King David who was in despair as long as his son was alive, imploring Jehovah with incessant prayers; but stopped thinking about him as soon as he was dead. That is why countless people endure countless lasting evils like lameness, poverty, low rank, ugliness and bad living conditions with perfect indifference, and do not even feel them anymore, like wounds that have scarred over, simply because they know that inner or outer necessity shows that nothing can be done about them; while more fortunate people cannot imagine how anyone can put up with the situation. It is the same with external necessity as it is with internal necessity: nothing reconciles us so well as a clear awareness of it. If we clearly recognize our failings and weaknesses as well as our good qualities and strengths, once and for all, if we plot our goal accordingly and accept what we cannot do; then this is the surest way of escaping (as far as possible, given our individuality) the bitterest of all sufferings, that of dissatisfaction with ourselves, which is the inevitable result of our ignorance about our own individuality, our false conceit, and the presumptuousness that results.

---

[a] Θυμὸν ἐνὶ στήθεσσι φίλον δαμάσαντες ἀνάγκῃ. (*Animo in pectoribus nostro domito necessitate.*)

Ovid's verses can be applied very well to the bitter topic of self-knowledge[a] that we are recommending:

> The best aid to the spirit is what has broken the torturous bonds
> That entangle the heart, and destroyed them once and for all.[b]

That much concerning the *acquired character*, which is not as significant for ethics proper as it is for life in the world. But it is associated with the intelligible and empirical character as a third category, and we had to undertake a somewhat detailed discussion of it in order to clarify how the will is subject to necessity in all of its appearances, while in itself it can nonetheless be considered free and even omnipotent.

363

§ 56

The entire visible world is the appearance, expression and image of this freedom, this omnipotence, and it develops progressively in accordance with the laws entailed by the form of cognition; but this freedom can also express itself anew, and indeed in precisely its most perfect appearance, where the completely adequate recognition of its own essence has arisen. It does this either by willing here, at the peak of clarity and self-consciousness, the same thing that it willed blindly and without self-awareness (in which case cognition in the individual, as in the whole, could only ever be a *motive* for it); or conversely, this freedom can express itself when cognition becomes a *tranquillizer* that placates and abolishes all willing. This is what we referred to before in general terms as the affirmation and negation of the will to life, which, as a general and not particular expression of the will with respect to the behaviour of the individual, does not disruptively modify the development of character and is not expressed in particular actions. Rather it vividly expresses the maxim that the will has freely adopted, in accordance with the cognition it has now attained, and it expresses this either through an increasingly strong emergence of the way of acting exhibited so far, or, conversely, by abolishing it. – Our task in developing this theme more clearly has been facilitated and assisted by the discussions of freedom, necessity and character that have since intervened. Our task will be easier still if we postpone it once more, and first direct our consideration to life itself, whose willing or non-willing is the great question, and indeed attempt to find out in general what really becomes of the will itself (which

---

[a] *Selbsterkenntniß*
[b] *Optimus ille animi vindex laedentia pectus / Vincula qui rupit, dedoluitque semel.* [*Remedia Amoris* (*Remedies of Love*), 293, slightly adapted]

is indeed the innermost essence of this life) through its affirmation, in what way and to what extent this affirmation satisfies or indeed can satisfy the will; in short, and in the most general and essential terms, what we can regard as its situation in this, its own world, a world that belongs to it in every respect.

To begin with, I would like to recall the discussion from the end of the Second Book, a discussion that was occasioned by the question raised there about the goal and purpose of the will; rather than answering this question, we saw how the will, at all levels of its appearance, from the lowest up to the highest, forgoes entirely any final goal or purpose. It is always striving, because striving is its only essence, and is not brought to an end by reaching any goal; it is therefore not capable of any ultimate satisfaction; obstacles can only detain it, while in itself it goes on to infinity. We saw this in the simplest of all the appearances of nature, in gravity, which does not stop striving and urging its way to an unextended central point (although it would negate itself and matter if it were ever to reach this point); gravity would not stop even if the whole universe were gathered up into a ball. We see this in other simple natural phenomena:[a] solidity strives to be fluid, whether by melting or dissolving, since its chemical forces can be free only in a fluid state: rigidity is the prison where they are held by the cold. Fluidity strives to be vaporized, and it passes into a vapour state as soon as it is freed from all pressure. No body is without an affinity,[b] i.e. without striving or without desire and appetite, as Jacob Böhme would say. Electricity transmits its inner self-dichotomy to infinity, even if the earth's mass absorbs the effect. As long as the pile keeps going, galvanism too is an aimless, endlessly repeated act of self-dichotomy[c] and reconciliation. The existence of the plant presents another example of a restless and insatiable striving, an incessant drive through higher and higher forms until the end point, the seed corn, becomes the beginning again: this is repeated to infinity: there is never a goal, never a final satisfaction, never a resting place. At the same time, we will remember from the Second Book that the many different forces of nature and organic forms struggle with each other for the matter in which they want to appear, since each only has what it has torn away from another; thus, there is a constant mortal struggle, and what emerges first and foremost is a resistance inhibiting the striving which is the innermost essence of all things. It urges in vain, but

364

365

---

[a] *Naturerscheinungen*
[b] *Verwandtschaft*
[c] *Selbstentzweiung*

its essence does not let it stop, it puts up a miserable struggle until this appearance perishes, at which point others eagerly grab its place and its matter.

We have long recognized that the striving that constitutes the kernel and the in-itself of everything is just what we call *will* when it appears in ourselves, which is where it manifests itself most clearly and in the full light of a most complete consciousness. When an obstacle is placed between it and its temporary goal, we call this inhibition *suffering*; on the other hand, the achievement of its goal is *satisfaction*, contentment, happiness. We could also apply this nomenclature to those appearances in the world that is devoid of cognition, appearances that are weaker in degree but identical in essence. We then see these in the grip of constant suffering, with no lasting happiness. All striving comes from lack, from a dissatisfaction with one's condition,[29] and is thus suffering as long as it is not satisfied; but no satisfaction is lasting; instead, it is only the beginning of a new striving. We see striving everywhere inhibited in many ways, struggling everywhere; and thus always as suffering; there is no final goal of striving, and therefore no bounds or end to suffering.

Although it takes close attention and effort to discover all this in the part of nature that is devoid of cognition, it stares us right in the face in the part of nature that *does* have cognition, in animal life, whose constant suffering is easy to prove. But we do not want to remain on these intermediate levels, we want to proceed to human life, where cognition is illuminated most brightly and everything stands out most clearly. This is because suffering becomes more apparent the more completely the will appears. Plants do not yet have sensibility, and thus do not have pain: both are present to a certain very small degree in the lowest animals, the infusoria and radiata. Even in insects, the ability to feel and to suffer is very restricted: only with the complete nervous system in the vertebrates is it present to a high degree, and this degree only increases with the greater development of the intellect.[30] An increase in pain[a] is directly correlated with an increase in clarity of cognition and an increase in consciousness; consequently, pain reaches its highest pitch in human beings, and even there continues to grow in proportion to cognition and intelligence; the man in whom genius dwells suffers the most. It is in this sense, namely in relation to the degree of cognition in general, not merely abstract knowledge,[b] that I understand and use that expression in Ecclesiastes: 'He that increaseth knowledge increaseth

366

[a] *Quaal*
[b] *Wissen*

sorrow.'[a] – This precise relation between the degree of consciousness and that of suffering was beautifully and intuitively expressed in a remarkable drawing by that philosophical painter or painting philosopher, *Tischbein*. The top half of the drawing shows women whose children are being taken from them, and who, in different groupings and attitudes, express deep maternal pain, anguish and despair in a variety of ways; the bottom half of the drawing shows, in the very same arrangements and groupings, sheep whose lambs are being taken away; every human head, every human position of the top half of the page has a corresponding analogy among the animals. As a result, you can see clearly how the pain that is possible in dull animal consciousness compares to the violent grief[b] that becomes possible only through clarity of cognition and consciousness.

This is why we want to observe the inner and essential fate of the will in *human existence*. Everyone will easily find the very same thing in the lives of animals, only expressed more or less weakly, and will also find enough in the suffering animal world to convince himself how essential *suffering is to all life*.

§ 57

The will appears as individual on every level illuminated by cognition. The human individual discovers his own finitude in infinite space and infinite time, and thus learns that he is vanishingly small compared to these. He is thrown into space and time and, given their boundlessness, his existence has only a relative rather than absolute *when* and *where*: his position and duration are finite parts of a boundless infinity. – He only truly exists   367 in the present, and the unchecked flight of the present into the past is a continuous passage into death, a constant dying; this is because his past life, aside from its eventual consequences for the present and the testimony it provides about the individual's will, is already completely dead, killed off, it is no more: thus on a completely rational level, he should be perfectly indifferent as to whether the content of that past was pleasure or pain. The present is continually passing through his hands into the past: the future is completely unknown and always brief. Thus his existence, seen only from the formal side, is a continuous plunging of the present into the dead past, a continuous dying. But if we now look at it from the physical side as well, it is clear that just as we know that walking is a continuously checked

---

[a] *Qui auget scientiam, auget et dolorem.* [(Ecclesiastes 1:18). Schopenhauer uses the term 'Koheleth' for this book of the Bible]

[b] *Quaal*

falling, the life of our body is only a constantly checked dying, a constant postponement of death: finally, even our mental activity is a continuously delayed boredom. Every breath we take wards off the perpetual onslaught of death; in this way, we struggle against death at every moment, and again at greater intervals, with every meal, every sleep, every time we warm ourselves, etc. Death has to win in the end: because we have been cast into death ever since birth, and it is only playing with its prey for a while before devouring it. In the meantime, we go on with our lives with considerable interest and deep concern for as long as possible, just as someone might blow as big a soap bubble as they can, and try to get it to last for as long as possible, although being absolutely certain that it is going to burst.

Looking at the part of nature that is devoid of cognition, we already saw its inner essence to be a continual striving, without goal and without rest, and this is much more evident when we consider animals and human beings. Willing and striving constitute their entire essence, fully comparable to an unquenchable thirst. But the basis of all willing is need, lack, and thus pain, which is its primordial destiny by virtue of its essence. If on the other hand it lacks objects to will, its former objects having been quickly dispelled as too easily achieved, it is seized with a terrible emptiness and boredom: i.e. its essence and its being itself become an intolerable burden to it. Thus, its life swings back and forth like a pendulum between pain and boredom;[31] in fact, these are the ingredients out of which it is ultimately composed. This has also been very fancifully expressed by saying that after people had placed all the pain and suffering in hell, nothing was left for heaven except boredom.

But the perpetual striving that constitutes the essence of every appearance of the will obtains its first and most universal foundation at the higher levels of objectivation from the fact that the will appears there as a living body with the iron command to be fed; and this commandment gets its force from the fact that this body is nothing other than the objectified will to life. A human being, as the most perfect objectivation of that will, is for that reason also the neediest of all beings: he is concrete willing and needing through and through, he is the concretion of a thousand needs. He stands with these upon the earth, left to his own devices, uncertain about everything except his needs and wants:[32] accordingly and for the most part, the whole of human life is consumed by worries about how to go on existing in the face of such difficult demands, worries that assert themselves afresh every day. Directly connected to this is the second demand, the propagation of the race. At the same time the human being is threatened on all sides by the most diverse dangers, and it takes constant vigilance to escape them.

He goes on his way with a cautious step, looking around anxiously because he is accosted by a thousand accidents and a thousand enemies. Thus it was in the wild, thus is it in civilized life; he has no security:

> Oh, in what darkness of life, in what great dangers,
> We pass our time, as long as it lasts!
>
> Lucretius, II.15[a,33]

For the vast majority of people, life itself is nothing but a constant struggle for this same existence, with the certainty of losing it in the end. But what enables them to survive this miserable struggle is not so much a love of life as it is the fear of death, which nonetheless stands inexorably in the background, and can step forward at any moment. – Life itself is a sea full of reefs and maelstroms that a human being takes the greatest care and caution to avoid; he uses all his efforts and ingenuity to wend his way through, while knowing that even if he is successful, every step brings him closer to the greatest, the total, the inescapable and irreparable shipwreck, and in fact steers him right up to it, – to death: this is the final goal of the miserable journey and worse for him than all the reefs he managed to avoid.

369

Now it is well worth noting right away that on the one hand, the pains and sufferings of life can easily grow to the point where even death (the whole point of life being the avoidance of death) becomes desirable, and people freely embrace it; and again on the other hand, that as soon as people get some respite from needs and sufferings, boredom is so close that they need to take up some pastime. What keeps all living things busy and in motion is the striving to exist. But when existence is secured, they do not know what to do: that is why the second thing that sets them in motion is a striving to get rid of the burden of existence, not to feel it any longer, 'to kill time', i.e. to escape boredom.[34] We see this in almost everyone who is secured from worries and wants; once they have rid themselves of all other burdens, they become burdens to themselves, and see every hour that passes as a gain, which is to say everything that shortens the very life that they have spent all their energies so far in sustaining for as long as possible. Boredom is certainly not an evil[b] to be taken lightly: it will ultimately etch lines of true despair onto a face. It makes beings with as little love for each other as humans nonetheless seek each other with such intensity, and in this way it becomes the source of sociability.[35] For reasons of

---

[a] *Qualibus in tenebris vitae, quantisque periclis | Degitur hocc' aevi, quodcunque est!* [Lucretius, *De rerum natura (On the Nature of Things)*, II. 15–16]
[b] *Uebel*

political prudence, public precautions are always taken against it, as against other universal calamities; that is because this evil can drive people to the greatest licentiousness as much as its opposite extreme, famine: bread and circuses[a] is what the people need. Philadelphia's strict penitentiary system makes boredom into an instrument of punishment, through loneliness and inactivity: and it is so horrible that it has already driven convicts to suicide. Just as need is the constant scourge of the people, boredom is the scourge of the respectable world. In middle-class life it is represented by Sunday, just as want is represented by the other six days of the week.[36]

Absolutely every human life flows between willing and attaining. The nature of every desire[b] is pain: attainment quickly gives rise to satiety: the goal was only apparent: possession takes away the stimulus: the desire, the need re-emerges in a new form: if not, then what follows is dreariness, emptiness, boredom, and the struggle against these is just as painful as the struggle against want. – For desire and satisfaction to follow each other without too long or too short an interval in between reduces the suffering caused by both to the smallest quantity, and constitutes the happiest course through life. Apart from this, what we might call the best part of life and the purest joy it affords, is pure cognition to which all willing is foreign: pleasure in beauty, a true delight in art; this experience lifts us out of real existence and changes us into disinterested[c] spectators. But because it requires rare talents, it is only granted to extremely few people, and even to these it is only like a passing dream: moreover, the higher intellectual powers these people possess make them susceptible to much greater suffering than duller minds could feel, and they feel lonely among beings markedly different from themselves: this offsets their advantage. But purely intellectual pleasures are inaccessible to the vast majority of people; most people are almost entirely incapable of experiencing the joy that lies in pure cognition: they are completely given over to willing. So if anything is to gain their sympathy and *interest* them, it must (and this is already clear from the meaning of the word) somehow arouse their *will*, even if its relation to the will is distant and merely theoretical; but the will can never be kept entirely out of play, because for most people, existence is much more about willing than about cognition: action and reaction are their only element. The naïve expression of this situation can be gleaned from trivialities and everyday occurrences:[d]

---

[a] *panem et Circenses* [from Juvenal, *Satires* X, 81]
[b] *Wunsch*
[c] *antheilslose*
[d] *Erscheinungen*

370

371

for instance, people write their names on popular sites that they visit, in order to react to the place and have an effect on it since it does not have an effect on them. Further, it is not easy for them to just look at a strange and rare animal, but they have to annoy it, tease it, and play with it, just to experience action and reaction; but this need to excite the will is seen most particularly in the invention and pursuit of card games, which really reveal the truly deplorable side of humanity.

But whatever nature or good fortune might have done, whoever you are and whatever you possess, you cannot ward off the pain that is essential to life:

> Peleus' son groaned aloud, lifting his eyes to heaven.[a]

And again:

> I was indeed the son of Zeus, son of Kronos, and nonetheless
> Endured unspeakable misery.[b,37]

The perpetual efforts to banish suffering do nothing more than alter its form. This is originally lack, need, worries over how to sustain life. If (and this is extremely difficult) we are successful in driving out pain in this form, then it immediately appears in a thousand others, varying, according to age and circumstances, as sex drive, passionate love, envy, jealousy, hatred, anxiety, ambition, greed, illness, etc., etc. If it ultimately cannot find any other form in which to appear, then it comes in the sad grey garments of satiety and boredom, and we then try hard to fend it off. Even if we finally succeed in driving these away, it can hardly be done without letting the pain back in one of its previous forms and so beginning the dance all over again; because every human life is thrown back and forth between pain and boredom. As depressing as this discussion is, I will also call attention to an aspect of the situation that offers consolation, and perhaps even allows us to achieve a Stoic indifference towards our own, present troubles. This is because our impatience with these troubles comes primarily from the fact that we recognize them as accidental, introduced by a chain of causes that could easily have been otherwise. For instance, we do not tend to worry about immediately necessary and completely universal troubles, e.g. the necessity of age and death and a host of daily inconveniences. It is rather the thought that the circumstances bringing some suffering to us 372

---

[a] Πηλειδης δ' ωμωξεν, ιδων εις ουρανον ευρυν. (*Pelides autem ejulavit, intuitus in coelum latum.*) [Homer, *Iliad*, XXI, 272]

[b] Ζηνος μεν παις ηα Κρονιονος, αυταρ οιζυν | Ειχον απειρεσιην. (*Jovis quidem filius eram Saturnii; verum aerumnam* | *Habebam infinitam.*) [Homer, *Odyssey*, XI, 620]

in particular are in some way accidental – this is what gives them their sting. But when we have recognized that pain as such is essential to life and unavoidable, and the only element of chance is the shape or form in which pain presents itself, that our present suffering occupies a space which, if vacated, would be immediately filled by a new suffering that is being kept at bay by the present one, that fate cannot really affect us in essential matters – if we have recognized all this, then this reflection, if it becomes an active conviction, could bring about a significant measure of Stoic equanimity and lessen our anxious concern for our own well-being. But in fact such a capable mastery of reason over the immediate feelings of suffering is seldom, if ever, to be found.

Incidentally, this discussion of the unavoidability of pain, of how one type displaces another, how the new one is drawn in by the departure of the old, might even lead to the paradoxical though not unreasonable hypothesis that the amount of pain essential to every individual is predetermined by his nature, and this amount cannot fall short or be exceeded, however much the form of suffering might change. This would mean that a person's suffering or well-being would not be determined externally at all, but instead it would be a function of that pre-set amount or arrangement. It certainly might increase or decrease at different times due to physical constitution, but overall it would remain the same and be nothing other than what is called temperament, or more precisely, as Plato expressed it in the first book of the *Republic*, the degree to which someone might be εὐκολος or δυσκολος, i.e. of an easy or difficult nature.[a] – A familiar experience speaks in favour of this hypothesis, the experience that great suffering makes us incapable of feeling lesser sufferings, as does the opposite experience, that in the absence of great suffering even the smallest annoyances pester and annoy us; but even more, experience also shows us that if a great misfortune – the sort that we shudder even to imagine – were really to take place, nonetheless, as soon as we had withstood the first sufferings, our frame of mind would remain largely the same. The converse is true as well, that after we achieve a long-desired happiness, generally and in the long run we do not feel markedly better and more content than we did before. Only the moment in which the change takes place touches us with any unusual strength as deep distress or sheer joy; but both evaporate quickly, because they rest on an illusion. They do not come from any current pleasure or pain, but only from our anticipation that a new future has opened up for us. The suffering or joy can take on such exaggerated forms

373

[a] *leichten oder schweren Sinnes*

only because it is on loan from the future, and consequently cannot last. – According to our present hypothesis, feelings of suffering or well-being resemble cognition in that the greater part is subjective and determined *a priori*. We could cite as another proof the fact that people's high or low spirits are obviously not determined by external circumstances, by wealth or status, since we encounter at least as many happy faces among the poor as among the rich. Further, the motives that give rise to suicide are so wildly different that we cannot cite any source of unhappiness that would be great enough to lead to suicide in any character with much probability; and few sources are trivial enough that something just as trivial has not already caused suicides. Now even if we do not always experience the same degree of cheerfulness or sadness, we will attribute it on this view not to any change in external circumstances but rather to our inner condition, our physical constitution. Because when there is an actual (though of course only temporary) increase in our cheerfulness, even to the point of joyfulness, it tends to emerge without any external occasion.[38] Of course, we frequently think that our pain comes only from particular, external conditions, and we are visibly oppressed or saddened only by these: we then believe that if only these conditions were removed the greatest contentment would necessarily follow. But this is an illusion. The overall quantity of our suffering and well-being is, according to our hypothesis, subjectively determined at every point in time. In this respect, the external motive for sadness plays the same role that a blister remedy does on the body, drawing together all the bad humours that would have otherwise been scattered. If it were not for this particular external cause of suffering, the suffering that is grounded in our essence for a certain period of time (and is therefore irremovable) would be scattered in a hundred different places and appear in the form of a hundred little bouts of moodiness and depression over things we now overlook completely, because our capacity for pain has already been reached by this major source of evil, and this has concentrated all the otherwise diffused sufferings into one point. This corresponds to the observation that when a fortunate outcome lifts a central, oppressive worry from our chests, its place is immediately filled by another worry, whose entire content had already been present, but could not enter consciousness *as* a worry because there was no room for it there; the content of the worry remained on the extreme horizon of consciousness as a dark, unobserved, and obscure shape. But now that there is room, this ready-made content comes right in and ascends the throne of the ruling (πρυτανεύουσα) worry of the day: even if its content is much more meagre than that of the evaporated worry, it still knows how to puff itself up so that it seems to

374

equal it in size, and so it can fill the whole throne as the main worry of the day.[39]

Excessive joy and acute pain are always and only to be found in the same person: because they determine each other reciprocally, and are also both conditioned by great mental activity. As we have already found, they are not produced merely by what is present, but rather by an anticipation of the future. But since pain is essential to life and the degree of pain is determined by the nature of the subject, sudden alterations, which always come from 375 outside, cannot really alter the degree of pain; so immoderate joy or pain is always based on an error and a delusion: and consequently both of these mental over-exertions can be avoided through insight. Immoderate joy (*exultatio, insolens laetitia*) is always based on the delusion that you have found something in life that is not really there, namely lasting gratification of your agonizing, constantly reoccurring desires or worries. People must inevitably be brought around later from each particular delusion of this type, and when it fades they must pay for it with sufferings as intense as the joys caused by its appearance. In this respect it is just like a height that you can only get down from by falling; that is why it should be avoided: and every sudden, excessive pain is just such a fall from this sort of height, the disappearance of this sort of delusion, and thus is conditioned by it. Consequently, both could be avoided if people were always able to survey things with perfect clarity and in a broader context, and were constantly on guard against painting things in the colours we only wish they had. The principal aim of Stoic ethics is to free the mind from all such delusions and their consequences, and give it an imperturbable equanimity instead. Horace is filled with this insight in the well-known ode:

Always remember to stay calm in times of trouble and in happier times to keep a heart that controls the overpowering joy.[a]

But for the most part we close our eyes to the recognition – which is like bitter medicine – that suffering is essential to life, and thus does not flow in upon us from the outside, but that all people carry within themselves an unconquerable source of suffering. We always look instead for an external, particular cause as a sort of pretext for the pain that will never go away; like free men who set up an idol in order to have a master. We strive tirelessly from desire to desire, and even when every achieved satisfaction proves nevertheless to be unsatisfying (however much it promised), quickly

---

[a] *Aequam memento rebus in arduis | Servare mentem, non secus in bonis | Ab insolenti temperatam | Laetitia.* – [*Odes*, II. 3]

revealing itself for the most part itself as a shameful error, we still do not see that we are drawing water with the vessel of the Danaids; we hurry on to new desires instead: 376

> As long as we lack what we desire, it seems to surpass
> All else; but when it's attained we desire another;
> And we are always caught in a similar thirst after life.
> Lucretius, III, 1095[a],[40]

So it continues, either to infinity or, more rarely, when a certain strength of character is present, until we come to a desire that cannot be fulfilled or relinquished: and then we have what we are looking for, as it were, namely something other than our own nature[b] that we can always blame as the source of our suffering. This puts us at odds with our fate, but it also reconciles us to our existence, since it frees us again from the recognition that suffering is essential and true satisfaction impossible in this existence. The consequence of this final type of development is a somewhat melancholy disposition, always carrying a single, great pain and consequently devaluing all smaller sorrows or joys; and this makes a more worthy appearance than the continuous grasping after new mirages, which is much more common.

§ 58

All satisfaction,[c] or what is generally called happiness,[d] is actually and essentially only ever *negative* and absolutely never positive. It is not something primordial that comes to us from out of itself, it must always be the satisfaction of some desire. This is because a desire, i.e. lack, is the prior condition for every pleasure. But the desire ends with satisfaction and so, consequently, does the pleasure. Thus satisfaction or happiness can never be anything more than the liberation from a pain or need: and this includes not only every actual, manifest suffering, but also every desire whose importunity disturbs our peace, and in fact even the deadly boredom that turns our existence into a burden. – But it is so hard to succeed at anything or to get anything done: difficulties and endless troubles stand in the way of every plan, obstacles pile up with every step. But if we suc- 377 ceed in overcoming them in the end, we never gain anything more than

---

[a] *Sed, dum abest quod avemus, id exsuperare videtur | Caetera; post aliud, quum contigit illud, avemus; | Et sitis aequa tenet vitai semper hiantes.* [Lucretius, *De rerum natura* (*On the Nature of Things*): in fact see III. 1082–5]
[b] *Wesen*
[c] *Befriedigung*
[d] *Glück*

liberation from some suffering or desire, and so we find ourselves just the way we were before we had the desire. – Only lack, i.e. pain, is ever given to us directly. Our cognition of satisfaction and pleasure is only indirect, when we remember the sufferings and privations that preceded them and ceased when they appeared. That is why we do not really notice or value the possessions and the advantages we actually have, but think that they represent the necessary course of things: this is because they only make us happy negatively, by warding off suffering. We can only feel their value after we have lost them: because lack, privation, suffering are positive and announce themselves directly. That is why we enjoy remembering needs, illnesses, wants and similar things that we have survived, because this is the only way for us to enjoy our present possessions. Nor can it be denied that in this respect, from the standpoint of egoism (which is the form of the will to life), the sight or description of other people's suffering gives us the same sort of satisfaction and pleasure; Lucretius put this nicely as well as candidly at the beginning of his second book:

> It is a joy to stand at the sea, when it is lashed by stormy winds,
> To stand at the shore and to see the skipper in distress,
> Not that we like to see another person in pain,
> But because it pleases us to know that we are free of this evil.[a]

Nonetheless, we will see later on that this type of pleasure, through such indirect recognition of our well-being, lies very near the source of true and positive malice.[b]

That all happiness is of a negative rather than positive nature, and for this reason cannot give lasting satisfaction and gratification, but rather only ever a release from a pain or lack, which must be followed either by a new pain or by *languor*, empty yearning and boredom – this is proven in art, that true mirror of the essence of the world and of life, and in poetry[c] in particular. Epic or dramatic compositions[d] can only ever present a struggle, striving, or fight for happiness, never enduring or complete happiness itself. They lead their heroes through a thousand difficulties and dangers up to the goal: but as soon as this is reached, the curtain quickly falls. Because now there is nothing more left to show than that the bright and shining goal that the hero thought would give him happiness has only been a mockery, and that

378

---

[a] *Suave, mari magno, turbantibus aequora ventis,* | *E terra magnum alterius spectare laborem:* | *Non, quia vexari quemquam est jucunda voluptas;* | *Sed, quibus ipse malis careas, quia cernere suave est.* [Lucretius, II. 1–4]

[b] *Bosheit*

[c] *Poesie*

[d] *Dichtung*

after reaching it he is no better off than he was before. True and lasting happiness is not possible, so it cannot be a subject for art. Of course the purpose of the idyll is in fact to describe just this: but you can also see that the idyll cannot be sustained. In the hands of the poet it always becomes either an epic – and then only a very insignificant one, strung together out of petty sufferings, petty joys and petty endeavours (this is most frequently the case) – or it becomes merely descriptive poetry, depicting the beauty of nature. This is actually pure cognition free from the will, which is in point of fact the only real happiness that is not preceded by suffering or need or necessarily followed by remorse, suffering, emptiness or weariness: but this happiness can fill only isolated moments, not the whole of life. – What we see in poetry we find again in music; in melody we again recognize the universal expression of the innermost history of will as it is conscious of itself, the most secret living, longing, suffering and joy, the ebbs and flows of the human heart. Melody is always a departure from the tonic through a thousand strange mazes to the point of the most painful dissonance, until finally it finds the tonic again, which expresses the satisfaction and calming of the will; but there is nothing further to be done with the will after this, and to continue any longer in the tonic would only lead to an annoying and vacuous monotony corresponding to boredom.

Everything that these remarks should clarify, the unattainable nature[a] of lasting satisfaction and the negativity of all happiness, is explained by what we showed at the end of the Second Book: namely that the will, which is objectified in human life as it is every appearance, is a striving without aim and without end.[b] We find this endlessness stamped on every element of its whole appearance, from the most universal form of appearance, time and space without end, up to the most perfect of all appearances, human life and striving. – We can assume three theoretical extremes to human life and regard them as its actual components. First, the violent willing, the great passions (*raja-guna*). This is evident in great historical characters, and is described in epic and drama; but it can manifest itself in a narrower sphere as well, since the size of objects is measured by how much they move the will, not by their external proportions. Next we have the second extreme, pure cognition, the comprehension of the Ideas conditioned by the liberation of cognition from the service of the will: the life of the genius (*sattva-guna*). Finally, the third, the greatest lethargy of the will and of cognition bound up with it, empty longing, life-chilling boredom

379

---

[a] *Unerreichbarkeit*
[b] *ohne Ziel und ohne Ende*

(*tama-guna*).[41] The life of the individual, far from remaining fixed in one of these extremes, only rarely touches on them, and is mostly just a stronger or weaker approximation of one or the other of these aspects, a needy willing of petty objects that always returns and thus escapes from boredom. – It is truly unbelievable how vacuously and meaninglessly (viewed from the outside) and how dismally and insensibly (viewed from the inside) life flows away for the vast majority of human beings. It is a feeble yearning and a torment, a dream-like whirl through the four ages of life through to death, accompanied by a series of trivial thoughts. They are like mechanical clocks that are wound up and go without knowing why; whenever someone is begotten and born, the clock of human life is wound again so it can play the same hurdy-gurdy that has already been played countless times, movement by movement, beat by beat, with insignificant variations.[42] – Every individual, every human face and its life history is just one more short dream of the infinite spirit of nature,[a] the persistent will to life; it is just one more fleeting image jotted playfully on its infinite page, space and time, and is allowed an infinitesimal existence (compared with these), before it is erased to free up room. Nonetheless, and here is the troubling side of life, each of these fleeting images, these stale conceptions, must be paid for by the whole will to life in all of its vehemence, with many profound sufferings and ultimately with the long-feared arrival of a bitter death. That is why the sight of corpses makes us suddenly so serious.

Viewed overall and in a general manner, and extracting only the most significant features, the life of every individual is in fact always a tragedy; but worked through in detail, it has the character of a comedy. The urges[b] and the nuisances of the day, the restless taunts of the minute, the hopes and fears of the week, the accidents of every hour, all of which are brought about by chance playing practical jokes[43] – these are true comic scenes. But the unfulfilled desires, the thwarted striving, the hopes that have been mercilessly crushed by fate, the fatal errors of the whole of life, with increased suffering and then death at the end, this always makes for tragedy. So as if fate wanted to add mockery to the misery of our existence, our lives have to contain all the grief of a tragedy, but we cannot even assert our dignity as tragic players; instead, in the expanse of life's details we cannot escape the roles of foolish, comic characters.

[a] *Naturgeist*
[b] *Treiben*

But to whatever extent troubles both large and small fill every human life and keep it in a constant state of restlessness and movement, still they cannot conceal the inadequacy of life for spiritual fulfilment, its emptiness and shallowness, nor can they expel the boredom that is always ready to fill every pause granted by worry. Thus it happens that the human spirit, not satisfied with the worries, cares and occupations that the real world presents to it, creates for itself another, imaginary world in the form of a thousand different superstitions, and gets completely involved in this other world, wasting both time and energy, as soon as the real world allows people the peace and quiet they are entirely incapable of feeling. This is mostly the case among peoples whose lives are made easy by the mildness of the climate and the soil, above all the Hindus, and then the Greeks, Romans and later 381 the Italians, Spaniards, etc. – People create spirits, gods and saints in their own image; these then need a constant supply of sacrifices, prayers, temple decorations, vows and their fulfilment, pilgrimages, greetings, adornment with images, etc. Their service is entwined with reality, and indeed obscures it: every event in life is then taken to be an action of those beings: dealing with them takes up half of life, is a constant source of hope, and, through the charm of delusion, is often more interesting than dealing with actual beings. These imaginary beings are expressions and symptoms of the twofold needs of humans, partly for help and support, and partly for something to do and a source of diversion. This often acts precisely counter to our most urgent needs – in the case of an accident or some danger, precious time and energy is wasted on prayers and sacrifices instead of responding to the threat; but even then, they fulfil our second type of need all the more, through those fantasy conversations with an imaginary spirit world: and this advantage of all superstitions is nothing to sneer at.

§ 59

We have been investigating the primary, elementary characteristics of human life at the most universal level, with a view towards convincing ourselves *a priori* that human life is dispositionally incapable of true happiness, that it is essentially a multifaceted suffering and a thoroughly disastrous condition. Now we could arouse a much more vivid conviction in ourselves if we wanted to take a more *a posteriori* approach and deal with particular cases, evoking images and giving examples of the unspeakable misery that both history and experience show, wherever and however we look. But then there would be no end to this chapter, and we would be removed from the standpoint of universality that is essential to philosophy.

382 Besides, such a description could easily be considered a simple declamation over human misery, as has often been given, and so be accused of one-sidedness, because it takes its point of departure from particular facts. But our approach is free from such suspicions and reproaches, since it is cold and philosophical, starting out from the universal and demonstrating *a priori* the unavoidable suffering grounded in the essence of life. But *a posteriori* confirmation is easy to find. Everyone who has woken up from the first dreams of youth, has paid any attention to his own experience or that of other people, has looked into life, into the history of the past as well as the present age, and finally into the works of the great writers – such a person (unless the indelible imprint of some prejudice has crippled his judgement) will certainly recognize the result, that the human world is the realm of accident and error which have a mercilessly free hand in matters both great and small, and are joined by stupidity and evil in brandishing the whip: thus it is that everything better makes its way with difficulty, that nobility or wisdom rarely appear, have an effect, or receive an audience, and that the absurd and perverse assert their mastery in the realm of thought, the trite and the tasteless in the realm of art, and the evil and underhanded in the realm of deeds, with only brief interruptions. On the other hand, excellence of any kind is only ever an exception, one case in a million, and even when it manifests itself in some enduring work, then afterwards, once it has survived the rancour of its contemporaries, it continues in isolation; it is preserved like a meteorite that has come from a different order of things than currently prevails. – But as far as the life of the individual is concerned, every life history is a history of suffering, because the course of each life is[44] for the most part a continuous series of accidents both great and small; of course, people try to hide this as much as possible, because they know that others will rarely show sympathy[a] or compassion, and in fact will almost always find gratification in the thought of troubles that are not their own at the moment; – but perhaps there will never be a man who, clear-headed and sincere at the end of his life, would want to do it all again – he would much rather choose complete non-existence

383 instead. The essential content of the world-famous monologue in *Hamlet* is, if summarized: our condition is so miserable that complete non-being would be decidedly preferable. Now if suicide really offered this, so that the alternative 'to be or not to be' lay before us in the full sense of the words, then it would be the clear choice, a highly desirable completion

---

[a] *Theilnahme*

('*a consummation devoutly to be wish'd*').[a] But there is something in us telling us that it is not so; this is not the end, death is not an absolute termination. – In the same way,[45] what was already mentioned by the father of history* has not been disproved since, that no man has existed who has not wished more than once not to live through the following day. Accordingly, the much-lamented brevity of life might be the best thing about it.[46] – Finally, if we were to call everyone's attention to the terrible pains and suffering their lives are constantly exposed to, they would be seized with horror: and if you led the most unrepentant optimist through the hospitals, military wards, and surgical theatres, through the prisons, torture chambers and slave stalls, through battlefields and places of judgement, and then open for him all the dark dwellings of misery that hide from cold curiosity, and finally let him peer into Ugolino's starvation chamber,[47] then he too would surely come to see the nature[b] of this best of all possible worlds.[c] Where else did *Dante* get the material for his hell if not from this actual world of ours? And a proper hell it became too. On the other hand, when he came to the task of describing heaven and its joys, he had an insurmountable difficulty before him; because our world offered him absolutely no material for doing so. That is why instead of giving us the joys of paradise, all he could do was to repeat the instruction imparted to him there by his ancestor, his Beatrice, and various saints. This is sufficiently instructive as to the nature[d] of this world.[48] Of course, as with all inferior goods, human life is covered with false glitter on the outside: what suffers always hides itself; and conversely,   384 people like to show off whatever glamour and glitter they can afford, and the more that inner contentment eludes them, the more they want other people to think of them as happy: this is how far stupidity will go, and other people's opinion is a principal goal of everyone's efforts, although the total nothingness[e] of this is already apparent from the fact that in almost all languages, vanity, *vanitas*, originally meant emptiness and nothingness. – But the miseries of life can grow so easily beneath all this deception that every day, death, which is normally feared more than anything, is eagerly embraced. Indeed, when fate wants to show all its tricks, it can bar even this refuge of the sufferer, and can deliver him, without hope, to slow and

---

* Herodotus [*Histories*] VII, 46.

[a] [Shakespeare, *Hamlet*, Act III, scene I]
[b] *Art*
[c] *meilleur des mondes possibles* [Leibniz, *Theodicy*, I, 8]
[d] *Art*
[e] *Nichtigkeit*

cruel torture at the hands of furious enemies. Then the tortured man will call in vain to his gods for help: he has been mercilessly surrendered to his fate. But this hopelessness is only the mirror of the invincibility of his will, as his person is the will's objecthood. – No external power can change or suppress this will, and no foreign power can free him from the pain that comes from life, which is the appearance of that will. Human beings are always thrown back on themselves, and this certainly holds for the most important case as well. In vain do they create gods for themselves in order to try to beg and wheedle out of them what only their own strength of will can accomplish. If the Old Testament made the world and human beings into the work of a God, the New Testament was compelled to let that God become a man in order to teach that holiness and redemption from the sorrows of this world can only come from the world itself.[49] For human beings, everything depends and will always depend on their will. Sannyasis, martyrs, saints of every faith and name have freely and gladly endured every torture because the will to life had abolished itself in them; and then they could welcome even the slow destruction of its appearance. But I do not want to anticipate a later discussion. – Still, I cannot hold

385 back from declaring here that *optimism*, where it is not just the thoughtless talk of someone with only words in his flat head, strikes me as not only an absurd, but even a truly *wicked* way of thinking, a bitter mockery of the unspeakable sufferings of humanity. – Do not think for a moment that Christian doctrine is favourable to optimism; on the contrary, in the Gospels, 'world' and 'evil'[a] are used as almost synonymous expressions.*

§ 60

We have completed the two discussions that needed to intervene, the first concerning the freedom of the will in itself along with the necessity of its appearance, the second concerning its fate in the world that mirrors its essence, given that it has to affirm or negate itself based on cognition of this world; now that this has been accomplished, we can further clarify the nature of the affirmation and negation themselves, having mentioned and explained them above in only very general terms; we will do this by looking at ways of acting (since this is the only way in which affirmation and negation are expressed) and by regarding this action with respect to its inner meaning.

* See chapter 46 of the second volume.

a *Uebel*

The affirmation of the will is the constant willing itself, undisturbed by any cognition, as it fills the lives of human beings in general. The human body is already the objecthood of the will as it appears at this level and in this individual; similarly, his willing, as it develops in time, is the paraphrase of the body, so to speak, the explanation of the meaning of the whole and its parts, and another way of presenting the same thing in itself that already appears in the body. Thus, instead of 'affirmation of the will', we could also say 'affirmation of the body'. The basic theme of all the various acts of will is the satisfaction of needs that are inseparable from the healthy existence of the body, are already expressed in it, and can be reduced to the preservation of the individual and the propagation of the species. But indirectly, this enables a great variety of motives to gain control over the will and to produce the most diverse acts of will. Each of these is only a specimen[a] or example of the will that appears here in general: what sort of specimen this is, what form the motive might take and impart to the satisfaction of needs – this is not essential. That willing in general occurs, and its degree of intensity, these are the issues here. The will can become visible only through motives, just as the eye can exercise its visual ability only in light. Generally speaking, a motive stands before the will as a many-sided Proteus: it always promises full satisfaction, that it will quench the thirst of the will; but if it does, it immediately appears in a new shape and begins moving the will all over again, always according to the degree of the will's intensity and its relation to cognition, which become manifest as empirical character through these very specimens and examples.

386

From the time they become conscious, human beings find themselves willing, and for the most part their cognition remains in constant relation to their will. First they try to fully understand the objects of their willing, then the means of attaining them. Now they know what they have to do, and they do not usually strive to know[b] anything else. They act and they press forward:[c] consciousness keeps them active and urges them on, always working towards the goal of their willing: their thinking concerns the choice of means to an end. For most human beings, this is what life is all about: they will, they know what they will, and they strive after it with enough success to protect them from despair and enough failure to keep them from boredom and its effects. A certain cheerfulness or at least composure emerges from this, which is not really changed by wealth or poverty: the rich and the poor do not enjoy what they have, since, as we

[a] *Probe*
[b] *wissen*
[c] *treibt*

showed, this affects people only negatively; rather they only enjoy what they hope to achieve through their efforts.[a] They press forward quite seriously, indeed with an air of importance: this is just how children approach their games too. – It is always exceptional when a life like this is disrupted by one of the modes of cognition that are independent of the service of the will and directed to the essence of the world in general, either the aesthetic call to contemplation, or the ethical call to renunciation. Most people are pursued through life by wants that do not allow them space for reflection. On the other hand, the will is often inflamed[50] to a degree that far surpasses the affirmation of the body, which then exhibits violent affects and powerful passions in which the individual does not just affirm his own existence but negates and tries to abolish that of others when they stand in his way.

387

In expending its own energy to preserve itself, the body demonstrates so minimal an affirmation that if it voluntarily stopped at this, we could assume that the death of the body would entail the extinction of the will that appears in it as well. But even the satisfaction of the sex drive goes beyond the affirmation of one's own existence, (which occupies such a small space of time) and affirms life for an indefinite time beyond the death of the individual. Nature, which is always true and consistent, and is here even naïve, shows us quite plainly the inner meaning of the act of procreation.[b] Our own consciousness, the intensity of the drive, teaches us that this act expresses the most decisive *affirmation of the will to life* purely and without further supplement (such as the negation of other individuals, for instance); and now, in time and in the sequence of causes, i.e. in nature, a new life appears as the result of the act: before the begetter the begotten appears, distinct from him in appearance but in itself, i.e. according to the Idea, identical to him. This is the act through which the generations[c] of living things bind themselves into a whole, and perpetuate themselves as such.[51] With respect to the begetter, procreation is only an expression, a symptom of his decisive affirmation of the will to life: with respect to the begotten, procreation is not the ground of the will that appears in him, since the will in itself recognizes neither ground nor consequent; rather it, like all causes, is only an occasional cause for the appearance of this will at this time in this place. As thing in itself, the will of the begetter is not different from the will of the begotten, since only the appearance is subject

---

[a] *Treiben*
[b] *Zeugungsaktes*
[c] *Geschlechter*

to the *principium individuationis*, not the thing in itself. With that affirmation, which goes above and beyond the individual body to the production
of a new one, suffering and death are affirmed again as well (since they
belong to the appearance of life), and the possibility of redemption, which   388
is brought about through the most perfect faculty of cognition,[a] is declared
fruitless for now. This is the deep reason for the shame associated with
copulation. – This view is presented mythically in the dogma of the Christian doctrine that we are all part of Adam's fall (which is obviously only the
satisfaction of sexual desire) and thereby guilty of suffering and death. That
religious doctrine transcends the consideration of things according to the
principle of sufficient reason, and recognizes the Idea of the human being.
The unity of this Idea is re-established out of the dispersion of humans
into countless individuals through the coalescing bond of procreation. On
this view, religious doctrine sees each individual as on the one hand identical with Adam, the representative[52] of the affirmation of life, and to this
extent as fallen into sin (original sin), suffering and death: on the other
hand, cognition of the Idea also reveals each individual to be identical with
the redeemer, the representative of the negation of the will to life, and to
this extent as part of his self-sacrifice, redeemed through his worthiness,[b]
and delivered from the bonds of sin and death, i.e. the world (Romans
5:12–21).

The Greek myth of Proserpina provides another mythological presentation of our view that sexual satisfaction is the affirmation of the will to life
beyond the life of the individual, a fall into life that is first consummated
by sexual satisfaction, as it were, or a renewed deliverance[c] to life. It was
still possible for Proserpina to return from the underworld as long as she
had not tasted its fruit, but she fell into it entirely by eating a pomegranate.
This sense of the myth emerges very clearly in Goethe's incomparable presentation, particularly with the sudden entrance of the invisible chorus of
the Parcae immediately after the eating of the pomegranate:

> You are ours!
> You should have returned without having eaten:
> And the bite of the apple makes you ours![d]

It is remarkable that *Clement of Alexandria* (*Stromata*, III, 15) describes
this using the same image and the same expression: 'Those who have

---

[a] *Erkenntnißfähigkeit*
[b] *Verdienst*
[c] *Verschreibung*
[d] [*Triumph der Empfindsamkeit* (*The Triumph of Sensibility*), Act IV]

389   made themselves eunuchs, free from all sin, for the sake of the kingdom of heaven, they are blessed, *because they keep themselves pure from the
world.*'[a,53]

Proof that the sex drive is the strongest and most decisive affirmation of
life comes from the fact that it is the ultimate purpose, the highest goal of
life in the natural human being,[54] as it is in the animal. Self-preservation
is his first striving, and as soon as he has seen to this he strives only for
the propagation of the race: as a merely natural being, he has no further
aspirations. Even nature, whose innermost essence is the will to life itself,
drives people to propagate with all its strength, as it drives animals. After
it has achieved its goal in the individual it is entirely indifferent to his
demise; nature, as the will to life, is only concerned with the preservation
of the species – the individual is nothing to nature. – Because the inner
essence of nature, the will to life, expresses itself most strongly in the sex
drive, Hesiod and Parmenides, the ancient writers and philosophers, said
very significantly that *Eros* was the first, the creator, the principle out of
which all things emerged. (See Aristotle's *Metaphysics*, I, 4.) Pherecydes said:
'Zeus transformed himself into Eros when he wanted to create the world'[b] –
Proclus in *Commentary on the Timaeus of Plato*, Book III. – We have recently
received a detailed treatment of this subject by *G. F. Schoemann, On the
love that creates the cosmos,*[c] 1852.[55] The *māyā* of the Indians too, whose
work and web is the entire illusory world, is paraphrased by *amor*.

The genitals are much more exclusively subject to the will and less
subject to cognition than any other external organ of the body: indeed,
the will shows itself almost as independent of cognition here as it does in
the parts of the body that work by mere stimuli and serve vegetative life or
reproduction, parts where the will works blindly, as it does in nature that
is devoid of cognition. This is because procreation is simply reproduction
that results in a new individual, reproduction to the second potency, as it

390   were, in the same way that death is only excretion to the second potency. –
As a result of all this, the genitals are the true *focal point* of the will and
consequently the opposite pole of the brain, the representative of cognition,
i.e. of the other side of the world, the world as representation. They are
the life-preserving principle, assuring endless life to time; it is this quality

---

[a]   Οἱ μεν ευνουχισαντες ἑαυτους απο πασης ἁμαρτιας, δια την βασιλειαν των ουρανων, μακαριοι
οὑτοι εισιν, οἱ του κοσμου νηστευοντες. (*Qui se castrarunt ab omni peccato, propter regnum coelorum,
ii sunt beati,* a mundo jejunantes.)

[b]   Εις ερωτα μεταβεβλησθαι τον Δια, μελλοντα δημιουργειν. (*Jovem, cum mundum fabricare vellet,
in cupidinem sese transformasse.*)

[c]   *De cupidine cosmogonico*

that led the Greeks to worship them in the phallus, and the Hindus in the lingam, which are therefore symbolic of the affirmation of the will.[56] On the other hand, cognition offers the possibility of the abolition of willing, redemption through freedom, and the overcoming and[57] annihilation of the world.

We already observed in detail at the beginning of this Fourth Book how the will to life in its affirmation must regard its relation to death, namely that it is not disturbed by death, because death is already included in life and belongs to it. It is fully balanced out by its opposite, procreation, which secures and guarantees immortal life to the will to life, in spite of the death of the individual; all of which the Indians express by giving the attribute of the lingam to Shiva, the god of death. We also argued there that someone with perfect presence of mind, who occupies the perspective of the decisive affirmation of life, can face death without fear. We will not discuss this any further at present. Most people occupy this perspective without clear presence of mind, and continuously affirm life. The world exists as a mirror of this affirmation, with countless individuals in endless time, endless space, and endless suffering, between procreation and death without end. – Yet there can be no further complaints about this from any of the parties involved: because the will performs the great tragedy and comedy at its own cost, and is its own spectator as well. The world is precisely what it is, because the will, whose appearance it is, is what it is, because that is what it wills. The justification for suffering is that the will affirms itself in this appearance too; and this affirmation is justified and balanced out by the fact that the will bears the suffering. This gives us a glimpse into *eternal justice* in general; later on we will come to recognize this more closely and clearly in its particulars as well. But first we must discuss temporal or human justice.* 391

§ 61

We remember from the Second Book that in the whole of nature, on all the levels of objectivation of the will, there must be a constant struggle between the individuals of all species, and this expressed an inner conflict within the will to life. Like all other phenomena, this is presented with greater clarity – and can be deciphered more thoroughly – on the highest level of objectivation. To this end, we now want to trace the source of *egoism*, the starting point for all struggle.

---

* See chapter 45 of the second volume.

We have called time and space the *principium individuationis*, because only through them and in them is a multiplicity of similar things possible. They are the essential forms of natural cognition, i.e. cognition that has sprouted[a] from the will. Thus the will will appear everywhere in the multiplicity of individuals. Of course this multiplicity does not affect it, the will as thing in itself, but rather only its appearances: the will is wholly and inseparably present in each of these, and sees itself surrounded by the endlessly repeated image of its own essence. But its only direct access to this essence, i.e. actual reality, is within itself. That is why everyone wants everything for themselves, wants to possess or at least control everything, and wants to destroy anything that opposes them.[58] In addition, in beings with cognition, the individual is the bearer of the cognitive subject, and this is the bearer of the world. In other words, the whole of nature outside the individual, including all other individuals, exists only in his representation, and he is always conscious of it only as his representation, which is to say only indirectly and as dependent on his own essence and existence; when his consciousness is destroyed, the world is necessarily destroyed for him as well, i.e. its being becomes equivalent to and indistinguishable from its non-being. Thus, every cognizing individual is in fact – and finds himself to be – the entire will to life, the in-itself of the world itself, the condition that completes the world as representation, and consequently a microcosm equal in value to the macrocosm. Nature itself, which is always and everywhere truthful, gives him this cognition spontaneously and independently of all reflection, as simple and immediately certain. Now the two necessary determinations mentioned above enable us to explain how every individual who is reduced to nothingness and disappears without a trace into the boundless world nevertheless makes himself the centre of the world, and privileges his own existence and well-being over that of everything else, and in fact, from a natural perspective, is ready to sacrifice all others for himself, ready to negate the world just to preserve his own self,[59] this drop in the sea, for a little while longer. This outlook is *egoism*,[b] which is essential to everything in nature, and is precisely why the inner conflict of the will with itself has such a terrible manifestation: because egoism has its continued existence[c] and essence in the opposition between microcosm and macrocosm, or in the fact that the *principium individuationis* is the form of the will's objectivation, which enables the will to appear in countless individuals in the same manner – and in fact both its sides (will and

[a] *entsprossen*
[b] *Egoismus*
[c] *Bestand*

392

representation) appear wholly and completely in each. Thus, while each individual is given immediately to itself as the entire will and the only representer,[a] everything else is first given to him only as his representation; that is why his own being[b] and its preservation are more important to him than everything else taken together. Everyone views his own death as the end of the world while being more or less indifferent about the deaths of his acquaintances, unless he is somehow personally involved.[60] At the highest level of consciousness, which is to say human consciousness, egoism (like cognition, pain and joy) must have reached the highest level as well, and the conflict between individuals (that it conditions) must be at its most terrible. And in fact, we see this everywhere before our eyes, in matters both great and small; sometimes we see it in its terrible aspect, in the lives of great tyrants and villains and in wars that devastate the world, and sometimes in its ridiculous aspect, where it is the subject of comedy and is particularly evident in self-conceit and vanity, which La Rochefoucauld grasped and presented abstractly[c] as no one else has done: we see it in world history and in our own experience. But it appears most clearly as soon as any group of people is released from all law and order: then at once we clearly see the war of all against all[d] that Hobbes described so perceptively in the first chapter of *De Cive*.[e] Not only do we see everyone trying to grab what they want from everyone else, but frequently one person will even completely ruin another person's happiness or life in order to increase his own well-being by some insignificant amount. This is the highest expression of egoism, whose appearances in this respect are surpassed only by those of genuine malice, which quite disinterestedly[f] tries to hurt and harm others in the absence of any personal advantage; we will be discussing this soon. – You may compare this exposition of the source of egoism with the presentation of the same thing in my prize essay *On the Basis of Morals*, § 14.[61]

We found above that suffering is an essential and unavoidable part of life, and as soon as it actually emerges in a particular form, one major source of suffering is *Eris*, the struggle between all individuals, the expression of the contradiction that afflicts the will to life from within, and which becomes manifest through the *principium individuationis*: fighting between beasts is an immediate and conspicuous, albeit cruel way of visualizing it. In this

393

---

[a] *das ganze Vorstellende*
[b] *Wesen*
[c] *in abstracto*
[d] *bellum omnium contra omnes*
[e] [See *De Cive* (literally 'On the Citizen'), I, 12: *bellum omnium in omnes*]
[f] *ganz uneigennützig*

primordial schism[a] there lies[62] an inexhaustible source of suffering in spite of the measures we take against it, measures that we will now consider more closely.

§ 62

We have already argued that the first simple affirmation of the will to life is simply the affirmation of one's own body, i.e. the presentation of the will through acts in time, to the extent that the body is already the spatial presentation of the same will through its form and purposiveness, and no further. This affirmation reveals itself as the preservation of the body through the use of its own forces. The satisfaction of the sex drive is directly linked to this and in fact it belongs to this satisfaction to the extent that the genitals belong to the body. That is why the *voluntary* renunciation of the satisfaction of this drive, when that renunciation is not grounded in any motives at all, is already a degree of the negation of the will to life,[63] the voluntary self-abolition of the will to life through the emergence of cognition operating as a *tranquillizer*. Accordingly, this kind of negation of one's own body already presents itself as a contradiction between the will and its own appearance. Even though here too, the body in its genitalia objectifies the will to propagate, propagation is nonetheless not willed. Precisely because it is the negation or abolition of the will to life, this kind of renunciation involves a difficult and painful self-overcoming; but more on this later. – Now the will presents a *self-affirmation* of the particular body in countless coexisting individuals, and because they are all characterized by egoism, the will very easily exceeds this affirmation in any given individual and becomes a *negation* of the same will as it appears in other individuals. The will of the first individual violates the boundaries of the other individual's affirmation of will. This occurs either when the first individual destroys or harms the other body itself, or when it forces the energies of that other body to serve its *own* will rather than the will that appears in the other body. Thus, when it takes the strength of the other's body from the will appearing in that body and uses it to enhance the strength that serves its *own* will over and above its own body, it is able to *affirm* its own will over and above its own body by negating the will that appears in another body. – This violation of the boundaries of someone else's affirmation of will has been clearly recognized for a long time, and

---

[a] *Zwiespalt*

its concept is denoted by the word *wrong*.ᵃ Both parties will instantly recognize the situation, not in the clear and abstract form we have given here of course, but as a feeling. When the sphere of some body's affirmation is violated by another individual's negation of it, the wronged party will feel this as an immediate mental injury which is entirely separate from and unlike any feeling of physical suffering that accompanies the deed, and also any irritation at the loss. On the other hand, the wrongdoer acquires the cognition that he is in himself the same will that also appears in that other, a will that affirms itself with such vehemence in the one appearance that, by transgressing the boundaries of its own body and its strengths, it comes to negate the will in the other appearance; consequently, regarded as will in itself, it struggles with itself through this very vehemence and tears itself apart; – I say that this cognition presents itself to him instantaneously, not abstractly,ᵇ but as an obscure feeling: and this is what people call pangs of conscience,ᶜ or more precisely in this case, the feeling of having *done wrong*.

We have analysed the concept of *wrong* in the most universal abstraction, but it expresses itself most perfectly, authentically, and palpably in concrete fashionᵈ in cannibalism. This is its clearest and most obvious form, the terrible image of the greatest conflict of the will with itself on the highest level of its objectivation, that of the human being. After this comes murder; when someone commits a murder he is seized instantly and with terrible clarity by those pangs of conscience whose meaning we have just given in dry and abstract terms, and which inflicts a life-long, incurable wound on any peace of mind. Our horror at a murder that has been committed, as well as our shrinking back in the face of a prospective murder are phenomena that accord with the boundless devotion to life pervading all living things, as the appearances of the will to life.⁶⁴ (Later on we will provide a more detailed analysis and conceptual clarification of the feeling that accompanies doing wrong or evil, the anguish of conscience.ᵉ) Intentionally mutilating or even injuring someone else's body – or indeed, any blow – can be seen as essentially the same as murder, differing only in degree. – Wrongdoingᶠ manifests itself further in the subjugation of other individuals, in forcing them into slavery, and finally in the assault on

---

ᵃ *Unrecht*
ᵇ *in abstracto*
ᶜ *Gewissensbiß*
ᵈ *in concreto*
ᵉ *Gewissensangst*
ᶠ *Unrecht*

396 somebody else's property, which, to the extent that we regard it as the fruit of their labour, is essentially the same as slavery, and is related to slavery as a simple injury is to murder.[65]

Property cannot be taken from anyone without *doing him wrong*, and according to our explanation of wrong, property can only be what someone has worked on personally and put his own energy into. Thus, when we take away someone's property, we take the energy in his body away from the will objectified in his body in order to make it serve the will objectified in someone else's body. So the wrongdoer violates the sphere of the other person's affirmation of will, not by assaulting the other person's body, but rather only by assaulting an inert thing entirely distinct from it, since the energy and labour of the other person's body are bound up and identified with this thing. From this it follows that all true, i.e. moral,[66] property rights are originally based solely and exclusively on the fact of working on something;[a] this was quite generally assumed even before Kant. In fact, the oldest of all codes of law put it very well and very clearly: 'The wise ones who know olden times declare that a cultivated field is the property of whoever cleared, refined and plowed the land; just as an antelope belongs to the first hunter to deal the fatal blow.' – *Laws of Manu*, IX, 44. – Kant's whole doctrine of right is a strange entanglement of mutually entailing errors, a fact that I attribute to the feebleness of his advanced age; this also explains why he grounds property rights in an initial seizure of property.[b] After all, why should simply declaring my will to keep other people from using an object all of a sudden give me a *right* to it? Clearly this declaration is first in need of legal grounding,[c] rather than Kant's assumption that it just *is* one. And how could people's actions be intrinsically (i.e. morally) wrong when they do not pay attention to claims grounded only in their own declaration to be the sole owner of the thing? How could this disturb anyone's conscience? It is obvious and easy to see that there could never be a *lawful seizure of property*, but only a lawful *acquisition or appropriation* of some object, by originally applying our own energy to it. Take the case of an object that has been worked on, improved, or guarded and protected from

397 mishap through someone's efforts, however small, even if they amounted to no more than plucking or picking up some wild fruit from the ground: someone who seizes this object clearly deprives the other of the results of the energy he has expended on it; he is making the other's body serve *his* will instead of its own, and is affirming his own will above and beyond

[a] *Bearbeitung*
[b] *Besitzergreifung*
[c] *Rechtsgrundes*

its appearance, to the point of negating the other's will, i.e. he is doing wrong.* – On the other hand, simply enjoying something without doing any work on it or safeguarding it against destruction gives us as little right to the thing as the declaration of our will to be its sole owner. Thus, when a family has hunted by itself in a district for even a hundred years without having done anything towards its improvement, then this family cannot keep out a newcomer who wants to hunt there too without morally doing wrong. There is absolutely no moral ground for the so-called right of preoccupation,[a] which holds that simply by virtue of having enjoyed a thing you can demand the exclusive right to its further enjoyment as an additional reward. The newcomer would have much more of a right to tell anyone whose claim rests merely on *this* right (the right of preoccupation): 'the very fact that you have been enjoying it for so long makes it right that others should enjoy it now'. There are no moral grounds for sole possession of any object that cannot be worked on or improved or secured against mishap, unless it is voluntarily relinquished by all other parties, for instance as a reward for service in another context; but this already presupposes a community governed by convention, the state. – The nature of the morally grounded right to property that we deduced above gives the owner just as unlimited a power over the object as he has over his own body; from which it follows that he can transfer his property to someone else, through exchange or donation, and the other person would then possess it with the same moral right as he did.

When it comes to *doing* wrong in general, this happens through either *violence* or *cunning*[b] and these are essentially the same from a moral perspective. First, in the case of murder, it makes no difference morally whether I avail myself of poison or a knife; and it is the same with every bodily injury. Other cases of wrong can all be reduced to the scenario of me, the wrongdoer,[67] forcing someone else to serve my will instead of his own and to act according to my will instead of his own. Using violence, I achieve this through physical causation; using cunning, however, I achieve it by means of motivation, i.e. causation that has passed through cognition. That is, I achieve it by supplying the other person's will with *illusory motives* that

398

---

* Thus, a foundation for natural property rights does not require the assumption that there are two parallel foundations for rights, rights based on *detention* along with rights based on *formation*; the latter is always sufficient. Only the name *formation* is not really appropriate, since the effort expended on an object need not always involve forming it in some way.

[a] *Präokkupations-Recht*
[b] *List*

lead him to follow *my* will while he thinks he is following his *own*. Since cognition is the medium of motives, I can only do this by falsifying his cognition, and this is a *lie*. Lies are always aimed at influencing another person's will, not his cognition alone and as such. Lies influence cognition only as a means, namely to the extent that cognition determines the will. My lies need a motive of their own, since they come from my will: but this motive can only be some other person's will, not his cognition in and of itself. As such, his cognition can never influence *my* will, and thus can never move it or be a motive for its goals. Only another person's willing and doing can be a motive, and thereby (hence indirectly) the other person's cognition. This is true not only of lies that are obviously self-interested, but also of lies that spring from pure malice, which only wants to glory in the painful consequences of the errors it causes in the other person. Even a windbag's sheer boastfulness[a] intends to exert some degree of influence over another person's willing and doing, by generating respect or raising himself in that person's opinion. It is not in itself wrong to simply refuse a truth, i.e. a statement in general, but it is wrong to put out a lie. You do not wrong a lost traveller by refusing to point him in the right direction; but you do if you point him in the wrong direction. – From what we have said it follows that every *lie* as such, just like every act of violence, is a *wrong*, because its aim is to extend the control of my will over other individuals and thus to affirm my own will by negating theirs, just as in the case of violence. – But the most perfect lie is the *broken contract*, because this clearly and completely unites all the stipulations we have mentioned. By entering into a contract, the other person's promise to act[b] is immediately and avowedly the motive for my present action. The promises are formally and deliberately exchanged. Each party is assumed to be in control of the truth of the claims he has made. If the other party breaks the contract, then he has deceived me; and by supplying my cognition with illusory motives he has steered my will according to his own intentions, has extended the control of his will over that of another individual, which is to say he has committed an absolute wrong. This is the ground of the moral legitimacy[c] and validity of *contracts*.

For the perpetrator, wrongdoing through violence is not as *ignominious*[d] as doing wrong through *cunning*,[e] because the former is a sign

---

[a] *die bloße Windbeutelei*
[b] *die fremde verheißene Leistung*
[c] *moralische Rechtmäßigkeit*
[d] *schimpflich*
[e] *List*

of physical strength, which the human race always finds impressive.[68] But because it takes a roundabout path, cunning betrays weakness and degrades the perpetrator as a physical and moral being. On top of this, lies and deception can only succeed when the one who employs them wins trust by professing disgust and contempt for them, so his triumph rests on the fact that he is credited with an honesty that he does not have. – The deep disgust that perfidy, disloyalty and treachery always excite is based on the fact that loyalty and honesty are the bonds that reunite (albeit externally) the will that has been splintered into the multiplicity of individuals; and thus they set a limit to the consequences of the egoism that results from the splintering. Disloyalty and treachery tear apart this last, external bond and give boundless scope to the consequences of egoism.[69]

In connection with our mode of investigation, we have found the content of the concept of *wrong* to be the structure of an individual's action in which he extends the affirmation of the will appearing in his body to the point where it becomes a negation of the will appearing in another individual's body. Using completely general examples, we established the boundary where the sphere of wrong begins by determining its gradation from the highest to the lower degrees with a few main concepts. It followed from this that the concept of *wrong* is the original and positive one. The counter-concept *right* is negative and derivative. So we must keep to the concepts, not the words. In fact, we could never talk about *right* if there was no wrong. The concept of *right* contains only the negation of wrong, and it includes every action that does not exceed the boundary presented above, i.e. any action that is not the negation of the other's will through the stronger affirmation of my own. With respect to *morality* pure and simple, that boundary splits the realm of possible actions into the wrong and the right. As long as an action does not intrude into the sphere of another person's affirmation of will by negating it in the manner discussed above, it is not a wrong. So for instance denying help to those in urgent need, calmly observing someone starve to death while you have more than enough, although cruel and diabolical, are not wrong: but we can be absolutely certain that anyone who is capable of this degree of unkindness and harshness will certainly commit any wrong as soon as his wishes demand it and no constraint is in the way.

The concept of *right*, as the negation of wrong, has its principal application and doubtless also its origin in the cases where an attempted wrong is resisted with violence; and since this resistance cannot itself be wrong, it is right. This is true even if it involves an act of violence that would

400

401 have been wrong on its own, taken out of context, and is only justified here by its motive, i.e. it becomes right. When an individual goes so far in the affirmation of his *own* will that he encroaches on the sphere of the affirmation of will essential to *my* person as such, and in doing so negates it, my resisting this encroachment is just the negation of that negation, and to this extent nothing more on my part than the affirmation of the will that appears essentially and originally in my body and is already implicitly[a] expressed through the mere appearance of this body; consequently it is not wrong but *right*. This means: I have the *right* to negate that other negation with the force I need to suppress it, which we can easily see might go as far as killing the other individual whose incursion as an encroaching external force can be resisted with a somewhat greater counter-force without the resistance being wrong, but rather right. This is because everything that happens on my side falls exclusively within the sphere of the affirmation of will that is essential to my person as such and is already expressed in it (this being the scene of the struggle), and does not encroach into that of the other, and is consequently only the negation of the negation, which is to say an affirmation that is not itself a negation. Thus *without doing wrong*, I can *compel* the other will to abstain from its negation of my will as this appears in my body and in the use of my body's forces for maintaining my body, without negating any other will that observes a similar limitation. In other words, I have to this extent a *right of compulsion*.[b]

In all cases where I have a right to use compulsion, which is to say a perfect right to use *violence* against another person, I can use *cunning* against the other's violence when the circumstances allow without doing wrong; consequently, I have an actual *right to lie to the same extent that I have a right to use compulsion*. So when someone is searched by a highway robber, he has a perfect right to assure the robber that he is not carrying any other possessions: likewise someone who tells a lie in order to lock a burglar into the cellar at night. Someone who is led to captivity by robbers, for instance by Barbary pirates,[c] has the right to kill them, not only with open violence but also using underhanded tricks, in order to free himself. –

402 For the same reason, a promise is not binding if it was exacted through compulsion, using direct bodily violence, because the person compelled in this way has a perfect right to free himself by killing, not to mention cheating, the perpetrators. Someone who cannot retrieve stolen property by force is not acting wrongly when he retrieves it through cunning. Indeed,

---

[a] *implicite*
[b] *Zwangsrecht*
[c] *Barbaresken*

if someone gambles with money that was stolen from me, I have the right to use false dice against him, because anything that I win back already belongs to me. Anyone wanting to deny this would have to deny even more the legitimacy[a] of the ruses adopted in wartime,[b] which is the violent form of lying,[c] and proof of the saying of Queen Christina of Sweden: 'The words of men are not good for anything, and their deeds are hardly to be trusted.'[70] – So sharply does right border on wrong. But I consider it superfluous to prove that all this is in full agreement with what was said above about the illegitimacy of lying and the use of force: this also serves to explain the unusual theories of the white lie.[*,d,71]

According to all we have said, wrong and right are merely *moral* determinations, i.e. they have validity with respect to the consideration of human action as such, and in reference to the *inner meaning of this action in itself.* There are two ways in which this registers itself immediately in consciousness. First, there is the inner pain that accompanies wrongdoing, and which is the wrongdoer's consciousness (through a mere feeling) of the excessive strength of his affirmation of will, a strength that went so far as to negate the appearance of the other's will. Second, there is the fact that although the perpetrator and the victim are certainly distinct as appearances, they are identical in themselves. Later, I will be in a position to give a more thorough explanation of the inner meaning of all anguish of conscience. However, the wronged party is painfully aware of the negation of his will as it is expressed through his body and its natural wants (for whose satisfaction nature refers him to his body's powers); and at the same time, he is also aware that he could, without doing wrong, repulse that negation by any means, if he did not lack the power. This purely moral meaning is the only meaning that right and wrong have for human beings *as* human beings, rather than as citizens of a State; consequently it exists even in the state of nature, in the absence of any positive law, and constitutes the foundation and the content of all that (for this reason) has been called *natural right*, or even better, moral right, since its validity does not extend to what is undergone,[e] to outer reality, but rather only to the deeds and

403

---

* A further discussion of the doctrine of right I am presenting here can be found in my prize essay *On the Basis of Morals*, § 17, pp. 221–30 of the first edition [see Hübscher *SW* 4, 216–26, and Cambridge edition, 207–15]

[a] *Rechtmäßigkeit*
[b] *Kriegslist*
[c] *thätliche Lüge*
[d] *Nothlüge*
[e] *Leiden*

the self-cognition of the person's own will that grows out of these deeds and is called *conscience*.[72] But in a state of nature, it cannot assert itself in every case to be valid for others externally and to restrain them so that right will prevail over might. In the state of nature, it depends on everyone in every case not *doing* wrong, but in no way does this spare them in all cases from *being* wronged, something that depends on their contingent, external strength. Thus the concepts of right and wrong are certainly also valid for the state of nature and are not remotely the products of convention; but they are valid there purely as *moral* concepts for everyone's self-cognition of their own will. On the scale that gauges the extremely different degrees of strength with which the will to life affirms itself in human individuals, the concepts of right and wrong represent a fixed point, like the freezing point on a thermometer, namely the point where the affirmation of one's own will turns into a negation of someone else's. In other words, it indicates through wrongdoing the degree of its intensity, united with the degree to which cognition is caught in the *principium individuationis* (which is the form of cognition that stands entirely in the service of the will). But anyone who wants to deny the purely moral consideration of human action or put it to the side, choosing to regard action only with respect to its outer efficacy and results, such a person can certainly (like *Hobbes*) treat right and wrong as conventional, arbitrary designations that do not exist anywhere outside of positive law; we can never use outer experience to teach this person something that is not a part of outer experience. In his book, *On the Principles of the Geometers*,[a] this very same *Hobbes* offers a really quite remarkable demonstration of his absolutely empirical way of thinking, by denying the whole of genuine, pure mathematics and stubbornly claiming that the point has extension and the line has breadth; and since we can never show him a point without extension or a line without breadth, we have as little a chance of teaching him the *a priori* nature of mathematics as we would with the *a priori* nature of right, because he will have nothing to do with non-empirical cognition.

The pure *doctrine of right*[b] is thus a chapter in *morals*,[73] and relates directly and exclusively to what people *do*, not to what they *suffer*.[c] This is because only deeds express the will, and the will is morality's sole concern. Suffering is just an event, and morality can take note of this only indirectly, namely to prove that it is not wrong to do something in order to avoid being wronged. – This chapter in morality would contain a precise determination

404

---

[a] *De Principiis Geometrarum* [The full title of the work is *De principiis et ratiocinatione geometrarum*]
[b] *Rechtslehre*
[c] *das Leiden* [also translatable as 'what they undergo']

of the border up to which an individual can go in affirming the will that is already objectified in his body, before it turns into a negation of that same will as it appears in another individual; it would also describe the actions that transgress this boundary, and are consequently wrong, which means they can be resisted without committing another wrong. So one's own *deeds* always remain the focus of attention.

But now *being wronged* appears as an event in outer experience, and as we have said, it is the clearest manifestation of the conflict of the will to life against itself. It emerges from the multitude of individuals and from egoism, both of which are conditioned by the *principium individuationis*, the form of the world as representation for the cognition of the individual. We have also seen above that a very large part of the suffering that is essential to human life has an ever-flowing source in that conflict between individuals.

All these individuals share the faculty of reason, which enables them not only to recognize the particular case (as with animals), but also to achieve an abstract overview of the whole, the total context. Now this faculty of reason quickly gave people insight into this source of suffering and made them concerned to diminish it, or even remove it where possible, through a collective sacrifice that would nonetheless be outweighed by the collective advantage that ensued. As pleasant as it may be to the egoism of an individual to do wrong in certain cases, still, it necessarily correlates with another individual's experience of *being* wronged, and this is a source of considerable pain to that other individual. Now reason, which takes in the whole picture, emerged from the one-sided standpoint of the individual to which it belonged, and momentarily liberated itself from its attachment to this individual. This freed it up to see that the pleasure one individual gets in doing wrong is always outweighed by the relatively greater pain another individual experiences in being wronged. It discovered that, since everything was being left to chance, everyone was afraid that he would experience the pain of being wronged much more frequently than the occasional pleasure of doing wrong. From this, reason recognized that the best and only means of reducing the suffering spread out amongst everyone, and also of distributing it as evenly as possible, would be to spare everyone the pain of being wronged by having everyone also renounce the pleasure of doing it. – The mechanism for achieving this is the *political contract*[a] or the *law*. This mechanism was easily devised and gradually perfected by

[a] *Staatsvertrag*

egoism, which, with the use of reason, methodically abandoned its one-sided standpoint. The origin of the political contract or the law which I have given here was already presented by Plato in the *Republic*. In fact, that origin is essentially unique and determined by the nature of the object. Nor is there any country where the state could have arisen in any other way, because this type of origin, this goal, is precisely what makes it a state in the first place; but it is all the same whether the condition of the people before the state was that of a collection of independent savages (anarchy), or a group of slaves under the arbitrary rule of a stronger party (despotism). In both cases the state did not yet exist: it only arose by common consent, and the state is more or less perfect depending on the extent to which the consent is tainted with anarchy or despotism. Republics tend towards anarchy, monarchies towards despotism, and the constitutional monarchy, which was then devised as a middle ground, tends towards factional control. To found a perfect state, you must start by creating beings whose nature allows them all to sacrifice their own well-being for the public good. Until then, something can be achieved by having *one* family whose well-being is inseparable from that of the country; so that they cannot promote the one without the other, at least as far as the most important issues are concerned. This is what gives the hereditary monarchy its advantage and its strength.[74]

406

Now if morality is concerned exclusively with *doing* right and wrong, and if it can precisely demarcate the limits of action for someone who is determined to do no wrong, then conversely, political science,[a] the theory of legislation, is exclusively concerned with *suffering* from wrong. This theory would not be interested in *doing* wrong, if suffering from wrong were not its necessary correlate. This is the enemy it is working against, and so the focus of its attention. In fact, if we could think of someone *doing* wrong in a way that did not involve another party *being* wronged, the state, to be consistent, could not prohibit such a deed. – Now the object under consideration for *morality*, the only thing morality takes to be real, is the will, the disposition.[b] It follows that morality considers a will determined to do wrong and held back and rendered ineffective only by an external power to be equivalent with the actual commission of wrong; accordingly, it will condemn one who wills in this way as unjust[c] from its seat of judgement. On the other hand, the state takes absolutely no notice of the will or the disposition merely as such; it only cares about the *deed* (whether it be attempted or executed), because the correlate of doing, on

[a] *Staatslehre*
[b] *Gesinnung*
[c] *ungerecht*

the other side, is *suffering*: so the deed, the event,[a] is the only thing that the state takes to be real: the disposition, the intention is investigated only to the extent that it can shed light on the meaning of the deed. Thus the state does not forbid anyone from thinking incessantly about murdering and poisoning someone as long as it is sure that fear of the sword and the wheel will keep this will constantly in check. It is not the state's business to eradicate foolish plans, wrongful tendencies, evil dispositions, but only to counter every possible motive for wrongdoing with a stronger motive for failing to do wrong, in the form of inevitable punishment. Accordingly, the criminal code aims to be a complete register of counter-motives for all the criminal actions presumed possible, – in the abstract,[b] to be applied concretely[c] to cases that occur.[75] Now political science, or legislation, will borrow from morality this chapter containing the doctrine of right and use it for its own purpose; this is the chapter that discusses the inner meaning of right and wrong and also determines the precise boundary between them. But legislation will borrow this simply and solely for its reverse side; that is, it takes all the boundaries that morality decrees to be inviolable if you do not want to *do* wrong, and views them the other way around, as boundaries whose violation cannot be allowed if you do not want to *be* wronged, and from which you have a *right* to drive others back: which is why these boundaries are barricaded on the passive side with laws. So, just as the historian is rather wittily called an inverted prophet, the theorist of rights[d] can be called an inverted moralist; and the doctrine of right[e] in its true sense (i.e. a doctrine of the *rights* to which you can lay claim) is an inversion of the chapter of morality that demonstrates the inviolable rights. The concept of wrong and its negation, right, which is originally *moral*, becomes *juridical* by transferring the starting point from the active to the passive side, which is to say through inversion. This, along with Kant's doctrine of right, which falsely derives from the categorical imperative the establishment of the state as a moral duty, has given rise even recently to the very peculiar and mistaken notion that the state is an institution for fostering morality, that it emerges from the striving for morality, and that it is thus erected against egoism. As if the eternally free will, the inner disposition that alone can be moral or immoral could be modified from the outside and induced to change! Still more mistaken is the theory that

[a] *Begebenheit*
[b] *in abstracto*
[c] *in concreto*
[d] *Rechtslehrer*
[e] *Rechtslehre*

408   the state is the condition for freedom in a moral sense, and thus a condition for morality: after all, freedom lies beyond appearances, to say nothing of human institutions. As we have said, the state is so far from being directed against egoism in general and as such, that the reverse is in fact true: the state emerges out of a cumulative, collective egoism that is fully aware of itself as such, and proceeds methodically from a one-sided standpoint to that of the universal. The state is set up under the correct assumption that pure morality, i.e. morally grounded rightful action, cannot be expected; otherwise, of course, the state itself would be quite superfluous. So the state, in endeavouring to further the common good, is not directed against egoism but only against the detrimental effects of egoism, which emerges from the multitude of egoistic individuals and impacts them all reciprocally, disturbing their well-being. Thus *Aristotle* even said (*Politics*, III): 'The end of the state is the good life . . . by which we mean a happy and honourable life.'[a],[76] And *Hobbes* gave an entirely correct and unexceptionable account of the origin and function of the state, just as it was also described in the old foundation of all state law and order, 'public security should be the first law'.[b],[77] – When the state fully achieves its goal, it will present the same appearance that would be expected if perfect justice[c] governed everybody's disposition. But the inner essence and origin of the two appearances will be the reverse. In the latter case, to be precise, the situation would be that nobody wanted to *do* wrong; but in the former case it would be that nobody wanted to *be* wronged, with the means to this end fully in effect. So the same line can be drawn from opposite directions, and a predator with a muzzle is just as harmless as a grass-eating animal. – But the state cannot go beyond this point: it cannot show a face[d] comparable to one based in universal and mutual benevolence and love. As we have just seen, it could not by nature prohibit any wrongdoing that did not have a corresponding

409   victim on the other end, and simply because this is impossible, it prohibits all wrongdoing. Conversely, given its tendency to promote the general welfare, it would very gladly arrange for everyone to *experience* good works and charitable deeds of all sorts if these did not have an indispensable correlate in the *performance* of good works and charitable deeds. But then every citizen of the state would want to take a passive role in this, nobody

---

[a]   Τελος μεν ουν πολεως το ευ ζην· τουτο δε εστιν το ζην ευδαιμονως και καλως. (*Finis civitatis est bene vivere, hoc autem est beate et pulchre vivere.*) [See *Politics*, III, 9, 1280b39 and 1281a1–2]
[b]   *salus publica prima lex esto* [After Cicero, *De legibus* (*On the Laws*), III, 3, 8: *salus populi suprema lex esto*]
[c]   *Gerechtigkeit*
[d]   *Erscheinung*

would want to be active, and there would be no reason to expect one citizen rather than another to play the active part. Thus only the negative can be *enforced*, and that is *right*; we cannot enforce the positive, which people have called duties of love or imperfect duties.

As we have said, legislation borrows from morality the pure doctrine of right, or the doctrine of the nature of, and boundary between, right and wrong, in order to use the reverse side for its own purpose (which is foreign to that of morality), which is to establish both positive legislation and a method for maintaining it, i.e. the state. Positive legislation is thus an application of the reverse side of the purely moral doctrine of right. This application can take place in the light of the distinctive conditions and circumstances of a particular people. But only when the positive legislation is essentially and thoroughly determined under the guidance of the pure doctrine of right, with this doctrine providing a demonstrable ground for each of its statutes – only then is the resulting legislation actually *positive law*,[a] and the state a *legal*[b] association, a *state* in the true sense of the word, a morally admissible institution, not an immoral one. Otherwise, the positive legislation lays the foundation for a *positive wrong*, and it is itself a publicly admitted, enforced wrong. Every despotism is like this, as are the constitutions of most Mohammedan kingdoms and parts of many other constitutions, e.g. serfdom, soccage,[c] and so on. The pure doctrine of right, or natural right, or better yet moral right is the basis of every just,[d] positive legislation, although always through inversion, just as pure mathematics is the basis of every branch of applied mathematics. The most important points of the pure doctrine of right, as philosophy has to deliver it to legislation for that purpose, are the following: (1) the explanation of the inner and true meaning and origin of the concepts of right and wrong,   410 and their application and position within morality. (2) The derivation of property rights. (3) The derivation of the moral validity of the contract; since this is the moral foundation of the state contract. (4) The explanation of the origin and purpose of the state, of the relation of this goal to morality and, as a result of this relation, the purposive transfer of the moral doctrine of right to legislation, through inversion. (5) The derivation of criminal law.[e] – The remaining contents of the doctrine of right are merely the application of these principles, the closer determination of the boundary

[a] *Recht*
[b] *rechtlicher*
[c] *Frohn*
[d] *rechtlichen*
[e] *Strafrechts*

between right and wrong for all possible situations in life, which are thus united and classified under certain perspectives and headings. The manuals of pure law[a] are basically in agreement about these particular doctrines: they only read differently in the principles, because these principles are always connected with some philosophical system. Having discussed the first four of these main points briefly and in general, although distinctly and clearly in relation to our own system, we still have to consider criminal law.[b]

Kant makes the fundamentally false claim that there is no perfect right to property outside of the state. According to our deduction above, there is property in the state of nature as well, with perfectly natural, i.e. moral right, a right that cannot be transgressed without doing wrong, but can be defended to the utmost without doing wrong. On the other hand it is certain that there is no *criminal law* outside of the state. All right to punish[c] is grounded in positive law alone, which has determined a punishment *before* the offence; the threat of this punishment should serve as a counter-motive, outweighing any possible motives for committing the offence. This positive law should be regarded as having the sanction and acknowledgement of all the citizens of the state. It is thus grounded in a common contract, which the members of the state are obliged to fulfil under all circumstances – they are obliged to inflict the punishment on the one hand and to accept it on the other. Thus, this acceptance is rightly enforceable. Consequently, the immediate *purpose of punishment* in the particular case is the *fulfilment of the law as a contract*. But the only purpose of the *law* is to *deter* people from encroaching on the rights of others: after all, people united themselves into a state, renounced wrongdoing, and assumed the burden of maintaining the state so that everyone could be protected from being wronged. Thus the law and its implementation, i.e. punishment, are essentially directed to the *future*, not the *past*. This distinguishes *punishment* from *revenge*, which is motivated solely by the event, i.e. what has already taken place, as such. When you retaliate for a wrong by inflicting pain without any future purpose, this is revenge; it can have no goal other than that of comforting yourself for your own suffering by looking at the suffering you have caused in someone else. This is wickedness and cruelty and it is ethically unjustifiable. If someone wrongs me, this in no way authorizes me to wrong him. Repaying evil with evil, with no other purpose, is neither moral nor otherwise justifiable

411

[a] *Recht*
[b] *Strafrechte*
[c] *Recht zu Strafen*

through any rational ground, and the right of retaliation,[a] placed as the self-sufficient and ultimate principle of criminal law, is senseless. Thus, Kant's theory of punishment as mere retribution for the sake of retribution is utterly groundless and wrong-headed. And yet it still haunts the writings of many doctrines of right under all sorts of fancy phrases that amount to empty verbal rubbish, such as: the punishment atones for the crime, or neutralizes and cancels it out, and so forth. But nobody has the authority to set himself up as a purely moral judge and avenger, to inflict pain on others for their misdeeds, and to exact penance. In fact, this would be a highly presumptuous piece of arrogance; thus the biblical: 'Vengeance is mine, saith the Lord, I will repay.'[b] People certainly have the right to concern themselves with the security of society: but this can only happen by banning all behaviour designated by the word 'criminal', preventing it through counter-motives in the form of threatened punishments; and these threats can only be effective when they are carried out, in spite of having failed to deter the crime. It is so universally acknowledged, indeed it is such a self-evident truth that the purpose of punishment – or more precisely of penal law – is to deter crime, that in England it is expressed even in   412 the very old formula of indictment, which the Crown attorney still uses in criminal cases, and which ends in the following manner: 'if this be proved, you, the said N.N. ought to be punished with pains of law, to deter others from the like crimes in all time coming'.[c,78] If a ruler wants to pardon a justly condemned criminal, his minister will object that the crime would be quickly committed again. – Punishment is distinct from revenge in that it has a purpose for the future, and punishment has this purpose only when it is carried out *in fulfilment of a law*. Only by announcing itself to be necessarily in effect for every future case does the law retain its strength as a deterrent, which is its purpose. – At this point, a Kantian would be sure to object that, according to this view, the punished criminal is used 'merely as a *means*'. Now the phrase that no Kantian ever tires of repeating, that 'you should treat people only as an end, never as a means', certainly sounds very important, and this recommends it to people who like formulas that relieve them of the need to think any further. But examined closely, it is a very vague and indeterminate claim and it achieves its aim very indirectly, and any case it is applied to needs first to be specifically clarified, determined and modified; taken universally, the claim is insufficient, uninformative and problematic as well. The murderer who is condemned to death by law

[a] *jus talionis*
[b] [Romans 12:19; also Deuteronomy 32:35]
[c] [Schopenhauer quotes this in English]

must now certainly and perfectly rightly be used as a mere *means*. He has disrupted public security, the principal goal of the state; in fact, unless the law is put into effect, he has abolished it; and consequently he himself, his life, his person, must now be the *means* of fulfilling the law and through it the re-establishment of public security. It is perfectly right to do so, to carry out the political contract that he himself entered into, to the extent that he is a citizen; according to this contract, he, in order to enjoy security for his life, his freedom and his property, had pledged his life, his freedom and his property for the security of all, a pledge that he has now forfeited.

413

There is, of course, nothing really new about the theory of punishment presented here, a theory that any healthy reason will find immediately convincing; it is just an old theory that had almost been supplanted by new errors, and this required me to present it as clearly as possible. The same thing is already essentially contained in what Pufendorf says in *On the Duty of Man and Citizen,*[a] Book 2, ch. 13. Hobbes agrees with it as well in *Leviathan*, chs. 15 and 28. In our day it has been famously championed by *Feuerbach.*[79] Indeed, it was already articulated by ancient philosophers: Plato presents it clearly in *Protagoras* (p. 114, ed. Bip.[b]), as well as in *Gorgias* (p. 168),[c] and finally in the eleventh book of the *Laws* (p. 165).[d] Seneca expresses Plato's opinion and the theory of all punishment perfectly, in just a few words: 'No wise man punishes because a wrong has been done, but rather in order that it should not be done' (*On Anger*, I, 16).[e]

Thus, in the state, we have become familiar with the mechanism by which egoism, armed with reason, tries to avoid its own negative consequences, consequences that backfire on it; and now each promotes the welfare of all because they see it as comprising their own. If the state fully achieved its goal, then it would unite all the strength of humanity in itself and would, so to speak, increasingly know how to make the rest of nature useful, ultimately removing all kinds of evil[f] to bring about something approaching a utopia. Of course not only is the state still very far from this goal, but there would still exist countless evils that are absolutely essential to life; and finally, even if they were all cleared away, the vacated space would be immediately occupied by boredom, which would keep us suffering just as much ever. And additionally, the state will never fully

---

[a] *De officio hominis et civis*
[b] [See *Protagoras* 324a–b. Here and elsewhere, Schopenhauer refers to the Bipont edition of Plato]
[c] [*Gorgias* 525a–b]
[d] [The discussion is actually from Book IX of Plato's *Laws*, 854d–e]
[e] *Nemo prudens punit, quia peccatum est; sed ne peccetur* (*De ira*, I, 16 [in fact I, 19, 7])
[f] *Uebel*

abolish quarrels between individuals; after they have been eliminated in great matters they will continue to vex in petty ones. And finally, if Eris has been driven happily from within, she will appear from without: when she has been banished in the form of a conflict between individuals through the institution of the state, she will return externally as war between nations and demand on a large scale and in a single blow, as an accumulated debt, the bloody sacrifices that prudent measures had withheld from her on a smaller scale. Even supposing that all this was finally overcome and put to the side through millennia of accumulated lessons in prudence, the end result would be the true over-population of the whole planet, a terrible evil that only a bold imagination can bring before the imagination.[*],[80]

414

§ 63

We have become familiar with *temporal justice*, which has its seat in the state, as either retributive or punitive; and we have seen that this becomes justice only when it takes the *future* into account. Any punishment or retribution for an outrage is unjustifiable if it lacks reference to the future; it only compounds the first evil[a] by adding a second that lacks any sense or significance. But the situation is entirely different with *eternal justice*, which we mentioned earlier and which governs the world, not the state; it is not dependent on human institutions, not subject to chance or deception, not uncertain, unstable or subject to error, but rather infallible, steadfast and secure. – The concept of retribution already entails temporality: which is why *eternal justice* cannot be retributive, as this would require time; it cannot permit any delays or reprieves, nor can it appeal to time to balance a bad deed with a bad result. Punishment must be tied to the offence to the point where the two become one.

Do you think that crimes fly to the gods on wings, and someone must then record them there on the tablet of Jupiter, and that Jupiter looks at them and administers justice for men? Not even the whole of heaven would be big enough to contain the sins of men, if Jupiter were to write them all down, nor would he be able to review them and assign a punishment to each. No! The punishment is already here, if you would only see it. (Euripides, quoted in Stobaeus, *Eclogues* I, ch. 4[b],[81])

---

[*] See chapter 47 of the second volume.

[a] *Uebel*

[b] Δοκειτε πηδᾳν τ᾽ ἀδικήματ᾽ εις 9εους | Πτεροισι, κἀπειτ᾽ εν Διος δελτου πτυχαις | Γραφειν τιν᾽ αυτα, Ζηνα δ᾽ εισορωντα νιν | Θνητοις δικαζειν; Ουδ᾽ ὁ πας ουρανος, | Διος γραφοντος τας βροτων ἁμαρτιας, | Εξαρκεσειεν, ουδ᾽ εκεινος αν σκοπων | Πεμπειν ἑκαστῳ ζημιαν· αλλ᾽ ἡ Δικη

415   It will soon be fully clear to anyone who has grasped the complete thought
       we have been developing that such eternal justice is really part of the essence
       of the world.

           The world in all the multiplicity of its parts and forms is the appearance,
       the objecthood of the one will to life. Existence itself as well as the mode
       of existence, in the whole and in each of the parts, all comes from the will
       alone. It is free, it is omnipotent. The will appears in everything, precisely
       as it determines itself, in itself and outside of time. The world is only the
       mirror of this willing: and all finitude, all suffering, all the misery the world
       contains belongs to the expression of what it wills; it is so because the will
       wills it so. Thus, with the strictest right, every being supports existence in
       general, both the existence of its species and the existence of its distinctive
       individuality, just as it is, in its surroundings as they are, in a world as it
       is, ruled by accident and error, temporal, transient, always suffering. And
       everything that happens to the individual – indeed everything that *can*
       happen – is always right. Because the will is his, and as the will is, so is the
       world. The responsibility for the existence and the condition of this world
       can only be borne by the world itself, and no other; for how could anyone
       else take it upon themselves? – If you want to know[a] what humanity,
       morally considered, is worth overall and in general, just look at the fate
       of humanity overall and in general. It is want, misery, sorrow, trouble and
       death. Eternal justice is at work: if human beings were not on the whole
       worthless, then their fate would not be on the whole so sad. In this sense we
416   can say: the world itself is the world tribunal, the Last Judgement.[b] If we
       could put all the misery of the world on *one* side of a scale, and all the guilt
       of the world on the other, the pointer would certainly vouch for this.[82]

           But of course the world does not present itself to the cognition of the
       individual as such (a cognition that has arisen from the will in order to serve
       it) in the same way that it eventually reveals itself to the investigator, that is,
       as the objecthood of the one and only will to life that he himself is. Instead,
       the eyes of the crude individual are clouded, as the Indians say, by the
       veil[c] of *māyā*: it is not the thing in itself that shows itself to the individual,
       but only appearances in time and space, in the *principium individuationis*

| Εντανθα που 'στιν εγγυς, ει βουλεσθ' ὁραν. (*Volare pennis scelera ad aetherias domus* | *Putatis,
illic in Jovis tabularia* | *Scripto referri; tum Jovem lectis super* | *Sententiam proferre? – sed mortalium*
| *Facinora coeli, quantaquanta est, regia* | *Nequit tenere: nec legendis Juppiter* | *Et puniendis par est.
Est tamen ultio,* | *Et, si intuemur, illa nos habitat prope.*) [More correctly *Eclogues* I, ch. 3, quoting
Euripides, *Melanippe*]
[a] *wissen*
[b] *Weltgericht*
[c] *Schleier*

and in the rest of the forms of the principle of sufficient reason: and in this form of his limited cognition, he does not see the essence of things, which is one, but rather only appearances, which are separated, disconnected, innumerable, highly dissimilar, and in fact opposed. Thus pleasure appears to him to be one thing and sorrow something entirely different, this human being appears as a torturer and murderer, that person a martyr and victim, evil[a] is one thing and trouble[b] another. He sees one person living in happiness, abundance and pleasure, while at this same person's door another is dying a miserable death from want and cold. Then he asks: where is retribution? And he himself, in the most violent urges of the will that is his origin and his essence, seizes the pleasures and delights of life, embraces them firmly, and does not know that through this very act of his will he is seizing and clutching to himself all the pains and miseries of life, the very sight of which strikes him with such terror. He sees the trouble, he sees the evil in the world: but he is very far from recognizing that both are only different sides of the single appearance of the one will to life; he considers them very different, in fact entirely opposed, and often tries to escape trouble, his own individual suffering, through evil, i.e. by causing other people to suffer, trapped as he is in the *principium individuationis*, deceived by the veil of *māyā*. – Just as a captain sits in a boat, trusting the weak little vessel as the raging, boundless sea raises up and casts down howling cliffs of waves; so the human individual sits calmly in a world full of sorrow, supported by and trusting in the *principium individuationis*, which is how the individual cognizes things as appearance. The boundless world, everywhere full of suffering, with its infinite past and infinite future, is alien to him – in fact, it is a fairy tale: his vanishing little person,[c] his unextended present, his momentary comfort, these alone have reality for him: and he does everything he can to maintain these as long as a more adequate cognition does not open his eyes. Until then, he has only an utterly dark presentiment[d] in the innermost depths of his consciousness that all of this is not really foreign to him but in fact connected with him in such a way that the *principium individuationis* cannot protect him. From this presentiment comes that indelible *dread*[e] shared by all humans (and perhaps even the more intelligent animals) and that seizes them so suddenly when some chance event leaves them in confusion about the *principium*

417

[a] *das Böse*
[b] *das Uebel*
[c] *seine verschwindende Person*
[d] *Ahndung*
[e] *Grausen*

individuationis – when the principle in some one of its forms seems to have suffered an exception: for instance, if it seems that some alteration has taken place without a cause, or a dead person has returned, or the past or the future are somehow present in any other way, or the distant is near. This sort of thing gives people a tremendous fright[a] because they are thrown into sudden confusion over the forms of cognition of appearances, which is the only thing keeping their own individuality separate from the rest of the world. But this separation itself lies only in appearance and not in the thing in itself, which is precisely the basis for eternal justice. – In fact, all temporal happiness stands on ground that has been undermined, and all prudence[b] wanders over the same ground. These protect the person from mishaps and supply him with pleasures; but the person is mere appearance: its distinction from other individuals – and its freedom from their sufferings – are both based on the form of appearance, the *principium individuationis*. From the perspective of the true nature[c] of things, everyone must regard all the sufferings of the world as his own; in fact, he must regard all merely possible suffering as actual, so long as he is the steadfast will to life, i.e. so long as he affirms life with all his strength. For cognition that sees through the *principium individuationis*, a happy life in time, as a gift of chance or effect of prudence, in the midst of the sufferings of countless others, – all this is just a beggar dreaming he is king, a dream from which he must awake to discover that it was only a fleeting illusion that had separated him from the suffering of his life.

418

Eternal justice will always elude an outlook ensnared in cognition that follows the principle of sufficient reason, the *principium individuationis*; this outlook will miss eternal justice entirely, unless it is salvaged through something like a fiction. Such an outlook sees evil people who commit cruelties and atrocities of every sort living happy lives and passing out of the world unchallenged. It sees the oppressed dragging on to the bitter end with lives full of suffering, without avenger or vindicator in sight. But eternal justice will only be understood and grasped by someone who transcends cognition that is guided by the principle of sufficient reason and bound to individual things, and who recognizes the Ideas, sees through the *principium individuationis*, and becomes aware that the forms of appearance do not apply to things in themselves. This person, by virtue of the same cognition, will be the only one capable of understanding the true essence of virtue, as it will soon be revealed to us in connection with the

[a] *Entsetzen*
[b] *Klugheit*
[c] *Wesen*

present line of discussion, although this cognition in the abstract[a] is not necessary at all for the actual practice of virtue. It will be clear to anyone who has achieved such cognition that the will is the in-itself of all appearance, and that all the misery imposed on others and experienced by himself, all the evil and the trouble, only ever affect one and the same being. This is true even if two beings present themselves in appearance as entirely different individuals, and even if their appearances are far apart in time and space. He sees that the difference between the one who metes out suffering and the one who must endure it is only phenomenal and does not concern the thing in itself, which is the will that lives in both. This will is deceived by the cognition that is bound in its service, and fails to recognize itself; trying to increase well-being in *one* of its appearances, it produces vast amounts of suffering in *another*, and so, in the violence of its impulses, it sinks its teeth into its own flesh, not knowing that it is only hurting itself, and revealing in this way, through the medium of individuation, its inner conflict with itself. The tormenter and the tormented are one. The   419 former is mistaken in thinking he does not share the torment, the latter in thinking he does not share the guilt. If both were made aware of this, the one who imposes the suffering would recognize that he lives in all things that suffer pain in this whole wide world, things that, if endowed with reason, would wonder in vain why they were called into existence for so much suffering, not understanding what is at fault. And the tormented party would see that all evil that is or ever was committed in the world flows from the will that comprises *his* essence as well, that appears in *him* as well; and through this appearance and its affirmation, he takes upon himself all the suffering that comes from such a will, and that it is right for him to endure it as long as he *is* this will. – The prophetic writer Calderón speaks from this recognition in *Life is a Dream*:

> Because the greatest offence of man,
> Is that he was born.[b]

And how could it not be an offence, given that it is followed by death in accordance with an eternal law? Calderón has merely expressed the Christian dogma of original sin in this verse.[83]

Vivid recognition of eternal justice, of the balancing scale inseparably connecting the evil of the offence[c] with the evil of the punishment,[d,84]

[a] *in abstracto*
[b] *Pues el delito mayor* | *Del hombre es haber nacido.* [*Life is a Dream*, (*La vida es sueño*), Act I, scene 2]
[c] *malum culpae*
[d] *malo poenae*

requires a complete transcendence of individuality and the principle of its possibility. Like pure and clear cognition of the essence of all virtue, to which it is related and which will be the next topic of discussion, recognition of eternal justice will always be inaccessible to most people. – Thus, the wise forefathers of the Indian people articulated it directly in the *Vedas*, i.e. the esoteric doctrines of wisdom (which are only permitted to the three reborn castes), at least as far as it can be grasped by concepts and language, and their imagistic, rhapsodic manner of presentation allows; but in the folk religion, or exoteric doctrine, the forefathers have communicated it only through myth. We find the direct presentation in the *Vedas*, the fruit of the highest human cognition and wisdom. The essence of this work has finally come to us in the *Upanishads*, which are the greatest gift of this century; it is expressed in many forms, but particularly when all the beings of the world, living and lifeless, are led in succession past the gaze of the disciples, while a certain word is pronounced over each of them, a word that has become a formula and as such is called *Mahavakya*:[a],[85] *Tatoumes*, or more correctly *tat tvam asi*, which means: 'You are that.'*– This great piece of wisdom is translated for the people (to the extent that they can grasp it, given their limitations) into the sort of cognition that complies with the principle of sufficient reason. Of course this piece of wisdom, purely and in itself, is completely foreign – even contradictory – to the nature of such cognition; such cognition cannot accommodate this wisdom, it could only accept a surrogate in the form of myth. Myth was a sufficient guide to action, since it illuminates the ethical meaning of action, albeit through pictorial representation in the manner of cognition that is eternally foreign to this meaning (i.e. according to the principle of sufficient reason). This is the purpose of religious doctrines, which are all mythological cloaks for truths that are inaccessible to the untutored human senses. In this sense,[86] mythology could be called, as Kant would say, a postulate of practical reason: but considered as such it has the great advantage of containing only elements that lie before our eyes in the real world, which is to say it can cover all its concepts with intuitions. We are referring here to the myth of the transmigration of the soul. It teaches that you must atone for all the suffering you inflict on other creatures over the course of your life by enduring precisely the same suffering in a following life in this very same world; it goes so far as to say that anyone who kills even an animal will

---

* *Oupenk'hat*, Vol. I, pp. 60ff. [*Chāndogya Upanishad*, 6, 8, 7]

a [*Mahāvākya*, great saying]

have to be born at some point in the infinity of time as precisely this sort of animal, and suffer the same death. It teaches that wicked behaviour will lead to a future life as a suffering and despised creature in this world, being reborn into the lower castes, or as a woman, or an animal, as pariah or Chandala, as a leper, a crocodile, etc. All the misery threatened by this myth is reinforced through real world perceptions[a] of suffering beings that do not   421
know[b] what they have done to deserve their misery, and the myth needs no other hell to support it. But, on the other hand, it promises as a reward that you will be reborn in a better, nobler form, as Brahman, as sage, as saint. The highest reward that can be expected from the noblest deeds and the fullest resignation, a reward that a woman can also receive after she has freely died on the funeral pyre of her husband in seven successive lives, and that also comes to people whose pure mouths have never spoken a single lie, – this reward is something that the myth can express only negatively in the language of this world, through the frequent promise of never being reborn again: 'you will not assume existence in appearance again':[c] or as it is expressed by the Buddhists who do not themselves believe in either the *Veda* or the caste system: 'You will achieve nirvana, i.e. a state in which four things are lacking: birth, ageing, sickness and death.'

There has never been and will never be a myth that is bound up so strongly with a philosophical truth accessible to so few as this ancient doctrine of the noblest and oldest of peoples; however degenerate they might now be in many respects, this wisdom, in the form of a universal folk belief, still rules and has decisive influence on life today as much as it had four thousand years ago. That is why Pythagoras and Plato already admiringly adopted this insurpassable instance[d] of mythic presentation, passed down from India or Egypt,[87] revered it, applied it, and believed it themselves, although we do not know how far their beliefs went. – We, on the other hand, send English clergymen[e] and Moravian[f] linen-weavers out to the Brahmans now out of compassion and want them to know better and to understand that they are made of nothing and should be grateful and pleased about it.[88] But the same thing happens to us that happens to someone who fires a bullet at a rock. Our religions will absolutely never take root in India: the ancient wisdom of the human race will not be

---

[a] *Anschauungen*
[b] *wissen*
[c] *Non adsumes iterum existentiam apparentem* [*Oupnek'hat* I, 97: *Chāndogya Upanishad*, 8, 15]
[d] *non plus ultra*
[e] [Schopenhauer uses the English term]
[f] *Herrnhuterische*

displaced by the events in Galilee. On the contrary, Indian wisdom flows back to Europe and will change the very foundations of our knowledge[a] and thought.[89]

§ 64

But we now want to proceed from our presentation of eternal justice, which has not been mythic but rather philosophical, to the related consideration of the ethical significance of action and of conscience, which is the merely felt cognition of that significance. – At this point, however, I will first call attention to two peculiarities in human nature that can help clarify how everyone is conscious, at least in the form of an obscure feeling, of the essence of this eternal justice and of the unity and identity of the will in all its appearances, which is the basis for eternal justice.

After someone commits an evil deed, not only the aggrieved party (who is animated mostly by a thirst for revenge) but even spectators who are completely indifferent derive satisfaction when they see the one who inflicted pain suffering precisely the same amount of pain in return – and this satisfaction is entirely independent of the state's purpose in punishing (as we have demonstrated it), which is the basis of criminal law. I think this is simply an expression of precisely that consciousness of eternal justice, although it is immediately misunderstood and falsified by the unclarified intellect. Caught in the *principium individuationis*, this intellect falls into an amphiboly of concepts and demands of appearance that which applies only to the thing in itself. It does not see the extent to which the offending and the offended parties are one, and that it is the same being which, failing to recognize itself in its own appearance, suffers the misery as well as the guilt. Rather, this intellect demands to see pain inflicted on the very same individual bearing the guilt. – Take someone who manifests an exceptional degree of wickedness, something that can certainly be found in many people without being paired with other qualities that this particular man has as well, such as an intellectual power far surpassing that of other people, and which enables him to impose untold suffering on millions of others, for instance as world conqueror – most people would demand that such a person atone for all this suffering by somehow, somewhere, suffering an equal amount of pain. This is because people do not recognize that the tormenter and tormented are in themselves one; and that the very same will through which they live and exist appears in the tormenter as well,

[a] *Wissen*

and achieves the clearest revelation of its essence precisely through him. They do not realize that the will suffers in the oppressor just as it does in the oppressed, and in fact it suffers more in the former, to the extent that consciousness there has a greater clarity and the will a greater vehemence. – This more profound recognition – which is no longer caught in the *principium individuationis* and which gives rise to all virtue and magnanimity – no longer fosters a temperament disposed to retribution, a fact to which Christian ethics bears witness, since this ethics blankly forbids evil to be repaid with evil and leaves eternal justice to the realm of the thing in itself, which is different from the realm of appearance. ('Vengeance is mine, saith the Lord, I will repay,' Romans 12:19.)

There is a much more striking, albeit much less common feature of human nature that expresses this desire to draw eternal justice into the realm of experience, i.e. of individuation; this trait also demonstrates a felt consciousness that, as I expressed it above, the will to life performs the great tragedy and comedy at its own cost, and that one and the same will lives in all appearances. This feature, I say, is the following. We sometimes see a man so profoundly infuriated by a great injustice[a] he has experienced, or perhaps only witnessed, that he deliberately and irretrievably dedicates his whole life to taking revenge on the person who committed the atrocity. We see him spend years looking for a powerful oppressor, for instance, and finally kill him, only to die on the scaffold himself, as he had foreseen; in fact, he often does not even try to avoid his own death, since he valued his life only as a means for revenge. – You find examples of this amongst the Spanish in particular.* Now if we look carefully at the spirit of this quest for retaliation, we find that it is very different from common vengefulness,   424 which wants to reduce the suffering it experiences by looking at suffering it has caused: in fact, we find that the purpose of this quest does not deserve to be called revenge so much as punishment. This is because it truly intends to set an example which will have an effect on the future, an example that is indeed devoid of any selfish purpose for either the avenging individual (who is destroyed in the attempt) or for society (which secures its own safety through laws). This punishment comes from the individual, not the state; it does not fulfil any law, but instead always concerns a deed that the state could not or would not punish, and whose punishment it condemns.

---

* That Spanish Bishop who, during the last war [1808–1814], simultaneously poisoned himself and the French generals at his table, should be included here, along with many events in that war. You also find examples in Montaigne, Book 2, ch. 12.

[a] *Unbild*

It seems to me that the indignation that would drive a man so far beyond the boundary of any self-love springs from the deepest consciousness that he is himself the entire will to life (a will that appears in all beings through all times) and that the most distant future belongs to him in the same way the present does, and thus cannot be a matter of indifference. Affirming this will, he nonetheless demands that the drama which is a presentation of its essence never exhibit such a terrible injustice again. He wants to frighten anyone who might commit an atrocity in the future through the example of a revenge that thwarts any line of defence, since the avenger is not afraid to die. The will to life, although still affirming itself here, no longer depends on the particular appearance, the individual, but instead includes the Idea of humanity, and wants to keep the appearance of this Idea purified of such a monstrous and revolting injustice. It is a rare, highly significant, even sublime character trait that leads an individual to sacrifice himself by striving to make himself into the arm of eternal justice,[a] the true essence of which he still does not correctly see.

§ 65

All our observations so far concerning human action have paved the way for our final discussion; they have greatly facilitated the task of bringing to abstract and philosophical clarity, and establishing as part of our central line of thought, the true ethical significance of the actions that are described in life with the terms *good* and *evil*, and are thus made perfectly intelligible.

425

But first, I want to trace the concepts of *good* and *evil* back to their true meanings; oddly enough, contemporary philosophical authors treat these concepts as simple and thus incapable of analysis.[90] I want to trace back the meanings of these concepts so that people do not keep labouring under the delusion that they contain more than is really the case, and that they state everything they need to in and of themselves. I can do this because I do not intend to hide behind the word *good* in ethics any more than I hid behind the words *beautiful* and *true* earlier on, acting as if, by adding the suffix '-ness'[b] (which has a particular solemnity[c] these days and is supposed to help out in so many cases) and pulling a serious face, I have done anything more in pronouncing such words than simply state three very broad, abstract and thus completely insubstantial concepts, which

---

[a] *Gerechtigkeit*
[b] [In German, the words for beauty, truth and goodness all end with the suffix '-heit', whose closest English equivalent is '-ness']
[c] σεμνότης

have very different origins and meanings. Is there anyone familiar with the contemporary literature and who has not grown sick of these three words, however unimpeachable their original references might have been, after he has seen for the thousandth time how people who are incapable of thought believe they only need to bring forth those three words with open mouths and the air of an enthusiastic sheep, to be speaking great wisdom?

We have already explained the concept of the *true* in the essay *On the Principle of Sufficient Reason*, ch. 5, §§ 29ff. The content of the concept *beautiful* was made genuinely clear for the first time in the Third Book, taken as a whole. Now we want to trace the concept of *good* back to its meaning, which is easily done. This concept is essentially relative, and designates the *suitability*[a] *of an object to any particular effort of the will.* So anything that is agreeable to the will in any one of its expressions, that is conducive to its purpose, is intended in the concept of *good*, however different such things might be in any other way. That is why we talk about good food, good roads, good weather, good weapons, good omens, etc., in short, we call everything good that is just as we want it to be; that is why something can be good for one person but the opposite for another. The concept of the good falls into two sub-categories, namely that of directly satisfying some present will, and that of satisfying it only indirectly, sometime in the future: in other words, the pleasant and the useful. – When we discuss beings without cognition, the opposite concept is expressed through the word *bad*,[b] and less frequently and more abstractly through *troublesome*,[c] which means everything that is not conducive to the striving of the will in each case. As with all other beings that can entertain relations with the will, people also called human beings *good* if they were advantageous, favourable, and friendly to the goals that were being willed at the moment, with the same meaning, and always maintaining the relativity that is seen for instance in the expression: 'this is good for me but not for you'. Now it was in some people's character not to get in the way of the endeavours of the will of others, but rather to promote them, and they were thus thoroughly helpful, benevolent, friendly and charitable; they were called *good* human beings, because of the way their actions related to the wills of others in general. As far as the opposite concept is concerned, German speakers (and French speakers too, for the last hundred years or so) use a different word (namely *böse*,[d] *méchant*) to describe beings with cognition (animals and people)

426

---

[a] *Angemessenheit*
[b] *schlecht*
[c] *Uebel*
[d] [evil]

from the word used to describe beings without cognition; by contrast, almost no other language makes this distinction: κακος, *malus, cattivo, bad*, are used for human beings as well as inanimate things if they oppose the goals of a definite, individual will. Thus, having started entirely from the passive aspect of the good, our discussion could only take up the active aspect later, when it was no longer investigating the activities[a] of humans designated as *good* in relation to others, but in their own right. In particular, it could explain both the purely objective respect that such good actions inspire in others, as well as the characteristic gratification that human beings who are called good feel about themselves, since they purchase this feeling through a different sort of sacrifice. On the other hand, our discussion could also explain the inner pain that accompanies an evil disposition, however many advantages this disposition might bring to the person who fosters it. This is the origin of ethical systems, both philosophical ethics as well as ethics grounded in religious doctrine. Both sorts have always tried somehow to connect happiness with virtue, philosophical systems using either the principle of contradiction or the principle of sufficient reason, which is to say either by identifying happiness with virtue or by making the one a consequence of the other, always sophistically. In religious systems, the two are connected by the claim that there exist worlds different from the one we can possibly cognize in experience.*,[91] But in the course of our discussion, the inner essence of virtue will prove to be a striving that tends in a direction diametrically opposed to that of happiness, i.e. of well-being and life.

427

---

* We note in passing that what gives every positive religious doctrine its great strength, the main point by which it takes firm possession of people's minds, is wholly and exclusively its ethical aspect. But the ethical content does not take hold directly as such, but rather by joining forces with the rest of the mythological dogma distinctive to the doctrine, and insinuating itself as if only the myth could explain it. This goes so far that, although the ethical meaning of the action [*Handeln*] is not remotely explicable according to the principle of sufficient reason (each myth rather following this principle), nevertheless, the faithful consider the ethical meaning of action to be inseparable from their myth, even to the point of unity, and see every attack on the myth as an attack on justice and virtue. This goes so far that with the monotheistic peoples, atheism, or godlessness has become a synonym for an absence of all morality. The priests welcome such conceptual confusion, and only in consequence could that horrible monster, fanaticism come into existence and rule, not just over specific, particularly wrong-headed and evil individuals, but also over entire peoples. It finally embodied itself in the West in the form of the Inquisition, something which, to the credit of humanity, only took place once in its history; according to the most recent and definitively authentic reports, in Madrid alone over the course of 300 years 300,000 people were painfully killed at the stake for reasons of faith (and in the rest of Spain there were many similar spiritual dens of murderers): a fact that all zealots should be immediately reminded of as soon as they want to make themselves heard.

[a] *Handlungsweise*

Given what we have said, the *good*, according to its concept, is a relative thing,[a] which is to say that every good is[92] essentially relative: because its essence is to exist only in relation to a desiring will. *Absolute good* is thus a contradiction: highest good or *summum bonum* mean the same thing, denoting properly an ultimate satisfaction for the will, following which there will be no new willing, an ultimate motive whose accomplishment will give lasting satisfaction to the will. But according to the discussion   428
so far in this Fourth Book, such a thing is unthinkable. It is no more possible for some satisfaction to stop the will from willing new things than it is for time to begin or end. The will can have no lasting fulfilment that gives perfect and permanent satisfaction to its strivings. It is the vessel of the Danaids: there is no highest good, no absolute good for the will, but rather only ever a temporary good. But if we would like to retain an old expression out of habit, giving it honorary or *emeritus* status, as it were, we might figuratively call the complete self-abolition and negation of the will, the true absence of will,[b] the only thing that can staunch and appease the impulses of the will forever, the only thing that can give everlasting contentment, the only thing that can redeem the world, all of which we will discuss at the end of our whole investigation – we might call this the absolute good, the *summum bonum*. We can look upon it as the one radical cure for the disease against which all other goods – such as fulfilled wishes and achieved happiness – are only palliatives, only anodynes. In this sense, the Greek τέλος, like the *finis bonorum*, correspond even better to what we are discussing.[93] – So much concerning the words *good* and *evil*; now, to the matter itself.

If a human being is always inclined to do *wrong* as soon as the opportunity exists and no outside force restrains him, then we call him *evil*. Given our explanation of wrong, this means that this person not only affirms the will to life as it appears in his own body, but goes so far in this affirmation as to negate the wills that appear in other individuals. This is apparent in his demand that the strengths of others serve his own will, as well as his desire to eradicate the existence of others if they oppose the endeavours of his own will. This ultimately springs from a high degree of egoism, whose nature[c] we have described above. Two things are immediately apparent here: *first*, that an extremely violent will to life expresses itself in such a human being, a will that goes far beyond the affirmation of his own life; and *second*, that his cognition, devoted entirely to the principle of sufficient

[a] τῶν πρός τι
[b] *Willenslosigkeit*
[c] *Wesen*

429   reason and caught in the *principium individuationis*, remains fixed in the
total distinction between his own person and all others, the distinction put
in place by the *principium individuationis*. Thus, he only looks to his own
well-being, and is perfectly indifferent to that of everyone else; he treats
their existence as entirely foreign to his own and separated from him by a
wide gulf; in fact, he really looks on them only as masks, lacking reality. –
And these two characteristics are the basic elements of the evil character.

   This great violence of willing is already immediately and in and of itself
a constant source of suffering. First, because all willing as such comes from
want, and thus from suffering (which is why, as we recall from the Third
Book, the momentarily silencing of all willing, which begins as soon as we
give ourselves up to aesthetic contemplation as the pure, will-less subject of
cognition – the correlate of the Idea – is one of the main components of the
pleasure we feel in the beautiful). Second, because the causal connection
between things ensures that most desires must remain unfulfilled, and the
will is much more often thwarted than satisfied; as a result, violent and
profuse willing always entails violent and profuse suffering. This is because
all suffering is nothing other than unfulfilled and thwarted willing; even
the pain that results when the body is injured or destroyed is only possible
as such because the body is nothing but the will itself become object. – And
since profuse and violent suffering is inseparable from profuse and violent
willing, even the facial expressions of highly evil people bear the stamp
of inner suffering: even if they achieve external happiness, people like this
always look unhappy, except when they are caught in some momentary
glee or are acting insincerely. This inner misery is absolutely and directly
essential to them, and it ultimately gives rise to the selfless pleasure they
experience in the suffering of others, a pleasure that is not a function of
mere egoism; this is true *malice*[a] and increases to the point of *cruelty*.[b,94]
In cruelty, the suffering of others is no longer a means to achieving the
will's own purposes, but rather has become an end in itself. A more detailed
explanation of this phenomenon is as follows. Because the human being
430   is an appearance of the will illuminated by the clearest cognition, he
always measures the real and felt satisfaction of his own will against the
merely possible satisfaction that cognition presents to him. From this
comes envy: every deprivation is made infinitely worse by other people's
pleasure, and eased by the knowledge[c] that other people are undergoing

---

[a] *Bosheit*
[b] *Grausamkeit*
[c] *Wissen*

the same deprivation. The evils[a] that everyone experiences and that are inseparable from human life do not sadden us very much: it is the same with those that are a function of the climate or the entire country. Calling to mind sufferings greater than our own soothes our pain: the sight of other people's suffering alleviates our own. If someone is filled with an extremely violent impulse of the will and, burning with greed, wants to take hold of everything to slake the thirst of his egoism, in doing so he must necessarily experience the fact that all satisfaction is only illusory and that acquisition does not achieve what desire had expected, namely the ultimate quenching of the fierce impulse of the will. Instead, the fulfilment of a wish only alters its shape, so now it spreads its misery in a new form; and in fact, when all wishes are finally exhausted, the will retains its impulses even in the absence of any known motives, and these impulses announce themselves with incurable misery through a feeling of the most horrible desolation and emptiness. All of this is perceived only to a lesser degree at the usual levels of willing, and produces a common degree of dejection; but in someone in whom the appearance of the will rises to the point of exceptional malice, there will necessarily arise an excess of inner suffering, eternal unrest, incurable pain. He will try indirectly to find the relief that is not accessible directly; to be specific, he will try to mitigate his own sufferings through the sight of other people's, which he also recognizes to be the expression of his own power. The suffering of others now becomes for him an end in itself, a sight that he glories in: and thus arises the appearance of genuine cruelty, the thirst for blood that is so often seen in history, in the Neros and the Domitians, in the African Deys, in Robespierre, etc.

Vengefulness is already related to malice,[95] since it repays evil with more evil, not for the sake of the future (which is the nature[b] of punishment), but rather only because of what has happened, past events as such, and thus unselfishly, not as a means, but rather as an end, in order to glory in the suffering the avenger has personally caused to the offending party. What distinguishes revenge from pure malice and excuses it to some extent is the appearance of right; to be precise: if the same act that is now an act of vengeance were legal – i.e. carried out according to a previously determined and known rule in a sanctioning social context – it would be punishment, and thus right.

We have described a suffering that springs from the same root as malice, namely the extremes of a violent will, and thus is inseparable from it; but a

431

---

[a] *Uebel*
[b] *Charakter*

completely different and distinctive pain is associated with malice as well, a pain that can be detected in every evil action, whether it be a mere injustice committed out of egoism, or pure malice[96] itself; it is called either the *pang of conscience* or the *anguish of conscience*, depending on how long it lasts. – Anyone who has kept the themes of this Fourth Book fresh in his mind – and in particular the truth presented at the beginning, that for the will to life, life itself (as its image or mirror) is always certain – and who also recalls the presentation of eternal justice, such a person will find that, given these observations, the pangs of conscience can only mean the following – i.e. its content, expressed abstractly, is as follows. Two aspects can be distinguished in the following explanation, although these aspects coincide entirely and must be thought as completely united.

However densely the mind of someone evil is enveloped in the veil of *māyā*, i.e. however firmly he is caught in the *principium individuationis*, seeing his own person as utterly distinct and separated from everyone else by a wide gulf (cognition that he firmly embraces, because it is the only viewpoint that will serve and support his egoism, since this cognition is almost always corrupted by the will) – nevertheless, a secret presentiment arises in the innermost part of his consciousness, a presentiment that this order of things is merely appearance, and that, in itself, it is completely different. It makes him suspect that, to whatever extent time and space might present him as completely distinct from other individuals and divide him from these others and the countless miseries they suffer, indeed that he causes them to suffer, and present these as entirely foreign to him, nonetheless, in himself and apart from representation and the forms of
432 representation, it is one will to life that appears in them all, and which here, failing to recognize itself, turns its weapons against itself; through the very act of trying to increase the well-being of one of its appearances, this will imposes the greatest sufferings on another. The evil person suspects that he is this very will in its entirety, and is thus not only the tormenter but the tormented as well, and that it is only a delusional dream, whose form is space and time, that separates him and keeps him free from the other's suffering; but the dream vanishes and in reality he must pay for pleasure with misery, and all the suffering that he considered only as a possibility, in fact concerns *him*, as the will to life, since possibility and actuality, proximity and distance in time and space differ from each other only from the perspective of the cognition of the individual, only by means of the *principium individuationis*, not in themselves. It is this truth that is expressed mythologically – i.e. in conformity with the principle of sufficient reason and translated into the form of appearance – as transmigration

of the soul: but it has its purest and most unadulterated expression in precisely that obscurely felt but inconsolable misery that is called anguish of conscience.[a] – This, however, arises from a *second* immediate recognition as well, which is intimately connected to that first, namely recognition of the strength with which the will to life affirms itself in the evil individual, a strength that goes far beyond his individual appearance to the point of completely negating the same will as it appears in another individual. The inner horror that the evildoer experiences following his own deed, a horror that he tries to conceal even from himself, contains, along with that presentiment of the nothingness[b] and merely illusory nature of the *principium individuationis* and the distinction it posits between himself and others, the recognition of the intensity of his own will, of the violence with which he has grasped life and attached himself to it, this very life whose terrible aspect he has seen before him, through the agony of those he has oppressed, and with which he is nonetheless so closely entwined that he has himself given rise to its greatest terrors as a means to the more complete affirmation of his own will. He recognizes himself to be the concentrated appearance of the will to life, feels the extent to which he has been cast into life and the countless sufferings that are essential to it, since life has infinite time and infinite space in which to annul the distinction   433 between possibility and actuality and to transform all the miseries that he now merely *recognizes* into miseries that he can actually *feel*. The millions of years of constant rebirth exist only in theory, just as the whole past and future are only notional: only the present fills time and is the form of the appearance of the will, and time is always new for the individual: it always finds itself newly created. This is because life is inseparable from the will to life, and its form is only the now. Death (you will excuse the repetition of the simile) is like the setting of the sun that only seems to be devoured by night, but in truth, as the source of all light, burns without pause, bringing new days to new worlds, forever rising and forever setting. Beginnings and endings concern only the individual, through the medium of time, the form of this appearance for representation. Only the will lies outside of time, Kant's thing in itself, and its adequate objecthood, Plato's Idea. This is why suicide is not a solution: what each person *wills* in his innermost being, that is what he must *be*: and what he *is*, that is what he *wills*. – But, besides the merely felt cognition of the illusoriness and the nothingness of the forms of representation that separate individuals,

[a] *Gewissensangst*
[b] *Nichtigkeit*

there is the self-cognition of one's own will itself and its degrees, and this gives pangs to conscience. The course of life elaborates the image of the empirical character whose original[a] is the intelligible character, and the evil person is shocked by this image; it is all the same whether it is brought out in large features, so that the world shares his horror, or in small ones, that he alone can see, because he is the only one it directly concerns. The past, being mere appearance, would be indifferent and could not disturb anyone's conscience if the character did not feel itself to be free from all time and unchangeable by time, as long as it does not negate itself. That is why events from the distant past still weigh heavily on the conscience. The prayer: 'lead me not into temptation' means 'do not let me see who I am'. – In the violence with which the evil person affirms life, a violence that presents itself to him in the suffering he imposes on others, he estimates

434   how far he is from abandoning and negating that very will, which is the only possible redemption from the world and its miseries. He sees the extent to which he belongs to the world, and how tightly he is bound up with it: his *recognition* of the sufferings of others was not able to move him: he is cast into life and the *feeling* of suffering. It is an open question whether this suffering will ever break and overcome the violence of his will.

This explanation of the meaning and inner essence of *evil*, which, as a mere feeling, i.e. *not* as clear and abstract cognition, forms the content of the *anguish of conscience*, will become clearer and more complete from an investigation of the *good*, provided that the investigation is carried out in precisely the same way, viewing it as a characteristic of the human will, and finally investigating the complete resignation and holiness that comes from goodness once it attains its highest degree. Opposites always shed light on each other and the day reveals both itself and the night, as Spinoza wisely remarked.

§ 66

A morality without grounding,[b] which is to say mere moralizing, can never be effective, because it does not motivate. But a morality that *does* motivate can do so only by influencing self-love.[c] And what results from this has no moral value. It follows from this that true virtue cannot arise from morality or abstract cognition in general, but must come from intuitive cognition that recognizes in another individual the same essence as in its own.[97]

[a] *Original*
[b] *Begründung*
[c] *Eigenliebe*

Virtue does indeed come from cognition, but not from abstract cognition that can be communicated through words. If it did, then it could
be taught, and the abstract explanation we are giving here of the essence
of virtue and the cognition that grounds it would improve the ethics of
anyone who understands us. But this is by no means the case. Ethical
lectures and sermons are as little capable of producing a virtuous person
as aesthetics, from Aristotle's onward, has ever made a poet. Concepts are
barren when it comes to the true and inner nature[a] of virtue, just as they
are for art, and can only be used in an absolutely subordinate way, as tools
for elaborating and safeguarding things that we already know and have
resolved upon. *Velle non discitur.*[b] In point of fact, abstract dogmas have
no influence on virtue, i.e. on goodness of disposition: false dogmas do not
disturb it and true ones do little to promote it. And, in all honesty, it would
be very bad if the most important aspect of a person's life, its eternally valid
ethical worth, were to depend on something whose attainment is as subject
to chance as dogmas, theological doctrines, or philosophemes. The only
value dogmas have for morality is that they provide a schema or formula
for virtuous people whose cognition is already derived from elsewhere (as
we will soon discuss); such people can then use this formula to articulate a
(mostly fictitious) account of their own non-egoistic deeds for the benefit
of their own reason. They do not *comprehend* the true essence of their
non-egoistic deeds, but they are used to being satisfied with the account
they give.

But of course dogmas can have a powerful influence on *action*, on
external deeds, just as customs and examples can (the latter because the
ordinary human being is aware of the weaknesses in his judgement and does
not trust it, but instead only follows his own or other people's experience).
But none of this alters anyone's disposition.* Abstract cognition only ever
gives motives and, as we showed above, motives can only alter the direction
of the will, not the will itself. But any cognition that can be communicated
can act on the will only as a motive: so however much the will is guided by
dogmas, what the person really wills overall remains the same. The person
has simply received different ideas concerning the means for achieving it,
and imaginary motives direct him just like actual ones. Thus, for instance,
with respect to his ethical worth, it is all the same whether he gives large

435

---

* They are just *opera operata* [good works for the sake of merit] as the church would say, that do
  nothing unless grace sends the faith that leads to rebirth. More on this later.

[a] *Wesen*

[b] [willing cannot be taught: Seneca, *Epistles* 81, 13]

presents to people in need, firmly convinced that he will be repaid tenfold in a future life, or if he uses the same sum to improve an estate that will carry interest – later, of course, but all the more securely and substantially. And someone who delivers a heretic to the flames for the sake of orthodoxy is just as much a murderer as a bandit who kills for a reward; and in fact, according to inner circumstances, he is just as much a murderer as someone who massacres Turks in the Promised Land, if he also really does it because he thinks it will earn him a place in heaven. These are people who only care about themselves, about their egoism, just like the bandit, and they differ from the bandit only in the absurdity of their methods. – As I have already said, only motives can affect the will from the outside, and these alter only the way it expresses itself, never the will itself. *Velle non discitur.*

When someone appeals to dogmas in doing good deeds, we must distinguish whether these dogmas are the true motives or whether, as I said above, they are nothing more than an ostensible account that the person uses to try to satisfy his own reason concerning a deed that emanates from a completely different source. He does the deed because he is *good*, but does not know how to explain it properly because he is no philosopher; still, he would like to have something to think. But the difference is very difficult to discover, because it lies at the depths of his soul. Thus we can almost never morally[98] judge other people's deeds properly, and very seldom our own. – The deeds and the patterns of behaviour[a] of both individuals and peoples can be profoundly modified by dogmas, examples and customs. But in themselves, all deeds (*opera operata*) are just empty images that acquire moral significance only by virtue of the disposition that produces them. This disposition, however, can really be exactly the same through very different outer appearances. Someone who dies on the wheel can be just as wicked as someone who dies peacefully in the bosom of his family. The same ground of malice can express itself in *one* people in the crude characteristics of murder and cannibalism, and in *another* subtly and softly, in miniature,[b] through court intrigues, tyrannies and petty cabals of all sorts: the essence is the same. It is conceivable that all crime could be prevented by a perfect state, or perhaps merely by universal faith in a system of rewards and punishments after death. Politically, much would be gained – morally, nothing at all, just that life would be less of a mirror to the will.

Thus, a truly good disposition, disinterested[c] virtue, and nobility of mind do not begin with abstract cognition, but do nonetheless begin with

---

[a] *Handlungsweisen*
[b] *en miniature*
[c] *uneigennützige*

436

437

cognition – namely, an immediate and intuitive cognition that cannot be reasoned for or reasoned away, a cognition that cannot be communicated precisely because it is not abstract. This cognition must come from each person, and thus is not truly and adequately expressed in words, but only in deeds, in actions, in the course of a person's life. We, who are looking to virtue for a theory and must express abstractly the essence of the cognition that grounds it, we, nonetheless, will not be able to provide the cognition itself in this expression, but rather only the concept of it. We always begin with action, which is the only way this cognition becomes visible, and we refer to action as its only adequate expression, which we now interpret and analyse, i.e. we describe in abstract terms what really takes place in it.

Now before we start talking about genuine *goodness*, in contrast to what we presented of *evil*, we must, as an intermediate step, touch on the simple negation of evil: this is *justice*.[a] The nature of right and wrong has been sufficiently explained above, so here we can briefly say that someone who freely recognizes and acknowledges the exclusively moral boundary between wrong and right, even when it is not secured by a state or any other form of force, and, in accordance with our explanation, will never let the affirmation of their own will go to the point of negating the will presented in another individual, – such a person is *just*. He will not impose suffering on other people to enhance his own well-being:[99] i.e. he will not commit crimes, he will respect other people's rights and property. – We see now that for someone who is just, the *principium individuationis* is no longer the absolute barrier that it is for someone who is evil; that, unlike with someone evil, he does not affirm the appearance of his own will alone and negate all others; that other people are not just masks for him, entities whose essence is entirely different from his own. Instead, he shows in his way of acting[b] that he *recognizes* his own essence (namely the will to life as thing in itself) in foreign appearances that are given to him as mere representations, and thus rediscovers himself in these other appearances to a certain extent, namely that of doing no wrong, i.e. failing to cause harm.[100] This is the extent to which he sees through the *principium individuationis*, the veil of *māyā*: and to this extent, he equates the essence outside of himself with his own: he does not harm it.

If we look at the innermost nature of this justice, we see that it already contains the resolution not to affirm your own will to the point where it

438

---

[a] *Gerechtigkeit*
[b] *Handlungsweise*

negates other appearances of the will by forcing them to serve yours.[101] You will want to do as much for others as they do for you. At its highest level, this just disposition is only ever paired with genuine goodness (which is no longer merely negative), and goes so far as to cause a person to question his right to inherited property and want to maintain his body only by his own strength, mental and physical, to see every service rendered to him, every luxury, as a reproach, and finally to accept poverty freely. Thus, after *Pascal* turned to asceticism, he stopped letting people serve him, although he had plenty of servants: without regard for his constant illnesses, he made his own bed, fetched his own meals from the kitchen, etc. (*Life of Pascal, By his Sister*,[a] p. 19). Along the very same lines, it is reported that many Hindus,[102] even Rajas, only use their wealth to support their families, their court and their servants, and very scrupulously follow the maxim of eating nothing other than what they themselves have personally grown and harvested. But this rests on a certain misunderstanding: it is precisely because the individual is rich and powerful that he can render the whole of human society these enormous services that compensate for the inherited wealth whose security he owes to society. In truth, the excessive justice of these Hindus goes beyond justice, it is genuine renunciation, negation of the will to life, asceticism, which we will discuss last. Conversely, doing nothing and living on inherited wealth and other people's exertions without accomplishing anything can certainly be seen as morally wrong, even if it must remain right according to positive laws.

439

We have found that voluntary justice has its most intimate beginnings in an ability to see through the *principium individuationis* up to a point, while an unjust person remains completely trapped in this principle. This ability to see through the *principium individuationis* can take place not only up to the point required for justice, but to a greater extent as well, and this leads to positive benevolence and beneficence, to loving kindness.[b,103] And this can happen regardless of how strong and energetic the will appearing in such an individual might be in itself. Cognition can always act as a counterbalance, teaching him to resist wrong and giving rise to every degree of goodness, even resignation itself. Thus, the good human being can by no means be considered an originally weaker appearance of the will than the evil one; rather, cognition gains mastery in him of the blind impulses of the will. There are certainly individuals who only seem to be good-natured because of the weakness of the will that appears in them: but they are soon

---

[a] *Vie de Pascal, par sa soeur* [the actual title is: *Vie de Pascal, écrit par Madame Périer sa soeur*]
[b] *Menschenliebe*

exposed by their inability to overcome themselves to any great extent in order to carry out a just or good deed.

Let us take the rare and exceptional case of a human being in possession of a considerable income, who uses very little of it for himself and gives everything else to those in need, renouncing many pleasures and comforts. If we want to clarify this human being's deeds, then, apart from any dogma he might use to make himself intelligible to his own reason, we find, as the simplest, most general expression, the essential character of his way of acting,[a] that he *makes less of a distinction than is usually made between himself and others.* This holds true even though the distinction is so great in many other people's eyes that the suffering of others is a source of direct pleasure for malicious people, while unjust people[104] see it as a welcome means of promoting their own well-being; this holds true even though people who are merely just find it enough not to cause suffering; it holds true even though most people generally know[b] and are familiar with the countless sufferings of others in their vicinity and do not decide to alleviate them, because doing so would require some sacrifices[c] on their part. Although in each of these cases, a powerful distinction seems to be in effect between one's own I and that of others, this difference is not so significant for the noble-minded sort of person we are discussing. The *principium individuationis*, the form of appearance, no longer has him quite so tightly in its grip; the suffering he sees in others affects him almost as much as his own, so he tries to establish an equilibrium between the two, giving up pleasures and undertaking renunciations to alleviate other people's suffering. He is aware that the difference between himself and others, which is so great a gulf for the evil person, belongs only to a fleeting and illusory appearance: he recognizes, immediately and without inference, that the in-itself of his own appearance is the in-itself of other people's too, that it is the will to life, and that it constitutes the essence of every single thing and is alive in all things; indeed, he recognizes that this extends even to animals and the whole of nature: which is why he does not want to hurt animals either.*,[105]

440

---

* People's rights to the lives and powers of animals are based on the fact that, because suffering increases along with the increase in the clarity of consciousness, the pain that animals suffer in death or work is not as great as that which humans suffer by doing without meat or animal power. This is why people can affirm their existence to the point of negating the existence of an animal, and the will to life as a whole suffers less than if we acted the other way around. This also determines the extent to which people can make use of animals without doing wrong, an extent that is often exceeded,

[a] *Handlungsweise*
[b] *wissen*
[c] *Entbehrung*

Such a person is as little capable of letting other people starve while he himself has enough to spare as anyone would be of going without food one day so that the next day they could have more than they could enjoy. The veil of *māyā* has become transparent for this person, who is practised in works of love, and the delusion of the *principium individuationis* has deserted him. He recognizes himself, his will, in every being, and so in suffering beings as well. He is free of the perversity with which the will to life, failing to recognize itself, enjoys deceptive and fleeting pleasures in the one individual here, by suffering and starving in *another* one there, causing misery and enduring misery and not realizing that, like Thyestes, it is greedily consuming its own flesh. So it laments the undeserved suffering at one point and it commits outrages without fear of Nemesis at another, always and always only because it fails to recognize itself in the other appearance. Trapped in the *principium individuationis*, which is to say in the mode of cognition governed by the principle of sufficient reason, it does not perceive eternal justice. To be cured of this delusion and deception of *māyā* and to perform works of love are one and the same. But the latter is the inevitable symptom of that cognition.

The *good conscience*, the satisfaction we feel after every unselfish deed, is the opposite of the pangs of conscience whose origin and meaning were explained above. A good conscience comes from the fact that unselfish deeds, arising out of the immediate recognition of our own essence in other appearances, confirm the recognition that our true self does not exist only in the single appearance of our own person, but in every living thing. This makes the heart feel larger, in the same way that it contracts in egoism. Egoism concentrates our interest on the single appearance of our own individual, and cognition shows us the countless dangers that keep threatening this appearance; anxiety and concern become the fundamental tones of our mood. But in the same way, the recognition that all living things are part of our own intrinsic essence extends our interest to cover the whole of life, expanding our hearts. By diminishing our interest in our own self, our anxious self-solicitude is attacked at its root and confined: hence the peaceful, confident cheerfulness that a virtuous disposition and good conscience brings, a cheerfulness that appears more distinctly with every good deed, since every good deed is one more confirmation for ourselves of the reason for our mood. The egoist feels he is surrounded by alien

particularly with beasts of burden and hunting dogs. Societies for the Prevention of Cruelty to Animals are especially directed against these activities. In my opinion, this right does not extend to vivisection, particularly of the higher animals. On the other hand, an insect does not suffer from death as much as humans suffer from being stung. – Hindus fail to see this.

and hostile appearances, and all his hopes rest on his own well-being. The good person lives in a world of friendly appearances: the well-being of each of these appearances is his own well-being. Even if the recognition of the overall lot of humanity does not make his mood a happy one, the lasting recognition that his own being is in all living things lends his mood a certain constancy and even cheerfulness. This is because an interest that extends to countless appearances cannot be alarmed like an interest that is concentrated on a single *one*. The chance events that take place among the totality of individuals balance each other out, while those that befall the single individual bring good or bad luck.[106]

If other people lay down moral principles as prescriptions for virtue and laws to be followed, I on the other hand, cannot do this, as I mentioned above, since I do not have any laws or 'oughts' to present to the eternally free will. On the other hand, that aspect of my discussion that corresponds to and is somewhat analogous with that prescriptive project is the purely theoretical truth (and the whole of my presentation can be seen as merely a development of this truth), namely that the will is the in-itself of every appearance, and as such is itself free from the form of appearance, and thus from all multiplicity.[107] With regard to acting, I do not know how this truth can be expressed in a worthier manner than through that formula from the *Veda* already quoted: '*Tat tvam asi!*' ('You are that!')[108] Anyone who, with clear cognition and firm inner conviction, is able to declare this to himself about every being he encounters is certain of all virtue and bliss, and is on the direct path to redemption.

In the final part of my presentation, I will show how love, whose origin and essence we know to involve seeing through the *principium individuationis*, leads to redemption, namely the complete abandonment of the will to life, i.e. all willing, but also how another path, a path which, though not as smooth, is more frequently travelled, can bring a human being there. But before coming to this final theme I will first discuss and explain a 443 paradoxical claim, not because it is paradoxical but because it is true and is part of the complete thought I am presenting. It is this: 'All love (αγαπη, *caritas*) is compassion.'

§ 67

We have seen how justice comes from an ability to see through the *principium individuationis* to a lesser degree; and at a higher degree, this ability gives rise to a genuinely good disposition that manifests itself as pure, i.e. unselfish love of others. This is realized most perfectly when it equates the other individual and his fate with its own: but it can go no further than this, because there is no ground for preferring another individual over yourself. Of course if there is a threat to the collective well-being or the lives of the majority of individuals, this can outweigh any concern over your own individual welfare. In such a case, the character who has achieved the highest goodness and the most perfect magnanimity will sacrifice his life completely for the good of many others: this is how Codrus died, as well as Leonidas, Regulus, Decius Mus, Arnold von Winkelried, and everyone else who freely and consciously goes to a certain death for the sake of family or fatherland.[109] Also on this level is everyone who willingly suffers and dies for asserting claims that are in the collective interest of humanity and are part of the human patrimony, i.e. key, universal truths and the eradication of great errors: this is how Socrates died, as well as Giordano Bruno[110] and the many heroes of truth who met with death at the stake at the hands of the priests.

With respect to the paradox mentioned above, we should recall that earlier we found suffering to be essential and inseparable from life as a whole, and that every wish stems from a need, a lack, a suffering, which means that every satisfaction is only the removal of a pain, not a source of positive happiness, that joys certainly deceive desires by putting themselves forward as positive goods when in truth their nature is solely negative, only the termination of an evil.[a] The only thing that goodness, love and nobility can do for other people is alleviate their suffering, and consequently the only thing that can ever move them to perform good deeds and works of charity is the *cognition of other people's suffering*, which is immediately intelligible from one's own suffering and the two are considered the same.[b] From this, however, it follows that the nature of pure love (αγαπη, *caritas*) is compassion – compassion that alleviates the suffering that belongs to every unsatisfied desire, be it great or small. Thus, we will not hesitate to contradict *Kant* directly, who would only acknowledge true goodness and virtue as such when they emerge from abstract reflection, and in fact from the concept of duty and the categorical imperative, and who describes the feeling of compassion as a weakness, absolutely not as a virtue. We will say, in direct contradiction to Kant: the mere concept is as barren for true virtue as it is for true art: all true and pure love is compassion, and all love that is not compassion is selfishness.[c] Selfishness is ερως; compassion

444

---

[a] *Uebel*
[b] *gleichgesetzt*
[c] *Selbstsucht*

is αγαπη.[a] The two are frequently combined. Even true friendship is always a mixture of selfishness and compassion: the selfish component comes from our pleasure in the presence of the friend, whose individuality corresponds to our own, and this almost always constitutes the greatest part of friendship; compassion is apparent in our heartfelt participation in the friend's well-being and woe, and the selfless sacrifices made on account of the latter. Even Spinoza says 'Benevolence is nothing but a desire born of compassion'[b] (*Ethics*, III, Prop. 27, Cor. 3, Scholium).[III] As confirmation of our paradoxical claim we might note that the tones and words of the language and caresses of pure love are entirely in line with those of compassion: and also, in passing, that in Italian the word *pietà* means both compassion and pure love.

This is also the place to discuss one of the most striking peculiarities of human nature, that of *weeping*, which, together with laughing, is one of the expressions that distinguish us from animals. Weeping is certainly not a straightforward expression of pain, because people will weep at the slightest pain. In my opinion, we never weep right away when we feel pain, but only 445 when it is repeated in reflection. We pass from the sensation of pain, even if it is physical, to a mere representation of it; then we find our own situation so deserving of compassion that we firmly and sincerely believe that if another person were in it, we ourselves would be filled with compassion and love and would be ready to help. Now, however, we ourselves are the object of our own sincere compassion; with the most helpful and obliging of dispositions, we now find ourselves the ones in need of help; we feel that we are enduring more than we could see anyone else endure. In this peculiarly involved frame of mind, where the immediate feeling of suffering is perceived only via a double detour, imagined to be someone else's, sympathized with as such, and then suddenly perceived directly as our own again, – nature relieves itself by way of this peculiar physical convulsion. – Thus, *weeping* is *compassion for ourselves*, or compassion that has been directed back to its point of origin. As such, it is conditioned by a capacity for love and compassion, and also by the faculty of imagination: which is why hard-hearted people and those lacking imagination do not weep very easily, and weeping is even seen as a sign of a certain degree of goodness in a character; it can disarm anger because we feel that anyone who can still weep must also necessarily be capable of love, i.e. of compassion for other people, because this leads to the mood conducive to weeping

---

[a] [The Greek words for different kinds of love are usually transliterated as *eros* and *agape*]
[b] *Benevolentia nihil aliud est, quam cupiditas ex commiseratione orta*

in the way just described. – Petrarch describes the welling up of his own tears, with naïve and true feelings, in a manner completely in line with the explanation we have been offering:

> As I wander deep in thought,
> I am taken with *such a strong compassion for myself,*
> That I often must weep aloud;
> Which I am not otherwise inclined to do.[a]

446   What we have said is further confirmed by the fact that children in pain usually only weep when someone pities[b] them, which is to say not because of the pain but rather because of their idea[c] of the pain. – When we are moved to weep by someone else's suffering rather than our own, it is because we either vividly imagine ourselves in the place of the person who is suffering, or we see in the person's fate the lot of all humanity, and thus primarily our own, which means that in a very roundabout way we are still really only weeping for ourselves, feeling compassion for ourselves. This seems to be one of the main reasons for the general and therefore natural tendency to weep when someone dies. It is not his loss that causes the mourner to weep: he would be ashamed of such egoistic tears, but is instead sometimes ashamed of *not* weeping. At first of course he is lamenting the lot of the dead person: but he even weeps in cases where the person died after a long, difficult and incurable bout of suffering that made death a desirable release. He is mainly overcome with compassion for the lot of all humanity, which is cast into finitude, for the fact that every life, however ambitious and productive, must be extinguished and come to nothing. Above all, he sees his own lot in that of all humanity, and the more so the closer he was to the one who died, and thus most of all if it was his father. Even if age and illness had made life a misery to the father, and his helplessness had made him a heavy burden to the son, the son will nonetheless weep bitterly over the death of his father, and for the reasons we have given.*,[112]

---

* See chapter 47 of the second volume. It is hardly necessary to recall that the whole system of ethics presented in outline in §§ 61–7 has a more complete and detailed presentation in my prize essay *On the Basis of Morals.*

[a] *I vo pensado: e nel pensar m'assale* | Una pietà si forte di me stesso, | *Che mi conduce spesso,* | *Ad alto lagrimar, ch'i non soleva.* [*Il Canzoniere*, Canzone 21: Schopenhauer gives a prose translation in a footnote added in edition C (1859)]
[b] *beklagt*
[c] *Vorstellung*

§ 68

After this digression on how pure love is identical with compassion, and how compassion turned back onto the individual is the symptom of the phenomenon of weeping, I will take up the thread of our earlier discussion   447
of the ethical meaning of action; I will now show how from the same source that gives rise to all goodness, love, virtue and nobility there ultimately emerges also what I call the negation of the will to life.

We saw earlier that hatred and malice are conditioned by egoism and that these are based on cognition caught up in the *principium individuationis*. We also found that seeing through that *principium individuationis* is the origin and essence both of justice and, when it goes further, of love and nobility at the very highest levels. By eradicating the distinction between one's own individual and that of others, this is the only thing that makes possible and explains perfect dispositional goodness that goes as far as the most disinterested[a] love and the most generous self-sacrifice for the sake of others.

But if this seeing through the *principium individuationis*, this immediate cognition of the identity of the will in all of its appearances, is present at a high degree of clarity, then it will at once show an even greater influence on the will. If the veil of *māyā*, the *principium individuationis*, is lifted from a human being's eyes to such an extent that he no longer makes the egoistic distinction between his person and that of others,[b] but rather takes as much interest in the sufferings of other individuals as he does in his own, and is not only exceedingly charitable but is actually prepared to sacrifice his own individual as soon as several others can be saved by doing so, then it clearly follows that such a human being, who recognizes himself, his innermost and true self in all beings, must also regard the endless suffering of all living things as his own, and take upon himself the pain of the whole world. No suffering is foreign[c] to him anymore. All the miseries of others that he sees and is so rarely in a position to alleviate, all the misery he learns about indirectly or in fact only knows to be possible, all these affect his spirit as if they were his own. He no longer bears in mind the changing well-being and woe of his own person, as is the case with the human being still trapped in egoism; as he sees through the *principium individuationis*, everything is equally close to him. He recognizes the whole, comprehends   448
its essence, and finds that it is constantly passing away, caught up in vain

---

[a] *uneigennützigsten*
[b] *zwischen seiner Person und der fremden*
[c] *fremd*

strivings, inner conflict, and perpetual suffering. Wherever he looks, he sees the sufferings of humanity, the sufferings of the animal kingdom, and a fleeting, fading world. But this is now all just as close to him as only *his* own person is to the egoist. Given what he knows about the world, how could he affirm this very life by constant acts of will, binding himself ever closer to it, embracing it ever more tightly? If the one who is still caught in the *principium individuationis*, in egoism, recognizes only particular things and their relations to his own person, and these things are ever renewed sources of *motivation* for his willing, conversely, a recognition of the whole, of the essence of things in themselves such as we have described, becomes the *tranquillizer* of all and every willing. The will begins turning away from life: it shrinks from each of the pleasures in which it sees life being affirmed. A human being achieves the state of voluntary renunciation, resignation, true composure,[a] and complete will-lessness.[b] – But for those of us who are still caught in the veil of *māyā*, we sometimes gain a very intimate recognition of the nothingness and bitterness of life in the form of our own painful sufferings or our vivid recognition of the sufferings of others, and we would like to take the sting out of desire and prevent any suffering from coming in, to cleanse and sanctify ourselves through complete and lasting renunciation – but then we are quickly enmeshed in the delusion of appearance once more, and its motives put the will back into motion: we cannot tear ourselves away. The temptations of hope, the flatteries of the present, the sweetness of pleasure, the well-being that falls to our personal lot amid the distress of a suffering world ruled by chance and error, all this pulls us back and fastens our bonds once more. Thus Jesus says: 'It is easier for a camel to go through the eye of a needle, than for a rich man to enter into the kingdom of God.'[c]

If we compare life to a circular path made of red-hot coals with a few cool places, where we are forced to keep going around and around the circle, someone entrapped in delusion is comforted by the coolness of the place where he is standing at the moment or that he sees nearby, and he begins running over the path. But someone who has seen through the *principium individuationis* and recognizes the essence of things in themselves, and thus the whole, is not susceptible to such comfort: he sees himself on all points of the circle simultaneously, and steps away. – His will reverses course, and no longer affirms his own being, mirrored in appearance,

449

---

[a] *Gelassenheit*
[b] *Willenslosigkeit*
[c] [Matthew 19:24. Schopenhauer gives an unusual version of this famous passage. Apparently reading Greek *kamilos* for *kamêlos* in the original, he has 'anchor cable' [*Ankertau*] instead of the expected 'camel']

but negates it instead. The phenomenon in which this is revealed is the transition from virtue to *asceticism*. Specifically, he is no longer satisfied with loving others as himself and doing as much for them as for himself; instead, he has conceived a loathing for the essence that is expressed as his own appearance, the will to life, the kernel and essence of that world he recognizes as a miserable place. Accordingly, he renounces the essence that appears in himself and is already expressed through his body, and his deeds now belie his appearance and come into open contradiction with it. Since he himself is essentially nothing other than an appearance of the will, he stops willing anything, is careful not to let his will attach itself to anything, and tries to steel himself with the greatest indifference towards all things. – His body, healthy and strong, expresses the sex drive through its genitalia; but he negates the will and belies the body: he does not will sexual satisfaction under any conditions. Voluntary, perfect chastity is the first step in asceticism or negation of the will to life. By means of chastity, asceticism negates an affirmation of the will that goes beyond individual life,[113] and proclaims that the will appearing in the body abolishes itself along with the life of this body. Nature, always true and naïve, states that the human race would die out if this maxim were universal: and given what was said in the Second Book about the inter-connectedness of all the appearances of the will, I think I can assume that when the highest appearance of the will has fallen away, then animal existence, its weaker reflection, will fall away as well, just as the half-shadows disappear along with the full light. If cognition were entirely abolished, the rest of the world would fade into nothing too, because there is no object without a subject. I would even refer to a passage in the *Veda* where it states: 'As hungry children press around their mother in this world, all beings await the holy sacrifice.'[a] (*Asiatic Researches*, Vol. 8, Colebrooke, *On the Vedas*, the excerpt from *Sama-Veda*: also in Colebrooke's *Miscellaneous Essays*, Vol. I, p. 88.)[114] Sacrifice means resignation in general, and the rest of nature must wait to be redeemed by human beings, who are both priest and sacrificial victim. Indeed, it is a truly remarkable fact, well worth mentioning, that this thought was also expressed by the admirable and incalculably profound Angelus Silesius in the little verse entitled 'Man brings everything to God'; it goes:

> Man! Everything loves you; everything throngs to you:
> Everything flows to you, in order to achieve God.[b]

450

---

[a] [See *Chāndogya Upanishad* 5, 24, 5. Schopenhauer annotated his copy of the 1819 first edition with the reference '*Oupnek'hat* I, 50']

[b] [*Der Cherubinische Wandersmann*, I, 275]

But an even greater mystic, Meister Eckhart, whose marvellous writings are finally available to us in the edition by Franz Pfeiffer (1857), says (p. 459), entirely in keeping with the present discussion: 'I confirm this with Christ, since he says: and I, if I be lifted up from the earth, will draw all men unto me (John 12:32). So the good men should carry all things up to God, their first origin. The masters prove to us that all creatures are made for the sake of man. This is proved in all creatures by each creature using another: oxen use grass, fish use water, birds use air, animals use the forest. Thus are all creatures useful to the good man: the good man carries one creature in another to God.' He wants to say: in exchange for redeeming the animals in and with themselves, human beings make use of them in this life. – It seems to me that the difficult passage in the Bible, Romans 8:21–4, should be interpreted in this sense.

Buddhism too does not fail to mention this theme: for instance, when Buddha, still as Bodhisattva, saddled his horse for the last time in his flight from his father's residence into the wilderness, he spoke this verse to his horse: 'You have existed a long time in life and in death; but now you should stop carrying and dragging things about. Take me away from here 451   this one last time, O Kanthaka,[a] and when I have achieved the Law (have become Buddha), I will not forget you.' (*Foe Koue Ki*, trans. Abel Rémusat, p. 233.)[115]

Asceticism is further manifested in voluntary and intentional poverty, which does not arise only accidentally,[b] by giving away property to alleviate other people's suffering, but as a goal in itself, and should serve as a constant mortification of the will, so that no satisfaction of wishes, the sweets of life, can excite the will loathed by self-knowledge.[c] Anyone who has reached this point will continue to sense a tendency for all sorts of willing, since he is still an animated body and concrete appearance of the will: but he intentionally suppresses[d] this by compelling himself not to do anything he really wants to do, and instead doing everything he does not want to, even when this serves no further purpose other than to mortify the will. Since he himself negates the will that appears in his own person, he will not resist it when someone else does the same to him, i.e. does him wrong;[116] that is why he welcomes every bit of suffering that comes to him from the outside, through chance or by someone's malicious actions, every harm, every injury, every disgrace, every insult: he receives them cheerfully, as an opportunity for assuring

---

[a] *Kantakana*
[b] *per accidens*
[c] *Selbsterkenntniß*
[d] *unterdrückt*

himself that he no longer affirms the will; rather, he cheerfully sides with everyone hostile to the expression of the will that is his own person. This is why he endures such insults and suffering with inexhaustible patience and gentleness, unaffectedly repays all evil with good, and does not allow the fire of rage to be rekindled within him any more than the flames of desire. – As he mortifies the will itself, he also mortifies its manifestation, its objecthood, the body: he feeds it meagrely, so that its exuberant thriving and prospering will not revive or stir up the will, of which he is merely the expression and mirror. So he takes to fasting, he takes to castigation and self-torture in order to keep breaking and deadening the will through constant deprivation and suffering, since he recognizes and abhors the will as the source of his own suffering existence and that of the world. – When death finally arrives to dissolve the appearance of that will whose essence had already died here long ago through voluntary self-negation, with the exception of the feeble remnant that appeared as the vitality of this body, this death is highly welcome and will be received cheerfully as a longed-for redemption. Death, in this case, does not just bring an end to appearance, as in other cases; rather, the essence itself is abolished, that essence that led only a feeble existence in and through appearance;*,[117] and this last, brittle bond has now been broken too. When someone comes to an end in this manner, the world comes to an end at the same time.

452

And what I have described here with a feeble tongue and general terms is not some philosophical fable I invented about the present: no, it was the enviable life of a great many saints and beautiful souls[a] among the Christians, and even more among the Hindus and Buddhists,[118] as well as among practitioners of other faiths. Despite the vast differences in the dogmas imprinted on their reason, these people conducted their lives in ways that gave identical expression to the inner, immediate, intuitive cognition from which all virtue and holiness spring. Because here too, we see the distinction between intuitive and abstract cognition, a distinction that has been so important, and that has extended to all aspects of our discussion, but that has received too little attention so far. When it comes to cognition of the essence of the world, there is a wide gulf between the

---

* This thought is expressed in a nice parable in the ancient philosophical Sanskrit writing *Sankhya Karika* [*Sānkhya Kārikā*, 67]: 'Nonetheless, the soul remains a while clothed in the body; just as a potter's wheel continues to turn after the pot has been finished, because of the push it received earlier. Only when the enlightened soul is separated from the body, and nature ends for it, does complete redemption come.' Colebrooke, *On the Philosophy of the Hindus: Miscellaneous Essays*, Vol. I, p. 259. Also in the *Sankhya Carica* by Horace Wilson, § 67, p. 184.

[a] *schöner Seelen*

two kinds of cognition that only philosophy can traverse. In fact, everyone is conscious of all philosophical truths on an intuitive level or in concrete fashion:[a] but to bring these truths to abstract knowledge,[b] to reflection, is the business of philosophers, who should do, and can do, nothing else.

453   This might be the first time that the inner nature[c] of holiness, self-denial, asceticism, and the mortification of one's own will has been expressed abstractly, cleansed of all mythology, as the *negation of the will to life*, which comes on the scene after complete recognition of its own essence has become a tranquillizer of all willing. On the other hand, all of those saints and ascetics have recognized it directly and expressed it through deeds; although they have the same inner recognition, they articulate it in very different ways, according to the dogma each has rationally accepted. This leads Indian, Christian and Lamaist saints to account for their own deeds in very different ways, but this does not matter in the least. A saint can be full of the most absurd superstitions, or conversely he can be a philosopher: it makes no difference. Only his deeds confirm him to be a saint: because morally, his deeds do not come from abstract cognition, but from an intuitively grasped, direct cognition of the world and its essence, and he filters this through some dogma only to satisfy his reason. That is why it is just as unnecessary for the saint to be a philosopher as it is for a philosopher to be a saint: just as it is completely unnecessary for a perfectly beautiful person be a great sculptor or a great sculptor to be beautiful. In general, it is strange to demand that a moralist not recommend any virtues other than the ones he himself possesses.[119] To use concepts that abstractly, universally and clearly reflect the whole essence of the world, and to transcribe a reflected image of the world into permanent concepts that are always available to reason: this and nothing else is philosophy. I recall the passage from Bacon of Verulam quoted in the First Book.[d]

   But the description I gave above of the negation of the will to life or the conduct[e] of a beautiful soul, of a resigned, voluntarily penitent saint, was itself only abstract, universal, and therefore cold. Since the cognition that gives rise to the negation of the will is intuitive and not abstract, it is not expressed perfectly through abstract concepts either, but rather only through deeds and conduct. Thus in order to get a better understanding of what we expressed philosophically as the negation of the will to life,

[a] *in concreto*
[b] *Wissen*
[c] *Wesen*
[d] [See 109 above]
[e] *Wandel*

people will need to familiarize themselves with examples from experience   454
and reality. Naturally, we will not encounter these in everyday experience:
'because everything of excellence is as difficult as it is rare',[a] as Spinoza
put it most excellently. So unless a particularly lucky fate makes us an
eyewitness, we must content ourselves with the biographies of such people.
Indian literature, as we know from the little that has been translated so
far, is very rich in descriptions of the lives of saints, penitents, Samanas,[120]
sannyasis, etc. Even the famous *Mythology of the Hindus*[b] by Madame de
Polier, although certainly not admirable in every respect, contains many
excellent examples of this sort (particularly in the thirteenth chapter of the
second volume). Among Christians too, there is no lack of examples of
what we are describing. Just read the (often poorly written) biographies
of the people who are sometimes termed holy souls, sometimes pietists,
quietists, pious enthusiasts, etc. Collections of such biographies have come
out at various times, such as Tersteegen's *Lives of Holy Souls*,[c] Reiz's *Histories
of People Who Have Been Born Again*,[d] and in our times a collection by
Kanne that contains some good along with a lot that is bad, one good part
in particular being the 'Life of Beata Sturmin'. The life of St Francis of
Assisi certainly belongs here too, this true personification of asceticism and
model for all mendicant friars. His life, described by his younger contemporary, St Bonaventure, who is also famous as a Scholastic, has recently
been republished: *Vita S. Francisci a S. Bonaventura concinnata* (Soest,
1847), shortly after the appearance in France of a thorough, detailed biography that drew on all sources: *History of St. Francis of Assisi*[e] by Chavin
de Mallan (1845). – As an oriental parallel to these monastic writings we
have the highly worthwhile book by Spence Hardy, *Eastern Monachism,
an account of the order of mendicants founded by Gotama Budha* (1850).[f]
It shows us the same phenomenon[g] in different attire. You also see how
little it matters whether it comes from a theistic or atheistic religion.[121] –   455
But I can recommend the autobiography of Madame de Guyon in the highest terms, as a particular, carefully detailed example and factual description
of the concepts I am advancing. The memory of this great and beautiful

---

[a] *Nam omnia praeclara tam difficilia quam rara sunt.* [*Ethics*, V, Prop. 42, Schol.]
[b] *Mythologie des Indous*
[c] *Leben heiliger Seelen*
[d] *Geschichten der Wiedergeborenen*
[e] *Histoire de S. François d'Assise*
[f] [The book is by Robert Spence Hardy and is entitled: *Eastern Monachism: An Account of the Origin,
Laws, Discipline, Sacred Writings, Mysterious Rites, Religious Ceremonies and Present Circumstances of
the Order of Mendicants*]
[g] *Sache*

soul always fills me with awe; to get to know her and to do justice to her
disposition, allowing for the superstitions of her reason, must be gratifying
to every person of a better sort, while the book will always be discredited
by common thinkers, i.e. the majority. This is because always and everywhere, people can only find value in things that are somewhat analogous
with themselves, things for which they at least have a weak talent. This
holds for intellectual as well as ethical matters. To a certain extent, we could
even consider the famous French biography of Spinoza as a relevant example, if we use the excellent introduction to his unsatisfying essay *Treatise
on the Improvement of the Intellect*[a] as a key to it. I can also recommend this
text as the most effective means I know of soothing the storms of passion.
Finally, even the great Goethe, as Greek as he was, did not consider it
beneath himself to show us this most beautiful side of humanity in the
clarifying mirror of poetry, by presenting an idealized life of Fräulein Klettenberg, in *Confessions of a Beautiful Soul*, and later, a historical report of it
in his own biography. Besides this, he recounted the life of St Philippo Neri
on two different occasions.[122] – The history of the world will, and indeed
must, always remain silent about these people whose conduct is the best
and only adequate illustration of this important point in our discussion.
This is because world history has a completely different, indeed opposite
content: it is not the negation and abandonment of the will to life, but
rather precisely its affirmation and appearance in countless individuals –
an affirmation and appearance in which its self-dichotomy emerges in full
clarity at the highest peak of its objectivation. What world history places
before our eyes is sometimes the ascendancy of the individual through
his cleverness, sometimes the violence of the crowds through their mass,
sometimes the power of chance, which has been personified into fate, but

456   always the futility and nothingness[b] of the whole of striving. But we are not
here to trace the thread of appearances through time; as philosophers, we
want to investigate the ethical meaning of actions and take this as the only
standard for what is meaningful and important to us. We will not let the
permanent majority of the vulgar and insipid prevent us from acknowledging that the greatest, most important and most significant appearance that
the world can show us is not someone who conquers the world, but rather
someone who overcomes it; and this is, in fact, nothing other than the
quiet, unnoticed life of someone who has achieved the cognition that leads
him to renounce and negate the will to life that fills all things and drives

[a]   *De Emendatione Intellectus*
[b]   *Nichtigkeit*

and strives in all things. The freedom of this will first emerges in him alone, making his deeds anything but ordinary. Thus, as badly written as these biographies usually are, and even though they are mixed with superstition and nonsense, the significance of the material makes these descriptions of the lives of holy, self-denying human beings incomparably more instructive and important for the philosopher than even Plutarch and Livy.

We will go a long way towards a fuller and more detailed understanding[a] of what we are calling (in the abstraction and universality of our mode of presentation) the negation of the will to life, if we also consider the ethical injunctions issued in this regard by people filled with its spirit. These will also demonstrate how venerable our view is, however new its purely philosophical expression might be. Christianity is closest to us; its ethics are entirely in the spirit of our present discussion, and lead not only to the highest degree of loving kindness[123] but also to renunciation. This final aspect was already clearly present in embryonic form in the writings of the Apostles, although it was fully developed and explicitly articulated only later. We find the Apostles prescribing: love of our neighbour as ourselves; beneficence; repayment of hatred with love and good deeds; patience; gentleness; the tolerance of all possible insults without resistance; abstinence in eating for the suppression of desire; resistance to the sex drive (complete resistance, if possible). We already see here the first stages of asceticism, or the genuine negation of the will, this last expression meaning just what in the Gospels is called denying the self and taking the cross upon oneself (Matthew 16:24–5; Mark 8:34–5; Luke 9:23–4; 14:26–7, 14:33).[124] This tendency was soon developed further, and gave rise to penitents, anchorites and monasticism; this origin, in itself pure and holy, was for this reason utterly unsuitable for the vast majority of people, and therefore what developed from it could only be hypocrisy and abomination: the abuse of the best is the worst of abuses.[b,125] In more highly developed Christianity, we see that *ascetic* seed coming into full blossom through the writings of the Christian saints and mystics. Along with the purest love, they also preach full resignation, voluntary and complete poverty, true composure,[c] perfect indifference towards all worldly things, the deadening of one's will and rebirth in God, the complete forgetting of one's own person and absorption into the intuition of the divine. A complete presentation of this is found in Fénélon's *Explanation of Maxims of the Saints concerning*

457

---

[a] *Kenntniß*
[b] *abusus optimi pessimus*
[c] *Gelassenheit*

the Inner Life.[a] But certainly, nowhere is the spirit of this development of Christianity so perfectly and powerfully expressed as in the writings of the German mystics, which is to say Meister Eckhart, and in the justly famous book *The German Theology*;[b] in his preface, Luther wrote that no other book, except for the Bible and Augustine,[126] taught him as much about the nature of God, Christ and humanity as this book did, – nonetheless we did not receive Meister Eckhart's true and genuine text until *Pfeiffer*'s 1851 Stuttgart edition.[127] It presents injunctions and doctrines that arise from a deep and most intimate conviction, and offers the perfect explanation of what I have presented as the negation of the will to life. Thus, one must get to know it more closely before one can dispute it with Jewish-Protestant confidence.[128] Tauler's *Imitation of Christ's Life of Poverty*,[c] together with his *Marrow of the Soul*[d] are written in the same exceptional spirit, although they are not to be valued quite as highly as that other work. In my opinion, the teachings of these true Christian mystics bear the same relation to the teachings in the New Testament that spirits of wine bear to wine itself. Or: what is visible to us in the New Testament as if through veils and mist confronts us in the works of the mystics, uncovered and in full clarity. Finally, one could regard the New Testament as the first consecration and the mystics as the second – small and great mysteries.[e,129]

But in the ancient Sanskrit works we find the phenomenon that we are calling the negation of the will to life developed more fully, presented more vividly, and expressed in a more comprehensive manner than could be the case in the Christian church and the Western world. The fact that this important ethical view of life could still be decisively expressed and continuously developed there is perhaps due mainly to the fact that it is not restricted by a completely alien element, which is what the Jewish doctrine is within Christianity. The sublime author of Christianity had to adapt and accommodate himself, in part consciously and in part perhaps even unconsciously to this Jewish doctrine. Christianity is put together from two very heterogeneous components; the purely ethical component is what I would call the primarily, or even exclusively Christian element, and I would distinguish it from the Jewish dogmatism with which it is found. If, as has often been feared, and particularly at present, that excellent and salutary religion were ever to be entirely corrupted, I would locate the reason solely

---

[a] *Explication des maximes des Saints sur la vie intérieure*
[b] *Die deutsche Theologie*
[c] *Nachfolgung des armen Lebens Christi* [The title should read: *Von der Nachahmung des armen Lebens Christi* but was not in fact written by Tauler]
[d] *Medulla animae*
[e] σμικρα χαι μεγαλα μυστηρια [Ceremonies celebrated by the Athenians in March and October]

in the fact that it does not come from a simple element, but rather from two originally heterogeneous elements that have only been brought together in the course of world history. The dissolution would come from these elements breaking apart due to their unequal relations and reactions to the spirit of the contemporary age; but after this, the ethical component would nevertheless necessarily remain intact, because it is indestructible. – Although our acquaintance with Hindu literature is still very imperfect, we find its ethics expressed in a most diverse and powerful manner in the *Vedas, Puranas,* poetic works, myths, legends of the holy men, maxims, and rules of life,*,a and we see prescribed: love of the neighbour with a complete denial of all self-love; love not at all restricted to the human race, but rather encompassing all living things;[130] beneficence to the point of giving away one's hard-won daily earnings; unlimited patience with all insults; repaying everything evil, however bad, with goodness and love; free and cheerful endurance of every disgrace; abstinence from the consumption of animals; complete chastity and renunciation of all pleasure^b for those who strive for true holiness; throwing away all possessions, abandoning every home and all relations, deep and total solitude spent in silent contemplation with voluntary penitence and terrible, slow self-torture to completely mortify the will, which finally goes to the point of voluntary death by starvation, or by meeting crocodiles head-on, by throwing yourself over the sacred precipice in the Himalayas, by being buried alive in a grave,[131] or also by throwing yourself under the wheels of the immense cart that drives around with divine images amid the singing, jubilation and dancing of the bayaderes. And as degenerate as this people might be in many respects, these four thousand year-old injunctions are still followed, even to the furthest extremes in certain individuals.**,132 What has been practised for so long among a people that numbers into the millions, while imposing

459

460

---

* See for instance the *Oupnek'hat, studio Anquetil du Perron,* Vol. 2, no. 138, 144, 145, 146 [i.e. the *Jábála, Paramahamsa, Áruneya* and *Kena Upanishads*] – *Mythology of the Indians,* by Madame de Polier, Vol. 2, chs. 13–17. – *Asiatisches Magazin,* by Klaproth, in the first volume: 'Ueber die Fo-Religion' ['On the Fo-Religion']; and also 'Bhaguat-Geeta' or 'Gespräche zwischen Kreeshna und Arjoon' ['*Bhagavadgītā* or *Dialogues between Krishna and Arjuna*']; in the second volume: 'Moha-Mudgava' [correctly *Moha-Mudgara*] – And *Institutes of Hindu-Law, or the ordinances of Menu* [correctly *Manu*] from the Sanskrit by Wm. Johns, German by Hüttner (1797); particularly the sixth and twelfth chapters. – Finally, many places in the *Asiatic researches.* (In the past forty years the Indian literature in Europe has grown to such an extent that if I wished to complete this note from the first edition it would fill several pages.)

** In the procession of the Juggernaut [*Jagan-nātha*] in June of 1840, eleven Hindus threw themselves under the cart and were instantly killed. (Letter of an East Indian landowner in the *Times* from 30 December 1840.)

^a *Lebensregeln*
^b *Wollust*

the most difficult sacrifices,[133] can really not just be an arbitrary whim, but must have grounds in human nature.[a] But you cannot wonder enough at the similarities you find when you read about the life of a Christian penitent or saint and that of an Indian. The two have exactly the same strivings and inner lives, despite such fundamentally different dogmas, customs and environments. Their injunctions are also the same: so for instance, Tauler speaks of the total poverty that you are supposed to seek, which consists in fully relinquishing and abandoning everything that might provide comfort or worldly pleasure, clearly because all this is a constant source of nourishment for the will, while the intention is to deaden it completely. And as the Indian counterpart, we see Fo[b] telling the sannyasi, who is supposed to be homeless and without belongings, that he should not lie down under the same tree too often lest he develop a preference or inclination for that tree. The Christian mystics and the teachers of the Vedanta philosophy also agree that all external works and religious practices are to be regarded as superfluous for someone who has achieved perfection.[134] – So many points of agreement in spite of such different times and peoples is a factual proof that what is expressed here is not some craze or eccentricity, as optimistic platitudes would have it, but rather an essential side of human nature that rarely comes forward only because of its excellence.

I have now provided the sources where people can familiarize themselves directly, using instances drawn from life, with the phenomenon in which the negation of the will to life presents itself. This is, in many ways, the most important point of our whole investigation: nonetheless, I have mentioned it only in general terms, since it is better to refer to people who speak from immediate experience than to lengthen this book unnecessarily by offering a feeble repetition of what they have said.

461   I will only add a few more things to the general description of the situation. We saw above that the evil person suffers constant, searing, inner misery through the violence of his will, and that when all objects of willing are exhausted, he finally cools the vicious thirst of his self-will in the sight of other people's pain. In comparison, if the negation of the will has arisen in someone, that person is full of inner joy and true heavenly peace, however poor, joyless and deprived his situation might look from the outside. This is not the restless impulse of life, the cry of jubilation that is conditioned by a preceding or succeeding bout of violent suffering, which constitutes

[a] *Wesen der Menschheit*
[b] [i.e. Buddha]

the behaviour of someone with a lust for life. Rather, it is an imperturbable peace, a profound calm and inner serenity; and when we behold this person with our eyes or in our imagination, we cannot help feeling the greatest longing, since we acknowledge that this alone is in the right and infinitely superior to everything else, and our better spirit calls to us the great 'Dare to know'.[a] We feel very keenly that every fulfilled wish we wrest from the world is really like alms that keep the beggar alive today so that he can starve again tomorrow; resignation on the other hand is like an inherited estate: it frees its possessor from all cares forever.

We may recall from the Third Book that the aesthetic pleasure in the beautiful largely consists in the fact that we have entered into a state of pure contemplation, momentarily suppressing all willing, i.e. all desires and concerns. We are free of ourselves, as it were; we are no longer the individual correlated with the individual thing, whose cognition is at the behest of its constant willing, for whom objects become motives; we are instead the eternal subject of cognition, cleansed of the will,[b] correlated with the Idea. And we know[c] that these moments, when we are released from the cruel impulses of the will and emerge from the heavy ether of the earth, are the most blissful ones we experience.[d] We can gather from this how blissful life must be for someone whose will is not merely momentarily placated, as it is in the pleasure of the beautiful, but calmed forever, indeed extinguished entirely except for the last glowing spark that sustains the body and is extinguished along with it. Such a person who, after many bitter struggles with his own nature, has ultimately prevailed completely, remains as only a pure, cognizing being, as an untarnished mirror of the world. Nothing can worry him anymore, nothing more can excite him, because he has cut all the thousands of threads of willing that keep us bound to the world and which, in the form of desires, fears, envy and anger, drag us back and forth amid constant pain. He gazes back calmly and smiles back at the phantasm of this world that was once able to move and torment his mind as well, but now stands before him as indifferently as chess pieces after the game is over, looking like discarded masks the morning after Carnival, although their forms taunted and disturbed us the night before. Life and its forms merely glide before him, like a fleeting appearance, like a gentle morning dream that floats by someone who is half awake, where reality is already shining through and cannot deceive anymore. And just like this dream, life

462

[a] *sapere aude*
[b] *willensreine*
[c] *wissen*
[d] *kennen*

and its forms finally disappear without any violent transition. From these considerations we can learn to understand what *Guyon* means when, at the end of her autobiography, she often expresses herself as follows: 'Everything is indifferent to me: I *cannot* will anything any longer: I often do not know whether or not I exist.' – In order to express how, after the will dies out, there can be nothing bitter about the death of the body (which is, of course, only the appearance of the will, and thus loses all meaning when the will is suppressed), and this death is in fact very welcome, – I may be permitted to record the words of that holy penitent herself, although they are not used in a very graceful manner: 'the high noon of glory: a day no longer followed by night; a life that no longer fears death, even in death itself: because death has overcome death, because whoever has suffered the first death will no longer feel the second death'[a] (*Life of Madame de Guyon*,[b] Vol. 2, p. 13).

In the meantime, we must not think that, after cognition has become a tranquillizer of the will and given rise to the negation of the will to life, it will never falter and that it can be relied upon like inherited property. Rather, it must constantly be regained by steady struggle. Since the body is the will itself, but in the form of objecthood or as appearance in the world as representation, then as long as the body lives, the whole will to life still exists as a possibility[c] and constantly strives to enter actuality and flare up again in all its blazing heat. Thus we find that the peace and blissfulness we have described in the lives of saintly people is only a flower that emerges from the constant overcoming of the will, and we see the constant struggle with the will to life as the soil from which it arises; on earth nobody can have lasting peace. This is why the history of the inner life of the saints is full of spiritual struggles, temptations, and the desertion of grace, i.e. of that mode of cognition that renders all motives ineffective, that serves as a universal tranquillizer to quell all willing, providing the most profound peacefulness and opening the door to freedom. Thus we also see people who have succeeded at some point in negating the will bend all their might to hold to this path by wresting renunciations of every sort from themselves, by adopting a difficult, penitent way of life and seeking out everything they find unpleasant: anything in order to subdue the will that will always strive anew. Hence, because they already recognize the value of

463

---

[a] *Midi de la gloire; jour où il n'y a plus de nuit; vie qui ne craint plus la mort, dans la mort même: parceque la mort a vaincu la mort, et que celui qui a souffert la première mort, ne goutera plus la seconde mort.*

[b] *Vie de Mad[ame] de Guion* [*Vie de Madame de Guion, écrite par elle-même*, Cologne, 1720. See II, 2, p. 13]

[c] *ist... seiner Möglichkeit nach da*

redemption, their anxious concern to hold on to this achieved salvation,[a] the scruples of conscience at every innocent pleasure or every small impulse of their vanity; and here too, vanity is the last thing to die, since it is the most indestructible, most active, and the most foolish of all the tendencies of humanity. – I have often used the expression *asceticism*, and I understand by it, in the narrow sense, this *deliberate* breaking of the will by forgoing what is pleasant and seeking out what is unpleasant, choosing a lifestyle of penitence and self-castigation for the constant mortification of the will.

Now if we see someone who has already achieved the negation of the will taking measures to maintain himself in that state, then suffering in general, as it is meted out by fate, offers a second way (δευτερος πλους[*,135]) of achieving this. Indeed, we can assume that most people can only come to it in this way, and that it is the personal *experience* of suffering – not just the *recognition* of suffering – that most frequently leads to a full resignation, often not until the presence of death. Only a very few people find it enough to begin with pure cognition which, seeing through the *principium individuationis*, first produces the most perfect goodness of disposition and universal human kindness, ultimately enabling them to recognize all the suffering in the world as their own, thus bringing about the negation of the will. Even with people who have approached this point, it is almost always the case that their own tolerable situation, the flattery of the moment, the temptation of hope, and the always recurring chance to satisfy the will, i.e. desire, will be constant obstacles to negating the will and constant temptations to affirming it again. That is why, in this respect, people have personified all those temptations as the devil. For the most part, the will must be broken by personal experience of great suffering before its self-negation can come into play. Then we see a man who has gone through all the stages of increasing difficulty[136] brought to the brink of despair amid the most violent resistance, – we see him suddenly retreat into himself, recognize himself and the world, change his whole being, raise himself above himself and all suffering; purified and sanctified by this suffering, with unassailable peace, blissfulness and sublimity, we see him willingly[b] renounce everything that he had previously desired with such violent intensity, and cheerfully embrace death. This silver gleam is the negation of the will to life, i.e. redemption, that suddenly emerges from

464

---

* Concerning δευτερος πλους see Stobaeus, *floril[egium]*, Vol. 2, p. 374. [δευτερος πλους, literally 'second voyage', also used by Plato, *Phaedo*, 99c–d]
a *Heil*
b *willig*

the purifying[a] flame of suffering. Sometimes, we even see people who had been extremely evil being purified or chastened to this degree by the most profound pain: they have become different people, and are completely transformed. Even their earlier misdeeds do not disturb their conscience any longer, although they willingly repent for them with death, and are glad to see an end to that appearance of that will which they now find alien and abhorrent. In his immortal masterpiece, *Faust*, the great Goethe has given us a clear and vivid portrayal of the negation of the will that is produced by great unhappiness and despair of any deliverance, specifically in the story of Gretchen's suffering; and this is the only poetic description of the phenomenon that I know. It is a perfect, classic example of the second path leading to the negation of the will; unlike the first, this path does not proceed through pure cognition of the suffering of a whole world that one freely takes upon oneself, but rather through the feeling of one's own boundless pain. Of course a large number of tragedies ultimately lead their heroes (whose wills tend to be violent) to this point of total resignation, where the will to life typically comes to an end, along with its appearance: but I know of no portrayal that brings what is essential about this transformation so clearly before our eyes and in a way so free from all extraneous elements as the one I have mentioned in *Faust*.

465

In real life, we see that unfortunate people who have to drink to the dregs the greatest amounts of suffering and face a shameful, violent and often miserable death on the scaffold, fully lucid but deprived of all hope, are quite often transformed in this way. Of course we cannot assume that there is as great a difference between their character and that of most people as their fate would imply; this fate can be mostly attributed to circumstances. Nonetheless, they are guilty and evil to a considerable degree. But after complete hopelessness has set in, we see many of them transformed in the way we have described. Now they exhibit genuine goodness and purity[137] of mind, true horror at any deed that is the least bit evil or uncaring: they forgive their enemies, even those who caused them to suffer innocently, and not merely verbally and with a sort of hypocritical fear of the judge of the underworld, but in fact and with inner conviction, not with a view to any revenge. In fact, their sufferings and death ultimately become precious to them, because the negation of the will to life has emerged. They often repudiate any help offered to them and die gladly, peacefully, blissfully. Life's final secret has been revealed to them in

---

[a] *läuternden*

the excess of their pain, namely the fact that trouble[a] and evil, suffering and hatred, the tormenter and the tormented, however different these appear to cognition that follows from the principle of sufficient reason, are in themselves one, the appearance of that one will to life that objectifies its conflict with itself by means of the *principium individuationis*. They have come to recognize both sides in full measure, the evil and the troubling, and since they see the ultimate identity of the two, they now repudiate both at the same time and negate the will to life. It is, as I have said, a matter of complete indifference which myth or dogma they give to their reason to account for their transformation and for this intuitive and immediate cognition.

Matthias Claudius undoubtedly witnessed this sort of a change of heart,[b] when he wrote the remarkable essay that stands in the *Wandsbeck Messenger*[c] (pt. I, p. 115) under the title 'History of the Conversion of ***[d]' and ends in the following manner: 'The human way of thinking can go from one point on the periphery to the opposite point and back to the first again, if circumstances trace the arc in this way. And these alterations are not particularly great or interesting in human beings. But that *remarkable, catholic, transcendental alteration*, where the entire circle is torn beyond repair and all the laws of psychology become vain and empty, where the coat of skins[e] is taken off, or at least turned inside out, and the scales fall from people's eyes, this is such that everyone who is somewhat conscious of the breath in his nose leaves his father and mother if he can hear and experience something certain about it.'[138]

The proximity of death and hopelessness is not absolutely necessary for such a reformation[f] through suffering. Even without it, great misfortune and pain can lead to the violent obtrusion of cognition of the conflict of the will to life with itself, and the nothingness of all striving becoming evident. That is why we have often seen people who have led a very turbulent life in the grips of passion, kings, heroes, soldiers of fortune, suddenly change,[g] embrace resignation and penitence, and become hermits or monks. This is true of all genuine accounts of conversion,[h] for instance that of Ramon Llull who had courted a beautiful woman for a long time, and was finally

466

[a] *Uebel*
[b] *Sinnesänderung*
[c] *Wandsbecker Bote*
[d] *Bekehrungsgeschichte* des ***
[e] *Rock von Fellen*
[f] *Läuterung*
[g] *andern*
[h] *Bekehrungsgeschichten*

allowed into her bedroom; he was looking forward to the fulfilment of all his wishes when she opened her corset and showed him her breast that had been horribly eaten up with cancer. From this moment on, as if he had looked into hell, he was a convert, leaving the court of the King of

467 Majorca and going into the wilderness to do penance.* This account of a conversion is very similar to that of the Abbé de Rancé, which I recounted briefly in chapter 48 of the second volume.ª We can observe that in both cases, conversion was occasioned by a transition from a lust for life to a loathing of it, and this serves to explain the striking fact that the most cheerful, sensual, frivolous nation in Europe, which has the greatest lust for life, i.e. France, is the nation that gave rise to the strictest monastic order by far, i.e. the Trappist, re-established by Rancé after its decline, and which retains its purity and fearful strictness to the present day, in spite of revolutions, changes in the church, and ingrained unbelief.[139]

Cognition of the natureᵇ of this existence, such as we mentioned above, can nonetheless recede again with whatever occasioned its arrival, and the will to life can re-emerge together with the previous character. Thus we see the passionate Benvenuto Cellini transformed in this manner, once in prison and another time with a serious illness, but he relapsed into his old condition after the suffering had disappeared. In general, the negation of the will does not follow from suffering with anything like the necessity of an effect from its cause, but rather the will remains free. In fact, this is the only place where its freedom emerges directly into appearance: which explains why Asmusᶜ expressed so strong an astonishment over 'transcendental alteration'. For all suffering, we can think of a will that is superior to it in intensity and is unconquered by it. Thus, in the *Phaedo*, Plato tells about people who feast, drink, and enjoy aphrodisia up to the moment of their execution, affirming life to the point of death.ᵈ In the person of the Cardinal Beaufort,** Shakespeare puts before our eyes the horrible end of a reprobate who dies full of despair, since neither suffering nor death

468 can break a will whose violence extended to the most extreme wickedness. The more violent the will, the more glaring the appearance of its conflict, and consequently the greater the suffering. A world that represented the

* Brucker, *History of Philosophy*, Vol. IV, part I, p. 10.
** *Henry VI*, part 2, Act 3, scene 3.

ª [See Hübscher *SW* 3, 725. As Schopenhauer recounts it, Rancé entered the room of his lover and struck his foot against her severed head, an experience which brought about a conversion]
ᵇ *Beschaffenheit*
ᶜ [The pen-name of the poet Matthias Claudius]
ᵈ [See 116e]

appearance of an incomparably more violent will to life than in the present world would exhibit that much more suffering: it would be a *hell*.

Because all suffering is mortification and a call to resignation, it has the potential to be a sanctifying force; this explains why great unhappiness and deep pain in themselves inspire a certain respect. But the sufferer only becomes truly awe-inspiring when he reviews the course of his life as a chain of suffering, or laments a great and incurable pain, without actually looking at the concatenation of circumstances that have plunged his particular life into sorrow, or stopping at the specific, great misfortune that befell him: – because up to this point, his cognition still follows the principle of sufficient reason and clings to the individual appearance; he still wills life, only not under the conditions he has encountered. He only becomes truly awe-inspiring when he lifts his gaze from the particular to the universal, when he views his own suffering as a mere example of the whole and, becoming a genius in the ethical sense, treats it as *one* case in a thousand, so that the whole of life, seen essentially as suffering, brings him to the point of resignation. This is why we are filled with awe in Goethe's *Torquato Tasso* when the princess discusses at length how her life and the lives of her family members have always been sad and joyless, and she is looking entirely to the universal in doing so.

We always picture very noble characters as having a certain air of quiet sadness, which is anything but constant sullenness over the vexations of daily life (this would be an ignoble feature and make us suspect an evil disposition). Rather, emerging from cognition, it is a consciousness of the nothingness of all goods and the suffering of all life, not only the noble character's own life. Of course such cognition can be first aroused by the suffering such characters have experienced themselves, particularly by a single great suffering. In the same way, a single unrealizable desire brought Petrarch to that state of resigned sorrow over the whole of life that speaks   469 to us so movingly in his works; the Daphne he chased had to vanish from his hands in order to leave behind the immortal laurels in place of herself. When the will has been broken to a certain extent by such a great and irrevocable refusal of fate, almost nothing more is willed, and the character shows itself as gentle, sad, noble and resigned. When grief ultimately has no further determinate object, but rather spreads itself over the whole of life, then it is to a certain extent a withdrawal into self,[a] a retreat, a gradual disappearance of the will whose manifestation, the body, is subtly but in its innermost essence undermined by it. In this, the person feels a certain

---

[a] *In-sich-gehen*

loosening of his bonds, a gentle foretaste of the death that proclaims itself as the simultaneous dissolution of the body and the will. That is why this grief is accompanied by a secret joy, and it is this, I believe, that the most melancholy of all peoples call 'the joy of grief'.[a] But the reef of *sensibility*[b] lies here too, in both life itself and in its poetic portrayal. When people are always complaining and always lamenting without steeling themselves and raising themselves to a state of resignation, then earth and heaven are both lost at the same time and watery sentimentality[c] is all that is left. Only when suffering assumes the form of absolute and pure cognition, so that, as tranquillizer of *the will*, it leads to true resignation, – only then is it the path to redemption and thus worthy of honour. Here we feel a certain respect at the sight of everyone who is very unfortunate, and this is related to the respect commanded by virtue and nobility, while at the same time, our own fortunate situation seems like a reproach. We cannot help viewing suffering, both our own and that of others, as at least a possible approach to virtue and holiness, and conversely viewing pleasure and worldly gratifications as a retreat from this. This reaches the point where anyone who suffers greatly in body or severely in mind, or even someone who simply undertakes, by the sweat of his own brow, manual labour of a kind that demands the greatest exertion, who is visibly exhausted but goes patiently on without complaining – I say, if we pay close attention to someone like this, he looks somewhat like an invalid undertaking a painful cure; he endures the pain caused by the cure willingly and even with satisfaction, since he knows that the greater his suffering, the greater the destruction of the morbid matter,[d] and that his present pain is therefore an index of his cure.

470

Given everything said so far, the negation of the will to life, which is what people call utter resignation or holiness, always comes from the tranquillizer of the will, and this is recognition of the will's inner conflict and its essential nothingness, which expresses itself in the suffering of all living things. The difference that we have presented by means of two paths is whether this recognition is called into existence by suffering that is merely and purely *cognized*, and which is freely approached by our seeing through the *principium individuationis*, or whether, on the other hand, recognition comes from one's own immediate *feeling* of suffering. True salvation, redemption from life and from suffering, is unthinkable without the complete negation of the will. Until then, everyone is only this will itself

---

[a] [Schopenhauer uses the English term]
[b] *Empfindsamkeit*
[c] *Sentimentalität*
[d] *Krankheitsstoff*

whose appearance is a passing existence, an always futile, always thwarted striving, and the world we have described as full of suffering; everyone belongs to this world, irrevocably and in the same way. We discovered earlier that for the will to life, life is always a certainty, and its only true form is that of the present, from which nobody ever escapes, since birth and death prevail in appearance. The Indian myth expresses this by saying: 'they are reborn'. The meaning of the great ethical difference between characters is that the evil person is infinitely remote from achieving the cognition that results in the negation of the will, and is thus *actually* abandoned to all the misery that appears in life as *possible*, since even the present, happy state of his person is only an appearance and deception of *māyā* made possible by the *principium individuationis*, the happy dream of a beggar. The suffering that he inflicts on others in the violence and ferocity of his will's impulses is the measure of the suffering he experiences himself, which cannot break his will or lead to ultimate negation. On the other hand, all pure and true love, and indeed all free justice, comes from seeing through the *principium individuationis*; and when this is achieved with full clarity, it leads to perfect sanctification and redemption, the phenomenon of which is the state of resignation we described above, the imperturbable peace that accompanies it, and the greatest joyfulness in death.*

471

§ 69

This should suffice, within the scope of our method of investigation, for a description of the negation of the will to life. This negation is the only act of the freedom of the will that emerges into appearance; it is thus what Asmus has called a transcendental alteration.[140] Nothing can be more different from this negation than *suicide*, the voluntary abolition of the individual appearance of the will. Far from being a negation of the will, this is a phenomenon of a strong affirmation of will. This is because negation is not essentially an abhorrence of the *suffering* of life, but an abhorrence of its *pleasures*.[141] The person who commits suicide wills life,[a] and is only unsatisfied with the conditions under which life has been given to him. Thus, when he destroys the individual appearance he is relinquishing only life, not the will to life. He wills life, wills the unimpeded existence and affirmation of his body, but the tangle of circumstances does not allow him

---

* See chapter 48 of the second volume.

[a] *will das Leben*

this and he undergoes great suffering. The will to life as such finds itself so totally constrained in this particular appearance that it cannot develop its striving. So it reaches a decision in accordance with its intrinsic essence, an essence that lies beyond the forms of the principle of sufficient reason, and which is therefore indifferent to every individual appearance, since it itself remains unmoved by all coming into existence and passing away, and is the innermost aspect of the life of all things. The act of suicide also finds support from the very same firm and inner certainty that prevents us all from living in constant terror of death, namely the certainty that the will will never lack for appearance. The will to life appears just as much in this self-killing (Shiva) as it does in the ease and comfort of self-preservation (Vishnu) and in the pleasure of procreation (Brahma). This is the inner meaning of the *unity of the Trimurtis*, which each human being is in his entirety, although in time it raises sometimes one and sometimes another of its three heads. – Suicide is related to the negation of the will in the same way that the individual thing is related to the Idea. The person who commits suicide negates only the individual, not the species.[142] We have already found that for the will to life, life is always a certainty, and suffering is essential to life, so it follows that suicide, the wilful destruction of one single appearance that leaves the thing in itself untouched, just as the rainbow remains stable however rapidly the drops that support it at any given moment might change, is a futile and foolish act. But besides this, it is the masterpiece of *māyā*, the most glaring expression of the contradiction of the will to life with itself. We already recognized this contradiction in the lowest appearances of the will, in the constant struggle between all the expressions of natural forces and all organic individuals over matter, time and space; and we saw this conflict become increasingly apparent, with terrible clarity, on each progressive level of the objectivation[143] of the will. On the highest level, which is the Idea of humanity, it reaches the point where it is not only the individuals presented in the same Idea that try to annihilate one another, but the single individual actually declares war on himself, and the violence with which he wills life and fights against the restrictions on life, against suffering, brings him to destroy himself. Through an act of will, the individual will abolishes the body, which is simply its own manifestation,[a] before suffering can break it. A person who commits suicide stops living precisely because he cannot stop willing, and the will affirms itself here through the very abolition of its appearance, because it can no longer affirm itself in any other way. But the very suffering

---

[a] *Sichtbarwerdung*

that he avoids so emphatically could, in the form of a mortification of the will, have led to self-negation and redemption; which is why, in this respect, someone who commits suicide is like a sick person who, having started undergoing a painful operation that could cure him completely, does not allow it to be completed and would rather stay sick. Suffering approaches and, as such, introduces the possibility of negation of the will; but he repudiates it by destroying the body, the appearance of the will, so that the will might remain unbroken. – This is the reason why almost all ethics,[144] philosophical as well as religious, condemn suicide, although they can only give strange, sophistical grounds for doing so. But if purely moral incentives have ever kept any human being from suicide, the inner meaning[a] of this self-overcoming (regardless of the concepts his reason clothed it in) is the following: 'I do not want to avoid suffering, because it can help suppress the will to life (whose appearance is so miserable) by strengthening the recognition that is beginning to stir in me of the true essence of the world, so that this recognition can ultimately become a tranquillizer of my will and redeem me forever.'

From time to time, everyone hears about a case where suicide extends to the children: the father kills the children he loves so much, and then himself. Now keeping in mind that conscience, religion and all established ideas have taught him to recognize murder as the worst of crimes, and yet he commits it anyway, in the hour of his own death, without any possible egoistic motive, the deed can only be explained by assuming that the individual's will recognizes itself directly in the children, but is nonetheless caught in the delusion that takes appearance for essence in itself; deeply affected by the recognition of the misery of all life, he now means to annul the essence along with the appearance, and in this manner rescue himself and his children (who he sees as a repetition of his own life) from existence and its miseries. – An analogous error would be someone believing he is accomplishing the same thing as voluntary chastity by thwarting the aims of nature in insemination, or even, in consideration of the inevitable suffering of life, by promoting infanticide, rather than doing all he can to safeguard life for everything that is crowding into it. Since the will to life is the sole metaphysical entity or thing in itself, where it exists, no violence can break it; the only thing violence can do is to destroy its appearance in a particular place, at a particular time. The will to life itself cannot be suppressed by anything except *cognition*. That is why the only path to salvation is for the will to appear without restraints, so that it can *recognize*

---

[a] *Sinn*

its own essence in this appearance. Only as a result of this recognition can the will abolish itself and in so doing put an end to suffering too, since suffering is inseparable from the will's appearance. But this is not possible by way of physical violence, such as the destruction of the seed, or by killing infants, or committing suicide. Nature leads the will to the light, because it is only in the light that it can find its redemption. Thus the goals of nature must be promoted in every way as soon as the will to life, which is nature's inner essence, has arrived at a resolution.[145] –

There is a form of suicide that seems completely different from the usual kind, although this new form might still not be well enough established. It is the death by voluntary starvation that emerges at the highest levels of asceticism, although its appearance is always accompanied by a lot of religious enthusiasm and even superstition, and this serves to obscure it. But it seems that the complete negation of the will can reach the point where even the will needed to maintain the vegetative functions of the body through nutrition can fall away. Far from stemming from the will to life, in this kind of suicide an ascetic of this type stops living simply because he has stopped willing altogether. It is not really conceivable that he would die in any way other than starvation (unless prompted by a particular superstition), because the intention of shortening misery would actually involve a degree of affirmation of the will. The dogmas that fill the reason of such a penitent mirror back his delusion that a higher sort of being has commanded him to fast, which is what his inner tendency drives him to. Older examples of this can be found in the *Breslauer Sammlung von Natur – und Medicin-Geschichte*, September 1719, pp. 363ff.; in Bayle's *Nouvelles de la république des lettres*, February 1685, pp. 189ff.; in Zimmermann, *On Loneliness*,[a] Vol. 1, p. 182; in the *Histoire de l'académie des sciences* of 1764, a report by Houttuyn, which is repeated in the *Sammlung für praktische Aerzte*, Vol. 1, p. 69. Later reports can be found in Hufeland's *Journal für praktische Heilkunde*, Vol. 10, p. 181, and Vol. 48, p. 95; also in Nasse's *Zeitschrift für psychische Aerzte*, 1819, part 3, p. 460; in the *Edinburgh Medical and Surgical Journal*, 1809, Vol. 5, p. 319.[b] In 1833, all the newspapers reported that in January, the English historian, Dr Lingard, died in Dover of voluntary starvation; according to later reports it was not him but rather a relative.[146] Nonetheless, most of these reports portrayed the individuals

475

[a] *Ueber die Einsamkeit*
[b] [Other titles translate as: *Breslau Collection of Natural and Medical History* (full title *Sammlung von Natur – und Medicin – wie auch hierzu gehörigen Kunst – und Literatur-Geschichten*); *News of the Republic of Letters*; *Annals of the Academy of Sciences*; *Collection for Practising Doctors*; *Journal of Practical Medicine*; *Journal for Psychiatric Doctors*]

as insane, and now it is no longer possible to learn the extent to which this might have been the case. But I will provide a new report of this kind, if only to ensure the preservation of one of the rare examples of the moving, remarkable and extraordinary phenomenon of human nature that at least appears to belong where I would like to put it, and would otherwise be very difficult to explain. This recent account is reported in the *Nürnberger Korrespondent* from 29 July 1813 in the following words:

'It is reported from Bern that in a thick forest near Thurnen, a small cabin was found in which lay a male corpse that had been decaying for approximately one month. The clothes could give little information about the status of their owner. Two very fine shirts lay beside him. The most important element was a Bible that had white sheets inserted into it which had been partially written on by the dead man. There he reports the day he departed from his house (without specifying where that was), and then he said that he had been driven by the spirit of God into the wilderness to pray and to fast. He had already fasted for seven days on his journey here: then he had eaten again. When he settled in, he began fasting again, and for as many days again. Every day was indicated by a mark, and five were found after which the pilgrim presumably died. A letter was also found addressed to a minister concerning a sermon that the dead man had heard him give; only the address was missing from this as well.' – There may be many intermediate stages and combinations of these two types of voluntary death, the one from the extremes of asceticism and the usual one from despair, and these combinations are certainly difficult to explain. But the human spirit[a] has depths, entanglements, and regions of darkness that are extremely difficult to unfold and shed light on.

476

§ 70

We have now finished presenting what I have been calling the negation of the will. This might be thought at odds with the earlier discussion of the necessity that accrues to motivation as much as it does to every other form of the principle of sufficient reason. As a result of this necessity, motives, like all causes, are merely occasional causes by means of which the essence of character develops and reveals itself with the necessity of a law of nature. This is why we have flatly denied the existence of freedom

[a] *Gemüth*

as *liberum arbitrium indifferentiae*.[a] Far from wanting to rescind[b] this, I am calling it back to mind. In truth, genuine freedom, i.e. independence from the principle of sufficient reason, accrues only to the will as thing in itself, not to its appearance, the essential form of which is everywhere the principle of sufficient reason, the element of necessity. The only time this freedom can manifest itself directly in appearance as well is when it brings to an end the thing that appears; and because the mere appearance, the living body, being a rung in the chain of causes, still continues to exist in time (which contains only appearances), it stands in contradiction to the will that manifests itself through this appearance, since the will negates what the appearance expresses. In such a case, the genitals, for instance, as the manifestation of the sex drive, are present and healthy; nonetheless, sexual satisfaction is not willed, even most inwardly. The whole body is nothing but the visible expression of the will to life, and

477   nonetheless the motives that correspond to this will are no longer effective. In fact, there is a dissolution of the body, an end to the individual that is both total and welcome, leading to a great inhibition of the natural will. The contradiction between our claim, on the one hand, that there is a necessary determination of the will through motives in accordance with character, and our claim, on the other hand, that it is possible to completely abolish the will, is only the repetition in philosophical reflection of a *real* contradiction which comes when the freedom of the will in itself, a freedom that knows no necessity, interferes directly in the necessity of its appearance. The key to reconciling these contradictions is that the state in which the character is removed from the power of the motive does not proceed immediately from the will, but rather from an altered mode of cognition. As long as we are only dealing with cognition that is caught up in the *principium individuationis* and follows the principle of sufficient reason, the motive has an irresistible force; but when we see through the *principium individuationis*, we immediately recognize the Ideas, indeed the essence of things in themselves, as being in everything the same will, and from this cognition comes a universal tranquillizer of willing; individual motives become ineffective, because the mode of cognition that corresponds to them retreats, obscured by an entirely different mode of cognition. Thus, character can never be altered partially; instead, with the consistency of a law of nature, character must realize itself as a whole in the particular individual whose appearance it is: but this very whole, the character itself,

---

[a] [Free choice of indifference]
[b] *aufheben*

can be fully abolished by the alteration in cognition described above. This abolition is what Asmus gazed at with wonder and dubbed the 'catholic, transcendental alteration', mentioned above: it is the very same thing[147] the Christian church has so aptly called *being born again*,[a] and it calls the cognition that gives rise to it the *effect of divine grace*.[b] – However, since we are not talking about an alteration but rather a complete abolition of the character, then however different the characters concerned might have been before this abolition, their actions[c] look very similar afterwards, although they *speak* very differently, according to their different concepts and dogmas.

It is in this sense that the old philosopheme[d] of the freedom of the will, which is both constantly disputed and constantly asserted, is not without grounds, and the church dogmas of being born again and the effect of divine grace are not without sense and meaning. But now we see them unexpectedly collapse into the same thing, and we can also understand what the most excellent Malebranche could mean in (correctly) saying: 'freedom is a mystery'.[e] The reason is that what the Christian mystics call the *effect of divine grace* and being *born again* are, for us, the immediate expression of the *freedom of the will*. It only occurs when the will, gaining cognition of its intrinsic essence, obtains by this means a *tranquillizer*, which deprives *motives* of their effectiveness, an effectiveness that falls within the sphere of a different mode of cognition, one whose objects are only appearances. – The possibility of a freedom that expresses itself in this way is the greatest advantage of being human, and one that animals will always lack because it requires a careful and deliberate reason[f] that can survey the whole of life, abstracted from any present impression. Animals lack any possibility of freedom, just as they lack any possibility of an authentic, which is to say a careful and deliberate ability to choose following a complete conflict of motives, which must be abstract representations for this to happen. Thus the hungry wolf sinks its teeth into the flesh of its quarry with all the necessity of a rock falling to earth, and there is no possibility of it recognizing that it is the mauled as well as the mauler. *Necessity* is the *kingdom of nature*; *freedom* is the *kingdom of grace*.

478

---

[a] *Wiedergeburt*
[b] *Gnadenwirkung*
[c] *Handlungsweise*
[d] *Philosophem*
[e] *La liberté est un mystère* [wrongly attributed to Malebranche, as also on the title page and final page of *FW* (see Hübscher *SW* 4, 1 and 98; Cambridge edition of *The Two Fundamental Problems of Ethics*, 31 and 109)]
[f] *Besonnenheit der Vernunft*

Now as we have seen, the *self-abolition* of the will begins with cognition, but cognition and insight as such are independent of free choice;[a] consequently, that negation of the will, that entrance into freedom cannot be forced by any intention or resolution, but rather emerges from the innermost relation of cognition to willing in human beings, and thus arrives suddenly, as if flying in from outside. That is precisely why the church calls it the *effect of divine grace*; but just as the church thinks that this is still dependent on the acceptance of grace, the effect of the tranquillizer is also ultimately an act of the freedom of the will.[b,148] And since the effect of divine grace fundamentally alters and reverses the whole essence of a person so that he no longer wills what he used to will so violently and a new human being truly takes the place of the old, the church calls this *being born again*. For what the church calls the *natural man*, to which it denies all capacity for goodness, is that very will to life that must be negated if redemption from an existence such as ours is to be achieved. Behind our existence lies something else and it only becomes accessible to us when we shake off the world.[149]

Christian doctrine symbolizes *nature*, the *affirmation of the will to life*, using *Adam*, because it focuses on the Idea of human beings in their unity, not the individual in accordance with the principle of sufficient reason; the sin that we inherited from Adam, i.e. our unity with him in the Idea, which is expressed temporally through the bond of procreation, causes us all to share in suffering and eternal death. Conversely, Christian doctrine symbolizes *grace*, the *negation of the will, redemption*, in the form of God become man, who, being free from all sinfulness, i.e. from all life-will,[c] cannot have arisen from that most decisive affirmation of the will as we did, and cannot have a body like ours, which is to say a body that is nothing but concrete will through and through, appearance of the will. Rather, being born from a virgin, he has only an illusory body.[d] This was the belief of the Docetae, i.e.[150] several of the Church Fathers who were very consistent on this point. It was taught by Appelles in particular, and Tertullian rose up against both Appelles and his followers as well. But even Augustine comments on the passage, Romans 8:3: 'God sending his own Son in the likeness of sinful flesh',[e] saying: 'For it was not sinful flesh, since he was not born from lust of the flesh: but the shape of the sinful flesh did cling

[a] *Willkür*
[b] *Freiheitsakt des Willens*
[c] *Lebenswillen*
[d] *Scheinleib*
[e] *Deus filium suum misit in similitudinem carnis peccati.*

to him, because it was mortal flesh' (*On 83 Questions*, question 66).[a] In his work known as the *opus imperfectum*,[b] I, 47, Augustine also teaches that 480 the original sin is both sin and punishment. It is already present in new-born infants, but only shows itself when they have grown. Nonetheless, the origin of this sin can be derived from the will of the sinner. This sinner was Adam, but we all existed in him: Adam became unhappy, and in him we have all become unhappy. – The doctrine of original sin (the affirmation of the will) and redemption (negation of the will) is really the great truth that makes up the core of Christianity; the rest of it is mostly only wrapping, coverings and appendages. Accordingly, we should always interpret Jesus Christ universally, as the symbol or personification of the negation of the will to life, not as an individual, according to either his mythological history in the Gospels or the presumably true history that grounds it. It is difficult to be completely satisfied with either the one or the other. It is merely the vehicle of that first interpretation for the people, who always require something factual. – The fact that contemporary Christianity has forgotten its true meaning and has degenerated into trite optimism is of no concern to us here.[151]

It is moreover an original and evangelical Christian doctrine that Augustine, with the approval of the heads of the church, defended against the platitudes of the Pelagians, and which *Luther* made it his principal goal to re-establish and cleanse of errors, as he explicitly describes in his book *On the Bondage of the Will*,[c] – it is, namely, the doctrine that the *will is not free*, but rather originally subject to a propensity for evil. This is why its works are always sinful and defective, and can never satisfy justice, and why ultimately it is never these works, but rather faith alone that makes blessed; but this faith itself does not emerge from resolutions or free will, but rather from the *effect of divine grace*, which comes to us as if from outside, without any effort on our part. – The crude and trite opinion of the present day conceals this last, truly evangelical dogma, or rejects it as absurd, just as it does the dogmas mentioned above, because, in spite of Augustine and Luther, it is fond of homely Pelagian common sense,[d] which is the same as contemporary rationalism.[152] It considers these profound doctrines, which 481 are distinctive and essential to Christianity in the narrowest sense, to be antiquated, while at the same time it adheres only to the dogmas that

---

[a] *Non enim caro peccati erat, quae non de carnali delectatione nata erat: sed tamen inerat ei similitudo carnis peccati, quia mortalis caro erat. Liber 83 quaestiones* qu. 66
[b] ['unfinished work', entitled *Against Julian of Eclanum*]
[c] *De servo arbitrio*
[d] *Pelagianischen Hausmannsverstand*

482   originated in and are retained from Judaism, dogmas that are associated with Christianity for merely historical reasons,*,¹⁵³ and treats these as the main point. – But in the doctrine mentioned above we recognize the truth that is in complete agreement with the results of our investigations. We see, namely, that genuine virtue and holiness of mind do not first arise from deliberate free choice[a] (works) but rather from cognition (faith), and this is the same conclusion we reached along our principal line of reasoning. Works come from motives and deliberate decisions, and if this was what led to blessedness, then however we look at it, virtue would never be anything except a prudent,[b] methodical, far-seeing egoism. – The Christian church, however, promises blessedness to the following kind of faith: just as we are all sinful because of the fall of the first man and have been cast into death and decay, we are all redeemed only through grace and by having the divine mediator take over our tremendous guilt, and this entirely without

---

*   That this is very much the case is evident from the fact that all the contradictory and incomprehensible elements contained in the system of Christian dogmatics (consistently systematized by Augustine), which have led straight to the opposing Pelagian platitudes, disappear as soon as we abstract away from the fundamental Jewish dogma and see human beings not as the work of someone else, but rather of their own wills. Then everything is at once clear and correct: then there does not need to be freedom in the *operari* [acting], because it lies in the *esse* [being], which is where sin lies too, as original sin; but the effect of divine grace is our own. – The present-day, rationalist view, on the other hand, considers many doctrines of Augustinian dogmatism grounded in the New Testament to be completely untenable, or even outrageous, for instance predestination. As a result, people reject what is authentically Christian, and return to crude Judaism. But the miscalculation or the primal defect of Christian dogmatics lies where it is never looked for, namely precisely in what it treats as settled and certain and removes from all investigation. If this is taken away, then the whole dogmatics is rational, because that dogma ruins theology just as it ruins all the other fields of knowledge [*Wissenschaften*]. If you study the Augustinian theology in the books *The City of God* (particularly in Book 14), you experience something analogous to what happens when you try to stand a body upright whose centre of gravity lies outside of it: however you try to turn it or position it, it keeps falling over. Here too, in spite of all the efforts and sophisms of Augustine, the guilt of the world as well as its misery always fall back on God, who made everything and everything that is in everything, and also knew how things would turn out. I have already established in my prize essay *On the Freedom of the Will* (ch. 4, pp. 66–8 of the first edition [See Hübscher, *SW* 4, 66–8; Cambridge edition, 84–6]) that Augustine himself was aware of this difficulty and very puzzled by it. – In the same way, the contradiction between God's goodness and the misery of the world, and also between the freedom of the will and divine foreknowledge is the inexhaustible theme of a controversy lasting for almost a hundred years between the Cartesians, Malebranche, Leibniz, Bayle, Clarke, Arnauld, and many others. The only dogma that the disputants consider as certain is the existence of God along with his attributes, and they spin in an endless circle by trying to bring these things into harmony, i.e. to solve the arithmetical problem that never works out but whose remainder appears sometimes here, sometimes there, after it has been hidden elsewhere. It never occurs to anybody to look for the source of the predicament in the basic assumption, although it is palpably evident. Only with Bayle do we notice that he notices this.

[a]   *Willkür*
[b]   *kluger*

any merit on our (the person's) part. What can result from a person's intentional deeds (those determined by motives), namely his works, can, by their very nature, never justify us, simply because they are *intentional deeds*, carried out according to motives, *opus operatum*. In this faith it is clear from the start that our condition is originally and essentially incurable and that we need to be *redeemed* from it; also, that we ourselves are essentially evil and are bound to evil so tightly that the works we perform according to laws and precepts,[a] i.e. according to motives, could never remotely satisfy justice, nor could they redeem us; rather, redemption is to be won only through faith, i.e. through an altered mode of cognition, and this faith itself can only come from grace, as if from the outside. This means that salvation is something entirely alien to our person, and it points to the fact that salvation requires us to negate and abolish precisely this person. Works, the observance of the law as such, could never justify, because they are always actions that take place according to motives. *Luther* expects (in his book, *A Treatise on Christian Liberty*[b]) that once faith has set in, good works will result from it entirely on their own, as symptoms, as the fruits of faith; they make absolutely no intrinsic claim to merit, justification or   483
reward, but rather they take place completely freely and gratuitously. – We also showed how seeing through the *principium individuationis* ever more clearly leads at first only to free justice, but then to love, to the point of completely abolishing egoism, and finally to resignation or the negation of the will.

I have introduced these Christian dogmas, dogmas that are intrinsically foreign to philosophy, only in order to show that the ethics that emerges from our whole investigation, and that is in precise agreement with and connected to all the aspects of it, is really nothing new, even if it is expressed in a new and unheard-of manner. Rather, it is in complete agreement with the whole of authentic Christian dogma, and was already contained and present in this dogma itself at every essential point. In the same way, it is in just as complete an agreement with the doctrines and ethical precepts that were again expressed in a completely different form in the sacred books of India. At the same time, by recalling the dogmas of the Christian church, we were able to explain and elucidate the apparent contradiction between the necessity that accrues to all expressions of character given certain motives (the kingdom of nature) on the one hand, and the freedom of the will in itself to negate itself and to abolish the character along with all the necessity

[a] *Vorschrift*
[b] *De libertate Christiana*

that accrues to motives grounded in character (the kingdom of grace) on the other hand.

§ 71

As I conclude the fundamental features of ethics as well as the complete development of the single thought that I set out to communicate, I certainly do not wish to conceal an objection concerning the final part of my presentation. In fact, I will even show that this objection lies in the nature[a] of the matter at hand and is absolutely impossible to remedy. The objection is that once our investigation has finally succeeded in placing before our eyes, in the phenomenon of perfect holiness, the negation and abandonment of all willing, and in so doing, the redemption from a world whose entire being is presented to us as suffering, then this will seem like a transition into an empty *nothing*.[b] I must begin by noting that the concept of *nothing* is an essentially relative one, and always refers to something particular that it negates.[c] People (namely Kant) have ascribed this quality only to the *nihil privativum*, which is indicated by a '−' in contrast to a '+', where the '−' can be made into a '+' by looking at things from the opposite perspective; they oppose the *nihil privativum* to the *nihil negativum*,[d] which would be nothing in every respect, and is illustrated with the example of a logical contradiction that cancels itself out. But considered more closely, an absolute nothing, a true *nihil negativum* is not even conceivable; instead, everything of this sort, when regarded from a higher standpoint or subsumed under a broader concept, is always just another *nihil privativum*. Every nothing is a nothing only in relation to something else and presupposes this relation, and thus presupposes the 'something else'. Even a logical contradiction is only a relative nothing. It is not a thought of reason, but it is not for that matter an absolute nothing. It is a compound of words, an example of the unthinkable that logic needs in order to establish the laws of thought. Thus, if we need an example for this purpose, we will keep hold of nonsense as the positive we are looking for and pass over sense as the negative. Thus, when subordinated to a higher concept, the *nihil negativum* or absolute nothing will appear as a mere *nihil*

484

---

[a] *Wesen*
[b] *Nichts*
[c] *negirt*
[d] ['Privative nothing' and 'negative nothing': see Kant, *Critique of Pure Reason*, A291–2 / B347–9. Kant explains *nihil privativum* as 'a concept of the absence of an object, such as a shadow or cold' and *nihil negativum* as 'the object of a concept that contradicts itself . . . because the concept is nothing, the impossible, like a rectilinear figure with two sides']

privativum or relative nothing which could always change signs with what it is negating, so that the former could be thought as negation, while it itself could be thought as position.[a] This is in agreement with the results of the difficult dialectical investigation of nothing that Plato conducts in the *Sophist* (pp. 277–86, Bipont): 'We have shown that the nature of *the different* is, and is parcelled out over the whole field of beings *in relation to one another*, and of every part of it that is set in contrast to that which is we have dared to say that precisely that is really *that which is not.*'[b,154]

485

What is generally accepted as positive, which we call *what is*[c] and whose negation has its most general meaning in the concept we express as *nothing*,[d] is precisely the world of representation, which I have established to be the objecthood of the will, its mirror. This will and this world are what we ourselves are, and representation in general belongs to them as one of their aspects: the form of this representation is space and time, and thus everything that has being from this standpoint must have a position in space and time. Concepts belong to representation too, the material of philosophy, and finally so do words, the signs of the concepts. The negation, abolition,[e] and turning around of the will is also an abolition and disappearance of the world, its mirror. If we are not looking at this mirror anymore, then it is futile to ask where it has turned to and to complain that, since it no longer has a where and a when, it is lost in nothing.[155]

If the opposite point of view were possible for us, it would involve reversing the signs and showing that what is being for us is nothing, and what is nothing for us is being. But as long as we are ourselves the will to life, we can only recognize and indicate that last thing negatively, because here in particular, Empedocles' old principle[156] that like can only recognize like deprives us of all cognition. But on the other hand, this principle does ultimately make possible all our actual cognition (i.e. the world as representation or the objecthood of the will) because the world is the self-cognition of the will.

---

[a] *Position*
[b] Την του ἑτέρου φυσιν αποδειξαντες ουσαν τε, και κατακεκερματισμενην επι παντα τα οντα προς αλληλα, το προς το ον ἑκαστου μοριον αυτης αντιτιθεμενον, ετολμησαμεν ειπειν, ὡς αυτο τουτο εστιν οντως το μη ον. (*Cum enim ostenderemus,* alterius *ipsius naturam esse, perque omnia entia divisam atque dispersam* in vicem; *tunc partem ejus oppositam ei, quod cujusque ens est, esse ipsum revera* non ens *asseruimus.*) [*Sophist,* 258d–e]
[c] *das Seiende*
[d] *Nichts*
[e] *Aufhebung*

Nonetheless, if someone persisted in demanding positive cognition of what philosophy can express only negatively, as the negation of the will, then all we could do would be to point out the state experienced by everyone who has achieved a perfect negation of the will, and that has been called ecstasy, rapture, enlightenment,[a] unity with God, etc. But this state cannot really be called cognition, because it no longer has the form of subject and object, and also because it is accessible only to one's own experience and not to experience that can be communicated beyond that.

486 But we who are firmly entrenched in the standpoint of philosophy must content ourselves here with negative cognition, satisfied in having reached the final boundary stone of the positive. Thus, if we have recognized the intrinsic essence of the world as will, and have seen in all its appearances only the will's objecthood, and have followed this from the impulses of the dark forces of nature (impulses that are devoid of cognition) up to the most conscious of human actions, – if we have recognized all this, we will certainly not evade the consequence that along with the free negation, the abandonment, of the will, all those appearances are also abolished, those constant urges and drives that have no goal or pause, that operate on all the levels of objecthood in which and through which the world exists, the manifold forms that follow each other in succession, the will's whole appearance and ultimately its universal forms as well, time and space, and also its final fundamental form, subject and object. No will: no representation, no world.

Only nothing remains before us. But our nature, which resists this melting away into nothing, is really only the will to life which we ourselves are, as it is our world. The fact that we hate nothing so much is nothing more than another expression of the fact that we will life so much, and we are nothing other than this will and know[b] nothing other than it. – But if we turn our eyes away from our own petty concerns and limitations[c] and look instead at those who have overcome the world, those in whom the will, achieving full self-cognition rediscovers itself in everything and then freely negates itself, and which then only needs to wait for the last trace of the will to disappear along with the body that it animates, – then, instead of the restless impulses and drives, instead of the constant transition from desire to fear and from joy to suffering, instead of the never-satisfied and never-dying hope which are the elements that make up the life-dream of the human being who wills – instead of all this, we are shown the

[a] *Erleuchtung*
[b] *kennen*
[c] *Dürftigkeit und Befangenheit*

peace that is higher than all reason, we are shown that completely calm sea of the mind, that profound tranquillity, imperturbable confidence and cheerfulness, whose mere glint in a countenance such as those portrayed by Raphael or Correggio is a complete and reliable gospel: only cognition remains, the will has vanished. But then we look with deep and painful longing at this state which puts the miserable and incurable nature of our own condition into sharp relief. Nevertheless, this consideration is the only one that can give us lasting comfort when we have truly recognized, on 487 the one hand, that incurable suffering and endless misery are the appearance of the will, of the world, and have seen, on the other hand, the world melting away with the abolition of the will, leaving only empty nothing before us. We can look at the lives and the conduct of saints; of course we rarely encounter them in our own experience, but they are brought before our eyes in their recorded histories as well as in art, which is vouchsafed by the mark of inner truth; and this is how we must drive away the dark impression of that nothing that hovers behind all virtue and holiness as the final goal, and that we fear the way children fear darkness. We must not evade it through myths and meaningless words as the Indians do, words such as 're-absorption into *Brahman*',[a,157] or the *Nirvana* of the Buddhists. Instead we confess quite freely: for everyone who is still filled with the will, what remains after it is completely abolished is certainly nothing. But conversely, for those in whom the will has turned and negated itself, this world of ours which is so very real with all its suns and galaxies is – nothing.[*,158]

---

[*] This is precisely the Pradschna-Paramita of the Buddhists, the 'beyond of all knowledge', i.e. the point where subject and object are no more. (See J. J. Schmidt, *Ueber das Mahajana und Pradschna-Paramita* [*On the Mahāyāna and Prajña-Pāramitā*])

[a] *das* Brahm

Critique of the Kantian Philosophy

*C'est le privilège du vrai génie, et surtout du génie qui ouvre une carrière,
de faire impunément de grandes fautes.*

Voltaire

['It is the privilege of true genius, and above all the genius who opens
a new path, to make great errors with impunity.' *Siècle de Louis XIV*,
chap. 32].

It is much easier to indicate errors and mistakes in the work of a great mind   491
than to give a clear and complete account[a] of its value. This is because
the mistakes are specific and finite and we can review each one, whereas
it is a mark of genius that the excellence of its works is unfathomable
and inexhaustible; they will not become obsolete, but will continue to
be instructive for centuries on end. The perfected masterpiece[b] of a truly
great mind will always have so profound and far-reaching an effect on the
entire human race that we cannot calculate how far geographically and
temporally its illuminating influence will extend. This will always be the
case, because however rich and accomplished the age might be in which
the masterpiece appeared, genius will always rise up like a palm tree above
the ground in which it is rooted.

But such profound and far-reaching effects cannot appear very quickly,
because there is such a vast distance between the genius and the usual run
of humanity. The knowledge[c] that this one person derives directly from life
and the world in the course of a *single* lifetime, knowledge that he acquires
and presents to others as a finished product, cannot become the immediate
property of humanity: humanity's capacity[d] to receive this knowledge does
not equal his capacity to provide it. Rather, having endured struggles with

[a] *Entwicklung*
[b] *Meisterstück*
[c] *Erkenntniß*
[d] *Kraft*

492   unworthy opponents who would contest the immortal one's very right to
live from the moment he is born, and would like to nip in the bud the
salvation[a] of humanity (like the snake in Hercules' cradle) – even after all
that, each piece of knowledge must first meander through the detours of
innumerable false interpretations and distorted applications, has to survive
attempts to amalgamate it with old errors, and so struggle on until a
new and unprejudiced generation comes its way. Even in its youth this
generation will gradually receive the content from that source through a
thousand diverted streams, assimilate it little by little, and so come to share
in the blessing[b] that should flow to humanity from this great spirit. Thus,
the education of the human race plods slowly on, the education of the weak
and unruly pupil of genius. – Thus too, the entire force and importance of
Kant's doctrine will only be revealed in the course of time, when one day
the *Zeitgeist* itself, transformed little by little under the influence of this
doctrine and altered in its most important and innermost aspect, will be
living testimony to the power[c] of that intellectual giant.[d] But it would be
presumptuous of me to anticipate this here, and I have no desire to take
on the thankless role of Calchas and Cassandra. Only, given what I have
been saying, I might be allowed to regard Kant's works as still very new,
while many people these days already see them as obsolete; they dismiss
these works, setting them aside or putting them behind them, as people
say.[1] This encourages others to become impertinent; they ignore Kant's
works altogether and keep philosophizing about God and the soul with
brazen audacity, using the presuppositions of the old dogmatic realism and
its scholasticism; – this is like trying to validate alchemical theories in the
context of modern chemistry. – Of course Kant's works do not need my
feeble eulogy; they will themselves be a source of eternal praise to their
master and will always have a place on this earth, if not in their letter then
certainly in their spirit.

However, if we look back at the immediate effect of Kant's doctrine,
at the efforts and events in the sphere of philosophy since then, we will
certainly find confirmation of a very disheartening remark of Goethe's:
'just as water that has been displaced by a ship immediately falls back into
place behind it; so too when great minds have pushed errors to the side
493   and made room for themselves these errors naturally close very quickly
behind them again'. (*Poetry and Truth*,[e] part 3, p. 521.) Nonetheless, this

---

[a] *Heil*
[b] *Wohlthat*
[c] *Gewalt*
[d] *Riesengeist*
[e] *Dichtung und Wahrheit*

period of time is only an episode that must be attributed to the fate of every new and great piece of knowledge, as mentioned above; and this episode is now unmistakably nearing its end, since the soap bubble that people kept blowing up is finally bursting. People are becoming generally aware that true and serious philosophy is still where Kant left it. For my part, I cannot see that anything has happened in philosophy between Kant's time and my own, so I will take up directly from him.[2]

My aim in this appendix is really only to justify the doctrine I have presented in the work itself, to the extent that the work disagrees with – or even contradicts – many aspects of Kant's philosophy. But I must say a few words on this score, since however different the content of my line of reasoning is from that of Kant, it has clearly been very heavily influenced by Kantian ideas, it necessarily presupposes them, and takes them as its point of departure. And I confess that, next to the impressions gained from the world of intuition, I owe what is best in my own development to the works of Kant, just as much as I do to Plato and the sacred texts of the Hindus. – Nevertheless, there are points where I do come into conflict with Kant, and I can only justify myself by showing that he was mistaken in these matters and by revealing the mistakes he has made. Accordingly, throughout this appendix I will need to proceed against Kant in a thoroughly polemical and serious way, exerting myself to the utmost. This is the only way to grind down the errors that cling to Kant's doctrine, allowing the truth of this doctrine to shine all the more brightly and endure all the more securely. Thus, it should not be expected that my sincere and deep feelings of respect for Kant will extend to his weaknesses and mistakes as well, and that I will expose these with the most cautious forbearance; this sort of prevarication would weaken and blunt my presentation. People might need to be treated with such forbearance while they are still alive, since human frailty cannot bear to see even the most just of its errors refuted in the absence of any mollification and flattery, and even then bears it badly enough; and at the very least, a teacher for the ages and benefactor of humanity deserves indulgence for his human frailties, so as to avoid causing him any pain. But the dead have cast this weakness aside: their merit[a] is established, and time will keep it increasingly free of overestimation and detraction. Their mistakes must be separated out, rendered harmless, and then consigned to oblivion. That is why in the polemic I am about to strike up against Kant I will be looking only at his mistakes and weaknesses; I will treat these with hostility and wage a merciless war of annihilation against them. I will be careful not to go easy on them or to conceal them; rather, I will

494

_____
[a] *Verdienst*

place them in the brightest light, in order to be that much more certain of destroying them. This is why I do not feel I am being unjust or ungrateful to Kant. But meanwhile, to guard against any semblance of malice in the eyes of other people, I will begin by focusing on the respect and gratitude I feel so deeply towards Kant; I will do so by briefly describing his main contributions, as I see them, and from so general a standpoint that I will not have to mention the points on which I will later have to contradict him.

Kant's greatest merit is to distinguish between appearance and thing in itself – by proving that the *intellect* always stands between us and things, which is why we cannot have cognition of things as they may be in themselves.[3] Kant was led down this path by *Locke* (see *Prolegomena to Any Future Metaphysics*, § 13, note 2). Locke had established that secondary qualities of things, such as sound, smell, colour, hardness, softness, smoothness, and the like are grounded in the affections of the senses and do not belong to objective bodies, to the things in themselves; he instead attributed only primary qualities to these things, i.e. qualities that presuppose only space and

495 impenetrability, which is to say: extension, shape, solidity, number, mobility. But this fairly obvious Lockean distinction stops at the surface of things and was only a youthful prelude, as it were, to the Kantian distinction. Kant started from an incomparably higher standpoint, and showed that what *Locke* had considered to be primary qualities,[a] i.e. qualities of things in themselves, belong only to the way in which things appear in our faculty of apprehension;[b] and this is the case precisely because we have *a priori* cognition of its conditions, space, time and causality. Thus, *Locke* took the thing in itself and subtracted the part that the sense organs play in appearance; but *Kant* subtracted the role of brain functions too (although not by that name), which gave infinitely greater meaning and a much more profound significance[c] to the distinction between appearances and things in themselves. To do so, he had to separate very clearly between our *a priori* and our *a posteriori* cognition, something that had not yet been done with proper rigour and thoroughness, or with a clear consciousness: and this, accordingly, became the chief import[d] of his profound investigations. – Here we want to note right away that Kant's philosophy has a threefold relation

[a] *qualitates primarias*
[b] *Auffassungsvermögen*
[c] *Sinn*
[d] *Hauptstoff*

to that of his predecessors: first, it confirms and expands on *Locke*, as we have just seen; second, it corrects and makes use of *Hume*, and we find this expressed most clearly in the preface to the *Prolegomena* (which is the finest and most comprehensible of all Kant's major works, and is read far too infrequently, since it makes the study of his philosophy much easier); third, it has a decidedly polemical and destructive relation to the philosophy of Leibniz and Wolff. People ought to be familiar with all three doctrines before going on to study Kant's philosophy. – Now if, as we said above, the distinction between appearance and the thing in itself, which is to say the doctrine that ideal and real are entirely different, is the basic feature[a] of Kant's philosophy, then the claim put forward soon afterwards, that these two are in a relation of absolute identity, is sad proof of Goethe's remark that I mentioned earlier; and even more so since the claim was based on nothing but the windbag's boasts[b] of intellectual intuition and was thus only a return to the vulgarity of common opinion, masked by an imposing façade of high-minded airs, bombast and gibberish. It became the worthy point of departure for the even cruder nonsense of the clumsy and mind-less[c] *Hegel*. – We have described how Kant separated appearance from the thing in itself, a distinction based in profundity and thoughtfulness[d] far more firmly than everything that had happened before; and its results were of infinite importance.[4] With complete originality and in an entirely novel way, Kant discovered, from a new angle and along a new path, the same truth that Plato tirelessly repeats, usually expressing himself, in his own language, as follows: this world that appears to the senses does not have true being, but is instead only an incessant becoming, it is and it is not, and apprehending[e] it does not involve cognition so much as delusion. Plato also expresses this mythologically at the beginning of the seventh book of the *Republic*, which I already mentioned in the Third Book of the present text as the most important passage in all Plato's works; there he says that the people who are chained firmly in a dark cave would not see either the true, original light or real things, but rather only the dim light of the fire in the cave and the shadows of real things that pass by this fire behind their backs: they would think that shadows were reality and true wisdom consisted of determining the succession of the shadows. – The same truth, presented in yet another, completely different way, is also a principal doctrine of

496

---

[a] *Grundzug*
[b] *Windbeutelei*
[c] *Geistlosen* [or 'spiritless', 'lacking spirit', presumably a reference to Hegel's concept of *Geist* (spirit)]
[d] *Besonnenheit*
[e] *Auffassung*

the *Vedas* and *Puranas*; this is the doctrine of *māyā*, which simply means what Kant called appearance in contrast to the thing in itself: because the work of *māyā* is declared to be precisely the visible world in which we exist, a magic trick, an insubstantial,[a] intrinsically inessential semblance[b] comparable to an optical illusion or a dream, a veil wrapped around human consciousness, something that can be said both to be and not to be with equal truth and equal falsity. – Kant not only expressed this same doctrine in a completely new and original manner, but also made it into an established and incontrovertible truth through the calmest and most sober presentation, while both Plato and the Indians only grounded their claims in a general world-view, articulating these claims as direct expressions of their consciousness, and presenting them more mythically and poetically than clearly and philosophically. In this respect they are related to Kant just as the Pythagoreans, Hicetas, Philolaus and Aristarchus[5] (who claimed that the earth rotates around the sun) are related to Copernicus. This sort of clear knowledge[c] and calm, level-headed[d] presentation of the dream-like constitution of the whole world is really the basis for the whole of Kant's philosophy, it is its soul and its very greatest merit. Kant accomplished this by taking apart the whole machinery of our cognitive faculty, which brings about the phantasmagoria of the objective world, and displaying it piece by piece, with admirable dexterity and clarity of mind.[e,6] All previous Western philosophies look indescribably clumsy compared to Kant; they fail to recognize this truth, which is why they always really speak as if they were dreaming. Kant was the first to wake them abruptly from this dream, which is why the last of the sleepers (Mendelssohn)[7] called him the universal destroyer.[f] He showed that the laws that govern existence[g] (i.e. experience in general) with staunch necessity cannot be used to deduce or explain *existence itself*, and that the validity of these laws is thus only relative, i.e. they arise only after existence, the world of experience in general, is already posited and present, and that consequently these laws cannot be our guide when we set about explaining our own existence or the existence of the world.[8] All previous Western philosophers imagined that these laws, which connect appearances to each other and all of which – time and space

[a] *bestandloser*
[b] *Schein*
[c] *Erkenntniß*
[d] *besonnene*
[e] *Besonnenheit*
[f] *Allzermalmer*
[g] *Daseyn*

as well as causality and inference[a] – I collect together under the rubric of the principle of sufficient reason, – all previous Western philosophers imagined that these laws were absolute and not conditioned by anything at all, eternal truths,[b] and that the world itself existed only as a result of and in conformity with them, and believed, accordingly, that they must be the key for solving the whole riddle of the world. The assumptions made for this purpose, which Kant criticized under name of the ideas of reason, really only served to raise mere appearance, the work of *māyā*, Plato's   498 world of shadows, to the position of sole and highest reality, and to posit appearance as the true and innermost essence of things, hence making true cognition of this essence impossible: i.e. in a word, putting the dreamers even more soundly to sleep. Kant showed that those laws, and consequently the world itself, are conditioned by the subject's mode of cognition, from which it follows that, however much people kept researching and reaching conclusions with this as their guide, they did nothing to advance the main issue, i.e. cognition of the essence of the world in itself and outside of representation, but instead only went round and round like a squirrel in a wheel. We can thus compare the dogmatists, taken altogether, with people who think that they will come to the end of the world if they keep going straight on for long enough. But then Kant sailed around the world and showed that because it is round, we will not escape by moving horizontally, but it might not be impossible if we move vertically. You could also say that Kant's doctrine makes us realize that we need not look beyond[c] ourselves for the beginning and the end of the world, but rather within.[9]

But all this rests on the fundamental distinction between dogmatic and *critical* or *transcendental philosophy*. Anyone wanting to clarify this with an example can do so quite readily by reading an essay by *Leibniz* as a specimen of the dogmatic philosophy, an essay that goes by the name 'On the ultimate origination of things'[d] and was first published in the Erdmann edition of Leibniz's philosophical works, vol. I, p. 147. It gives a proper, realist-dogmatic, *a priori* demonstration of the origin and excellence of the world using the ontological and cosmological proofs, on the grounds of the eternal truths.[e] – It is admitted once in passing that experience reveals the exact opposite of the excellence of the world demonstrated here, but experience is given to understand that it knows nothing of the matter

---

[a] *Schlussfolge*
[b] *aeternae veritates*
[c] *außer*
[d] *De rerum originatione radicali*
[e] *veritates aeternae* [the Latin phrase occurs twice more in this paragraph]

and should keep its mouth shut when philosophy has spoken *a priori*. –

499 With *Kant, critical philosophy* comes on the scene as the adversary of this entire method; critical philosophy conceives its problem to be precisely those eternal truths that serve to support all such dogmatic structures; it investigates their origin and finds it to be in people's heads. They stem from forms specifically belonging to these heads and are carried around inside of them for the purpose of apprehending an objective world. So here in the brain is the quarry that supplies the matter for that proud dogmatic construct. To achieve this result, critical philosophy must *go above and beyond* the eternal truths on which all dogmatism has so far been grounded, in order to make these into its objects of investigation; but in so doing, it has become *transcendental* philosophy. From this it follows further that what we recognize as the objective world does not belong to the essence of things in themselves, but rather only to its *appearance*, and is conditioned by those very forms that lie *a priori* in the human intellect (i.e. the brain), and thus that the world can contain nothing but appearances.[10]

Of course Kant did not realize that appearance is the world as representation, and the thing in itself is the will. But he showed that the appearing world is conditioned by the subject as much as it is by the object; and by isolating the most general forms of its appearance, i.e. of representation, he showed that we do not just come to have cognition of these forms and comprehend[a] their complete conformity to law by proceeding from the object; we cognize these forms just as well when we proceed from the subject, and we can do so because they really constitute the boundary between object and subject and are thus common to both; and Kant concluded that when we follow this boundary we do not get to the inside of either the object or the subject, and consequently we never gain cognition of the essence of the world, the thing in itself.

As I will soon show, Kant did not deduce the thing in itself properly but rather by means of an inconsistency, and he had to repent for this in the form of frequent and overwhelming attacks on this principal aspect of his doctrine. He did not directly recognize the will as the thing in itself, but he did take a huge, revolutionary step in the direction of this recognition, by demonstrating that the undeniable, moral[11] meaning of human action

500 is utterly different from and independent of the laws of appearance, and never explicable from these, but rather is something that touches directly on the thing in itself: this is the second main point of view with respect to his merit.

[a] *übersehe*

We can see the third main point of view as the complete overthrow of the scholastic philosophy, a term I would like to use as a general designation for the whole period beginning with the Church Father, Augustine, and ending shortly before Kant. *Tennemann* very accurately gives the principal characteristic of scholasticism as the guardianship of the established religion[a] over philosophy, which really has nothing left to do except to confirm and elaborate the chief dogmas that religion prescribes for it: the true scholastics, up to Suarez, confess this without disguise: subsequent philosophers do so more unconsciously or at least without admitting that this is happening. Scholastic philosophy supposedly lasted until only about a hundred years before Descartes, who then supposedly inaugurated a whole new epoch of free enquiry, independent of all positive religious doctrine; but this in fact cannot be attributed to Descartes and his followers;[*,12] we can attribute to them only an illusion of this or at most an attempt[b] at it. Descartes was an extremely great man, and he accomplished a great deal, making allowances for his time. But if we do not make such allowances, and instead measure him according to this liberation of thought from all

501

---

* Bruno and Spinoza are completely excluded from this characterization. They each stand independent and alone, and belong to neither the century nor the part of the world that repaid the one with death and the other with persecution and ignominy. Their miserable existences and efforts in the West are like those of a tropical plant in Europe. Their true, spiritual homeland would be the banks of the sacred Ganges: there they would have led peaceful and honoured lives, among like-minded people. – Bruno was burned at the stake for his book, *Della causa principio ed uno* [*On the Cause, the Principle and the One*] where, in the opening verses, he clearly and beautifully expresses how lonely he feels in his century; and at the same time he shows a presentiment of his fate, which makes him hesitate in his descriptions until he is overcome by that drive, so strong in noble spirits, to communicate what he knows to be true:

> *Ad partum properare tuum, mens aegra, quid obstat;*
>   *Seclo haec indigno sint tribuenda licet?*
> *Umbrarum fluctu terras mergente, cacumen*
>   *Adtolle in clarum, noster Olympe, Jovem*

> [What prevents you from giving birth, my suffering mind,
> Do you too offer your work to this unworthy age?
> When shadows sway over lands themselves, lift up
> Your peaks, my Olympus, into high heavens above.]

Anyone who reads his principal work, like the rest of his Italian writings (which used to be so rare, but are now available to all through a German edition), will discover, as I did, that of all the philosophers, he is the only one to approach Plato when it comes to injecting the philosophical with a strong display of poetic power and tendency, which he uses to particularly dramatic effect. Just imagine the tender, spiritual, and thoughtful being presented to us in his writings in the hands of the coarse, furious priests who were his judges and executioners, and thank time itself for bringing in a brighter and milder century so that the posterity whose curses should reach those diabolical fanatics is in fact our present era.

[a] *herrschenden Landesreligion*
[b] *Streben*

fetters and the beginning of a new period of impartial and independent investigation that he has been credited with, we are forced to discover that, given the scepticism that he never took seriously and thus abandoned so quickly and easily, he in fact has the air of *wanting* to suddenly throw off all the fetters of his earlier indoctrination into opinions belonging to his age and nation; but he only *seems*[a] momentarily to do so, only to take these opinions back up again at once and adhere to them all the more strongly; and it is the same with all of his successors up to Kant. Goethe's verses are most applicable to a free and independent thinker[b] of his breed:

> If Your Grace will allow this analogy,
> He seems like a long-legged cicada to me,
> That jumps and keeps jumping while flying along,
> Then returns to the grass and resumes its old song.[c]

Kant had reasons for making it seem as if *he* meant to do the same. But the ostensible leap that was permitted him (because everyone knew it led back to the grass) turned into a flight this time; and now the people standing below can only look up, but they cannot capture him again.

    Thus, Kant dared to produce a doctrine demonstrating that the dogmas which had supposedly been proven so often were in fact unprovable. He dealt the death blow to speculative theology and the rationalist psychology associated with it. They have disappeared from German philosophy since then, and we must not be misled by the fact that the word is sometimes retained after the subject has been abandoned, or that some impoverished professor of philosophy thinks first of his fear of his master and leaves the truth to look after itself. The scope of Kant's merit can only be assessed by someone who has observed the pernicious influence of those concepts on the natural science, as well as the philosophy, of all the writers of the 17th and 18th centuries, even the very best of them. There has been a striking change of tone and metaphysical background in German scientific writings since Kant: before Kant things were as they still are in England. – This merit of Kant's is connected to the fact that[13] all the previous philosophy of the ancient, medieval and modern periods was thoroughly dominated by blind adherence to the laws of appearance, the elevation of these laws into eternal truths, and the consequent transformation of transient appearance into the true essence of the world; in short, this philosophy was dominated

---

[a] *zum Schein*
[b] *Selbstdenker*
[c] [*Faust*, ' Prologue in Heaven']

by a *realism* whose delusions were undisturbed by reflection.[a] *Berkeley*, like *Malebranche* before him, had recognized the one-sided nature of this – indeed, its falseness – and was not able to reverse it, because his attack was limited to a *single* issue. So it was left to *Kant* to help the fundamental idealistic insight, which in the whole of non-Islamicized Asia is indeed essentially one of religion, to gain dominance in philosophy at least in Europe. Before Kant, we were *in* time, now time is in us, etc.[14]

That realistic[15] philosophy even treated ethics in accordance with the laws of appearance, laws that it conceived as being absolute and valid even for things in themselves. Thus ethics was grounded sometimes on the doctrine of happiness,[b] sometimes on the will of the Creator of the universe, and ultimately on the concept of perfection.[c] In and of itself, this concept is completely empty and vacuous, since it designates a mere relation that derives its meaning only from what it is applied to; 'being perfect' does not mean anything more than 'corresponding to some concept that was presupposed and given', a concept that must therefore be presented in advance, and without which perfection is an abstract quantity and consequently meaningless in itself. Now if we wanted to presuppose tacitly the concept of 'humanity', and thus posit as a moral principle an aspiration for the perfection of humanity, all this amounts to is 'people should be what they should be' – which leaves us just no wiser[d] than before. 'Perfect' is practically synonymous with 'numerically complete',[e] since it means that all the predicates found in the concept of the species are represented – which is to say are really extant – in some given case or individual. Thus, if used absolutely and in the abstract,[f] the concept of 'perfection' is a vacuous word, and so is talk of the 'most perfect being' and suchlike. All this is mere verbiage. Nevertheless, the concept of perfection and imperfection was current coin in the previous century; in fact, it was the pivot point that almost all moralizing and even theologizing turned on. Everyone had it on their lips, and it ended up being a real nuisance. We see even the best writers of the age, such as Lessing, entangled in and struggling with perfections and imperfections in the most pitiful way. At the same time, any thinking person must have had at least a vague sense that there is no positive content to the concept of perfection, since, like an algebraic function, it indicates a

503

---

[a] *Besinnung*
[b] *Glücksäligkeitslehre*
[c] *Vollkommenheit*
[d] *klug*
[e] *vollzählig*
[f] *in abstracto*

mere relation in the abstract.[16] – Kant, as I already mentioned, completely separated the great and undeniable ethical significance of actions from appearance and its laws, and showed the former to be directly concerned with the thing in itself, the innermost essence of the world, in contrast to the latter, i.e. time and space and everything that fills them and is arranged in them according to causal laws, which are seen as an insubstantial and chimerical[a] dream.

The little I have said in no way exhausts the topic, but might be enough to testify to the fact that I acknowledge Kant's great merit, and I have done this both for my own satisfaction and also because justice demands that these merits be called to mind by anyone who wants to follow me in relentlessly exposing his flaws, which I will now proceed to do.

---

504   The fact that Kant's great achievements were necessarily accompanied by great mistakes can be assessed in a purely historical way by noting that although he effected the greatest revolution in philosophy and brought an end to fourteen centuries of scholasticism (understood in the broader sense I have given), truly inaugurating an entirely new, third epoch in philosophy; nonetheless, the immediate result of his appearance was almost exclusively negative, not positive. This is because he did not establish a complete new system for his followers to maintain for some limited period of time; consequently, although everyone clearly recognized that something major had taken place, no one really knew what it was. They certainly saw that the whole philosophical enterprise to date[17] had been a futile dream, and that a new age had now awoken from this dream, but they did not know what to believe in next. A great emptiness, a great need had opened up and this aroused a general interest, even from the public at large. Men without any conspicuous talent felt inspired, although without being impelled by any inner drive or feeling of strength (a feeling that can express itself at inauspicious times as well, as with Spinoza); they made a variety of weak, absurd and occasionally crazy experiments that came to the notice of the newly attentive public who listened with the sort of patience only to be found in Germany.

The same thing must have happened at some point in nature as well, when a great revolution transformed the entire face of the earth, when land and sea exchanged places and the ground was levelled to allow for a new creation. It took a long time after that for nature to give rise to a new series of permanent forms, each in harmony with itself and with

---

[a] *bestand- und wesenloser*

the others: strange and monstrous organized forms[a] emerged that were not in harmony with themselves or with each other and could not last long; but their remains are still in existence, and are precisely what have provided us with a memorial of the fluctuation and experimentation of nature recreating itself anew. – Since, as we all know, Kant has initiated a very similar crisis and an age of monstrous creations[b] in philosophy, it can be inferred that his merit was not absolute but rather suffered from gross defects, and must have been negative and one-sided. We will now search for these defects.

505

To begin with, we want to scrutinize and make clear to ourselves the fundamental thought that is the point[c] of the whole *Critique of Pure Reason*. – Kant adopts the standpoint of his predecessors, the dogmatic philosophers, and shares the following assumptions with them. (1) Metaphysics is the science of what lies beyond the possibility of all experience. – (2) This can never be discovered using principles that are themselves derived from experience (*Prolegomena*, § 1); rather, only what we know[d] *prior to*, and thus *independently of* all experience can go beyond possible experience. – (3) Some principles of this kind are really to be found within our reason, and they are comprehended under the term 'cognition from pure reason'. – This is the extent to which Kant makes common cause with his predecessors, but at this point he parts ways. His predecessors say: 'these principles, or cognition from pure reason, are expressions of the absolute possibility of things, eternal truths,[e] sources of ontology; they stand above the world-order as fate[f] stood above the gods of the ancients'. Kant says: these are mere forms of our intellect, laws that do not concern the existence of things but rather our representations of them; thus, they are valid only for our apprehension[g] of things and cannot extend further than the possibility of experience, as was the intention according to article 1 above. The very fact that these forms of cognition are *a priori*, since this can be the case only by virtue of their subjective origin, separates us forever from cognition of the essence in itself of things and limits us to a world of mere appearances, so that we cannot have cognition of how things might be in themselves *a posteriori*, let alone *a priori*. Metaphysics is therefore impossible and into its

[a] *monströse Organisationen*
[b] *ungeheuren Ausgeburten*
[c] *Absicht*
[d] *wissen*
[e] *aeternae veritates*
[f] *Fatum*
[g] *Auffassung*

506 place steps a critique of pure reason. Here, Kant achieves a complete victory over the old dogmatism; which is why all attempts at dogmatism since then have had to adopt a completely different method from earlier ones: I will now proceed to a justification of my own attempt in accordance with the expressed intention of the present critique. Specifically, a closer examination of the argument above reveals that its very first basic assumption[a] is a begging of the question;[b] this lies in the claim (which is laid out with particular clarity in *Prolegomena*, § 1): 'the source of metaphysics absolutely cannot be empirical, its principles and fundamental concepts can never be taken from either inner or outer experience'. Yet absolutely nothing is offered in defence[c] of this cardinal claim except an etymological argument from the word 'metaphysics'. But in truth, the situation is as follows: the world and our own existence are necessarily given to us as a riddle. Now it is assumed without further ado that the solution to this riddle cannot come from a thorough[d] understanding of the world but instead must be sought in something entirely different from the world (since this is what it means to be 'outside the possibility of all experience'); moreover, everything that we could somehow grasp[e] *immediately* must be excluded from this solution (since this means possible experience, inner as well as outer); instead, we must look for the solution mediately, namely by means of inferences from universal principles *a priori*. But after the main source of all cognition had been thus excluded and the direct path to the truth obstructed, we need not wonder that dogmatic efforts failed and that Kant could demonstrate the necessity of this failure; it had been assumed in advance that metaphysics was identical with *a priori* cognition. But for this to be the case, we would have first needed proof that the material for solving the riddle of the world could not possibly be contained in the world itself, but instead could only be looked for outside of the world, in something that could only be reached under the guidance of those forms we are conscious of *a priori*. But as long as this is unproven, we have no grounds for ruling out the richest of all sources of cognition (namely inner and outer experience), and

507 restricting ourselves to contentless forms just when we are faced with the most important and difficult of all tasks. This is why I say that the solution to the riddle of the world must come from an understanding of the world itself; that the task of metaphysics is not to skim over that experience in which the world exists, but rather to understand it from the ground up,

---

[a] *Grundannahme*
[b] *petitio principii*
[c] *Begründung*
[d] *gründlichen*
[e] *Kenntniß*

since both outer and inner experience are certainly the main sources of all
cognition; that it is therefore only possible to solve the riddle of the world
by linking outer experience to inner experience in the right way and at
the right point, and thus effecting a connection between these two such
different sources of cognition; still, this can only take place within certain
limits that are inseparable from our finite nature, so that we obtain a proper
understanding of the world, but without achieving a complete and self-
sufficient explanation of its existence, an explanation that does away with
all further problems. Thus 'it is possible to go forward up to a point',[a] and
my path lies between the earlier dogmatic doctrine of omniscience[b] and the
despair of Kantian critique. But the important truths that Kant discovered,
truths that brought down the earlier metaphysical systems, have provided
the data and material for my own. Compare what I say about my method
in chapter 17 of the second volume. – So much about Kant's fundamental
thought: now we want to consider how he goes about this as well as the
details of the project.[18]

─────────

Kant's style throughout bears the mark of a superior mind, a genuine, solid
individuality,[c] and an entirely extraordinary intellectual prowess;[d] the character of this style might be aptly described as a *brilliant dryness* that allowed
him to grasp concepts firmly, select them with the greatest assurance, and
scatter them freely here and there, to the astonishment of the reader. I find
the same brilliant dryness in Aristotle's style, although it is much simpler. –
Nonetheless, Kant's mode of presentation[e] is often unclear, indeterminate,
inadequate, and at times obscure. This last is certainly excused in part
by the difficulty of the subject-matter and the profundity of the thought;
but[19] someone with lucid knowledge[f] who is basically clear in his own
mind about what he thinks and wants would never write unclearly or
advance fluctuating, indeterminate concepts. Moreover, he would never
amass extremely difficult, complex foreign expressions and then use them
incessantly, the way Kant took words and formulas from ancient and even
scholastic philosophy and joined them together for his own purposes, as
is the case with 'transcendental unity of apperception' for instance, or
the way he always uses the phrase 'unity of synthesis'[g] where just plain

508

[a] *est quondam prodire tenus* [Horace, *Epistles* 1, I, 32]
[b] *Allweisheitslehre*
[c] *Eigentümlichkeit*
[d] *Denkkraft*
[e] *Vortrag*
[f] *ganz deutlich weiß*
[g] *Einheit der Synthesis*

'unification'[a] would do. Such a person would not keep explaining what he has already explained once, which is what Kant does, for instance with notions like the understanding, the categories, experience, and other main concepts. Such a person would certainly not keep repeating himself and yet still leave the same passages obscure every time he presents a thought that he has already presented a hundred times; instead, he would state his position once, clearly, thoroughly, and exhaustively, and leave it at that. 'The better we understand an issue, the more we are determined to express it in a single way' says Descartes in his fifth letter.[b,20] But the greatest problem with Kant's occasionally obscure delivery is that it acted as 'an example whose vices are easy to imitate'[c] and was indeed misinterpreted to the point where it played the role of a corrupting authority.[d] The public had been compelled to realize that what is obscure is not always senseless: so senseless things immediately took refuge behind obscure modes of presentation. *Fichte* was the first to seize upon this new privilege and make vigorous use of it; *Schelling* was at least his equal in this, and soon they both were overtaken by a host of hungry scribblers devoid of both spirit and honesty. Still, it was *Hegel* who ultimately showed the greatest audacity in dishing out pure nonsense, slapping together senseless, raving tangles of verbiage such as had only ever been heard in lunatic asylums; he became the instrument of the most ponderous, universal mystification that the world has ever seen, and this with a degree of success that will seem utterly incredible to posterity and will remain a monument to German foolishness.[e] In vain did *Jean Paul* write his fine paragraph: 'Higher appreciation of philosophical insanity from the lectern and of poetic insanity in the theater' (*Aesthetic Finishing School*[f]); since *Goethe* had already written in vain:

509

> Such gibberish is what we expect from a fool
> And with fools there is no intervening.
> When people hear words they assume as a rule
> That behind them is some sort of meaning.[g]

---

[a] *Vereinigung*

[b] *Quo enim melius rem aliquam concipimus, eo magis determinati sumus ad eam unico modo exprimendam.* [Descartes, *Letters*, I]

[c] *exemplar vitiis imitabile* [Horace, *Epistles*, 1, 19, 17]

[d] *verderblicher Autorisation*

[e] *Niaiserie*

[f] *ästhetische Nachschule* [*Kleine Nachschule zur ästhetischen Vorschule* (*Little Finishing School to the Aesthetic Preparatory School*) is part of Jean Paul's *Vorschule der Ästhetik*]

[g] [*Faust* I, 2563–6]]

But let us turn back to *Kant*.[21] It must be admitted that there is nothing about him of grandiose, ancient simplicity, of naïvety, ingenuousness or candour.[a] His philosophy finds no analogy in Greek architecture, which presents large, simple proportions that can be taken in at a single glance. It is much more reminiscent of Gothic architectural design, since an entirely unique peculiarity of Kant's spirit is a strange delight in *symmetry* that loves to take a colourful multiplicity and bring it into order, and then repeat the order in sub-orders, and so on indefinitely, just as in Gothic churches. In fact, he sometimes pursues this until it becomes a game, indulging this inclination so far that he does clear violence to the truth, which he treats in the way that old-fashioned gardeners treat nature, creating symmetrical avenues, squares and triangles, trees shaped like pyramids and spheres, and hedges in orderly curves. I will support this with facts.

After treating space and time in isolation, and then disposing of the whole world of intuition that fills space and time, the world in which we live and exist, with the meaningless words 'the empirical content of intuition is *given* to us' – then, in a *single* leap, Kant suddenly arrives at the *logical foundation of his whole philosophy, the table of judgements*. From this he deduces twelve categories, an even dozen, symmetrically arranged under four headings, which later become a terrible Procrustean bed into which he violently forces everything in the world and everything that happens in human beings; he will recoil from no act of violence, he will scorn no sophism, just to keep repeating the symmetry of that table wherever he goes. The first thing to be symmetrically deduced from it is the pure physiological table of the universal principles of natural science, namely: axioms of intuition, anticipations of perception, analogies of experience, 510 and postulates of empirical thought in general. Of these principles, the first two are simple, but the last two symmetrically emit three little shoots apiece. The simple categories were what he calls *concepts*; but the principles of natural science are *judgements*. According to his supreme guide to all wisdom, namely that of symmetry, the series is now to prove fruitful in *inferences*,[b] and this is indeed what happens, once again in a measured and symmetrical way. This is because, just as experience along with its *a priori* principles arose for the *understanding* through the application of the categories to sensibility, likewise the *ideas* of reason come about by applying *inferences* to the categories, a transaction that *reason* carries out according to its supposed principle of seeking the unconditioned. This takes place

---

[a] *ingénuité, candeur*
[b] *Schlüssen*

as follows: the three categories of relation provide the only three possible types of major premise[a] for inferences, and the inferences will accordingly be of three types, each of which can be viewed as an egg from which reason hatches an idea: from the categorical mode of inference comes the idea of the *soul*, from the hypothetical comes the idea of the *world*, and from the disjunctive comes the idea of *God*. In the middle one, the idea of the world, the symmetry of the table of categories is repeated yet again, since its four headings produce four theses, each of which has a symmetrical counterpart in the form of an antithesis.

   We certainly pay a tribute of wonder to the combination – which is, in truth, a highly astute one – that called forth this elegant structure; and we will continue our thorough investigation of its foundations and its component parts. – But first, the following remarks are in order.

It is astonishing how Kant goes on his way without further reflection, attending to his symmetry and arranging everything accordingly, but failing to consider any of the objects treated in this way on its own. I will explain more carefully. After looking at intuitive[b] cognition only in mathematics, he completely neglects all the other areas of intuitive[c] cognition that place the world before us, focusing exclusively on abstract thinking; but any meaning or value abstract thinking has comes first from the intuitive world, and this world is infinitely more significant, universal, and richer in content than the abstract part of our cognition. In fact, and this is a major point, he never clearly distinguished between intuitive and abstract cognition, a failing that mired him in insoluble, internal contractions, as we will see later. – After disposing of the entire world of the senses with the meaningless 'it is given', he makes, as we said, the logical table of judgements into the foundation stone of his edifice. But he does not give a moment's thought to what really lies before him. These forms of judgements are certainly *words* and *combinations of words*.[d] But it really ought to have been asked what these words immediately stand for: and then it would have been discovered that it is *concepts*. The next question would then have been as to the nature[e] of *concepts*. The answer to this would have revealed the relation these have to the intuitive representations

---

[a] *Obersätzen*
[b] *intuitive*
[c] *anschauliche*
[d] *Wortverbindungen*
[e] *Wesen*

in which the world exists:[a] then intuition would have distinguished itself from reflection. This would have required an investigation, but not simply into the manner in which pure and merely formal *a priori* intuition enters into consciousness – it would necessarily have led to an investigation of how its content, empirical intuition, enters consciousness as well. But this would have shown the role the *understanding* plays in all this, and thus in general what the *understanding* really is, and what, on the other hand, is meant by *reason*, the critique of which was being written here. It is really quite remarkable that he never once determines this final point in a proper and satisfactory manner; rather, he comes up with incomplete and erroneous explanations, and these only occasionally, as is required in a given context, which completely contradicts Descartes' rule, cited above.[*,22] For example, on p. 11/V 24 of the *Critique of Pure Reason*,[23] reason is the faculty of *a priori* principles; on p. 299/V 356 he once again says that reason is the faculty of *principles*, and that it is opposed to the understanding which is the faculty of *rules*! Now, you would think that there must be a world of difference between principles and rules, such as would justify the assumption of a special cognitive faculty for each. But this vast different is supposed to lie in the simple fact that *rules* are cognized *a priori* through pure intuition or the forms of the understanding, and principles only come *a priori* from mere concepts. We will return to this arbitrary and unacceptable distinction later, with the Dialectic. On p. 330/V 386, reason is the faculty of inferring:[b] he often describes mere judgement (p. 69/V 94) as an affair of the understanding. But this really just means: judgement is an affair of the understanding, as long as the basis of judgement is empirical, transcendental,[24] or metalogical (essay *On the Principle of Sufficient Reason*, §§ 31, 32, 33);[25] but when it is logical, as is the case with inference, then a very special, vastly superior cognitive faculty is at work, and that is reason. Indeed, even further, at p. 303/V 360, it is argued that the conclusions[c] drawn immediately from a proposition are still a matter of the understanding, and only those involving an intermediate

512

---

* It can be noted here that I always cite the *Critique of Pure Reason* according to the page numbers of *the first edition*, since these numbers are always provided in the Rosenkranz edition of the collected works: in addition, I will give the page numbers of the fifth edition proceeded by 'V'; all the other editions from the second onward are the same and have the same page numbers. [The first edition of the *Critique of Pure Reason* is nowadays customarily referred to as A, the second through fifth editions as B. So Schopenhauer's references represented here in the form p. 11/V 24 are equivalent to A11 / B24 etc.]

a *dasteht*
b *schließen*
c *Folgerungen*

concept are carried out by reason; and the example given is that if we take the claim 'all humans are mortal', the conclusion 'some mortal beings are human beings' is drawn by the mere understanding. On the other hand, 'all scholars are mortal' would require an entirely different and vastly superior faculty, that of reason. How was it possible for a great thinker to come up with something like this! On p. 553/V 581, reason is suddenly the persisting condition of all voluntary[a] actions. On p. 614/V 642 it consists in being able to give an account of our assertions: p. 643, p. 644/V 671, 672, it consists in uniting the concepts of the understanding into ideas, just as understanding unites the manifold of objects into concepts. On p. 646/V 674, it is nothing other than the faculty of deriving the particular from the universal.

513   *Understanding* is constantly being explained in new ways as well, in seven passages in the *Critique of Pure Reason*. On p. 51/V 75 it is the faculty of bringing forth representations itself. On p. 69/V 94 it is the faculty of judging, i.e. of thinking, i.e. of cognition through concepts. On p. 137 of the fifth edition it is the faculty of cognitions in general. On p. 132/V 171, it is the faculty of rules. But on p. 158/V 197 we read: 'it is not only the faculty of rules, but also the source of principles,[b] in accordance with which everything stands under a rule'; and nonetheless it was opposed to reason above, because only reason was the faculty of principles.[c] On p. 160/V 199, the understanding is the faculty of concepts: but on p. 302/V 359, it is the faculty of the unity of appearances by means of rules.

The explanations I have provided of those two cognitive faculties are solid, clear, determinate, simple, and moreover in full agreement with the way language has been used by all peoples at all times. Accordingly, I do not need to defend my explanations against such truly confused and groundless remarks,[d] even if they do come from Kant. I have only mentioned these as examples of my criticism that Kant pursued his symmetrical, logical system without giving enough thought to the objects he was dealing with.

Now as I said above, if Kant had enquired seriously into the extent to which two such different cognitive faculties (one of which is the distinguishing feature of humanity) can be known,[e] and what reason and understanding mean in the linguistic usage of all peoples and all philosophers, then he would never have divided reason into a theoretical and a

---

[a] *willkürliche*
[b] *Grundsätze*
[c] *Principien*
[d] *Rede*
[e] *sich zu erkennen geben*

practical component, and this on no better authority than the scholastic distinction between the *intellectus theoreticus* and *practicus* (a distinction that was used in an entirely different sense) nor would he have made practical reason the source of virtuous action. Likewise, before Kant so carefully separated the concepts of the understanding (by which he understood sometimes his categories and sometimes all other common concepts) from the concepts of reason (his so-called ideas), and made both into the material for his philosophy, which for the most part dealt only with the validity, use and the origin of all these concepts; – before doing this, as I said, he really ought to have investigated what a *concept* was in the first place. But unfortunately even an investigation as necessary as this was omitted entirely, which was a major contributing factor in the disastrous confusion of intuitive and abstract cognition, as I will soon show. – The same lack of adequate deliberation that made him ignore questions such as: 'what is intuition?', 'what is reflection?', 'what is a concept?', 'what is reason?', 'what is the understanding?' – also allowed him to ignore other issues that were just as urgently in need of investigation, issues such as: 'what do I call the *object*[a] that I distinguish from *representation*?', 'what is existence[b]?', 'what is an object[c]', 'what is a subject?', 'what is truth, illusion, error?' – But he pursued his logical schema and his symmetry without stopping to reflect or look around. The table of judgements should and must be the key to all wisdom.

514

I mentioned above that Kant's chief merit was to distinguish between appearance and thing in itself, stating that this entire visible world is appearance, and thus denying the laws of appearance any validity outside of appearance itself. But it is remarkable that[26] he did not derive this merely relative existence of appearance from the simple, undeniable truth that lay so close at hand, '*no object without a subject*'. This would have allowed him to demonstrate that, because the object only ever exists with reference to a subject, it is at its very root dependent on and conditioned by the subject; consequently, it is mere appearance and does not exist unconditionally or in itself. Kant did not do justice to *Berkeley*, who had already made this important claim into the foundation stone of his philosophy, thus earning himself an immortal place in our memory. Still, Berkeley did not draw the proper conclusions from this claim, and as a result, people generally

[a] *Gegenstand*
[b] *Daseyn*
[c] *Objekt*

failed to understand him or did not pay him enough attention. In my first edition I explained Kant's avoidance of this Berkeleyan proposition as a clear case of timidity[a] in the face of resolute idealism which, at the same time, I found distinctly articulated in many passages of the *Critique of Pure Reason* as well, and this led me to accuse Kant of contradicting himself. 515 This criticism was sound enough, coming from someone familiar only with the second edition of the *Critique of Pure Reason*, or the five editions printed after that, as was the case with me at that time. But later, when I read Kant's main work in the already rare first edition, I was delighted to see all these contradictions disappear; I found that even if Kant did not use the exact formula 'no object without subject', he nonetheless declares just as resolutely as Berkeley and I have done that the external world in space and time is just a representation of the cognitive subject. So, for instance, on p. 383 of that text he says without reservation 'If I were to take away the thinking subject, the whole corporeal world would have to disappear, as this is nothing but the appearance in the sensibility of our subject and one mode of its representations.' But in the second edition he suppresses the whole passage from pp. 348–92 which gives a beautifully clear presentation of his resolute idealism, and he brings in a lot of contradictory assertions instead. This resulted in the circulation of a disfigured and corrupted text of the *Critique of Pure Reason* from 1787 to 1838; the book became self-contradictory, and could not have made complete sense to anyone. I have written more about this in a letter to Professor Rosenkranz, speculating about the reasons and the weaknesses that could have moved Kant to disfigure his immortal work in this way. Professor Rosenkranz included the most important section of the letter in his introduction to the second volume of his edition of Kant's collected works, and I refer to it here.[b] In 1838, Professor Rosenkranz was persuaded by my claims[c] to restore the *Critique of Pure Reason* to its original form by having the *first* edition of 1781 printed in the aforementioned second volume, thus rendering philosophy an inestimable service, perhaps even rescuing the most important work in German literature from destruction; and he should always be remembered for this. But nobody should imagine himself acquainted with the *Critique* 516 *of Pure Reason* or believe that he has a clear idea of Kant's doctrine if he

[a] *Scheu*
[b] [See Karl Rosenkranz and Friedrich Wilhelm Schubert (eds.), *Immanuel Kant's Sämmtliche Werke* (Leipzig: Leopold Voss, 1838), vol. 2, xi. For Schopenhauer's letter see *GB*, 165–8. Schopenhauer later sent an extensive list of textual differences he had discovered between the editions of the *Critique* (see *GB*, 168–74) for which Rosenkranz expresses his thanks (op. cit., xv).]
[c] *Vorstellungen*

has only read the second edition or one of the editions to follow that; this is simply impossible, because he has read only a garbled, corrupted, and in some respects inauthentic text. It is my duty here to state this firmly, as a warning to everyone.

The manner in which Kant introduces the *thing in itself* stands in undeniable contradiction to the resolutely idealistic fundamental insight so clearly articulated in the first edition of the *Critique of Pure Reason*, and doubtless this is the chief reason why he suppressed the main idealist passage in the second edition and declared his frank opposition to Berkeley's idealism; but in doing so, he simply made his work incoherent, and could not remedy its principal defect. This defect, as everyone knows, is the way he chose to introduce the thing in itself – an unacceptable way, as was demonstrated extensively by G. E. Schulze in *Aenesidemus*, and was soon acknowledged as the untenable point of his system. The issue can be clarified quite briefly. Although the fact was hidden under many twists and turns, Kant grounded the presupposition of the thing in itself in an inference according to the law of causality, namely that empirical intuition, or more precisely the *sensation*[a] in our sense organs that generates empirical intuition, must have an external cause. But according to his own, correct, discovery, we are familiar with the law of causality *a priori*; consequently it is a function of our intellect, and thus *subjective* in origin; further, the sensory sensation[b] itself to which we apply the law of causality is undeniably *subjective*, and finally even space, in which we locate the cause of the sensation as an object by application of this law, is an *a priori* and thus *subjective* form of our intellect. Accordingly, the whole of empirical intuition remains on strictly *subjective* ground;[c] it is simply an event within us, and there is nothing independent of and entirely different from it that can be imported as a *thing in itself* or verified as a necessary presupposition. In truth, empirical intuition is and remains merely our representation: it is the world as representation. We can arrive at the essence in itself of this world only along the completely different path I have introduced. This alternative path involves appealing to self-consciousness, which announces the will as the 'in-itself' of our own appearance. But at this point, the thing in itself becomes something entirely different in kind[d] from representation and its elements, as I have argued.

517

---

[a] *Empfindung*
[b] *Sinnesempfindung*
[c] *Grund und Boden*
[d] *ein . . . toto genere Verschiedenes*

As I said, this great defect in the Kantian system was demonstrated quite early, and it is an illustration of a splendid Indian proverb: 'no lotus without a stem'. The stem here is the flawed deduction of the thing in itself: but only the manner of the deduction, not the acknowledgement of a thing in itself for a given appearance. *Fichte*, however, misunderstood it to be the latter, which he was able to do only because he was not interested in truth but in causing a stir to further his own personal goals. Accordingly, he was thoughtless and foolhardy enough to deny the thing in itself altogether, and to set up a system in which not only the merely formal aspect of representation is deduced from the subject *a priori*, as with Kant, but even the material aspect, the entire content of representation is supposedly deduced as well. In doing so, he reckoned quite correctly on the general lack of judgement and foolishness[a] of the public, who took bad sophisms, pure hocus-pocus, and absurd claptrap for proof; so that he succeeded in attracting public attention away from Kant and towards himself, and directing German philosophy onto a path where it was later advanced by Schelling before finally achieving its goal in the absurd Hegelian pseudo-sagacity.[b]

Now I return to Kant's great error touched on above, the fact that he did not properly distinguish intuitive from abstract cognition, which gave rise to a fatal confusion that we must consider more closely. If he had clearly distinguished intuitive representations from concepts thought merely in the abstract,[c,27] then he would have kept them straight and would always have known which of the two he was dealing with. Unfortunately this is not what happened, although criticisms have not yet been voiced on this account, and might therefore be unexpected. The 'object of experience'[d] he is always talking about, the true object[e] of the categories, is not the intuitive representation, but neither is it the abstract concept; it is different from both, and yet is both at the same time, and a complete absurdity.[f] As incredible as it seems, he lacked the clarity of mind[g] or else the good will[28] to straighten this out and explain clearly to himself and to others whether his 'object of experience,[h] i.e. of cognition resulting from the application of the categories' is the intuitive representation in space and time (my first

518

---

[a] *Niaiserie*
[b] *Afterweisheit*
[c] *in abstracto*
[d] *Objekt der Erfahrung*
[e] *Gegenstand*
[f] *Unding*
[g] *Besonnenheit*
[h] *Gegenstand der Erfahrung*

class of representations) or merely the abstract concept. He always had in mind something intermediate between the two, however strange this may be, and this caused the unhappy confusion that I must now bring to light: to which end I will have to review the entire doctrine of elements in general.

––––––––––

The *Transcendental Aesthetic* is work of such extraordinary merit that it alone could serve to immortalize the name of Kant. Its proofs are so persuasive that I number its doctrines[a] among the irrefutable truths; they are undoubtedly also some of the richest in consequences, and can therefore be considered as that rarest of things in this world, a true and great discovery in metaphysics.[29] Kant provided rigorous proof that we are *a priori* conscious of a portion of our cognitions, a fact that admits of no other explanation than that they make up the forms of our intellect; indeed, this is not so much an explanation as a clear statement of the fact itself. The reason is that *a priori* does not mean anything other than 'not acquired through experience, and thus not coming to us from the outside'. But what is present in the intellect without having come from the outside is just what belongs to it originally and intrinsically,[b] its own essence. And if this intrinsic aspect consists of the general manner in which all its objects must present themselves to it, this entails that these are the forms of its cognition, i.e. the fixed and established manner in which it performs this function. Accordingly, 'cognitions *a priori*' and 'the intellect's own   519 forms' are fundamentally just two ways of saying the same thing, and thus to a certain extent synonymous.[30]

I cannot think of anything that I would get rid of in the doctrine of the Transcendental Aesthetic, but there are a few things I would add. In particular, Kant did not finish his train of thought, since he did not reject the whole Euclidean method of demonstration, even after saying on p. 87/V 120 that all geometric knowledge[c] is immediately evident in intuition. It is quite remarkable that even one of his opponents, and in fact the most astute of them all, G. E. Schulze (*Critique of Theoretical Philosophy*,[d] II, 241), drew the conclusion that Kant's doctrine would give rise to an entirely different treatment of geometry than the usual one. He meant this to be an apagogic proof against Kant, but in fact he unwittingly began a war

[a] *Lehrsätze*
[b] *das ihm selbst ursprünglich Angehörige*   .
[c] *Erkenntniß*
[d] *Kritik der theoretischen Philosophie*

against the Euclidean method. A point of reference for this is § 15 in the First Book of the present text.[31]

After the comprehensive discussion in the Transcendental Aesthetic of the universal *forms* of all intuition, you would expect at least some explanation of their *content*,[a] of the way *empirical* intuition enters our consciousness, the way cognition of this whole world arises within us, a world we find so real and so important. But Kant's doctrine does not really have anything more to say on this score than the frequently repeated but meaningless expression: 'The empirical aspect of intuition is *given* to us from the outside.' – So here too Kant is able to leap from the *pure forms of intuition* straight over to *thinking*, to the Transcendental Logic. At the very beginning of this section (*Critique of Pure Reason*, p. 50/V 74), where Kant cannot help touching on the material content[b] of empirical intuition, he makes his first false step or commits the πρῶτον ψεῦδος.[c] 'Our cognition,' he says, 'has two sources, namely receptivity of impressions and spontaneity of concepts: the first is the capacity for receiving representations, the second is the capacity for cognizing an object by means of these represen-

520   tations: through the former an object is given to us, through the latter it is thought.'[d] – That is false: because it would entail that the *impression*,[e] which is the only thing we are merely receptive to, and which therefore comes from without and is all that is really '*given*', is already a *representation* or even an *object*. But the impression is nothing more than a mere *sensation*[f] in the sense organs, and it is only by using the *understanding* (i.e. the law of causality) and space and time, the forms of intuition, that our *intellect* transforms this mere *sensation* into a *representation*, which now exists as an *object*[g] in space and time and can be distinguished from the latter (from the object) only by appealing to the thing in itself, and is otherwise identical with it. I have presented this process in detail in my essay *On the Principle of Sufficient Reason*, § 21. This completes the business of both the understanding and intuitive cognition, and it does not need concepts or thought for this purpose; thus even animals have these representations. If concepts and thought are added, which can certainly be attributed to spontaneity, then *intuitive* cognition will be abandoned entirely and a completely different class of representations, namely non-intuitive ones,

---

[a] *Inhalt* ['content' translates *Inhalt* below unless otherwise stated]
[b] *Gehalt*
[c] [first false step or mistaken premise: Aristotle, *Prior Analytics* II, 18, 66a16]
[d] [Schopenhauer's gloss is a departure from Kant's text, although he does not change the meaning]
[e] *Eindruck*
[f] *Empfindung*
[g] *Gegenstand*

abstract concepts, will enter consciousness. This is the activity of *reason*, and the content of rational thought comes exclusively from the intuitions that precede it and from comparisons between these and other intuitions and concepts. But this is how Kant imports thought into intuition and lays the ground for the fatal confusion of intuitive and abstract cognition that I am criticizing at present. He allows intuition, taken on its own, to be devoid of understanding, purely sensuous, and thus merely passive; and an *object*ᵃ is grasped only through thought (category of the understanding): and this is how he brings *thought into intuition*. But then again the object of *thought*ᵇ is an individual, real object;ᶜ and this deprives thought of its essential character of universality and abstraction and entails that thought has individual things rather than universal concepts for its object;ᵈ in doing this, Kant again brings *intuition into thought*. This gives rise to the fatal confusion I mentioned, and the consequences of this first false step extend over his entire theory of cognition. The complete confusion of intuitive 521 representation with abstract representation runs through the whole theory and creates a sort of intermediate between the two,³² which he describes as the object of cognitionᵉ through the understanding and its categories, and calls this cognition *experience*. It is difficult to believe that Kant himself could have had in mind anything wholly determinate or truly clear with this object of the understanding:ᶠ I will now prove this by way of the immense contradiction that runs through the whole of the Transcendental Logic, a confusion that is the true source of the obscurity enveloping it.

To be precise: in the *Critique of Pure Reason* on pp. 67–9/V 92–4; pp. 89, 90/V 122, 123; and further on V 135, 139, 153, he repeats and insists: the understanding is not a faculty of intuition, its cognition is not intuitive but rather discursive; the understanding is the faculty of judging (p. 69/V 94), and a judgement is mediate cognition, the representation of a representation (p. 68/V 93); the understanding is the faculty of thinking, and thinking is cognition through concepts (p. 69/V 94); the categories of the understanding are by no means the conditions under which objectsᵍ are given in intuition (p. 89/V 122), and the intuition has absolutely no need of the functions of thinking (p. 91/V 123); our understanding can only think, not intuit (V, pp. 135, 139). Further, in the *Prolegomena*, § 20:

ᵃ *Gegenstand*
ᵇ *Gegenstand des* Denkens
ᶜ *Objekt*
ᵈ *Objekt*
ᵉ *Gegenstand der Erkenntniß*
ᶠ *Gegenstand des Verstandes*
ᵍ *Gegenstände*

intuition, perception, *perceptio*, belong exclusively to the senses; judging belongs to the understanding alone; and §22: the business of the senses is to intuit, that of the understanding is to think, i.e. to judge. – Finally, in the *Critique of Practical Reason*, fourth edition, p. 247 (Rosenkranz edition p. 281):[33] understanding is discursive, its representations are thoughts, not intuitions. – All of these are Kant's own words.

It follows that this intuitive world would exist for us even if we had no understanding at all, that it comes into our heads in an entirely inexplicable manner that Kant frequently refers to with his remarkable expression: 'intuition is *given*', without ever offering any further explanation of that indeterminate and figurative expression.

522   All these passages stand in the most glaring contradiction to the whole of the rest of his doctrine of the understanding, its categories, and the possibility of experience, as presented in the Transcendental Logic. To be specific: in *Critique of Pure Reason*, p. 79/V 105, through its categories, the understanding brings unity to the manifold of *intuition*, and the pure concepts of understanding apply *a priori* to objects of *intuition*.[a] On p. 94/V 126, 'the categories are conditions of experience, whether of *intuition* or of the thinking that is encountered in it'.[b] On V, p. 127, the understanding is the originator of experience. On V, p. 128, the categories determine the *intuition* of objects,[c] on V, p. 130, everything that we represent as combined[d] in an object[e] (which is of course something intuitive and not something abstract) must first be combined by an act of understanding. On V, p. 135, understanding is explained all over again as the faculty of combining *a priori*, and of bringing the manifold of given representations under the unity of apperception: but, according to all linguistic usage, apperception is not the thinking of a concept, it is *intuition*. On V, p. 136 we find a supreme principle of the possibility of all intuition in reference to the understanding. On V, 143, a heading even states that all sensuous intuition is conditioned by the categories. In the same place, the *logical function of judgement* also brings the manifold of given *intuitions* under an apperception in general, and the manifold of a given intuition necessarily stands under the categories. On V, p. 144 unity enters into *intuition* through

[a] *Gegenstände der Anschauung*
[b] [Schopenhauer quotes this passage inaccurately. It should read: the categories 'must be recognized as *a priori* conditions of the possibility of experiences (whether of the intuition that is encountered in them, or of the thinking)'. Schopenhauer's version of this passage is actually quite misleading, since it implies that thinking is encountered in intuition, which Kant would vigorously deny]
[c] *Gegenstände*
[d] *verbunden*
[e] *Objekt*

the understanding, by means of the categories. On V, p. 145, the thinking of the understanding is explained in a very strange way as synthesizing, combining and ordering the manifold of *intuition*. On V, p. 161, experience is possible only through the categories, and consists in the connection[a] of *perceptions,* which are then certainly intuitions. On V, p. 159, categories are *a priori* cognitions of objects of intuition[b] in general. – Further, both here and V, p. 163 and p. 165 present a key doctrine of Kant's, the doctrine *that the understanding is what first makes nature possible,* by prescribing to it laws *a priori* and directing it according to its (the understanding's)   523 lawlikeness, etc. But nature is certainly something intuitive and not an abstraction; the understanding must therefore be a faculty of intuition. On V, p. 168 it is said that the concepts of the understanding are the principles of the possibility of experience, and this is the determination of appearances in space and time in general; and these appearances are certainly present in intuition. Finally, on pp. 189–211/V 232–56 there is an extended proof (whose falsity is demonstrated in detail in my essay *On the Principle of Sufficient Reason,* § 23),[34] that neither the objective succession nor the simultaneity of objects of experience[c] is perceived through the senses, but instead is brought into nature only through the understanding, and nature itself becomes possible in this way. But it is certain that nature, the sequence of events and the simultaneity of states, is purely intuitive and not merely an abstract thought.

I invite anyone who shares my admiration for Kant to reconcile these contradictions[35] and show that Kant had something quite clear and determinate in mind with his doctrine of the object of experience[d] and the way it is determined through the activity of the understanding and its twelve functions. I am convinced that the contradiction I have shown, which runs through the entire Transcendental Logic, is the reason why its presentation is so obscure. Kant was himself obscurely conscious of the contradiction and struggled with it inwardly, but nevertheless would not or could not raise it to clear consciousness; so he cast a veil over it for himself and for other people and used all sorts of surreptitious means to evade it. We might also deduce from this the fact that he made the cognitive faculties into a very strange and complicated machine, with so many wheels, such as the twelve categories, the transcendental synthesis of imagination, inner sense, the transcendental unity of apperception, as well as the schematism of the

[a] *Verknüpfung*
[b] *Gegenstände der Anschauung*
[c] *Gegenstände der Erfahrung*
[d] *Objekt der Erfahrung*

pure concepts of the understanding, etc. And in spite of this great apparatus, there is never an explanation of the intuition of the external world, which is certainly a primary concern in our cognition; rather, this urgent demand is always rejected in an extremely shabby manner with the same, meaningless, metaphorical expression: 'empirical intuition is given to us'. On p. 145 of the fifth edition we also learn that that empirical intuition is given through the object,[a] which must therefore be something different from the intuition.

Now if we try to discover Kant's innermost view[b] on the matter, a view that he does not express very clearly himself, we find that this sort of object[c] (which is different from *intuition* but is not for that matter a *concept*) is for him the true object for the understanding,[d] and that it is really the strange presupposition of such an unrepresentable object[e] that first makes intuition into experience. I believe that Kant was ultimately driven by an old, deeply ingrained prejudice – one that resists all investigation – into assuming that there is such an *absolute object*,[f] which is an object in itself, i.e. without a subject. This object is by no means the *intuited object*;[g] instead, it is added in thought to intuition through the concept, as something that corresponds to the intuition. When this takes place, the intuition becomes an experience and has value and truth, which are a function of its reference to a concept. (This is diametrically opposed to our presentation, which holds that the concept acquires value and truth only from the intuition.) The true function of the categories is to add this object[h] to intuition in thought, an object that is not capable of direct representation. 'Only through intuition is the object[i] given, which is then thought in accordance with the categories' (*Critique of Pure Reason*, first edition, p. 399).[36] This is made particularly clear in a passage on p. 125 of the fifth edition: 'The question now is whether *a priori* concepts do not also precede, as conditions under which alone something can be, if *not intuited*, nonetheless *thought* as *object* in general',[j] which he affirms. This clearly shows the source of the error and the confusion that surrounds it. Because

---

[a] *Objekt*
[b] *Meinung*
[c] *Objekt*
[d] *Gegenstand für den Verstand*
[e] *Gegenstand*
[f] *eines . . . absoluten Objekts*
[g] *das* angeschaute Objekt
[h] *Objekt*
[i] *Gegenstand*
[j] Gegenstand *überhaupt*

the *object* as such[a] only ever exists for *intuition* and in intuition: it may be completed by the senses, or, in their absence, by the imagination.[b] On the other hand, what is *thought* is only ever a universal non-intuitive *concept*, which can at best be the concept of an object in general:[c] but thinking refers 525 only mediately to *objects*,[d] through the mediation of concepts, and these objects themselves are and remain *intuitive*. This is because our thinking does not serve to give reality to intuitions: intuitions have their reality in themselves, to the extent that they are capable of it (empirical reality); rather, our thinking serves to unite what is common to intuitions, and their results, in order to preserve them and manipulate them more easily. But Kant ascribes objects[e] themselves to *thought*, in order to make experience and the objective world dependent on the *understanding*, without letting this be a faculty of *intuition*. In this respect he certainly distinguishes intuiting from thinking, but he makes individual things into the object,[f] partly of intuition, partly of thought. But in fact they are only the former: our empirical intuition is immediately *objective* precisely because it emerges from the causal nexus. It has things[g] immediately as its object,[h] and not representations distinct from things. Individual things are intuited as such in the understanding and through the senses: the *one-sided* impression on the senses is immediately completed by the imagination. But as soon as we turn to *thought*, we leave individual things behind, and concern ourselves with general concepts that are devoid of intuitions, even if we then go on to apply the results of our thinking to the individual things. If this is kept in mind, we clearly see how unacceptable it is to assume that the intuition of things only obtains reality and becomes an experience through thinking these very things, a thinking that involves the application of the twelve categories. Rather, empirical reality and consequently experience is already given in the intuition itself: but the intuition too can only come about by applying cognition of the causal nexus (which is the sole function of the understanding) to the sensory sensation.[i] Accordingly, intuition is truly intellectual,[j] which is precisely what Kant denies.

[a] *Gegenstand als solcher*
[b] *Einbildungskraft*
[c] *Gegentande überhaupt*
[d] *Gegenstände*
[e] *Gegenstände*
[f] *Gegenstand*
[g] *Dinge*
[h] *Gegenstand*
[i] *Sinnesempfindung*
[j] *intellektual*

The assumption of Kant's that I am at present criticizing can found in the passages cited, but it is also articulated in a particularly clear manner at the very beginning of § 36 of the *Critique of the Power of Judgement* as well as in the *Metaphysical Foundations of Natural Science*, in the note to the first explanation of 'Phenomenology'. But it is stated most clearly, and with a naïvety that, given the difficulty of the point, Kant would be the last person to hazard, in a book by a Kantian, namely Kiesewetter's *Outline of a Universal Logic*,ᵃ third edition, part I, p. 434 of the argument, and part II, §§ 52 and 53 of the argument. It is also in Tieftrunk's *Laws of Thought in a Purely German Garb*ᵇ (1825). This really shows how the disciples of any given thinker become the magnifying glass for his errors when they fail to think for themselves. Having settled on his doctrine of the categories, Kant presents it very gingerly. His disciples on the other hand set off with foolhardy assurance, and thus make its falsity obvious.[37]

Given what we have said, Kant does not really consider the objectᶜ of the categories to be the thing in itself, but rather its nearest relation:[38] it is the *object in itself*,ᵈ which is an object that does not need a subject; it is an individual thing that is not in space and time, because it is not intuitive; it is the object of thoughtᵉ without being an abstract concept. So Kant actually makes a three-way distinction: (1) representation; (2) the object of representation;ᶠ (3) the thing in itself. The first is the business of sensibility, which Kant sees as comprising (in addition to sensation) space and time as pure forms of intuition. The second is the business of the understanding, which adds it in *thought* through its twelve categories. The third lies beyond all possibility of cognition. (As an example of this, see p. 108 and p. 109 of the first edition of the *Critique of Pure Reason*.) But there are no grounds for distinguishing between representation and the object of representation: Berkeley had already proven this, and it emerges from the whole of my presentation in the First Book (particularly chapter 1 of the supplement), and even from Kant's own, fully idealistic fundamental point of view in the first edition. But if we do not want to consider the object of representation as a representation, thereby equating the two, then the object of representation must be assimilated to the thing in itself: in the end, this depends on the sense given to the word 'object'.ᵍ But one thing is always certain: if we

---

ᵃ *Grundriss einer allgemeinen Logik*
ᵇ *Denklehre in rein Deutschem Gewande*
ᶜ *Gegenstand*
ᵈ *Objekt an sich*
ᵉ *Gegenstand des Denkens*
ᶠ *Gegenstand der Vorstellung*
ᵍ *Gegenstand*

think clearly and carefully, we will not find anything except representation and thing in itself. The source of Kant's errors is the unjustified insertion of that hybrid, the object of representation; but when this is taken away, the doctrine of the categories as *a priori* concepts falls too, because they do not add anything to intuition and are not valid of the thing in itself; rather they only enable us to think of those 'objects of representations' and thus transform representation into experience. This is because every empirical intuition is already experience, but every intuition that comes from sensory sensation is empirical. By means of its sole function (*a priori* cognition of the law of causation), the understanding refers this sensation to its cause; and in this way the cause presents itself in space and time (forms of pure intuition) as the object of experience,[a] a material object[b] persisting in space through all of time, but always remaining a representation, like space and time themselves. If we want to get beyond this representation, we come to the question of the thing in itself; and the answer to this question is the theme of my entire work, as it is the theme of all metaphysics in general. The error of Kant's that I have presented here is related to the mistake I criticized earlier, that he does not provide a theory of the origin of empirical intuition but rather takes this as *given*, without further comment. He identifies it with mere sensory sensation (to which he adds only the forms of intuition, space and time) and comprehends both under the name of sensibility. But these materials do not give rise to objective representation; for this, a sensation must be referred to its cause, which involves the law of causation and therefore the understanding. Without this, sensation remains merely subjective and fails to position any object[c] in space, even when the space has been assigned to the sensation. But for Kant, the understanding cannot be used for intuition: the understanding must limit itself to *thinking* if it is to remain within the Transcendental Logic. This is related to another one of Kant's errors: that he left it to me to provide the only valid proof for what he correctly knew to be the *a priori* character of the law of causality, namely a proof from the possibility of[39] objective, empirical intuition itself. In place of this, he gave a manifestly false proof, as I have already shown in my essay *On the Principle of Sufficient Reason*, § 23.[40] – From what we said above, it is clear that Kant's 'object of representation'[d] (2) is composed of elements stolen partly from representation (1) and partly from the thing in itself (3). If experience really only came about when the understanding applied

527

528

---

[a] *Gegenstand der Erfahrung*
[b] *materielles Objekt*
[c] *Objekt*
[d] *Gegenstand der Vorstellung*

twelve different functions, in order to *think* objects[a] through twelve *a priori* concepts (the objects having previously been merely intuited) – then every real thing as such would have to have a large number of determinations that could not possibly be thought away, because, like space and time, they were given *a priori*. In fact, these determinations would be an essential part of the thing's existence,[b] but without being derivable from the properties of space and of time. But we only come across one comparable determination: that of causality. Materiality is based on this, since the essence of matter consists in activity,[c] and it is causality through and through (see vol. II, chap. 4). But only materiality distinguishes the real thing from the fantasy image,[d] which really is a mere representation. The persistence of matter[e] gives the thing material permanence[f] through time, while its forms change in accordance with causality. All other aspects of the thing are either the determinations of space or time, or its empirical qualities, and all of these lead back to its efficacy[g] and are thus more precise determinations of causality. But causality already comes into empirical intuition as a condition, making this the business of the understanding; the understanding already makes intuition possible, but does not contribute anything to experience and its possibility apart from the law of causality. What fills the old ontologies, apart from what is stated here, is nothing but the relations of things to each other or to our reflection, and scrambled-up farrago.

The groundlessness of the doctrine of the categories is already apparent in Kant's manner of presentation.[h] What a distance between the Transcendental *Aesthetic* and the Transcendental *Analytic* in this respect! In the *former*, what clarity, determinateness, assurance and firm conviction, openly expressed and unerringly communicated! Everything is luminous, no dark and hidden recesses remain: Kant knows what he wants, and knows that he is right. In the *latter*, on the other hand, everything is obscure, con-
529 fused, indeterminate, fluctuating and uncertain, progress is timid, full of apologies and appeals to what is to come, or even what is being held back. Besides, the entire second and third sections of the Deduction of the Pure Concepts of the Understanding were completely altered in the second edition, because they did not satisfy even Kant; they are entirely

---

[a] *Gegenstände*
[b] *Daseyn*
[c] *Wirken*
[d] *Phantasiebilde*
[e] *die Materie, als beharrend*
[f] *Beharrlichkeit*
[g] *Wirksamkeit*
[h] *Vortrag*

different from the first edition, but not for that matter any clearer. We see Kant really fight against the truth so that he can assert the tenets[a] he has already adopted. In the Transcendental *Aesthetic*, all of his propositions are genuinely proven from undeniable facts of consciousness; but when we look closely at the Transcendental *Analytic*, we find mere assertions that it is and must be thus. Style is the physiognomy of the mind, so here as everywhere, the presentation bears the mark of the thinking that gave rise to it. – We should also note that whenever Kant wants to explain something more precisely by way of an example, he almost always uses the category of causality, and what he says turns out to be correct, – but this is because the law of causality is the real and the only form of the understanding, and the other eleven categories are only blank windows. The deduction of the categories is simpler and more straightforward in the first edition than in the second. He is concerned to show how the understanding, given an intuition from sensibility, produces experience by thinking the categories. In doing so, he repeats the terms 'recognition', 'reproduction', 'association', 'apprehension', and 'transcendental unity of apperception' *ad nauseam*, without gaining any clarity. But most striking of all is the fact that throughout this explanation he never once touches on the issue that must be the first thing on everyone's mind, the relation between sensory sensation and its external cause. If he does not want to admit there is a relation, then he would have to deny it explicitly; but this he does not do. So he creeps around the issue, and all Kantians have crept right behind him. The secret motive behind this is that he is saving the causal nexus, under the name of 'ground of appearance', for his false deduction of the thing in itself: but also, this relation to a cause would make intuition intellectual, and this he cannot concede. In addition, he seems to have been afraid that if we allow for a causal nexus between sensory sensation and object,[b] the object would immediately become a thing in itself, and this would introduce Lockean empiricism. But this difficulty is eliminated if we bear in mind that the law of causality has just as subjective an origin as sensory sensation itself, and furthermore, that one's own body already belongs to representation, to the extent that it appears in space. But Kant's fear of Berkeleyan idealism prevented him from admitting this.

530

The essential operation of the understanding by means of its twelve categories is repeatedly given as 'the combination of the manifold of intuition': but Kant never properly explains or shows what this manifold of intuition

[a] *Lehrmeinung*
[b] *Objekt*

is before the understanding combines it. Now time and space (in all of its three dimensions) are *continua*, i.e. their parts are all originally combined, not separate. But they are the general forms of our intuition: thus everything that is presented (that is: given) in them also appears originally as a *continuum*, i.e. all its parts appear already combined and do not require an additional combination of the manifold. But if you want to interpret that unification of the manifold of intuition by saying that I refer the different sensuous impressions of an object[a] to only this one object, and so, for instance, in viewing a bell, I recognize that it is one and the same body that affects my eye as yellow, my hands as smooth and hard, my ear as sonorous – then this is really a *consequence* of *a priori* cognition of the causal nexus (this real and only function of the understanding). By virtue of this cognition, all those different effects on my different sense organs lead me only to their common cause, namely the constitution of the body that stands before me, so that my understanding apprehends the unity of the cause as a single, intuitively presented object, regardless of the diversity and multiplicity of the effects. – Kant gives an excellent recapitulation of his doctrine in the *Critique of Pure Reason*, pp. 719–26, or V 747–54, where he describes the categories, perhaps more clearly than elsewhere, as 'the mere rule of the synthesis of that which perception may give *a posteriori*'. He seems to be thinking of something like the construction of a triangle, where the angles give the rule for constructing[b] the sides: at least this picture gives us the best explanation for what he says about the function of the categories. The introduction to the *Metaphysical Foundations of Natural Science* contains a long note that also provides an explanation of the categories, saying that they 'are indistinguishable from the formal actions of the understanding in judgements' except that in the latter, the subject and predicate can always trade places, if need be; so in this note, judgement in general is defined as 'an action through which the given representations first become cognition of an object'.[c] According to this, animals would not be able to have any cognition of objects, since they do not make judgements. In general, according to Kant, there are only concepts – not intuitions – of *objects*.[d] I, on the other hand, say: objects exist in the first instance for intuition alone, and concepts are always abstractions from this intuition.[41] Thus, abstract thinking must be closely guided by the world that is present in intuition, since concepts only get their content through

531

[a] *Objekt*
[b] *Zusammensetzung*
[c] *Objekt*
[d] *Objekten*

their reference to this world. Nor can we assume that there is *a priori* any determinate form for concepts other than a capacity for reflection in general, the essence of which is the formation of concepts, i.e. abstract, non-intuitive representations, and this is the sole function of *reason*, as I have shown in the First Book. Accordingly, I ask that we throw away eleven of the categories and keep only causality, yet realize that its activity is really the condition of empirical intuition, which is thus not merely sensuous[a] but rather intellectual, and that the object[b] intuited in this way, the object of experience,[c] is the same as representation, which is distinct only from the thing in itself.

After repeated study of the *Critique of Pure Reason* at different stages of my life, a conviction has urged itself on me concerning the origin of the Transcendental Logic, and I will share it here since it is very useful   532 in understanding that section. The only discovery that is grounded in an objective standpoint and the highest human reflection is the *aperçu* that we have *a priori* cognition of time and space. Pleased by this happy discovery, Kant wanted to pursue this vein even further, and his passion for architectonic symmetry provided him with a guide. Just as he had found a pure *a priori* intuition underlying empirical *intuition*, as a condition, likewise, he thought, certain *pure concepts* would surely act as presuppositions in our cognitive faculty, laying the ground for empirically acquired *concepts*. Further, actual empirical thought would be possible only by way of pure *a priori* thought, a thought that would itself be entirely devoid of objects,[d] and would need to take them from intuition. Just as the *Transcendental Aesthetic* establishes an *a priori* foundation for mathematics, logic must have one as well, and accordingly the former received a symmetrical counterpart[e] in the form of a *Transcendental Logic*. From this point on, Kant was no longer unbiased, no longer in a position to conduct pure research and observation of what is present in consciousness; instead he was directed by a presupposition and in pursuit of a purpose,[f] namely that of finding what he had presupposed. This would enable him to use his happy discoveries in the Transcendental Aesthetic to erect a second storey in the form of an analogous, i.e. corresponding, symmetrical Transcendental Logic. For this, he hit upon the table of judgements, from which he formed the

[a] *sensual*
[b] *Gegenstand*
[c] *Objekt der Erfahrung*
[d] *Gegenstände*
[e] *Pendant*
[f] *Absicht*

table of categories (as well as he could) as the doctrine of the twelve pure concepts *a priori*, which are supposed to be the condition of our *thinking* precisely those *things* whose *intuition* is conditioned *a priori* through the two forms of sensibility. So now there was a *pure understanding* to correspond symmetrically to the *pure sensibility*. After this, he was struck by another consideration that offered him a way of increasing the plausibility of the matter at hand, namely the assumption of the *schematism* of the pure concepts of the understanding. But this most clearly betrayed the course of his procedure, a procedure of which even he was unconscious. Specifically, since he was bent on finding an *a priori* analogue for every empirical function of the cognitive faculty, he noticed that another intermediate is very frequently, if not always, to be found between our empirical intuition and our empirical thought (which is completed by abstract, non-intuitive concepts), since every now and then we try to return to intuiting from abstract thinking. But we really only try this to convince ourselves that our abstract thinking has not strayed too far from the secure ground of intuition, becoming too high-flown or even turning into mere verbiage. This is something like the situation when we walk in the dark and occasionally reach out to touch the wall that guides us. Similarly, we return only tentatively and momentarily to intuiting, by conjuring up in imagination[a] an intuition corresponding to the concept that engages us at the moment, although it can never be completely adequate to the concept, and is just a temporary *representative* of it: I have already said what needs to be said on this point in my essay *On the Principle of Sufficient Reason*, § 28.[42] Kant calls a passing phantasm[b] of this sort a *schema* in contrast to the perfected image in fantasy,[c] and says that it is, as it were, a monogram of the imagination.[d] He claims that, just as this sort of a thing stands midway between our abstract thinking of empirically acquired concepts and our clear intuitions that take place through the senses, there are similar *schemata of the pure concepts of the understanding* existing *a priori* between pure sensibility (the *a priori* faculty of intuition) and the pure understanding (thus the categories), which is the *a priori* faculty of thought. Kant describes each of these schemata as monograms of the pure imagination *a priori*, and assigns each of them to its corresponding category in the strange chapter 'On the schematism of pure concepts of the understanding', which is infamous for its excessive obscurity, because nobody has ever been any the wiser for

533

---

[a] *in der Phantasie hervorrufen*
[b] *Phantasma*
[c] *Phantasie*
[d] *Monogramm der Einbildungskraft*

reading it. But its obscurity is dispelled when it is seen from the standpoint given here; and this is also where we see more clearly than anywhere else the intentions behind his method and the resolution made in advance to find what corresponds to the analogy and what can serve the cause of architectonic symmetry. In fact the whole thing starts to verge to a certain extent on the comical. Since he assumes that the empirical schemata (or representatives of our real concepts in fantasy) will have analogous schemata in the pure (*contentless*) *a priori* concepts of the understanding (categories), he overlooks the fact that the purpose of such schemata is entirely absent here. This is because the purpose of the schemata in empirical (actual) thought is based solely on the *material content* of such concepts; specifically, since these concepts are deduced from empirical intuition, we can help and orient ourselves when we are thinking abstractly by casting an occasional, fleeting glance back at the intuition from which concepts are taken, to assure ourselves that our thought still has real content.[a] But this necessarily presupposes that the concepts we are concerned with come from intuition, and it is a mere glance backwards at their material content, or in fact just something to help us in our weakness. So this obviously and necessarily does not work with *a priori* concepts that are utterly devoid of content, because these concepts do not emerge out of intuition but rather approach it from within so as to acquire content in the first place; consequently, they do not have anything to look back on. I have gone into so much detail because this is precisely what throws light on the secret course of Kant's philosophizing, which is that Kant, having happily discovered the two *a priori* forms of intuition, now takes analogy as his guide and tries to give an *a priori* analogue for every determination of our empirical cognition; in the schemata, this even extends to a merely psychological fact. Meanwhile the apparent profundity and the difficulty of the presentation serve to conceal from the reader that its content remains a totally arbitrary assumption that is wholly incapable of proof. And someone who has finally penetrated into the sense of such a presentation will be easily led to believe that this hard-won understanding is actually a conviction of the truth of the matter. But if Kant had been unbiased, engaging in pure enquiry here as he did with the discovery of *a priori* intuition, he would necessarily have discovered that what is added to a pure intuition of space and time when an empirical intuition comes from it, is on the one hand sensation, and on the other hand cognition of causality, which transforms the mere sensation into an objective empirical intuition. But for precisely that reason cognition of

534

535

[a] *Gehalt*

causality is not borrowed and learned from sensation in the first place; rather, it is present *a priori* and is precisely the form and function of the pure understanding. It is the pure understanding's only form and function, but it is so rich in results that all our empirical cognition rests on it. – If, as has often been said, an error is only fully refuted when its origin has been established psychologically, I believe that I have accomplished this in the discussion above with respect to Kant's doctrine of the categories and their schemata.[43]

_____

After introducing such major mistakes into the first simple outlines of a theory of the faculty of representation, Kant arrived at a variety of complicated assumptions. First of all, there was the synthetic unity of apperception: a very strange thing, very strangely presented. 'The "I think" must be able to accompany all my representations.' 'Must – be able to': this is a problematic-apodictic enunciation; in plain language, a claim that takes away with one hand what it gives with the other. And what is the meaning[a] of this claim that balances on such a fine point? – That all representing is thinking? – No it is not, and this would have been disastrous; there would then be nothing but abstract concepts, and least of all any pure intuition that is free from reflection and the will, like that of the beautiful, the deepest grasp of the true essence of things, i.e. their Platonic Ideas.[44] And then animals would have to think or they would not be able to represent. – Or could the claim mean something like: no object without a subject? If so, it is very badly expressed, and would come too late. If we summarize Kant's claims we will find that what he understands by the synthetic unity of apperception is something like the extensionless centre of the sphere of all our representations, whose radii converge on it. It is what I call the subject of cognition, the correlative of all representations, and it is at the same time what I have described and discussed in detail in chapter 22 of the second volume as the focal point where the rays of brain activity converge. I refer to that here, so as not to repeat myself.[45]

536

_____

It follows from the critique given above that I reject the entire doctrine of the categories and regard it as one of the baseless assumptions with which Kant burdened the theory of cognition.[46] This also follows from my demonstration of the contradictions in the Transcendental Logic, contradictions that

[a] *Sinn*

stem from confusing intuitive cognition with abstract cognition, and also from my demonstration that there is no clear and distinct concept of the nature[a] of the understanding or of reason – instead, Kant's writings offer us only incoherent, inconsistent, inadequate and incorrect remarks concerning those two faculties of mind. Finally, it follows from the explanations of these same faculties that I myself have given in the First Book and the supplemental materials, and in even greater detail in the essay *On the Principle of Sufficient Reason*, §§ 21, 26 and 34,[47] explanations that not only fully agree with the clarified concepts of both of those cognitive powers, but are themselves distinct and determinate, proceed clearly from considerations of the nature of our cognition, and are manifest in the linguistic usage and the writings of all times and peoples. These explanations can be defended against Kant's very different presentation mainly by exposing the errors of that presentation. – But now since Kant bases his entire theory of thought – indeed his entire philosophy – on the table of judgements, and this table is in itself basically correct, it is incumbent on me to demonstrate how these universal forms of all judgements arise in our cognitive faculty, and bring them into agreement with my description of this faculty. – Throughout this discussion I will always use the concepts of understanding and reason in the way I have explained them, so I will assume that the reader is familiar with this.

An essential difference between my method and that of Kant is the   537
fact that he begins with mediated, reflected cognition, while I start from immediate and intuitive cognition. He can be compared to someone who measures the height of a tower from its shadow, while I am like the person who puts the measuring stick right up against it. That is why philosophy for him is a science *from*[b] concepts, while for me it is a science *in* concepts, drawn from intuitive cognition (the only source of all evidence) and grasped and formulated in universal concepts.[48] He skips over this whole intuitive, multifaceted world around us, a world that is rich in meaning, and keeps to the forms of abstract thinking; this presupposes (although Kant never states as much) that reflection is the ectype of all intuition, and thus that everything essential in intuition must be expressed in reflection, and indeed in very condensed forms and features that are for this reason easy to overlook, and consequently that the essential and lawlike features of abstract cognition furnish us with all the strings that set the colourful puppet show of the intuitive world into motion before our eyes. – If

[a] *Wesen*
[b] *aus*

only Kant had expressed this supreme principle of his method clearly and
followed it consistently, he would at least have needed to keep the intuitive
separate from the abstract, and we would not have needed to struggle with
insoluble contradictions and confusions. But we see from the way he carries
out his task that he had a very foggy conception of this principle of his
method, and as a result we still have to guess what it is even after a thorough
study of his philosophy.

As far as the stated method and basic maxim itself is concerned, it has
many strengths and it is a brilliant thought. The essence of all science
consists in uniting an endless manifold of intuitive appearances under
comparatively few abstract concepts. We then use these concepts to construct a system in which all those appearances are fully under the control
of our cognition, and we can explain what happens and determine what is
going to happen. The sciences divide the extensive sphere of appearances
among themselves according to the particular and diverse types of these
538 appearances. Now it was a bold and lucky thought to isolate what is absolutely essential in concepts as such, independent of their content, in order
to discover the forms of all thought and thus learn also what is essential
to all intuitive cognition and consequently to the world as appearance.
Since it would be necessary, this essential element could be discovered *a
priori*, which means it would have a subjective origin and would serve
Kant's purposes. – Now before going any further, there should also have
been an investigation into the relationship between reflection and intuitive
cognition (which of course would presuppose the sort of clear separation
of the two that Kant never made), into the manner in which reflection
reproduces and stands in for intuitive cognition, whether it does so purely,
or whether it is altered and rendered somewhat unfamiliar by taking on
its (reflection's) own forms, whether the form of abstract, reflective cognition is determined more by the form of intuitive cognition, or by its own
intrinsic, irrevocable character, that of reflection, so that even the very heterogeneous elements in intuitive cognition can no longer be distinguished
as soon as it enters reflective cognition, and conversely many distinctions
that we perceive in the reflective mode of cognition have in fact originated
in reflective cognition and do not indicate any corresponding differences
in intuitive cognition. Now an investigation such as this would have shown
that intuitive cognition undergoes almost as much of an alteration when
it is assimilated into reflection as food does when it is assimilated into
the animal organism, since its forms and mixtures are determined by the
organism itself, and their composition makes it impossible to recognize the
character of the food; – or (because this is saying a little too much) such

an investigation would have at least shown that the relationship between intuitive cognition and reflection has nothing in common with the way objects are mirrored in water, and hardly resembles the relation objects have to their shadows, since shadows give only a few external outlines, uniting the greatest multitude of things in the same shape, and also giving the most dissimilar things the same outline; and so it is not possible to reconstruct the shapes of things completely or with any confidence from their shadows.

The whole of reflective cognition, or reason, has only one main form, and this is the abstract concept; this form is distinctive to reason itself, and does not have any immediately necessary connection with the intuitive world. Thus, the intuitive world exists for animals in the complete absence of reflective cognition, and the form of reflection would have fitted it just as well even if it had been entirely different. But the unification of concepts into judgements has certain determinate and lawful forms discovered through induction and which constitute the table of judgements. These forms are for the most part derived from the reflective mode of cognition itself, and thus directly from reason, especially to the extent that they arise through the four laws of thought (which I call metalogical truths) and through the maxim of all and none.[a] Others of these forms are grounded in the intuitive mode of cognition and thus in the understanding, but they do not on that account provide any information about an equal number of particular forms of the understanding; rather, they can be derived entirely from the one and only function of the understanding, namely immediate cognition of cause and effect. Still others of these forms have ultimately arisen from the encounter and combination of the reflective and intuitive modes of cognition, or rather from the integration of the latter into the former. I will now review each of the moments of judgement in turn and show how each one originates in the sources mentioned above. It follows straight from this that the categories cannot be deduced from these, and the assumption that they exist is just as groundless as their presentation has been found to be confused and self-contradictory.

(1) The so-called *quantity* of judgements stems from the essence of concepts as such, and is consequently grounded only in reason and has absolutely no immediate connection to understanding and intuitive cognition. – As I explained in the First Book, it is an essential aspect of concepts as such that they have an extension, a sphere, and that the broader, less determinate concept encompasses the narrower, more determinate one.

---

[a] *dictum de omni et nullo* [See note above on § 9, 71]

The narrower concept can therefore be separated out as well, either by
being marked out as the undetermined part of the broader concept in
general, or by being given a particular name that determines it and distinguishes it off completely. The judgement that completes this operation in
the first case is a particular one, in the second case a universal; for instance,
the same part of the sphere of the concept 'tree' can be isolated through a
particular or through a universal judgement, namely: 'some trees have oak
galls' or: 'all oaks have oak galls'. – The difference between the two operations is very small, and indeed only made possible by the richness of the
lexicon in a given language. Nonetheless, Kant declared that this difference
reveals two fundamentally different actions, functions, or categories of the
pure understanding, which is supposed to determine experience *a priori* by
means of these very things.

Finally, a concept can be used to achieve a determinate, individual,
intuitive representation, the concept itself being derived[a] from this representation, and at the same time from many others: this is what happens
in the singular[b] judgement. Such a judgement only indicates the border
between abstract and intuitive cognition, into which it passes directly: 'this
tree here has oak galls'. – Kant created a special category from this as well.

After what has been said, there is no need here for further polemics.

(2) In the same way, the *quality* of judgements falls completely within the
province of reason and does not adumbrate any law of the understanding
that makes intuition possible, i.e. it makes no reference to this. The nature
of abstract concepts is precisely the essence of reason itself, understood
objectively, and as we explained in the First Book, it involves the possibility
of uniting and dividing the spheres of the concepts; the universal laws[c] of
identity and contradiction rest on this possibility as their presupposition,
and I attribute *metalogical* truth to these laws because they come purely from
reason and are not to be explained any further. They determine that what
is united must remain united and what is divided must remain divided,
and thus that what is posited cannot at the same time be cancelled again;
they presuppose the possibility of connecting and dividing the spheres
of concepts, i.e. they presuppose the possibility of judgement. But the
form of judgement lies simply and solely in reason; unlike its *content*, this
form is not taken over from the understanding's intuitive cognition, which
accordingly does not offer any correlate or analogy for it. After intuition has
arisen through the understanding and for the understanding, its existence

---

[a] *abgezogen*
[b] *einzelne*
[c] *Denkgesetze* [laws of thought]

is complete, it is not subject to any doubts or errors, and it is a stranger to both affirmation and negation. This is because it speaks for itself and, unlike the abstract cognition of reason, it does not have its value and substance[a] merely in reference to something outside of itself, in accordance with the principle of sufficient reason of cognition. It is nothing but reality, and all negation is foreign to its nature:[b] this can only be added in thought by reflection, but for that very reason always remains within the realm of abstract thought.

To the affirmative and negative judgements Kant adds infinite judgements, using a whim of the old scholastics, an overly subtle and imaginary stopgap that does not even need discussion, a blank window like many others he brings in for the sake of his symmetrical architectonic.

(3) Kant brought together three entirely different characteristics of judgements under the very broad concept of relation, and we must examine them each in turn if we are to understand[c] their origin.

(a) In general, the *hypothetical judgement* is the abstract term for that most universal form of all our cognition, the principle of sufficient reason. In my 1813 essay on this principle I showed that it has four very different meanings and that in each of these it stems from a different power of cognition and concerns a different class of representations. This makes sufficiently clear that the hypothetical judgement in general, this universal form of thought, cannot simply arise out of the understanding and its category of causality, as Kant would have it, but rather that the law of causality which I have shown to be the pure understanding's sole form of cognition is only one of the modes of the principle of sufficient reason, a principle that encompasses all pure or *a priori* cognition; in each of its meanings, however, this principle is expressed by this hypothetical form of judgement. – Here we see quite clearly how elements of cognition[d] with very different origins and meanings nonetheless, when thought by reason in the abstract,[e] appear in one and the same form, a combination of concepts and judgements; they can no longer be distinguished in this form – they can only be distinguished by abandoning abstract cognition completely and returning to intuitive cognition. Thus, the method adopted by Kant of beginning from the standpoint of abstract cognition in order to find the elements and the innermost mechanism of even intuitive cognition was

542

---

[a] *Gehalt*
[b] *Wesen*
[c] *erkennen*
[d] *Erkenntnisse*
[e] *in abstracto*

completely the wrong way around. Furthermore, my whole introductory essay *On the Principle of Sufficient Reason* is in a certain sense just a thorough discussion of the meaning of the hypothetical form of judgement; and so I will not dwell on this any longer here.

(b) The form of the *categorical judgement* is nothing other than the form of judgement in general, in the truest sense. This is because, strictly speaking, judgement means nothing more than thinking the combination or the irreconcilability of conceptual spheres: thus the hypothetical and the disjunctive combinations are not really special forms of judgement, because they are only applied to judgements that are already complete and in which the combination of concepts remains unaltered, namely the categorical. But they connect these judgements together again, since the hypothetical form expresses their mutual dependence and the disjunctive their irreconcilability. But mere concepts have only *one* type of relation to each other, namely the one expressed in the categorical judgement. The intersection[a] and the complete separation of the conceptual spheres (i.e. affirmation and negation) are the more precise determination or the subspecies of this relation, and Kant made these into special categories under a completely different heading, that of *quality*. The intersection and separation are subdivided further, according to whether the spheres intersect completely or only partially, and this determination constitutes the *quantity* of the judgements, which Kant again made into a special heading of categories. Thus, he separated things that are very closely related or indeed identical, easily grasped modifications of the only possible relations of mere concepts to each other, and conversely he united very heterogeneous things under the heading of relation.

Categorical judgements have the laws[b] of identity and contradiction as their metalogical principle.[49] But there are different *grounds* for connecting conceptual spheres, and these grounds are what give *truth* to the judgement (the judgement being nothing but this very connection); consequently, the truth of the judgement can be logical or empirical or transcendental or metalogical; this was explained in the introductory essay, §§ 30–3,[50] and does not need to be repeated here.[c] But it shows just how diverse immediate cognition can be, given that it is all presented abstractly[d] by combining the spheres of two concepts as subject and predicate, and that no single function of the understanding can be proposed as corresponding to and

543

---

[a] *Ineinandergreifen*
[b] *Denkgesetze*
[c] [See Introduction above, xviii–xix]
[d] *in abstracto*

producing this combination. For instance, the judgements: 'water boils', 'the sine measures the angle', 'the will decides', 'work is distracting', 'it is difficult to make distinctions'; – all of these express the most diverse relations in the same logical form, which once again confirms for us how wrongheaded a beginning it is to adopt the standpoint of abstract cognition in order to analyse immediate, intuitive cognition. – The categorical judgement only emerges from actual cognition in the understanding (in my sense) when the judgement expresses causality; but this is the case even with judgements that indicate a physical quality. When I say: 'this body is heavy, hard, fluid, green, acidic, alkaline, organic, etc.' – this always indicates the body's activity,[a] which is to say cognition that is possible only through the pure understanding. But after this was expressed abstractly through subject and predicate, as were a lot of things utterly different from it (for instance the subordination of highly abstract concepts), these purely conceptual relations were transferred back to intuitive cognition, and it was thought that the subject and predicate in the judgement must have their own distinctive correlate in intuition, that of substance and accident. Later I will show that the concept of substance has no true content other than that of the concept of matter. Accidents, for their part, mean exactly the same thing as types of effects, so the supposed cognition of substance and accident is still only the pure understanding's cognition of cause and effect. But we discussed how the representation of matter really originates in our First Book, § 4, and more clearly in the essay *On the Principle of Sufficient Reason*, at the end of § 21, p. 77.[51] To a certain extent, we will be able to see this even more closely when we investigate the principle that substance is permanent.

544

(c) *Disjunctive judgements* come from the law of excluded middle, which is a metalogical truth. For this reason, they belong entirely to pure reason and do not have their origin in the understanding. So, to deduce the category of community[b] or *reciprocal causation*[c] from them is an absolutely glaring example of the violence to the truth Kant sometimes allows himself just to satisfy his desire for architectonic symmetry. The fatal flaws in this derivation have already been demonstrated on a number of levels and it has been frequently and justifiably criticized, particularly by *G. E. Schulze* in his *Critique of Theoretical Philosophy*[d] and by *Berg* in his *Epicritique*

---

[a] *Wirken*
[b] *Gemeinschaft*
[c] *Wechselwirkung*
[d] *Kritik der theoretischen Philosophie*

of Philosophy.[a] – What analogy is there really between the problematic[b] determination of a concept through mutually exclusive predicates and the thought of reciprocal causation? They are in fact completely at odds, because when one of the two disjuncts is actually posited in the disjunctive judgement, the other is necessarily suppressed. On the other hand, if two things are thought of as being in a relation of reciprocal causation, positing the one necessarily entails positing the other and vice versa. Thus the true, logical analogy of reciprocal causation is doubtless the vicious circle,[c] where the ground is also the grounded and the other way around, as is supposedly the case with reciprocal causation. And just as logic rejects the vicious circle, metaphysics bans the concept of reciprocal causation. In all seriousness, I now want to show that there is no such thing as reciprocal causation in the true sense of the term,[52] and although people like to use the concept (precisely because the thought is so vague), closer examination shows it to be empty, false and unreal. First of all, let us think about what causality really is, using the discussions in the introductory essay, § 20, and also in my prize essay *On the Freedom of the Will*, chap. 3, pp. 27ff., and finally in the fourth chapter of our second volume.[53] Causality is the law according to which emerging *states* of matter determine their position in time. Causality deals only with states, and in fact it really only deals with *alterations* and has nothing to say about either matter as such or permanence without alteration. *Matter* as such does not fall under the law of causality, since it does not become or pass away, and neither does the entire *thing*, as it is generally known; only *states* of matter do. Further, the law of causality has nothing to do with *permanence*, because when nothing is *altered* there is no *activity*[d] or causality, but rather an enduring state of rest. But if this is altered, then the newly arising state is itself either permanent or it is not, and leads directly to a third state. The necessity with which this takes place is precisely the law of causality, which is a form of the principle of sufficient reason and is thus incapable of further explanation, because the principle of sufficient reason is the very first principle of all explanation and all necessity. It is clear from this that the existence of cause and effect is closely connected and necessarily related to *temporal order*. Only to the extent that state A precedes state B in time, and their succession is necessary rather than contingent, i.e. not just a sequence[e] but a consequence;[f] – only to this

545

[a] *Epikritik der Philosophie*
[b] *offengelassenen*
[c] *circulus vitiosus*
[d] *Wirken*
[e] *Folgen*
[f] *Erfolgen*

extent is state A the cause and state B the effect. But the concept of *reciprocal causation* entails that they are both causes and effects of each other, and this is to say that they both occur both earlier and later, which is an absurdity.[a] We cannot accept that both *states* are simultaneous, and indeed necessarily simultaneous; if they necessarily belong together and exist simultaneously, they constitute only *one* state. And since the persistence of this one state requires the continuing presence of all its determinations, we are no longer dealing with alteration and causality but rather with duration and rest. The only thing that can be said about this is that when *one* determination of the whole state is altered, the resulting state cannot last, but rather becomes the cause of the alteration of all the other determinations of the first state, and this gives rise to a new, third state. All of this takes place according to the simple law of causality alone, and does not provide any basis for a new law, that of reciprocal causation.

546

In addition, I will flatly assert that the concept of *reciprocal causation* is not attested by a single example. Everything that might be offered in its defence is either in a state of rest (and since the law of causality has meaning only with respect to alterations it does not apply in this case), or is an alternating succession of mutually conditioning states with the same name, and which can be explained perfectly well with simple causality. An example of the first phenomenon is when a scale is at rest because there are equal weights on each side: there is no activity[b] here, because there is no alteration: it is in a state of rest. Gravity is equally distributed; it strives (like every body supported at its centre) but it cannot express its force through any effect.[c] Removing *one* of the weights gives rise to a second state which is the immediate cause of a third, the sinking of the other weight, but all this takes place in accordance with the simple law of cause and effect and does not need a special category of the understanding, or even a special name. An example of the second phenomenon is a fire that continues to burn. Oxygen combined with the combustible body causes heat, which in turn causes that chemical combination to re-emerge. But this is nothing other than a chain of causes and effects whose links might alternate but nonetheless have the *same name*: the burning A gives rise[d] to free heat B, and this gives rise to a new burning C (i.e. a new effect that has the same name as cause A, but is not the same thing), this then gives rise to a new heat D (which is not really identical with effect B, but is only the same in

[a] *Ungedanke*
[b] *Wirken*
[c] *Wirkung*
[d] *bewirkt*

547   concept, i.e. has the *same name* as this effect) and so on and so on. A good
      example of what people generally call reciprocal causation can be seen in
      von Humboldt's theory of the desert (*Views of Nature*[a]), 2nd edition, vol. 2,
      p. 79). It does not rain in deserts, but it does rain in the wooded mountains
      that border them. This is not caused by mountains attracting the clouds;
      rather, the column of heated air that rises up from the sandy plains prevents
      the droplets of vapour from disintegrating, and drives the clouds upwards.
      The vertically rising air current is weaker in the mountains, the clouds
      drop, and the cooler air produces rain. Thus, the absence of rain in the
      desert is in a relation of reciprocal causation with the absence of plant
      life: it does not rain, because the heated expanse of sand radiates more
      heat, and it is due to this lack of rain that the desert does not become a
      steppe or a grassy corridor. But this is clearly just another succession of
      causes and effects with the same name, as in the earlier example, and not
      essentially different from simple causality.[54] The same thing happens with
      the swinging of a pendulum and in fact with the self-maintenance of the
      organic body as well: here, it is also the case that each state leads to a new
      one and is in turn brought about by it, the two states being of the same
      type but different things. But here the situation is more complicated, since
      the chain is made up of many sorts of links, not just two, so that a link
      with the same name will only reoccur after many others have intervened.
      However, all we are ever confronted with is an application of the single and
      simple law of causality, which gives the rule for the sequence of states; we
      are not faced with anything that can be grasped only through a new and
      special function of the understanding.

      Or does anyone suggest proving the concept of reciprocal causation by
      pointing out that action and reaction[b] are equal to each other? But this is
      for precisely the reason I urge so strongly and have discussed in detail in the
      essay *On the Principle of Sufficient Reason*, namely that the cause and the
      effect are not two bodies, but rather two successive states of bodies, and that
      consequently all of the bodies concerned are implicated in each of the states;
      thus, the effect, which is to say the newly emerging state, a collision for
548   instance,[55] extends to both bodies in the same proportion. So the colliding
      body is altered just as much as is the body collided with (each in proportion
      to its mass and velocity[56]). If anyone wants to call this reciprocal causation,
      then all causation[c] is reciprocal causation, and we do not need any new
      concepts much less a new function of the understanding on this account;

      [a] *Ansichten der Natur*
      [b] *Wirkung und Gegenwirkung*
      [c] *Wirkung*

rather we are only left with a superfluous synonym for causality.[a] But this is the very position Kant thoughtlessly expounds in the *Metaphysical Foundations of Natural Science*, where the proof of the fourth proposition of mechanics begins: 'all external causation[b] in the world is reciprocal causation'. So how is the understanding supposed to contain different *a priori* functions for simple causality[c] and for reciprocal causation?[d] – or in fact, how is the real succession of things supposed to be possible and cognizable only by means of causality, and their simultaneity possible and cognizable only by means of reciprocal causation? But if all causation[e] were really reciprocal causation, then succession and simultaneity would be the same thing, and everything in the world would happen at once.[57] – If there were true reciprocal causation, then a perpetual motion machine[f] would be possible and even *a priori* certain: but instead, the claim that it is impossible is based *a priori* in the conviction that true reciprocal causation does not exist, and that the understanding does not have a form for such a thing.[58]

Even Aristotle denies reciprocal causation in the true sense: he notes that two things can indeed cause one another reciprocally, but only when each is understood in a different sense, for instance when one acts on the other as a motive while the second acts on the first as a cause of motion. We find the same language in two passages: *Physics*, bk II, chap. 3, and *Metaphysics*, bk V, chap. 2. 'Many things are the causes of each other; so for instance gymnastics is the cause of bodily strength, and this is the cause of gymnastics. But it is not in the same way; rather the one is the end and the other the beginning of the process.'[g] Moreover, if he did accept the existence of true reciprocal causation then he would state it here, since in both passages he is trying to enumerate all possible types of causes. In the *Posterior Analytics*, bk II, chap. 11 he mentions a cycle of causes and effects, but not reciprocal causation.   549

(4) The categories of *modality* have an advantage over all the others in that each expresses something really corresponding to the form of judgement from which it is derived. This is almost never the case with the

---

[a] *Kausalität*
[b] *Wirkung*
[c] *Kausalität*
[d] *Wechselwirkung*
[e] *Wirkung*
[f] *perpetuum mobile*
[g] Εστι δε τινα και αλληλων αιτια· οιον το πονειν αιτιον της ευεξιας, και αυτη του πονειν· αλλ' ου τον αυτον τροπον, αλλα το μεν ως τελος, το δε ως αρχη κινησεως. (*Sunt praeterea quae sibi sunt mutuo causae, ut exercitium bonae habitudinis, et haec exercitii: at non eodem modo, sed haec ut finis, illud ut principium motus.*) [*Physics* II, 3, 195a8–11; *Metaphysics* Δ (V), 2, 1013b9–11]

other categories, which are for the most part deduced from the forms of judgement with the most arbitrary violence.

It is perfectly true that the concepts of possibility, actuality and necessity give rise to the problematic, assertoric and apodictic forms of judgement. But it is not true that these concepts are the understanding's special and original forms of cognition and are incapable of further derivation. Rather, they come from the single and original form of all cognition, a form that we are thus conscious of *a priori*, the principle of sufficient reason; indeed cognition of *necessity* follows directly from this principle. On the other hand, the concepts of contingency, possibility, impossibility and actuality only come about through the use of reflection. That is to say, there is no sense in which they come from a *single* mental power, the understanding; instead, they come from the conflict between abstract and intuitive cognition, as will soon be seen.

My claim is that the notion of necessity and that of consequence from a given ground are fully interchangeable and completely identical. We can never cognize – or even think – something as necessary unless we see it as the consequence of a given ground: and the concept of necessity entails nothing more than this dependence, this notion of being posited through something else, and this inevitability of being its consequence. It follows from this that the concept of necessity arises and exists solely and exclusively through the use of the principle of sufficient reason. And so, according to the different forms of this principle, there is a physical necessity (of effect from a cause), a logical necessity (through the ground of cognition, in analytic judgements, inferences, etc.), a mathematical necessity (according to the ground of being in space and time), and finally a practical necessity, which does not refer to determination through a supposed categorical imperative, but rather to an action that emerges necessarily according to present motives and a given empirical character. – But everything necessary is only relative, since it presupposes a ground from which it follows: absolute necessity is a contradiction. – As for the rest, I refer to § 49 of the essay *On the Principle of Sufficient Reason*.[59]

Contingency[a] is the contradictory opposite, i.e. the negation of necessity. The content of this concept is therefore negative; specifically, it is nothing more than absence of the connection expressed by the principle of sufficient reason. This is why even the contingent is only ever relative: specifically, it is contingent only in reference to something that is *not* its ground. Every object of any sort, e.g. everything that takes place in the

550

[a] *Zufälligkeit*

actual world, is always simultaneously necessary and contingent: *necessary* in relation to the one thing that is its cause; *contingent* in relation to everything else. This is because its contact with everything else in time and space is a mere coincidence[a] without any necessary connection: hence the words contingency,[b] συμπτωμα, *contingens*.[60] Something absolutely contingent is therefore just as unthinkable as something absolutely necessary. This is because the former would be an object that is not in a ground/consequent relation with any other object. But the fact that such a thing is unimaginable is simply a negative expression of the content of the principle of sufficient reason, which must be overturned in order to conceive of something absolutely contingent. But then it would have lost all meaning too, since meaning accrues to the concept of contingency only in reference to that principle, and means that two objects do not relate to each other as ground and consequent.

To the extent that nature is an intuitive representation, everything that happens in nature is necessary because it follows from its cause. If we consider the individual thing in relation to things that are not its cause, then we recognize it as contingent; but this is already an abstract reflection. If we abstract even further and completely remove a natural object from its causal relations to everything else, and thus from its necessity and contingency, then this type of cognition is concerned with the concept of the *actual*.[c] This concept considers only the *effect*[d] without looking into 551 its cause, in relation to which it is called *necessary*, while it is *contingent* in relation to everything else. All this is ultimately based on the fact that the modality of the judgement does not refer to the objective constitution of things so much as to the relation our cognition has to them.[61] But since everything in nature follows from a cause, then everything *actual* is also *necessary*, but only to the extent that it is *at this time*, and *in this place*, because determination through the law of causality extends no further than this. However, if we leave intuitive nature and turn to abstract thought, we can represent to ourselves in reflection all the natural laws – we are familiar with some of these *a priori* and some *a posteriori* – and this abstract representation contains everything that is in nature at *any* time and in *any* place, but abstracted from every particular place and time: and this sort of reflection is precisely what brings us into the broad realm of *possibility*. But even here there is no room for *impossibility*. It is evident

---

[a] *Zusammentreffen*
[b] *Zufall*
[c] *Wirklichen*
[d] *Wirkung*

that possibility and impossibility exist only for reflection,[62] for the abstract cognition of reason, and not for intuitive cognition, although it is the pure forms of intuitive cognition that give reason the determinations of possibility and impossibility. Possibility and impossibility are metaphysical or merely physical according to whether the laws of nature from which we begin thinking about possibility and impossibility, are known[a] *a priori* or *a posteriori*.

This explanation needs no proof because it is based directly on cognition of the principle of sufficient reason and the development of the concepts of necessity, actuality and possibility; furthermore, it demonstrates with sufficient clarity that there was absolutely no reason for Kant to assume three special functions of the understanding for these three concepts, and that here again he did not allow any scruples to disturb him in carrying through with his architectonic symmetry.

552   In addition, Kant made the major mistake of confusing the concept of necessity with the concept of contingency, although he was simply following the precedent of earlier philosophy which misused abstraction in the following manner. It was obvious that something follows inevitably when its ground is posited, i.e. it cannot fail to be, and is thus necessary. But people stopped with this last provision alone and said: something is necessary if it cannot be otherwise, or if its opposite is impossible. They failed to consider the ground and the root of such necessity, and overlooked the concomitant relativity of all necessity, thus creating the entirely unthinkable fiction of something *absolutely necessary*, i.e. something that exists with the inevitability of a consequent from a ground, but without being a consequent from a ground, and is thus not dependent on anything. But this addition is asking for the absurd,[b] because it contradicts the principle of sufficient reason. People nonetheless took this fiction as their point of departure and declared, in diametric opposition to the truth, that everything posited through a ground is contingent; this is because they saw the relativity of its necessity and compared it with that completely unfounded and self-contradictory notion of an *absolute* necessity.[*,63] Kant

---

* See Christian Wolff's *Rational Thoughts Concerning God, World, and Soul* [*Vernünftige Gedanken von Gott, Welt und Seele*], §§ 577–9. – It is strange that the only thing he describes as contingent is what is necessary according to the principle of sufficient reason of becoming, i.e. what happens according to causes, and on the other hand he acknowledges as necessary what is necessary according to the other forms of the principle of sufficient reason, e.g. what follows from the *essentia* (definition), and thus analytic judgements as well as mathematical truths. He says that this is because only the law

[a] *erkannt*
[b] *eine absurde Petition*

retains this fundamentally wrongheaded definition of contingency and uses it as an explanation in the *Critique of Pure Reason*, V, pp. 289–91, p. 243; also V, p. 301, pp. 419, 458, 460; also V, pp. 447, 486, 488.[a] This lands him in the most obvious self-contradiction, since at p. 301 he says: 'everything contingent has a cause', adding: 'something is contingent whose non-existence is possible'. But if something has a cause, it cannot possibly fail to exist: therefore it is necessary. – Incidentally, this whole incorrect explanation of necessity and contingency already comes from Aristotle, from *On Generation and Corruption*,[b] book II, chaps. 9 and 11, where something is described as necessary when its non-existence is impossible: it is opposed to something whose existence is impossible, and between these two are the things that can exist or not exist, i.e. what comes into existence and what passes away, and these would then be contingent. According to what we have said before, it is clear that this explanation, like so many others in Aristotle, has come about by adhering to abstract concepts and failing to refer back to the concrete and intuitive, although this is the source of all abstract concepts and must function as a check on them. 'Something whose non-existence is impossible' – this can always be thought in the abstract:[c] but if we take this over to what is concrete, real, intuitive, we do not find anything that can illustrate the thought, even as a possibility, – other than what we have just described as the consequent of a given ground, whose necessity, however, is relative and conditioned.[64]

I will take this opportunity to add another couple of remarks concerning these modal concepts. – Since all necessity is based on the principle of sufficient reason and is for that reason relative, all *apodictic* judgements are originally *hypothetical*, according to their ultimate meaning. They become *categorical* only through the introduction of an *assertoric* minor, which is to say in the conclusion of a syllogism.[d] If this minor is still undecided, and if this indecision is expressed, the result is a *problematic* judgement.

What is apodictic in general (as a rule) – a law of nature – is always only problematic in reference to a particular case, because the condition

of causality gives an infinite series, while the other types of sufficient grounds [*Gründen*] provide finite ones. Nonetheless, this is not remotely the case with the forms of the principle of sufficient reason in pure space and time, but only with logical grounds of knowledge: but Kant considered mathematical necessity to be this sort of a logical ground. – Compare the essay *On the Principle of Sufficient Reason*, § 50.

[a] [This somewhat garbled list amounts to the following in today's standard system of referencing: B289–91; A243 / B301; A419 / B447; A458 / B486; A460 / B488]
[b] *De generatione et corruptione*
[c] *in abstracto*
[d] *Schlußsatz*

that sets the case under the rule must first actually appear. And the other way around, what is necessary (apodictic) in the particular as such (each particular alteration, made necessary by its cause), is itself only problematic when expressed overall and in general. This is because the emerging cause only concerns the particular case, and the apodictic, always hypothetical judgement only ever expresses general laws, and does not directly express particular cases. – All this is grounded in the fact that possibility exists only in the sphere of reflection and for reason, while actuality exists in the sphere of intuition and for the understanding; and necessity exists for both. In fact, the difference between necessity, actuality and possibility really only exists in abstraction[a] and notionally; in the real world they all collapse into one. This is because everything that takes place does so *necessarily*; since it takes place from causes and these have causes of their own; the whole course of events of the world, great as well as small, forms a tight chain of necessarily unfolding events. Consequently, everything actual is at the same time necessary, and in reality there is no difference between actuality and necessity, and similarly none between actuality and possibility. This is because what has not happened, i.e. has not become actual, was also not possible, because the causes without which it could never have taken place did not themselves take place, nor could they have taken place in the great chain of causes: it was therefore an impossibility. Every event is thus either necessary or impossible. All this is nonetheless true only of the empirically real world, i.e. of the complex of particular things, and thus of what is completely particular or individual as such. But if, on the other hand, we use reason to consider things in general and grasp them abstractly, then necessity, actuality and possibility separate out again. We cognize everything that is in accordance with the *a priori* laws of our intellect as possible in general; we cognize what corresponds to the empirical laws of nature as possible in this world, even if it has never actually happened, and we thus clearly distinguish the possible from the actual. In itself, the actual is of course always necessary as well, but it is understood as such only by someone who is aware of its cause: apart from this, it is and is called contingent. This consideration also gives us the key[65] to that dispute concerning the possible[b] between the Megaric Diodorus and Chrysippus the Stoic which Cicero reports in the book *On Fate*.[c] Diodorus says: 'only what becomes actual was possible: and everything actual is also necessary'. – Chrysippus on the other hand says: 'there is much that is

---

[a] *in abstracto*

[b] *contentio* περι δυνατων

[c] *de fato*

possible that never becomes actual: because only the necessary becomes actual'. – We can explain this to ourselves in the following way: actuality is the conclusion of an inference for which possibility supplies the premises. But this inference required the minor premise in addition to the major: only together do they provide complete possibility. The major gives a merely theoretical, general possibility in abstraction: but this in itself does not make anything remotely possible, i.e. capable of becoming actual. For this we need the minor, which gives possibility in the particular case by bringing it under the rule. This is precisely how the particular case at once becomes actuality. For instance:

> Major: All houses (and consequently my house too) can burn.
> Minor: My house is on fire.
> Conclusion: My house is burning.

Every universal claim, and thus every major, only ever determines things (with respect to actuality) under some presupposition, and thus hypothetically. For instance, the ability to burn presupposes being on fire. This presupposition is furnished by the minor. The major always loads the cannon but only after the minor provides a match is there a shot, the conclusion. This is true without exception of the relation between possibility and actuality. But since the conclusion, which expresses actuality, always follows *necessarily*, then everything actual must also be necessary, from which it can be seen that being necessary only means being the consequent of a given ground: with actuality, this ground is a cause, which is why everything actual is necessary. Accordingly, we see the concepts of possibility, actuality and necessity collapsing together and not only the last presupposing the first, but the other way around as well. What keeps them apart is the constraint placed on our intellect by the form of time: because time is the intermediary between possibility and actuality. We have perfect insight into the necessity of a particular event, given knowledge[a] of all its causes: but the conjunction of all these different and mutually independent causes appears *contingent* to us, indeed their mutual independence is precisely the concept of contingency. But since each of them was the necessary consequent of *its* cause, and the chain of causality has no beginning, then contingency proves to be a merely subjective phenomenon[b] that arises from the limitation of the horizon of our understanding, and is thus just as subjective as the optical horizon where the sky meets the earth.[66] –

[a] *Erkenntniß*
[b] *Erscheinung*

Since necessity is the same thing as being a consequence from a given ground, it must appear as a particular type of necessity with each form of the principle of sufficient reason; its opposite must be the possibility and impossibility that arise only when reason considers objects abstractly. Thus, the four types of necessity mentioned above are opposed by the same number of types of impossibility: physical, logical, mathematical and practical. It might also be noted that if we remain entirely within the province of abstract concepts, possibility always adheres to the more general concept and necessity to the narrower one: for instance 'an animal *can* be a bird, fish, amphibian, etc.' – 'a nightingale *must* be a bird, a bird *must* be an animal, an animal *must* be an organism, an organism *must* be a body'. – This is really because logical necessity, which is expressed in the syllogism, proceeds from the universal to the particular and never the other way around. – By contrast, in intuitive nature (representations of the first class) everything is genuinely necessitated by the law of causality. Only reflection can come in and interpret it as contingent at the same time (by comparing it with what did not cause it) and as purely and simply actual (by disregarding all causal connections). The concept of *actuality* is only really found in this class of representations, as the derivation of the word from the concept of causality already shows.[a] – The third class of representations, that of purely mathematical intuition, has nothing but necessity, provided one remains strictly within its limits. Here as well, possibility arises only in reference to the concepts of reflection: for instance, 'a triangle *can* be right-angled, obtuse, equiangular, but *must* have three angles that equal two right angles'. So you only get to *possibility* by passing from the intuitive to the abstract.

557   After this presentation, which presupposes that we keep in mind both the essay *On the Principle of Sufficient Reason* as well as what we said in the First Book of the present work, I hope there will be no more doubts about the true and very diverse origins of the forms of judgement presented to us in the table of judgements, nor any further doubts that the twelve special functions of the understanding that are offered to explain them constitute an unjustifiable and groundless assumption. This last point is reinforced by a number of specific and obvious remarks. For instance, it takes a real passion for symmetry and a real faith[b] in the guidance it provides to assume that affirmative, categorical and assertoric judgements are so fundamentally

---

[a] [The German term for actuality is *Wirklichkeit*, and is related to *Wirkung* which means effect]
[b] *Vertrauen*

different as to justify an entirely distinctive function of the understanding for each.

Kant himself reveals that he is conscious of the untenable nature of his doctrine of the categories through the fact that in the second edition of the third chapter of the Analytic of Principles (*phaenomena et noumena*) he omits several long passages from the first edition (namely pp. 241, 242, 244–6, 248–53) that exposed the weaknesses of that doctrine too openly. So for instance he himself says on p. 241 that he has not defined the individual categories because he could not define them even if he wanted to, since they are not capable of definition; – in doing so he had forgotten that on p. 82 of the same first edition he had said: 'I deliberately spare myself the definition of these categories, although I should like to be in possession of them.' This was thus – if I may be pardoned for saying so[a] – a lot of hot air. But he let this final passage stand. And thus all those passages that he subsequently and discretely omitted show that he did not have anything clear in mind with the categories, and that the whole doctrine stands on unstable legs.[67]

This table of categories is supposed to be the guide for all metaphysical, indeed all scientific inquiry (*Prolegomena* § 39). And in fact it is not only the basis of the whole Kantian philosophy and the model[b] for all its symmetry, as demonstrated above, but it really became the Procrustean bed onto which Kant forced every possible consideration with a violence that I will now consider more closely. But with such an opportunity what were the 'imitators, servile herd'[c] to do! We have seen. That violence is exercised in ignoring and forgetting the meanings of the expressions indicated by the headings, forms of judgements and categories, and retaining only the expressions themselves. These have their origins partly in Aristotle's *Prior Analytics*, I, 23 (on the quality and the quantity of the terms of the syllogism[d]), but were chosen arbitrarily,[68] because the scope of the concepts certainly could have been described very differently than with the term *quantity*, although this particular term matched its object better than the rest of the headings of the categories did. Even the word *quality* was clearly only chosen due to the custom of opposing quantity to quality, because quality is certainly an arbitrary enough name for affirmation and negation.

558

---

[a] *sit venia verbo*

[b] *Typus*

[c] *imitatores, servum pecus* [Horace, *Epistles*, I, 19, 19]

[d] περι ποιοτητος και ποσοτητος των του συλλογισμου ὁρων (*de qualitate et quantitate terminorum syllogismi*) [Deussen and Hübscher suggest *Prior Analytics* I, 29, 45b15 as the correct reference – though the wording Schopenhauer gives is not found there, only a mention of ποιότης or 'quality']

But now every observation Kant makes, every quantity in time and space, every possible quality of things, physical, moral, etc. is put under those category headings, regardless of whether these things have anything even remotely in common with those headings of the forms of judgement and thought – that is, anything except the accidental, arbitrary name. All the respect that is otherwise due to Kant must be kept in mind here to stop us from using harsh terms to voice our indignation over this procedure. – The next example is provided directly by the pure physiological table of general principles of natural science. What in the world does the quantity of judgements have to do with the fact that every intuition has an extensive magnitude? What does the quality of judgements have to do with the fact that every sensation has a degree? – Rather, the former is based on the fact that space is the form of our outer intuition, and the latter is nothing more than an empirical and moreover completely subjective perception, drawn from a consideration of the constitution of our sense organs. – Further-

559 more, the table that lays the ground for rational psychology (*Critique of Pure Reason*, p. 344/V 402) introduces the *simplicity* of the soul under qual-ity. But this is just a quantitative property and has absolutely no relation to affirmation or negation in judgement. Nevertheless, quantity is supposed to be occupied by the *unity* of the soul, although this is already included in simplicity. Then modality is forced into this in a ridiculous manner; namely, that the soul is related to[a] *possible* objects. But 'being related' belongs to relation;[b] only this is already occupied by substance.[69] Then the four cosmological ideas, which are the content of the antinomies, are traced back to the headings of the categories; we will discuss this more fully later, when we examine these antinomies.[70] Several examples that are perhaps even more glaring are provided by the table of the *categories of freedom* in the *Critique of Practical Reason*! – And again in the first book of the *Critique of the Power of Judgement*, which goes through the judgement of taste according to the four headings of the categories. And finally in the *Metaphysical Foundations of Natural Science*, which is divided entirely according to the table of categories, which might be the main cause of the falsity that is sometimes mixed up with what is true and excellent in this important work. Just look, at the end of the first chapter, at how the unity, multi-plicity, and totality of the directions of lines are supposed to correspond to categories that are so named according to the quantity of judgements.

---

[a] *stehe im Verhältniß zu*
[b] *Verhältniß gehört . . . zur Relation*

The principle of the *permanence of substance* is derived from the category of subsistence and inherence. But we are only familiar with this from the form of categorical judgements, i.e. from the combination of two concepts as subject and predicate. How violently this great metaphysical principle is made to depend on the simple, purely logical form! But this is only a matter of form[a] and for the sake of symmetry. The proof given here for this principle entirely disregards its supposed origin from the understanding and the category, and proceeds from the pure intuition of time. But this proof is completely wrong as well. It is false to say that there is *simultaneity* and *duration* in mere time: these representations only arise after *space* has been unified with time, as I have already shown in the essay *On the Principle of Sufficient Reason*, § 18,[71] and more thoroughly in § 4 of the present text; both explanations are presupposed for an understanding of what follows. It is false that time itself *remains*[b] through all change: rather, time is precisely what is fluid: time that remains is a contradiction. Kant's proof is untenable, however much he defended it with sophisms: indeed, it lands him in the most obvious contradiction. After he has falsely established *simultaneity* as a mode of time (p. 177/V 219), he says (p. 183/V 226) entirely correctly: '*Simultaneity* is not a *modus* for time itself, in which no parts are simultaneous but rather all succeed one another.' – In truth, space is just as implicated as time in simultaneity. This is because if two things are simultaneous without being the same thing, then they are divided by space; if two states of a *single* thing are simultaneous (for instance, the glowing and the heating of iron), then they are two simultaneous effects of a *single* thing, and presuppose matter which presupposes space. Strictly speaking, simultaneity is a negative determination which signifies only that two things or states are not divided in time, and that we must look elsewhere to find a way of distinguishing between them. – Certainly our cognition of the permanence of substance, i.e. of matter, must rest on an *a priori* insight, since it is indubitable and thus cannot be drawn from experience. I deduce it from the fact that the principle of all becoming and passing away, the law of causality of which we are *a priori* conscious, essentially concerns only *alterations*, i.e. the successive *states* of matter. It is, for this reason, limited to form and leaves *matter* untouched; matter is thus present in our consciousness as the enduring foundation of all things; it is not subject to becoming or passing away and thus always exists. A deeper argument for the permanence of substance, one that is drawn from an analysis of our

[a] *pro forma*
[b] *bleibe*

intuitive representation of the empirical world in general, can be found in our First Book, § 4, where it is shown that the essence of *matter* consists in
561 the complete *unification of space and time*,[72] a unification that is possible only by way of the representation of causality, and consequently only for the understanding. This is because the understanding is nothing but the subjective correlative of causality, and thus only knows matter as active,[a] i.e. as causality through and through, and thinks of being and activity[b] as one and the same thing, as is already implied in the word *actuality*.[c] Inner unification of space and time, – causality, matter, actuality, – are thus one and the same thing, and the subjective correlate of this single thing is the understanding. Matter must carry within itself the conflicting properties of the two elements from which it arises; the representation of causality is what eliminates the contradiction between the two and makes their coexistence[d] intelligible to the understanding, since matter exists only through and for the understanding, and the whole faculty of understanding consists in the cognition of cause and effect. Thus the unstable flux of time unifies itself for the understanding in matter, appearing as the change of accidents in the rigid immobility of space, an immobility that is presented as the permanence of substance. If substance passed away as accidents do, then appearance would be completely torn away from space and belong only to time: the world of experience would be dissolved through the destruction of matter, annihilation. – Thus, the principle of the permanence of substance that everyone recognizes as *a priori* certain must be deduced and explained from the role that *space* plays in matter, i.e. in all appearances of actuality (since space is the opposite and the reverse of time and thus, in itself and apart from any association with time, has nothing to do with change); but it cannot be deduced from mere time, to which Kant for this purpose absurdly attributed *duration*.[e],[73] –

   In the essay *On the Principle of Sufficient Reason*, § 23,[74] I demonstrated in detail why the following proof for the necessity as well as the *a priori* nature of the law of causality from the merely temporal sequence of events
562 was incorrect, so I will simply mention it.[*] The same thing holds for the

---

[*] My refutation of Kant's proof might be compared with that of *Feder*, in *On Time, Space, and Causality* [*Ueber Zeit, Raum und Kausalität*] § 28; and that of G. E. *Schulze*, in *Critique of Theoretical Philosophy* [*Kritik der theoretischen Philosophie*] vol. 2, pp. 422–42.

[a] *wirkend*
[b] *Wirken*
[c] *Wirklichkeit*
[d] *Zusammenbestehn*
[e] *Bleiben*

proof of reciprocal causation, the concept of which I have just exposed as unreal. – We have already said what we needed to say about modality, and we will now proceed to a consideration of its principles. –

There are quite a few more details in the course of the Transcendental Analytic that I would want to refute, but I am afraid of trying my readers' patience so I will leave them to think these over on their own.[75] In the *Critique of Pure Reason* we are constantly confronted with Kant's major and fundamental mistake, which I have already criticized in detail, the failure to distinguish between abstract, discursive cognition and intuitive cognition. This is always spreading obscurity over Kant's entire theory of the faculty of cognition, so that the reader never knows what is under discussion at any given time. The reader does not understand but only speculates, trying to apply what Kant says alternatively to thinking and to intuition, and always remaining undecided. Kant's astonishing lack of reflection concerning the essence of intuitive and abstract representation leads him in the chapter 'On the distinction of all objects into *phenomena* and *noumena*' (as I will now discuss in greater depth)[76] to make the monstrous claim that without thinking, which is to say without abstract concepts, there is no cognition of objects, and that because intuition is not thinking, it is not cognition at all and is nothing more than a mere affection of sensibility, mere sensation! But even more, he claims that intuition without a concept is completely empty, while concept without intuition is still something (p. 253/V 309). This is the exact opposite of the truth, because concepts get their meaning and content only from their relation to intuitive representations, from which they are abstracted and derived, which is to say constructed by omitting everything inessential. Accordingly, if concepts are deprived of their foundation in intuition, they are empty and unreal.[77] On the other hand, intuitions have immediate and considerable meaning in themselves (the will, the thing in itself, is even objectified in them): they are their own representatives,[a] speak for themselves, and their content is not simply borrowed, as is the case with concepts. This is because they are governed by the principle of sufficient reason only in the form of the law of causality; as such, it determines only their position in space and time, and does not condition their content or their meaningfulness, as is the case with concepts, where the principle of sufficient reason serves as the basis of cognition.[78] And it seems as though Kant really meant to distinguish between intuitive and abstract representations here: he reproaches Leibniz and Locke, saying that the former made everything into abstract representations and the latter made

563

---

[a] *vertreten sich selbst*

everything into intuitive ones. But he never actually makes this distinction: and even though Locke and Leibniz really did make those mistakes, Kant himself is weighed down with a third mistake that encompasses the other two, namely that of mixing the intuitive and the abstract to produce a monstrous hybrid, an absurdity that cannot possibly be clearly represented, and which could only serve to confuse and bewilder students and put them at odds with each other.

But thought and intuition are certainly kept more distinct in the chapter we have mentioned, 'On the distinction of all objects into *phenomena* and *noumena*', than they are anywhere else: only they are distinguished here in a way that is fundamentally false. Specifically, Kant states, p. 253/V 309: 'If I take all thinking (through categories) away from an empirical cognition, then no cognition of any object at all remains; for through mere intuition nothing at all is thought, and that this affection of sensibility is in me does not constitute any relation of such representation to any object at all.' – To a certain extent, this claim contains all of Kant's errors in a nutshell: it brings to light his misconception of the relation between sensation, intuition and thought, his consequent identification of intuition (whose form is supposed to be space – and indeed in all three dimensions) with the simple, subjective sensation in the sense organs, while allowing an object to be cognized through thought alone (conceived in a manner distinct from intuition). I, on the other hand, say: objects[a] are initially the objects of intuition,[b] not

564   of thought, and all cognition of *objects*[c] is itself originally and intrinsically intuition. It is certainly not mere sensation, and in fact the understanding already proves that it is active in this. The *thought* that is added only with human beings, not with animals, is just abstraction from intuition; it does not give any fundamentally new cognition, and does not posit objects that were not already there. Rather, it only alters the form of the cognition already acquired through intuition, making it into abstract cognition in concepts, whereupon its intuitive nature[d] is lost[79] but its combination becomes possible, and this broadens its applicability immeasurably. The *matter*[e] of our thinking on the other hand is nothing other than our intuitions themselves, and not something that intuition does not already contain and that is only added through thought. Thus the matter of everything present in our thought must be capable of demonstration in

---

[a]   *Objekte*
[b]   *Gegenstände der Anschauung*
[c]   *Gegenständen*
[d]   *Anschaulichkeit*
[e]   *Stoff*

our intuition; otherwise it would be an empty thought. However much this matter is worked on and transformed through thought, we must still be able to reconstitute this matter and to lead thought back to it, just as a piece of gold might ultimately be reduced from all its solutions, oxidations, sublimations and combinations, and presented once more, reguline and undiminished. But this could not be the case if something – and indeed the most important element – had been added to the object by thought itself.

The whole chapter on the amphiboly that follows this is just a critique of the Leibnizian philosophy, and as such is largely correct, although it has all been ordered and arranged with an eye to architectonic symmetry, which serves as the guide here as well. So, to bring out the analogy with the Aristotelian organon, a transcendental topic is set up that consists in regarding each concept from four perspectives in order to establish which cognitive faculty it belongs to. But these four perspectives are adopted entirely capriciously, and we would be equally justified in adding ten more: the fact that there are four of them corresponds to the category headings, and thus the principal Leibnizian doctrine is divided among them as much as possible. Through this critique, to a certain extent, things were branded as natural errors of reason when they were really just false abstractions on the part of 565 *Leibniz*, who dished up his own, strange inventions instead of learning from his great philosophical contemporaries, Spinoza and Locke.[80] The chapter on the amphiboly of reflection ultimately claims that there could possibly be a type of intuition that is completely different from our own, but one to which our categories nonetheless apply.[81] The objects[a] of that supposed intuition would be the *noumena*, things that we can only *think*, but are in fact completely problematic, since we do not have the intuition that would give such thought meaning; as a result, the object[b] of that thought would be nothing but an entirely undetermined possibility. I have cited passages above which show that Kant contradicted himself by sometimes positioning the categories as the condition for intuitive representation, and sometimes as a function of merely abstract thought. They have only the latter meaning here, and it seems as if Kant wanted to ascribe a merely discursive thinking to them. But if this were really what he meant, then he would have needed to characterize thinking in general at the beginning of the Transcendental Logic before specifying the different functions of thinking in such detail, and consequently distinguish thought from intuition; and he should have

[a] *Objekte*
[b] *Gegenstand*

shown what sort of cognition is given in mere intuition and what sort of new cognition is added with thought. Then we would have known what Kant was really talking about, or rather, he would have talked about things much differently; specifically, he would have talked about intuition at one point and thought at another, instead of always dealing with something intermediate[a] between the two, which is an absurdity.[b] Then there would not be that great gap between the Transcendental Aesthetic and the Transcendental Logic, where, after presenting the mere form of intuition he disposes of its content, the whole of empirical perception, with a simple 'it is *given*' and does not ask how it comes about, *whether with or without the understanding*. Instead, he jumps to abstract thought; not even to thought in general, but straight to certain forms of thought, and does not say a single word about the nature of thought, the nature of concepts, the relation of abstract and discursive cognition to concrete and intuitive cognition, the difference between human and animal cognition, or the nature of reason.[82]

566

The difference between abstract and intuitive cognition, which Kant entirely overlooks, was the very one that ancient philosophers indicated as *phainomena* and *nooumena*;[c],* the opposition and incommensurability between these terms proved very productive in the philosophemes of the Eleatics, in Plato's doctrine of Ideas, in the dialectic of the Megarics, and later in the scholastics, in the conflict between nominalism and realism. This latter conflict was the late development of a seed already present in the opposed tendencies of Plato and Aristotle. But Kant, who completely and irresponsibly neglected the issue for which the terms *phainomena* and *nooumena* were already in use, then took possession of the terms as if they were stray and ownerless, and used them as designations of things in themselves and their appearances.

—————

After having to reject Kant's doctrine of the categories just as he himself rejected that of Aristotle, I nevertheless want to suggest a third way of achieving what they intended. What they were both looking for under the

---

* See Sextus Empiricus, *Pyrrhoniae hypotyposes* [*Outlines of Pyrrhonism*], Bk. I, chap. 13, νοουμενα φαινομενοις αντετι9η Αναξαγορας (*intelligibilia apparentibus opposuit Anaxagoras*) ['Anaxagoras opposed what is thought to what appears' – an approximation to what Sextus says]

[a] *Mittelding*
[b] *Unding*
[c] φαινομενα *und* νοουμενα

rubric[a] of the categories was the most general concepts under which people had to subsume all things, different as they are, concepts through which everything in existence would ultimately be thought. This is why Kant conceived of them as the *forms* of all thought.

Grammar is to logic as clothing is to the body. So, these very highest concepts, this ground bass of reason that supports all specific thought and without which thinking cannot take place – should they not ultimately rest on concepts which, precisely because of their exceeding universality (transcendentality), are not expressed in individual words but rather in whole classes of words? After all, one of them is already thought with each word (whatever it may be) – so should we not look for their definition in grammar rather than in a dictionary? Should they not ultimately be those distinctions of concepts which make the word that expresses them either a noun or an adjective, a verb or an adverb, a pronoun, a preposition, or some other particle, in short the parts of speech?[b] After all, these indisputably describe the forms that all thought must initially assume and in which it immediately moves. This is why they are the essential linguistic forms, the basic components of every language, and we cannot imagine a language that does not at least consist of nouns, adjectives and verbs. To these basic forms would then be subordinated the forms of thought that are expressed through their inflection, which is to say through declension and conjugation, where it does not generally matter whether this is designated with the help of an article or a pronoun. We nonetheless want to examine the matter somewhat more closely, and raise the question anew: what are the forms of thought?

(1) Thought consists completely and exclusively of judgements: judgements are the threads of its entire fabric. Without the use of verbs, our thinking does not advance, and as soon as we use verbs we are judging.

(2) Every judgement consists of cognizing the relation between a subject and a predicate, which the judgement separates or unites with a number of restrictions. It unites them by acknowledging the actual identity of the two, an identity that can only take place when the concepts are interchangeable; then in recognizing that the one is always thought in the other but not conversely, – this in the universal, affirmative proposition; and then in recognizing that the one is sometimes thought along with the other, in the particular, affirmative proposition. The negative proposition takes the opposite course. Accordingly, we must be able to find the subject, predicate

567

[a] *Namen*
[b] *partes orationis*

and copula in every judgement (the copula being either affirmative or negative), even when these are not individually designated by their own word, although this is typically the case. Often a *single* word signifies both predicate and copula, such as: 'Caius ages'; sometimes a *single* word stands in for all three, like *concurritur*, i.e. 'the armies are engaged in close combat'. This shows that the forms of thought are not to be found so directly and straightforwardly in words, or indeed in the parts of speech. The same judgement can be expressed in different languages, or even with different words or different parts of speech in the same language, and yet the thought remains the same, and consequently so does its form: because the thought could not remain the same if the forms of thought were themselves different. But the verbal structure could certainly be different while the thought, or the form of the thought, remains the same, because this is just the outer clothing on the thought, although this thought is inseparable from *its* form. So grammar only explains the clothing on the forms of thought. The parts of speech can therefore be derived from the original forms of thought themselves, forms that are independent of all language: their function is to express these with all their modifications. They are the instruments of the forms of thought, the clothing that must fit their structure perfectly so that the structure can be recognized in it.

568

(3) These actual, unchanging, original forms of thought are of course those of Kant's *logical table of judgements*; except that this table has windows that are left blank for the sake of symmetry and the table of categories, and these must be removed; likewise the false arrangement. Thus:

(4) (a) *Quality*: affirmation or negation, i.e. combination or separation of concepts: two forms. It attaches to the copula.

(4) (b) *Quantity*: the concept of the subject is accepted entirely or in part: totality[a] or multiplicity. Individual subjects also belong to the first: 'Socrates' means: 'all Socrateses'. Thus only two forms. It attaches to the subject.

(4) (c) *Modality*: really has three forms. It determines the quality as necessary, actual or contingent. Consequently, it also attaches to the copula.

These three forms of thought stem from the laws of contradiction and identity. But what comes from the principle of sufficient reason and the law of the excluded middle is:

(4) (d) *Relation*. This only appears when we make judgements about completed judgements, and it can only consist in stating either the

---

[a] *Allheit*

dependence of one judgement on another (even when both are   569
plural) and consequently in combining them in a *hypothetical*
proposition; or in stating that judgements exclude each other, and
consequently in separating them in a *disjunctive* proposition. It
attaches to the copula, which in this case separates or combines the
completed judgements.

The *parts of speech* and the forms of grammar are thus ways of expressing
the three components of judgement, which is to say the subject, predicate
and copula, as well as the possible relations between these, and thus the
forms of thought just mentioned and the more precise determinations and
modifications of these forms. Nouns, adjectives and verbs are thus essential,
basic components of language in general, which is why they are necessarily
to be found in all languages. Nonetheless, we can imagine a language
in which adjectives and verbs are always mixed together, as occasionally
happens in every language. In the meantime it can be said: nouns, articles
and pronouns are for expressing the *subject*; – adjectives, adverbs and
prepositions are for expressing the *predicate*; – and for expressing the *copula*
there are verbs, and verbs already contain the predicate (with the exception
of *to be*[a]). Philosophical grammar teaches us the precise mechanism for
expressing the forms of thought; similarly, logic tells us about the operations
with the forms of thought themselves.

Note. As a cautionary note concerning a false path and an illustration
of what was said above, I mention *S. Stern's Provisional Foundations for a
Philosophy of Language*[b] (1835) which is a thoroughly unsuccessful attempt
to construct the categories from grammatical forms. He gets thought completely mixed up with intuition, and therefore wants to deduce the would-
be categories of intuition (rather than the categories of thought) from the
forms of grammar; accordingly, he puts the grammatical forms in direct
relation to *intuition*. He is caught up in the great mistake of thinking
that *language* refers directly to *intuition* instead of referring directly only
to *thought* as such, and thus to *abstract concepts*, and to intuition only by
means of these; but its relation to intuition leads to a complete alteration of
the form. What is present in intuition certainly does become an object of
thought, as do the relations that arise from time and space; thus there must
also be linguistic forms to express it, although only ever in the abstract,[c]   570
as concepts. Concepts are always the primary material of thought, and the
forms of logic refer only to these, they never refer *directly* to intuition.

[a] *esse*
[b] *Vorläufige Grundlage zur Sprachphilosophie*
[c] *in abstracto*

Intuitions only ever determine the material truth of propositions, never the formal truth, which is directed according to logical rules alone.[83]

———————

I return to Kant's philosophy, and come to the *Transcendental Dialectic*. Kant opens this section with an explanation of *reason*, the faculty that is to play the leading role here since only sensibility and the understanding have appeared on stage so far. I have already discussed Kant's different explanations of reason, including the one given here, that 'it is the faculty of principles'. Now we are told that all the *a priori* cognition we have been considering so far, cognition that makes both pure mathematics and pure natural science possible, provides only *rules* and not *principles*. This is because it comes from intuitions and forms of cognition, not from pure *concepts*, and these are required in order to be called principles. Accordingly, a principle should be cognition *from pure concepts*, yet nonetheless *synthetic*. But this is simply impossible. Only *analytic* propositions can come from mere concepts. If concepts are to be combined synthetically and indeed in an *a priori* manner, then this combination must necessarily be mediated by a third thing, by a pure intuition of the formal possibility of experience, just as synthetic judgements *a posteriori* are mediated by empirical intuition. Consequently, a synthetic *a priori* proposition can never come from mere concepts. But in general the only thing we are conscious of *a priori* is the principle of sufficient reason in its different forms, and thus no synthetic judgements are possible *a priori* other than those that come from what gives content to that principle.

Nevertheless, Kant finally comes forward with a supposed principle of reason that meets his demands, but with only this *one*, from which other corollaries follow. It is the proposition that Christian Wolff established and explained in his *Cosmologia*, section I, chap. 2, § 93, and in his *Ontologia*, § 178. Earlier, under the name of Amphiboly, strictly Leibnizian philosophemes were regarded as natural and necessary errors of reason and criticized as such; and now the very same thing happens with the philosophemes of Wolff.[84] Kant's presentation of this principle of reason is murky and obscure: he is unclear, indeterminate and cuts it up in pieces (p. 307/V 364, and p. 322/V 379); but expressed clearly, it is as follows: 'If the conditioned is given, then the totality of its conditions must be given as well, and thus the *unconditioned* too, through which alone every totality is complete.' The apparent truth of this proposition is most obvious when the conditions and the conditioned are conceived as links in a hanging chain whose uppermost end cannot be seen, so it could continue on to infinity. But since the chain hangs rather than falls, there must be *one* link on top that comes first and is somehow fastened down. Or more concisely: reason would like to have a starting point for the causal chain that goes back to infinity; it would find this convenient. But we want to test this proposition against itself, not against images.[85] It is certainly synthetic, because analytically nothing follows from the concept of the conditioned except that of a condition. But it is not true either *a priori* or *a posteriori*; rather, it obtains its illusion of truth in a sly and very subtle way that I must now reveal. Our immediate and *a priori* cognition is expressed in the principle of sufficient reason in its four forms. All abstract expressions of the principle of sufficient reason are already borrowed from this immediate cognition, and are thus mediated: their corollaries are even more so. I have already mentioned above how *abstract* cognition often unites the manifold of *intuitive* cognition into a *single* form or a *single* concept in such a way that it can no longer be differentiated. Thus, abstract cognition is to intuitive cognition as a shadow is to the real objects whose great diversity it reproduces in a *single*, all-encompassing outline. Now the supposed principle of reason uses this shadow. In order to deduce the unconditioned from the principle of sufficient reason, with which it is in direct contradiction, it cleverly abandons the direct, intuitive cognition of the content   572 of the principle of sufficient reason in its individual forms, and uses only the abstract concepts that are drawn from it and have value and meaning only through it, in order somehow to smuggle its unconditioned into the broad scope of those concepts. Its method is most clear when clothed in dialectical terms: for instance: 'If there is a conditioned, then its condition must be given as well, and indeed fully, which is to say completely, which means the totality of its conditions, and consequently (if they form a series) the whole series, and consequently the beginning of the series, and thus the unconditioned.' – But it is already false that the conditions of a conditioned can as such form a *series*. Rather, the totality of the conditions for each conditioned must be contained in its *most proximate* ground,[a] the ground from which it follows immediately and which is a *sufficient* ground only in this way. So for instance, the different determinations of the state that is the cause, all of which must come together before the effect appears.[86] But the series, the chain of causes for instance, arises only when we regard what had just been the condition as a conditioned, at which point the whole operation starts all over again and the principle of sufficient reason reappears with its demands. But there can never be a genuinely successive

[a] *Grunde*

series of conditions for a conditioned, a series that would exist merely as such and for the sake of what is finally and ultimately conditioned. Rather, there is always an alternating series of conditions and conditioned, and with each link that is set aside the chain is interrupted and the demands of the principle of sufficient reason are completely withdrawn; it starts up again when the condition becomes a conditioned. Thus the principle of *sufficient* reason[a] only ever demands the completeness of the *most proximate* condition, never the completeness of a *series*. But this very concept of the completeness of the condition leaves undetermined the question of whether this is supposed to be simultaneous or successive; and since the latter is now chosen, the demand arises for a completed *series* of conditions following one another. Only an arbitrary abstraction would allow us to

573 view a series of causes and effects as a series of pure causes that exist only for the sake of the final effect and are thus called for as its *sufficient* ground. But a closer and more level-headed[b] deliberation that descends from the indeterminate universality of abstraction to particular, determinate reality shows however that the demand for a *sufficient* ground extends only to the completeness of the determinations of the *most proximate* cause, not to the completeness of a series. The demand of the principle of sufficient reason is completely extinguished in every given sufficient ground. It starts all over from the beginning as soon as this ground is in turn regarded as a consequent, but it never directly demands a series of grounds. If, on the other hand, we do not go straight to the issue but remain within abstract concepts instead, then those distinctions disappear: a chain that alternates between causes and effects, or between logical grounds and consequences, will pass for a chain of pure causes or grounds for the final effect, and the *completeness of the conditions* that allow a ground to be *sufficient* in the first place appears as the completeness of those series of pure grounds that exist only for the sake of the final consequent. Then the abstract principle of reason[c] struts right in, issuing its demand for the unconditioned. But we do not need a critique of reason with antinomies and their solution to see that this is invalid; we only need a critique of reason understood in my sense, namely an investigation of the relation between abstract cognition and immediate, intuitive cognition, an investigation that proceeds by descending from the indeterminate generality of the former to the fixed determination of the latter. It follows from this that the essence of reason

[a] [In Schopenhauer's usage the German term for this principle, *Satz vom Grund*, often does not include the term 'sufficient' – but it does so here with emphasis: *Satz vom* zureichenden *Grunde*]
[b] *besonnener*
[c] *Vernunftprincip*

certainly does not consist in a demand for the unconditioned, because as soon as it proceeds with full deliberation it will necessarily discover for itself that an unconditioned is a total absurdity. As a cognitive faculty, reason is only ever concerned with objects;[a] but everything that is an object for the subject is necessarily and irrevocably subordinate to and in line with the principle of sufficient reason, with regard to what precedes as much as with regard to what follows.[b] The validity of the principle of sufficient reason is so firmly entrenched in the form of consciousness that we simply cannot objectively imagine anything from which a 'why' could not be fur-   574 ther demanded, which is to say we cannot imagine an absolute Absolute[c] that would stop us in our tracks.[d] The fact that someone or other finds a place where he feels comfortable, comes to a stop, and chooses to call it 'the Absolute' cannot be held up against this irrefutable, *a priori* certainty, even if he puts on very high-minded airs. And in fact all the talk about the Absolute, which has been the almost exclusive theme in all the philosophy attempted since Kant, is nothing but the cosmological argument *incognito*. Since Kant filed suit against this argument it has been outlawed, stripped of its rights, and unable to show its true face, so it appears in all sorts of disguises: sometimes it looks very high-minded, clothed in intellectual intuition or pure thought; sometimes it looks like a dubious vagabond that gets what it needs partly by begging and partly with threats in the more unassuming philosophemes. But if my dear sirs absolutely must have an Absolute, then I will supply them with one that satisfies all requirements for such a thing much better than the misty forms they dream up: it is matter. Matter is uncreated and imperishable, and is thus truly independent, that which is in itself and is grasped through itself,[e] and everything emerges from its womb and everything returns to it: what more could you want in an Absolute? – But to people who are unmoved by any critique of reason we should rather call out:

> Are you not like women who return
> and yet again return to their first word,
> though we reason with them for hours?[f]

Factual proof that a retreat to an unconditioned cause or first beginning is certainly not grounded in the essence of reason is provided by the fact

---

[a] *Objekten*
[b] *a parte ante . . . a parte post*
[c] *absolutes Absolutum*
[d] *wie ein Brett vor dem Kopf*
[e] *quod per se est et per se concipitur*
[f] [Schiller, *Wallensteins Tod* (*Wallenstein's Death*), II, 3]

that the original religions[a] of our race, the religions that still have the greatest number of followers in the world, Brahmanism and Buddhism, neither know nor admit such assumptions; instead, they follow the series of mutually conditioning appearances to infinity. The note given below with the critique of the first antinomy is relevant to this issue; in addition, people can refer to Upham's *Doctrine of Buddhaism* (p. 9) and in general to any authentic report on Asian religions. Judaism should not be identified with reason.[87] –

Kant does not mean to assert that his supposed principle of reason is objectively valid, but only subjectively necessary; he deduces it, even as such, only from a shallow sophism, p. 307/V 364. Specifically, we try as hard as possible to subsume every known truth under a more general truth, and this is supposedly nothing other than the very hunt for the unconditioned that we presupposed. But this really amounts to nothing more than the fact that we make use of reason (i.e. the faculty of abstract, universal cognition that distinguishes reflective, linguistically capable, thinking people from animals, the slaves of the present), using it for the purpose of simplifying our cognition through a comprehensive view of things. This is because the use of reason consists precisely in our cognition of the particular through the general, the case through the rule, and this through the more general rule, and thus in our attempts to gain the most general point of view. This sort of comprehensive overview facilitates and perfects our cognition to such an extent that it gives rise to the great difference between animal and human life, and again between the lives of the educated and those of vulgar people. Now the series of *grounds of cognition* that exist only in the realm of the abstract, i.e. reason, certainly always ends in something that cannot be proven, i.e. in a representation that is not further conditioned by this form of the principle of sufficient reason, which is to say in an *a priori* or *a posteriori* directly intuitive ground of the highest proposition in the inferential chain. I have already shown in § 50 of the essay *On the Principle of Sufficient Reason*[88] that here the series of the grounds of cognition really passes over into the series of the grounds of becoming or of being. But if we want to insist on this circumstance in order to prove the existence of the unconditioned in accordance with the law of causality, even if it is only as a demand, then this is possible only if we fail to distinguish between the forms of the principle of sufficient reason, and instead cling to the abstract expression and get them all mixed up. Kant even tried to ground this confusion in a simple wordplay between *universalitas*

---

[a] *Urreligionen*

and *universitas*,[a] p. 322/V 379.[89] – It is therefore fundamentally false that our search for higher grounds of cognition, more general truths, comes from presupposing an object that is by its very nature[b] unconditioned, or that has anything at all in common with such an object. How could it be essential for reason to presuppose something that it must know to be an absurdity as soon as it thinks about it? Rather, we can never show that the concept of the unconditioned originated anywhere other than in the inertia of the individual who wants to use it to get rid of all further questions, his own as well as those of other people, albeit without any justification.

Kant himself of course denies objective validity to this supposed principle of reason, yet he holds it to be a necessary, subjective presupposition; he thus introduces an insoluble dichotomy into our cognition and soon allows it to become increasingly evident. To this end, he develops that principle of reason further, on p. 322/V 379, according to his beloved architectonic-symmetrical method. From the three categories of relation come three types of inference, each of which provides a guide for looking for a particular type of unconditioned, of which there are again three: the soul, the world (as object in itself and self-contained totality), and God. Now this quickly points to a greater contradiction, albeit one that Kant ignored because it would be quite dangerous for the symmetry: two of these unconditioneds are in fact themselves conditioned by the third. Specifically, the soul and the world are conditioned by God, the cause that created them: thus, they do not share with God the predicate of being unconditioned, which is what is at issue here, but rather only the predicate of being inferred from principles of experience that are above and beyond the realm of the possibility of experience.

Setting this aside, we find that the three unconditioned things which (according to Kant) reason must always encounter when following its essential laws are the three, principal, pivotal issues for all philosophy that have arisen under the influence of Christianity, from the scholastics up through Christian Wolff.[90] As accessible and familiar as these concepts have become through all these philosophers, and even now through the philosophers of pure reason, this in no way establishes that, in the absence of revelation, these concepts necessarily proceed from the development of anyone's reason, as a product characteristic of its essence.[91] To establish this, we would need to initiate a historical enquiry into whether the ancient and the non-European peoples (and in particular the Hindustani and some of

577

[a] ['universality' and 'allness']
[b] *seinem Daseyn nach*

the most ancient Greek philosophers) really acquired these concepts, or whether (just as the Greeks rediscovered their own gods everywhere) we have charitably ascribed these concepts to them by quite falsely translating the Hindu Brahma and the Chinese Tian as 'God'. We could see if it is not rather the case that genuine theism can be found only in Judaism and the two religions that arose from it, religions whose followers have, for this very reason, grouped together the practitioners of all the other religions as 'heathen'.[a] – This, by the way, is an exceptionally naïve and crude term that should be banned, at least from scholarly works, because it equates Brahmans, Buddhists, Egyptians, Greeks, Romans, ancient Germans, Gauls, Iroquois, Patagonians, Caribbeans, Tahitians, Australians, etc., and lumps them all together. A term like 'heathen' is appropriate for a preacher, but it should be immediately expelled from the scholarly world; it can go to England and settle down in Oxford. – It is an established fact that Buddhism in particular, the religion with the greatest number of adherents on earth, is devoid of theism and in fact detests it. As far as Plato is concerned, my opinion is that he owes his occasional bouts of theism to Judaism. This is why Numenius (according to *Clement of Alexandria, Stromata*, I, chap. 22, Eusebius, *Preparation for the Gospel*,[b] xii, 12, and Suidas, under 'Numenius') called him the Greek-speaking Moses:[c] 'Because what is Plato but an Attic-speaking Moses?';[d] and accused him of having stolen (αποσυλησας) his doctrines of God and the creation from the Mosaic texts. *Clement* often refers to the fact that Plato was familiar with Moses and used him, for instance *Stromata*, I, 25. – V, chap. 14, § 90 etc., – *The Paedagogus*, II, 10 and III, 11, and also in the *Exhortation to the Heathen*,[e] chap. 6. There, after spending the previous chapter monkishly scolding and deriding all of the Greek philosophers for not having been Jews, he praises only Plato and breaks into pure exaltation over the fact that because Plato learned his geometry from the Egyptians, his astronomy from the Babylonians, magic from the Thracians, and much else from the Assyrians, he likewise received his theism from the Jews: 'I know your teachers, even if you wanted to hide them, . . . your belief in God came from the Hebrews.'[f] A moving scene of recognition. – But I find an unusual confirmation of

578

[a] *Heiden*
[b] *Praeparatio evangelica*
[c] *Moses graecisans*
[d] Τι γαρ εστι Πλατων, η Μωσης αττικιζων;
[e] *Cohortatio ad Gentes*
[f] Οιδα σου τους διδασκαλους, κὰν αποκρυπτειν εθελης, . . . δοξαν την του θεου παρ αυτων ωφελησαι των Εβραιων (*tuos magistros novi, licet eos celare velis, . . . illa de Deo sententia suppeditata tibi est ab Hebraeis*)

the matter in the following. According to Plutarch (*On Marius*) and even better, according to Lactantius (I, 3, 19)[a] Plato thanked nature for the fact that he was a human being and not an animal, a man and not a woman, a Greek and not a barbarian. Now in Isaac Euchel's *Prayers of the Jews*,[b] from the Hebrew, second edition, 1799, p. 7, there is a morning prayer in which the Jew thanks and praises God for making him a Jew and not a heathen, a freeman and not a slave, a man and not a woman.[92] – Such a historical investigation would have preserved Kant from the unfortunate necessity in which he is now involved, in allowing these three concepts to have arisen necessarily from the nature of reason, and also would show that they are untenable and cannot be grounded in reason. This makes reason itself sophistical since at p. 339/V 397 he says: 'They are sophistries not of human beings but of pure reason itself, and even the wisest of all human beings cannot get free of them; perhaps after much effort he may guard himself from error, but he can never be wholly rid of the illusion, which ceaselessly teases and mocks him.' Accordingly, these Kantian 'ideas of reason' can be compared to the focal point in which the converging, reflected rays from a concave mirror come together a couple of inches from its surface, which, by an unavoidable process of the understanding, results in the presentation of an object that is a thing without reality.[93]

But the word 'ideas' was a very unfortunate choice for those three supposedly necessary productions of pure, theoretical reason; it was torn out of Plato, who used it to designate the imperishable forms that, multiplied in time and space, are imperfectly visible in the countless, individual, transient things. This would make Plato's Ideas entirely a matter of intuition,[c] as is indicated quite distinctly by the very term that he chose, which could only be adequately translated through things that are intuitive or visible. And yet Kant used it to designate things that lie so far beyond any possibility of intuition that even abstract thinking can only partially capture them. Plato was the first to introduce the term 'Idea', and over the past twenty-two centuries it has consistently retained his meaning. Not only all the philosophers of antiquity, but also all the scholastics and even the Church Fathers and the theologians of the Middle Ages, used it exclusively with this Platonic meaning, namely in the sense of the Latin word *exemplar*, as *Suarez* explicitly introduced in his twenty-fifth *Disputation*, section 1. – It is bad enough that the English and the French were later led by the poverty of their languages to misuse this word, but this is of no real significance.

579

---

[a] [*Divine Institutes*, Book 3, 19.17]
[b] *Gebeten der Juden*
[c] *durchaus anschaulich*

Kant misused the word *idea* by giving it a new meaning, one that shares with Plato's Ideas (as well as with all possible chimeras) the trivial common ground of not being an object of experience, although there is absolutely no justification for doing so. But since a couple of years of misuse pales in comparison with the authority of many centuries, I have always used the word in its ancient, original, Platonic meaning.[94]

──────────────

The first edition of the *Critique of Pure Reason* contains a much more thorough and detailed refutation of *rational psychology* than the second and subsequent editions, so we certainly need to use the first edition here. Overall, this refutation has great merit and there is a lot of truth to it. Nonetheless, I firmly believe that it was only for the sake of symmetry that Kant derived the necessity of the concept of the soul from those paralogisms; he did this by applying the demand for the unconditioned to the concept of *substance*, which is the first category of relation, and he claimed, accordingly, that this is how the concept of the soul arises in any faculty of speculative reason. If the concept of the soul really did originate in the presupposition of a final subject of all predicates of a thing, then we would assume that not only human beings but every inanimate thing necessarily has a soul, since even inanimate things require a final subject of all their predicates. Overall, Kant makes use of a completely unacceptable expression when he speaks of a something that can exist only as a subject and not as a predicate (e.g. *Critique of Pure Reason*, p. 323/V 412; *Prolegomena*, §§ 4 and 47), although a precedent for this can already be found in Aristotle's *Metaphysics*, IV, chap. 8. Absolutely nothing exists as both subject and predicate, since these expressions belong exclusively to logic and signify the relation of abstract concepts to each other. Their correlates or representatives in the intuitive world would be substance and accident. But if this is the case, we do not need to look any further for something that only ever exists as substance and never as accident, since we have it immediately in matter. Matter is the substance of all qualities of things, and these are its accidents. Retaining Kant's expression (an expression that we have just criticized), matter is really the final subject of all predicates of every empirically given thing, namely what remains after we have discounted all of its qualities of every sort. And this is true of human beings as it is of animals, plants and stones, and it is so obvious that it takes a determined refusal not to see it. I will soon show that matter is really the prototype of the concept of substance. – But subject and predicate are to substance and accident just as the principle of sufficient reason in

580

logic is to the law of causality in nature, and it is just as unacceptable to confound or equate the latter pair as it is to mix up the former. But in the *Prolegomena*, § 46 Kant takes just such a confusion or equation to its limit, so as to allow the concept of the soul to arise from the final subject of all predicates and from the form of a categorical inference. In order to expose the sophistry[a] of these paragraphs you simply need to bear in mind that subject and predicate are purely logical determinations that apply only and exclusively to abstract concepts, and this according to their relation in judgement; on the other hand, substance and accident belong to the intuitive world and its apprehension in the understanding, but they are found there only as identical with matter and form or quality. We will say more about this soon.

581

The opposition that led to the assumption of two fundamentally different substances, body and soul, is in fact an opposition of objective and subjective. When people objectively grasp themselves in external intuition, they discover a spatially extended and thoroughly corporeal being. If, by contrast, they grasp themselves merely in self-consciousness, which is to say purely subjectively, they discover something that simply wills and represents, free of all forms of intuition, which is to say lacking any of the qualities that apply to bodies. Now they form a concept of the soul, like all the transcendent concepts that Kant calls ideas, by applying the principle of sufficient reason, the form of all objects, to something that is not an object, and in fact to the subject of cognition and of willing.[95] Specifically, they regard cognition, thought and willing as effects; they look for the cause of these effects and, being unable to assume that it is the body, they posit a cause that is entirely different from the body. This is how the first and the last of the dogmatists prove the existence of the soul: Plato does it in *Phaedrus*, and Wolff is still doing the same thing, namely starting from thinking and willing as the effects that lead to this cause. Only after this hypostatization of a cause corresponding to the effect had given rise to the concept of an immaterial, simple and indestructible being, did this school of thought develop and demonstrate this concept from that of *substance*. But they had already gone out of their way to form this concept ahead of time for this very purpose, using the following noteworthy ruse.

The representation of matter is given along with the first class of representations, i.e. representations of the real, intuitive world, because the law of causality governing that first class determines changes of state, and these changes themselves presuppose something permanent that is being

---

[a] *Sophistikation*

582 changed. When discussing the principle of the permanence of substance above, I drew on earlier passages to show that this representation of matter arises in the understanding (for which alone it exists) because time and space are inwardly united through the law of causality (the understanding's only form of cognition). Space assumes a role in this product in the permanence of *matter*, and time assumes a role in the changes of *state*. Purely on its own, matter can only be thought in the abstract[a] and not intuited, because its appearance to intuition is always already in form and quality. *Substance* is another abstraction from this concept of *matter*, and consequently a higher genus. It arises from the fact that people allow only the predicate of permanence to remain in the concept of matter, and think away all its other essential qualities, extension, impenetrability, divisibility, etc. Like every higher genus, the concept of *substance* contains *less in itself* than the concept of *matter*: but, it does not for that reason contain *more under itself*, as is always otherwise the case with higher genera, since it does not include any lower genera other than matter. Instead, matter remains the only true sub-species of the concept of substance, the only thing that can be proved to illustrate it and realize its content. Reason typically produces higher concepts through abstraction in order to think these concepts simultaneously in several different sub-species, sub-species that are differentiated through secondary determinations; but this typical function is quite out of place here, and consequently the abstraction is either completely pointless and futile, or there is an ulterior motive[b] behind it. This becomes apparent when a second sub-species of substance is coordinated with its true sub-species, matter; this second sub-species is the immaterial, simple, indestructible substance of the soul. But the surreptitious nature of this concept is already present in the illegitimate and illogical development of the higher concept *substance*. When reason proceeds in a lawlike manner, the only way it forms higher, generic concepts[c] is by placing the concepts of several species[d] next to each other, comparing them, and proceeding discursively; by leaving out their differences and retaining their agreements, reason obtains the generic concept that encompasses all the concepts of the species but contains less than they do. It

583 follows from this that species concepts must always precede the generic concept. In the present case, however, it is the other way around. The concept of matter existed before the generic concept of *substance*, and there

---

[a] *in abstracto*
[b] *Nebenansicht*
[c] *Geschlechtsbegriff*
[d] *Artbegriffe*

was no reason, and consequently no justification, for forming the generic concept of substance out of the concept of matter by arbitrarily leaving out all but one of its determinations. The second, false sub-species was slipped in later, by being placed next to the concept of matter. But all that needed to happen in order to form this sub-species was explicitly to negate what was already tacitly omitted from the higher generic concept, namely extension, penetrability, divisibility. So the concept of *substance* was formed only as a vehicle for surreptitiously slipping in the concept of immaterial substance. Consequently, it cannot be anything like a valid category or a necessary function of the understanding: in fact it can be easily dispensed with, because its only true content is contained in the concept of matter; compared to matter it is itself only a great void with nothing to fill it except the surreptitiously inserted secondary genus of *immaterial substance*, and it was formed only to accommodate this. Thus, rigour demands that it be rejected entirely and the concept of matter be put in its place wherever it occurs.

The categories were a Procrustean bed for every possible thing; but the three types of inference play that role only for the three so-called ideas. The idea of the soul had been compelled to discover its origin in the categorical form of inference. The focus here is on the dogmatists' views[a] about the world-whole[b] to the extent that we conceive it (as object in itself) as between two boundaries, that of the smallest of things (the atom) and that of the largest (the boundaries of the world in space and time). These boundaries must stem from the form of the hypothetical syllogism. No special compulsion is needed for this, because the hypothetical judgement gets its form from the principle of sufficient reason, and all these so-called ideas – not simply the cosmological idea – in fact come from unreflectively and unconditionally applying this principle and then subsequently and arbitrarily laying it to the side. Specifically, the principle of sufficient reason only ever authorizes a search for the dependence of one object on another, until the power of imagination is finally exhausted and the journey comes to an end. But all this loses sight of the fact that each object, and indeed the whole series of objects and the principle of sufficient reason itself, are involved in a much greater and more intimate dependency, namely a dependency on the cognitive subject; in fact, the principle of sufficient reason is valid only

584

---

[a] *Vorstellungen*
[b] *das Weltganze*

for the objects of a subject, i.e. representations, since it determines the position of these objects in space and time. Moreover, since the form of cognition from which the cosmological ideas are deduced here, namely the principle of sufficient reason, is the origin of all overly-subtle hypostases, no sophisms are needed in this case, but they are needed that much more in order to classify these ideas according to the four headings of the categories.

(1) The cosmological ideas with respect to time and space, which is to say the ideas of the boundaries of the world in both time and space, are boldly regarded as determined through the category of *quantity*, a category that they clearly have nothing in common with except the fact that logic accidentally indicates the scope of the concept of the subject in judgement with the word *quantity*; but this is just a metaphorical expression, and another could have been chosen just as easily. But this is sufficient licence, given Kant's passion for symmetry, for using the happy accident of this nomenclature and linking it up with the transcendental dogmas of the extension of the world.

(2) Even more boldly, Kant links the transcendental ideas concerning matter with *quality*, i.e. affirmation or negation in a judgement, a move that is not even grounded in an accidental similarity of terms, because the mechanical (not chemical) divisibility of matter refers specifically to its quantity and not its *quality*. But even more, this whole idea of divisibility is not remotely a consequence of the principle of sufficient reason, and yet all the cosmological ideas are supposed to flow from this principle, as the content of the hypothetical form. Kant relies on the claim that the relation of part to whole is that of condition to conditioned, which is indeed a relation according to the principle of sufficient reason, yet this claim is a subtle but groundless piece of sophistry. The relation of part to whole rests instead on the principle of contradiction. This is because the whole does not exist through the parts nor the parts through the whole, but both necessarily exist together because they are the same thing and any separation between them is arbitrary. According to the principle of contradiction, this is based on the fact that when the parts are thought away, the whole is thought away too, and vice versa. But it is certainly not based on the parts as a *ground* conditioning the whole as a *consequent*, so that we would be driven, according to the principle of sufficient reason, to find the ultimate parts which we could then use as the ground for understanding the whole. – Here the love of symmetry overpowers even difficulties of this magnitude.

(3) The idea of the first cause of the world would properly belong under the heading of *relation*. But Kant has to reserve this for the fourth heading,

that of modality, or else nothing would be left for it. So he forces this idea under the heading of modality by saying that what is contingent (i.e. every consequent from its ground, as he explains, in diametric opposition to the truth) becomes necessary through the first cause. – So for the sake of symmetry, the concept of *freedom* appears as the third idea, which really only means the idea of the cause of the world, since this is the only thing that fits here, as is clearly stated in the remark to the thesis of the third conflict.[a] The third and fourth conflicts are thus fundamentally tautological.

But as far as all this is concerned, what I have found and what I have to say is that the entire antinomy is just a shadow-boxing, a mock battle. Only the claims of the *antitheses* are really based in the forms of our cognitive faculty, or to put it objectively, in the necessary, *a priori* certain, most universal laws of nature. So their proofs alone proceed from objective grounds. By contrast, the claims and the proofs of the *theses* have only subjective grounds, and are based only on the weakness and overly subtle reasoning of the individual. The individual's power of imagination exhausts itself in an infinite regress, so it stops this regress through arbitrary assumptions that it glosses over as well as it can; and in addition to all this, the individual's power of judgement has been disabled by early and firmly imprinted prejudices in these matters.[96] This is why the proofs for the thesis in all four conflicts are only ever sophistical, while those for the antithesis are the inevitable conclusions of reason from the laws of the world as representation, laws that we are conscious of *a priori*. It cost Kant a great deal of effort and artfulness[b] to maintain the thesis and have it appear to attack an opponent endowed with original force. His first and usual trick is that he does not bring out the crux of the argument,[c] as one does when one is conscious of the truth of a proposition, and thus present it in as isolated, naked and clear a way as possible; instead, he supports both sides with the same argument, hidden beneath and mixed up in a torrent of superfluous and long-winded sentences.

The theses and antitheses that appear in conflict here are reminiscent of the 'just argument' and the 'unjust argument'[d] that Socrates presents as quarrelling in Aristophanes' *The Clouds*. Nonetheless, this similarity extends only to the form, not the content, as is claimed by those who would ascribe a moral influence to these most speculative of all questions

586

---

[a] [i.e. the Third Antinomy of Pure Reason]
[b] *Kunst*
[c] *nervus argumentationis*
[d] δικαιος und αδικος λογος [See *Clouds* 112–18 and 889–1104]

in theoretical philosophy, and thus seriously consider the thesis to be a 'just argument' and the antithesis an 'unjust argument'. But I will not cater to such limited and backwards little minds here; I will honour the truth more than I honour them, and reveal Kant's proofs of the individual theses as sophisms, while the proofs for the antitheses are completely honest and accurate, and rest on objective grounds. – I will assume throughout this investigation that the reader has Kant's antinomies on hand.

If the proof of the thesis in the first conflict is allowed to be valid, it proves too much, since it applies to time itself just as much as it does to any change in time, and thus proves that time itself must have a beginning, which is absurd. Besides, the sophism consists of the fact that instead of the series of states lacking a beginning, which was initially at issue, we are now suddenly talking about the series lacking an end (being infinite), and 587 something is proven that nobody doubts, that the idea of completeness logically contradicts this endlessness, and yet every present is the end of the past. But we can always *conceive*[a] of the end of a beginning-less series without detracting from its lack of a beginning, just as conversely, we can *conceive* the beginning of an endless series. But nothing at all is brought forward to counter the actually correct argument of the antithesis, that the alterations of the world absolutely and necessarily presuppose an infinite, *regressive* series of alterations. We can conceive the possibility that the causal series will one day end up in an absolute standstill, but we cannot remotely conceive the possibility of an absolute beginning.[*]

With respect to the spatial boundaries of the world, it is proven that if the world is supposed to be a *given whole*, it must necessarily have boundaries: this conclusion is true, only its first link was precisely what needed to be proven, and yet is still unproven. Totality presupposes boundaries

---

[*] The assumption that the world is bounded in time is certainly not a necessary thought of reason, and this can even be proved historically, since the Hindus never taught such a thing even in their popular religion, much less in the *Vedas*. Instead, they tried to express the infinity of this world of appearance, this insubstantial, inessential web of *māyā*, mythologically, through a monstrous chronology; specifically, they very cleverly stressed the relativity of all periods of time in the following myth (Polier, *Mythologie des Indous* [*Mythology of the Hindus*], vol. 2, p. 585). The four ages, the last of which is our own, collectively comprise 4,320,000 years. Each day of the creator Brahma has 1000 such periods of four ages of the world, and each of his nights has another 1000. His year has 365 days and just as many nights. He lives 100 of his years, always creating: and when he dies, a new Brahma is immediately born and so on from eternity to eternity. The same relativity of time is also expressed through a special myth from the *Puranas*, which is recounted in Polier's work, vol. 2, p. 594. In these myths, a Raja visits Vishnu for a few minutes in his heaven, and upon returning to earth afterwards finds that several million years have gone by and a new age has appeared, because each one of Vishnu's days is equal to 100 recurrences of the four ages.

[a] *denken*

and boundaries presuppose totality: but here they are both presupposed arbitrarily. – The antithesis, however, does not provide as satisfactory a proof for this second point as for the first, because the law of causality　588 furnishes necessary determinations with respect to time but not space; in fact, it gives us the *a priori* certainty that no filled time could ever be bordered by a prior, empty time, and no alteration could ever be the first, but it does not assure us that a filled space cannot be next to an empty space. To this extent, no decision concerning the latter would be possible *a priori*. Nonetheless, the difficulty in conceiving of the world as bounded in space lies in the fact that space itself is necessarily infinite, and that a bounded, finite world within it, however big it might be, becomes infinitely small, and the imagination finds an insurmountable obstacle in this disproportion, since it can only choose between a conception of the world as infinitely large or infinitely small.[97] The philosophers of antiquity already saw this: 'Metrodorus, the head of the school of Epicurus, taught that it is absurd that only a single ear of corn would come from a big field, and only a single world would arise in the infinite',[a] Stobaeus, *Eclogues* I, chap. 23. – Thus, many of them taught (as follows immediately from this), that 'in the infinite there are infinitely many worlds'.[b,98] This is the sense of Kant's argument for the antithesis too, only he ruined it with his stilted, scholastic presentation. The same argument could also be used against the world having boundaries in time, if a much better argument did not already exist, using causality as a guide. With the assumption of a world bounded in space, the unanswerable question further arises of what priority or privilege the filled part of space would have over the infinite, empty space. Giordano Bruno gives a thorough presentation of the arguments for and against the finitude of the world in his book *On the Infinite, Universe and Worlds*,[c] and his account is well worth reading. Incidentally, Kant himself claimed seriously and from objective grounds that the world is infinite in space, in his *Natural History and Theory of the Heavens*, part II, chap. 7.[d] Aristotle acknowledges the same thing in *Physics*, III, chap. 4, a chapter which, along with the ones that follow, is well worth reading with regard to this antinomy.[99]

---

[a] Μητροδωρος, ὁ καθηγητης Επικουρου, φησιν ατοπον ειναι εν μεγαλω πεδιω ἑνα σταχυν γεννηθηναι, και ἑνα κοσμον εν τῳ απειρῳ (*Metrodorus, caput scholae Epicuri, absurdum ait, in magno campo spicam unam produci, et unum in infinito mundum*) [Again, Schopenhauer's reference to *Eclogues* is slightly inaccurate: see I, ch. 22]

[b] απειρους κοσμους εν τῳ απειρῳ (*infinitos mundos in infinito*) [ibid.]

[c] *Del infinito, universo e mondi*

[d] [*Allgemeine*] *Naturgeschichte und Theorie des Himmels* [see Ak 1: 306–31]

589   In the second conflict, the thesis becomes immediately involved in a none-too-subtle begging of the question[a] since it begins: '*Every composite*[b] substance is composed of simple parts.' From this arbitrary assumption of a composite nature[c] it is then of course very easy to prove the simple parts. But the proposition at issue, that 'all matter is composite', remains unproven because it is just a groundless assumption. The opposite of the simple is not the composite, but rather the extended, that which has parts, the divisible.[d] What is in fact tacitly assumed here is that the parts existed before the whole and were pieced together in order to create the whole, because this is what the word 'composite' means. But this cannot be asserted any more than the opposite. All that divisibility means is the possibility of breaking the whole into parts, not that the whole is composed of parts or came about this way. Divisibility only claims the parts with respect to what follows; being composite claims them with respect to what precedes.[e] There is essentially no temporal relation between the parts and the whole, rather, they condition each other and are to this extent always simultaneous: because the spatially extended thing exists only to the extent that both are there. Therefore what Kant says in the remark on the thesis, 'Properly speaking, one should call space not a *compositum* but a *totum* etc.',[f] is entirely true of matter as well, which is simply space made perceptible.[100] – On the other hand, the infinite divisibility of matter asserted by the antithesis follows *a priori* and incontrovertibly from the infinite divisibility of space, which it fills. There is absolutely nothing to contest this proposition; thus, even Kant presents it as the objective truth, on p. 513/V 541, after he has stopped acting like a spokesman for 'unjust argument'[g] and is speaking seriously in his own voice. Likewise, in the *Metaphysical Foundations of Natural Science* (p. 108, first edition) the proposition, 'matter is divisible to infinity', is stated as established truth at the top of the proof of the first proposition of Mechanics, after it had appeared and was proven as the fourth proposition of Dynamics.[h,101] But Kant ruins the proof of the antithesis here with his confused presentation and useless stream of words, slyly intending that the evidentness[i] of the

---

[a] *petitio principi*
[b] *zusammengesetzte*
[c] *Zusammengesetztseyn*
[d] *das Extendirte, das Theilehabende, das Theilbare*
[e] *a parte post . . . a parte ante*
[f] [not a composite, but a whole: see A439 / B466]
[g] αδικος λογος
[h] [Ak. 4: 503 and 537]
[i] *Evidenz*

antithesis not cast too heavy a shadow over the sophisms of the thesis. –   590
Atoms are not a necessary idea of reason; they are just a hypothesis for
explaining the differences in the specific gravity of bodies. The fact that
there is a different explanation that is even simpler and better than the
theory of atoms is something Kant himself showed in the Dynamics of his
Metaphysical Foundations of Natural Science,[a] and before him Priestley, *On
Matter and Spirit*, section 1. In fact, the basic idea can already be found in
Aristotle, *Physics*, IV, 9.[102]

The argument for the third thesis is a very subtle sophism; it is really
Kant's supposed principle of pure reason itself, completely untouched and
unchanged. It tries to prove the finitude of the series of causes from the fact
that a cause, in order to be *sufficient*, must contain the complete sum of the
conditions that give rise to the resulting state, the effect. But the argument
takes this completeness of the determinations that are *simultaneously* present
in the state that is the cause, and in its place substitutes the completeness
of the *series* of causes through which that state itself is first actualized.
And because completeness presupposes that something is self-contained,[b]
and this in turn presupposes finitude, the argument uses this to deduce the
existence of a first cause that closes the series and is therefore unconditioned.
But the sleight of hand is clear. In order to grasp state A as the sufficient
cause of state B, I presuppose that it contains the completeness of the
requisite determinations whose collective presence inevitably gives rise to
state B. This totally satisfies my requirement that it be a *sufficient* cause,
and is not directly connected with the question of how state A itself was
actualized; this question belongs to an entirely different investigation, one
in which I now regard this very same state A as an effect rather than a
cause, so that a different state must now relate to it just as it related to B.
But the presupposition of the finitude of the series of causes and effects,
and accordingly the presupposition of a first beginning, does not appear
to be at all necessary in any of this, any more than the presence of the
present moment presupposes a beginning of time itself.[103] Instead, this
presupposition is added only by the laziness of the speculating individual.   591
The fact that this presupposition lies in accepting a cause as *sufficient ground*
is thus both surreptitiously introduced and false, as I have already shown in
detail in my consideration of the Kantian principle of reason that coincides
with this thesis. In the remarks, Kant has the nerve to illustrate the claim
of this false thesis by citing the act of rising from a chair as an example of

---

[a] [See Ak. 4: 532–3]
[b] *Geschlossenheit*

an unconditioned beginning – but it is just as impossible to rise without a motive as it would be for a ball to roll without a cause. I certainly do not need to prove the groundlessness of his appeal to ancient philosophers, an appeal that arises from his feeling of weakness, by citing Ocellus Lucanus, the Eleatics, etc. not to mention the Hindus. Just as before, there are no objections to the argument of the antithesis.[104]

As I have already noted, the fourth conflict is in fact tautological with the third. Even the proof of the thesis is essentially the same as the previous proof. Its claim, that every conditioned presupposes a complete *series* of conditions, a series that therefore ends with the unconditioned, is a begging of the question[a] and must be immediately denied. No conditioned presupposes anything other than its condition; the fact that this is itself conditioned gives rise to a new investigation that is not directly contained in the first one.

It cannot be denied that the antinomy has a certain plausibility: nonetheless, it is strange that no other part of the Kantian philosophy has met with so little opposition, or indeed has received so much recognition as this highly paradoxical doctrine. Almost all philosophical factions and textbooks have accepted its validity, and have repeated and even elaborated on it. At the same time, almost all of Kant's other doctrines have been contested – and there has never been a lack of warped minds who have rejected even the Transcendental Aesthetic. But the unanimous acclaim that the antinomy has received might ultimately stem from the fact that some people get a sense of inner contentment when they observe the point where the understanding is really supposed to come to an end by running into something that simultaneously is and is not – a point, accordingly, where they are actually confronted with the sixth stunt of Philadelphia, in Lichtenberg's broadside.[b],[105]

592

If we investigate the true sense of Kant's *critical resolution* of the cosmological conflict that now follows, it is not what he says it is, namely the solution to the conflict through the disclosure that both sides proceed from false presuppositions, where both are wrong in the first and second conflicts but right in the third and fourth; rather, it is in fact a confirmation of the antitheses through the explanation of their claims.

---

[a] *petitio principii*
[b] [In 1777 in Göttingen Lichtenberg exhibited a satirical poster, 'Lichtenberg's Avertissement', mocking Jacob Philadelphia's forthcoming exhibition, which was allegedly of scientific experiments, as a show of absurd magic tricks. The 'sixth stunt' is a 'metaphysical' one 'in which he shows that something actually can be and not be at the same time. It requires great preparation and expense, but he performs it for just one Thaler in honour of the University.']

First Kant asserts in this solution something that is clearly false, that both sides proceed from the presupposition, as a major premise, that when the conditioned is given, so is the completed (which is to say closed) *series* of its conditions. Only the *thesis* bases its claims on this proposition, Kant's pure principle of reason; the antithesis on the other hand always explicitly denies it and claims the opposite. Kant further burdens both sides with the presupposition that the world exists in itself, i.e. independent of cognition and the forms of this cognition: but once more, this assumption is made only by the thesis; it provides so little support for the claims of the antithesis that it is in fact completely incompatible with it. This is because the concept of an infinite series directly contradicts the idea that the series is completely given: thus it is an essential aspect of the series that it exist only in relation to the process of going through it,[a] but not independently of this. On the other hand, the presupposition of determinate boundaries entails the presupposition that a whole exists for itself and independent of any measurement that is carried out. Thus, it is only the thesis that falsely presupposes a world-whole[b] existing in itself, i.e. given prior to any cognition, and to which cognition is merely added. The antithesis is in fundamental conflict with this presupposition from the start, because the infinity of the series, which it asserts only under the direction of the principle of sufficient reason, can exist only to the extent that the regress is complete, not independently of this. Just as an object in general presupposes a subject, an object determined as an *endless* chain of conditions necessarily presupposes a mode of cognition that corresponds to it in the subject, namely the *continuous pursuit* of links in the chain. But this is just what Kant gives and often repeats as the solution to the conflict: 'the infinity of the size of the world only exists *through* the regress, not *prior* to it'. This solution to the conflict is thus really only a decision in favour of the antithesis, whose assertion already entails this truth, making it utterly incompatible with the assertions of the thesis. If the antithesis had claimed that the world consisted of an infinite series of grounds and consequents and was nonetheless independent of representation and its regressive series, and thus existed in itself and constituted a given whole, then it would have contradicted not only the thesis but itself as well. This is because an infinity can never be *completely* given, nor can an *endless* series exist (except to the extent that it is endlessly traversed[c]), nor can something

593

[a] *Durchgehn*
[b] *Weltganzen*
[c] *durchlaufen*

boundless constitute a whole. Kant claims that this presupposition misled both sides, but it actually belongs only to the thesis.

Aristotle already subscribed to the doctrine that an infinite could never be in actuality,[a] i.e. actual[b] and given, but could rather be only potentially.[c] 'The infinite cannot exist in actuality: . . . but rather an infinite that exists in actuality is impossible',[d] *Metaphysics*, K, 10. – Further: 'There is no infinity in actuality, but there is in possibility with reference to division', *On Generation and Corruption*, I, 3.[e] – He explains this at great length in *Physics* III, 5 and 6, where he gives just the right solution to all the antinomic oppositions. He presents the antinomies in his concise manner and then says: 'an intermediary (διαιτητου) is required': after which he gives the solution that the infinite, in space as well as in time and in division, is never *prior* to regress or progress but rather is *in* them. – Thus, the truth already lies in the correct understanding of the concept of the infinite. We misunderstand ourselves when we think we can conceive infinity of any sort as something objectively present and complete, and independent of regress.[106]

594   In fact, starting with Kant's solution to the conflict and proceeding backwards, the claim of the antithesis follows directly. Namely, if the world is not an unconditioned whole and does not exist in itself but rather only in representation, and if its series of grounds and consequents do not exist *prior* to the regress of its representations but rather only *through* this regress, then the world cannot contain any determinate or finite series, because their determination and limitation would have to be independent of representation, which would only be added on: rather, all its series must be endless, i.e. cannot be exhausted by any representation.

On p. 506/V 534, Kant wants to prove the transcendental ideality of appearance by showing that both sides are incorrect, and begins: 'If the world is a whole existing in itself, then it is either finite or infinite.' – But this is false: a whole existing in itself certainly cannot be infinite. – Rather, that ideality can be deduced from the infinity of the series in the world in the following manner: if the series of grounds and consequents in the world has no end at all, then the world cannot be a whole given independently of representation, because such a thing always presupposes

---

[a] *actu*
[b] *wirklich*
[c] *potentiâ*
[d] Ουκ εστιν ενεργειᾳ ειναι το απειρον· . . . αλλ᾽ αδυνατον το εντελεχειᾳ ον απειρον (*infinitum non potest esse actu: . . . sed impossibile, actu esse infinitum*) [*Metaphysics* K (XI), 10, 1066b11–18]
[e] κατ᾽ ενεργειαν μεν γαρ ουδεν εστιν απειρον, δυναμει δε επι την διαιρεσιν (*nihil enim actu infinitum est, sed potentia tantum, nempe divisione ipsa*) *De generat[ione] et corrupt[ione]*, I. 3 [318a20–1]

determinate boundaries, just as by contrast an infinite series presupposes an infinite regress. Thus the presupposed infinity of the series must be determined through the form of ground and consequent, and this must be determined through the subject's mode of cognition; thus the world as it is cognized exists only in the representation of the subject.

Whether Kant himself knew that his critical resolution of the conflict was really a claim in favour of the antithesis, I cannot say. It all depends on whether what Schelling somewhere very perceptively calls Kant's system of accommodation extended this far, or whether Kant's mind here was fettered by an unconscious accommodation to the influence of his time and circumstances.

The solution to the third antinomy, which is concerned with the idea   595
of freedom, deserves special consideration; in particular, we find it quite remarkable that it is precisely here, with the idea of *freedom*, that Kant was forced to speak at greater length about the *thing in itself*, which until now had been seen only in the background. We find this easy to understand, since we have recognized the thing in itself as the *will*. This is really the point where Kant's philosophy leads to my own, or where mine grows from the stem of Kant's. Anyone who pays close attention to the *Critique of Pure Reason*, pp. 356 and 537/V 564 and 565 will be convinced of this. Just compare these passages with the introduction to the *Critique of the Power of Judgement*, pp. xviii and xix of the third edition, or p. 13 of the Rosenkranz edition, which even says: 'The concept of freedom in its object (this is certainly the will) can make a thing representable in itself but not in intuition; the concept of nature on the other hand can certainly make its object representable in intuition, but not as thing in itself.'[a] But in particular just read § 53 of the *Prolegomena* concerning the solution to the antinomies and then tell me honestly whether everything said there does not sound like a riddle to which my own doctrine is the key. Kant did not complete his thinking: all I have done is to see his business through.[b] Accordingly, I have taken what Kant said only with regard to human appearances and applied it to appearances in general, since these differ from human appearances only in degree. Specifically, I have said that their intrinsic essence is absolutely free, i.e. that it is a will. How fruitful this

---

[a] [See Ak. 5: 175. Schopenhauer alters the arrangement of Kant's sentence and interpolates his own remark 'this is certainly the will']
[b] *Sache*

insight is in connection with Kant's doctrine of the ideality of space, time and causality is shown in my work.[107]

596 Kant never devoted a special argument to the thing itself nor did he derive it explicitly. Rather, whenever he needs it, he quickly infers it from the fact that appearance (which is to say the visible world) must certainly have a ground, an intelligible cause that is not itself appearance and thus does not belong to possible experience. He does this after constantly insisting that the categories, and thus the category of causality too, could only ever be applied to possible experience: they are merely forms of the understanding that serve to spell out the appearances in the sensible world and have absolutely no meaning above and beyond this, etc. In this way, he prohibits their application to things beyond experience in the strongest terms, and correctly explains and simultaneously disposes of all previous dogmatism as originating in a transgression of this law. Kant's unbelievable inconsistency on this point was soon noticed by his first opponents and was used to attack his philosophy in ways that it could not defend itself against. We certainly do apply the law of causality *a priori* and before experience to the alterations we sense with our sense organs: but for this very reason, the law of causality has just as subjective an origin as the sensations themselves, and therefore does not lead to the things in themselves. The truth is that representations cannot be transcended by way of representations: they are a closed whole and offer no resources of their own that would lead to the essence of the thing in itself, an essence that is entirely different in kind[a] from them. If we were beings[b] who were only able to represent, then the path to things in themselves would be completely closed to us. Only the other side of our own essence[c] can shed light on the other side of the essence in itself of things. This is the path I have taken.[108] Nonetheless, there are extenuating factors that we can cite in favour of Kant's derivation of the thing in itself (a derivation that even he had prohibited), and these are the following. Kant does not posit the object as simply and absolutely conditioned by the subject and vice versa, as truth would demand, rather, he posits only the manner of the object's appearance as conditioned by the subject's forms of cognition, which we are thus also conscious of *a priori*. But what is cognized only *a posteriori* is, in contrast to this, the immediate effect of the thing in itself, which becomes an appearance only when it passes through those forms of appearance that are given *a priori*. From this standpoint, it is in some respects explicable how Kant could have failed to

[a] toto genere *verschiedenen Wesen*
[b] *Wesen*
[c] *Wesen*

notice that being an object in general is already entailed by the form of appearance, and is just as much conditioned by the being of the subject in general as the object's mode of appearance is conditioned by the subject's forms of cognition. Thus, if we assume a thing in itself, it absolutely cannot be an object, which Kant nonetheless always presupposes it to be; rather, such a thing in itself must lie in a realm that is entirely different in kind from representation (cognition and being cognized), and thus is the last thing that could ever be derived from the laws governing the connection of objects among themselves.

The same thing that happened to Kant with the *a priori* nature of the law of causality happened again with the proof for the thing in itself; in both cases the doctrines are correct but their proofs are false: they are both correct conclusions from false premises. I have retained them both, but have grounded them with certainty and in an entirely different manner.[109]

I have not brought in the thing in itself surreptitiously nor have I deduced it according to laws that exclude it, since they already belong to its appearance. Nor have I come to it in a roundabout way. Rather, I have proven it immediately at the point where it immediately lies, in the will that reveals itself to everyone immediately as the in-itself of his own appearance.

The concept of *freedom* also comes from this immediate cognition of one's own will in human consciousness, because the will as world-creator, as thing in itself, is certainly free from the principle of sufficient reason and with it all necessity, and thus absolutely independent, free and even omnipotent. Of course this is true only of the will in itself, not of its appearances, the individuals who are already inalterably determined by the will itself as its appearances in time. But in ordinary consciousness, as opposed to philosophically enlightened consciousness, the will is straight away confused with its appearance and what belongs to the former is attributed to the latter, which gives rise to the illusion[a] of the individual's unconditioned freedom. Thus, Spinoza is right when he says that if a thrown stone were conscious, it too would believe it was flying of its own free will. This is because the one and only free will is the in-itself even of the stone; but here where the will appears as a stone, it is already fully determined, just as it is in all its appearances. But we have already discussed all this in sufficient detail in the main part of this work.

By misunderstanding and overlooking this immediate emergence of the concept of freedom in every human consciousness, Kant now (p. 533/V

[a] *Schein*

561) posits the origin of that concept in a very subtle speculation through which the unconditioned (which reason is always supposed to seek) allows for the hypostatization of the concept of freedom, and even the practical concept of freedom is supposed to be grounded in this transcendent idea of freedom alone. In the *Critique of Practical Reason* § 6, and p. 185 of the fourth edition, p. 235 of the Rosenkranz edition,[a] he deduces this last concept in yet another manner, from the fact that it is presupposed by the categorical imperative: for the sake of this presupposition, that speculative idea is supposed to be the primary source of the concept of freedom; and this is where it really becomes meaningful and is applied. But in fact neither is the case. This is because the least refined[b] human beings are the ones who are most vividly convinced by the delusion[c] that individuals are perfectly free in their particular actions, and these are people who have never really thought about it, which means that it is not grounded in any speculation, although it is often taken over by speculation. On the other hand, only philosophers are free from this delusion and in fact only the most profound of them, as well as the most thoughtful and enlightened Church authors.[110]

Given all that has been said, the origin of the concept of freedom is by no means essentially an inference, either from the speculative idea of an unconditioned cause, or from the fact that the categorical imperative presupposes it. Rather it comes immediately from the consciousness in which everyone instantly recognizes himself without further ado as the *will*, i.e. as that which, as thing in itself, does not have the form of the principle of sufficient reason, and which itself does not depend on anything while everything else depends on it, but without at the same time recognizing himself with philosophical criticism and reflection as a determinate appearance of this will – one could say act of will – that has already emerged in time, and as distinct from the will to life itself. Thus, instead of recognizing his whole being as an act of his freedom, he instead looks for freedom in his particular actions. I refer to my prize essay on the *Freedom of the Will* on this point.[111]

Now if, as he pretends here, and even seems to have done on earlier occasions, Kant had simply deduced the thing in itself (and that, moreover, with the massive inconsistency of an inference that he himself completely prohibited); – what a strange accident it would be that here, where he first really approaches the thing in itself and sheds light on it, he immediately recognizes in it the *will*, the free will that declares its presence in the world

599

<hr/>

[a] [Ak. 5: 29–30 and 103]
[b] *rohesten*
[c] *Wahn*

only through temporal appearances! – So although it cannot be proven, I think it is likely that whenever Kant spoke about the thing in itself, he was already thinking obscurely of the will in the darkest depths of his mind. There is evidence for this in the preface to the second edition of the *Critique of Pure Reason*, pp. xxvii and xxviii, and in the Rosenkranz edition, p. 677 of the Supplements.[a][112]

Moreover, it is precisely this intended solution to the supposed third conflict that gives Kant the opportunity to express very eloquently the most profound thoughts of his philosophy. So in the whole of section six of the Antinomies of Pure Reason, but above all the presentation of the opposition between the empirical and intelligible character, pp. 534–50/V 562–78, which I consider one of the most excellent things anyone has ever said (a parallel passage in the *Critique of Practical Reason* can be seen as a supplemental explanation of this passage: pp. 169–79 of the fourth edition, or pp. 224–31 of the Rosenkranz edition).[b] Still, this makes it all the more regrettable that this is not where it should be, since on the one hand, it cannot be found in the way indicated by the presentation, and thus could be deduced in another way; and on the other hand it does not fulfil the purpose it is there for, namely the solution of the supposed antinomy. The intelligible ground of appearance, the thing in itself, is deduced from appearance through the inconsistent application of the category of causality over and above all appearance, an application we have criticized in sufficient detail. In this case, the human will (which Kant gives the utterly unjustifiable title of 'reason', an unforgivable breach of all linguistic usage) is set up as this thing in itself with an appeal to an unconditioned 'ought', the categorical imperative, which is postulated without further ado.

Instead of all this, the honest and open procedure would have been to start off immediately from the will, to prove this as the in-itself of our own appearance, one that we cognize without any mediation, and then to give the presentation of the empirical and intelligible character. We would explain how all actions, though necessitated[113] by their motives, are nonetheless necessarily and absolutely ascribed to their author alone, both by him and by anyone else judging the actions, and are considered as belonging exclusively to him, so that he is treated as guilty or meritorious accordingly. – This alone was the straight path to the cognition of that which is not appearance and consequently not to be discovered according

600

---

[a] [i.e. B xxvii–xxviii. Rosenkranz printed as Supplements passages that are exclusively found in the B edition]
[b] [Ak. 5: 94–100]

to the laws of appearance, but instead reveals and objectifies itself and can be cognized through appearance: the will to life. This would then have to have been presented, merely by analogy, as the in-itself of every appearance. But then of course it could not have been said (p. 546/V 574) that only sensuously conditioned faculties are conceivable in inanimate nature, and even in the animal kingdom. In Kant's language this is really to say that an explanation according to the law of causality exhausts even the innermost essence of those appearances, so that in their case, the thing in itself is very inconsistently abolished. – The entire concept of the thing in itself was distorted by the fact that Kant presented it in the wrong place, and deduced it in a correspondingly roundabout way. Since the will or thing in itself is found in the course of a search after an unconditioned cause, it emerges in relation to appearances as a cause to an effect. But this relation takes place only within appearance, and thus already presupposes appearance; it cannot connect it to something outside of it that is entirely different from it in kind.[a]

Furthermore, Kant fails to achieve the intended goal, the solution to the third antinomy through the resolution that each side is true in a different sense; this is because neither the thesis nor the antithesis mentions things in themselves, but only appearance, the objective world, the world as representation. What the thesis wants to show through its demonstrable sophism is absolutely nothing other than the fact that this (appearance) contains unconditioned causes, and this is also what the antithesis correctly denies. Thus the whole presentation of the transcendental freedom of the will (to the extent that it is a thing in itself), a presentation given in justification of the thesis, however excellent it is in itself, is nevertheless really a jump into a different domain.[b] The transcendental freedom of the will presented here is certainly not the unconditioned causality of a cause, which is what the thesis claims, because a cause must essentially be an appearance, not something entirely different in kind that lies beyond all appearance.

When we speak of cause and effect, the relation of the will to its appearance (or of the intelligible character to the empirical) should never be introduced, as happens here, because it is completely different from a causal relation.[114] But it is also stated quite correctly in the solution to the antinomy that a human being's empirical character, like all other causes in nature, is inalterably determined, and thus actions necessarily follow it

601

[a] toto genere *von ihr verschieden*
[b] μεταβασις εις αλλο γενος [see Aristotle *De caelo* (*On the Heavens*), I, 1, 268b1]

in accordance with external influences. Thus, regardless of any transcendental freedom (i.e. the independence of the will in itself from the laws of the connections of its appearance), nobody has the ability to begin a series of actions from himself alone; and yet this is what the thesis asserts. Thus, freedom has no causality, because only the will is free, and it lies outside of nature or appearance; the latter is only ever its objectivation, but does not stand in a relation of causality to it, since this sort of a relation is found only within appearance, and thus already presupposes it. The causal relation cannot include appearances themselves or connect them with something that is explicitly not an appearance. The world itself can be explained only from the will (since the world is precisely the will itself, to the extent that the will appears) and not through causality. But causality is the only principle of explanation *in the world*, and everything takes place only in accordance with the laws of nature. Thus, right lies entirely on the side of the antithesis, which sticks to what is at issue and uses the principle of explanation that is valid in this case, and therefore needs no justification.[a] The thesis, by contrast, is supposedly extracted from its difficulties by a justification that begins by skipping to something completely different from what was in question, and then adopts a principle of explanation that cannot be applied there.

602

As we have already said, the fourth conflict is, in its deepest sense, tautological with the third. In its solution Kant develops the untenability of the thesis even further: he does not offer any reason for its truth and its supposed compatibility with the antithesis, just as, conversely, he cannot find any reason for opposing the antithesis. He introduces the assumption of the thesis very imploringly, yet he himself calls it (p. 562/V 590) an arbitrary presupposition whose object might very well be intrinsically impossible, and makes an utterly impotent attempt to find it a little haven somewhere in which it will be safe from the sweeping power of the antithesis, so as not to reveal the nothingness of his favourite pretence that there are necessary antinomies in human reason.

———————

This is followed by the chapter on the transcendental ideal, which brings us right back to the rigid scholasticism of the Middle Ages. You would think you were listening to Anselm of Canterbury himself. The *ens realissimum*,[b] the sum total[c] of all realities, the content of all affirmative propositions,

[a] *Apologie*
[b] [most real being]
[c] *Inbegriff*

comes into view, and in fact with the claim that it is a necessary idea of reason! – For my part, I have to admit that my faculty of reason is incapable of such a thought, and I cannot form any determinate ideas from the words that describe it.

Furthermore, I have no doubt that Kant was compelled only by his passion for architectonic symmetry to include this strange chapter, a chapter that was unworthy of him. The three main objects of the scholastic philosophy (and this, as we have said, can be broadly construed as continuing all the way to Kant), the soul, the world and God, are supposed to be deduced from the three possible major premises[a] of inferences, although it is clear that they have only come – and indeed *can* only come – from the unconditioned use of the principle of sufficient reason. But after the soul 603 was forced into the categorical judgement, and the hypothetical was used for the world, nothing was left for the third idea except the disjunctive major premise. Luckily, some preparatory work was found in this sense, namely the *ens realissimum* of the scholastics along with the ontological proof for the existence of God put forward in rudimentary form by Anselm of Canterbury and then perfected by Descartes. Kant was very happy to make use of this, and it stirred up memories of an earlier, youthful Latin work. But he made an extremely great sacrifice in this chapter for the sake of architectonic symmetry. Flying in the face of all truth, the notion[b] (we must say grotesque notion) of a sum total of all possible realities is made into an essential and necessary thought of reason. In order to deduce it, Kant seized on the pretence that our cognition of individual things comes from a progressive limitation of universal concepts, and consequently of the most universal one of all, the one containing all of reality *within itself*.[c] In the process, he contradicts his own doctrine as much as he contradicts the truth, because our cognition works precisely the other way around, departing from the particular and being broadened into the universal; all universal concepts arise through an abstraction from real, particular things that are cognized intuitively, and this can continue up to the most universal concept of all, which then encompasses everything under it, but almost nothing *within it*. With this, Kant sets the operation of our cognitive faculty on its head, and could therefore certainly be accused of giving rise to the philosophical charlatanism that has become famous in our day. Instead of recognizing concepts as thoughts abstracted from things, this charlatanism reverses the situation, putting concepts first and viewing things only as

[a] *Obersätzen*
[b] *Vorstellung*
[c] *in sich*

concrete concepts; it puts forward a world turned upside down,[a] a piece of philosophical buffoonery that naturally met with general acclaim.[115] –

If we assume that everyone's reason must or at least could attain the concept of God without an act of revelation, this could clearly happen only if guided by causality; and this is obvious enough not to require any proof. Even Christian Wolff says (*General Cosmology*,[b] preface, p. 1): 'In   604 natural theology, we logically prove the existence of the highest being from cosmological principles. The contingency of the universe and of the order of nature together with the impossibility of (pure) chance are the steps one uses to climb from this visible world to God.'[c] And Leibniz before him had already said, with reference to the law of causality: 'We could never prove the existence of God without this great principle'[d] (*Theodicy*, § 44). And likewise in his argument with Clarke, § 126: 'I will go so far as to say that the existence of God could never be proven without this great principle.'[e,116] By contrast, the thought developed in this chapter is so far from being essential and necessary to reason that it can instead be regarded as a proper specimen[117] of the monstrous products of an age that was led by peculiar circumstances into the strangest deviations and nonsense. This was the age of scholasticism, which is without equal in the history of the world and can never return. At its apex, this scholasticism certainly produced the principal proof for the existence of God from the concept of the *ens realissimum*, and used the other proofs only secondarily, as accessories. But this is just a method of teaching, and does not prove anything about the origin of theology in the human mind. Here, Kant took the procedure of the scholastics for a procedure of reason, which is something he does quite frequently. If the essential laws of reason truly dictated that the idea of God came from the disjunctive syllogism in the form of an idea of the most real of all beings, then this idea would certainly have appeared in the philosophers of antiquity too. But there is not a trace of an *ens realissimum* in any of the ancient philosophers; several of them certainly speak about a creator of the world, although only as something that gives form to an independently existing matter, a demiurge,[f,118] though they infer this

---

[a] *verkehrte Welt*
[b] *Cosmologia generalis*
[c] *Sane in theologia naturali existentiam Numinis e principiis cosmologicis demonstramus. Contingentia universi et ordinis naturae, una cum impossibilitate casus, sunt scala, per quam a mundo hoc adspectabili ad Deum ascenditur.*
[d] *Sans ce grand principe nous ne pourrions jamais prouver l'existence de Dieu.*
[e] *J'ose dire que sans ce grand principe on ne saurait venir à la preuve de l'existence de Dieu* [Leibniz–Clarke Correspondence, § 126]
[f] δημιουργος

solely and exclusively on the basis of the law of causality. Indeed, Sextus Empiricus (*Against the Mathematicians*,[a] IX, § 88) presents an argument of *Cleanthes*, which some people take to be the ontological proof. This it is not, it is rather only an inference from an analogy: since experience tells us that *one* being in the world is always better than another, and although humans complete the series as the best of all, they nonetheless have many failings, there must therefore be even better beings and finally a being who is the best of all (κρατιστον, αριστον[b]), and this would be God.[119]

605

As to the detailed refutation of speculative theology that now follows this, I have only briefly to say that it, like the entire critique of the three so-called ideas of reason, and thus the whole Dialectic of pure reason, is to a certain extent the goal and purpose of the whole work; nonetheless, this polemic does not really have a universal, enduring,[120] or purely philosophical interest, as the preceding doctrinal sections do, i.e. the Aesthetic and the Analytic. Rather, its interest is more temporal and local, since it stands in a special relation to the principal moments of philosophy that were dominant in Europe until Kant, and Kant earned everlasting acclaim by completely overthrowing them with this polemic. He eliminated theism from philosophy, since philosophy is a science and not a dogma and only has room for what is either empirically given or can be established by tenable proofs. Of course this is true only of real philosophy, philosophy that is taken seriously and founded on the truth alone; it has nothing to do with the joke that is university philosophy, in which speculative theology plays the same principal role now as it ever did, and in which the soul makes an unceremonious appearance as a known character just as before. This is the philosophy that is endowed with salaries, royalties, and even councillor's titles and, looking proudly down from its heights, has been completely oblivious to little people like me these past forty years; it would be thrilled to be free of old Kant and his Critiques so it could drink Leibniz's health with fervent enthusiasm.[121] – We can note further that, just as Kant was admittedly brought to his doctrine of the *a priori* nature of the concept of causality by *Hume's* scepticism in reference to that concept, so Kant's critique of all speculative theology might have been inspired by Hume's critique of all popular theology, a critique that Hume had set out in his *Natural History of Religion* (which is well worth reading) and the *Dialogues*

606

-----

[a] *Adversus Mathematicos*
[b] [the strongest, the best]

on Natural Religion; Kant might actually have wanted to supplement these. That former text of Hume's is really a critique of popular theology, showing how pitiful it is and pointing by way of contrast to rational or speculative theology as genuine and respectable. But Kant exposes the groundlessness of this second type of theology, leaving popular theology untouched and even showing it in a dignified form, as a faith based on moral feeling. The pseudo-philosophers[a] later twisted this into perceptions of reason,[b] consciousnesses of God, or intellectual intuitions of the supersensible, the divine, and the like; but Kant, tearing down old and venerable errors and knowing the danger of the business, had only intended to substitute a pair of weak and temporary props by way of moral theology, so that the collapsing edifice would not fall on him and he would have time to get away.[122]

As far as the execution of this scheme is concerned, nothing like a critique of reason was needed to refute the *ontological* proof for the existence of God; even without presupposing the Aesthetic and Analytic, it is very easy to show that this ontological proof is nothing more than a sophistical[c] and utterly unconvincing play of concepts. There is already a chapter in Aristotle's organon that provides such a perfect refutation of the onto-theological proof, it is as if it had been written for this purpose. It is the seventh chapter of the second book of the *Posterior Analytics*, and it says explicitly, among other things, that 'existence does not belong to the essence of a thing'.[d]

The refutation of the *cosmological* proof is just a specific application of the doctrine of the *Critique* presented to this point, and there is nothing to be said against it. – The *physico-theological* proof is a mere amplification of the cosmological proof, which it presupposes, and is only thoroughly refuted in the *Critique of the Power of Judgement*.[123] With this in mind, I refer my reader to the heading: 'Comparative Anatomy' in my work *On the Will in Nature*.

Kant, as I said, was only concerned with speculative theology in his   607
critique of these proofs, and limited himself to the academy.[e] If, on the other hand, he had kept an eye on life and popular theology as well, he would have had to add a fourth proof to the other three, the proof that

---

[a] *Philosophaster*
[b] *Vernunftsvernehmungen*
[c] *spitzfündiges*
[d] το δε ειναι ουκ ουσια ουδενι: d.h. *existentia nunquam ad essentiam rei pertinet* [*Posterior Analytics* II, 7, 92b13–14]
[e] *Schule*

really stirs the great masses and, in Kant's technical vocabulary, would most appropriately be called the *ceraunological* proof.[a] It is the proof grounded in the human feeling of helplessness, impotence and dependence in the face of the infinitely superior, inscrutable and mostly ominous powers of nature. Added to this is the natural human tendency to personify everything, and finally also the hope of achieving something with pleas, flattery and even gifts. In every human endeavour there is something outside our power and beyond our calculations: the gods originated in the wish to win this over for ourselves. An old saying[b] of Petronius' is: 'fear first creates gods in the world'.[c] Hume mainly criticizes this proof, and in the writings mentioned above he appears very much as a forerunner of Kant. – Kant put the professors of philosophy to shame once and for all with his critique of speculative theology: these professors are paid by Christian governments, and are not allowed to abandon the main article of faith.[*] So how do these gentlemen look after themselves? – They simply claim that the existence of God is self-evident. – Oh really! After the ancient world performed miracles to prove it, at the cost of its conscience, and the modern world enlisted[d] the ontological, cosmological and physico-theological proofs, at the cost of its understanding, – these good gentlemen find it to be self-evident. And it is from this self- evident God that they go on to explain the world: that is their philosophy.

608

Before Kant, there was a real and established dilemma between materialism and theism, i.e. between the assumption that the world was created by blind chance and the assumption that it was created by an external, ordering intelligence with purposes and concepts, nor was there a third thing.[e] This is why atheism and materialism were the same thing: it is why there were doubts as to whether there could really be atheists, i.e. people

---

[*] Kant said: 'It is quite absurd to expect enlightenment from reason and yet to prescribe to it in advance on which side it must come out.' (*Critique of Pure Reason*, p. 747/V 775.) On the other hand, the following naïvety is a statement of a philosophy professor in our age: 'If a philosophy denies the reality of the basic ideas of Christianity, it is either false or, *even if true, nonetheless unusable –*' *scilicet* [in other words] for philosophy professors. It was the late Professor Bachmann who, in the *Jena'schen Litteraturzeitung* [*Jena Literary Journal*] of July 1840, no. 126, exposed his colleagues' maxim so indiscreetly. In the meantime, it is worth noting as a characteristic of university philosophy that if the truth will not fit in or comply, it is unceremoniously shown the door with a 'Go away, truth! We can't *use* you. Do we owe you anything? Do you pay us? – Then go!'

[a] [proof from fear; *keraunos* in Greek is a thunderbolt, especially as the weapon of the god Zeus]
[b] *Wahrwort*
[c] *Primus in orbe Deos fecit timor* [*Fragments*, 27, 1]
[d] *ins Feld gestellt*
[e] *neque dabatur tertium* [from *tertium non datur*, the standard Latin expression of the law of excluded middle]

who genuinely believe that blind chance could effect such an extravagantly purposive order in nature, particularly in organic nature: see for instance Bacon's *Essays* (*Sermones Fideles*), essay 16, 'On Atheism'. In the opinion of both the great masses and the English, who are entirely on the side of the great masses (the 'mob'[a]) in such matters, this is still the case, even with their most famous scholars. Just look at R. Owen, *Comparative Osteology*[b] (1855), preface, pp. 11–12, where he still stands before the old dilemma between Democritus and Epicurus on the one hand and on the other hand an *intelligence*,[c] in which 'the *knowledge* of a being like man arose before man appeared'.[d] All purposiveness must come from an *intelligence*: he never dreamt of doubting this. Yet in the somewhat modified preface read before the *Académie des Sciences* on 5 Sept. 1853 he said, with childish naïvety, 'teleology or scientific theology':[e] these are precisely one and the same thing to him! (*Comptes rendus*, Sept. 1853). If something in nature is purposive, then it is intentional, a work of deliberation, of intelligence. But of course, what does the *Critique of the Power of Judgement* or even my book *On the Will in Nature* matter to an Englishman like this or to the *Académie des Sciences*? These gentlemen do not look so far beneath themselves. These 'enlightened colleagues'[f] despise metaphysics and 'the German philosophy'[g] – they stick to spinning-wheel philosophy.[h] But the validity of this disjunctive major premise, this dilemma between materi-   609 alism and theism, rests on the assumption that the world that lies before us is the world of things in themselves, and that consequently there is no order of things other than the empirical order. But after Kant made the world and its order into mere appearances whose laws rest primarily on the forms of our intellect, the existence and essence of things and of the world no longer needed to be explained on the analogy of alterations that we perceive or effect in the world, nor did what we see as means and ends need to have arisen in consequence of such cognition. So by depriving theism of

[a] [Schopenhauer uses the English term]
[b] *Ostéologie comparée* [The full title of this work is *Principes d'ostéologie comparée*]
[c] [Schopenhauer uses the French term]
[d] *La* connaissance *d'un être tel que l'homme a existé avant que l'homme fît son apparition.*
[e] *La téléologie, ou la théologie scientifique*
[f] *illustres confrères*
[g] *die* philosophie allemande
[h] *Rockenphilosophie* [Günter Zöller points out that Schopenhauer's reference is to *Rocken*, 'distaff' or 'spinning wheel', and offers the translation 'spinning-wheel philosophy' (See 'Note on Text and Translation', in Arthur Schopenhauer, *Prize Essay on the Freedom of the Will* (Cambridge: Cambridge University Press, 1999), p. xxxviii). An earlier translation had 'petticoat philosophy', based on the wrong assumption that this compound contained the word *Rock*, 'petticoat'. A 'distaff' philosophy carries the connotation of 'women's gossip' or 'old wives' tales'. See the classic dictionary by Grimm and Grimm, *Deutsches Wörterbuch* (Leipzig: Hirzel, 1893), Vol. 8, 1104]

its foundation through his important distinction between appearance and thing in itself, Kant also opened the path to completely different and more profound explanations of existence.[124]

In the chapter on the final aim of the natural dialectic of reason, the three transcendent ideas are said to have value as regulative principles in advancing our understanding[a] of nature. But this can hardly have been serious on Kant's part. At any rate, no expert on nature will doubt the opposite, namely that these presuppositions are impediments, and deadly for all investigations in nature. To test this with an example, just think whether the assumption of a soul, as an immaterial, simple, thinking substance would have helped with the truths that *Cabanis* presented so well, or with the discoveries of *Flourens*, Marshall *Hall*, or Charles *Bell*; or whether it would have represented the worst sort of obstacle.[b] Indeed, Kant himself said (*Prolegomena* § 44), that 'the ideas of reason are contrary to and obstructive of the maxims for the cognition of nature by reason'.[c] –

It is certainly not the least of the merits of Frederick the Great that Kant was able to develop and was allowed to publish the *Critique of Pure Reason* under his reign. Under any other regime, a salaried professor would hardly have dared to do such a thing. Kant had to promise the successor to this great king not to write anymore.[125]

---

610   I could perhaps forgo a critique of the ethical part of the Kantian philosophy, since I provided a more detailed and thorough critique in the *Two Fundamental Problems of Ethics* twenty-two years after this one (first) appeared. But this critique from the first edition should be retained, at least for the sake of completeness, and moreover it can serve as a fitting introduction[d] to that later and much more thorough critique, to which I therefore principally refer the reader.[e,126]

In keeping with the love of architectonic symmetry, there must be a counterpart[f] to theoretical reason. The term is provided by the *intellectus practicus* of the scholastics, which is itself derived from Aristotle's νοῦς

---

[a] *Kenntniß*
[b] [Nineteenth-century physiologists who worked on the brain and nervous system. Hall is referred to in § 23 above (141). Schopenhauer makes positive use of the findings of all these authors at various points throughout his writings. It is notable, however, that in *WWR* 2, ch. 20 he criticizes Flourens for taking an anachronistic Cartesian position (Hübscher *SW* 3, 300ff.)]
[c] [Ak. 4: 331]
[d] *Prolusion*
[e] [For the more thorough critique, see *BM*, ch. 2 (Cambridge Edition of *The Two Fundamental Problems of Ethics*, 123–80)]
[f] *Pendant*

πρακτικος, (*De anima*, III, 10, and *Politics*, VII, chap. 14: 'For reason is both practical and theoretical'[a]).[127] Nonetheless, something quite different is signified here: not the reason directed towards technical matters intended by Aristotle. Instead, practical reason appears here as the source and origin of the undeniable ethical significance of human action, as well as of all virtue, magnanimity,[b] and every attainable degree of saintliness.[c] Accordingly, everything supposedly comes from *reason* alone and needs nothing else. Acting rationally would be the same as acting in a virtuous, noble or saintly manner: and acting selfishly, maliciously or viciously would just be acting irrationally. Meanwhile, all epochs, all peoples and all languages have always distinguished sharply between these things and thought of them as completely different, just as everyone who has not been versed in the language of the newer schools continues to do, i.e. the entire world with the exception of a small handful of German scholars. The rest of the world thinks of virtuous conduct and a rational life[d] as two completely different things. It would be very degrading[e] and perhaps even blasphemous to consider the sublime founder of the Christian religion, whose life is set up as a model for all virtue,[128] as the *most rational* person of all, and it would be almost just as bad if it was said that he only prescribed the best instructions for an entirely *rational life*. Moreover, anyone who follows these precepts and, instead of thinking of himself and his own future needs, only ever thinks about remedying the greater present needs of others, and in fact gives all his possessions to the poor before going on his way without any means of support, to preach the virtue that he himself practises; everyone rightly honours such a person, but who would venture to praise him as the pinnacle of *rationality*? And finally, when Arnold von Winkelried, with excessive magnanimity, caught all the enemy spears with his own body in order to secure victory and salvation for his countrymen, who would praise this as an extremely *rational* deed? – On the other hand, if we see a person who from his youth has given exceptional thought to how to secure for himself the means for a carefree livelihood, for maintaining his wife and children, for providing for his good name and winning external honours and distinctions, and in the process has not been led astray or misguided by the charm of present pleasures, or the thrill of defying the arrogance of the

611

---

[a] ὁ μεν γαρ πρακτικος εστι λογος, ὁ δε θεωρητικος [*Politics* VII, 14, 1333a25; also *De anima* (*On the Soul*) III, 10, 433a14]

[b] *Edelmuth*

[c] *Heiligkeit*

[d] *Lebenslauf*

[e] *unwürdigen*

powerful, or the desire to avenge any wrongs or undeserved humiliations he has suffered, or by the attractions of useless aesthetic or philosophical preoccupations, or by travel abroad, – never letting any of this or anything similar cause him to lose sight of his goal, but rather working towards it single-mindedly and with the greatest dedication: who would venture to deny that such a philistine is extraordinarily *rational*? This is true even if he were to permit himself a couple of harmless expedients that are not particularly praiseworthy. In fact we can go further: if a villain, working with deliberate shrewdness and a well-conceived plan, were to obtain wealth, honour, and even thrones and crowns, and then with the most refined cunning surround and overpower each neighbouring state in turn to become a world conqueror, not letting himself be diverted by any considerations of justice[a] or humanity, but instead stamping out and crushing everything that opposes his plans with brutal consistency, plunging millions of people into misery of every sort without compassion,[b] condemning them to bloody deaths while heaping regal rewards on his followers and helpers, always protecting them, never forgetting them, and thus attaining his goal: who does not see that someone like this will necessarily operate in an extremely rational manner? That just as a powerful understanding was needed to draw up the plans, a perfect mastery of *reason* – indeed a specifically *practical reason* – was needed to carry them out? – Or are the precepts that the clever, consistent, thoughtful and far-sighted Machiavelli gave to the prince somehow *irrational*?*

612

Just as malice is perfectly compatible with reason, and in fact only really becomes terrible in conjunction with it, magnanimity for its part is sometimes combined with a lack of reason. An instance of this would be the action of Coriolanus, who, after having spent years expending all his strength in avenging himself against the Romans, when the time finally came, let himself be moved by the entreaties of the Senate and the tears of his mother and wife to relinquish the revenge that he had prepared so

---

* Incidentally, Machiavelli's problem was to answer the question of how the prince can *unconditionally* retain the throne, in the face of enemies from within and without. Thus, he was not remotely concerned with the ethical problem of whether a prince, being a man, should or should not want anything like this. Rather, he was only concerned with the purely political problem of how the prince can make it come to pass, *if* this is what he wants. He answers this in the manner of someone giving instructions for playing chess, where it would be silly to regret any failure to answer the question whether it is morally advisable to play chess in the first place. It would make as much sense to reproach Machiavelli for the immorality of this work as it would be to reproach a fencing master for not starting his lessons with a moral lecture against murder and manslaughter.

[a] *Recht*
[b] *ohne Mitleid*

carefully and for so long. Indeed, since this brought down the justified anger of the Volscians upon him, he died for those Romans whose ingratitude he knew and had been so intent on punishing. – Finally, for the sake of completeness we will mention that reason can very easily be united with a lack of understanding. This is the case when a stupid maxim is chosen but then carried out consistently. An example of this would be the Princess Isabella, the daughter of Philip II, who vowed not to change into a clean shirt as long as Ostend was not conquered, and kept her word for three years.[129] All vows are generally of this sort, since they arise from a lack of insight in accordance with the law of causality, i.e. a lack of understanding. Nonetheless, if your understanding is limited enough to have made them, it is rational to carry through with them.

In keeping with what we have said, we also see the writers immediately before Kant opposing conscience, as the seat of moral impulses,[a] to reason: so for instance *Rousseau*, in the fourth book of *Émile*: '*Reason* deceives us, but *conscience* never deceives us' and somewhat further: 'It is impossible to explain the immediate principle of conscience by drawing conclusions from our nature, since this principle of *conscience* is independent of *reason* itself.' And further: 'My natural feelings spoke for the common good, my *reason* related everything to myself... You can try as hard as you like to ground virtue in *reason* alone, but what solid basis can we give it?'[b] – In the *Reveries of a Solitary Walker*,[c] Fourth Walk, he says: 'I have always found it preferable to solve all difficult moral questions through the dictates of *conscience* rather than according to the light of *reason*.'[d] – Indeed, even *Aristotle* said explicitly (*Ethica Magna*, I, 5), that the virtues have their seat in the 'irrational part of the soul' and not in the 'rational part'.[e] In accordance with this, *Stobaeus* (*Eclogues*, II, chap. 7), speaking about the Peripatetics, says: 'They believed of ethical virtue that it concerns the irrational part of the soul, because as far as the present observation is concerned, they assume that the soul consists of two parts, a rational and an irrational part, and to the rational part belong: magnanimity, level-headedness, astuteness, wisdom, memory, a skill at learning, and the like. On the other hand, the

613

---

[a] *Regungen*

[b] *La* raison *nous trompe, mais la* conscience *ne trompe jamais.... Il est impossible d'expliquer par les conséquences de notre nature le principe immédiat de la* conscience *indépendant de la* raison *même.... Mes sentimens naturels parlaient pour l'intérêt commun, ma* raison *rapportait tout à moi... On a beau vouloir établir la vertu par la* raison *seule, quelle solide base peut-on lui donner?*

[c] *Rêveries du promeneur*

[d] *Dans toutes les questions de morale difficiles je me suis toujours bien trouvé de les résoudre par le dictamen de la* conscience, *plutôt que par les lumières de la* raison.

[e] *im* αλογω μοριω της ψυχης (*in parte irrationali animi*) *und nicht im* λογον εχοντι (*in parte rationali*) [See *Ethica Magna* (or *Magna Moralia*, now not thought to be by Aristotle) I, 5, 1185b4–13]

irrational part contains: temperance, justice, courage, and the rest of what are called the ethical virtues.'ᵃ And *Cicero* argues at length (*The Nature of the Gods*ᵇ III, chaps. 26–31) that reason is the necessary means and instrument of all crimes.¹³⁰

614

I have declared *reason* to be the *faculty of concepts*. This very special class of universal, non-intuitive representations, which are symbolized and established only through words, is what distinguishes human beings from animals and makes us masters of the earth. Animals are slaves of the present and their motives are directly connected to sensibility; thus, they are moved or repelled by these motives with the same necessity as iron is by a magnet; by contrast, reflectivenessᶜ has arisen in humans through the gift of reason. It is this that allows us to look forward and backward and to get a comprehensive view of our lives and the ways of the world; it allows us to be independent of the present, to approach things deliberately, thoughtfully and systematically, to do evil as well as good. But what we do, we do with absolute self-consciousness. We know exactly what our will decides, what it will choose each time, and what other choice was possible under the circumstances; we come to know ourselves through this self-conscious willing and we reflect ourselves in our deeds. Reason can be called *practical* when it is connected with human action in all these ways: it is theoretical only to the extent that the objects of its concern do not have reference to the actions of the thinker, but are of merely theoretical interest to him, and very few people are capable of this. What is called *practical reason* in this sense is basically signified by the Latin term *prudentia* (prudence, circumspection) which, according to Cicero (*The Nature of the Gods*, II, 22), is an abbreviated form of *providentia*.ᵈ,¹³¹ By contrast, when the term *ratio* is used to discuss a power of the mind, it generally refers to theoretical reason proper, although the ancients did not observe this distinction very rigorously. – For the vast majority of people, reason tends in an almost

---

ᵃ Την ηθικην αρετην ὑπολαμβανουσι περι το αλογον μερος γιγνεσθαι της ψυχης, επειδη διμερη προς την παρουσαν θεωριαν ὑπεθεντο την ψυχην, το μεν λογικον εχουσαν, το δ'αλογον. Και περι μεν το λογικον την καλοκαγαθιαν γιγνεσθαι, και την φρονησιν, και την αγχινοιαν, και σοφιαν, και ευμαθειαν, και μνημην, και τας ὁμοιους· περι δε το αλογον, σωφροσυνην, και δικαιοσυνην, και ανδρειαν, και τας αλλας τας ηθικας καλουμενας αρετας. (*Ethicam virtutem circa partem animae ratione carentem versari putant, cum duplicem, ad hanc disquisitionem, animam ponant, ratione praeditam, et ea carentem. In parte vero ratione praedita collocant ingenuitatem, prudentiam, perspicacitatem, sapientiam, docilitatem, memoriam et reliqua; in parte vero ratione destituta temperantiam, justitiam, fortitudinem, et reliquas virtutes, quas ethicas vocant.*) [p. 83 of *Eclogues*, ch. 6, not ch. 7]

ᵇ *de Natura Deorum*

ᶜ *Besonnenheit*

ᵈ [foresight, precaution]

exclusively practical direction. If this is abandoned too, then thought loses its control over action, which means: 'I know what is best and approve of it, but the worse is what I do'[a] or[132] 'in the morning I make plans and in the evening I make a fool of myself.'[b] If a human being's actions are not guided by thought but instead by the impression of the present, almost as with animals, then he is called *irrational* (which does not carry with it any accusation of moral depravity), although what he lacks is not really reason but rather its application to action; it can be said in a way that his reason is merely theoretical and not practical. At the same time, he can be a very good sort of person,[c] as many are, who cannot look on others' unhappiness without helping, even to the point of sacrifice, but who still does not pay his debts. Irrational characters like this are incapable of committing major crimes, because they find the requisite discipline, disguise and self-control impossible. Yet they are unlikely to achieve any great degree of virtue, because no matter how naturally inclined they are to the good, they cannot prevent the isolated vicious and malicious outbursts that every human being is subject to, and are compelled to act on them since reason does not present itself in its practical capacity in order to counter these outbursts with inalterable maxims and fixed precepts.

Finally, *reason* shows itself as quite specifically *practical* in properly rational characters who are thus typically referred to as practical philosophers and are characterized by an extraordinary equanimity in both unpleasant and pleasant circumstances, an even temper, and a firm persistence once a decision has been reached. In fact it is the prevalence of reason in them, i.e. a cognition that is more abstract than intuitive, and thus an ability to survey the whole of life by means of concepts, in general and overall, that acquaints them with the disappointment of the momentary impression, the volatility of all things, the brevity of life, the emptiness of pleasure, the fickleness of fortune, and the great as well as trivial tricks of chance. This is why nothing unexpected happens to them, and what they know in the abstract[d] does not surprise and disconcert them when they encounter it in reality and in particular cases, which is what happens with characters who are not so rational. The present, the intuitive, the actual has such force over these other characters that cold, colourless concepts retreat into the background of consciousness and, forgetting precepts and maxims, they are at the mercy of affects and passions of every sort. At the end of the First

615

616

[a] *Scio meliora, proboque, deteriora sequor.* [Ovid, *Metamorphoses*, VII, 20, slightly adapted]
[b] *Le matin je fais des projets, et le soir je fais des sottises.*
[c] *ein recht guter Mensch*
[d] *in abstracto wissen*

Book I already argued for my view that Stoic ethics was originally nothing
but a set of instructions on how to lead a genuinely rational life in this
sense. There are many passages where Horace repeatedly praises this too.
His *Nil admirari*[a] also belongs here, as well as the Delphic motto: 'nothing
in excess'.[b] It is absolutely wrong to translate *Nil admirari* as 'Admire nothing'. This expression of Horace's does not concern the theoretical so much
as the practical, and really means 'do not value anything unconditionally,
do not become smitten with anything, do not believe that the possession
of any given object can bring happiness: every unutterable longing for an
object or state is only a teasing chimera, and you can free yourself from
this longing just as completely and much more easily through a clarified
knowledge[c] than you would if you achieved possession of it'. Cicero uses
admirari in this sense too, in *On Divination*,[d] II, 2. What Horace means
is thus the fearlessness[e] and imperturbability[f] as well as dispassionateness[g]
which Democritus had already praised as the highest good (see Clement
of Alexandria, *Stromata* II, 21, and compare Strabo, I, pp. 98 and 105).[h,133]
It is really not a matter of virtue and vice in such rationality of conduct,
but this practical use of reason is what gives people their real advantage
over the animals, and this is the only respect in which it is meaningful and
permissible to talk about human dignity.[i]

     In all cases that we can describe or imagine, the difference between
rational and irrational action comes down to the question of whether the
motives are abstract concepts or intuitive representations. That is why the
explanation I gave of reason is in precise agreement with the linguistic
usage of all times and peoples, which itself certainly cannot be considered
contingent or arbitrary. Instead, we must realize that it comes from the
difference between mental faculties, a difference that everyone is conscious
of and that is reflected in language, even if people do not raise it to the clarity of an abstract definition. Our ancestors did not create words that were
617 undefined and senseless, words that would somehow lie ready for philosophers to come along centuries later and decide what should be thought
with them. Rather, our ancestors used their words to designate well-defined

[a] [Let nothing make you lose your composure: *Epistles*, I, 6, I]
[b] Μηδεν αγαν
[c] *verdeutlichte Erkenntniß*
[d] *de divinatione*
[e] αθαμβια
[f] ακαταπληξις
[g] αθαυμασια
[h] [Strabo, *Geography*, I, 3, 16 and 21]
[i] *Würde*

concepts. The words are not ownerless, and to assign to them a completely different meaning from what they have had so far would be to misuse and take liberties with them, so that everyone could use any word in whatever way they pleased, which would necessarily result in boundless confusion. *Locke* already demonstrated extensively that most philosophical disagreements come from the incorrect use of words. As evidence, just glance at the scandalous misuse that intellectually sterile pseudo-philosophers these days make of the words substance, consciousness, truth, etc.[134] And the explanations and assertions of all philosophers from all ages (with the exception of the most recent) concerning reason are in agreement with my explanation, as is the conception[a] prevailing among all peoples of this human prerogative. Just look at what Plato called reason or the rational part of the soul[b] in the fourth book of the *Republic* and in countless other passages scattered throughout his writings, what Cicero said in *The Nature of the Gods*, III, 26–31, what Leibniz and Locke said about this in the passages already cited in the First Book. The list of citations would go on forever if we wanted to show that all philosophers before Kant generally discussed reason in the sense I use, even if they did not know how to explain its essence with perfect distinctness and clarity by tracing it back to a single point. What people right before Kant understood by reason can be seen in two treatises by Sulzer from the first volume of his assorted philosophical works: the first being 'Analysis of the Concept of Reason',[c] the second being 'On the Mutual Influence of Reason and Language'.[d,135] If, by contrast, you read about how reason has recently been discussed due to the influence of the Kantian error, an error that then grew like an avalanche, then you would have to assume that all the sages of antiquity as well as all philosophers prior to Kant had no reason at all, because the immediate perceptions, intuitions, apprehensions[e,136] and intimations of reason that   618 have now been discovered were as foreign to them as the sixth sense of bats is to us. And as far as I am concerned, I must admit that I, with my limited abilities, cannot grasp or imagine a reason that immediately perceives or even observes or intellectually intuits the supersensible, the Absolute (along with the lengthy narratives that accompany it) in any way other than as the sixth sense of bats. But we must say this in favour of the invention or discovery of a reason like this, which instantly and immediately perceives

---

[a] *Begriff*
[b] λογιμον oder λογιστικον της ψυχης
[c] *Zergliederung des Begriffes der Vernunft*
[d] *Ueber den gegenseitigen Einfluss von Vernunft und Sprache*
[e] *Vernehmungen*

whatever one wants it to, that it is an incomparable expedient[a] for most easily extracting oneself and one's favourite fixed ideas from the world, in spite of all the *Kants* and their critiques of reason. The invention itself and the reception it has met with do honour to the age.

Thus, all philosophers of all ages have had a basically correct idea of what is essential to *reason*[b] (το λογιμον, ἡ φρονησις, *ratio, raison*, reason), although their knowledge was not sufficiently determinate and they failed to trace it back to a single point; by contrast, they were not as clear with respect to the *understanding*[c] (νους, διανοια, *intellectus, esprit*, intellect, understanding). In consequence, they frequently mistook the latter for reason, which is why they never achieved a fully complete, uncontaminated and straightforward explanation of its essence. The concept of reason received a completely foreign secondary meaning in the Christian philosophers, through its contrast with revelation, and many people, with this in mind, have rightly claimed that we can know from reason alone (i.e. without revelation) that we have a duty to be virtuous. This consideration was certainly influential, even on Kant's presentation and choice of terms. But that contrast is really of positive, historical significance and is thus foreign to philosophy, which must be kept free from it.

We might have expected Kant to begin his critiques of theoretical and practical reason with a description of the nature[d] of reason in general; after having determined the genus, he might then have been expected to proceed to an explanation of the two species, demonstrating how the one reason expresses itself in two such different ways, and yet, by retaining its main character, proves to be the same in both. But we find nothing of this. I have already shown how inadequate, indecisive and discordant the explanations are that he occasionally gives in passing of the faculty that he is criticizing in the *Critique of Pure Reason*. *Practical* reason is already to be found unannounced in the *Critique of Pure Reason*; and then in the critique devoted to it, it is treated as an established fact, without further explanation or justification[e] and without any concern for the (thoroughly trampled upon) linguistic usage of all times and peoples or the conceptual determinations of the greatest, earlier philosophers. Particular passages suggest that on the whole Kant believed the essential characteristic of reason to be cognition of *a priori* principles. Now since knowledge[f] of

619

---

a *expédient*
b *Vernunft* [Schopenhauer ends the ensuing list of equivalents with the English word 'reason']
c *Verstand* [In the list here Schopenhauer gives the English words 'intellect' and 'understanding']
d *Wesen*
e *Rechenschaft*
f *Erkenntniß*

the ethical significance of action does not originate empirically, it too is a *principium a priori* and therefore comes from reason, which is to this extent *practical.* – I have already said enough about the fallacious nature of this explanation of reason. But even apart from this, think of how superficial and unfounded it is to take independence from experience as the only characteristic feature uniting these most heterogeneous things, and in the process ignoring the fundamental and immense distance that exists between them in other respects. Even assuming, although not admitting, that knowledge[a] of the ethical significance of action arises from an imperative within us, an unconditioned *ought*, how fundamentally different this would be from those universal *forms of cognition* that Kant proved we are *a priori* conscious of in the *Critique of Pure Reason*, a consciousness that allows us to express in advance an unconditioned *must* that is valid for all possible experience. The difference between this *must*, this necessary form of the object that is already determined in the subject, and that moral *ought* is so vast and striking that we can accept their unification under the rubric of 'non-empirical modes of cognition' as a clever comparison,[b] but not as a philosophical justification for equating their points of origin.

Moreover, the birthplace of this child of practical reason, the *absolute ought* or categorical imperative, is not the *Critique of Practical Reason* but rather the *Critique of Pure Reason*, p. 802/V 830. The birth is a violent one, and succeeds only with the forceps of a '*hence*',[c] which brashly and boldly (we should really say shamelessly) installs itself between two wildly different and unconnected propositions in order to join them as ground and consequent. Specifically, Kant begins with the proposition that we are determined not just by intuitive motives but by abstract ones as well, expressing himself in the following manner: 'it is not merely that which stimulates the senses, i.e. immediately affects them, that determines human choice, but we have a capacity to overcome impressions on our sensory faculty of desire by representations of that which is useful or injurious even in a more remote way; but these considerations about that which in regard to our whole condition is desirable, i.e. good and useful, depend on reason.' (Perfectly true: if only he always spoke this rationally about reason!) '*Hence* (!) this also yields laws that are imperatives, i.e. objective laws of freedom, and that say what ought to happen, even though perhaps it never does

620

[a] *Erkenntniß*
[b] *witziges Gleichniß*
[c] *Daher*

happen . . .'ᵃ –! So without further legitimationᵇ the categorical imperative springs into the world to lead its regiment with its *unconditioned ought*. But this is a sceptre made of iron wood, because the concept of *ought* absolutely and necessarily refers to the threat of punishment or a promised reward, as a necessary condition, and it cannot be separated from this without being annulled and deprived of any meaning: hence an *unconditioned ought* is a contradiction in terms.ᶜ This error must be censured, however closely related it might otherwise be to Kant's great service to ethics, which consisted in freeing ethics from all principles of the world of experience, and especially from every direct or indirect doctrine of happiness,ᵈ and correctly showing that the kingdom of virtue is not of this world. This merit is so much the greater since all the ancient philosophers with the single exception of Plato, namely the Peripatetics, Stoics and Epicureans, tried very different tricks to make virtue and happiness either mutually dependent by way of the principle of sufficient reason, or identical with each other by way of the principle of contradiction. The same criticism applies equally to all philosophers of the modern era up to Kant. So he deserves high praise for this: however, justice requires us to remember both that the presentation and execution of his ethics often does not correspond to its tendency and spirit, as we will see shortly, and also that, even so, he was not the very first person to purge virtue of all principles of happiness. In the *Republic* in particular, which tends along precisely these lines, Plato had already explicitly taught that virtue is to be chosen for itself alone, even when it is inexorably linked with unhappiness and disgrace. Even more, Christianity preaches a completely unselfish virtue that is to be practised¹³⁷ not for the sake of compensation in the afterlife but rather without any reward, out of a love for God, to the extent that it is not works which justify but rather only the faith that virtue accompanies as a mere symptom, and thus appears completely gratuitously and of its own accord. Just read Luther's *Treatise on Christian Liberty*.ᵉ I will not take the Indians into account at all; their holy books consistently describe the hope of a reward for one's works as the path of darkness that can never lead to blessedness.ᶠ But Kant's doctrine of virtue is not so pure: or rather, its presentation remains far behind its spirit, and has in fact fallen prey to

621 (margin)

ᵃ [Schopenhauer substitutes his own emphases for those of Kant in this citation. The parenthetical remarks are his own interpolated commentary]
ᵇ *Beglaubigung*
ᶜ *contradictio in adjecto*
ᵈ *Glücksäligkeitslehre*
ᵉ *de libertate Christiana*
ᶠ *Säligkeit*

inconsistencies. He turns next to the notion of the *highest good*, in which we find virtue married with happiness. The *ought*, which was initially so unconditional, goes ahead and postulates a condition in order to free itself of its inner contradiction, which is a burden it cannot live with. Happiness in the highest good is certainly not supposed to be the real motive for virtue: it stands there nonetheless, like a secret article whose presence turns the rest of the contract into a mere sham. It is not actually the reward of virtue, but rather a free gift that virtue furtively seeks out after performing its work. You can convince yourself of this by looking at the *Critique of*   622 *Practical Reason* (pp. 223–66 of the fourth edition, or pp. 264–95 of the Rosenkranz edition).[a] His whole moral theology has the same tendency, which is why morals in fact destroy themselves through moral theology. I will say it again: any virtue that is practised for the sake of some reward is based on a cunning, methodical, far-sighted egoism.

The content of the absolute *ought*, the principle of practical reason, is the famous: 'act so that the maxim of your willing can always at the same time be valid as the principle of a universal law'. – This principle gives someone who wants a regulative[b] for his own will the task of seeking out a regulative for everyone's will. – Then there is the question of how this is to be found. To find the rule for my conduct I clearly should not look only to myself, but to the totality of all individuals. Then my goal becomes the well-being of everyone, without distinction, instead of my own well-being alone. But it is still a question of well-being. I then discover that everyone can be equally well off only when each person makes other people's egoism the limit of his own. From this of course it follows that I should not injure anyone, because then (since this principle is assumed to be universal) I will not be injured either; but this is the only reason why I, given that I am looking for a moral principle and do not have one yet, can wish this to be a universal law. But clearly this leaves the desire for well-being, i.e. egoism, as the source of this ethical principle. This would be an excellent foundation for a theory of the state[c] but it does not work as a foundation for ethics. This is because anyone who is looking to this moral principle to determine a regulative for the will of all is himself in need of regulative; otherwise he would be indifferent to everything. But this regulative can only be that of his own egoism, since this is the only thing that other people's behaviour has any bearing on; thus his will can refer to other people's actions only by way of his own egoism and with respect to it, and these actions will

[a] [Ak. 5: 124–48]
[b] *Regulativ*
[c] *Staatslehre*

623

not be a matter of indifference to him. Kant himself very naïvely lets this be known on p. 123 of the *Critique of Practical Reason* (p. 192 of the Rosenkranz edition), where he explains the search for the maxim for the will in the following way: 'If everyone looked with complete indifference on the need of others, and if *you belonged* to such an order of things, would you be in it with the assent of your will?'[a] – 'How rashly we sanction a law that is unfair to ourselves!'[b] would be the rule for the acquiescence in question. Likewise, in the *Groundwork to the Metaphysics of Morals*, p. 56 of the third edition, p. 50 of Rosenkranz: 'A will that decided not to help anyone in need would conflict with itself, since many cases could arise *in which one would need the love and sympathy of others*', etc. Looked at closely, this ethical principle is thus nothing other than an indirect and hidden expression of the simple old principle: do not do to others what you would not have done to you[c] and therefore refers primarily and directly to passivity, to suffering, and to deeds only by means of this. Thus, as we have said, it would be an extremely useful guide for setting up a state, which is established to prevent the *suffering that results from wrongdoing*[d] and tries to secure the maximum sum of well-being for one and all. But in ethics, where the object of investigation is the *deed as a deed* and in its direct significance for the *doer* – but not its consequence, suffering, or its relation to others – such a consideration is absolutely not permitted, since it basically amounts to a principle of happiness, which is to say egoism.

This is why we cannot share Kant's joy over the fact that his principle of ethics is not material, i.e. does not posit an object as a motive, but is instead merely formal, corresponding symmetrically to the formal laws we learned about in the *Critique of Pure Reason*. It is clearly not a law but only a formula for finding a law; and not only did we already have this formula more quickly and clearly in the old 'do not do to others what you would not have done to you',[e] but analysis reveals that it only ever gets its content by reference to one's own happiness, and thus it can only serve rational egoism, which is the origin of all legal constitutions as well.

624

There is another error, one that everyone finds offensive, and so it is frequently the object of criticism and was once parodied in an epigram by Schiller. It is the pedantic tenet[f] that if a deed is to be truly good and

---

[a] [Ak. 5: 69. Next quotation from Kant Ak. 4: 423]
[b] *Quam temere in nosmet legem sancimus iniquam* [Horace, *Satires* I, 3, 67]
[c] *quod tibi fieri non vis, alteri ne feceris*
[d] *des Unrechtleidens*
[e] *quod tibi fieri non vis, alteri ne feceris*
[f] *Satzung*

deserving, it must be performed solely out of respect for recognized law and the concept of duty, and according to a maxim that reason is conscious of in the abstract,[a] not from any inclination, not from any feeling of goodwill towards others, not from any tender-hearted compassion, sympathy or feelings from the heart which (according to the *Critique of Practical Reason*, p. 213, p. 257 of the Rosenkranz edition)[b] right-thinking individuals will find positively annoying, something that confuses their well-considered and deliberate maxims. Rather, the deed must be done reluctantly and with self-restraint. Remember too that hope for a reward is not supposed to be at issue here, and you can see the absurdity of this demand. But more importantly, it runs completely counter to the true spirit of virtue: it is not the deed that has merit, but rather the willingness to perform[c] it, the love that produces it and without which it would be a dead work. This is why Christianity rightly teaches that all outer works are worthless if they do not come from that true disposition that consists of genuine willingness and pure love, and that it is not accomplished works (*opera operata*) that bring blessedness and redemption but rather faith, the true disposition that is granted only by the Holy Spirit, not the free and deliberate will that looks only to the law. –

Kant's demand that every virtuous action take place coldly and without (indeed against) any inclination, from pure, deliberate respect for the law and in accordance with its abstract maxims, is tantamount to the claim that every true work of art must come from a well-considered application of aesthetic rules. The one is just as perverse as the other. The question, already canvassed by Plato and Seneca, of whether virtue can be taught, is to be answered in the negative. In the end, people must decide to accept the following insight (an insight that gave rise to the Christian doctrine of Providence[d] as well): primarily and according to its inner nature, virtue, like genius, is innate, and just as the collective efforts of all professors of aesthetics cannot give anyone the ability to produce works of genius, i.e. true works of art, professors of ethics and preachers of virtue cannot turn an ignoble character into one that is virtuous and noble, which is much more obviously impossible than changing lead into gold. The search for an ethics and a supreme principle of ethics that would have practical influence and really transform and improve the human race is just like the search for the philosopher's stone. – At the end of our Fourth Book we discussed in

625

---

[a]　*in abstracto*
[b]　[Ak 5: 118]
[c]　*Gernthun*
[d]　*Gnadenwahl*

detail the possibility that someone might nonetheless experience a complete change of sensibilities[a] (rebirth), not by way of abstract cognition (ethics) but rather by way of intuitive cognition (effect of grace[b]); and the content of that Book spares me the need to spend any longer on this discussion here.

Finally, Kant also reveals his complete failure to grasp the true meaning of the ethical content of action in his doctrine of the highest good as the necessary unification of virtue and happiness, with virtue making you worthy of happiness. But this already invites the logical reproach that the concept of worthiness, which sets the standard, already presupposes an ethics as *its* standard, which therefore cannot be derived from it. In our Fourth Book we saw that when genuine virtue attains its highest level, it leads ultimately to a complete renunciation where all willing comes to an end: happiness, by contrast, is a satisfied willing, and the two are thus fundamentally incompatible. Anyone who understands my presentation will need no further argument for the complete perversity of this Kantian view of the highest good. And I do not have a negative presentation here apart from and in addition to my positive presentation.

So we encounter Kant's passion for architectonic symmetry in the *Critique of Practical Reason* too, since he has styled it after the *Critique of Pure Reason* with the same headings and forms, the obvious arbitrariness of which is particularly visible in the table of the categories of freedom.

———————

626 The *Doctrine of Right*[c] is one of Kant's last works, and it is so weak that, although I reject it completely, I think polemics against it are superfluous; it will have to die a natural death from its own weakness, just as if it were the work of an ordinary mortal and not a great man. So I will do away with the negative procedure with respect to the *Doctrine of Right* and refer instead to the positive, which is to say the brief outline laid out in our Fourth Book. I can offer just a couple of general remarks on Kant's *Doctrine of Right* here. The mistakes that I criticized in the *Critique of Pure Reason* as clinging to Kant everywhere can be found in such superabundance in the *Doctrine of Right* that you often think you are reading a satirical parody of Kant's style, or at least listening to a Kantian. But the two main errors are these. He wants (and many people have since wanted) to distinguish sharply between ethics and a doctrine of right, without making the latter

[a] *Sinnesänderung*
[b] *Gnadenwirkung*
[c] *Rechtslehre*

dependent on positive legislation, i.e. arbitrary force, but instead allowing the concept of right to exist *a priori* and purely for itself. However, this is not possible, because action, apart from its ethical significance and apart from the physical relation to others and thus to physical force, does not even possibly allow for a third perspective. Consequently, when Kant says: 'duty of right[a] is what *can* be coerced',[b] this '*can*' might either be understood physically, in which case all rights are positive and arbitrary and every arbitrary act[c] that enforces them is right; or the '*can*' might be understood ethically, which brings us straight back to the sphere of ethics. So with Kant, the concept of right hovers between heaven and earth, and has no ground to set foot on; with me, it belongs in ethics. Secondly, his determination of the concept of right is completely negative and therefore unsatisfying:* 'Right is what is consistent with the mutual compatibility and coexistence[d] of the freedoms of individuals according to a universal law.'[e] – Freedom (here the empirical, i.e. physical freedom, not the moral[138] freedom of the will) means not being obstructed, and is thus a mere negation. This is just what compatibility and coexistence mean as well: all we have here are negations, no positive concepts, and in fact we would not have any experience of what is really at issue if we did not already know it in some other way. – As these ideas are developed, the most perverse views arise, such as the view that there is absolutely no property right in the state of nature, i.e. outside the political state,[f] which really means that all rights are positive and thus natural right is based on positive right, although it should be the other way around. Further, we find legal acquisition[g] grounded in seizure of property;[h] the ethical obligation to set up a civil constitution; the grounds for the right to punish,[i] etc., all of which, as I have said, I do not think worthy of any special refutation. In the meantime, these Kantian errors have had a very detrimental influence, obscuring and confusing truths that have long been known and stated, and giving rise to strange theories and a lot of writing and fighting. Of course this cannot last for long, and we

627

---

* Although the concept of right really is a negative one, in contrast to the positive starting point of wrong, the explanation of these concepts cannot for that reason be entirely negative.

[a] *Rechtspflicht*
[b] [See Ak. 6: 220]
[c] *Willkür*
[d] *Zusammenbestehn*
[e] [See Ak. 6: 230]
[f] *Staat*
[g] *rechtliche Erwerbung*
[h] *Besitzergreifung*
[i] *Strafrecht*

already see truth and sound reason[a] making inroads again. One sign in particular of this last trend, in contrast to the many crazy theories, is J. C. F. Meister's book *Natural Right*,[b] although I do not for this reason regard the book as a model of achieved perfection.

After what I have said so far, I can also be very brief concerning the *Critique of the Power of Judgement*. You have to admire how Kant, to whom art certainly remained completely foreign, and who to all appearances had little susceptibility for beauty, and in fact most likely never had the opportunity to see a significant work of art, and, finally, who even seemed never to have heard of Goethe, the only other person in either the century or the nation who could be put by his side as a fellow giant, – as I say, it is admirable that, given all this, Kant could render such a great and lasting service to the philosophical consideration of art and of the beautiful. This service lies in the fact that as much as people had contemplated art and beauty, it had only ever been from an empirical standpoint, using facts to discover the quality that distinguished an object considered *beautiful* from other objects of the same type. Following this path, people would start with particular claims and then proceed to more general ones. They tried to distinguish true[c] artistic beauty from false, and to find distinguishing characteristics of this truth[d] which could then serve as rules. What pleased people as beautiful and what did not, what we should therefore imitate, aim for, and what we should avoid, what rules should be established, at least negatively, and in short, what means there are for exciting aesthetic pleasure,[e] i.e. what conditions for aesthetic pleasure lie in the *object* – this was the almost exclusive theme of all investigations concerning art. Aristotle had taken this path, and even in most recent times people such as Hume, Burke, Winckelmann, Lessing, Herder, and many others are still on that path. In fact, the universality of the aesthetic propositions that were discovered ultimately led back to the subject, and it was noted that if we were sufficiently familiar with the effect on the subject, then we could determine *a priori* its cause in the object, which is the only procedure capable of giving this investigation scientific certainty. This occasionally gave rise to psychological discussions; in particular, this was

[a] *gesunde Vernunft*
[b] *Naturrecht*
[c] *ächte*
[d] *Aechtheit*
[e] *Wohlgefallen*

the intention of Alexander Baumgarten, who advanced a universal aesthetic of all beauty in which he began with the concept of the perfection of sensible cognition, which is to say intuitive cognition. But for him, the subjective aspect is concluded at once when this concept is established, and he proceeds to the objective aspect and associated practical considerations. – But here too, the merit was reserved for Kant, who initiated a serious and profound investigation into *the stimulus*[a] *itself* that leads us to call the object that occasions it *beautiful*, in order (if possible) to find its conditions and component parts in our mind. Thus his investigations went in an entirely subjective direction. This was clearly the correct path, because in order to explain an appearance given in its effects, we must first be completely familiar with this effect itself so that we can thoroughly determine the constitution of the cause. But Kant's merit in this regard did not really extend much further than indicating the correct path, and giving an example, in the form of a short-lived attempt, of roughly how it is to be followed. What he did give cannot be regarded as objective truth or a real   629
gain. He specified the method for this investigation, paved the way, but in other respects fell short of the goal.

In the 'Critique of Aesthetic Judgement', we are forced to note from the very beginning that Kant retains the method characteristic of his whole philosophy, a method that I have discussed thoroughly above. I mean the method of beginning with abstract cognition and going on to investigate intuitive cognition, so that the former serves as something like a *camera obscura* for him to receive and survey the latter. In the *Critique of Pure Reason*, the forms of judgement were supposed to have provided him with cognition of our whole intuitive world, and similarly in the 'Critique of Aesthetic Judgement' he does not begin with the beautiful itself, with intuitive, immediate beauty, but rather with the *judgement* concerning the beautiful, which is called by the very ugly name of a judgement of taste.[b] This he takes as his problem. In particular, his attention is drawn to the fact that such a judgement is clearly the expression of a process in the subject, but is nonetheless just as universally valid as if it concerned a quality of the object. This is what struck him, not the beautiful itself. He only ever begins with what other people say, with judgements about beauty, not with the beautiful itself. It is as if he knew about it only from hearsay, not directly. In almost the same way, a highly intelligent blind person could combine precise reports concerning colours into a theory. We can treat

[a] *Anregung*
[b] *Geschmacksurtheil*

Kant's philosopheme over beauty in almost the same way. Then we will find that his theory is highly ingenious, and in fact sometimes comes up with a general comment that is striking and true; but his real solution to the problem is so completely unacceptable and remains so far beneath the dignity of the topic that it would not occur to us to regard it as the objective truth. For this reason, I consider myself excused from providing a refutation of it, and here too I refer to the positive section of my work.

With respect to the form of his whole book we might note that it arose out of the idea[a] that the key to the problem of the beautiful could be found in the concept of *purposiveness*.[b] The idea is deduced, which is no difficult matter, as we have learned from Kant's successors. Cognition of the beautiful is now put in baroque unity with cognition of the purposiveness of natural bodies; both are placed within a *single* cognitive faculty called the *power of judgement*,[c] and the two heterogeneous topics are treated in the same book. Various symmetrical-architectonic amusements and diversions are then indulged with these three cognitive powers: reason, judgement and understanding; a passion for such diversions is very much in evidence all through this book, for example in the whole thing being forcibly adapted to the style of the *Critique of Pure Reason*, and particularly in the far-fetched antinomy of aesthetic judgement. The accusation of gross inconsistency could be levelled here, since, after Kant incessantly repeated in the *Critique of Pure Reason* that the understanding is the faculty of judgement, and after the forms of its judgement were made the cornerstone of all philosophy, a completely distinctive power of judgement now arises, entirely unlike the first. In the positive section of my work I already explained what I myself call the power of judgement, namely the ability to translate intuitive cognition into abstract cognition and then correctly apply the latter to the former.[139]

By far the best part of the 'Critique of Aesthetic Judgement' is the theory of the sublime: it is incomparably more successful than the theory of the beautiful. Not only does it provide the general method of investigation, as the theory of the beautiful does, but it also goes some way along the correct path, so that even if it does not exactly give the right solution to the problem, still it touches on it very closely.

Because of the simplicity of the subject matter, we can recognize in the 'Critique of *Teleological* Judgement', perhaps more than anywhere else, Kant's rare talent for twisting a thought back and forth and expressing it in many different ways until it turns into a book. The whole book

[a] *Einfall*
[b] *Zweckmäßigkeit*
[c] *Urtheilskraft*

says only this: although organized bodies necessarily seem to us as if they were composed according to a concept of purpose that preceded them, we are still not justified in assuming this to be objectively the case. Because things are given to our intellect from the outside and indirectly, it can have cognition only of their outer, not their inner side, not how they arise and exist; accordingly, it cannot grasp a certain constitution distinctive to the products of organic nature except by analogy, comparing them to works of intentional, human design whose constitution is determined through a purpose and the concept of this purpose. This analogy is sufficient to allow us to grasp the agreement of all its parts to the whole, and even provide us with a guide for their investigation. But this absolutely cannot be made into the actual explanatory basis for the origin and being of such bodies, because the need to conceive them this way arose subjectively. – Something like the preceding would be my summary of Kant's doctrine. It is already substantially present in the *Critique of Pure Reason*, pp. 692–702/V 720–30. But even here we find *David Hume* to be Kant's worthy forerunner in the recognition of *this* truth: he had sharply contested this assumption too, in the second section of his *Dialogues Concerning Natural Religion*. The difference between the Humean and the Kantian critiques of this assumption is mainly this, that Hume criticizes it as based in experience, while Kant, on the other hand, criticizes it as *a priori*. Both are correct, and their presentations complement each other. The essential aspect of the Kantian doctrine is in fact already expressed in Simplicius' commentary on Aristotle's *Physics*: '[Democritus and Epicurus] committed the error of thinking that everything that happens for the sake of a purpose could only rest on intention and deliberation, and yet they remarked that the products of nature did not come into being in this way'[a] (*Scholia on Aristotle*, Berlin edition, p. 354).[140] Kant was perfectly right about this. And after it had been shown that the concept of cause and effect could not be applied to the entirety of nature in general in its being, it was also necessary to show that the structure[b] of nature is not to be conceived as the effect of causes directed by motives (concepts of purpose). If you consider how plausible the physico-theological proof sounds, and the fact that even *Voltaire* considered it to be irrefutable, it was of the utmost importance to show that what is subjective in our apprehension[c] (Kant

631

---

[a] ἡ δε πλανη γεγονεν αυτοις απο του ἡγεισθαι, παντα τα ἑνεκα του γινομενα κατα προαιρεσιν γενεσθαι και λογισμου, τα δε φυσει μη οὑτως ὁραν γινομενα. (*Error iis ortus est ex eo, quod credebant, omnia, quae propter finem aliquem fierent, ex proposito et ratiocinio fieri, dum videbant, naturae opera non ita fieri.*)

[b] *Beschaffenheit*

[c] *Auffassung*

632   claimed this for space, time and causality) also extended to our judgements
concerning natural bodies; and thus, the need we feel to see them as
arising in a premeditated way, according to concepts of purpose, such
that *a representation of them would have preceded their being*, is of just
as subjective an origin as the intuition of space that presents itself so
objectively. Consequently, it cannot be considered as objective truth.[141]
Kant's presentation of the matter is excellent, apart from his exhausting
long-windedness and repetition. He claims correctly that we will never
succeed in explaining the constitution of an organic body from merely
mechanical causes, by which he means the unintentional, lawlike effects
of all the universal forces of nature. Nonetheless, I find another gap here.
Specifically, Kant denies the possibility of this sort of explanation merely
with respect to the purposiveness and apparent intentionality of *organic*
bodies. But we find that even where this does not occur, the explanatory
grounds of *one* region of nature cannot be transferred over to another;
rather, they abandon us as soon as we set foot in a new region, and
new principles emerge in their place, principles that we could never hope
to explain using the old ones. So the laws of gravity, cohesion, rigidity,
fluidity and elasticity are dominant in the region of true mechanism,
laws that in themselves (apart from my explanation of all natural forces
as lower levels of the objectivation of the will) exist as expressions of
forces that cannot be explained any further and constitute the principles
of all further explanation, which consists merely in a reduction to these.
If we abandon this region and come to the appearances of chemistry,
of electricity, magnetism, crystallization, then the former principles are
of no use at all; in fact, the former laws no longer hold, the former
forces are overpowered by others, and appearances contradict them directly,
following new fundamental principles which, like the first, are original
and inexplicable, i.e. cannot be traced back to more general ones. So for
instance we will never be able to explain even a salt dissolving in water,
not to mention more complicated chemical phenomena,[a] according to
genuinely mechanical laws. This has already been described in greater detail
in the Second Book of the present work. I think that a discussion like this
633   would have been very useful in the 'Critique of Teleological Judgement',
and would have shed considerable light on what was said there. Such a
discussion would have been particularly advantageous to Kant's excellent
suggestion that a deeper comprehension[b] of that intrinsic essence whose

[a] *Erscheinungen*
[b] *Kenntniß*

appearances are the things in nature would discover that one and the same ultimate principle is at work in both mechanical (lawlike) nature and its seemingly intentional operations, a single principle that could serve as the common explanatory ground of both. I hope I have given such a principle by establishing the will as the true thing in itself. Accordingly, and in general, our Second Book and its supplements and particularly my work *On the Will in Nature*[142] have perhaps served to deepen and clarify our insight into the inner essence of the apparent purposiveness, harmony and agreement of the whole of nature. For this reason, I have nothing further to say here on the subject. –

The reader who is interested in this critique of the Kantian philosophy should not fail to read the supplement provided under the heading 'Some Further Elucidations of the Kantian Philosophy' in the second section of the first volume of my *Parerga and Paralipomena*. It must be borne in mind that my writings, few as they are, were not all composed at the same time but rather successively, over the course of a long life and with much time intervening. Accordingly, one cannot expect that all the things I have said about some topic will be together in a single place.[143]

Variants in different editions

There were three editions of this work during Schopenhauer's lifetime:

A   1819: first edition of *The World as Will and Representation* (*Die Welt als Wille und Vorstellung: vier Bücher, nebst einem Anhange, der die Kritik der Kantischen Philosophie enthält, von Arthur Schopenhauer*. Leipzig: F. A. Brockhaus) [1819 appears on title page; in fact published at the end of 1818]

B   1844: second edition of *The World as Will and Representation*, volume I (*Die Welt als Wille und Vorstellung. Von Arthur Schopenhauer. Zweite, durchgängig verbesserte und sehr vermehrte Auflage. 1. Band* (Leipzig: F. A. Brockhaus)

C   1859: third edition of *The World as Will and Representation*, volume I (*Die Welt als Wille und Vorstellung. Von Arthur Schopenhauer. Dritte, verbesserte und beträchtlich vermehrte Auflage. 1. Band* (Leipzig: F. A. Brockhaus)

The text translated in this volume is that edited by Arthur Hübscher, *Arthur Schopenhauers Sämtliche Werke* (Mannheim: F. A. Brockhaus, 1988), vol. 2, which essentially follows edition C, though with later editorial changes introduced by Julius Frauenstädt in the first complete edition of Schopenhauer's works (1873), and by subsequent editors, some of which are noted here.

We chiefly catalogue changes that Schopenhauer made between A, B and C. Some passages from A were substantially modified, others were entirely deleted and do not occur at all in B or C.[1] But the majority of changes are

---

[1] Passages only in A are marked as *Zusatz* ('addition') in the critical apparatus used by Hübscher (vol. 7, 141ff.) and similarly marked in the apparatus used by Paul Deussen in his earlier edition of *Arthur Schopenhauers Sämtliche Werke* (1911–23), vol. 6. It should be noted that these are passages *printed* in edition A. They are *not* handwritten additions to Schopenhauer's copy of A (as is stated in the recent translation by Richard Aquila, *The World as Will and Presentation*, vol. 1 (New York: Pearson/Longman, 2008), xlii–xliii, 622 and *passim*). Hübscher also lists the more substantial

additional passages newly inserted in B, and more such passsages inserted in C.

It is neither useful nor possible (in a translation) to list all changes between the editions. Our policy has been in general not to comment in these notes on the following: minor changes to wording that have little or no effect on the overall train of thought; references to the second volume of *WWR*, which itself appeared only in 1844; references to other works by Schopenhauer that post-date A; section numbers for *WWR 1* itself (and cross-references employing them) which were lacking in A; Schopenhauer's Latin translations of passages which he had quoted in Greek and his footnotes providing German translations for passages in English, Spanish, etc. (inserted in C).

PREFACES TO THE FIRST, SECOND AND THIRD EDITIONS

1 In A and B: '14th century'.
2 Footnote added in C.
3 '(Written . . . 1818)' added in B.
4 Two footnotes, 'Fichte and Schelling' and 'Hegel', added in C.

FIRST BOOK: THE WORLD AS REPRESENTATION, FIRST CONSIDERATION

1 'It was already present . . . Descartes' point of departure' added in B.
2 Two sentences 'On the other hand, W. Jones . . . transcendental ideality' added in C. Schopenhauer gives the quote from Jones in the English.
3 In footnote reference in A: § 21 (of first edition of *FR*).
4 '(For more details on this . . . § 21, p. 77)' added in C.
5 Two sentences (one in German) 'This derivation of the fundamental . . . Rosenkranz edition, p. 372)' added in B.
6 Sentence 'But I have gone into this . . . (§ 21)' added in C, with minor changes to the following sentence.
7 'the upright appearance of objects . . . upside down' added in B.
8 'and finally the stereoscope' added in C.
9 In A and B, instead of '(as I have done here and in the other places referred to)': 'In the essay on colours.'
10 'Fichtean' added in B.
11 'This is its empirical reality' added in C.

passages that occur only in A as *Gestrichene Stellen* (deleted passages), in his vol. 7, 97–113. For direct acquaintance with the text of A, the facsimile edition *Faksimilenachdruck der 1. Auflage der Welt als Wille und Vorstellung*, ed. Rudolf Malter (Frankfurt am Main: Insel, 1987) is extremely useful. (There are other cases where later editions have incorporated Schopenhauer's handwritten annotations to his copies of B and C. Some instances of this are indicated in the notes here.)

12 'that is: the world has transcendental reality' added in C.

13 In A and B, after 'It is this:' 'we have imagination [*Phantasie*]'

14 Sentence 'The only certain criterion . . . perceptibly broken' absent in A. A shorter version is present in B, with a reference to *FR*, § 22.

15 'even our own body presents itself . . . supplied by touch' added in B.

16 In 'I have explained all this in great detail . . . I therefore refer the reader to these texts', the references to *FR* and the *Ethics* volume are added in C.

17 In A: 'Newton's'. At end of sentence 'which Newton's calculations later confirmed' added in B.

18 Sentence 'Strictly speaking, *cleverness* . . . in the service of the will' added in C.

19 'The 27th chapter of the supplementary volume is also devoted to this topic' added in B. All subsequent references to *WWR* 2 added in B (before which *WWR* 2 did not exist) will not be routinely annotated below.

20 In A and B the reference is to §§ 30ff. of *FR* (first edition).

21 In A, after 'windbags': 'But this should be regarded as a sheer idiosyncrasy, from which blame can accrue only to my feeble mind, never to such a powerful wisdom as theirs.'

22 In A, instead of 'This is how materialism's enormous begging of the question . . . the final link': 'This how the final link'.

23 Long passage 'So this is the absurdity of materialism . . . in accordance with law' added in C.

24 In A and B: 'it currently stands at fifty-something'.

25 Sentence 'Those who still take . . . predecessors have done' added in C.

26 In A, instead of 'most immediate': 'most developed'.

27 Sentence 'Those who are fond of . . . now takes the stage' added in B.

28 In A, instead of 'their irreconcilable opposition': 'their irreconcilable and greatest possible opposition.'

29 'and letting the object arise out of it' added in B. Also in A, instead of 'that is supposed to send forth the object': 'which is properly called idealism'.

30 In A, instead of 'illusory philosophy of J. G. Fichte', simply 'philosophy of J. G. Fichte'. And immediately following in A, instead of the sentence 'We must comment upon it in this context', the following longer passage: 'who appeared on the scene in our time, became famous and was forgotten within a few years I cannot acknowledge as genuine idealism Descartes' sceptical reflections on the reality of the external world, which he straight away left behind by taking a way out that, although forgivable for his time, was in itself silly. He thus suppressed the half-born thought which nonetheless, because the life of truth had stirred in it, lived on later, albeit still with the same half-nature [*Halbheit*] as Malebranche's occasional causes and Leibniz's pre-established harmony. Berkeley's great and true recognition (which neither he nor anyone else put to further use), that the object is nothing without the subject, and that the objective world thus consists in our representation, is not genuine idealism either. Both these philosophers are also dealing with an object in itself: Descartes and his followers with a world that is objective

in itself, Berkeley with a God who is objective in himself. – Fichte alone, then, was genuinely an idealist, and we must comment upon him in this context.'

31 In A, instead of 'the type of seriousness that . . . adapt themselves to circumstances': 'the type of seriousness that makes demands on all one's powers and is prepared to undergo everything in order to awaken inner conviction in others too'.

32 'because he possessed a striking talent for rhetoric' added in B.

33 'and thought, like all imitators . . . doing better than him' added in B.

34 Footnote here in A and B reads: 'This is clarified and expounded in the Appendix.'

35 Sentence 'Intuition is sufficient unto itself . . . but rather the thing itself' added in B.

36 'since every error has a poison inside it' added in C.

37 'both *will*' added in B.

38 'This is why the Greek and Italian . . . using words' added in B.

39 ὁ λογος, το λογιστικον added in B.

40 'rigorously' added in B.

41 Footnote added in C.

42 In A: § 29 (of first edition of *FR*).

43 'the concepts of *Ruminantia* . . . These are interchangeable concepts' added in B.

44 'because it is merely abstract knowledge . . . knows concretely' added in C.

45 'or in its application' added in C.

46 In A, instead of 'We are justified in treating logic on its own terms . . . rational or abstract sort. Accordingly [etc.]', the following version: 'For this reason logic must to an extent no longer be taught on its own and as a self-sufficient science, because as such it leads to nothing. Rather it must be presented in the context of philosophy as a whole, through its treatment of cognition, especially of the rational or abstract sort. To an extent [etc.]'. In B the same passage is retained with minor variations.

47 'the whole technique of reason emerges little by little from these' added in C.

48 In A and B, instead of 'The only practical use that can be made . . . (as a chapter in its book)': 'By no longer being presented as a special science, but rather in interconnection with the whole of philosophy (as a chapter in its book)'.

49 In A and B, instead of 'of Persian authors': 'of the Brahmins [*der Braminen*]'.

50 In A and B, instead of 'taken as a whole': 'much better than any other [science]'.

51 In A, after 'prior to all experience': '(the science that we should give the name "metaphysics", which is currently without an owner, since metaphysics of nature is already a tautology)'.

52 In A, after 'belongs to experience': 'Here I am completely ignoring philosophy and ethics, theory of right and aesthetics which are included in it: further on it will become apparent that in a certain respect it does belong to the sciences,

but yet in one principal point it is distinguished from all of them, and on that point is more in accord with the fine arts.'

53 'of self-satisfaction, of honour, of disgrace, of right, of wrong' added in B.

54 'why the English term . . . *continental*' added in B.

55 Sentence 'Similarly, it is no help . . . have the knack of it' added in B.

56 In A, instead of 'as Seneca claims in his book *On Mercy*': 'as an ancient writer claims'.

57 Sentence 'However, we just as often . . . correctly subsumed it' added in B.

58 In A, instead of 'such actual things': 'those real objects (intuitive representations)'.

59 Sentence 'All laughter is occasioned . . . explanation of the ridiculous' added in C.

60 In A, instead of 'whereas foolishness shows itself . . . judgements and opinions': 'whereas foolishness shows itself in actions, unless it only expresses its intention instead of actually carrying it out'.

61 Sentence 'The characteristic property . . . heart of the matter' added in B.

62 Sentence 'When, especially in political . . . depends on exactly these' added in C.

63 'to which we can also add . . . obscene (indecent) purposes' added in B.

64 Schopenhauer's texts A, B, C have 'parabola', but 'hyberbola' must be meant.

65 Paragraph 'Here I have treated . . . p. 134 (first edition)' added in C.

66 In A, instead of 'the series of alterations to the surface of the earth': 'the alterations to the surface of the earth, in so far as it is not organic'.

67 Two sentences 'All ultimate i.e. original evidentness . . . not transcendent cognition' added in B.

68 Several sentences from beginning of paragraph 'People often talk in lofty tones . . . an exclusively logical character' added in C.

69 'Then the laws governing it (Kepler's laws) were discovered' added in B.

70 In A and B, instead of 'The discovery of the hypothesis . . . expressing the given facts': 'Thus inferences alone were sufficient to discover the hypothesis'.

71 'and had telescopic eyes' added in C.

72 In A, instead of 'so-called metaphysical truths': 'genuinely metaphysical truths'.

73 'i.e. can neither come to be nor pass away' added in C.

74 In A, instead of 'that are in this sense called metaphysical': 'that are metaphysical'.

75 Sentence 'The most decisive step . . . 1852' added in C. A has instead: 'Professor Thibaut in Göttingen has performed a great service in his *Outline of Pure Mathematics* [*Grundriß der reinen Mathematik*], although I would like a much more decisive and thorough substitution of the evidentness of intuition in place of logical proof.

Professor Schweins in Heidelberg (*Mathematics for primary scientific instruction* [*Mathematik für den ersten wissenschaftlichen Unterricht*] 1810) has also declared himself against the Euclidean treatment of mathematics and attempted to move away from it. Only I find that his improvement reaches only as far as the presentation and not the method of treating mathematics itself, which still remains wholly Euclidean. He has certainly adopted a more coherent, more pragmatic approach rather than the fragmentary approach of Euclid, and that is definitely praiseworthy; but then he has abandoned Euclid's strict form without in the least moving away from his method as such, that is, logical proof in places where immediate evidentness would have been available. So all the objections made above against Euclid apply just as much to this treatment: truth comes in through the back door just as much, reveals itself accidentally [*per accidens*] in the case at hand, and is then pronounced as universally valid right away. Justification for this does not arise in such a procedure, because the connection between the conditions given in the theorem and the relations subsequently discovered does not become visible at all; it is just that we encounter both together on this occasion, and are provoked into the view that it will turn out that way on all occasions.'

76 In A, instead of 'and all subsequent geometrical truths . . . or even with itself': 'He proves the subsequent propositions from their consistency with the axioms and the inconsistency of their negation with them; and then each subsequent proposition from its consistency with the prior proposition and the inconsistency of its negation with it.'

77 In A, instead of 'geometry': 'mathematics'.

78 In A, instead of 'all empirical intuition, and most of experience': 'all experience'.

79 In A, instead of 'extremely small': 'infinitely small'. And the following clause 'although even here . . . deceived all at once' added in C.

80 Sentence 'Only in deliberately organized . . . formation of hypotheses' added in B.

81 In A and B, instead of: 'repeated experience brings induction . . . possibility of deception is negligible': 'repeated experience brings induction (i.e. cognition of the ground on the basis of the consequent) infinitely close to the evidentness of mathematics (i.e. cognition of the consequent on the basis of the ground), and the possibility of deception vanishes to an infinitely small magnitude'.

82 Three sentences 'But this possibility does still exist . . . on the right-hand side' added in C.

83 In A, after 'mathematics': 'metaphysics (pure natural science)'.

84 Sentence 'Kant's vague and indeterminate . . . p. 350 of the 5th edition' added in B.

85 Two sentences 'Error is therefore wholly . . . three species of error)' added in B. A has simply 'I redundantly add the following three examples which can also be viewed as representatives of the three species of error.'

86 'is often simply a false generalization and' added in B.

87 'and chemical properties' added in B.

88 Sentence 'Gravity for instance . . . a completely satisfactory explanation' added in B.

89 'although what is original in all appearances stems from it: the thing in itself' added in B.

90　In A and B, instead of 'In my essay . . . (§ 51)': 'In the introductory essay, § 57 [i.e. of the first edition of *FR*]'.

91　'I later provided . . . *Problems of Ethics*' added in C.

92　In A, instead of 'empirical': 'empirical and metaphysical'.

93　'by the example of Duns Scotus' added in C.

94　' "the end of all virtue . . . p. 138)' added in C.

95　Sentence 'This is why Antisthenes . . . or we must leave it' added in B.

96　' "cupidity and not poverty . . . fragment 25' added in C.

97　Sentence 'This is why Chrysippus claimed . . . the things of the world' added in C.

98　Footnote added in C.

99　Sentence 'Cicero's *Paradoxes* . . . Stoic point of view' added in C.

100　Sentence 'Similarly: . . . ibid., p. 104)' added in C.

SECOND BOOK: THE WORLD AS WILL, FIRST CONSIDERATION

1　In A Schopenhauer used a different passage as the epigraph for the Second Book:

> *Daß ich erkenne, was die Welt*
> *Im Innersten zusammenhält,*
> *Schau' alle Wirkenskraft und Samen,*
> *Und thu' nicht mehr in Worten kramen.*
> *Goethe*

[*Faust* I, lines 382–5: 'That I may discover what holds the world's innermost core together, see all its effective power and seeds, and no longer mess around with words']

He later found the passage from the German author and alchemist Agrippa von Nettesheim in a book he possessed by J. Beaumont, with a very long title that starts *Historisch- Physiologisch- und Theologischer Tractat von Geistern, Erscheinungen, Hexereyen, and anderen Zauber-Händeln . . .* [*Historical, Physiological and Theological Treatise on Ghosts, Apparitions, Bewitchings and other acts of magic . . .*]. In his own copy of *WWR* edition B (1844) Schopenhauer wrote a note that the extract comes from a letter by Agrippa quoted by Beaumont on p. 281. According to Edward Bentley, *Notes and Queries* 92 (1919), 119–20, the letter in question is to Aurelius ab Aquapendente, September 1527 (*Letters*, Book V, 14, part ii, p. 905 of Agrippa's *Opera*) in which Agrippa is explaining that 'books on magic, astrology, alchemy and the philosopher's stone are not be be understood literally, but are to be interpreted by a spirit within us'.

2　'unity of plan' [*unité de plan*] added in B.

3　Paragraph 'Now we are already in a position . . . before me have taken' added in C.

4　In A and B, instead of 'involuntary acts': 'so-called involuntary acts'.

5 Sentence 'This is specifically discussed . . . of the second edition' added in C.

6 In A and B, instead of '§§ 29ff.': '§§ 32ff. [of *FR*, first edition]'.

7 Seven sentences 'After all, what other sort of existence . . . immediately in our-selves as will' added in B.

8 In footnote: 'It is the same with Kepler's assertion . . . traverse their bases' added in B.

9 In A, instead of 'as well as the relevant discussions . . . pp. 178ff. of the first edition': 'what is said in the introductory essay [i.e. *FR*, first edition], § 46'.

10 In A, instead of 'functions' (here and later in the sentence): 'alterations'.

11 'and the concept of force is created from such cognition' added in C.

12 Four sentences 'It is a stimulus-response when . . . from a motive in cognition' added in B.

13 Sentence '*Marshall Hall* . . . (involuntary) nerves' added in B.

14 In A, instead of 'Several accounts have claimed that Diogenes . . . prussic acid kills by first paralysing the brain': 'Whether suicide has ever been committed in this way, I do not know; but one can see it being possible, and it would be a strong example of the influence of abstract motives, i.e. the superiority of genuinely rational willing over merely animal willing. That the cause of breathing is a motive, not a stimulus, and that breathing is mediated and con-ditioned by cognition (of the need for air) also has, incidentally, a physiological corroboration in the fact that it is conditioned by activity of the brain. Hence prussic acid kills by first paralysing the brain.'

15 Footnote added in B.

16 '(as with human desires, this striving is only intensified by obstacles)' added in B.

17 Footnote added in B.

18 Two sentences (one in German) 'Thus, as the necessity accruing to some cognition . . . not derivable from anything else' added in B.

19 The long passage 'Examples of the general method I have in mind here include . . . pretend they had nothing to do with it' added in C. In A and B, a short footnote: 'Examples of the general method I have in mind here are: Democritus' atoms, Descartes' vortex, Le Sage's mechanical physics, Reil's form and mixture as cause of animal life etc.'

20 '(for instance, magnetism from electricity)' added in B.

21 Sentence 'The scholastics had already . . . Disputatio XV, sect. I)' added in C.

22 'Even St. Augustine expressed . . . (*City of God*, XI, 28)' added in C.

23 Paragraph 'It is also worth noting that Euler saw . . . had already been debunked' added in B.

24 'since the relation between the part and the whole . . . apart from this form of intuition' added in B.

25 In A, instead of five sentences 'Thus one can say that if, impossibly, a single being . . . true and distinctive essence', a whole paragraph: 'This property of the will – that it is quite indifferent to the number of individuals in which any particular level of its objecthood is expressed, no matter whether they exist one after another or at the same time, that their infinite number never exhausts

it, while on the other hand *a single* appearance achieves as much as thousands in respect of its becoming visible – I would like to apply to this property an unusual and indeterminate word that is in fact badly regarded, but is fitting for a property in respect of which the will as thing in itself is utterly opposed to all the things in nature. I would like to call it the *magic* of the will; for in this concept we are thinking of something that, despite not being any natural force, and consequently not being subordinate to the laws of nature and restricted by them, nonetheless exerts an inner force [*Gewalt*] upon nature, just as the will as thing in itself does when, like a magician [*Zauberer*], it calls into visibility things that for us are of the greatest reality, but that in respect of the will are merely reflections of its essence – like the image of the sun in all drops of dew. It gives life to all these things without losing any part of its power, and their number exists only for the spectator, not for the will. – This use of the word *magic* is just a thoroughly casual comparison, though, and no more weight should be placed upon it, nor will further use be made of it.'

26 Sentence 'Diogenes Laertius provides . . . exist as their copies' added in B.

27 Sentence 'Take the earth away and the stone would not fall, although gravity would still be there' added in B.

28 In the sentence 'This distinction between the human species . . . than they are in humans', in A and B, instead of 'probably': 'without doubt'; mentions of 'birds', 'rodents' and 'higher animals' added in B. In footnote here, reference to Cuvier added in C.

29 'it is omnipresent' added in C.

30 In A, instead of 'three thousand years': 'twenty years'; and instead of 'plant': 'tree'. Footnote here added in B, except 'In the garden of Mr Grimstone . . . 1844' added in C.

31 In A, instead of 'metaphysical explanation': 'philosophical explanation'.

32 Two sentences (one in German) 'Nonetheless, a law of nature will . . . complete register of facts' added in C.

33 In A and B, instead of 'which it understands completely . . . reduce all others to it': 'to which it forcibly tries to reduce all others'.

34 In A, instead of 'of heavenly bodies': 'of the magnet'.

35 Four sentences 'Physiology's explanatory goal . . . pp. 306ff. of that work' added in B.

36 'It is well known that in recent times . . . renewed audacity' added in C.

37 'I will show that the life force certainly makes . . . much less animal life' added in C.

38 Sentence 'Aristotle's term "substantial form [*forma substantialis*]" . . . of the will in a thing' added in B.

39 'as "unity of plan", "uniformity of the anatomical element" [*l'unité de plan, l'uniformité de l'élément anatomique*]' added in B.

40 In A and B, instead of 'the philosophers of nature working within Schelling's school': 'those writers who in Germany today are called philosophers of nature'.

41 '(whose identity was established later)' added in C.

42 Sentence 'In China, on the other hand . . . *Yin* and *Yang*' added in B.

43 'in the *I Ching*' added in B.

44 'rather' and quotation '*Encheirisin naturae . . .* know not how' added in C.

45 ' "because if strife were not . . . *Metaphysics* B, 5' added in B.

46 In A, instead of 'revelation': 'visibility [*Sichtbarkeit*]'.

47 In A, instead of 'since every animal can maintain . . . the human race, which overpowers': 'but the human race overpowers'.

48 'and *man is a wolf to man* [*homo homini lupus*]' added in B.

49 Seven sentences 'Many insects (in particular the *Ichneumonidae* wasps . . . You can see the same thing even at the lowest levels' added in B – except the passage 'The bull-dog ant . . . 1855' added in C.

50 In A, instead of 'appearance': 'arena [*Schauplatz*]'.

51 Two sentences (one in German) 'This contradicts neither the law . . . the movement's cessation' added in B.

52 In A, instead of the two sentences 'Rather in the case of the planets . . . that we cannot see': 'Rather it is the original state of every heavenly body, which flies through infinite space until it comes into the sphere of attraction of a larger body that overpowers it and binds it to itself. This body itself also flies forwards until a larger one captures it.'

53 '(since in absolute space motion cannot be distinguished from rest)' added in B.

54 'i.e. presented for representation as an organ' added in B. Footnote here added in B, and references to second edition of *WN* (and *WWR* 2) added in C.

55 In A, instead of 'magnetic clairvoyance': 'animal magnetism [*thierischen Magnetismus*]'.

56 'which is now supposed to replace everything' added in B.

57 In A, instead of 'has already taken its definite and unalterable course': 'already has its definite and unalterable degree of objectivation'.

58 In footnote, sentence 'See Suárez . . . sections 7 and 8' added in C.

59 In A, instead of 'a hundredfold': 'tenfold'.

60 '(Platonic)' added in B; and again below in this paragraph.

61 Two sentences 'this basically stems from the fact . . . pursuit, anxiety and suffering' added in C.

62 '(Platonic)' added in B.

63 In footnote: references to 1st edition of *Critique of Pure Reason* added in B. In A: reference to *FR* is to § 46 (i.e. of *FR*, 1st edition).

64 Seven sentences (five in German) 'In animals we see the will to life . . . expressed in any other language' added in B.

65 Sentence 'Just as the same theme can be presented . . . very different life histories' added in B.

66 'and we see this consensus of nature everywhere' added in B.

67 'and its refrangibility' added in C.

68 'the hydrous cells in the stomach of a camel . . . desert' added in C; 'the sail of the nautilus . . . its little ship' added in B.

69 Footnote added in C.

70 Two sentences 'That harmony only goes far enough . . . not to the continuation of individuals' added in B.
71 Footnote added in B.
72 In A and B, instead of 'material cause': 'cause'.

THIRD BOOK: THE WORLD AS REPRESENTATION, SECOND CONSIDERATION

1 'which accordingly means: the will become object, i.e. representation' added in C.
2 In A, instead of 'particularly': 'unfortunately'.
3 Paragraph 'To bring Kant's language even closer to Plato's . . . in the Third Book' added in C.
4 Footnote added in C.
5 In A, instead of 'forty years': 'twenty years'.
6 Sentence 'Time is merely the scattered . . . αιωνος εικων κινητη ὁ χρονος' added in B – though with 'Plotinus' in B, changed to 'Plato' in C. Also 'moving' and κινητη added in C.
7 In A, instead of 'lower': 'imperfect'.
8 In A and B, instead of 'so that it is as if the object existed on its own, without anyone to perceive it, and we can no longer separate the intuited from the intuition': 'so that we now know only that intuition is occurring here [*hier angeschaut wird*], but no longer know who is the one that intuits, and cannot at all separate the intuited from the intuition'.
9 In A and B, instead of 'Thomas Paine's observation': 'the saying of Napoleon Buonaparte'.
10 Footnote added in B.
11 Paragraph 'Now anyone who has become so engrossed . . . (*Oupnek'hat*, I, 22)' and footnote added in C.
12 Two sentences 'Accordingly, the "expression of genius" . . . directed exclusively towards motives' added in B.
13 Sentence 'The fact that even today . . . and Germans in particular' added in B. In B, instead of 'almost half a century': 'that is, 33 years'.
14 'Horace calls it "amiable madness" . . . beginning of *Oberon*' added in B.
15 'Cicero too says: . . . And thin partitions do their bounds divide' added in C.
16 'Byron' added in B.
17 In A, instead of '250 million': 'millions'.
18 Two sentences 'Indeed, I do not want to fail to mention . . . abnormality that disposes one to madness' added in B.
19 'purely intellectual' added in B.
20 'when he enters an insane asylum' added in B.
21 'just as someone might remove a limb . . . replace it with a wooden one' added in B.
22 In A and B, instead of 'as a Platonic *Idea*, i.e. as a permanent form of this whole genus of things': 'as an *Idea*'.

23 'Platonic' added in C.

24 Three sentences 'It signifies eternal salvation . . . in orderly figures' added in B.

25 'which reaches a climax when they are transparent' added in B.

26 'and indeed on a large scale' added in B.

27 Footnote added in C.

28 'The view out over endless prairies . . . of the sublime' added in C.

29 Sentence 'Many objects of our intuition arouse the impression . . . are all of this type' and whole following paragraph 'Indeed, our explanation of the sublime . . . than as a sufferer' added in B.

30 'and in fact reject it' added in B.

31 'that we become *objective* in viewing it, i.e.' added in B.

32 Sentence 'According to Aristotle (*Metaphysics* XI, chapter 3) . . . House or Ring' and 'In any case' added in C.

33 'He says specifically: "But they define . . . perfect in themselves"' added in C.

34 In A and B, instead of 'the disclosure that the building is made of pumice-stone': 'the news that it is only made of wood'.

35 'that architecture operates not only mathematically but also dynamically, and' added in C.

36 Sentence 'Practical hydraulics offers . . . Trevi Fountain in Rome' added in B.

37 Sentence 'For the most part the scenic beauty . . . combination and variation' and 'These are the two conditions that landscape gardening promotes' added in B.

38 In A, instead of 'objectivation': 'objecthood [*Objektität*]'. This subsitution of terms occurs a dozen more times in the Third Book, and these are not separately annotated below.

39 In A, instead of 'paintings and sculptures of animals . . . with ancient animals etc.' 'paintings of animals'.

40 'but also without disguise, naïvely and openly . . . take an interest in animals' added in B.

41 In A, instead of 'and is called *Mahavakya*, the great word: "*tat tvam asi*"': '"Tatoumes", as the Persian translator writes it, or "Tutwa" as the English translator does'.

42 In A and B, instead of 'natural forces': 'natural laws'.

43 In A, instead of 'the possibility of cognition in general, the universal *How* . . . no exceptions': 'the cognition possible for the individual'.

44 'and "Yes, that was it!" is the reply of the knowing connoisseur' added in B.

45 In A, instead of 'Empedocles': 'Pythagoras'.

46 Footnote added in B.

47 '(although it is held by Xenophon's Socrates: Stobaeus, *Anthology*, vol. 2, p. 384)' added in 4th edition (Frauenstädt, 1873) on the basis of Schopenhauer's annotation in his copy of C.

48 Two sentences 'Grace presupposes as its condition . . . the will at the highest level of its objectivation' added in B.

49 'a Laocoön whose voice has stuck in his throat, *vox faucibus haesit*' added in B.

50 'Raphael's *Violin Player* in the Sciarra gallery in Rome' added in B.

51 'just as it makes no difference . . . made of gold or of wood' added in C.

52 Sentence 'Even the fleeting nature of the moment . . . particular to the Idea of its species' added in B.

53 'in Plato's sense' added in C.

54 Two sentences 'For what is modesty if not . . . being honest, not modest' added in B.

55 Sentence 'The *Idea* is unity shattered into multiplicity . . . unity before the fact [*unitas ante rem*]' added in C.

56 Three sentences 'Just read the complaints of the great minds . . . approval of the present, and vice versa' added in B.

57 'lying entirely outside of the artwork' added in B.

58 'the palm the symbol of victory, the mussel the symbol of pilgrimage' added in B.

59 Two sentences 'Meanwhile people generally take emblems to be . . . therefore merely *symbolic*' added in B, with 'Alciati' added in C.

60 'How well Kleist uses allegory . . . the whole of the earth"' added in B.

61 Four sentences 'I know of three extended allegorical works: . . . (as Hamlet would call him) has in mind' added in B.

62 Sentence 'The symbols we have mentioned . . . with an explicit moral' added in B.

63 'Since everything symbolic fundamentally rests on convention' added in C.

64 'who would guess, if they did not already know . . . hieroglyph through and through' added in B.

65 In A, instead of 'as the reliefs with the great sun-god Mithra, – always still being interpreted': 'as the Egyptian hieroglyphs are as pictorial representations'.

66 'For instance: . . . over the food-growing earth' added in B.

67 'Thus Schiller says . . . That alone will never age' added in C.

68 Sentence 'Just as a circle with a one inch diameter . . . know humanity in the one just as in the other' added in C.

69 In A, instead of 'intuits and describes only his own state': 'intuits only his own state and objectifies it [*ihn objektivirt*]'.

70 Seven sentences 'The whole achievement of this poetic genre . . . to its own consciousness' added in C.

71 Five sentences 'Over the course of a life, these two subjects . . . to the character of the elderly' added in B, with the passage 'Byron has expressed this well . . . High mountains are a feeling' added in C.

72 'that the unspeakable pain . . . of the world and of existence' added in B.

73 Four sentences 'By contrast, the demand for so-called poetic justice . . . as Calderón says with perfect frankness' added in C.

74 'Euripides' Phaedra, Creon in *Antigone*' added in B.

75 'as well as the *Women of Trachis*' added in B.

76 'likewise Corneille's *Cid* . . . relation of Max to Thecla' added in B.

77 'if it were nothing more, then the satisfaction . . . our being given voice' and 'Thus' added in B.

78 '(Platonic)' added in C.

79 'this is precisely why the effect of music . . . music speaks of the essence' added in B.

80 'it rises and falls only in large intervals . . . a bass transposed by a double counterpoint' added in C.

81 'also physically' added in C.

82 In A, instead of 'has a genuinely coherent consciousness': 'has a succession of mental developments'.

83 'Plato already describes music . . . *Laws*, VIII' added in B; 'and Aristotle too says . . . *Problems*, ch. 19' added in C.

84 'completely different one . . . what preceded it, and so' added in B.

85 The majority of a paragraph 'Therefore it does not express this or that individual and particular joy . . . when performed on instruments alone' and 'Given all we have said' added in C.

86 Sentence 'From this inner relationship of music to the true essence . . . the things he has in mind' and 'For' added in B, with slight expansion in C.

87 'and thus presents what is metaphysical . . . thing in itself for all appearance' added in B.

88 'the inner spirit of' added in C.

89 Three sentences 'This is because melodies are to a certain extent . . . gives *universalia in re*' added in B.

90 In A, instead of 'which allows it to pass before us like a paradise . . . removed from their pain. Similarly, its essential seriousness': 'and its essential seriousness'.

91 'Even repetition signs, including *da capo* . . . we must listen to it twice' added in C.

92 In A, instead of 'metaphysics': 'philosophy'.

93 'we cannot even compute a scale within which . . . one role and sometimes another' added in C.

94 Sentence 'We can think of Raphael's St Cecilia as a symbol of this transition' added in B.

FOURTH BOOK: THE WORLD AS WILL, SECOND CONSIDERATION

1 '("it is nothing but a negative expression . . . *Orations*, 5)' added in B.

2 Sentence 'This, by the way, can be dismissed . . . necessarily *has* become' added in B.

3 In A, instead of 'Shiva': 'Shiva, Rudra, Mahadeva [*Mahadäh*]'.

4 Sentence 'The present always exists . . . rainbow on the waterfall' and 'Because' added in C.

5 Six sentences 'Only the present is always there and fixed . . . happens to be precisely now"' added in C: except for the passage 'for the will, life is a certainty, and for life, the present is a certainty' which is present in A and B also.

6 Sentence 'Or: time is like an unstoppable stream . . . does not carry away' added in B.

7 In A, instead of 'objectivation': 'objecthood [*Objektität*]'.

8 Footnote added in C.

9 'and death annuls the deception . . . this is continued existence' added in C.

10 In A, instead of 'art arises from the actual existence of this degree of cognition': 'The actual existence of this degree of cognition produces art, and is then called genius.'

11 In A, instead of two whole paragraphs 'In 1840 [or in B 'In these recent years'] . . . unfathomable', and the first part of a third, 'If, in the same circumstances . . . would be a determination of the thing in itself', the following long passage: 'I also remind the reader of what I have said about this topic in the introductory essay [i.e. *FR*], § 46, and also in the Second Book of the present work. With that presupposed, the following remarks on the matter may enlighten further and make this important point clearer.

Innermost self-consciousness is the point at which the thing in itself, the will, makes a transition into appearance, into what can be cognized, and thus both meet together. The will lies outside the realm of the principle of sufficient reason, and thus outside the realm of necessity, while appearance lies entirely within it. Where philosophy has not yet taught anyone to distinguish the two, they are mixed up in thought and then the freedom of the will in itself is transferred to its appearance, i.e. to the will where it becomes cognizable. And this is the reason why some people, who have not yet had their judgement refined by philosophy, take the *liberum arbitrium indifferentiae* [free choice of indifference] to be an immediate fact of consciousness. Accordingly, they say in a particular case "this human being in this situation *can* act in such and such a way and also the opposite way". But their philosophical opponents say "He cannot act other than just this way."

The development of the concept of *being able* [*Können*], which really has a double meaning, can most usefully clarify the matter. To make the relationship simpler, let us first explain it with an example from inorganic nature. For an alteration to take place, i.e. for a cause to bring about an effect, always requires at least two bodies, and moreover two that are *different* in quality or motion: one on its own, or many together that are the same in every respect, will produce no alteration. So the state that is called a cause is a relation between different bodies, and the conditions that make up this relation are necessarily shared by both. E.g. if motion is to *happen*, one must always be moved, the other capable of movement. If fire is to occur, the one body must be oxygen, the other related to oxygen. We do not discover whether it is until it meets together with oxygen. Thus its *being able to burn* is doubly conditioned: first by its own constitution, and secondly by that of the medium around it. "It *cannot* burn" is ambiguous. It can mean "it is not combustible", or "the external conditions for burning (oxygen and temperature) are not present". What we see here in the case of the law of causality also applies to the law of motivation, motivation being only causality that has passed through cognition, or causality mediated by cognition. "This human being *cannot* do that" either means that the external conditions for such an action, that is, the external motives or the external power, are lacking, or it means that he himself is not capable of such an action even if the said conditions obtain. But the latter can also be expressed as "He does not *will* it". For the inner conditions are nothing other than his own constitution, his essence, i.e. his will. Now just as the chemical properties of a body become apparent only after it is tested against many reagents, or its weight after it has been balanced against others, so a human being's *internal ability* [*innere Können*], i.e. his willing, becomes apparent only after it has entered into conflict with motives (the motives here, like the reagents in the other case, being merely occasional causes) and after the sphere of his *external ability* has widened to an appropriate extent, becoming all the greater and clearer the more the sphere has widened. If it is really narrow, the human being lies in prison, alone. Then his inner ability cannot become public any more than the chemical properties of a body shut off from air and light.

But let a human being have wealth, have desires, have cognition of much misery in others. Now the sphere of his *external ability*, which is commonly just called ability, is wide enough and it must become apparent whether he would rather satisfy all his desires or lessen the misery of others. From this it will become clear what his *inner ability* is, i.e. what his willing is. It does indeed seem to the person himself and to others who judge unphilosophically, that he could do one thing as well as the other, and this seeming arises from the following: they are attached to the abstract concept *human being* [*Mensch*], and they cannot do otherwise, given that they want to make a judgement *a priori*, because it is only from concepts and not from real individuals that we can gain exhaustive cognition that provides content for analytic judgements. So they subsume the individual under that concept and transfer what holds of a human being in general – namely that he could act in both ways in such a case – to the individual, and ascribe to him a choice as yet undetermined by anything (*liberum arbitrium indifferentiae*). But if the individual had such a choice, he would have to be able to act one way today, and in the opposite way tomorrow under exactly the same circumstances. But then the will would have to be in time, and either it would have to be a mere appearance or time would have to pertain to the thing in itself; for alteration is possible only in time, and the conditions of inner ability, that is, the will, must have altered in this case, given that those of external ability are assumed to be the same. However, if the will as thing in itself is outside of time, as our entire account makes necessarily the case, then the conditions of inner ability can never alter, only those of external ability. So if the will of that individual were such as to prefer the lessening of others' sufferings over the increase of his own pleasures, then he would have done it yesterday when the external ability was there as it is today; and if he did not do it yesterday, then, since his inner ability has undergone no alteration, it is quite certain that he will not do it today either, i.e. he *cannot* do it. Thus as regards the outcome it is immaterial whether the inner or the outer conditions for the required action are absent: in both cases we say that the individual *cannot* perform this action. Although the term peculiar to the inner conditions for action is *willing*, we often use the term *being able* for them as well, indicating by this metaphor the necessity that the efficacy [*Wirken*] of the will has in common with the efficacy of nature. Just as a determinate level of the will's manifestation reveals itself in every natural force in accordance with unchangeable laws, so something of the same kind appears in every human individual too, and from it his deeds flow in accordance with a law that is equally strict, though not equally easy to apprehend and express. – This is also the reason why we demand of a dramatic author that each character he introduces should have the strictest coherence and unity with itself and carry it right through to the end.'

12 Whole paragraph 'The claim that the will is empirically free, a *liberum arbitrium indifferentiae*... I say he *cognizes* what he wills' added in B.

13 Two sentences ' "Since the word ηϑος (character)... II, ch. 7' added in B.

14 'predestination as a result of' added in B.

15 'at the centre of most of the controversies in the church' added in B.

16 'which shows that he preferred the truth over his fellow Stoics, who said that virtue can be taught' added in B.

17 In A, instead of 'To be effective, a motive does not just need to be present, it must be recognized': 'To what we earlier called external ability belongs not just the presence of conditions and motives, but also cognition of them'.

18 In A, instead of 'For the relationship between (for instance)... others in need': 'So, for example, it is not sufficient that the human being we earlier put forward as an example should possess wealth'.

19 In A, instead of sentence 'For this to happen, the motives must... present, intuitive apprehension': 'while the animal is determined not by the stronger, but always by the directly present motive. For in concrete terms [*in concreto*] only *one* motive ever has effect at a time, because intuitive representations are in a time sequence without any breadth. An animal, having only this kind of representations, is thus always determined by the representation present at a given time, provided it is a motive for its will at all, without reflection and without choice.'

20 In A, instead of 'This is the absolute *ability to choose*... In fact, people's deliberative capacity is one of the things': 'This is the determination of choice [*Wahlbestimmung*] which raises humans above animals and is one of the things'. The passage 'and causes us to credit ourselves with freedom of the will... i.e. a character' added in C.

21 'and are thus in an enviably carefree condition' added in B.

22 In A, instead of 'We have shown that the human deliberative ability is dependent... misled Descartes and Spinoza into identifying': 'We can now clarify the difference between animal and human decisions of the will with the help of an example, and at the same time dissolve one of the most famous arguments against the will's necessitation, which can indeed be dissolved only by starting from this point. I mean the very famous humorous example of the ass between two bundles of hay, which is ascribed to the scholastic Buridan, although it is supposedly not to be found in his extant writings. It is really a

significant argument against the dependency of the will, and Descartes and Spinoza ought to have taken more notice of it, as they both falsely identified'.

23 'although it is that of a true conclusion drawn from false premises' added in B.

24 In A, instead of five sentences and part of a sixth 'The dissimilarity we have demonstrated between the ways humans and animals... The causes of our pains and pleasures are not generally found in the real present', this longer passage: 'If opposing motives could cancel one another out in the way that two equally strong opposing cognitive grounds bring about absolute doubt, suspension of judgement [*suspensio judicii*], or in the way that equally strong causes working against one another mutually cancel their effect, resulting in a standstill – if opposing motives too could cancel one another in this way, then either the will must be free, in the sense of non-philosophers, i.e. self-determining without any ground, or Buridan's ass must die of hunger between two bundles of hay that are exactly the same and the same distance away, because of the lack of any ground that would draw him to one of them in preference to the other. But if we now look back to the difference we have just explained between human and animal cognition, we know that the conflict between two mutually excluding motives is in no way possible in the non-rational cognitive faculty of the animal, and we could never teach the ass that by seizing the one bundle of hay he will lose the other. For only one representation at a time is present to him and able to have efficacy as a motive; in this case it is the particular bundle of hay his eyes are directed at, the direction depending on the series of his preceding movements, and because of that his action here is also necessarily determined. – But if we now replace non-rational cognition with rational cognition, then abstract motives are effective in reflection, and there is the very real possibility of the will's being influenced independently of time, of there being consciousness of the mutual exclusion in a choice and of the conflict that results, and finally of forces that have totally equal weight. Then the standstill that occurs is immediately removed by an additional third reflection to the effect that, if no resolve at all is reached, not just one but both the objects of choice will be lost. This reflection becomes the motive for an enforced choice that is really blind, but which is so intolerable to reason that either it is driven by superstition to demand a pronouncement of fate and grasps after some kind of divination, mostly thought up on the spot specially for the case at hand; or alternatively, once reason has found itself to be inadequate for making the decision, it is intentionally set aside and the decision is left to an immediate impression of the present, as in the animal case, and so really left to chance. If this is thought of as fate, then this instance transforms back into the first.'

25 Three sentences 'In fact, when we are experiencing acute mental suffering... earlier, happier days' and 'Besides' added in B.

26 In A, instead of 'the law of causality': 'the principle of sufficient reason [*Satze des Grundes*]'.

27 'or even just enjoyable for himself. He will ... Many a person has no insight into these matters and will make all sorts of failed attempts' added in C.

28 'accordingly, nothing can give us greater peace of mind ... circumstances, which is fatalism' added in B.

29 'from a dissatisfaction with one's condition' added in B.

30 Two sentences (one in German) 'Plants do not yet have sensibility ... greater development of the intellect' added in C.

31 In A, instead of 'i.e. its essence and its being itself become ... pendulum between pain and boredom': 'because then its essence no longer expresses itself, it is not aware of its existence [*seines Daseyns nicht inne wird*]. So its life wavers back and forth between pain and boredom'.

32 'uncertain about everything except his needs and wants' added in B.

33 Sentence 'At the same time the human being is threatened ... vigilance to escape them' added in B. Next three sentences 'He goes on his way with a cautious step ... Lucretius, II.15' added in C.

34 Two sentences 'What keeps all living things busy ... "to kill time", i.e. to escape boredom' added in B.

35 Sentence 'It makes beings with as little love ... the source of sociability' added in B.

36 'bread and circuses is what the people need' and three sentences 'Philadelphia's strict penitentiary system ... the other six days of the week' added in B.

37 'And again: I was indeed the son of Zeus ... endured unspeakable misery' added in B.

38 Sentence 'Because when there is an actual ... any external occasion' added in B.

39 Two sentences 'This corresponds to the observation that ... as the main worry of the day' added in B.

40 Quotation 'For as long as we do not have ... Lucretius, III, 1095' added in B.

41 The parentheses '(*raja-guna*), (*sattva-guna*), (*tama-guna*)' added in B.

42 Sentence 'They are like mechanical clocks ... beat by beat, with insignificant variations' added in C.

43 'all of which are brought about by chance playing practical jokes' added in C.

44 In A, instead of 'every life history is a history of suffering, because the course of each life is': 'the observer will find that it is'.

45 Three sentences 'The essential content of the world-famous monologue ... not an absolute termination' and 'In the same way' added in C.

46 Sentence 'Accordingly, the much-lamented brevity of life might be the best thing about it' added in B.

47 'torture chambers' and 'and finally let him peer into Ugolino's starvation chamber' added in B.

48 Five sentences 'Where else did *Dante* get the material ... as to the nature of this world' added in B.

49 Sentence 'In vain do they create gods ... sorrows of this world can only come from the world itself' added in C.

50 In A, instead of the sentence 'Most people are pursued through life . . . reflection' and 'On the other hand, the will is often inflamed': 'Much more often the will is inflamed'.

51 Sentence 'This is the act through which . . . perpetuate themselves as such' added in B.

52 In A, instead of 'representative': 'symbol'; and the same again later in the sentence.

53 Paragraph 'It is remarkable that *Clement of Alexandria . . . pure from the world*''' added in C.

54 In A, instead of 'in the natural human being': 'in the purely sensual [*sinnlichen*] human being'; in next sentence, in A, instead of 'as a merely natural being': 'as a merely sensual being'.

55 Two sentences 'Pherecydes said . . . 1852' added in C.

56 'it is this quality that led the Greeks . . . the affirmation of the will' added in B.

57 'overcoming and' added in B.

58 In A, instead of three sentences 'Of course this multiplicity does not affect it . . . anything that opposes them': 'Each of them, considered in itself, is the whole will to life, which appears here at a determinate level of clarity, and expresses its whole essence, with all of its energy and forcefulness, to the degree in which is can become visible here. For this expression it needs only itself immediately, not other individuals outside itself.'

59 In A, instead of 'his own self': 'his own individual'.

60 Sentence 'Everyone views his own death . . . somehow personally involved' added in B.

61 Sentence 'You may compare this exposition . . . § 14' added in B.

62 In A and B, instead of 'and which becomes manifest through the *principium individuationis* . . . In this primordial schism there lies': 'Here there lies'.

63 In A and B: 'is already a degree of the negation of the will to life'. In C: 'is already negation of the will to life'. Hübscher retains the wording of A and B here.

64 Sentence 'Our horror at a murder . . . appearances of the will to life' added in B.

65 'which, to the extent that . . . injury is to murder' added in B.

66 In A and B, instead of 'moral': 'ethical'. There are some two dozen further instances of this substitution in § 62, which are not separately noted here.

67 In A, instead of 'First, in the case of murder, it makes no difference . . . all be reduced to the scenario of me, the wrongdoer': 'Setting aside the cases of murder and injury, this [doing wrong] always comprises me, the wrongdoer'.

68 'which the human race always finds impressive' added in C.

69 'so his triumph rests on the fact that he is credited with an honesty that he does not have' and two sentences 'The deep disgust that perfidy . . . consequences of egoism' added in B.

70 'which is the violent form of lying . . . and their deeds are hardly to be trusted''' added in B.

71 Footnote added in B.

72 In A, instead of 'the self-cognition of the person's own will that grows out of these deeds': 'the cognition of the person's own will that comes out of these deeds'. In B: 'the self-cognition . . . that comes out of these deeds'.

73 In A and B, instead of 'morals': 'ethics [*Ethik*]'. Schopenhauer uses 'morals' [*Moral*] for the philosophical discipline that studies morality and value. There are a dozen more identical substitutions in § 62, which are not separately noted below.

74 Four sentences 'Republics tend towards anarchy . . . its advantage and its strength' added in B and C. 'Until then . . . its advantage and its strength' only in C.

75 Sentence 'Accordingly, the criminal code . . . concretely to cases that occur' added in C.

76 Sentence 'Thus *Aristotle* even said . . . happy and honourable life"' added in B.

77 'just as it was also described . . . "public security should be the first law"' added in B.

78 Five sentences 'And yet it still haunts the writings . . . deter others from the like crimes in all time coming"' added in C. After 'all time coming' in Frauenstädt's edition (1873): 'If a prince wishes to pardon a criminal who has rightly been sentenced, his minister will make the objection that then this crime will soon be repeated' – added on the basis of Schopenhauer's annotation in his copy of C.

79 Sentence 'In our day it has been famously championed by *Feuerbach*' added in B.

80 Sentence 'Even supposing that all this was finally overcome . . . before the imagination' added in B. Footnote added in B.

81 Quotation 'Do you think that crimes fly to the gods . . . Stobaeus, *Eclogues* I, ch. 4' added in B.

82 The passage 'The responsibility for the existence and the condition . . . would certainly vouch for this' added in C, except sentence 'In this sense we can say: the world itself is the world tribunal, the Last Judgement' added in B.

83 In A, Calderon's thought is given only in German. In B, the Spanish is added in a footnote. In C, Spanish text with German in parenthesis. In A, instead of the two sentences, 'And how could it not be an offence . . . original sin in this verse': 'This thought is also the basis for the Christian dogma of original sin.'

84 'of the balancing scale inseparably connecting the evil of the offence with the evil of the punishment' added in C.

85 'and as such is called *Mahavakya*' added in B. Also in A, instead of 'more correctly *tat tvam asi*': 'or *tutwa*'.

86 Sentence 'This is the purpose of religious doctrines . . . untutored human senses' and 'In this sense' added in B.

87 'or Egypt' added in B.

88 'and to understand that they are made . . . pleased about it' added in C.

89 Two sentences 'Our religions will absolutely never take root . . . knowledge and thought' added in B.

90 'oddly enough, contemporary . . . incapable of analysis' added in B.

91 In footnote in A, instead of 'This goes so far that with the monotheistic . . . confusion, and only in consequence': 'only in consequence of this association of thoughts'.

92 In A, instead of 'Given what we have said . . . which is to say that every good is': 'Every good is'.

93 Sentence 'In this sense, the Greek τελος . . . to what we are discussing' added in B.

94 In A, instead of 'this is true *malice* and increases to the point of *cruelty*': 'this is called *cruelty*'.

95 In A, instead of 'malice': 'cruelty'.

96 In A, instead of 'malice': 'cruelty'.

97 Paragraph 'A morality without grounding . . . same essence as in its own' added in C.

98 In A and B, instead of 'morally': 'ethically'. Four other identical substitutions occur in § 66, and are not separately noted below.

99 'to enhance his own well-being' added in B.

100 'i.e. failing to cause harm' added in B.

101 In A, instead of 'not to affirm your own will . . . by forcing them to serve yours': 'not to affirm your own will over and above the appearance of the external body, by negating the appearances of the will in others and willing to force their bodies to serve your will instead of theirs'.

102 In A, instead of the sentence 'Thus, after *Pascal* turned to asceticism . . . p. 19)' and 'Along the very same lines, it is reported that many Hindus': 'This is why many Hindus'.

103 In A, instead of 'loving kindness [*Menschenliebe*]': 'love [*Liebe*]'.

104 In A, instead of 'for malicious people, while unjust people': 'for cruel people, while evil people'.

105 In footnote in A, instead of sentence 'Societies for the Prevention of Cruelty . . . against these activities': 'which is why there are laws [in B: 'laws and associations'] against this in England and North America'. Sentence 'In my opinion . . . the higher animals' and 'On the other hand' added in B.

106 Whole paragraph 'The *good conscience*, the satisfaction we feel . . . bring good or bad luck' added in B.

107 'and thus from all multiplicity' added in B.

108 In A, instead of '*Tat tvam asi!*': 'Tatoumes'.

109 'Leonidas, Regulus' added in B; 'family or' added in B.

110 In A, instead of 'as well as Giordano Bruno': 'as well as Jesus of Nazareth'.

111 Sentence 'Even Spinoza says . . . Scholium)' added in B.

112 Six sentences (five in German): 'This seems to be one of the main reasons . . . and for the reasons we have given' added in B. Footnote added in C.

113 In A, instead of 'beyond individual life': 'beyond the body'.

114 'also in Colebrooke's *Miscellaneous Essays*, vol. I, p. 88.)' added in B.

115 A long passage across three paragraphs 'Indeed, it is a truly remarkable fact, well worth mentioning, . . . Abel Rémusat, p. 233.)' added variously in B and C. 'But an even greater mystic, Meister Eckart . . . make use of them in this life' added in C. Whole paragraph 'Buddhism too does not fail . . . Abel Rémusat, p. 233.)' added in C.

116 'Since he himself negates the will . . . i.e. does him wrong' added in B.

117 Footnote added in B.

118 'and Buddhists' added in C.

119 Sentence 'In general, it is strange to demand . . . the ones he himself possesses' added in C.

120 'Samanas' added in C.

121 Five sentences 'The life of St Francis of Assisi . . . whether it comes from a theistic or atheistic religion' added in C.

122 Sentence 'Besides this, he recounted the life of St Philippo Neri on two different occasions' added in B.

123 In A and B, instead of 'loving kindness [*Menschenliebe*]': 'love [*Liebe*]'.

124 'this last expression meaning just what . . . 14:33)' added in B, except '14:26–27, 14:33)' added in C.

125 'the abuse of the best is the worst of abuses [*abusus optimi pessimus*]' added in C.

126 In A, after 'Augustine': 'whom he mentions, as an Augustinian, only in an honorary capacity [*honoris causa*]'.

127 'nonetheless we did not receive . . . 1851 Stuttgart edition' added in C.

128 Sentence 'Thus, one must get to know it . . . Jewish-Protestant confidence' added in C.

129 Three sentences 'In my opinion, the teachings of these true Christian mystics . . . small and great mysteries' added in C.

130 'love not at all restricted to the human race . . . all living things' added in B.

131 'by throwing yourself over the sacred precipice . . . buried alive in a grave' added in B.

132 Footnote added in B.

133 'while imposing the most difficult sacrifices' added in B.

134 Sentence 'The Christian mystics and the teachers . . . has achieved perfection' added in C.

135 Footnote based on a marginal note by Schopenhauer in his copy of C.

136 In A, instead of 'of increasing difficulty': 'of the greatest sufferings'.

137 'and purity' added in B.

138 Paragraph '*Matthias Claudius* undoubtedly witnessed . . . something certain about it"' added in B.

139 In A and B, instead of 'that of Ramon Llull who had courted a beautiful woman . . . to do penance': 'that of Ramon Llull, which one can read in Tiedemann's *Geist der spekulativen Philosophie* [*Spirit of Speculative Philosophy*], vol. 5, p. 59, and which is remarkable for the strange event that

occasioned it.' Footnote to Brucker added and remainder of paragraph 'This account of conversion . . . ingrained unbelief' also added in C.

140 'it is thus what Asmus has called a transcendental alteration' added in C.

141 Sentence 'This is because negation is not . . . abhorrence of its *pleasures*' added in C.

142 Sentence 'The person who commits suicide negates only the individual, not the species' added in C.

143 In A and B, instead of 'objectivation': 'objecthood [*Objektität*]'.

144 In A, instead of 'ethics': 'ethicists [*Ethiker*]'.

145 Paragraph 'From time to time, everyone hears . . . has arrived at a resolution' added in B.

146 'in the *Histoire de l'académie des sciences* . . . it was not him but rather a relative' added in B.

147 In A, instead of 'This abolition is what Asmus gazed at with wonder . . . it is the very same thing': 'This abolition is the very same thing'.

148 'but just as the church thinks . . . an act of the freedom of the will' added in C.

149 'For what the church calls the *natural man* . . . when we shake off the world' added in C.

150 'the Docetae, i.e.' added in B.

151 Eight sentences 'In his work known as the *opus imperfectum*, . . . is of no concern to us here' added variously in B and C. 'Accordingly, we should always interpret . . . is of no concern to us here' added in C. B has here: 'But contemporary Christianity has forgotten its true meaning and has degenerated into trite optimism.'

152 'in spite of Augustine and Luther . . . the same as contemporary rationalism' added in B.

153 Footnote added in B. A large part of the footnote text 'but the effect of divine grace is our own . . . Only with Bayle do we notice that he notices this' added in C.

154 'This is in agreement with . . . that which is not"' added in B.

155 'since it no longer has a where and a when' added in B.

156 In A, instead of 'Empedocles' old principle': 'the Pythagoreans' old principle'.

157 In A and B, instead of 're-absorption into *Brahman*': 're-absorption into the primal spirit [*den Urgeist*]'.

158 Footnote (absent in A, B, C) based on Schopenhauer's handwritten note in his copy of C.

APPENDIX: CRITIQUE OF THE KANTIAN PHILOSOPHY

1 'or putting them behind them, as people say' added in B. The following sentence 'This encourages others . . . context of modern chemistry' added in C.

2 Paragraph 'However, if we look back . . . so I will take up directly from him' added in B.

3 'by proving that the *intellect* . . . of things as they may be in themselves' added in C.

4 Eleven sentences 'Kant was led down this path by *Locke* . . . and its results were of infinite importance' added in B.

5 In A, instead of 'Philolaus and Aristarchus': 'and other ancient philosophers'.

6 Sentence 'Kant accomplished this by taking apart the whole . . . with admirable dexterity and clarity of mind' added in B.

7 '(Mendelssohn)' added in C.

8 Sentence 'He showed that the laws that govern . . . explaining our own existence or the existence of the world' added in C.

9 Sentence 'You could also say that Kant's doctrine . . . but rather within' added in B.

10 Paragraph 'But all this rests on the fundamental distinction . . . thus that the world can contain nothing but appearances' added in C.

11 In A and B, instead of 'moral': 'ethical'.

12 In footnote in A, instead of 'anyone who reads his principal work . . . through a German edition': 'Anyone who has the rare good fortune to read this, his principal work'.

13 Four sentences 'He dealt the death blow to speculative theology . . . things were as they still are in England' and 'This merit of Kant's is connected to the fact that' added in B.

14 In A, instead of 'in short, this philosophy was dominated by a *realism* . . . reflection' and three sentences '*Berkeley*, like *Malebranche* . . . Before Kant, we were *in* time, now time is in us, etc.', the following passage: 'in short, speaking as if in a dream was entirely dominant in scholasticism, especially the later kind that is called new philosophy. Still, it is not an exclusive characteristic of that philosophy, since the same objection can be made against the philosophemes of the Greeks, with the possible exception of those of the Eleatics and Plato. – Kant put an end to all this once and for all. Fully to gauge the magnitude of this achievement you need to undertake the thankless task of studying the old and new scholasticism that has cropped up in so many forms, particularly at the point at which its stupidity opened out to its fullest extent, in the Leibniz–Wolffian philosophy.'

15 'realistic' added in B.

16 Six sentences '"Perfect" is practically synonymous with "numerically complete" . . . indicates a mere relation in the abstract' added in C.

17 In A, instead of 'the whole philosophical enterprise to date': 'Scholasticism'.

18 Long paragraph 'To begin with, we want to scrutinize and make clear to ourselves the fundamental thought . . . how he goes about this as well as the details of the project' added in B.

19 In A, instead of 'Kant's style throughout . . . profundity of the thought; but': 'Kant's mode of presentation, although it bears the mark of genuine, solid individuality, and a quite extraordinary intellectual prowess, is nonetheless often unclear, indeterminate, inadequate'.

20 Sentence '"The better we understand an issue . . . Descartes in his fifth letter' added in C.

21 Six sentences (including Goethe quotation): 'But the greatest problem with Kant's occasionally obscure delivery . . . But let us turn back to *Kant*' added in B.

22 Footnote here added in B. But 'which completely contradicts Descartes' rule, cited above' added in C.

23 In A, the page reference here is simply 'p. 24'. Schopenhauer had not seen the first edition of the *Critique of Pure Reason* when A was published. Many subsequent references to the *Critique* were similarly altered in B, and are not noted separately below.

24 In A and B, instead of 'transcendental': 'metaphysical'.

25 In A and B, the reference is to '(introductory essay [*FR*, first edition], §§ 33, 24, 35)'.

26 In A, instead of 'But it is remarkable that': 'But it is very strange, and must be seen as his first mistake, that'.

27 In A, instead of a long passage across four paragraphs: 'In my first edition I explained Kant's avoidance of this Berkeleyan proposition . . . If he had clearly distinguished intuitive representations from concepts thought merely in abstract', the following passage: 'Thus, instead of making that proposition [No subject without object] the basis of his claims and showing the object *simply as such* to be immediately dependent on the subject, instead of moving towards his goal along this wide, straight road that lies before him, Kant turns on to a side route. That is, he makes the object dependent on the subject not through its being cognized as such and in general, but through the mode and manner of its being cognized. He shows laboriously how the subject anticipates all the object's modes of appearance, thus taking all of the *how* of appearance out of it, and leaving the object with only a completely obscure *what*. – This way of presenting things does have the particular, and great, merit of describing the boundary between subject and object, which is common to them both and can therefore be discovered equally by starting from the realm of the subject or from that of the object. But it also has a great disadvantage, which we shall examine next.

Kant chose this indirect procedure and was not decisive enough to say "No object without subject: this visible world is as such *representation*, as such dependent on the subject, and its laws will never reveal anything about that which is *not* representation and *not* dependent" – that he did not do this arose indisputably from the fact that he shrank from the accusation of idealism, and in his own mind rejected idealism as a view that would make the world into a mere play of shadows and leave no thing in itself remaining. By being careful and mindful of saving the thing in itself too early, he brought it about that instead of the thing itself he got only a wretched changeling which later brought him many inconveniences. If instead, when dealing with representation as such, he had abandoned the thing in itself to its fate, afterwards it would have found itself on its own by a completely different route, as will. His neglect of the direct procedure for showing the thoroughgoing dependence of the object on the subject, and his adoption of the indirect procedure, has a strange similarity with the practice he observes when proving the *a priori* status of the law of causality. In that case, instead of proving the point immediately as a condition of the possibility of all experience from the fact that all empirical intuition makes an immediate inference from the effect to the cause, he wants to show it by a side route, laboriously and pointlessly to boot, from the possibility of real succession. On this see the introductory essay [i.e. *FR*, first edition], § 24. – In the course of his investigation Kant rightly has no hesitation in saying: "All objects of an experience possible for us are mere representations, which, as they are represented, have no existence grounded in itself (*Critique of Pure Reason*, p. 519). [= B 518–19: all following references are to the B edition of the *Critique*, the only version Schopenhauer had access to at time of writing.] – "The objects of experience do not exist at all outside it. . . . In themselves, appearances, as mere representations, are real only in perception, which in fact is nothing but the reality of an empirical representation" (ibid., p. 521). – "Because the world does not exist at all in itself (independently of the regressive series of my representations)" (p. 533). – "Appearances as such are nothing outside our representations" (p. 535) – And for all that he was unable to make the straightforward and free decision to place the proposition "No object without subject" at the head of his philosophy, as consistency would have demanded, but took that arduous and misleading side route. This once again corroborates my accusation above that he lacked great simplicity and naïve candour: he prefers what is knotted, crooked, convoluted to what is simple and straight, and to great masses. The disadvantage of his procedure in this chief respect arises from the following. In the single proposition "No object without subject" the whole of the main content of the critical philosophy is present at *one* stroke. With that, all possible objects as such are already entirely dependent on the subject, and so are not things in themselves, but strictly just things for the subject, *representations*. And in fact this applies not only to things in space and time, but to any objects that are so much as possible, since they are always only for the subject, i.e. are only representations. Hence if there is to be a thing in itself – i.e. if the world is to be anything else besides *mere representation* – then this in-itself of the world must be something of an entirely different kind [toto genere *Verschiedenes*] from representation. But we cannot infer what it is by applying the laws for connecting representations (principle of sufficient reason). Rather we retrieve it immediately from our consciousness of our self [*Selbst*], which is also partly representation, an appearance among appearances and part of nature, but which on the other hand reveals itself immediately to consciousness not at all as representation, but rather as something entirely different in kind from representation, namely as *will*. And the *will* is the in-itself of the world, as I hope has been sufficiently shown in the present work. – However, by not taking this direct route, not showing the object as such as dependent on the subject, but instead laboriously making only the mode and manner of being an object dependent on the subject's mode of cognition, Kant obtains merely the result that things in themselves are not as we cognize them, but he still retains an *object*, a *representation*, a *noumenon*, as thing in itself. This is not sufficient, because no object is unconditioned, nor can it be a thing in itself, since it always presupposes the subject. But to make matters worse he reaches this noumenon as thing in itself simply by way of a crude inconsistency, by applying the principle of sufficient reason beyond appearance, an application that he himself has quite rightly forbidden. He later suffered attacks because of this that could never be rebutted, and his philosophy remained stuck in an internal contradiction. – His discoveries that the forms of all appearance are already present *a priori* in consciousness have great value in themselves and would have been an excellent achievement as an implementation of and accompaniment to the main proposition "No object without subject", and that is how I would like them to be regarded.

If Kant had made this main proposition his point of departure, he would hardly have ended up making the great error that we touched on above, of not separating intuition and concept, which resulted in a fatal confusion which we must now examine. The proposition "No object without subject" could easily have led him either to separate objects according to universal classes, or at least to make a sharp division between all intuitive representations and concepts that are merely thought abstractly'.

28 'or else the good will' added in B.

29 Sentence 'Its proofs are so persuasive . . . great discovery in metaphysics' added in B.

30 Five sentences 'Kant provided rigorous proof that . . . and thus to a certain extent synonymous' added in C.

31 After 'First Book of the present text', a paragraph in A: 'We can regard the Transcendental Aesthetic as the self-contained examination of what I presented in the introductory essay [*FR*] as the third class of representations. Would that Kant had also examined the other three classes in the same separate manner, and accordingly made a clean distinction between intuition and concept – and finally, when he explains (pp. 152–3) that we have cognition of ourselves only as appearance, would that he had made this clear by saying that the cognition we have of ourselves apart from intuition of our body, which he calls cognition through *inner sense*, is nothing other than the cognition of our individual willing, which is the will to life itself revealing itself not immediately, but only in acts of will, and hence in time. Then he would not have needed the expression "inner sense" either, an expression that is an utterly redundant and unprovable assumption, and in fact really contains a contradiction. G. E. Schulze (*Critique of Theoretical Philosophy* [*Kr(itik) d(er) theor(etischen) Phil(osophie)*], vol. 2, p. 643) had already quite rightly criticized this assumption of an inner sense, which since then has become very much in favour, and called for it to be abandoned. Yet the assumption was not made first by *Locke*, as Schulze thinks; rather, it is very old, perhaps first introduced by the Church Father Augustine, who sets out and explains inner sense in his book *On the Free Choice of the Will* [*de libero arbitrio*], II, 8. There is even

something similar that should be interpreted in this sense already in Aristotle's *On the soul* [*de anima*] III, 2.'

32 In A, instead of the long passage over two paragraphs: 'At the very beginning of this section (*Critique of Pure Reason*, p. 50/V 74) . . . The complete confusion of intuitive representation with abstract representation runs through the whole theory and creates a sort of intermediate between the two': 'In this section we find properly revealed the big mistake that I am concerned to criticize, the complete confusion of intuitive representation with abstract representation to create a sort of intermediate between the two.' The sentence 'I have presented this process in detail . . . § 21' added in C.

33 In A, instead of 'fourth edition, p. 247 (Rosenkranz edition p. 281)': 'p. 247'. A predates the Rosenkranz edition of Kant, as Schopenhauer makes clear in the text above. (For the Kantian passage see Ak. 5: 137.)

34 In A, the reference here is 'In the introductory essay [*FR*, first edition], § 24'.

35 In A, instead of 'contradictions': 'glaring contradictions'. In next sentence, instead of 'contradiction': 'monstrous contradiction'.

36 Sentence '"Only through intuition is the object given . . . p. 399)' added in C.

37 Long passage across two paragraphs 'This is made particularly clear in a passage on p. 125 of the fifth edition . . . His disciples on the other hand set off with foolhardy assurance, and thus make its falsity obvious' added in B.

38 In A, instead of 'Given what we have said, Kant does not really . . . but rather its nearest relation': 'This object, if not really the Kantian thing in itself, is rather its nearest relation'.

39 'the possibility of' added in C.

40 In B, instead of '§ 23': '§ 24'.

41 In A, instead of long passage across the three paragraphs 'So Kant actually makes a three-way distinction: (1) representation; (2) the object of representation; (3) the thing in itself. . . . I, on the other hand, say: objects exist in the first instance for intuition alone, and concepts are always abstractions from this intuition', the following shorter passage: 'On the other hand, if we give a general summary of Kant's purest pronouncements about it, the *thing in itself* proper is that which appears in space and time and all the forms of cognition, i.e. the thing whose becoming-visible [*Sichtbarwerden*] these appearances are, but which in itself is not subordinate to those forms. Construed in that way it leads by itself to something that is definitely not object or representation, but which makes up the essence of the world in so far as it is *not* representation. This, according to my account, is the *will*. Kant's thing in itself too, when construed in this pure and general manner, as that to which all *plurality* must be alien (because it is outside space and time), but which determines the particular essence of every thing, also takes us quite close to Plato's Ideas. These we have recognized as the different levels of the will's adequate objecthood [*Objektität*], as extensively discussed in our Second and Third Books. – Only Kant did not get so far with his presentation of the thing in itself, and this significance that it has can only have been at the basis his thoughts in an

unclear fashion, and it never came clearly into his consciousness. In most places he makes an inference to the thing in itself as the cause of appearance, applying the principle of sufficient reason in a way he himself forbids as transcendent. And then it coincides with that unhappy *object in itself,* that absurdity [*Unding*] that the understanding is supposed to add in thought to intuition so that it can become experience. It was this that hovered before him in his Deduction of the Categories, and all the contradictions that I have demonstrated in the Transcendental Logic arise out of this absurdity. It was also this absurdity that prevented him from reaching the clear recognition that every object exists only in relation to the subject, is a representation of the subject and is in any case either an intuition or an abstract, non-intuitive concept. Hence the complete confusion of these two things and the related contradictions we have demonstrated. These contradictions are accompanied by the following inference that flows from the same confusion: that if (according to p. 143) even empirical intuition comes to consciousness only through the categories of the understanding, but the understanding is supposed to be the faculty of *thinking,* then necessarily either animals think or they do not even have intuition. However, on the other hand, from the conflicting claim that occurs just as often – that intuition is *given* and the understanding with its categories contributes nothing to it – we can conclude that the categories are a redundant, baseless and empty hypostasis. For in that case the world of intuition stands there fully complete, independently of the understanding, and only abstract thinking is left over for the categories. But then abstract thinking must necessarily take its guidance from the world of intuition, not the other way round, as we are so often told in spite of this. Only if the world of *intuition* came into existence through the application of the categories would Kant be justified in saying that nature is guided by the understanding and its laws. But if the whole world of intuition is *given* as fully complete without the assistance of the understanding, then it must be the other way round, and thinking must be guided by experience. Then the understanding can have none of its concepts *a priori,* because otherwise it would not be in agreement with nature, unless we assume a pre-established harmony [*harmonia praestabilita*] between understanding and nature – an assumption as redundant as it is baseless, because it is simpler, and certain from everyone's inner experience, that abstract concepts come into existence in accordance with the world of intuition, by means of reflection. So once again the contradiction becomes apparent in Kant's assertions that it is the categories that determine nature, or experience, and yet that the understanding is not supposed to contribute anything to intuition. –'

42 In B, instead of '§ 28': '§ 29'.
43 Sentence 'Accordingly, I ask that we throw away eleven of the categories. . . from the thing in itself' and two whole paragraphs 'After repeated study of the *Critique of Pure Reason* . . . the categories and their schemata' added in B.
44 'Platonic' added in B.

45 In A, instead of three sentences 'If we summarize Kant's claims . . . I refer to that here, so as not to repeat myself': 'In addition Kant unfortunately never wanted to admit this truth clearly to himself. – Anyone who is not, shall we say, firmly resolved to find an almost bottomless profundity in that proposition [The "I think" must be able to accompany all my representations], will agree with me that the real sense of the proposition, or rather what prompts it, is that consciousness of the individual unity of the person accompanies all the person's cognitions, in that their succession depends upon it. Thus in so far as such succession is determined by the position of the person in the world, that individual unity is as it were the thread on which the successive perceptions row themselves up like pearls in a string and are held together and united into one single string. – At the same time it will be recalled from the Third Book of this work that we should regard this admixture of the consciousness of the person into cognition as a contamination [*Verunreinigung*] of cognition by the will, whose concretization [*Konkrescenz*] and appearance the person is. Hence cognition relates to the person only as long as it is in the service of the will, something that must end if there is to be aesthetic cognition, in which alone all is completely well with us. Then, in aesthetic cognition, i.e. cognition that is pure and free of the will, consciousness of personality disappears, recedes entirely, and in the process the individual who is having this kind of cognition is transfigured into the pure subject of cognition and the object that is intuited in this way is transfigured at the same time into its Idea. As expounded in that passage.'

46 'and regard it as one of the baseless . . . theory of cognition' added in B.

47 'and the supplemental materials . . . § 21, 26' added in B; 'and 34' added in C.

48 Sentence 'That is why philosophy for him is . . . and formulated in universal concepts' added in B.

49 Sentence 'Categorical judgements have . . . metalogical principle' added in B.

50 In A and B, instead of '§§ 30–3': '§§ 32–35'.

51 In A, instead of '§ 4, and more clearly in the essay . . . p. 77': 'pp. 11–16'. In B: '§ 4 (first edition, pp. 11–16)'.

52 In A, instead of 'and vice versa. Thus the true, logical analogy . . . I now want to show that there is no such thing as reciprocal causation in the true sense of the term': 'Moreover, I now want to show that there is no such thing as reciprocal causation'.

53 In A, instead of '§ 20, and also in my prize essay . . . our second volume': '§ 23'. In B: '§ 23, which I shall not repeat here'.

54 Six sentences 'A good example of what people generally call . . . different from simple causality' added in B.

55 'a collision for instance' added in B.

56 'and velocity' added in B.

57 Three sentences 'But this is the very position Kant thoughtlessly expounds . . . everything in the world would happen at once' added in B.

58 Sentence 'If there were true reciprocal causation . . . a form for such a thing' added in C.

59 Sentence 'As for the rest . . . *Sufficient Reason*' added in C.

60 In A, instead of '*contingens*': '*accidens*'.

61 Sentence 'All this is ultimately based . . . cognition has to them' added in B.

62 'for reflection' added in C.

63 In footnote in A and B, the final reference is 'Compare introductory essay, § 55 [i.e. of *FR*, first edition]'.

64 Three sentences 'Incidentally, this whole incorrect explanation . . . relative and conditioned' added in C.

65 In A and B, instead of eight sentences (six in German) 'In fact, the difference between necessity, actuality and possibility . . . and is called contingent' and 'This consideration also gives us the key': 'And this is the occasion of, and the key'.

66 Long passage 'We can explain this to ourselves in the following way . . . as subjective as the optical horizon where the sky meets the earth' added in B.

67 Paragraph 'Kant himself reveals that he is conscious . . . stands on unstable legs' added in B.

68 In A, instead of 'These have their origins partly in Aristotle's . . . but were chosen arbitrarily': 'But these were chosen arbitrarily'.

69 Six sentences (three in German): 'Rather, the former is based on the fact . . . already occupied by substance' added in B.

70 Sentence 'Then the four cosmological ideas . . . when we examine these antinomies' added in C.

71 In A and B, the reference here is 'in the introductory essay [*FR*, first edition], § 19'.

72 In A, instead of the longer passage 'Kant's proof is untenable, however much he defended it with sophisms . . . *unification of space and time*': 'Kant's proof is untenable, however much he defended it with sophisms. Yet the permanence of substance is by all means cognized *a priori* and as necessary, but this cognition first enters consciousness immediately and intuitively: it can be raised to mediate, abstract, reflective cognition only by deriving it from the truth expounded in the aforementioned passage of our First Book, that the essence of *matter* consists in the complete *unification of space and time*'.

73 In A, after '*duration*': 'the principle can be developed negatively from the law of causality that is known to us *a priori*, and whose validity we extend only to states, never to matter'.

74 In A and B, the reference here is to '§ 24' [of *FR*, first edition].

75 Sentence 'There are quite a few more details . . . think these over on their own' added in B.

76 In A, instead of 'leads him in the chapter . . . (as I will now discuss in greater depth)': 'leads him on pp. 309 and 314'.

77 In A, instead of 'from which they are abstracted . . . Accordingly, if concepts are deprived of their foundation in intuition, they are empty and unreal': 'they are only the representation of the latter, their reflection'.

78 In A, after 'the basis of cognition', the sentence: 'That fatal confusion of thinking and intuition stands out really glaringly in the proposition (p. 324

[i.e. B 324]): "that a concept has its *place* either in *sensibility* or in pure *understanding*." Schopenhauer's version is, however, a loose and misleading paraphrase of the passage in Kant's text.

79 'its intuitive nature is lost' added in C.

80 Paragraph 'But thought and intuition are certainly kept more distinct...added to the object by thought itself' and part of the next paragraph 'The whole chapter on the amphiboly... Spinoza and Locke' added in B.

81 In A, instead of the sentence 'The chapter on the amphiboly of reflection... categories nonetheless apply': 'Thought and intuition are kept more distinct than anywhere else in the chapter on the Amphiboly of the Concepts of Reflection, where it is ultimately claimed that there could possibly be a type of intuition that is completely different from our own, but one to which our categories nonetheless apply.'

82 In A, after 'or the nature of reason': 'After giving an extensive treatment to the categories and what follows from them, he patches in between them and intuition that additional absurdity, the schemata of the pure concepts of the understanding – which no human being can think of as anything determinate, and whose impossibility I have discussed sufficiently in the introductory essay [i.e. *FR* first edition], § 29.'

83 Whole section 'After having to reject Kant's doctrine of the categories just as he himself rejected that of Aristotle... forms of thought themselves' added in B, except sentence 'Grammar is to logic as clothing is to the body' added in C. Final note 'As a cautionary... according to logical rules alone' added in C.

84 Two sentences 'It is the proposition that Christian Wolff... philosophemes of Wolff' added in B.

85 'The apparent truth of this proposition is most obvious... But we want to test this proposition against itself, not against images' added in B, except sentence 'Or more concisely... it would find this convenient' added in C.

86 'all of which must come together before the effect appears' added in B.

87 Eight sentences 'And in fact all the talk about the Absolute... Judaism should not be identified with reason' added in B.

88 In A and B the reference here is to '§ 55 of the introductory essay [*FR*, first edition]'.

89 Sentence 'Kant even tried to ground... p. 322/V 379' added in B.

90 In A, instead of 'all philosophy that has arisen... up through Christian Wolff': 'Scholastic philosophy, the name that can be given, as we have said, to all European philosophy from the Church Father Augustine onwards, up through Christian Wolff'.

91 'as a product characteristic of its essence' added in C. In A here: 'which one could be inclined to deny precisely because it would lessen the value of the revelation, making it redundant'.

92 The passage 'by quite falsely translating the Hindu Brahma and the Chinese Tian as "God"' and twelve sentences 'We could see if it is not rather... a man

and not a woman' added partly in B and partly in C. 'This, by the way, is an exceptionally naïve . . . settle down in Oxford', 'the religion with the greatest number of adherents on earth', and 'and in fact detests it' added in C. Eight sentences (six in German) 'As far as Plato is concerned . . . a man and not a woman' added in C.

93 Sentence 'Accordingly, these Kantian "ideas of reason" . . . a thing without reality' added in C.

94 Sentence 'But since a couple of years . . . meaning' added in B, with 'Platonic' added in C.

95 In A, instead of long passage starting in previous paragraph 'If the concept of the soul really did originate . . . in fact to the subject of cognition and of willing': 'By contrast, in an unprejudiced investigation into the origin of this concept it will be found that, like all the transcendent concepts that Kant calls ideas, it only arises by applying the principle of sufficient reason, the form of all objects, to something that is not an object, and in fact to the subject of cognition and of willing.' Two sentences 'Retaining Kant's expression . . . refusal not to see it' added in C. Two sentences 'The opposition that led to the assumption . . . apply to bodies' added in C.

96 'and in addition to all this . . . prejudices in these matters' added in B.

97 'since it can only choose between a conception of the world as infinitely large or infinitely small' added in B.

98 'The philosophers of antiquity already saw this . . . infinitely many worlds"' added in C.

99 Four sentences 'With the assumption of a world bounded . . . with regard to this antinomy' added in B.

100 'What is in fact tacitly assumed here . . . space made perceptible' added in B; but in B, instead of 'and were pieced together in order to create the whole . . . with respect to what precedes [*a parte ante*]': 'something that can, however, no more be asserted than its opposite'.

101 'the proof of the first proposition of Mechanics . . . fourth proposition of Dynamics' added in B.

102 Three sentences 'Atoms are not a necessary idea of reason . . . *Physics*, IV, 9' added in B.

103 'and accordingly the presupposition of a first beginning' and 'any more than the presence of the present moment presupposes a beginning of time itself' added in C.

104 Two sentences 'I certainly do not need to prove . . . argument of the antithesis' added in B.

105 Paragraph 'It cannot be denied . . . Lichtenberg's broadside' added in B, except that the opening 'It cannot be denied that the antinomy has a certain plausibility: nonetheless' is added in C.

106 Paragraph 'Aristotle already subscribed . . . and independent of regress' added in B.

107 In A, instead of eight sentences 'This is really the point where Kant's philosophy leads to my own . . . is shown in my work': 'But Kant, though he by no

means starts from this idea [*Vorstellung*] is nonetheless brought near to the truth in a strange way.'

108 Five sentences 'We certainly do apply the law of causality . . . This is the path I have taken' added in B.

109 Paragraph 'The same thing that happened . . . in an entirely different manner' added in B.

110 In A, after 'Church authors': 'to the extent that they explain the will as necessarily subject to sin because of a depravity that extends from the first human being to all the rest, as free only to do evil, not to do good, and as quite powerless on its own to make justification and recompense; and they hold the freedom of the will to consist only in the freedom to sin (thus Luther and Melanchthon) and hope for redemption only through faith and grace: all of which we have examined sufficiently at the conclusion of the Fourth Book.'

111 'I refer to my prize essay on the *Freedom of the Will* on this point' added in B.

112 Sentence 'There is evidence for this . . . p. 677 of the supplements' added in B.

113 In A, instead of 'necessitated': 'conditioned and determined'.

114 In A, after 'from a causal relation': 'and indeed it can really be called a relation only metaphorically [*gleichnißweise*]'.

115 Four sentences (three in German) 'In order to deduce it, Kant seized . . . met with general acclaim' added in B.

116 'Even Christian Wolff says . . . from this visible world to God"' added in B. 'And Leibniz before him had already said . . . proven without this great principle"' added in C.

117 In A and B, instead of 'specimen [*Musterstück*]': 'masterpiece [*Meisterstück*]', evidently a printing error.

118 'although only as something . . . a demiurge' added in B.

119 'Indeed, Sextus Empiricus . . . and this would be God' added in C.

120 'enduring' added in C.

121 Three sentences 'He eliminated theism from philosophy . . . with fervent enthusiasm' added in C.

122 Four sentences 'We can note further that, just as . . . would have time to get away' added in B, except 'consciousnesses of God' and 'knowing the danger of the business' added in B.

123 In A, instead of '*Critique of Judgement*': '*Critique of Teleological Judgement*'.

124 Two paragraphs 'Kant, as I said, was only concerned . . . profound explanations of existence' and previous sentence 'With this in mind, I refer my reader to the heading: "Comparative Anatomy" in my work *On the Will in Nature*' added in B. But sentence 'In every human endeavour . . . for ourselves' added in C; in B, instead of 'an extravagantly purposive order': 'a purposive order'; '(the "mob")' added in C; 'even with their most famous scholars' and seven sentences 'Just look at R. Owen . . . they stick to spinning-wheel philosophy' added in C. And in the footnote beginning 'Kant said', in B Schopenhauer refrains from citing Professor Bachmann by name or citing his article.

125 In A, section ends at 'investigations into nature'. 'To test this with an example, just think . . . cognition of nature"' added in B; paragraph 'It is certainly not the least . . . not to write anymore' added in C.

126 In A, instead of paragraph 'I could perhaps forgo a critique . . . refer the reader': 'I now move on to the ethical part of the Kantian philosophy. Here it will not be necessary to go into the same degree of detail as above by following the guidance of his writings, partly because Kant's ethics can be reduced [*sich zurückführen läßt*] to a few principles, partly because the *Critique of Practical Reason* is an incomparably weaker work than his critique of theoretical reason. It was written at a time when Kant's mind was already starting to bear the traces of ageing that sadly are so strongly in evidence in his even later works. So in my negative presentation here I can be much briefer, referring back to the positive presentation, i.e. the ethical part of this present work of mine: "for the true is the index of itself and of what is false" [*est enim verum index sui et falsi*]'. In B, instead of 'twenty-two years after this one': 'three years ago'.

127 In A, instead of '(*De anima*, III, 10 . . . both practical and theoretical")': '(*De anima*, III, 6)'.

128 In A, instead of 'whose life is set up as a model for all virtue': 'who after a life entirely without blemish, full of renunciation and full of the highest loving kindness, set the seal on his teachings and intensified them by freely undergoing a wretched, torturous death'.

129 In A, instead of 'the Princess Isabella, the daughter of Philip II': 'that Spanish princess'; 'for three years' added in C.

130 Paragraph 'In keeping with what we have said . . . instrument of all crimes' added in B, except 'In accordance with this, *Stobaeus* . . . the ethical virtues' added in C.

131 'which, according to Cicero . . . *providentia*' added in B.

132 '"I know what is best and approve of it, but the worse is what I do" or' added in B.

133 Sentence 'Cicero uses *admirari* . . . II, 2' added in C; sentence 'What Horace means . . . pp. 98 and 105)' added in B.

134 Five sentences (four in German) 'Our ancestors did not create . . . consciousness, truth, etc.' added in B.

135 Sentence 'What people right before Kant . . . Reason and Language"' added in B.

136 'apprehensions' added in C.

137 In A, instead of 'Even more, Christianity . . . that is to be practised': 'Then Christianity proper also teaches a completely unselfish virtue that, according to the teachings of the purest and most genuine Christians, e.g. Luther, is to be practised'.

138 In A and B, instead of 'moral': 'ethical'.

139 'and then correctly apply the latter to the former' added in B.

140 Nine sentences 'Because things are given to our intellect from the outside . . . Berlin edition, p. 354)' added in B.

141 Two sentences (one in German) 'If you consider how plausible . . . as objective truth' added in B.

142 'and its supplements and particularly my work *On the Will in Nature*' added in B.

143 Paragraph 'The reader who is interested . . . together in a single place' added in C.

Glossary of names

ACHILLES, Greek mythological hero

ADAM, figure from the Hebrew Bible, first man

AGAMEMNON, Greek mythological hero, son of Atreus

AGRIPPA VON NETTESHEIM, Heinrich Cornelius (1486–1535), author, jurist, philosopher, physician and alchemist from Cologne

AHRIMAN, Middle Persian equivalent of Angra Mainyu, Zoroastrian evil spirit

AJAX, Greek mythological figure, son of Telamon and hero in Trojan War

ALBERTUS MAGNUS, SAINT (c.1200–80), Dominican bishop, German philosopher and theologian, applied Aristotle to Christian thought

ALCIATUS, ANDREAS (Alciati, Andrea) (1492–1550), Italian humanist

ALCINOUS, (second century), Middle Platonist philosopher

ALFIERI, COUNT VITTORIO (1749–1803), Italian dramatist, considered the founder of Italian tragedy

ANACREON (570–488 BC), Greek lyric poet

ANAXAGORAS (c.500–428 BC), pre-Socratic Greek philosopher

ANGELUS SILESIUS (Johannes Scheffler) (1624–77), German mystic and poet

ANQUETIL-DUPERRON, ABRAHAM HYACINTHE (1731–1805), orientalist, translator and editor of *Oupnek'hat*, a translation of the *Upanishads* into Latin (from Persian), a book which Schopenhauer acquired in 1813, and later referred to as the 'consolation of his life'

ANSELM OF CANTERBURY, SAINT (1033–1109), philosopher, theologian and Archbishop of Canterbury

ANTINOUS (110 or 111–30), famously beautiful Greek youth loved and deified by Roman Emperor Hadrian

ANTISTHENES (445–365 BC), Greek philosopher, student of Socrates, founder of Cynicism

APOLLO, Greek god of arts and sciences

APPELLES (Apelles) (mid-second century), theologian

ARISTARCHUS of SAMOS (310–230 BC), Greek astronomer and mathematician who argued that the sun not the earth was the centre of the universe

ARISTOPHANES (446–386 BC), Greek comic playwright

ARISTOTLE (384–322 BC), the great and immensely influential Greek philosopher

ARJUNA, hero in the Hindu epic *Mahābhārata* and the *Bhagavadgītā*

ARNAULD, ANTOINE (1612–94), French theologian, philosopher, mathematician

ASMUS (see CLAUDIUS, MATTHIAS)

ATE, Greek mythological figure, personification of the folly or ruinous actions of human beings

AUGUSTINE, SAINT (353–430), Church Father, Bishop of Hippo

BACCHUS (Dionysus), Graeco-Roman god of wine and madness

BACHMANN, Karl Friedrich (1785–1855), Professor in Jena, Hegelian

BACON [of Veralum], LORD FRANCIS (1591–1626), English philosopher, statesman, scientist, lawyer

BAUMGARTEN, ALEXANDER (1714–62), German philosopher and originator of the study of philosophical aesthetics

BAYLE, PIERRE (1647–1706), French writer of the Enlightenment, author of *Dictionnaire Historique et Critique* (*Historical and Critical Dictionary*)

BEATRICE (see PORTINARI, BEATRICE)

BEAUFORT, CARDINAL, character (Bishop of Winchester) in Shakespeare's *King Henry VI part II*

BELL, CHARLES (1774–1842), Scottish surgeon and anatomist, one of the founders of clinical neurology

BELLORI, GIAN PIETRO (1613–96), Roman biographer of seventeenth-century Italian Baroque artists

BERG, FRANZ (1753–1821), professor of theology at Würzburg, opponent of Schelling

BERKELEY, GEORGE (1685–1753), Bishop, Irish philosopher and proponent of idealism

BODHISATTVA, term meaning 'enlightened being' or 'wisdom-being', usually refers to the Buddha himself

BÖHME, JACOB (1575–1624), Lutheran mystic and theosophist born in Silesia

BONAVENTURA OF BAGNOREIGIO, SAINT (Giovanni Fidanza) (1221–74), scholastic philosopher, theologian and mystic

BOUTERWECK, FRIEDRICH (1766–1828), German aesthetician, professor of philosophy at Göttingen

BRAHMA, Hindu god of creation, one of the Trimurti

BRIGHELLA, stock comic character from Commedia dell'arte

BRUCKER, JOHANN JAKOB (1696–1770), German pastor and historian of philosophy

BRUNO, GIORDANO (1548–1600), Italian philosopher of nature, burned to death as a heretic

BUDDHA (Siddārtha Gautama) (sixth-fifth century BC), historical founder of the Buddhist religion

BUFFON, GEORGE-LOUIS LECLERC, COMTE DE (1707–88), French naturalist, progenitor of the concept of natural selection

BUHLE, JOHANN GOTTLIEB (1763–1821), German historian of philosophy

BURKE, SIR EDMUND (1729–97), Irish statesman and philosopher

BYRON, LORD GEORGE GORDON (1788–1824), British Romantic poet

CABANIS, PIERRE JEAN GEORGES (1757–1808), French physiologist, proponent of materialist view of consciousness

CALCHAS, Greek mythological prophet

CALDERÓN DE LA BARCA, DON PEDRO (1600–81), Spanish dramatist

CALIBAN, character in Shakespeare's *The Tempest*

CAMERARIUS, JOACHIM (1534–98), physician and botanist

CARRACCI, ANNIBALE (1560–1609), Italian Baroque painter

CASSANDRA, Greek mythological prophet

CECILIA, SAINT, patron saint of musicians

CELLINI, BENVENUTO (1500–71), Italian Renaissance artist, musician and auto-biographer

CERVANTES, MIGUEL DE (MIGUEL DE CERVANTES SAAVEDRA) (1547–1616), Spanish novelist, poet and playwright, author of *Don Quixote*

CHAMPOLLION, JEAN-FRANÇOIS (1790–1832), French classical scholar, philologist and orientalist who first deciphered the Egyptian hieroglyphs by translating parts of the Rosetta Stone

CHATIN, ADOLPHE GASPARD (1813–1901), French physician and botanist

CHAVIN DE MALLAN, biographer of Saint Francis of Assisi

CHLADNI, ERNST (1756–1827), German physicist and musician

CHRISTINA, QUEEN OF SWEDEN (1626–89), reigned from 1632 to 1654

CHRYSIPPUS (*c.*280–*c.*206 BC), Greek philosopher, head of the early Stoic school in Athens

CICERO, MARCUS TULLIUS (106–43 BC), pre-eminent Roman statesman and orator, who composed the first substantial body of philosophical work in Latin

CLARKE, SAMUEL (1675–1729), English philosopher

CLAUDIUS, MATTHIAS (pen-name Asmus) (1740–1815), German poet

CLEANTHES (330–230 BC), Stoic philosopher and head of the Stoic school in Athens

CLEMENT OF ALEXANDRIA (*c.*150–215), Christian Platonist philosopher

CODRUS (*c.*1089–1068 BC), last King of Athens, sacrificed himself to save the city

COLEBROOKE, HENRY THOMAS (1765–1837), English Indologist, translator of the *Upanishads*

COLUMBINE, stock comic character of a female servant from Commedia dell'arte

COPERNICUS, NICOLAUS (1473–1543), Polish astronomer whose theories revolutionized the study of the solar system

CORDELIA, character in Shakespeare's *King Lear*

CORIOLANUS, GAIUS MARCIUS, fifth-century BC Roman general

CORNEILLE, PIERRE (1606–84), French dramatist, one of the founders of French tragedy

CORREGGIO, ANTONIO ALLEGRI DA (1489–1534), Italian painter

CREON, Greek mythological king of Thebes, character in Sophocles' *Oedipus Rex* and *Antigone*

CUVIER, BARON FRÉDÉRIC VON (1769–1832), French naturalist and zoologist, helped establish the field of comparative anatomy

CYNICS, philosophical movement in Greece from mid-fourth century BC

DANAIDS, in Greek mythology, the fifty daughters of Danaus, forty-nine of whom murdered their husbands on their wedding night and were punished in the underworld by endlessly carrying water in a leaking sieve

DANTE, ALIGHIERI (1265–1321), Italian poet, author of the great trilogy *La Divina Commedia* (*The Divine Comedy*)

DAPHNE, Greek mythological figure of a nymph who is transformed into a laurel

DECIUS MUS, PUBLIUS, three Romans of the same name, legendary for sacrificing themselves for their city

DEMOCRITUS (*c.*460–370 BC), pre-Socratic philosopher, believed that matter is not infinitely divisible and named its smallest part 'atom'

DENNER, BALTHASAR (1685–1749), German late Baroque portrait painter

DESCARTES, RENÉ (1596–1650), French philosopher, important early modern rationalist philosopher who maintained a dualism between mind and body

DESDEMONA, character in Shakespeare's *Othello*

DEYS, rulers of Algiers and Tunisia under the Ottoman Empire (1671–1830)

DIOGENES LAERTIUS (between 200 and 500), Athenian historian of ancient philosophy, whose work *Lives of the Philosophers* is a rich source of knowledge about earlier thinkers

DIOGENES OF SINOPE (*c.*412–323 BC), Greek philosopher, Cynic

DOCETAE, early Christian adherents to Docetism, the belief that Jesus' physical body was an illusion

DOMITIAN, TITUS FLAVIUS (51–96), Roman emperor

DRYDEN, JOHN (1631–1700), English poet, literary critic, translator

DUNS SCOTUS (1266–1308), scholastic theologian and philosopher

ECKERMANN, JOHANN PETER (1792–1854), German poet and author of *Conversations with Goethe*

ELEATIC SCHOOL, Greek school of philosophers, followers of Parmenides of Elea (early to mid-fifth century BC), who argued against plurality and motion

EMPEDOCLES (*c.*495–*c.*435 BC), Greek philosopher, important for his cosmology

EPICTETUS (*c.*55–*c.*135), Greek Stoic philosopher

EPICURUS (341–270 BC), Greek philosopher, founder of the important school of Epicureanism

ERIS, Greek goddess of strife

EROS, Greek god of love

EUCHEL, ISAAC ABRAHAM (1758–1804), German Jewish author and scholar

EUCLID (third century BC), Greek mathematician, first axiomatic geometer

EULENSPIEGEL, TILL, fictional trickster figure originating in Middle Low German folklore

EULER, LEONHARD PAUL (1707–83), Swiss mathematician and physicist

EURIPIDES (*c.*480–406 BC), Athenian tragedian

EUSEBIUS OF CAESAREA (*c.*263–*c.*339), called 'Father of Church History'

FEDER, JOHANN GEORG HEINRICH (1740–1821), German eclectic philosopher, opponent of Kant

FÉNÉLON, FRANÇOIS (1651–1715), French Roman Catholic theologian, poet and writer, advocate of Quietism

FERNOW, KARL LUDWIG (1763–1808), German art critic and archaeologist

FEUERBACH, PAUL JOHANN ANSELM RITTER VON (1775–1833), German legal scholar

FICHTE, JOHANN GOTTLIEB (1762–1814), German philosopher, one of the chief figures in German Idealism in the period immediately after Kant, author of the *Wissenschaftslehre* (*Science of Knowledge*) and *System der Sittenlehre* (*System of Moral Philosophy*). Schopenhauer attended Fichte's lectures in 1811–13, but describes him as a pompous and inferior thinker

FLOURENS, MARIE JEAN PIERRE (1794–1867), French physiologist and brain scientist

FO, Chinese name for the Buddha

FRANCIS OF ASSISI, SAINT (1181–1226), founder of the Franciscans, patron saint of animals

FRANZ MOOR, character in Schiller's play, *The Robbers* (*Die Räuber*)

FREDERICK THE GREAT (Friedrich II) (1712–86), King of Prussia

GALIGNANI, GIOVANNI ANTONIO (1757–1821), Italian newspaper publisher

GOETHE, JOHANN WOLFGANG VON (1749–1832), poet, dramatist and scholar in many fields, Germany's greatest writer and prominent Enlightenment figure. Schopenhauer knew Goethe in the period 1813–14 and collaborated with him over his theory of colours

GORGIAS (*c.*487–376 BC), Greek pre-Socratic philosopher and Sophist

GOZZI, COUNT CARLO (1720–1806), Italian dramatist

GRACIÁN, BALTHASAR (1601–58), Spanish moralist, intensively studied and translated into German by Schopenhauer

GRETCHEN, character in Goethe's *Faust*

GRIMSTONE, WILLIAM, owner of a herbary in Highgate, London

GUYON, MADAME (Jeanne-Marie Bouvier de la Motte-Guyon) (1648–1717), French mystic and Quietist

HALL, MARSHALL (1790–1857), English physician and physiologist

HAMLET, the character in Shakespeare's play of the same name

HARDY, REV. ROBERT SPENCE, scholar of Buddhism

HAYDN, JOSEPH (1732–1809), Austrian classical composer

HEGEL, GEORG WILHELM FRIEDRICH (1770–1831), German philosopher, leading figure in the movement of German Idealism, author of *Phänomenologie des Geistes* (*Phenomenology of Spirit*) and *Enzyklopädie der Philosopischen Wissenschaften* (*Encyclopedia of Philosophical Sciences*), Professor of Philosophy in Berlin and dominant intellectual figure in the first four decades of the nineteenth century. Consistently critized and satirized by Schopenhauer as a charlatan

HELVÉTIUS, CLAUDE ADRIEN (1715–71), philosopher of the French Enlightenment

HERACLITUS (*c.*535–475 BC), Greek pre-Socratic philosopher

HERCULES, legendary Greek hero of great strength and prowess

HERDER, JOHANN GOTTFRIED VON HERDER (1744–1803), German philosopher, poet, translator and literary critic

HERODOTUS OF HALICARNASSUS (*c.*484–*c.*425 BC), ancient Greek historian and perhaps the first European historian

HESIOD (eight century BC), one of the earliest known Greek poets

HICETAS (*c.*400–335 BC), Greek Pythagorean philosopher

HIPPIAS OF ELIS (mid-fifth century BC), Greek pre-Socratic philosopher and Sophist

HIRT, ALOYS LUDWIG (1759–1837), German art historian and professor of art history

HOBBES, THOMAS (1588–1679), English philosopher

HOME, HENRY (Lord Kames) (1696–1782), Scottish Enlightenment philosopher

HOMER (fl. *c.*700 BC), the early ancient Greek poet, author of the epic poems the *Iliad* and the *Odyssey*

HOOKE, ROBERT (1635–1703), English natural philosopher and mathematician

HORACE (Quintus Horatius Flaccus) (65–8 BC), Roman poet, frequently quoted by Schopenhauer

HORATIO, character in Shakespeare's *Hamlet*

HOUTTUYN, MARTINUS (1720–98) Dutch naturalist

HOWITT, WILLIAM (1795–1879), novelist and explorer

HUFELAND, CHRISTOPH WILHELM FRIEDRICH (1762–1836), doctor

HUMBOLDT, ALEXANDER VON (1769–1859), German naturalist, explorer and biogeographer

HUME, DAVID (1711–76), the important Scottish philosopher, essayist and historian, admired by Schopenhauer

HÜTTNER, JOHANN CHRISTIAN, translated the book of Manu from English to German in 1797

IAGO, character in Shakespeare's *Othello*

IXION, Greek mythological figure who deceived the gods and is bound to a burning solar wheel for all eternity

JACOBI, FRIEDRICH HEINRICH (1743–1819), German polemicist, critic of Enlightenment and idealism

JEAN PAUL (Johann Paul Friedrich Richter) (1763–1825), German writer

JESUS CHRIST (4 BC–29/30), central figure of the Christian religion, in which he is considered the son of God

JOHN THE BAPTIST, Jewish preacher and prophet, contemporary and supporter of Jesus

JOHNSON, SAMUEL (1709–84), English man of letters, lexicographer and subject of famous biography by James Boswell

JONES, WILLIAM (1746–94), English philologist and orientalist, helped found the modern study of Sanskrit

JULIAN THE APOSTATE (331/332–363), Roman emperor

JUVENAL, DECIMUS IUNIUS (*c.*58–138), Roman satirist

KANNE, THOMAS ARNOLD (1773–1824), professor of Asian literature

KANT, IMMANUEL (1724–1804), German philosopher, commonly considered the greatest philosopher of modern times, a view Schopenhauer shares. Author of *Kritik der reinen Vernunft* (*Critique of Pure Reason*) (1781 and 1787), *Grundlegung zur Metaphysik der Sitten* (*Groundwork to the Metaphysics of Morals*) (1785) and *Kritik der praktischen Vernunft* (*Critique of Practical Reason*) (1788) among other works, Kant is the most important single influence on Schopenhauer, who especially admires his resolution of the problem of freedom and necessity and his idealist account of space and time, but is highly critical of many aspects of Kant's philosophy

KANTHAKA, the Buddha's horse

KEMBLE, CHARLES (1775–1854), British actor

KEPLER, JOHANNES (1571–1630), German mathematician and astronomer, key figure in the Scientific Revolution

KIESEWETTER, JOHAN GOTTFRIED KARL CHRISTIAN (1766–1819), German professor of philosophy, popularizer of Kant's philosophy

KING DAVID, figure from the Hebrew Bible, king of Israel

KING LEAR, character in Shakespeare's play of the same name

KLAPROTH, HEINRICH JULIUS (1783–1835), German orientalist

KLEIST, EWALD CHRISTIAN VON (1715–59), German poet

KLETTENBERG, SUSANNA KATHERINA VON (1723–1774), friend of Goethe

KOHELETH (Qohelet), main speaker in the book of Ecclesiastes

KOSACK, CARL RUDOLF (1823–69), professor of mathematics and physics at the Nordhausen Gymnasium

KRISHNA, Hindu god, hero of the *Bhagavadgītā*

LA ROCHEFOUCAULD, FRANÇOIS DE (1613–80), French writer, famous for his *Maxims*

LACTANTIUS (*c*.240–*c*.320), early Christian author

LAERTES, character in Shakespeare's *Hamlet*

LAMARCK, JEAN-BAPTISTE (1744–1829), French naturalist, formulated a theory of evolution

LAMPERT, JOHANN HEINRICH (1728–77), Swiss mathematician, physicist and astronomer

LAOCOÖN, Greek mythological figure, warned the Trojans against bringing the Greek wooden horse into Troy. He and his two sons were subsequently strangled by sea-serpents. The scene became the subject of a famous sculpture group

LAPLACE, PIERRE-SIMON (1749–1827), French mathematician and astronomer

LAVATER, JOHANN KASPAR (1741–1801), Swiss poet and physiognomist

LE SAGE, GEORGES-LOUIS (1724–1803), Swiss physicist

LEIBNIZ, GOTTFRIED WILHELM (1646–1716), German-born philosopher and mathematician, a leading figure in seventeenth-century intellectual life

LEONIDAS (*c*.540–480 BC), king of Sparta, known through his heroic death in the war against the Persians

LESSING, GOTTHOLD EPHRAIM (1729–81), German Enlightenment philosopher, dramatist and art critic

LICHTENBERG, GEORG CHRISTOPH (1742–99), German satirical writer, professor of philosophy at the University of Göttingen

LINGARD, DR JOHN (1770–1851), English Catholic historian

LIVY (Titus Livius) (59 BC–AD 17), Roman historian

LLULL, RAMON (1232–1315), Majorcan writer, mystic and philosopher

LOCKE, JOHN (1632–1704), English philosopher, empiricist, author of *An Essay concerning Human Understanding*

LUCRETIUS (Titus Lucretius Carus) (*c*.99–*c*.55 BC), Roman poet and philosopher

LUTHER, MARTIN (1483–1546), German Protestant theologian of great influence

MACHIAVELLI, NICCOLÒ (1469–1527), Florentine Renaissance diplomat, political philosopher

MAHOMET (see MOHAMMED), character in a play of the same name by Voltaire

MALEBRANCHE, NICOLAS (1638–1715), French theologian and Cartesian philosopher

MANU, Hindu half-divine progenitor of humanity

MARS, Roman god of war

MARSYAS, Greek mythological satyr, flayed by Apollo after losing a musical contest

MAX, character in Schiller's *Wallenstein*

MECKEL, JOHANN FRIEDRICH (1781–1833), German professor of pathology, anatomy and surgery at the University of Halle

MEISTER ECKHART (1260–1328), German theologian, philosopher and mystic

MEISTER, JOHANN CHRISTIAN FRIEDRICH (1758–1828), German professor of law

MENDELSSOHN, MOSES (1729–86), German Jewish Enlightenment philosopher

MENENIUS AGRIPPA (d. 493 BC), Roman patrician famed for comparing the social classes to parts of the body

METRODORUS OF LAMPSACUS (331–277 BC), Greek philosopher and major proponent of Epicureanism

MIDAS, Greek mythological king of Pessinus

MINERVA, Roman goddess of wisdom

MONTAIGNE, MICHEL EYQUEM DE (1533–92), French philosopher and essayist

MOSES, prophet of the Hebrew Bible

MOHAMMED (*c*.570–632), central figure of Islam, in which he is considered messenger and prophet of God

MÜNCHHAUSEN, KARL FRIEDRICH HIERONYMUS, FREIHERR VON (1720–97), German baron, military figure, story-teller

NASSE, CHRISTIAN FRIEDRICH (1778–1851), German physician and professor

NERI, SAINT PHILIP ROMOLO (1515–95), Italian priest, called 'Apostle of Rome'

NERO, LUCIUS DOMITIUS (37–68), Roman emperor famed for egoism and vanity

NEWTON, ISAAC (1632–1727), the great English mathematician, physicist and astronomer

NUMENIUS OF APAMEA (second century), Greek philosopher, forerunner of Neoplatonism

OCELLUS LUCANUS (fifth century BC), Pythagorean philosopher

OPHELIA, character in Shakespeare's *Hamlet*

ORMUZD, Middle Persian equivalent of Ahura Mazda, Zoroastrian deity, the one uncreated Creator

OSIANDER, FRANZ BENJAMIN (1759–1822), professor of medicine

OSSIAN, supposed narrator and author of ancient Gaelic poem cycle, later shown to be a modern creation

OVID (43 BC–AD17/18), Roman poet

OWEN, SIR RICHARD (1804–92), English zoologist and anatomist

PAINE, THOMAS (1737–1809) British radical pamphleteer, advocate of colonial American independence

PALMIRA, character in Voltaire's *Mahomet*

PANTALONE, stock comic character of miserly old man from Commedia dell'arte

PARIS, Greek mythological figure whose elopement with Helen was the immediate cause of the Trojan War

PARMENIDES OF ELEA (fifth century BC), Greek pre-Socratic philosopher

PASCAL, BLAISE (1623–62), French mathematician, physicist, Jansenist philosopher

PAUL, SAINT (died *c*.64), apostle and one of the first Christian theologians

PELAGIUS (fl. *c*.400), initiator of a movement in Christian thought that emphasized free will as opposed to divine grace

PERIPATETICS, ancient Greek school of philosophy dating from about 335 BC, founded by Aristotle

PERSEPHONE (Roman: Proserpina), Greek mythological goddess of earth's fertility, queen of the underworld

PETRARCH (Petrarca), FRANCESCO (1304–74), Italian poet and scholar

PETRONIUS (*c*.27–66), Roman courtier, assumed to be the author of the *Satyricon*

PETTIGREW, THOMAS (1791–1865), surgeon and antiquarian, expert on Egyptian mummies

PFEIFFER, FRANZ (1815–68), German literary scholar, philologist

PHAEDRA, Greek mythological figure, character in Euripides' *Hippolytus*

PHERECYDES (sixth century BC), early Greek thinker

PHILIP II (1527–98), king of Spain

PHILOCTETES, Greek mythological figure and character in Sophocles' play of the same name

PHILOLAUS (*c*.480–*c*.385 BC), Greek Pythagorean, pre-Socratic philosopher

PINDAR (522–443 BC), Greek lyric poet

PLATO (427–347 BC), the great Greek philosopher of immense influence on subsequent philosophy, and one of Schopenhauer's most important influences

PLAUTUS (*c*.254–184 BC), Roman playwright

PLINY THE YOUNGER (Gaius Plinius Caecilius Secundus) (*c*.61–112), Roman statesman and author

PLOUCQUET, GOTTFRIED (1716–90), German philosopher and logician

PLUTARCH (46–125), Graeco-Roman statesman and historian

POLIER, MARIE-ELISABETH DE (1742–1817) Swiss writer, orientalist

POPE, ALEXANDER (1688–1744), English poet

PORTINARI, BEATRICE (Bice di Folco Portinari) (1266–90), Florentine woman who inspired Dante

POUSSIN, NICOLAS (1594–1665), French painter

PRIESTLEY, JOSEPH (1733–1804), English theologian, philosopher and scientist

PRINCESS ISABELLA (Infanta Isabella Clara Eugenia) (1566–1633), daughter of Phillip II, ruler of the Spanish Netherlands

PROCLUS (412–85), Greek Neoplatonic philosopher and commentator on Plato

PROSERPINA (see PERSEPHONE)

PROTEUS, Greek mythological figure, early sea god

PUFENDORF, SAMUEL VON (1632–94), German political philosopher, statesman, historian

PYRRHO OF ELIS (*c.*360–*c.*270 BC), Greek philosopher, first Sceptic

PYRRHONISTS, sceptical school in ancient Greek philosophy

PYTHAGORAS (*c.*570–*c.*497 BC), early Greek sage, founder of Pythagorean tradition in philosophy

PYTHAGOREANS, Greek philosophers, mathematics and music theorists in the tradition founded by Pythagoras

RACINE, JEAN (1639–99), French dramatist

RAMEAU, JEAN-PHILIPPE (1683–1764), French Baroque composer and music theorist

RANCÉ, (Abbé) ARMAND JEAN LE BOUTHILLIER DE (1626–1700), abbot, founder of the Trappist Cistercians

RAPHAEL (1483–1520), High Renaissance Italian painter and architect

REGULUS (d. *c.*250 BC), Roman general and consul

REIL, JOHANN CHRISTIAN (1759–1813), German physician, physiologist, anatomist, psychiatrist, proponent of vitalism

REIZ, JOHANN HEINRICH (d. 1721), reformation minister

RÉMUSAT, JEAN PIERRE ABEL (1788–1832), French orientalist

RICHARD III, character in Shakespeare's play of the same name about the life of the fifteenth-century king of England

ROBESPIERRE, MAXIMILIEN FRANÇOIS MARIE ISIDORE DE (1758–94), French revolutionary leader, member of the Committee of Public Safety

ROLLA, the Inca hero in Richard Brinsley Sheridan's play, *Pizarro*

ROSENKRANZ, JOHANN CARL FRIEDRICH (1805–79), professor in Königsberg, editor of an important edition of Kant's works (1838–40)

ROSSINI, GIOANCHINO ANTONIO (1792–1868), Italian composer, primarily of opera

ROUSSEAU, JEAN-JACQUES (1712–78), French writer of the Enlightenment

RUISDAEL, JACKOB VAN (1628–82), Dutch landscape painter

SCHELLING, FRIEDRICH WILHELM JOSEPH VON (1775–1854), philosopher of German Idealism and Romanticism, criticized by Schopenhauer

SCHILLER, JOHANN CHRISTOPH FRIEDRICH (1759–1803), German poet, dramatist and aesthetician

SCHLEIERMACHER, FRIEDRICH DANIEL ERNST (1768–1834), German theologian and philosopher

SCHMIDT, J. J. (Isaac Jacob) (1779–1847), German orientalist

SCHOEMANN, GEORG FRIEDRICH (1793–1879), German professor of classical literature

SCHULZE, GOTTLOB ERNST (1761–1833), German professor, sceptical critic of Kant, and Schopenhauer's teacher at the University of Göttingen

SENECA, LUCIUS ANNAEUS (4 BC–AD 65), Roman poet and Stoic thinker, committed suicide at the instigation of Nero

SEXTUS EMPIRICUS (fl. *c.*200), Greek sceptical philosopher

SHAKESPEARE, WILLIAM (1564–1616), English dramatist and poet

SHIVA, Hindu god, the destroyer or transformer, one of the Triumurti

SHYLOCK, character in Shakespeare's *The Merchant of Venice*

SILENUS, Greek mythological follower of Dionysus

SIMPLICIUS (*c.*490–*c.*560), Neoplatonist philosopher, wrote extensively on Aristotle

SOCRATES (470–399 BC), Greek philosopher, teacher of Plato

SODEN, FRIEDRICH JULIUS HEINRICH, COUNT VON (1754–1831), playwright

SOPHOCLES (*c.*496–406 BC), Greek tragedian

SPINOZA, BENEDICT (Baruch) DE (1632–77), Jewish Dutch philosopher

STAHL, GEORG ERNST (1660–1734), physician, chemist and physiologist

STERN, SIGISMUND (1812–89), philosopher of language

STOBAEUS, JOANNES (fifth century), Neoplatonist, author of an anthology of excerpts from previous writers, valuable as a source book for ancient philosophy

STOICISM, school of Hellenistic philosophy dating from the early third century BC founded by Zeno of Citium in Athens

STRABO (63/64 BC–AD 24), Greek historian, geographer, philosopher

STURMIN, BEATA (1682–1730), German Quietist, mystic

SUÁREZ, FRANCISCO (1548–1617), Spanish philosopher and transmitter of medieval thought

SUIDAS (tenth century), supposed author of the Suda (Souda), Byzantine Greek historical encyclopaedia

SULZER, JOHANN GEORG (1720–79), Swiss mathematician and philosopher

SWIFT, JONATHAN (1667–1745), Anglo-Irish satirist, essayist, poet and political pamphleteer

TANTALUS, Greek mythological character who deceived the gods and served them his children, and was punished in the underworld by being forced to stand next to food and drink which would recede as he reached for them

TARTAGLIA, stock comic character from Commedia dell'arte, near-sighted with stutter

TAULER, JOHANNES (*c.*1300–61), German mystic and theologian

TENNEMANN, WILHELM GOTTLIEB (1761–1819), German historian of philosophy

TERSTEEGEN, GERHARD (1697–1769), German theologian and hymn writer, mystic

TERTULLIAN (*c*.160–*c*.220), theologian and early Church Father

THALES OF MILETUS (*c*.624–*c*.536 BC), pre-Socratic philosopher

THECLA, character in Schiller's *Wallenstein*

THYESTES, Greek mythological figure who unwittingly ate his own sons

TIEFTRUNK, JOHANN HEINRICH (1759–1837), German professor of philosophy

TISCHBEIN, JOHANN HEINRICH WILHELM (1751–1829), German painter, friend of Goethe

TREMBLEY, ABRAHAM (1700–84), Swiss naturalist

UGOLINO DELLA GHERARDSCA (*c*.1220–89), Italian nobleman who was imprisoned and starved to death. He appears in the lowest circle of Dante's Inferno

UPHAM, EDWARD (1776–1834), British orientalist

VAN DER WERFT, ADRIAN (1659–1722), Dutch painter

VICQ D'AZYR, FÉLIX (1746–94), French physician and anatomist and originator of the field of comparative anatomy

VIRGIL (Publius Vergilius Maro) (70–19 BC), leading Roman poet

VISHNU, Hindu god, the maintainer or preserver, one of the Trimurti

VOLTAIRE (François-Marie Arouet) (1694–1778), French thinker central to the Enlightenment

VOß, JOHANN HEINRICH (1751–1826), German-Slavic translator, poet and philologist

WENZEL, JOSEF (1768–1808), German doctor, author of work on the brain

WIELAND, CHRISTOPH MARTIN (1733–1813), German poet and writer

WILKINSON, SIR JOHN GARDNER (1797–1875), English Egyptologist

WILSON, HORACE HAYMAN (1786–1860), professor of Sanskrit at Oxford

WINCKELMANN, JOHANN JOACHIM (1717–68), German Hellenist, historian of ancient art, archaeologist

WINKELRIED, ARNOLD VON, Swiss hero of the battle of Sempach (1386)

WOLFF, CHRISTIAN (1679–1754), German Enlightenment philosopher

XENOPHON (*c*.431–355 BC), Greek soldier and writer, friend and student of Socrates

XERXES I (519–465 BC), king of Persia

ZENO OF CITIUM (333–264 BC), Greek philosopher, founder of the Stoic school

ZENO OF ELEA (*c*.490–*c*.430 BC), pre-Socratic Greek philosopher, famous for his paradoxes

ZEUS, Greek mythological figure, ruler of the gods

ZIMMERMANN, JOHANN GEORG RITTER VON (1728–95), Swiss doctor and philosopher

Index

Printed in Great Britain
by Amazon

65971223R00398